Policies for Prosperity

Policies for Prosperity

Essays in a Keynesian Mode

James Tobin

Edited by P. M. Jackson

The MIT Press
Cambridge, Massachusetts

First MIT Press edition, 1987

Typeset in 10pt Times Roman by
Photo·graphics, Honiton, Devon

Printed in Great Britain by
Whitstable Litho Printers Ltd., Whitstable, Kent

Library of Congress Cataloging-in-Publication Data
Tobin, James, 1918–
   Policies for prosperity.

   Includes index.
   1. Keynesian school of economics. 2. Supply-side economics—United States. 3. United States—Economic policy—1981–   . I. Jackson, P. M. (Peter McLeod) II. Title
HB99.7.T63 1987   330.15′6   87–2967
ISBN 0-262-20066-X

To BETTY,
who for forty years has tried to keep my
values true and my priorities straight,
this book is lovingly dedicated

Contents

List of Figures

List of Tables

Preface

This volume contains forty-three policy-oriented essays written over the past twelve years. They vary in length from 'op-ed' newspaper articles to long papers prepared for conferences, symposia, and edited books. They were usually addressed to audiences beyond the economics profession, and I believe they are on the whole accessible to interested readers whether or not they are proficient in economics. I cannot pretend they are as easy reading as a daily newspaper or a best-selling novel; they would not serve their purpose if they did not require and elicit some intellectual effort. Technical economics has been kept at a minimum, but economists, including undergraduate and graduate students, will see their tools in use, mostly implicitly but occasionally explicitly.

As the title of the book says, the essays are 'in a Keynesian mode'. They are almost all about macroeconomics, the behaviour of whole economies, a subject that dates from Keynes's great book of 1936. That is the year I began studying economics, and throughout my fifty years as student, teacher, scholar, and public servant, Keynes's ideas have strongly influenced me—without, I hope, enslaving me. In recent years Keynesian theories and policies have been under attack, both within the economics profession and in the wider arena of public opinion and politics. Many of the essays in this book concern the battle of ideas, and set forth my Keynesian point of view.

These essays were prepared for a wide variety of occasions, with different sponsors, audiences, and media of publication. Inevitably they contained repetitions of ideas, arguments, and expressions. While some redundancy has been eliminated, much remains. I thought it desirable that any essay republished should still be self-contained. Aside from some deletions of repetitive material and of remarks specific to the initial occasion or first publication, the essays are republished as initially presented, with editorial but not substantive corrections.

Professor Peter Jackson initially suggested assembling a collection of my policy-oriented essays for publication, and graciously volunteered to help me select them and prepare them for a book. I would not have taken the time to do so without his initiative and his editorial assistance. I like the idea, because the essays were so scattered among special publications that no one but me could see the unifying thematic message. Of course, I alone am responsible for everything in the book, including all the errors.

I am grateful also to Edward Elgar and his colleagues at Wheatsheaf Books Ltd for encouraging Peter Jackson and me in this undertaking, and for their patience with me.

My intellectual debts to students and colleagues at Yale and elsewhere are too numerous and diffuse to recount. Yale University, its Economics Department, and its Cowles Foundation for Research in Economics, my homes for many years, have as always provided me generous and invaluable intellectual and logistical support. Many of the essays here published were originally written when the late Laura Harrison was effectively and devotedly managing all the secretarial duties connected with my busy life of teaching, writing, speaking, and travelling. Her successor Marlene Feldman is following in her footsteps and has helped greatly to get this volume ready for the publisher.

PART I

Keynesian Economics: Theory and Policy

INTRODUCTION

John Maynard Keynes was born in 1883, and his revolutionary book *The General Theory of Employment, Interest, and Money* came out in 1936. The hundredth anniversary of his birth and the fiftieth birthday of his book were the occasions for many celebrations and appraisals. Chapters 1, 2, and 4 were prepared for three such occasions. By coincidence the United States Congress passed the Employment Act of 1946 just ten years after the publication of the book, which was surely the original source of the ideas that led the Congress to commit federal policies to the maintenance of 'maximum production, employment, and purchasing power'. I prepared Chapter 3 for a celebration of the fortieth anniversary of the Act. Together these four essays seek to introduce the reader to Keynesian ideas and policies as applicable to the 1980s.

The other two chapters of Part I are book review essays. Chapter 5, on Patinkin, is a vehicle for setting forth Keynes's views on money and their differences from classical and monetarist doctrines. Chapter 6, on Thurow, describes and criticizes the several anti-Keynesian movements of these years—what Thurow calls 'dangerous currents' in economics. The doctrinal battles are not just academic, because these modern anti-Keynesian currents have inspired government policies in the United States, the United Kingdom, and all over the world in the 1970s and 1980s.

1 Keynesian Policies in Theory and Practice*

I. THE TURNING OF THE TIDE

The 100th anniversary of the birth of John Maynard Keynes occurs, like the publication of his *General Theory*, during a world depression. History has contrived to call attention to Keynes just when his diagnoses and prescriptions are more obviously credible than at any other time since the Great Depression of the 1930s. The current depression is tragic, but the coincidence of timing may be fortunate. It should help revive the credibility of Keynesian analysis and policy both within the economics profession and in the broader public arena. It may even enhance the prospects for recovery in this decade, and for stability and growth in the longer run.

Of course we have a long way to go, both to restore prosperity to the world and to restore realistic common sense to discussion and decision about economic policy. But the beginnings of recovery that have brightened the economic news this year, mainly in the United States, can be credited to Keynesian policies, however reluctant, belated, or inadvertent. Our Federal Reserve finally took mercy on the economy about one year ago and suspended its monetarist targets. Its easing of monetary policy saved the world financial system from dangerous crisis and averted further collapse of economic activity. At the same time American fiscal measures began to exert a powerful expansionary influence on aggregate demand. This Keynesian policy was, of course, fortuitous in its timing and unintentional in its motivation. It was a combination of tax cuts, rationalized by anti-Keynesian supply-side arguments, and increased defence spending. Whatever one may think of the distributional equity and allocational

---

*September 1983, keynote address, forum on The Policy Consequences of John Maynard Keynes, Hofstra University, Hempstead, NY. In Harold Wattel, editor, *The Policy Consequences of John Maynard Keynes,* Armonk, NY: M.E. Sharpe Inc., 1985, pp. 1–21

efficiency of these measures, they are increasing private and public spending on goods and services and making jobs. Every business economist and forecaster knows that, even if his boss's speeches deplore federal deficits as the principal threat to recovery.

In the battle for the hearts and minds of economists and of the thoughtful lay public, the tide may also have turned. The devastating effects of Thatcher policies on the United Kingdom, and of Volcker policies in this country after October 1979, have opened many eyes and minds. The idea that monetary disinflation would be painless, if only the resolution of the authorities to pursue it relentlessly were clearly announced and understood, proved to be as illusory as Keynesians predicted. Monetarism, both of the older Friedman version stressing adherence to money stock targets and of the new rational expectations variety, has been badly discredited. The stage has been set for recovery in the popularity of Keynesian diagnoses and remedies. I do not mean to imply, of course, that there is some Keynesian truth vintage 1936 or 1961 to which economists and policy makers will or should now return, ignoring the lessons of economic events and of developments in economics itself over these last turbulent fifteen years. I do mean that in the new intellectual synthesis, which I hope and expect will emerge to replace the divisive controversies and chaotic debates on macroeconomic policies, Keynesian ideas will have a prominent place.

A strong case can be made for the success of Keynesian policies. Virtually all advanced democratic capitalist societies adopted, in varying degrees, Keynesian strategies of demand management after World War II. The period, certainly until 1973, was one of unparalleled prosperity, growth, expansion of world trade, and stability. Unemployment was low, and the business cycle was tamed. The disappointments of the 1970s—inflation, stagflation, recessions and unemployment resulting from anti-inflationary policies—discredited Keynesian policies. But, after all, the Vietnam inflation occurred when President Johnson rejected the advice of his Keynesian economists and refused to raise taxes to pay for his war. The recoveries of 1971–3 and 1975–9 ended in double-digit inflation in the United States. But the Yom Kippur War of 1973, OPEC, and the Ayatollah Khomeni were scarcely the endogenous consequences of those recoveries or of the monetary and fiscal policies that stimulated or accommodated them. Indeed the main reason for pessimism about recovery today is the likelihood that excessive caution, based on misreading of, or overreaction to the 1970s, will inhibit policy for recovery in the 1980s. If so we will pay dearly in unemployment, lost production, and stagnant investment to insure against another inflationary burst.

But if we Keynesians need feel no compulsion to be apologetic, neither are we entitled to be complacent. Keynes did not provide, nor did his various followers over the years, a recipe for avoiding unstable inflation at full employment. The dilemma, though it became spectacularly severe in the last fifteen years, is an old one. It was recognized and prophesied by Keynesians like Joan Robinson and Abba Lerner in the early 1940s, when commitments to full employment policies after the war seemed a likely prospect, and it was a practical concern of policy makers throughout the postwar period. It still remains the major problem of macroeconomic policy. Keynesians cannot accept—nor will, I think, the politics of modern democracies— the monetarist resolution of the dilemma, which amounts simply to redefining as full employment whatever unemployment rate, however high, seems necessary to insure price stability. But we cannot ignore the possible inflationary consequences of gearing macroeconomic policies simply to the achievement of employment rates that seem 'full' by some other criterion. The politics of modern democracies will not allow that, either. I shall return to this central issue later.

II. J. M. KEYNES ON MACROECONOMIC POLICY

It is time now to say more about what Keynesian policies are. Actually the *General Theory* itself contains little in the way of concrete policy recommendations; for the most part, those are left to be inferred by the reader. But Keynes was of course an active participant in policy debates in the United Kingdom in the 1920s and 1930s. One evident purpose of the *General Theory* was to provide a professional analytical foundation for the policy positions he had been advocating in those debates. Let me recall some of them.

Keynes opposed Britain's return in 1925 to the 1914 parity of sterling with gold and the United States dollar. His arguments were summarized in *The Economic Consequences of Mr Churchill*, who was Chancellor of the Exchequer at the time. More from shrewd realism than from theory, Keynes based his opposition on a view he held consistently thereafter and formally expounded in the *General Theory*, the downward inflexibility of money wages. He predicted, correctly in the event, that making wage costs fall to correct the overvaluation of the pound would be difficult, socially disruptive, and economically costly. He thought that workers and their unions would accept lower real wages accomplished by a lower exchange value of sterling and higher import prices while they would resist the equivalent adjustment via money wage cuts. Once the fateful decision he opposed was taken, moreover,

Keynes advocated government leadership in bringing about a smooth reduction of nominal wages. This advice too was ignored. Britain entered a long period of industrial strife, mass unemployment, and depression.

In 1929 the Liberal Party, led by Lloyd George, proposed during its unsuccessful electoral campaign a programme of public works to relieve unemployment. Keynes supported the proposal in his pamphlet with H. D. Henderson, *Can Lloyd George Do It?*. There and in his later testimony before the Macmillan Committee, Keynes refuted what came to be known as the 'Treasury View'. In modern parlance, this view was that public works outlays, financed by borrowing, would 'crowd out' private borrowing, investment, and employment one hundred per cent. The UK Treasury, like other exponents of crowding-out scenarios in other countries and at other times, made no distinction between situations of idle resources and those of fully employed resources. Keynes pointed out how public and private saving generated by public works activity, and overseas borrowing as well, would moderate the crowding out the Treasury feared, and how the Bank of England could be accommodative. Of course, only after the famous multiplier paper by Keynes's student R. F. Kahn, stimulated by this very controversy, could Keynes develop a full rationale of his position.

The reigning Governments would neither adjust the exchange rate nor adopt expansionary fiscal measures. Keynes was therefore led to favour for macroeconomic reasons a general tariff, in effect a devaluation of sterling for merchandise transactions only. When Britain was finally forced to devalue sterling in 1931, Keynes lost interest in the tariff, though one was enacted anyway. Keynes was, of course, quite aware of the 'beggar-my-neighbour' aspects of devaluations and tariffs, but in the British policy discussions he was a Briton. The *General Theory*, fortunately, is cast in a closed economy, interpretable as the whole world, and thus excludes nationalistic solutions.

The general characteristics of Keynes's policy interventions are clear from these examples. Keynes consistently focused on real economic outcomes, to which he subordinated nominal and financial variables, prices, interest rates, and exchange rates. Keynes naturally and unproblematically attributed to governments the power and the responsibility to improve macroeconomic performance. Keynes was a pragmatic problem solver, always ready to figure out what to do in the circumstances of the time. These characteristics carried through to his policy career after the *General Theory*, his effective contributions to British war finance and to international monetary architecture.

What does the *General Theory* itself say about policy? Fiscal policy, long regarded as the main Keynesian instrument, is introduced obliquely as a means of beefing up a weak national propensity to spend. Keynes warns against budget surpluses built by overprudent sinking funds. He advocates redistribution through the fisc in favour of poorer citizens with higher consumption propensities. He welcomes public investment but deplores the political fact that business opposition to productive public investments limits their scope; none the less intrinsically useless projects will enrich society if the resources directly and indirectly employed would otherwise be idle. Keynesian theory of fiscal policy was developed by others, notably by Alvin Hansen and the members of his Harvard Fiscal Policy Seminar.

Keynes was ambivalent on monetary policy. For fifteen or twenty years following publication of the *General Theory*, many economists, more in England than America, used the authority of the book to dismiss or downgrade the macroeconomic importance of money. Their reasons were, first, the apparent insensitivity of investment and saving to interest rates during the 1930s and, second, the observed insensitivity of interest rates to money supplies in the same period. Keynes's own views were more subtle. Though he was the originator of the 'liquidity trap' and exploited it in his theoretical attack on the 'classical' theory of unemployment, in his discussions of monetary policy he did not regard it as a typical circumstance or as an excuse for inaction by central banks. Neither did he regard investment decisions as beyond the reach of interest rates. His scepticism arose from his belief that the long-run expectations governing the marginal efficiency of capital are so volatile and unsystematic that central banks might well be unable to offset them by variation of interest rates. Yet he thought they should try, arguing for example that mature investment booms should be prolonged by interest rate reductions rather than killed by monetary tightening.

The same view led Keynes in the *General Theory* to advocate some 'socialization' of investment. This idea is not spelled out. Apparently Keynes had in mind not only public capital formation and tax policies affecting private investment, but more comprehensive, though cooperative, interventions in private investment decisions. Moreover, he had in mind not only cyclical stabilization but a long-run push to saturate the economy with capital and accomplish 'the euthanasia of the rentier'. Perhaps Jean Monnet's postwar 'indicative planning' in France, where government sponsored a coordinated raising of sights to overcome pessimism and lift investment, is an example of what Keynes had in mind. Perhaps some of the Swedish measures designed to make investment less pro-cyclical are another example.

Finally, I call attention to Keynes's habit of regarding wage determination as subject to 'policy'. This is evident in the *General Theory* as well as in the pamphleteering cited above. In the book Keynes discusses stable versus flexible money wages as an issue open to social choice. He regards cyclical stability of nominal wages not only as likely fact but as preferable to flexibility. In a famous passage he notes that monetary expansion and wage reduction are equivalent ways of attaining higher employment and observes that only 'foolish' and 'inexperienced' persons would prefer the latter to the former. His frequent references to 'wage policy' do not fit very well with his attempt at the outset of the *General Theory* to build his story of involuntary unemployment on the competitive foundations of Marshallian economics. But in policy matters Keynes was a shrewd and practical observer, and it would not be far-fetched to infer from his hints that he expected and advocated direct government interventions in the wage-setting process.

III. KEYNESIAN PRINCIPLES OF MACRO POLICY

The theory of macroeconomic policy, the subject of bitter controversy today, really developed after World World II and after Keynes's death. The principles of what came to be known as Keynesian policies were expounded in the postwar 'neoclassical synthesis' by Paul Samuelson and others. They occupied the mainstream of economics until the powerful monetarist and new classical counter-revolutions of the last fifteen years. They were the intellectual foundations of official United States policies in the Kennedy–Johnson years, when the media discovered them and somewhat misleadingly called them the 'New Economics'. They are expounded in the 1962 Economic Report of the Kennedy Council of Economic Advisers.

Let me review those principles, with particular reference to the items that are now particularly controversial, some of which are explicitly rejected by United States policy makers, as well as by those of other countries, notably the Thatcher government in the United Kingdom.

The first principle, obviously and unambiguously Keynesian, is the explicit dedication of macroeconomic policy instruments to real economic goals, in particular full employment and real growth of national output. This has never meant, in theory or in practice, that nominal outcomes, especially price inflation, were to be ignored. In the early 1960s, for example, the targets for unemployment and real GNP were chosen with cautious respect for the inflation risks. Today, however, a popular anti-Keynesian view is that macroeconomic policies can and should be aimed solely at nominal targets, for prices and/or nominal GNP, letting private 'markets' determine the consequences for real economic variables.

Second, Keynesian demand management is activist, responsive to the actually observed state of the economy and to projections of its paths under various policy alternatives. The anti-Keynesian counter-revolutionaries scorn activist macroeconomic management as 'fine tuning' and 'stop–go' and allege that it is destabilizing. The disagreement refers partly to the sources of destabilizing shocks. Keynes and his followers believe such shocks are endemic and epidemic in market capitalism, that government policy makers, observing the shocks and their effects, can partially but significantly offset them, and that the expectations induced by successful demand management will themselves be stabilizing. (Of course, Keynesians have by no means relied entirely on discretionary responsive policies; they have also tried to design and build automatic stabilizers in the fiscal and financial systems.) The opponents believe that government itself is the chief source of destabilizing shocks to an otherwise stable system, that neither the wisdom nor the intentions of policy makers can be trusted, and that stability of policies mandated by non-discretionary rules blind to actual events and forecasts are the best we can do. When this stance is combined with concentration on nominal outcomes, the results of recent experience in Thatcher's Britain and Volcker's America are not hard to understand.

Third, Keynesians have wished to put both fiscal and monetary policies in consistent and coordinated harness in the pursuit of macroeconomic objectives. Any residual scepticism of the relevance and effectiveness of monetary policy vanished early in the postwar era, certainly in the United States though less so in Britain. Keynesians have, of course, opposed the use of macroeconomically irrelevant norms like budget balance as guides to policy. They have, however, pointed out that monetary and fiscal instruments in combination provide sufficient degrees of freedom to pursue demand management objectives in combination with whatever priorities a democratic society chooses for other objectives. For example, Keynesian stabilization policies can be implemented with large or small government sectors, progressive or regressive tax and transfer structures, and high or low investment and saving as fractions of full employment GNP. In these respects latter-day Keynesians have been more optimistic than the author of the *General Theory*, believing that measures to create jobs do not have to be wasteful and need not focus exclusively on bolstering the national propensity to consume. The idea that the fiscal–monetary mix can be chosen to accelerate national capital formation, if that is a national priority, is a contribution of the so-called 'neoclassical synthesis'. Disregard of the idea since 1980 is the source of many of the current problems of United States macroeconomic policy, which may be not only inadequate to promote recovery but also perversely designed to inhibit national investment at a time when greater provision for the future is a widely shared social priority.

Fourth, as I observed earlier, Keynesians have not been optimistic that fiscal and monetary policies of demand management are by themselves sufficient to achieve both real and nominal goals, to obtain simultaneously both full employment and stability of prices or inflation rates. Neither are Keynesians prepared, as monetarist and new classical economists and policy makers often appear to be, to resolve the dilemma tautologically by calling full employment whatever unemployment rate results from policies that stabilize prices.

Every American administration from Kennedy to Carter inclusive, possibly excepting Ford, has felt the need to have some kind of wage–price policy. This old dilemma remains the greatest challenge; Keynesian economists differ among themselves, as well as with those of different macroeconomic persuasions, on how to resolve it. It may be ironically true that, thanks to good luck and to the severity of the depression, revival of inflation is unlikely during recovery in the 1980s just when policy makers are acutely afraid of it. The two late Eisenhower–Martin recessions of the late 1950s helped pave the way for an inflation-free Keynesian recovery in the early 1960s, and the Volcker depression may do the same. But it would be foolish to count on that, even more to assume the problem has permanently disappeared.

The need for a third category of policy instruments—in addition to fiscal and monetary, the 'wage policy' hinted in the *General Theory*— is clear to me. We can and should push other measures to reduce the expected value of the NAIRU (the non-accelerating inflation rate of unemployment). These include standard labour market, manpower, and human capital policies. They include attacks on the sacred cows of legislation that impart floors to some wages and prices and bias upward the price response to aggregate demand stimulus. They include encouragement to new arrangements for labour compensation, substituting shares in the performance and fortunes of employers for exclusive reliance on administered or negotiated scales of pay for labour time. They include measures to make collective bargaining more responsive to those workers with greater risks of unemployment. But even if everything is done that realistically can be done—politically and economically—on these fronts, I believe we will need incomes policies in our arsenal. The challenge is to design policies which labour and management will accept in the interests of better macroeconomic performance, policies which will not be so rigid and heavy handed in microeconomic impact as to entail severe costs in allocational efficiency. I myself believe that guideposts, to which compliance is induced by tax-based rewards, offer the greatest promise. But the subject is still wide open.

Until Keynesians design the instrument missing from their kit of tools, we cannot press with the full conviction and confidence merited by theory and history the superiority of Keynesian policies to the anti-Keynesian policies of recent experience.

IV. POLITICS AND IDEOLOGY

In the near half-century since the debut of the *General Theory*, Keynesian macroeconomics have been identified politically and ideologically with liberalism, in the modern rather than the nineteenth-century meaning of that word. Although prior to 1979 conservative governments—Republican in the United States and Conservative in Britain—practised Keynesian demand management, its main proponents have been liberal parties, Democratic in this country, Labour in the United Kingdom, social democratic parties elsewhere. Certainly Keynes has never been accepted in the ideological pantheon of business and finance, despite the efforts of groups like the Committee for Economic Development in the United States to define a pragmatic synthesis. The lines are drawn more sharply than ever now that conservative movements with ideologies explicitly condemning Keynes and Keynesian policies have gained influence and power.

The reasons for business interests to reject Keynes are not entirely clear. Keynes himself thought the implications of his theory were moderately conservative. He found no fault with the way capitalist systems allocated employed resources. (These days, with externalities more apparent and hazardous, he might be less confident.) He wanted to employ more resources—to the benefit of claimants to profits as well as to job seekers, as experience repeatedly testifies. The fiscal and financial shibboleths he challenged, and often ridiculed, were obstacles to general prosperity, not just to the well-being of workers. Compared with the revolutionary institutional changes threatened by other critics of capitalism's failures in the Great Depression, the reforms prescribed by Keynes were mild and conservative indeed. Perhaps the instinctive revulsion of conservatives was due to the suspicion that the liberation of government from traditional norms and the assignment to government of powers and responsibilities for overall economic performance would unleash a host of unpredictable social, political, and economic hazards. Perhaps businessmen feared that full employment would cost them more by tilting bargaining power toward labour than it would gain them in the fruits of prosperity. Perhaps they felt intuitively that they really were being displaced from the temples of their civilization.

Organized labour has found Keynesian economics selectively congenial. Its interest in jobs coincides with the full employment emphasis of Keynesian macroeconomic policies. But labour's support of price-increasing measures and unions' representation of senior employed workers at the expense of the unemployed worsen the trade-off agony and cripple full employment policies. Moreover, it has been difficult, to say the least, to obtain and maintain labour's acceptance of incomes policies. Political parties that espouse Keynesian policies are also those which depend on non-business interest groups for campaign support. The public does not make distinctions obvious to economists, and many associate Keynesian economics with all sorts of dubious microeconomic interventions.

There is, however, a sense in which Keynesian economics is a natural ally of liberalism. In the same passage where Keynes exonerated capitalism of allocational inefficiency, he faulted it for inequality of wealth as well as for chronic underemployment. There is nothing particularly Keynesian about the welfare state, which in greater or lesser degree has grown in every democratic capitalist country since World War II. Keynesian macroeconomists could take any side of controversies about social security, socialized medicine, food stamps, and the like. Nevertheless Keynesian economics at a minimum provides a licence for welfare state measures and other government efforts towards redistribution of wealth. The licence is the faith that macroeconomic stabilization and prosperity are compatible with a wide range of social policies, that modern capitalism and democracy are robust enough to prosper and progress while being humane and equitable. That faith conflicts with the visions of extreme Right and Left, which agree that extremes of wealth and poverty, of security and insecurity, are indispensable to the functioning of capitalism. Keynesian policies helped to confound those dismal prophecies in the past; I think they will do so again.

2 The Future of Keynesian Economics*

All these anniversaries are hard on old men. Three years ago it was the 100th anniversary of Keynes's birth, also Schumpeter's birth and Marx's death. Last year it was the centenary of the American Economic Association and the semicentennial of the Social Security Act. This year is the fortieth birthday of the Employment Act and the Council of Economic Advisers. Here we are observing the golden anniversary of the *General Theory*.

I note with some sadness that most of these zero mod 10 celebrations are occurring when the persons and institutions being remembered are not in great repute in the profession and the larger society. That gives these occasions an antiquarian, nostalgic, and apologetic character, and probably explains the advanced age of most of the speakers. I would really like to hear some twenty-eight-year-old speaker on the subject I have been assigned; he or she will have a lot more to do with the future of macroeconomics than I will.

It is something of an anniversary year for me too. I started studying economics as a college sophomore in 1936, and because my young tutor in Harvard College didn't know any better I cut my teeth on the *General Theory*. Some people think I learned nothing since.

REVOLUTION, COUNTER-REVOLUTION, AND SYNTHESIS IN MACROECONOMICS

Does Keynesian economics have a future? Observing the profession, I see signs that its recession has 'bottomed out', that some slight recovery has occurred. We should not expect recovery to the *status quo ante* 1968. That's not how intellectual cycles work. We do learn

---

*April 1986. Eastern Economic Association, Philadelphia. To be published in *Eastern Economics Journal*.

something from these swings, and new syntheses replace both the previous antitheses. The so-called neoclassical neo-Keynesian synthesis of the 1950s and 1960s differed from the neoclassical macroeconomic orthodoxy against which Keynes revolted and from the Keynesian revolution vintage 1940 as well. Today's new classical macro is not only a counter-revolution against the previous orthodox synthesis but an improved version of pre-Keynesian orthodoxy. Macroeconomics will never be the same as before Keynes, or as before Lucas.

The cycles in professional economics run parallel to fashions in politics and public opinion. Both are greatly influenced by salient events and simplistic explanations. The parallel is not reassuring to a profession with scientific pretensions. Keynesian theory and policy, as embodied in the synthesis mentioned above, were riding high in professional and public esteem during the euphoria of the mid-1960s about national economic performance. Subsequent inflation and stagflation brought massive swings to monetarism, new classical macro, and even supply-side economics.

However, the recessions after 1979, in America and Europe both, seemed to discredit the new classical–new monetarist view that disinflation will not be very painful or take very long if monetary contraction is pre-announced to be firmly irreversible. The stagnation of Europe throughout the 1980s under orthodox anti-Keynesian policies and the apparent potency of fiscal policy as demand stimulus in this country also breed doubts even among young theorists. At a more scientific level, new classical propositions have not passed econometric tests. Many macroeconomists today think that Keynes is not good theory but that good theory doesn't fit the facts. It remains to be seen how economic science will escape this impasse.

NEW CLASSICAL BUSINESS CYCLE THEORIES, REAL AND UNREAL

One reason Keynesian economics has a future is that rival theories of economic fluctuations do not.

The controversies of recent years focused on the inertia of nominal prices and wages and their rates of change, on the irrationality of adaptive expectations or of implicit or explicit contracts without complete indexation, on the Phillips Curve and the reality and durability of the policy trade-offs it once seemed to offer. The Lucas 'supply curve' offered an interpretation of Phillips-type statistical correlations that denied any real potency to monetary policy beyond those arising from monetary surprises leading to transient misperceptions of relative prices. Those failures and asymmetries of information were constitutionally too weak to support a theory of business cycles adequate to the stylized facts. You don't hear much about this kind of cycle theory these days. Indeed the old short-run Phillips Curve seems to have risen from the ashes.

New classical macro has had right along an alternative theory of business fluctuations, 'equilibrium' or 'real' business cycle theory. Cycles are just the appropriate movements incident to the economy's fully informed intertemporal general equilibrium. Money and other nominal variables are an irrelevant sideshow. The current preoccupation of new classical theorists and econometricians is to show how a purely real theory can account for the stylized facts.

Ironically, I have reflected, Keynes also had a purely real equilibrium theory, only his equilibria were demand-constrained underemployment situations. Preoccupation with the issues raised by the stickiness of nominal wages and prices in Keynes leads many modern economists, especially those who never read the book we are celebrating, to overlook Keynes's second argument about money wages. He asserted that flexibility of money wages would not remedy unemployment. There could still be deficiencies of aggregate demand in a world of wage and price flexibility. He used a very classical argument, namely that real demand should be independent of absolute prices. Early Keynesian cycle models were non-monetary, and that is why they were criticized and went out of fashion. They did allow scope for policy, that is, real fiscal demand stimulus, and in this respect of course they differ from the new classical models, in which labour markets are clearing all the time.

Interest rate and wealth effects apparently refute Keynes's neutrality argument. But those effects may be too weak to overcome the destabilizing expectational effects of price flexibility on aggregate demand. Deflation and even disinflation have negative effects on demand while they occur, effects that can be avoided only if nominal wages and prices *jump* to equilibrating values. Of course, the introduction of dynamics abandons Keynes's pretension to an equilibrium theory of unemployment. I personally do not regret that. Some years ago I set forth simple 'Keynesian models of recession and depression',[1] in which flexibility of prices could not avoid prolonged periods of unemployment in disequilibrium, or even guarantee the global stability of the full employment equilibrium.

I hazard the prediction that neither of the two species of 'business cycle theory' offered by new classical macroeconomics will be regarded as serious and credible explanations of economic fluctuations a few years from now. Whatever cycle theory emerges in a new synthesis will have important Keynesian elements. I will return later to a related but somewhat different theme of the *General Theory*, and to its relevance to the anti-Keynesian counter-revolution: the dependence of short-run aggregate demand on long-term investments whose outcomes are intrinsically unpredictable even as to probabilities. But first I want to make some comments on the methodological side of the new classical counter-revolution.

THE 'MICROFOUNDATIONS' METHODOLOGY OF MODERN MACROECONOMICS

The *General Theory* founded macroeconomics as a distinctive topic of theory and empirical inquiry. It established general equilibrium modelling as the way to study business cycles, monetary and fiscal policies, and other economy-wide events. Of course, this was lowbrow general equilibrium theory. Macro models took many shortcuts, made many simplifying assumptions; their structural equations were not necessary implications of highbrow general equilibrium theory, as set forth by Walras or later by Arrow and Debreu. Neither did they, as a general rule, violate the canons of such theory; I believe, though I will not argue the case tonight, that even sticky money wages can be defended from the charge of 'money illusion'.[2] The shortcuts and simplifications were and are inevitable costs of getting interesting and testable propositions, of which fullblown general equilibrium is virtually empty.

From Keynes on, macro model builders relied on the standard paradigms of neoclassical theories of the behaviour of individual agents in specifying their behavioural equations. If you doubt that, I recommend that you re-read, or read, Keynes's chapters on the propensity to consume; I doubt that any aspect of consumption and saving behaviour which students of the consumption function have raised in its fifty-year life is not foreshadowed in Keynes's initial discussion. But Keynes and his successors had to use and did use information and hypotheses about behaviour other than the implications of optimization theory. First, they could appeal to empirical observation, or to hunches about plausibility, to place restrictions on individual behaviours. Second, aggregate relationships are the results of diverse behaviours of multitudes of individual agents; a structural macro equation combines assumptions about individual behaviour and assumptions about aggregation. Third, macro modellers inject some realism about the institutions and economic structures of the economies they are describing. Those economies did not, do not, conform to the assumptions of highbrow general equilibrium, for example perfect and complete competitive markets. Pure theorists naturally found macro models aesthetically unappealing and intellectually confusing. But whom do the pure theorists consult at departmental lunches when they become, like other newspaper readers, curious about budget deficits and trade deficits?

'Microfoundations!' was the rallying cry of the methodological counter-revolution against Keynesian economics, really against all macroeconomics. Its protagonists complained of the absence of explicit derivations of macro behavioural equations from optimization; they proposed to build a new macro solidly and clearly based on individual rationality. Only relationships with those microfoundations, they said, could be expected to be stable over the range of applications—not just forecasts but also conditional forecasts of the effects of policy interventions and other exogenous variations—to which macroeconomics aspires. This counter-revolution has swept the profession until now it is scarcely an exaggeration to say that no paper that does not employ the 'microfoundations' methodology can get published in a major professional journal, that no research proposal that is suspect of violating its precepts can survive peer review, that no newly minted Ph.D. who can't show that his hypothesized behavioural relations are properly derived can get a good academic job.

After fifteen or twenty years of this methodological counter-revolution, where do we stand? What you gain on the swings you lose on the roundabouts. Aggregation is a tough problem, so it is just finessed. It's easy to display explicit microfoundations when you assume the whole private economy can be represented as one agent (or in the second semester as two who differ only in age and endowment). This agent, or the multitude of identical agents, operates in competitive markets with flexible prices, but of course there are no transactions in these markets (except in the second semester once every two-period lifetime). The immense volumes of transactions we actually observe in markets for assets and commodities are simply not explained. No heed is paid to all the problems of coordination and communication which concerned Keynes and other macro theorists—the differences between savers and investors, lenders and borrowers, bulls and bears, risk lovers and risk averters, and so on.

Why this 'representative agent' assumption is a less *ad hoc* and more defensible simplification than the dirty constructs of earlier macro modellers, and of today's macroeconometricians, is beyond me. I note some biases to which this methodology leads. The single-agent abstraction makes social welfare identical with the welfare of the individual agent. It excludes by definition any discrepancies between individual and social optima, in particular the deadweight losses due to involuntary unemployment, the market failure that motivated macroeconomics at its origins fifty years ago. The methodology treats government as an alien player in a two-person game with the anthropomorphic private sector, a game in which the government incomprehensibly tries to throw the private sector off its optimal solution while the private agent tries to outwit the evil or idiot policy maker. These biases work in a conservative and Panglossian direction, a political implication not present in abstract highbrow general equilibrium theory or asserted by its wiser architects and practitioners.

I exaggerate. An increasing number of theoretical papers using the new methodology attempt to model setups in which things do not work out for the best and in which government may even play some beneficently corrective role. I note, however, that this role is seldom a Keynesian one, because the distortion the government can correct is seldom a failure of markets to clear. Moreover, because of the methodology those papers are, like the ones that glorify the invisible hand, logical exercises rather than models that seriously try to describe real world economies.

In journals, seminars, conferences, and classrooms macroeconomic discussion has become a babble of parables. The parables are often specific to one stylized fact, for example the correlation of nominal prices and real output in cyclical fluctuations. Their usual inability to fit other stylized facts appears not to bother the authors of papers of this genre. The parables always rely on individual optimization, across time and states of nature. They differ in the arbitrary institutional restrictions they specify, on technology, markets, or information.

Even the individual's optimization problem is simplified and specialized in the interests of analytic tractability. Utility and production functions take parametric forms. By convention, equations are linear or log linear or are so approximated. The whole point of 'microfoundations' is to find stable relationships that survive policy variations, exogenous shocks, and the passage of time. But we have no basis for empirical confidence that an individual's utility function, for example, remains the same over his life, independently of his actual experience an environment. We certainly have no basis for assuming that a utility function with a constant rate of relative risk aversion is a stable basis for intertemporal choices and choices involving risk.

Today there is a big gulf between academic macroeconomics and the macroeconomics oriented to contemporary events and policies. If you were running the Congressional Budget Office or the Council of Economic Advisers, who would be of more use to you, an expert teller of parables or a practitioner of old-fashioned *IS/LM* and of structural econometric models built in its spirit? I think this gulf must and will narrow, and that is one reason I have hope for the future of Keynesian economics.

THE UNCERTAINTIES OF A HIGH-INVESTMENT ECONOMY

I now return from methodology to substance.

When Keynes was writing, 'equilibrium' in its complete and precise sense meant a repetitive steady state, indeed a stationary state without population growth and technical progress. Keynes observed that the propensity to save of an advanced capitalist economy was too high to permit a steady-state full employment equilibrium. There were two polar possibilities. One was to operate the economy with enough unemployment to reduce net saving to zero. (I note that it was this low-level steady state that Pigou contended could not be an equilibrium; his 'Pigou effect' article was entitled 'The classical stationary state'.) The other was to operate the economy at full employment with positive net investment and a growing capital stock. Keynes thought this was a scenario full of uncertainties, for reasons I am about to review.

First, however, I remind you that Harrod as early as 1939 lifted this discussion from stationary states to states of steady growth. He rephrased Keynes's problem as an excess of the 'warranted' over the 'natural' growth rate. As in Keynes, that discrepancy arises from a high propensity to save. Following Keynes, Harrod alleged that in this situation full employment would eventually become unsustainable because growth of capital faster than output would bring the marginal efficiency of capital to, potentially below, the liquidity floor to interest rates. He thought that full employment with high investment was a situation of knife-edge instability, from which any lapse would trigger the downward accelerator–multiplier spiral, an idea spelled out in more detail by Goodwin, Hicks, and others. Later and younger authors, including Robert Solow and myself, pointed out in the 1950s various ways in which this instability could be avoided. A point of agreement is that monetary policy would have to accommodate any decline in marginal efficiency of investment due to capital deepening; even if there were no liquidity trap, there still might be a problem of monetarism.

I note in passing that neither Keynes nor Harrod saw steady inflation as a way out of the liquidity trap. Why not? I think Keynes had a reason, as follows: if there were an inflationary trend, money wages would come to be indexed. They they wouldn't be sticky in the short run, and it would not be feasible to raise employment by price increases that reduce the real wage. Keynes thought of money wage stickiness as a desirable stabilizing feature of the economy.

Keynes's concerns about high national propensities to save do not, of course, seem as relevant today for the United States and for other mature economies that have found ways to sustain public and private consumption. Those institutions and measures are in a macroeconomic sense Keynesian, although we who took part in the postwar synthesis were anxious to free Keynesian economics from the taint of bias towards consumption and against capital formation. Anyway Japan and Germany and some other European countries still exhibit in the 1980s the high saving propensities that Keynes saw in the US and UK in the 1930s; they also exhibit the tendencies to stagnation he observed fifty years ago.

I come to my main point. In contemplating an economy dependent for short-run demand on high investment and capital growth, Keynes had in mind a more subtle and sweeping point than the ones considered by the growth and cycle theorists I have just mentioned. A repetitive stationary state involves very little risk, and what there is is *risk* in the sense of Frank Knight, calculable by probabilities and in principle insurable—one could also say calculable in the sense of J. M. Keynes's *Treatise on Probability*. Such a state Joseph Schumpeter called the 'circular flow' and found unexciting. A high-investment economy is necessarily travelling to *terrae incognitae*, with true Knightian or Keynesian *uncertainty*, distinguished from risk by the essential unknowability of the probabilities. The uncertainties come from new and untried technologies, factor proportions outside previous experience, and the dependence of the outcomes of current investment on the nature and size of future investment. All those uncertainties would be present even if full employment were perpetually maintained. They are compounded by the uncertainties of aggregate demand.

Keynes is quite explicit that the absence of complete futures markets leaves producers in doubt about future demands for their products. When a consumer skips lunch today in order to save for future consumption, she gives no signal to enable producers to prepare for her future consumption and to make the necessary investments. She saves in generalized financial form, completely free to decide later what goods she wants and when.

Attitudes, confidence, optimism, animal spirits affect investment when calculations are inconclusive. That is why Keynes thought investment was in large part exogenous, why he was not unreservedly sanguine about controlling investment by monetary policy via interest

rates, and why he suggested that some central organization of investment might be necessary to stabilize capitalist economies. Perhaps he
was thinking of something like the postwar French Plan, designed to
enable the various sectors of the economy to schedule their investments
within a common view of the macroeconomic future and with knowledge of the plans of their customers and suppliers. Maybe he was
thinking of coordination and planning initiatives like those of MITI
and the other institutions of 'Japan Inc.'.

A couple of summers ago I heard a leading younger macroeconomist
describe Keynesian theory as 'economics without expectations'. That
might be true of the fleshless formal models that some of us have
used and taught. It is not true of the *General Theory*, where long-
terms expectations play a decisive role. What is true is that Keynes does
not think these expectations can be endogenously generated, nor does
he think that everyone has, or is compelled by logic and evidence to
have, the same expectations of the same futures. Organized securities
markets offer little guidance to entrepreneurs and managers, he says,
because the dominant traders are oriented to short-term gains achieved
by anticipating the opinions of other traders rather than to long-term
fundamentals.

Keynes and Schumpeter were rivals; they disagreed on many things.
They are alike in emphasizing that capitalist growth—development in
Schumpeter's title—is qualitatively different from steady states or
circular flows.

Can it be that a society would choose a steady state with permanently
high unemployment to high-investment growth, preferring chronic
underutilization to the uncertainties of full employment and the saving
it would generate? It seemed unlikely until the mid 1970s and the
1980s. But Western Europe seems to be a case in point. Dominated
by Germany, Europe prefers to channel its saving propensities to
accumulation of secure claims against the rest of the world, the United
States in particular, or to waste them in high unemployment and
underachievement, rather than to accept the adventures of domestic
innovation and investment. The same can be said of Japan, where
growth is below potential even though enviably high. In these countries
the demand stimulus from exports, to the nations where they send
their savings, is the only kind of demand stimulus comfortable and
acceptable.

These low-level political, social, and economic equilibria are in an
important sense Keynesian. But they are also maintained by some of
the institutions Schumpeter foresaw in predicting the decay of capitalism, the excesses of the welfare state and of industrial relations that
tend to turn cyclical Keynesian unemployment into classical and

structural unemployment. Paradoxically the same conservative governments that appeal to those excesses and rigidities as excuses for the stagnation of their economies maintain them in force because they disarm the natural oppositions to their macroeconomic policies.

The United States is a different story. We are hardly a high-saving society in normal circumstances, and *our* conservative government has engaged in massive public dissaving. Thus we have created an outlet for some of the saving our friends abroad do not wish, or know how, to use. Infatuated with supply-side ideology, the Reagan Administration unintentionally adopted in extreme degree one of Keynes's remedies for high unemployment, high public and private consumption. Keynes would have regarded that as better than the chronic double-digit unemployment of the Europeans. But it certainly would not have been his preferred solution, because a much higher rate of domestically financed public and private capital formation was within our grasp. Keynes and Schumpeter both would have understood the lift of animal spirits brought by Reagan's presidency, and the enthusiasm it engendered in the business community. Unfortunately the potential of that euphoria has been wasted in the bizarre mix of monetary and fiscal policies of this decade.

Yes, Keynesian economics has a future because it is essential to the explanation and understanding of a host of observations and experiences, past and present, that alternative macroeconomic approaches do not illuminate. That includes the bearing of uncertainties and expectations on economic activity. It definitely includes business fluctuations, and fiscal and monetary policies.

NOTES

1. *American Economic Review*, May 1975, vol. LXV no. 2, 195–202, reprinted in my *Essays in Economics*, vol. 3, *Theory and Policy*, Cambridge, Mass.: MIT Press, 1982, Chapter 5.
2. *See* Chapter 4.

3 Fiscal and Monetary Policy under the Employment Act*

As we observe the fortieth birthday of the Employment Act, the auguries of its future are mixed. On the negative side, the objectives to which the Act committed federal economic policy—maximum employment, production, and purchasing power—command little support in word or deed among legislative and executive makers of policy. The Council of Economic Advisers, the major institution established by the Act to implement that commitment, has lost status and influence. Its attention has shifted to lesser goals. The Joint Economic Committee, more faithful to the original mandate but ever handicapped by its lack of legislative function, has difficulty getting its voice heard. The ideology dominating economic policy since 1980 rejects the premises of the Act, denying that federal interventions can improve the performance of the economy.

On the positive side, the economic climate over the foreseeable future is more clement than it has ever been since the twentieth birthday party. Nothing now on the horizon threatens the historically extraordinary series of external shocks that dominated the scene and preoccupied policy makers throughout the world from 1966 to 1981— notably the Vietnam War and the two oil crises of the 1970s. Now the OPEC cartel is collapsing and energy prices are falling. What is missing is commitment and confidence to take advantage of the benign climate of this decade.

Consider the complacency, resignation, and indifference with which the stagnation of the economy these last eighteen months has been accepted. The recovery that began in late 1982 stalled in June 1984 at 7 per cent unemployment, give or take a couple of tenths, and at about 80 per cent capacity utilization. My esteemed fellow CEA

*January 1968, Joint Economic Committee, US Congress, Symposium on the Fortieth Anniversary of the Employment Act, Washington, published in David Obey and Paul Sarbanes, eds., *The Changing American Economy,* Blackwell 1986, chapter 3. Also in *Challenge* May/June 1986, pp. 4–12, in shorter version titled 'High time to restore the Employment Act of 1946'.

alumnus Herbert Stein has interpreted the experience to signify that those numbers are equilibrium values, 'natural rates'. I was dismayed to find him subscribing to Panglossian macroeconomics. In my own view, this low-level stability reflects not an optimal equilibrium but the inadvertence or excessive caution of the monetary authorities. Certainly the architects of the Act, and those who took it seriously over its first quarter century, would not have been content. They would not brag about real GNP growth barely fast enough to keep high unemployment rates from rising further, nor congratulate themselves on avoiding outright recession. Observing that wage and price inflation rates are subsiding and seeing no bottlenecks or shortages on the economic landscape, they would wish to push the economy with deliberate speed towards higher utilization of its capacity to produce.

UNEMPLOYMENT AND INFLATION

The Employment Act did not specify any numerical target for unemployment. That was wise, because feasible targets have varied from time to time and will vary in future. Particular Administrations and Congresses may adopt and announce numbers—like the 4 per cent of the Kennedy years—but only as interim goals to be reconsidered with experience. It was a great mistake for the Congress to enshrine in the Humphrey–Hawkins Act numerical goals for unemployment and inflation that were in combination patently unachievable in the 1970s, in contrast to the 1960s. The result was that policy makers could ignore not only the numbers but the spirit that motivated them.

The Employment Act is directed first of all to fiscal and monetary policies affecting aggregate demand for goods and services. Inflation is the systemic constraint on the use of demand stimulus to lower unemployment and to increase utilization of productive capacity. All but one of the six recessions the United States has suffered in the last thirty years can be attributed to deliberate policies to restrict aggregate demand in order to bring inflation rates down. (The exception, in 1960, could be attributed to the alarm of policy makers over budget deficits and gold losses.) The counter-inflationary objectives were generally achieved, but with serious interruptions to economic growth and long intervals of high unemployment and excess capacity. Distaste for rising inflation rates, and indeed for persistent inflation above 5 per cent, is a strong revealed political preference of the American public. There is good reason, therefore, to keep enough slack in labour and product markets to avoid substantial risk of triggering a spiral of accelerating prices.

The natural rate of unemployment already mentioned is conceptually the lowest 'inflation-safe' rate obtainable by expansion of aggregate demand, the lowest rate that fiscal and monetary policies can be expected to achieve. Unemployment may be, and probably is, still excessive at that rate, but further reduction requires structural reform along with fiscal and monetary demand management.

It is important to be clear about what the inflation limits to demand management do and do not mean operationally. First, no one can be sure what the inflation hazards are at any unemployment rate in given circumstances, only that they are greater at 7 per cent than at 8 per cent and greater at 6 per cent than at 7 per cent. Second, no one can ever guarantee that there is zero inflation risk; it would be silly and wasteful to run the economy with so many resources idle that inflation risk was negligible. Third, the hazard to be avoided is a continuing, pervasive acceleration of prices. One-shot boosts of particular prices and even of general price indexes are bound to occur, especially in cyclical recoveries; they are not a problem even though they make statistical measures of annualized inflation rates temporarily high.

Today we do not know what the inflation-safe unemployment rate is, even if we could agree on how little inflation risk that concept should imply. I don't know; Herb Stein doesn't know; Paul Volcker doesn't know. The fact that inflation rates rose at successively higher unemployment rates—from 3–4 per cent in the late 1960s to 5 per cent in 1973 and 6 per cent in 1979—is doubtless an influential reason for caution today. However, I think this history is useless evidence for policy in this decade. It tells us nothing about normal labour and product markets today; if it describes any natural rate, it is the 'natural rate' of energy consumption and oil imports in the trying decade of the 1970s.

Now there is good reason to believe the natural rate of unemployment is well below the current rate of 7 per cent. Both wage inflation and commodity price inflation are still declining. Workers and their unions are still desperately afraid of losing jobs. Employers are scared of losing markets, and in many cases of going broke. Both are frightened of foreign competition. Changes in industrial structure and comparative advantage have hit particularly hard those industries and unions whose price and wage behaviour used to set extravagant patterns for a large part of the economy. So long as these benign conditions prevail, I think we should persist in gradually reducing the slack in the economy.

The situation today reminds me of the early 1960s. Two recessions in 1957–8 and 1960 had taken unemployment from around 4 per cent to 6 or 7 per cent and reduced inflation from a peak between 4 and 5 per cent in the mid 1950s to less than 2 per cent. Nevertheless, influential opinion in the Federal Reserve and elsewhere opposed measures to expand aggregate demand, on the grounds that they would be inflationary and that the increases in unemployment were structural rather than cyclical. These diagnoses and fears turned out to be groundless in the 1961–5 expansion, which lowered unemployment to 4 per cent without adding perceptibly to inflation. Although 4 per cent unemployment is not a realistic objective for aggregate demand policy now, we can surely lower the rate to 6 per cent or less.

The gains from completing the recovery and boosting the utilization of existing productive resources are insufficiently understood and appreciated. Unemployment is privation for those affected, often pushing them below the poverty line. Unemployment compensation does not make them whole, materially or psychologically. Most unemployed are not even eligible. But from a society-wide point of view, unemployment is a waste of productive resources, whether or not the individuals unemployed suffer hardships.

The unemployment rate is a convenient cyclical barometer of macroeconomic performance; production, capacity utilization, and income are all strongly negatively correlated with underutilization of labour. So is the overall incidence of poverty, far beyond the personal privations of those unemployed. Each point unemployment is lowered gains from 2 to 3 per cent of GNP, about $100 billion. Of that, some $40–50 billion would be saved by businesses, households, and governments—the federal deficit would go down by $25 billion—adding to domestic investment or diminishing overseas borrowing. No tax incentives or other supply-side nostrums could do as much for saving and investment. For this reason, the high employment commitment embodied in the Act of 1946 is important, indeed essential, for long-run growth.

DEMAND MANAGEMENT AND STRUCTURAL POLICIES

Why is unemployment so high at 'full employment?' That is, why is the inflation-safe unemployment rate so high? What explains its distressing and apparently inexorable upward drift these past twenty years? Perhaps the 'natural' rate is just a moving average of actual rates; perhaps the recessions engineered to cope with the inflationary shocks of the 1970s have left us an unpleasant legacy. Perhaps, as suggested above, the natural rate today is a lot lower than generally believed. Anyway, it is too high.

The time to fix the roof is when it is not raining. Structural unemployment, beyond the reach of macroeconomic demand policies, afflicts disproportionately certain vulnerable demographic groups, teenagers, young adults, minorities. Labour markets are very imperfectly competitive. The interests of unemployed outsiders are insufficiently represented in wage-setting decisions and negotiations, where the claims of insiders, senior job-holders, take excessive precedence. Prior to 1981, administrations and Congresses were at least concerned with these problems. They sought to ameliorate them by both labour market and wage–price policies, not very successfully to be sure. Those approaches are not fashionable today. But the problems are still there, and the issues will recur.

I suggest that this would be a good topic for major study by the Joint Economic Committee. The agenda could include a number of ideas how to lower the inflation-safe unemployment rate: improvements in public education; relaxation of minimum wage laws and other regulations that limit the downward flexibility of wages and prices; encouragement of labour contracts that relate wages to firms' revenues, profits, or labour productivity; penalizing by unemployment insurance surtaxes employers who raise wages while they are curtailing employment or while unemployment is high in their localities; annual economy-wide guideposts for wages and prices, with compliance induced by tax-based rewards and penalties.

DEMAND SIDE, SUPPLY SIDE

Clear thinking about macroeconomic policies requires distinction between aggregate demand and aggregate supply and between the effects of policies on demand and supply. Potential real GNP is the output the economy can produce with unemployment and capacity utilization at their inflation-safe rates. Its growth trend depends on the growth of productive resources, labour and capital, and on productivity-raising technological progress. Its level also depends, as noted above, on the amount of slack in the economy deemed necessary to contain inflation. Structural reforms, including 'supply-side' measures, may increase potential GNP and/or its growth rate. But experience suggests that such effects are small and slow, difficult to discern and predict. The sources of productivity growth are elusive; its decline in the 1970s remains a mystery to the leading students of the subject.

The supply-side measures of the 1980s have yet to bear fruit in potential GNP.

Actual real GNP fluctuates irregularly around the potential trend, generally in response to demand-side shocks or to policy-induced changes in aggregate demand. The two kinds of demand management policies available to the federal government are fiscal and monetary. Choices among the several fiscal and monetary instruments available may also affect potential GNP, in the future rather than contemporaneously. We must distinguish short-run demand stabilization from long-run growth in potential output, and sort out the effects of policies on these two goals.

FISCAL POLICY AS DEMAND MANAGEMENT

The sponsors of the Employment Act expected fiscal policy to be the main instrument of short-run demand management, and it was in fact actively used. In almost every recession prior to the most recent pair of 1979–82, fiscal stimulus, temporary or permanent, was deliberately applied to promote recovery. It took the form of extra purchases of goods and services (e.g. public works) or transfer payments (e.g. enlarged Social Security or unemployment benefits) or tax cuts. In 1964 income taxes were cut during a recovery, in order to keep it alive. On several occasions fiscal instruments were used to restrain aggregate demand during booms; taxes were increased sharply during the Korean War and belatedly during the Vietnam War.

Deliberate changes in budget programmes and revenue legislation, sometimes adopted in the interests of macroeconomic stabilization, are to be distinguished from the built-in automatic contributions of the federal budget to stability. Without programmatic or legislative actions, tax collections fall during recessions and rise during recoveries and booms; likewise certain expenditures, especially transfers to the unemployed, the poor, and other victims of hard times, move countercyclically. As a result, private purchasing power falls less than business activity in slumps and rises less in prosperities. Built-in stabilizers do not prevent or reverse cyclical swings, but they do reduce their amplitude.

The well-known counter-cyclical movements of federal budget deficits or surpluses are just the mirror image of the partial stabilization of private spending power. Large budget deficits have actually been passive symptoms of weakness in aggregate demand throughout the economy, rather than indicators of increased active fiscal stimulus. The 'high-employment budget deficit', now returned to popularity as the 'structural deficit', corrects for these cyclical effects, measuring what the budget outcome would be under existing programmes, entitlements, and tax codes if the economy were operating at a constant rate of utilization of potential output. Changes in this deficit (often a surplus in the past) are a fairly accurate measure of the changes in aggregate demand due to fiscal policy, whether for stabilization purposes or for other reasons.

The stronger are the built-in stabilizers, the less need there is to resort to discretionary changes in the structural budget in the interests of demand management. Presidents Kennedy and Johnson, seeking to reinforce the automatic stabilizers, proposed some semi-automatic triggers for altering certain taxes and expenditures for counter-cyclical stabilization, but Congress did not act upon their proposals.

The use of fiscal tools for demand management does not necessarily bias the federal budget either to chronically higher deficits or to chronically higher expenditures and taxes. It is true that the budget has been much bigger relative to the economy since World War II than before. This was due to the much larger permanent burdens of national and international security on the United States, and to the growth of Social Security, Medicare and Medicaid, and other transfer programmes. It is also true that the larger size of the budget, given that expenditures are stable or counter-cyclical and tax revenues are procyclical, both strengthened the built-in stabilizers and facilitated discretionary demand management. Until 1981 structural deficits were small, generally less than 1 per cent of potential GNP, and often negative. The public debt grew more slowly than the economy, falling from more than 100 per cent of GNP at the end of World War II to 25 per cent in the 1970s. The size and growth of the budget, expenditures and revenues both, raise political issues regarding the nation's priorities as between various public programmes and taxpayers' private interests. Those are quite separate from the uses of fiscal policies as instruments of macroeconomic management—functions that can be performed whether the federal budget is much larger or much smaller than it is today.

MONETARY POLICY AS DEMAND MANAGEMENT

Monetary policy, decided and executed by the Federal Reserve System, also operates on aggregate demand—though indirectly, by altering the availability and cost of credit to households, businesses, and state and local governments, by affecting the values of their existing assets and debts, nowadays by influencing the foreign exchange value of the dollar and the competitiveness of American products in world markets, and by influencing the expectations of economic actors about all these variables. In principle, within broad limits, anything that fiscal policy could do to aggregate demand monetary policy could also do, or undo. The two are substitutes for one another in demand management, although their side effects, including their implications for long-run growth of potential output, may be quite different. As policy instruments, they are also substitutes, in the sense that their settings are technically—and in the United States today also administratively and politically—independent. The Fed is not compelled to print money to finance government deficits; it is free to do the reverse, to monetize less public debt and tighten its policies when fiscal stimulus is strong.

The fact that the two kinds of policies are substitutes has an important implication that is insufficiently appreciated. In doses of equivalent effect on aggregate demand, fiscal and monetary policies have pretty close to identical effects on output relative to prices. The 'natural' rate limit to demand expansion remains about the same whether it is approached by monetary stimulus or fiscal stimulus. There is no way to twist the outcome more in favour of output and employment and against price and wage inflation by altering the mixture of monetary and fiscal dosages. In particular, in given circumstances of the economy there is nothing intrinsically more or less inflationary in monetary expansion than in equivalent fiscal stimulus. I will acknowledge one qualification to these propositions below, in discussing international implications of the fiscal–monetary mix, but the central point will stand.

Over the past forty years, particularly over the last fifteen, monetary policy has overtaken fiscal policy as the principal regulator of macro-economic performance. In the 1940s many Keynesian economists were, because of their reading of experience during the Great Depression, as sceptical of the potency of monetary measures as they were enthusiastic about the newfound potentials of fiscal management of aggregate demand. (They were misreading Keynes, in my opinion.) Until 1951, the Federal Reserve remained a prisoner of its wartime commitment to support federal securities prices at par; essentially there could be no independent monetary policy with interest rates thus frozen. Even after the Fed's liberation by the Accord of 1951, its strategy of 'leaning against' the cyclical winds was more a monetary built-in stabilizer than an active control of the economy. In the 1960s, and especially in the 1970s under the influence of monetarist critics, the Fed assumed a more active and independent role. The Fed is, after all, well positioned to be the major arbiter of macroeconomic developments. The Federal Open Market Committee has ten or more moves a year to the Congressional budget-makers' one.

THE DECLINE AND FALL OF COMPENSATORY FISCAL POLICY

In the past forty years discretionary active fiscal policy has fallen in the esteem of both policy makers and economists. Lags in decision making and implementation meant that expenditure changes, and even tax and transfer changes, were likely to take effect too late to do their intended good, and might even do harm. New theories, stressing the importance of expectations in the behaviour of consumers and businessmen, questioned the effectiveness of temporary fiscal measures. For example, the temporary income tax surcharges President Johnson belatedly persuaded Congress to pass in 1968 were judged to have disappointingly small effects on taxpayers' spending. The increasing complexity of the annual budget-making process in Congress in the 1970s produced delays that diluted the value of the macroeconomic considerations involved in the decisions. This was unfortunate and ironic, coming at the same time as procedural reforms designed to enhance the rationality of budget making by requiring Congress to decide consciously on the budget as a whole and by providing members of Congress via its new Budget Office better independent economic and budgetary intelligence than they ever had before.

At the same time, the grip of monetary policy on the economy was strengthening. As the Federal Reserve drifted towards monetarism and geared its policy to announced targets for growth of monetary aggregates, its policy was leaning much harder against all winds and was less accommodative to fiscal stimuli. The structure of the financial system became more monetarist too. The velocity of money became less responsive to interest rates, for several reasons. When nominal interest rates are high, businesses and households have strong incentives to economize their holdings of cash, irrespective of marginal changes in interest rates. Together with banks, they also have strong incentives to arrange *de facto* interest payments on their deposits, including transactions accounts. Now previous legal limits on interest payments to depositors are well on the way out.

However, the greatest blow to the use of fiscal policy in demand management came with the Reagan Administration's budgets beginning in 1981. Drastic tax cuts plus rapid build-up of defence spending, incompletely offset by cuts in civilian expenditures, generated deficits, actual and structural, far larger relative to the economy than in any previous peacetime experience. Federal debt rose to about 40 per cent of GNP in four years.

The Reagan budgetary programmes, as they were phased in over several years, were heavy stimuli to aggregate demand during the recovery that began in late 1982. This was counter-cyclical fiscal policy with a vengeance. Of course, it was serendipitous; the Administration officially scorned Keynesian ideas of demand management. The Reagan budgets had two quite different motivations. One was supply-side confidence that cuts in tax rates would tap vast reservoirs of work effort, saving, and enterprise, and thus greatly speed the growth of the economy and even balance the budget. Even if successful, this strategy had more to do with long-run potential GNP than with short-run demand-side recovery. The second was a political strategy designed to achieve the Administration's prime ideological goal, the shrinking of civilian government: cut taxes, then use the public outcry against the resulting deficits to bludgeon Congress into cutting non-defence spending.

The Gramm–Rudman 'solution' to the nation's deficit problem does not restore fiscal policy to effective partnership in demand management. On the contrary, it is likely to be the *coup de grace*— if it really takes effect, and at least as long as it lasts. Of course, it was already true that the sheer magnitude of the structural deficits ruled out counter-cyclical fiscal policy for all practical purposes; certainly any extra fiscal stimulus to combat recession is now unthinkable. Gramm–Rudman not only formalizes that incapacity but makes matters worse. In case weakness of the economy adds to prospective deficits, the legislation mandates additional expenditure cuts to meet the prescribed schedule for reduction of the deficit (actual, not structural). Such cuts would tend to make the economy weaker still. Thus the built-in fiscal stabilizers that served us well for forty years are to be replaced by mandatory destabilizers. There are, to be sure, some escape hatches in the law, but they are inadequate to prevent the perverse responses just described.

Over the foreseeable future, therefore, Federal Reserve monetary policy will be macroeconomic policy. Without built-in and discretionary fiscal stabilizers, the monetary authorities will have to act more boldly to preserve stability in the face of the inevitable surprises. Fortunately, since its policy shift in 1982, the Fed has become quite pragmatic.

In the 1970s, and especially in the three years after October 1979, the Fed imposed upon itself targets for the growth of intermediate monetary aggregates, *M-1*, *M-2*, and so on. Having staked its credibility to the financial markets on the realization of these targets, the Fed was reluctant to deviate from them even when adherence to them had unintended and unwelcome macroeconomic consequences. This dilemma became acute and dangerous in 1982, when an unanticipated and persistent decline in the velocity of money meant that sticking to the targets implied a further severe decline in nominal and real GNP. Eventually Paul Volcker and his colleagues chose the economy over *M-1*, to universal relief and with no loss of credibility. That policy shift turned the economy from recession to recovery, and since then Fed policy has been oriented more to macroeconomic performance as measured by variables that really matter—GNP, prices, exchange rates, interest rates—than to money stock growth targets. The Fed has recognized that velocity is volatile, the more so because of recent institutional, technological, and regulatory changes, and is prepared to adjust money growth to compensate for persistent velocity changes even if it requires transgressing and revising its *M* targets.

The Fed has, it is true, allowed the economy to stagnate over the last year and a half, but that seems to reflect its macroeconomic judgement rather than its concern for money stock targets *per se*. The corollary is that the Congress should make its own judgements about the desirable paths of real GNP and unemployment, and convey them to the Federal Reserve. After all, these are the most important economic decisions the federal government makes. Responsible elected officials should not evade them. Twice a year the Federal Reserve reports to Congressional committees its monetary targets for the coming quarters and its 'projections' for GNP, prices, and unemployment. Since the Fed has been shifting emphasis to macroeconomic performance and downgrading money stock growth, these projections can be interpreted as its basic targets. The committees should take them seriously in the hearings, both *ex ante* and *ex post*. (The economy fell short of the Fed's February and July projections for GNP in the second half of 1985.)

The immediate challenge is the transition to a tighter fiscal stance and to a better policy mix. It should not be allowed to bring on recession or prolong stagnation. If fiscal policy is about to be tightened severely, by Gramm–Rudman or by normal legislative process, the Fed should lower interest rates significantly, even if this requires unusually high money growth during the transition. If so, and only if so, will we reap the benefits of an improved mix of fiscal and monetary policy.

THE MONETARY–FISCAL MIX TODAY AND TOMORROW

Reaganomic fiscal policy led to an extreme monetary–fiscal mix, beyond feasible sustainable limits. Even while slack remained in the economy these past three years, the Federal Reserve felt it necessary from time to time to contain the speed of recovery propelled by massive fiscal stimulus. Thus real interest rates, even after-tax rates on US Treasury obligations, which had been elevated sky-high during the Fed's recessionary anti-inflation crusade after 1979–82, remained above the economy's long-run growth rate after the Fed shifted gears to recovery. This constellation is a recipe for unending and accelerating growth in ratios of federal deficits and debts to GNP. The high net interest costs of the debt alone guarantee such instability, which is of course accentuated by a 'primary' deficit (that is, on transactions unrelated to existing debt) of about $2\frac{1}{2}$ per cent of GNP. Although the 40 per cent debt/GNP ratio already reached is not itself disastrous, runaway growth of that ratio is not a viable long-run future.

As I stressed above, the same total dose of demand stimulus can be given in various mixtures of monetary and fiscal medicine. The short-run consequences for output, employment, and prices will be very much the same. Important side effects will be different. The principal differences are in the uses of national output, in particular the relative shares of private and public consumption, on the one hand, and real investment, on the other—to put it more basically, the relative shares of present- and future-oriented economic activities. Generally speaking, a loose-fiscal–tight-money policy mix, of which the 1980s present an extreme example, encourages present consumption relative to investment for the future.

I should at this point interject some caveats regarding the identification of future-oriented, growth-oriented, policy with tight budgets. Some deficit-increasing expenditures are future-oriented, for example public investments in infrastructure, research, education, and environmental protection. It would be silly to cut these out in blind ideological belief that only private capital formation matters to the future productivity of the economy. Those outlays should be considered on their merits, weighed against shopping centres and casinos in the private sector as well as against robots and computers. Robert Eisner is right about this, and the JEC could take the lead in insisting on capital accounting for the public sector in the United States, about the only civilized country where it is not done. Moreover, some deficit-increasing tax reductions increase private investment instead of, or along with, private consumption. Careful attention to the content of government budgets is essential to appraise the effects of particular fiscal–monetary mixes. These caveats do not, however, save the United States policy mix of recent years from the charge that it has been pro-consumption and anti-growth.

Comparing the year 1984 with 1978, the last preceding year of normal prosperity, I find that fully 97 per cent of the growth of real final sales (GNP less inventory investment) was destined for private consumption or government purchases of goods and services. The Reagan macroeconomic strategy failed completely in its objective of tilting the disposition of national output toward private investment in the interests of speeding up productivity growth. While increased domestic fixed investment did amount to about 23 per cent of the increment of real GNP, this was almost completely offset by the decline in Americans' foreign investment, that is, our net exports. Domestic capital formation mortgaged to foreigners will not benefit our children and our children's children.

While the tax legislation of 1981 (modified in 1982) gave incentives for private saving and investment, its immediate and direct effect was to add massively to the government's dissaving. The second effect swamped the first. Anyway, there is no evidence that the tax cuts enhanced households' propensity to save. Although new tax incentives may have helped revive business investment in 1983 and 1984—this too is debatable—high real interest rates worked the other way, especially on residential construction, which did not enjoy similar concessions.

The same recovery could have been engineered with much less fiscal stimulus, with deficits in the normal range of postwar experience, and with real interest rates several hundred basis points lower. There would have been more domestic investment and much more foreign investment; we would not have the large trade deficits that have crippled American manufacturing and agriculture.

These international implications of United States macroeconomic policies have been the most surprising and disturbing feature of recent experience. Although they corresponded qualitatively to economists' textbooks, we too were unprepared for their magnitudes. There is a powerful new mechanism by which high interest rates reduce demand for goods and services. It is a product of the regime of floating exchange rates, which replaced the Bretton Woods system of fixed parities in 1971–3, combined with the high international mobility of interest-sensitive funds, free of exchange controls, passing through worldwide markets of marvellous technical efficiency. In the 1980s high US interest attracted funds into dollars, appreciated the exchange value of the dollar, and made American goods uncompetitive at home and abroad. The excess of imports over exports (3 per cent of GNP) has become a major drag on aggregate demand and the source of counter-productive political pressures for protectionism.

At the same time, dollar prices of goods with unchanged foreign currency prices fell; since these have some weight in American price indexes, the appreciation of the dollar assisted our disinflation—accounting for perhaps 10 per cent of the decline in the Consumer Price Index from 1980 to 1984. This effect is an exception to the rule I stated above, that for given impact on aggregate demand the mix of outcomes between prices and quantities is independent of the mix of demand management policies. A loose-fiscal–tight-money mix does yield somewhat lower prices for the same output. However, this gain accrues only to the one country pursuing the policy. Our trading partners suffered extra temporary inflation because of the appreciation of the dollar, which inflicted on them higher local prices for goods (including oil wherever produced) invoiced in dollars. For the same reason, we will not be able to keep those disinflationary gains of recent years related to the appreciation of our currency. As the dollar depreciates and restores some of our lost competitiveness in world markets, we will have to pay back the disinflation we borrowed from our friends overseas. Consequently, the exception to the rule is not, in my opinion, a weighty justification for the bizarre policy mix the United States drifted into during this decade.

SUMMARY AND CONCLUSION

1. The objectives of the Employment Act should be restored to high priority in federal economic policy. It is high time to break the dismal upward trend of unemployment. The climate is favourable; the stagflationary shocks of the 1970s are behind us. Stagnation at 7 per cent unemployment is overcautious when no signs of inflationary pressure, either from wage costs or from demand, are visible. So long as these benign conditions obtain, federal demand management policies should aim gradually to reduce the unemployment and excess capacity rates. Under present circumstances, this task falls to Federal Reserve monetary policy.

2. Since 1982 the Fed has been gearing its policies less to money stock targets and more to macroeconomic performance. Its semi-annual projections of GNP can be taken as indicators of its desired path for the economy. Congress should welcome and reinforce this trend, make its own targets for the economy known to the Fed, and hold the Fed responsible for macroeconomic performance, as measured by variables that really matter: GNP growth, prices, unemployment.

3. The inflation-safe unemployment rate, though surely significantly lower than the current rate, can only be estimated with further experience in today's environment, and even then with uncertainty. It

is probably too high for the nation's economic health. Structural policies and reforms will be needed to make it possible for demand management policies to aim at lower rates of unemployment. These have to do with government regulations, labour and product markets, wage- and price-setting institutions. The JEC has an opportunity to contribute to the design of such structural changes. The time to fix the roof is when it is not raining.

4. The tight anti-inflationary monetary stance of 1979–82 and the Reaganomic fiscal programmes from 1981 on have given the United States an unprecedented, extreme, and bizarre mix of demand management policies. The tight-money–easy-budget combination is not viable in the long run. It results in real interest rates on public debt higher than the sustainable growth rate of the economy. This is a recipe for unending rise in the debt-to-GNP ratio, especially because the primary budget is also in deficit. The policy mix runs counter to long-run growth because it encourages present-oriented uses of GNP relative to future oriented ones. The mix has resulted in a large current account deficit in US international transactions, that is, in massive net borrowing from the rest of the world. Although the appreciation of the dollar bought us some extra disinflation, it was borrowed from our trading partners and will have to be repaid eventually. The temporary disinflationary gains do not justify our policy mix, nor should their reversal deter us from moving to a more normal and better mix or from completing our presently stalled recovery. A tighter-fiscal and easier-money mix will lower interest rates, depreciate the dollar, and improve the competitiveness of American industry and agriculture. It will also be better for long-run growth. All these consequences are to be welcomed.

5. Fiscal policy, once the mainstay of demand stabilization, is now the junior partner of monetary policy. The extreme size of current and prospective budget deficits, actual and structural, rule budgetary changes out as counter-cyclical tools. The Gramm–Rudman remedy is almost worse than the disease, since it mandates perverse pro-cyclical movements in fiscal stimulus. The Federal Reserve will need to be active and bold in order to keep the economy free of recession during the transition to tighter fiscal policy, *a fortiori* to complete the recovery and sustain growth.

6. Once the transition is made, there is good reason for optimism that the rest of the century can be one of stability and growth, the more so if pragmatic realism is substituted for ideology in the management of the economy. As an aged veteran soldier of the cause of the Employment Act, I am unavoidably dismayed by the wholesale

dismissal on all sides of pre-1980 ideas and policies. I look forward to the day when some of the forgotten 'oldie goldies' will be rediscovered and hailed as 'new'.

4 On the Theoretical Foundations of Keynesian Economics*
(Comment on Lord Kaldor's 'Keynesian Economics after Fifty Years')

I deeply appreciate the honour of participating in this celebration, especially because I cut my teeth on the *General Theory*. A Harvard sophomore all of eighteen years, I was just beginning study of economics when my young tutor said 'Here's a new book, maybe quite important, just published in England. Let's you and I read it for tutorial this year.' Not knowing enough to be properly scared, I plunged in. It was an exciting time in that Cambridge too; the contagion spread to undergraduates. Here was an intellectual revolution challenging encrusted and irrelevant orthodoxy, opening intriguing avenues for young minds, and promising to save the world.

Thanks to that initiation, I spent a large part of my career on Keynesian economics—trying to tidy it up and provide more solid foundations for key equations, giving it empirical content, applying it in policy, teaching it, and defending it against infidels. Much of my work was critical of Keynes in detail, but I think it was faithful in spirit. Though I dislike being pigeon-holed, I wear the label Keynesian with pride, especially nowadays.

Discussing Nicky Kaldor's paper is a particular honour. From my student days on, I learned from every article of his I read; there were many, and many more I should have read. I learned even when I disagreed. In those cases I later found deeper messages that had escaped me at first, an experience also common in reading Keynes. Kaldor, like Keynes, has combined imaginative and perceptive theorizing, intense concern for real world events, and resourceful contributions to public policy. His paper today, like his extensive testimony to the

*July 1983, Keynes Centenary, Kings College, Cambridge. Published in David Worswick and James Trevithick, editors, *Keynes and the Modern World*, Cambridge: University Press, 1984, pp. 28–37. New title.

Select Parliamentary Committee, shows how he just keeps rollin' along.

Keynesian economics has been suffering hard times, both in the public arena and in the economics profession. Stagflation, misread to discredit Keynesian theories and policies, is an obvious reason. It has intensified professional scepticism of long standing. Kaldor's paper refers to the chronic professional turbulence about the *General Theory*, and I take this as my topic also.

Why all this turbulence? he asks. Basically, I think, it stems from the evident discrepancy between Keynes's propositions and the theoretical paradigm central to our discipline. That is the theory of general competitive equilibrium, in which rational individuals optimize and markets for all commodities are simultaneously cleared by prices. In the Walrasian model no lapses from full employment, let alone permanent equilibria with excess supplies, can occur.

This construction, for sociological and psychological reasons that I will not elaborate, has a powerful fascination for the best analytical minds attracted to our discipline, especially those of post-Depression vintage. Theorists whose trained instincts lead them to presume that the Invisible Hand really works cannot credit the massive market failures alleged by the *General Theory*. They presume instead that Keynesian propositions rest on attribution of irrational behaviour to economic agents—for example, money illusion or misperception of government policy—and accordingly dismiss them.

The so-called neoclassical synthesis of earlier postwar decades never effected a complete reconciliation. In recent years of disillusionment with government interventions of all kinds, faith in the optimality of 'market solutions' solidified. Scepticism of the 'microfoundations' of macroeconomics grew, and heavier burdens of proof were loaded on allegations of market failures. Modern classical theorists bring to the fray more powerful ammunition than Keynes's classical targets and opponents of five decades ago.

Keynes did indeed allege massive systemic market failure, orders of magnitude more serious than the items in the standard welfare economics catalogue of exceptions to the optimality of market outcomes. According to Keynes, interconnected failures occur both in labour markets and in capital markets. I condense and paraphrase. Workers are unemployed even though they are willing to work for real wages no greater than their marginal productivities, and even though they and their employers would willingly buy the products of their labour if the capital markets correctly matched interest rates to intertemporal preferences.

General equilibrium theory itself has been refined and elaborated in the years since the *General Theory* appeared. Walras's conjectures have been rigorously proved, but with considerable sacrifice of their applicability. As a succession of notable theorists—Wald, Arrow, and Debreu are important names—made Walras's vision rigorous, they had to introduce restrictive assumptions that made the Invisible Hand less reliable than Smith or Walras or Marshall or Pigou or Hayek thought. It is easier now than it was for Keynes in 1936 to describe in the language of the paradigm itself the sources of his alleged market failures. Yet even if, as Kaldor says, Keynes was no student of Walras, he understood surprisingly well his own heresies.

Keynesian market failures may be ascribed to several complementary sources: (1) the incompleteness of markets, in particular the absence of most 'Arrow–Debreu' markets for future and contingent deliveries; (2) the intrinsic indeterminacy of the expectations on which agents must act in the absence of those markets; (3) the essential non-neutrality of money, which indeed would have no function in a full Walras–Arrow–Debreu world; (4) interdependence among individuals in utilities or preferences, a phenomenon arbitrarily excluded from individualistic general equilibrium models; and (5) imperfections of competition, such that many agents are not price takers but price makers.

Keynes was quite explicit about all of these except the fifth. Kaldor makes that last one, imperfect competition, the sole genesis of macroeconomic difficulties. Pure competition implies full employment equilibrium, he says, while imperfect competition implies Keynesian macroeconomics. He therefore blames Keynes for failing to see, or at least to say clearly, that his General Theory requires microfoundations encompassing increasing returns to scale and consequently monopoly, oligopoly, or monopolistic competition.

Why did Keynes not exploit the microeconomic revolution fomented by his own colleagues and disciples in the same years he was revolutionizing macroeconomics? That certainly is a puzzle, as Kaldor says. To try to win the game on the other side's home field and with their book of rules was a mistake. But faithful neoclassicals on both sides of the Atlantic had no compunctions in dismissing imperfect competition from microeconomic theory as a trivial exception proving the rule of pure competition. They probably would not have found Keynes's macroeconomics any more appealing if he had based it on imperfect competition. I agree with Kaldor that imperfections of competition are necessary at some stages of Keynes's argument; I am not sure they are sufficient. Anyway, the other four departures from modern Walrasian conditions are also essential, and I suspect sufficient to generate some kind of macro difficulties even if all extant markets were properly flexprice-cleared.

Kaldor admiringly cites Martin Weitzman's observation that constant returns to scale implies that any unemployed worker can employ himself by replicating in microcosm the economy from which he has been excluded. This shows, according to Kaldor and Weitzman, that increasing returns technology is a necessary condition of unemployment. But doesn't the unemployed worker need the other factors of production? And if he has the wealth or credit to obtain their services, what prevents the unemployed from likewise establishing individually or collectively enterprises with U-shaped cost curves in industries with either homogeneous or differentiated products?

Weitzman's construction is one of a number of ingenious non-Walrasian parables in the current literature. They have the virtue of showing how Keynes-like problems can arise among rational optimizing agents. They generally show how an economy may get stuck in an inferior member of a family of equilibria. But these stories are usually told wholly in terms of real variables, and in my opinion miss the essential monetary and intertemporal features of macroeconomics.

I return to the four items in the above list which, I argue, are reasonably explicit in the *General Theory*. On the first, the absence of markets for most future and contingent commodities, it is sufficient to quote Keynes:

An act of individual saving means—so to speak—a decision not to have dinner today. But it does *not* necessitate a decision to have dinner or to buy a pair of boots a week hence or a year hence or to consume any specified thing at any specified date. Thus it depresses the business of preparing today's dinner without stimulating the business of making ready for some future act of consumption. It is not a substitution of future consumption-demand for present consumption-demand—it is a net diminution of such demand ... If saving consisted not merely in abstaining from present consumption but in placing simultaneously a specific order for future consumption, the effect might indeed be different. For in that case the expectation of some future yield from investment would be improved, and the resources released from preparing for present consumption would be turned over to preparing for the future consumption.

The trouble arises, therefore, because the act of saving implies, not a substitution for present consumption of some specific additional consumption which requires for its preparation just as much immediate economic activity as would have been required by present consumption equal in value to the sum saved, but a desire for 'wealth' as such, that is for a potentiality of consuming an unspecified article at an unspecified time.

The non-neutrality of money has two dimensions in Keynes:

1. Prices are generally quoted, whether in organized markets or by

price makers and negotiators, in the society's nominal unit of account. So are numerous financial assets and debts—there are well-developed futures markets for currency. This is a natural feature of a monetary economy, for it enables the society to reap the 'public good' fruits of using a common unit of account. But it does contribute to inertia in nominal wealth holdings and debts, and if prices are themselves decision variables for individual agents, to inertia in nominal price paths.

2. Money and other nominally denominated assets are imperfect substitutes for other stores of value, including real goods. The stocks of money and other nominal assets, inside and outside, and the expectations of their real rates of return, affect demands for commodities for consumption and investment. The so-called classical dichotomy is a misleading guide to monetary analysis and policy. It certainly cannot apply to conventional central bank operations or to the asset exchanges by which commercial banks and other financial institutions alter the volume of deposits. These are not equivalent to simple and universal changes in the unit of account; they do not alter proportionately all existing individual positions with respect to present and future money.

Keynes stressed the incalculable uncertainties of returns to long-term investments, and the consequent element of exogeneity in the states of business confidence—'animal spirits'—that drive capital investment. The point has long been rightly emphasized in Cambridge, England, notably by Joan Robinson and Kaldor. I think it was not sufficiently acknowledged across the Atlantic. Two uncertainties are involved. One concerns future demands for and earnings from specific capital goods now put in place, as indicated in the quotation above. The other concerns asset prices. What savers are willing to pay for assets today depends on their guesses of what future buyers will pay them, which in turn depends on their guesses, etc. Bubble phenomena are endemic and epidemic. Keynes's discussion has a modern ring. Consider the current vogue of overlapping generation models, where each generation, in order to consume in retirement, must sell its assets to the next. Recent statistical studies, moreover, find that stock and bond prices are much more volatile than justified by the variability of pay-outs.[1]

Although Keynes, like modern classical macroeconomists, saw the importance of expectations, he would dissent from their faith that 'rational' expectations can take the place of the missing markets. This is a principal reason why in Keynesian economics, in contrast to monetarism old and new, exogenous demand shocks are an important source of business fluctuations, why instability does not arise solely from erratic government policy, and why there is opportunity and need for compensatory demand management. As Kaldor emphasizes, moreover, growth in potential supply does not automatically generate the demand to purchase it.

I included interdependence of utilities as the fourth item in my list because of the role it plays in Keynesian wage theory, which I discuss below. Some hint of it may also be detected in Keynes's propensity to consume, which he regarded as a social–psychological phenomenon rather than a simple aggregation of individual behaviours. General equilibrium models conventionally stick to individualism, because externalities in preferences or technologies are analytically inconvenient. But rationality does not exclude dependence of one consumer's preferences on the actual consumptions of others.

Why are labour markets not always cleared by wages? Keynes begins the *General Theory* with this central question. His answer is usually interpreted to depend on an *ad hoc* nominal rigidity or stickiness in nominal wages, and thus to attribute to workers irrational 'money illusion'. This interpretation, for which sympathetic expositors of Keynes bear no little responsibility, is the main reason neoclassical theorists reject Keynesian macroeconomics.

I now think, however, that Keynes provides a theory free of this taint. At least he almost does, and the gap can be filled with the help of Kaldor's recommendation of attention to non-competitive elements in labour and product markets. This is not to say that a permanent equilibrium with involuntary unemployment can be proved. That is not an important operational issue. It is enough that inertia in nominal wage and price paths last long enough for unemployment to be a serious social problem and a costly economic waste, and for demand management policies to work.

The several elements in such a theory are these:

1. Wages are set or bargained in the nominal unit of account. As Keynes was aware, things would be different if they were set in terms of commodities labour produces or fully indexed to consumer goods prices.
2. Wage setting is decentralized.
3. Workers are principally concerned with relative wages—here enters interdependence of utilities. An economy-wide increase in prices reduces all real wages proportionately, and that makes it more acceptable to every group of workers than a local reduction in their money wages, which they perceive as damaging their

relative position. Evidence accumulated in labour economics strongly supports Keynes's observation of the crucial importance of relative wages.

These three assumptions together explain, without resort to any 'money illusion' at all, why it is easier, as Keynes saw as early as his criticism of Mr. Churchill's return to the old gold parity, to lower real wages by raising prices than by lowering money wages. The argument is perfectly clear in the *General Theory*. I don't know why it is so widely ignored.

But the argument is not complete. The three assumptions do not explain why unemployed workers would not prefer jobs at lower relative money and real wages to idleness, or why employers would not hire them or threaten to hire them in place of relative-wage-conscious employees. This would happen if labour markets were competitive wage-auction markets. In fact, another well-established finding of labour economists is that queues at factory gates have little direct effect on wages paid inside. Wage patterns do not give way until employers are in such financial straits that insiders' jobs are credibly in jeopardy. But for the power of the insiders we need explanations that Keynes did not provide, except for hints that he really had in mind wage-setting mechanisms other than auction markets.

Kaldor informs us of Keynes's interesting distinction between an 'entrepreneur economy' and a 'cooperative economy'. The former is characterized by large-scale production units hiring large numbers of wage labourers. That implies wage scales which are decision or negotiation variables—that already gives them inertia. Furthermore, workers are not hired or rehired daily but with mutual expectations of continuity. Trained on the job, they acquire individually and, I stress, collectively firm-specific human capital. Heavy turnover disrupts teamwork and damages productive efficiency. Inside workers can exploit this fact even without union organization or the threat of unionization—better with than without. Whether by contract or by unilateral decision of the employer, periodic revision of wage scales always involves implicitly or explicitly negotiation with existing employees. In this way increasing returns to scale and non-competitive features of 'markets' are the missing but essential ingredients of Keynes's theory of nominal wage inertia.

The case can be further strengthened by noting the prevalence of non-competitive average-cost-based pricing of products. These prices too are made, not taken, and here too a case can be made for rationality of behaviour apparently deviant from Walrasian assumptions. For example, oligopolistic rivals cannot know for sure whether a drop in sales or orders is local or sectoral or economy-wide (a type of confusion Robert Lucas, the leading new classical theorist, exploits in a different context). The rivals therefore are reluctant to cut margins and prices for fear of triggering price warfare. Their behaviour in turn strengthens labour's resistance to wage cuts.

Excess capital capacity, highly correlated with unemployment of labour, is a problem for equilibrium theorists. They can scarcely argue that machines and plants are unemployed because they prefer job search or the dole. It could be argued that technological complementarity idles capacity whenever employment falls for whatever reason. But factor substitutability, usually assumed in neoclassical models, is frequently feasible. Entrepreneurs expecting fluctuations in labour supplies and real wages would plan installations to allow such substitutions. Keynes worried about this problem in his appendix on marginal user cost. His idea was that entrepreneurs would keep capacity idle in bad times because using it would impair its productivity in a more remunerative future. This was not a convincing resolution of a puzzle he trapped himself into by insisting on competitive product markets where firms continuously equate price and marginal cost.

Keynes's theory of wages and unemployment involved a second argument, the proposition that downward flexibility of money wages would not in any case eliminate unemployment due to deficiency of aggregate demand. Product prices would just chase wages down, and no incentive to expand output and employment would arise. The standard criticism has been that this is true, as Keynes himself appears to admit later in the book, only in the liquidity trap—and not even then if the Pigou–Patinkin real balance effect works. The latter is dubious: differences in marginal propensities to consume from wealth between debtors and creditors could swamp the stimulus of increased real value of base money and public debt. More important in practice, the very process of deflation or disinflation may, as Keynes observed, move demands for commodities and labour perversely—a destabilizing effect that can occur even if nominal interest rates have plenty of room to fall. It is no accident that even in the good old days when agriculture unsuccoured by governments was the main industry and occupation, when prices and wages were much more flexible, deflationary times were hard times.

Once it is recognized that for whatever reason money wages and prices cannot and do not continuously clear markets, then some substitute or supplementary mechanism of equating demand and supply must come into play. A great contribution of the *General Theory*, foreshadowed of course by Richard Kahn, was recognition that quantity adjustments will play this role, and development of the calculus of quantity adjustment for the system as a whole. Recent rediscovery by mathematical economists under the label 'disequilibrium theory' adds precious little of macroeconomic significance to what Keynes and Keynesians long knew. Keynes's principle of effective demand says it all quite clearly: your demand is constrained by what you actually can sell, not determined by what you would like to sell and buy at prevailing prices. Walrasian critics to the contrary, it was not a vulgar mistake for Keynes to relate consumption to realized income rather than to wage rates and prices.

I agree with most of what Kaldor says concerning the 'monetarist counter-assault'. It was indeed a tactical mistake for Keynes and Keynesians to acquiesce, uncritically and inadvertently, in the formulation that the stock of money M is an exogenous policy-determined variable. It was especially a mistake when M was identified empirically with aggregates consisting largely of 'inside' money, and when central banks themselves were not playing by monetarist rules but were 'leaning against the wind'. It was also clearly a mistake for open economies committed to fixed exchange parities. Endogeneity of M's explained many of the pseudo-reduced-form correlations that helped to popularize Milton Friedman's monetarism. But perhaps more than Kaldor realizes, the mistakes were corrected and his points made in the debates on monetarism in the United States in the 1960s.

I interject here a Keynesian point of practical relevance in the 1930s, and quite possibly today. It relates to asymmetries of expectations and perceived risks as between savers and investors, lenders and borrowers. Keynes would not have approved the current fashion of models where all agents are identical in tastes, expectations, and circumstances (except for age in some models). They leave unexplained the great bulk of daily transactions on financial markets. He was worried that lenders' expectations of restoration of 'normal' interest rates would keep long rates high in the depression, whereas borrowers had no equivalent expectations of normal earnings to justify borrowing and investing at such rates. At the time short rates were so close to zero that monetary authorities could not bring further downward pressure on long rates via short rates. But I have the impression that Keynes regarded lenders' expectations and fears as an obstacle to recovery independent of the floor to short rates. A similar asymmetry of expectations appears to be an obstacle to recovery now, in the United States anyway, intensified by lenders' fears that expansionary monetary measures spell future inflation and by the central banks' fears of those fears.

The interest-elasticity of the demand for money was, I think, not as irrelevant to the monetarist debates as Kaldor says. It is the shape of the Hicksian *LM* curve that matters, for the effects of fiscal policies and the responses of the economy to real demand shocks and to financial shocks. The shape depends jointly on the interest-elasticities of money demands and supplies; supply elasticities depend both on the behaviour of depository institutions and on the policies of central banks. I do agree, however, that this aspect of the monetarist–Keynesian debate is less crucial than the questions of unemployment, inflation, and demand management to which most of Kaldor's paper and my discussion are addressed.

On the compatibility of full employment and price stability Kaldor leaves us up in the air when he says, 'The solution ... may require far-reaching changes in the institutional arrangements concerning the division of the national product between the different groups and classes ...'. Earlier he quotes a stronger statement to the same effect published in *The Times* of London in 1943 and generally attributed to Joan Robinson. This is still the major dilemma of policy. As any economics student can expatiate in an exam paper, incomes policies entail distortions and deadweight losses. But those have to be weighed against the social costs of the massive market failures to which Keynes and Keynesian economics call attention.

As positive theory, Keynesian macroeconomics has one immense advantage over its old and new classical rivals: it can explain, and they cannot, the main repeatedly observed characteristics of business fluctuations. As guide to policy, Keynesian macroeconomics can claim considerable credit for the successful performance of capitalism since World War II. Keynesian ideas will survive the counter-revolutions. The synthesis that emerges from their challenges will, I expect, be more theoretically acceptable to the profession than the earlier 'neoclassical synthesis'. The crisis in economic theory is as much one of microeconomics as of macroeconomics, and it will have to be resolved by systematic rebuilding on non-Walrasian foundations.

NOTE

1. *See* Chapter 26.

5 Patinkin on Keynes's Monetary Thought*

It is a truly amazing story. He was a renowned teacher, scholar, and writer, an influential commentator on world affairs, an expert always consulted by his government, an intellectual active in partisan politics, a successful operator in business and finance, and much more. At the age of forty-seven, he had just published his *magnum opus*, a two-volume treatise setting forth his mature conclusions on the entire range of his scientific expertise. The eagerly awaited work excited great interest in his profession, but considerable criticism too. The author himself was dissatisfied. Even before the ink was dry, he was changing his mind and working on the sequel. This task became a corporate enterprise, engaging not only the critical wisdom of his peers but the loyal enthusiasm of one of the most remarkable concentrations of talented young scholars in academic history. Seminars and lectures quickly turned from glosses on the completed work to draft chapters of the new. Over five years of constant conversation and correspondence, the master, his young disciples, and selected critics, friendly and not so friendly, argued out the new doctrines. He and his disciples never doubted they were at last figuring out how the world really works, solving puzzles that had stumped their predecessors for a century. They did not rely on experimental findings, statistical inference, historical study, or mathematical innovation, but on sheer logic and insight. Their parochial confidence that truths worth knowing arose inside a circle of a forty-mile radius would have been ridiculous arrogance had it not been so nearly justified. Finally, the new book appeared and wrought the revolution its makers anticipated, not only commanding the attention of the profession worldwide for decades to come, but profoundly influencing the policies and politics of nations.

The two books were, of course, Keynes's *Treatise on Money* (1930)

*February 1981, *Journal of Political Economy*, vol. 89, no. 1, pp. 204–7. Review of Don Patinkin, *Keynes's Monetary Thought: A Review of Its Development*, Durham, NC: Duke University Press, 1976.

and his *General Theory* (1936). The publication of *The Collected Writings of John Maynard Keynes* by the Royal Economic Society makes available many details of the story, and more are accessible in unpublished documents among the Keynes Papers in the Marshall Library at Cambridge. It is the good fortune of the profession that a great monetary theorist, Don Patinkin, has undertaken active research in the history of monetary theory and in particular on Keynes. In the brief volume under review he traces Keynes's monetary and macroeconomic thought through his three major works, beginning with the *Tract on Monetary Reform* (1923), stressing the story sketched above of the two later books. Keynes's multiple roles in science and public life make for an engrossing case study of the interactions of theoretical developments with the events, problems, and policy controversies of the times. The intellectual and personal relationships of Keynes to his older colleagues (Pigou, Robertson, Hawtrey, Hayek), to his young disciples at Cambridge (Kahn, Joan Robinson, Austin Robinson, Sraffa) and at Oxford (Harrod, Meade), and to others (including Kaldor, Lerner, Myrdal, Ohlin, Hicks) are a fascinating episode in the sociology of scholarship. Patinkin's concise narratives whet the appetite, and he refers us to works by Winch, Moggridge, and Howson for full meals.

Here Patinkin's main emphasis is on theory. He clearly explains and compares propositions of the three books and related articles, and he seeks reasons for the changes. Most readers will be particularly interested in Patinkin's views of what Keynes 'really meant' in the *General Theory*. With admirable restraint, Patinkin refrains from interpreting or appraising Keynes from the hindsight of today's theory and knowledge, even his own.

The *Tract* Patinkin finds fascinating on the national and international problems and policies of the era, but in monetary economics he finds it a routine recital of the Cambridge version of the quantity theory. The *Treatise* he finds dull and mechanical—'a Keynes out of character, a Keynes attempting to act the role of a Professor, and a Germanic one at that' (p. 24). The famous Fundamental Equations are fundamentally flawed, and the objective of explaining output fluctuations is bound to elude a theory that is designed to explain prices and profits for given output but lacks equations for output determination. It is this gap that led Keynes to the theory of effective demand, in Patinkin's view the central insight of the *General Theory*. For the *General Theory* and for Keynes's lifetime contribution Patinkin is a great enthusiast. In these days, when Keynes's standing with the profession and with the general public is cyclically low, when the man's writings and influence are blamed for all the world's ills, students and young economists will gain valuable perspective from Patinkin's book.

On the main points of interpretation I agree with Patinkin. (1) The pretension to establish an equilibrium with involuntary unemployment, which puts off so many economists instilled with neoclassical instincts, should not be taken seriously. Keynes is really describing an economy in disequilibrium, or in a succession of constrained temporary equilibria, using comparative statics as the analytical language of the day. His strong conviction and his true message are that the automatic self-righting mechanisms of whole economies are slow, weak, and unreliable. Excess supply can persist for long periods, whether one calls the situation equilibrium or not. (2) Keynes did not assume either money wage rigidity or money illusion. He did contend that wages would adjust downward slowly—more slowly than prices could move upward. And he was sceptical of the employment effects of economy-wide wage reduction. As Patinkin says, he regarded wage and price deflation as the equivalent of monetary expansion. Neither might be capable of lowering interest rates enough to revive investment in depressed times. (3) Keynes emphasizes non-policy disturbances to the economy, real as well as monetary. The 'state of long-term expectation' by entrepreneurs and investors is a major determinant of effective demand. Since these expectations relate to essentially unknowable and non-probabilistic future events, including the expectations of future entrepreneurs and investors, they are arbitrary and volatile. Keynes also stresses, as in the *Treatise*, the importance of differences of view between savers and investors, or bulls and bears, or lenders and borrowers. (4) The Hicksian *IS/LM* apparatus captures beautifully the general equilibrium character of Keynes's vision, but its concise formalism does not do justice to the above insights and others. (In early drafts of the book and in lectures Keynes wrote symbols for expectations or 'state of the news' as arguments of functions, but they were not in the book for Hicks to find.)

My differences from Patinkin's observations are minor. (1) He describes (p. 81) the financial side of the *General Theory* as a three-asset model (money, bonds, equities), in contrast to the two-asset model (money, equities) of the *Treatise*. This seems to be stretching things. It seems to me that the *General Theory* really has only two assets (money, everything else). Anyway, there is only one endogenous interest rate, that to which the estimated marginal efficiency of capital is to be equated by variation of investment—a stock-flow confusion, as Lerner observed early on. In treating the portfolio choice between equities and fixed-money-value assets and in considering the way the market brings together 'bulls' and 'bears', I think the *Treatise* is superior, dealing with more interesting and important matters than speculation about bond interest rates. (2) Patinkin notes with favour (p. 36) that the *Treatise* abandoned the quantity-theory presumption, followed in the *Tract*, that monetary measures first alter the quantity of money and only then, via this medium, affect spending, profits, prices, and output. In the *Treatise* central bank operations change interest rates and thereby affect all the variables, including the quantity of money, simultaneously. The *General Theory* appears to be a step backward in this respect. (3) Patinkin allows himself to wonder (p. 110) about Keynes's omission of wealth, in distinction from capital gains, as a determinant of consumption. Keynes in fact does recognize life-cycle effects, and he would properly not wish to count planned or expected accumulations of savings as another determinant. But why does he not recognize real gains or losses on money balances? The answer is not clear. Perhaps it is because none of Keynes's theoretical work contemplates drastic or continuing one-way price change. As in other monetary theory of the day, the *quaesitum* was the determination of the equilibrium value of money, that is, the price level, not the inflation rate or any other dynamic price path. Given this mind-set, Keynes might naturally regard short-run price variation as too transient and reversible to enter consumers' reckoning of wealth. The same mind-set must be the reason Keynes did not see inflation as a way of lowering real interest rates even when nominal rates were close to their floor. (4) Greater stress might be placed on Keynes's uncritical acceptance of the neoclassical competitive model. By assuming that firms are price takers in auction markets rather than price setters in monopolistic competition or oligopoly, he made it harder to sustain his vision of persistent disequilibrium, with failures of coordination, communication, and adjustment. Imperfect competition was the other revolution in economics in the 1930s; one of its sites was Keynes's Cambridge, and two of its agents, Joan Robinson and Sraffa, were in his group. Yet for some mysterious reason the two revolutions were never meshed.

Keynes planned, Patinkin reports, to write a book of 'Footnotes to the *General Theory*', but was never able to do so. The fourth book, Patinkin feels, would have been one of continuation and clarification of the third. Keynes had no reason to rethink the *General Theory* as he had the *Treatise*.

Which of the several Keynesian traditions today is authentic? Any or all? Patinkin does not enter this dangerous terrain. We can hope he will tell us on some other occasion. Meanwhile we can look forward to more books that combine, as this one does, fascinating narrative, economic history, history of thought, and lucid exposition of difficult theory.

6 Fashionable Challenges to Keynesian Economics*
(Thurow's *Dangerous Currents*)

These days the media, hungry for novelty and conflict, dramatize economists' disagreements and oversimplify economic issues. In the early 1960s journalists baptized the Keynesian proposals of President Kennedy's advisers 'the New Economics' and exaggerated their novelties, their claims, and their successes. When LBJ's Vietnam adventure substituted inflation for unemployment as the salient economic problem, the media discarded the New Economics in favour of Milton Friedman's monetarism. In the 1970s the 'supply side' (ironically, the term originated with derisive intent by Herbert Stein put the ideas he was ridiculing on the map) became the vogue, making Arthur Laffer with his cocktail-napkin curve the star economist of the business convention circuit. Monetarism and supply-side economics were both, in different ways, counter-revolutions against Keynesian economics, itself an intellectual revolution only forty years old but now routinely modified in editorials and political oratory by the adjective 'discredited'.

A third counter-revolution is more solidly based in the discipline but has also infiltrated the public arena. This is the new classical macroeconomics, associated with the idea of 'rational expectations'. The Panglossian conclusion of this theory is that macroeconomic performance is always as good as it can be under the circumstances and certainly cannot be improved by the usual Keynesian monetary and fiscal tools. A fourth reaction against Keynesian economics is more old-fashioned. Orthodox economists, financiers, and politicians are hammering away against government deficits and debt, as they have consistently since the days of Keynes and FDR. Reaganomics is a loose amalgam of these four quite disparate anti-Keynesian doctrines.

Only a handful of the 20,000 members of the American Economic Association are, like Lester Thurow, visible participants in this sort

---

*November 1983, *Harper's* pp. 64–8. Review of Lester Thurow, *Dangerous Currents: The State of Economics*, New York: Random House, 1983. © 1983 by *Harper's Magazine*. All rights reserved. Reprinted by special permission.

of commentary and controversy. Thurow is a professional economist of stature and achievement; specialists read, discuss, and respect his academic papers and books. At the same time, congressional committees seek his testimony, popular magazines and newspapers print his articles, *Newsweek* subscribers read his columns, journalists report his views, lay audiences listen to his speeches. Thurow is extraordinarily gifted in turning sophisticated economic analysis into graceful and accessible language.

This kind of double life has a long and distinguished tradition in economics. Most of the durable scientific content of the discipline originated in interpretations of current events and emerged from controversies over public policy. Adam Smith was attacking mercantilism, David Ricardo was promoting free trade and sound money, John Maynard Keynes was tangling with F. A. Hayek and the British Treasury about causes and cures for unemployment. Professional economics, ideology, political economy, and economic politics are intertwined. The ideas of economists shape the thinking of politicians and influential citizens, sometimes directly, more often osmotically and subtly. Economists' interests and opinions, in turn, respond to events and to public opinion. Below the tip of the iceberg, the everyday research and teaching of the profession goes on, shaping the views of students who will become managers, bankers, bureaucrats, voters, and congressmen, and determining the trained instincts of economists who will staff government agencies and Wall Street firms and provide the quotes on yesterday's statistics for *The New York Times* and the *Wall Street Journal*. Classrooms, textbooks, professional journals, and technical research reports reflect the same doctrinal currents that have dominated recent public discussion.

Thurow's new book calls them 'dangerous currents', hazardous to public policy today and tomorrow, and to the health of the profession itself. He sounds an urgent alarm, directed to both his fellow economists and the general public. Economics is becoming sterile, concerned not with the real world but with never-never lands constructed for its own intellectual convenience. Conclusions valid for those imaginary lands are disastrously false guides to policy in the United States or other actual economies. Developing this thesis, Thurow attacks all of the anti-Keynesian doctrines enumerated above. This does not mean he is an uncritical Keynesian; as his other writings have demonstrated, he fits no stereotype.

In Thurow's view, the several dangerous currents spring from a common source central to the discipline of economics. This is the paradigm of 'competitive equilibrium', of 'price-auction markets', in

Thurow's phrase. It goes back to Adam Smith's Invisible Hand, one of the Great Ideas of intellectual history: individuals act rationally, selfishly, and myopically, but the collective result is to maximize the wealth of nations. This miracle is accomplished by competition in free markets. In such 'price-auction' markets, supplies and demands are continuously equated by prices, which in turn give consumers, producers, investors, and workers all the signals needed for them to take individually and socially optimal actions. No central planning is required; indeed government intervention beyond the definition and enforcement of property rights and contracts is socially counter-productive. In the realm of ideology and politics, this idea has flourished as the economic content of nineteenth-century liberalism and twentieth-century conservatism. In the discipline of economic theory, it has been rigorously stated and proved, the necessary and sufficient conditions precisely spelled out and the many qualifications duly noted.

In its more austere and abstract guise, competitive-equilibrium theory became the paradigm that justifies the claim of economics to be a 'hard' social science, in contrast to its 'soft' neighbours. As in Adam Smith, resources are efficiently allocated by auction markets where prices freely move to match demands and supplies. There are as many markets and prices as commodities, and they are all 'cleared' simultaneously. For many economists, perhaps more today than ever before, this construction is the presumptive reference point. The burden of proof is on anyone who says that real world markets fail to yield socially optimal outcomes or that government interventions can ever improve welfare. If improvements were possible, wouldn't rational people voluntarily make deals that would leave them mutually better off?

Against this presumption, Keynes always had hard sledding. He said that workers were unemployed even though they were willing to work for real wages no greater than their productivity, and to buy now or in the future the products of their labour. Theorists who presume that workers and employers behave rationally and that markets clear smoothly were and still are incredulous that such massive market failures could occur. It was hard for them to explain away so spectacular an example as the Great Depression. But as it receded in memory, the presumption in favour of the Invisible Hand gained adherence both inside the profession and outside. Confronted with apparent evidence that people do not behave rationally, individually or collectively, that markets are not competitive, that most markets are not cleared by flexible prices, and that many markets do not even exist, true believers contrive involved explanations to reconcile the

observations with the model of competitive voluntary market equilibrium. For example, unemployment is explained away as the preference
of the unemployed for leisure, or for time to look for better jobs, or
for unemployment compensation.

It is this latter-day development—taking the competitive–equilibrium
model more literally and uncritically than economists ever did before—
that Thurow challenges. As he points out, the faith is not supported
by any evidence that the actual economy is any better described as a
set of simultaneously cleared 'price-auction markets' than it was
before—quite the contrary. It has simply gained credence from the
facile view that J. M. Keynes and policies he inspired are to blame
for the inflation and stagflation of the last fifteen years. Thurow also
suggests that economists are not immune to the tides of influential
non-professional opinion and to temptations to say things lay audiences
like to hear.

The theme of the book is that economics based on the 'price-
auction' paradigm is irrelevant as science and dangerous as policy.
Innocent readers will, I fear, have a hard time distilling this important
message from Thurow's prose; it is scattered through the book, not
delivered centrally and coherently. If they become sceptical of the
Invisible Hand ideology so prevalent today in various guises, if they
become more pragmatic and less ideological on policy issues, the book
will have succeeded. Professional readers will see the essential thesis,
all right. Their most likely reaction is to ask what paradigm, what
method, Thurow proposes in place of what seems to them the only
game in town. That is unfair. It's enough for this one book to sound
the alarm, in the hope of converting some young economists from
blind religion to open-minded research. In the final chapter Thurow
suggests that economists have much to learn from the allegedly softer
social sciences, and that counsel of humility is good advice.

The central message of the book is interspersed with Thurow's own
substantive economics, his own criticisms of and counter-arguments to
the several 'dangerous currents', his interpretations of the stagflation
of the 1970s and other recent history, his scepticism of modern
econometric methodology, and his own findings on earnings inequality
and human capital. These passages, especially the last topic, are not
well organized or well integrated with the main theme. The best of
them and the most germane is Chapter 7, a carefully argued explanation
of why labour 'markets' diverge from the competitive-market model
in ways that involve no irrationality of behaviour yet support Keynes's
basic propositions about unemployment.

This reviewer, like any other professional reader, could mention many disagreements over details. Much of the controversy about contemporary macroeconomic theory and policy concerns the reconciliation of low unemployment with low inflation. Monetarists and new classical economists minimize the conflict. They would aim for low inflation, confident that competitive markets will yield unemployment as low as workers really want. Keynesians see a much more intractable and painful conflict of objectives, for reasons Thurow explains fully and eloquently. In a world where prices are not determined in impersonal auction markets but set by managers of large firms to cover full costs plus normal profits, where oligopolies and monopolies rather than numerous competitors characterize many industries, where wage scales are established by large employers or by long contracts negotiated with unions, and where governments guarantee floors for farm prices, prices rise more readily than they fall, and patterns of inflation stubbornly persist even in hard times. It is difficult to keep inflation under control by monetary measures alone without considerable sacrifice of employment and production. Witness the reluctance of all the governments represented at the Williamsburg summit in May to stimulate recovery, for fear of re-igniting inflation. Incomes policies—ranging from informal guideposts for wage and price increases to full-scale controls—have been advocated and used to mitigate the conflict. Thurow, however, gives them short shrift, for reasons I find unconvincing, and he offers no alternatives.

Thurow's critiques of the 'dangerous currents' contain some flaws. I will mention three. First, readers will be confused by his dual use of the term 'supply side'. It appears first in Chapter 3, where the author discusses supply-price factors in inflation: wage pushes, commodity shortages, and OPEC shocks. These non-monetary sources of price increases have nothing to do with the dangerous doctrinal current discussed in Chapter 5—supply-side economics, the intellectual rationale for Reagan's tax and budget strategies. Second, that chapter blames equilibrium 'price-auction' economics for the extremes of the Laffer Curve and Kemp–Roth–Reagan legislation. This is unfair, because many theorists and practitioners of 'price-auction' economics would not subscribe to the exaggerated empirical estimates of incentive effects characteristic of the supply-side movement or approve of the regressive distributional consequences.

Third, Chapter 6 betrays a shocking misunderstanding of the rational expectations school. Thurow says on p. 143: 'Rational expectationists (such as Lucas and Sargent) also differ from the supply-siders and the monetarists in that they believe that monetary policies have little impact on inflation. Like the supply-siders, rational expectationists believe that government cannot improve the workings of the equilibrium price-auction market, but unlike supply-siders they also believe that government cannot systematically damage the performance of the market . . . [and] don't believe that economic performance can be systematically improved by removing government interference.' This incredible paragraph has got it all wrong.

Macroeconomists of the rational expectations school are monetarists, indeed more Catholic than the pope. They believe that increases and decreases of money supplies are wholly reflected in inflation and deflation and have no other effects for good or ill. They believe that non-monetary policies and events (for example, tax changes and OPEC shocks) have no significant effects on overall price levels, as distinguished from the relative prices of different commodities, but can have important real consequences. Robert Lucas *et al.* say that policies that change money stocks have no *real* effects if anticipated by the public, because rational private agents in auction markets will simply and instantaneously raise or lower their dollar wages and prices until the real (i.e. purchasing-power) quantity of money remains the same. By the same token, correctly perceived monetary policies have no effects on production, employment, real interest rates, or other real variables.

Monetary operations have real effects only temporarily, according to this theory, only when the public is confused about what the monetary authority (the Federal Reserve in the United States) is doing or intending to do. Indeed, it is precisely this theory that was the intellectual foundation for the recent 'credible threat' strategies of disinflation in the United Kingdom and the United States: if Margaret Thatcher and Paul Volcker make clear that money growth will be curtailed relentlessly whatever the consequences for production and employment, then price and wage inflation will fall so fast that production and employment will not suffer significant damage.

However, again contrary to Thurow, rational expectations theory does not necessarily exclude supply-side reforms. The theory does not deny that fiscal measures and other *real* government interventions or their removal can affect real economic performance. They cannot make employment more or less full à la Keynes, to be sure, because labour markets, like all other markets, are assumed always to be in price-cleared equilibrium. But they can conceivably improve or worsen the efficiency with which the economy uses its fully employed resources.

While these surprising errors do not impair the validity of Thurow's basic criticism of the school, they will unfortunately damage their credibility.

Reaganomics and its several doctrinal elements are not doing well these days. The stock of supply-side economics has plummeted as rapidly as it rose. Monetarism, having brought the United States and world economies to the brink of disaster in 1982, until to almost universal relief the Federal Reserve suspended its monetarist targets, has also waned in professional and public popularity. Well-advertised, relentless monetary disinflation turned out to be much more painful in unemployment, excess capacity, and lost production than rational expectations theory implied. Older contestants, Keynesians and old-fashioned fiscal conservatives, are back in the centre of the arena. The fickle sensitivity of profession and public to current events and fashions may now be working in favour of Thurow's message. But it is no less timely and important.

PART II
Reaganomics

INTRODUCTION

The election of 1980 brought to Washington a President and Administration ideologically committed to radical change in economic and social policy. Nothing so momentous had occurred in American politics since Franklin Delano Roosevelt. Although conservative counter-revolutions were taking place in other advanced capitalist democracies too, the Reagan revolution was different because of the unique strand of 'supply-side' economics contained in its package of conservative ideologies. Part II contains nine of my writings on the events, controversies, doctrines and policies of the Reagan era to date. It begins with the most recent, an assessment of Reaganomics prepared for a Canadian audience.

The five 1981 pieces that follow, I like to think, demonstrate that I understood pretty well from the beginning the objectives, strategies, and probable consequences of the Administration's policies. However, I initially took at face value the Administration's structural budget estimates, only later realizing that the Administration was underestimating the growth of spending, especially for defence and for interest on the public debt, as well as overestimating economic growth, as I did appreciate. Chapters 13 and 14 concern the radical change in fiscal policy effected by the Reagan budgets and the corresponding tight monetary policy resulting from the central bank's fear that fiscal stimulus was excessive. Analysis of these policies continues in Parts III and IV.

In critically discussing Reagan's fiscal policy, I have tried to maintain perspective and balance. Deficit spending is not the unmitigated disaster many critics saw in it, as long as the economy is underemployed and capable of responding to demand stimulus by extra production and employment rather than by inflation. However, the same recovery could occur by expansionary monetary policy, were the Federal Reserve willing to engineer it, together with the more moderate federal budgets of the thirty-five years before 1981. The Reagan–Volcker mix of fiscal and monetary policies had massive and unhealthy side effects for the dollar, for US foreign transactions, for world interest rates, and for the shortage of national saving in the United States. The unending growth of federal debt and deficits, faster than US Gross National Product, implied by this policy mix could not be viable in the long run. It is now in the process of being corrected, although by excessively draconian procedures that threaten the health of the economy and the effectiveness of essential government programmes.

President Reagan describes the outcomes of his policies as an 'economic miracle'. As prelude to this Part, I present here several charts comparing economic developments during five years of Reaganomics with those of the first five years of the Kennedy–Johnson Administrations two decades before.

January 1961 and January 1981 are similar in several respects. Each time the political party of the Administration changed, and the new Administration consciously emphasized the change in economic philosophy and strategy. The new direction taken in 1981 was in most ways the opposite of 1961, and was also a more radical departure from the past. In each case the new President inherited a troubled economy. Kennedy was inaugurated at the trough of the second of two 'back-to-back' recessions, 1957–8 and 1960, Reagan during the brief interlude between the recessions of 1980 and 1981–2. In both cases these recessions were in considerable degree the by-products of anti-inflationary monetary policies.

The nine charts that follow compare the paths of key macroeconomic variables over the two periods, beginning two years (eight quarters or 24 months) before inauguration and extending six years beyond (23 quarters or 71 months after period zero, the quarter or month of inauguration).

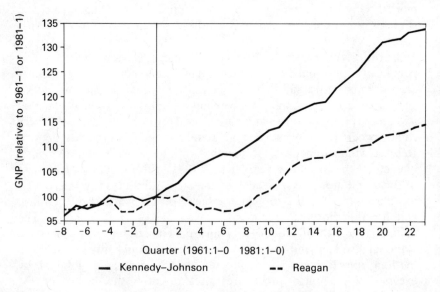

Figure 1   Gross national product ($1982)

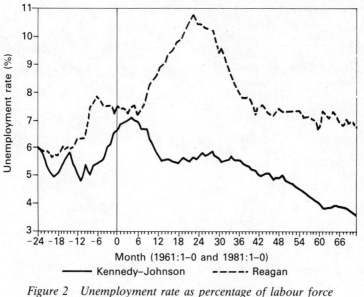

Figure 2   Unemployment rate as percentage of labour force

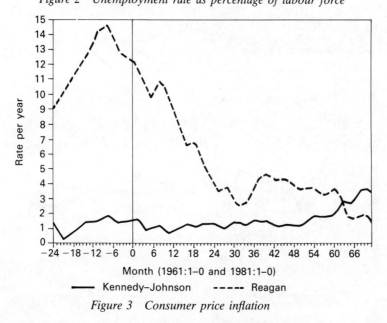

Figure 3   Consumer price inflation

Note: *The Figure shows monthly smoothed estimates of the inflation rate of the Consumer Price Index. The estimate is the percentage increase over the same month a year before in a three-month moving average of the Index centred on the current month. The inflation rate inherited by Reagan was much higher than that inherited by Kennedy. During Reagan's first six years it came down ten percentage points; during the first five Kennedy–Johnson years it increased slightly, but in 1965 was well below the 1985 rate. Of course, during the Johnson Vietnam War period 1966–9, the inflation rate rose three percentage points. The beginning of the rise in 1966 can be seen in the Figure.*

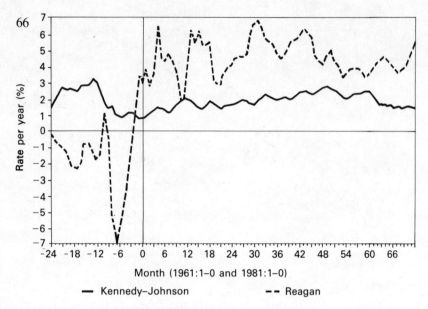

Figure 4   Real short-term interest rate

Note: The 'real interest rate' here plotted is the difference between the average rate per annum on three-month Treasury Bills for the month and a smoothed estimate of inflation in the Consumer Price Index for the same month. The estimate is the one depicted in Figure 3 and explained in its note.

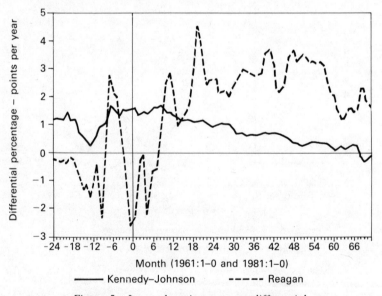

Figure 5   Long–short interest rate differential

Note: The difference between long and short interest rates is generally thought to be related to predominant market expectations, hopes, and fears of movements of interest rate levels. A positive differential is indicative of sentiment that nominal rates will be higher in future, possibly because inflation is expected to be higher, possibly because real rates are expected to move up.

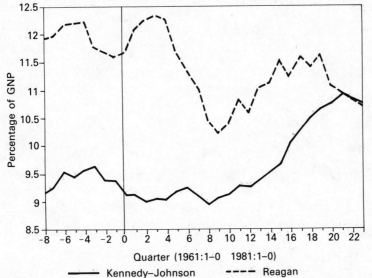

Figure 6   Gross fixed investment (non-residential)

Note: Gross private investment in fixed non-residential capital was a larger share of GNP in the late 1970s and 1980s than in the 1960s. During the 1961–6 period this share increased relative to the previous decade, partly because of the introduction of the Investment Tax Credit and accelerated depreciation. See also Figure 7.

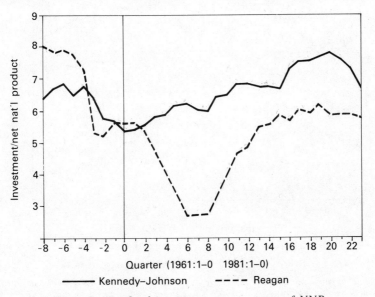

Figure 7   Net fixed investment as percentage of NNP

Note: Here, unlike Figure 6, fixed investment includes residential as well as non-residential capital formation. But the major difference is that net investment is smaller than gross investment by the Capital Consumption Allowance (adjusted for inflation), an estimate of economic depreciation calculated by the Department of Commerce for the National Income and Product Accounts. Net National Product is smaller than GNP by the same amount. Comparison of Figures 7 and 6 confirms the widespread impression that much more of gross investment in the more recent period is acquisition and replacement of short-lived equipment.

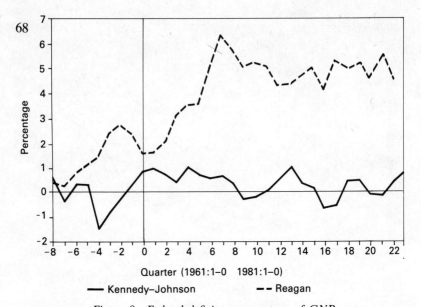

Figure 8 Federal deficit as percentage of GNP

Note: The Reagan fiscal revolution is dramatically depicted here. About half of national private net saving is offset by federal dissaving.

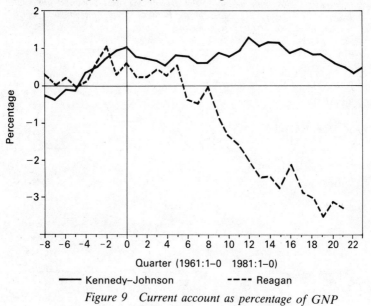

Figure 9 Current account as percentage of GNP

Note: The chart pictures the net surplus or deficit of the United States in current transactions with the rest of the world. The current account covers exports and imports of goods and services, including income received and paid on past investments. A surplus increases the net stock of claims of US entities against the rest of the world, and a deficit decreases that element of national wealth. During the 1980s much of the accumulation of national wealth in the form of domestic fixed capital (Figures 7 and 8) has been offset by decumulation of the country's net foreign assets.

7 Reagonomics in Retrospect

Rarely in a democracy does a new government take office determined to change course radically, and endowed with the electoral mandate to enable it to do so. Franklin Roosevelt in 1933 and Lyndon Johnson in 1965 were the only United States Presidents in my lifetime who had and used this opportunity, until Ronald Reagan was inaugurated in 1981. Most Administrations veer only moderately from the established compromise consensus they inherit. Their minor course adjustments reflect the difference from their predecessors and opponents in the balance of interests in the coalition that elected them. Leaders like FDR, LBJ, and Reagan—and across the sea, Margaret Thatcher—manage to shift bodily the whole path of policy. After them, the centrist consensus from which successors will deviate is forever different.

Ronald Reagan came to Washington with a strong and distinctive social and economic ideology. Roosevelt and Johnson, pragmatists both, were definitely not ideologues. They responded decisively and imaginatively to the situations they confronted; the New Deal and the Great Society were not preordained by any long-held doctrinal beliefs of their builders. Liberalism, in its twentieth-century meaning, is a loose set of attitudes and values rather than a coherent ideology. But there is a ready-made right-wing ideology, and Reagan came to Washington in 1981 with programmatic agenda conceived in its image.

THE ECONOMIC IDEOLOGY OF THE REAGAN ADMINISTRATION

What was the economic ideology President Reagan brought to Washington?

*March 1986, lecture at University of Western Ontario Centre for American Studies, unpublished. Revised February 1987.

Basically, of course, it was the ancient theme of nineteenth-century 'liberalism', celebrating the miracle of Adam Smith's Invisible Hand, the virtues of free markets, free enterprise, and *laissez faire*. It has long been espoused by the Right in the United States. After the Second World War conservative intellectuals, business leaders, and politicians rallied to this flag even when it was outside the general consensus. Barry Goldwater was their hero in 1964, but Johnson clobbered him. Ronald Reagan became a public figure and a potential political leader by his talent for communicating the ideology on radio, television, and in person under the sponsorship of General Electric.

The Invisible Hand
Free market ideology is an extravagant version of the central paradigm of economic theory. The modern theory of general competitive equilibrium and its theorem that such an equilibrium is in some sense a situation of optimal social welfare make rigorous the intuitive conjectures of Adam Smith and subsequent classical and neoclassical economists. Economists know the restrictive conditions of these proofs; they can list the standard caveats and qualifications. These are lost in the arena of politics and public opinion, and they are increasingly glossed over by economists themselves. At the same time and for the same reasons that conservative ideology was gaining in public favour, its counterpart in economic theory was being more and more uncritically accepted throughout the economics profession.

Every ideological movement has its own version of history. As Reagan tells it, the US economy was a shambles when he came to its rescue in 1981. All the blame he laid to federal economic policies under previous Administrations since the Second World War: chronic deficits, over-taxation, large and growing government, loose monetary policy, macro-economic 'fine tuning', intrusive regulation, bureaucratic waste, misguided welfare handouts, and so on. In this story there is no credit for the remarkable performance of the economy in the 1950s and 1960s and no acknowledgement of the roles of OPEC, the Iranian revolution, and other external shocks in the 1970s.

Government as Leviathan
In renascent conservative doctrine, government 'is the problem, not the solution'. In the 1970s this message found receptive ears in a populace disillusioned by Vietnam, Watergate, and the economic disappointments of the decade. Government regulations and taxes, according to candidate and President Reagan, shackle the energies and initiatives of the citizens. Government, especially central govern-ment, has become a Leviathan, devouring the resources of the nation.

Government has expanded far beyond its proper functions of national defence, internal order, protection of property rights, and enforcement of contracts. Government has no business redistributing income and wealth, beyond minimal 'safety nets' for the truly poor and disadvantaged. Even these needs should be met primarily by private charity, supplemented by local governments.

The objective of highest priority for the Reagan Administration has been from the beginning to reduce the size of the federal government and budget relative to the economy. This implied severe cuts in federal civilian spending, because Reagan was also committed to a sharp increase in military expenditures. The non-defence budget, it is true, had been growing faster than GNP. This was almost entirely in social security benefits, for old age and disability and for Medicare, health insurance for the aged, introduced by Lyndon Johnson in 1966. These are universal entitlements, not needs tested, and the growth of spending for them had been closely matched by earmarked payroll taxes. Social security growth reflected a combination of demographic trends, economic developments, fiscal miscalculations, and political generosities, notably on the part of the Nixon–Ford Administrations and their Democratically controlled Congresses. The experts in the Reagan team knew these facts, but the President preferred to ignore them and talk about the excessive size of the budget as a whole.

The Strategy of Cutting Taxes First
The idea that the federal budget must stop growing faster than GNP was not new; both Presidents Ford and Carter had committed themselves to this objective. Reagan, however, was ready to slaughter cows that previous Administrations and Congresses regarded as politically sacred. He was also ready to follow a strategy that his predecessors eschewed as unsound. That was to cut taxes first, accept the resulting deficits, and use the abhorrence of deficit spending, among politicians, financiers, and the general public, as a bludgeon to force Congress to cut civilian spending. Cutting the budget, civilian spending and taxes both, was and is the prime goal.

Only a conservative Republican President could have adopted this strategy without provoking an outraged response from the financial community, and negative reactions in financial markets. Such responses forced Jimmy Carter to modify several of his proposed budgets. For example, when his budget for fiscal year 1979 was proposed in January 1978, it showed a deficit of $60 billion. The outcry forced Carter to submit a revised budget with a much lower expected deficit, abandoning some expenditure initiatives and scaling down some tax cuts. While Reagan and his spokesmen have always given lip service to the old conservative orthodoxy of budget balance, it has always been a distinctly subordinate objective. The President has often explained the strategy of lowering taxes first by saying that the way for parents to keep kids from overspending is to cut their allowances.

The strategy did not work quite the way President Reagan had hoped. Although Congress acquiesced in drastic cuts in civilian spending, other than for social security entitlements, these were insufficient to bring the federal deficit under control. What the President did succeed in doing was to make politically impossible any major restoration of federal tax revenues. His landslide victory in 1984 over Walter Mondale, who courageously but recklessly told the electorate that taxes would have to go up, closed that road to fiscal sanity for the foreseeable future. What the President eventually lost to his Congressional opponents was about half of his ambitious build-up of defence spending. Even so, the 'unacceptably large' deficits continued. The Gramm–Rudman Act of 1985 acknowledged the impasse. Its purpose was to force the President and Congress to agree on how to eliminate the deficit over five fiscal years 1987–91 or else face mindlessly automatic cuts in both defence and civilian spending, cuts that neither side would like.

Supply-side economics and the budget
Supply-side economics gave Reagan another argument for reducing taxes faster than he could hope to lower expenditures. This argument is not wholly consistent with the strategy just discussed, but ideology and political economics do not have to be consistent. The argument was that cutting tax rates would actually raise tax revenues, a claim that made famous the economist who made it famous. Arthur Laffer drew his curve on a cocktail napkin for the instruction of Congressman Jack Kemp. The curve dramatized the incontrovertible truth that beyond some point a rise in tax rates will discourage taxable activities so much that revenues actually decline. Laffer and Kemp jumped to the unsupported conclusion that US rates were already there. This assertion was naturally an instant sensation in conservative political and business circles, lending as it did apparent scientific authority to something they wanted very much to believe. Ronald Reagan believed it, and he still does. Raising taxes, he continues to say, will be devastating to the economy. Economic growth propelled by tax cuts, he continues to say, will balance the budget. Members of his Administration who thought otherwise and had the courage to speak up—like Martin Feldstein, who never bought the Laffer line, and David Stockman, who once did but learned better—are now in private life.

Supply-side fiscal economics as espoused by Laffer, Kemp, and Reagan is reminiscent of extravagant claims advanced by some Keynesian enthusiasts that tax cuts would pay for themselves in revenues generated by expansion of economic activity. The expansion they had in mind was 'demand-side'. The scenario was that in an economy with excess unemployment and redundant industrial capacity, the spending of tax cuts would prime the pump. Sober Keynesians believed that tax cuts—or additional government expenditure—would stimulate activity in a slack economy, but not by enough to avoid an increase in the deficit.

The label 'supply side', which had a great deal to do with the attention the doctrine rapidly received, was coined satirically by Herbert Stein in order to distinguish what he called supply-side fiscalism from the old Keynesian demand-side brand. There are in logic several differences. From a demand-side viewpoint, additional government spending is at least as expansionary as private spending, mostly only on consumption, induced by tax reductions. The supply-siders, however, contend that both cutting tax rates and *reducing* public spending are stimulative. The supply-side recipe is supposed to give private individuals greater after-tax incentives to work, save and invest, innovate, and take risks—not to consume. These responses are supposed to augment productivity and raise the economy's capacity to produce from a given employed labour force, while demand-side fiscal stimuli are intended to raise the economy's production from given capacity by employing more of the available labour force. Laffer's theory, if valid, should work even if unemployment were at and remained at its full employment minimum, while a Keynesian fiscal prescription is intended only as therapy for recession or tonic for an uncompleted recovery.

These differences did not prevent the supply-side protagonists from claiming the 1964 Kennedy–Johnson tax cut as a precedent, even though its motivation and success were demand-side and even though there is no credible evidence that by itself it led to net reduction of the deficit. Nor has logic prevented them from staking claim to the 1983–85 US recovery, even though that fits a standard Keynesian scenario.

There is of course a less flamboyant, less novel, and more professional supply-side economics, namely good straight microeconomics. Economists of all shades of opinion recognize that taxes and transfers have incentive and disincentive effects. This has been recognized in policy too, for example the Investment Tax Credit introduced in the Kennedy Administration and the sliding scales relating welfare benefits and food stamps to recipients' own resources, introduced under

Johnson and Nixon. Martin Feldstein joined the Reagan Administration
after leading for a decade important research on the effects of taxation
of capital income on investment and saving. The Reagan ideologues
had the directions of effects right; the trouble was, as Charles Schultze
observed, that they multiplied reasonable empirical magnitudes tenfold.

Monetarism
Monetarism was another ingredient in the triumphant conservative
ideology of 1981. Strict control of money supply growth was accepted
as necessary and sufficient for disinflation; the Federal Reserve should
stick to non-inflationary M targets and hit them. Supply-siders were
somewhat uncomfortable, fearful that the Fed would not accommodate
the expansion their own policies would generate. The Administration
tried feebly to argue that monetary stringency would take care of
prices while supply-side stimuli raised output. Inflation is, after all,
'too much money chasing too few goods', and their policies would
shrink the money and multiply the goods!

Later the supply-siders became downright hostile to the Fed. They
blamed Paul Volcker, the Chairman of the Federal Reserve Reagan
inherited from Jimmy Carter but reappointed, for the incomplete
success of their programme. They joined their voices to those of some
Keynesians in urging more accommodative monetary policy and lower
interest rates. Unlike the Keynesians, they also attacked the present
international monetary regime, floating exchange rates, and called for
return to the gold standard or the Bretton Woods fixed-parity system
or some variant. This always had been a plank in the platform of the
original supply-side guru Robert Mundell and his popularizer Jude
Wanniski, who were very imporant influences on Kemp, Stockman,
and Laffer. The President has flirted publicly with this idea, but the
pragmatists of his Administration have so far kept it from becoming
serious policy. The ambivalence of the Reaganomics intellectuals
towards monetarism and floating exchange rates sets some distance
between them and the world's leading conservative economist, Milton
Friedman.

Supply-side thinking differentiates Reaganomics also from the more
orthodox conservatism guiding the policies of other governments these
days, notably in Japan, West Germany, which sets the tone for Europe,
and the United Kingdom. Those governments share Reagan's faith in
laissez-faire, but they also subscribe to traditional budgetary prudence
and firm monetarism. Reaganomics enthusiasts cite the greater recovery
of the United States since 1982 as proof of the superiority of their
brand of conservatism over the conventional variety.

MACROECONOMIC MANAGEMENT 1981–5

In 1981 Congress adopted the President's economic and budgetary programmes to an amazing degree. The Democrats retained nominal control of the House and a near majority of the Senate. But, bulldozed by their disastrous defeat in the Presidential election, they submitted with docility and me-too-ism. Tax cuts amounting to about 3 per cent of GNP were passed, to be phased in over three years. Simultaneously, a build-up of defence spending, designed to raise it eventually from 5.5 per cent to 8 per cent of GNP, was begun. (As the Administration points out, defence would still be 2–3 percentage points lower relative to GNP than in the 1950s and 1960s.) Civilian budget cuts were passed almost equal in eventual magnitude to the defence increases. Entitlements were still growing, however. The Administration made some noises about taking them on, but drew back when the flak made clear that social security was one ancient monument the opposition could and would defend.

The official 1981 forecasts of the economy and the budget were very rosy. In part, they were phoney, as Stockman has admitted in his unguarded interview at the time with an *Atlantic* writer, for which the President took him to the proverbial woodshed, and in great detail in his later book. In part, they reflected an unjustified optimism about the economy, shared by most private forecasters at the time.

In October 1979 Paul Volcker had instituted a strict monetarist regimen designed to rid the economy of the high inflation accompanying the second oil shock. A recession began in spring 1980—contributing to the defeat of Jimmy Carter—but there was a slight recovery at the end of the year. Anyone who understood Volcker's policy should have known that this was a temporary blip: I did understand the Fed's intentions. Recession resumed with a vengeance only months after the inauguration, too late to be taken into account in the budget and economic prospectuses of the new Administration.

Later in 1981, people began to recognize realities: Deficits of a new order of magnitude were in prospect. Moreover, they were not just cyclical; they were structural, that is, they would continue even when the economy was operating, and generating government revenues, at normal rates of unemployment and capacity utilization. One big reason was the growth of interest payments on federal debt. High interest rates were in part the consequence of the unprecedented fiscal stimulus, superimposed on the Fed's monetary policy. High interest payments, in turn, enlarge the deficit—altogether, a vicious spiral.

Alarm in the financial community and in Congress about prospective deficits did inspire some serious efforts to contain them. In 1982

Congress passed, and the President reluctantly signed, the Tax Equity and Fiscal Responsibility Act (TEFRA), enhancing revenues and in particular taking back some of the more egregious goodies given corporations by the Economic Recovery Tax Act of 1981 (ERTA). Furthermore, in one of the finer examples of statesmanlike cooperation between Congress and the Executive, between parties, and among interest groups, a blue-ribbon commission chaired by Alan Greenspan arrived at compromise recommendations to assure the 'solvency' of social security. The package was enacted in 1983, containing both benefit reductions, payroll tax increases, and other provisions projected to put the account in the black for several decades ahead. Indeed the Social Security Trust Fund will contribute surpluses up to 2 per cent of GNP to the unified federal budget in the 1990s. In almost every year after 1981, Congress has nibbled at the deficit, making expenditure cuts and also 'enhancing revenues', to use the obligatory euphemism for tax increases. These efforts have added up, until now even without Gramm–Rudman the structural deficit would be declining.

The Federal Reserve reversed policy in late summer 1982, and the recession ended a few months later. There were several reasons for the reversal. The downturn, which took unemployment close to 11 per cent, three and a half points higher than on inauguration day in January 1981, was deeper and faster than the Fed had expected. An unexpected slowdown in the velocity of money had made the Fed's monetary growth targets more restrictive than the Fed had intended. Third World debtor countries and the banks in the United States and other advanced countries who had lent to them were on the brink of a financial crisis. Congress, by passing TEFRA, was showing some appreciation of the federal budgetary problem and withdrawing some of the fiscal stimulus that the Fed regarded as excessive.

In 1983 and 1984, after Volcker had turned the economy around, the 1981 tax and defence expenditure programmes were coming into force and delivering a massive fiscal stimulus to aggregate demand. This was well-timed Keynesian recovery policy of unprecedented magnitude. Of course, it was quite serendipitous. The Administration had not expected a recession in the first place, and had on principle repudiated counter-cyclical demand management. Fortunately for business activity, taxpayers appeared not to realize that the cuts they were enjoying were supply-side measures designed to be saved rather than spent. Defence procurements and contracts percolated through the economy too. The fiscal stimulus to demand led to such rapid recovery at some times that the Fed felt it necessary to apply the monetary brakes. As a result real interest rates, i.e. market rates corrected for inflation, remained high, certainly much higher than if the same recovery had been driven by monetary policy combined with pre-1981 budget policies.

The United States drifted into a bizarre and extreme mix of tight monetary and easy fiscal policies, with several unpleasant consequences: the federal debt would be growing faster than GNP as far as the eye could see, because interest on the debt alone was increasing the debt faster than the sustainable growth rate of the economy, while expenditures other than debt interest would exceed revenues even when the recovery was complete. High interest rates induced a net capital inflow and appreciated the dollar enough to yield an equivalent current account deficit. As a result, the recovery was unbalanced; manufacturing industries and agriculture suffered formidable international competitive disadvantage, while services and other non-tradables sectors flourished. Pressures for protection of jobs and markets in the disadvantaged sectors threatened the political consensus that had long supported a liberal US commercial policy.

Let no one underestimate the drastic nature of the change in fiscal policy in 1981. While the federal government seldom ran surpluses in the last forty years, before 1981 its deficits were modest, virtually always less than 2 per cent of GNP, compared with the 4 and 5 per cent deficits of the Reagan years. Before 1981, cyclical recoveries brought deficits down close to zero, and the structural 'high unemployment' budget was often in surplus. Now we have *structural* deficits of 3 to 4 per cent of GNP. Before 1981, the debt/GNP ratio had declined, from more than 100 per cent at the end of the Second World War to 25 per cent in the 1970s. Five years of Reaganomics have raised it almost to 40 per cent. That figure is not itself a catastrophe, but the prospect that it will rise and accelerate endlessly portended future disaster.

Proponents of the 'political business cycle' hypothesis will cite the first Reagan Administration as a stunning confirmation. Nearly two years of painful disinflationary recession were followed by recovery through election day 1984. Poor Jimmy Carter had recovery first, then a new surge of inflation, then recession throughout his campaign for re-election. Reagan's success, however, was another example of his incredible luck. As argued above, the decisive demand management policies were Volcker's, not those of either President. And Reagan's fiscal contributions to recovery were unintentional. No matter. In 1984 Reagan ran on his restoration of prosperity, as if 1981–2 had occurred on some predecessor's watch. Actually the unemployment rate was the same in October 1984, just before the election, as it had been in December 1980, just before Reagan's inauguration.

WHERE DO WE STAND TODAY?

The unfinished recovery
The economy is still not fully recovered. The United States has done better than the six other 'economic summit' nations. But through 1986 unemployment remained nearly a point higher than at the peak of Jimmy Carter's recovery in 1978–9, two points higher than at Nixon's peak in 1973, and the same as at the peak of the short-lived recovery in 1981. Utilization of industrial capacity stayed around 80 per cent, compared to 85–7 per cent in previous prosperities.

The decline in the inflation rate is the great victory—it is 4 per cent or even lower now, compared to 9 or 10 per cent after the two oil shocks of the 1970s (year-to-year changes of GNP deflator). Persons with long memories may recall that inflation rates of 4 to 5 per cent were considered intolerable before 1973 and were indeed the occasion for counter-inflationary policies. But few have quarrelled with Paul Volcker's decision to declare victory in the war on inflation when it got below 5 per cent. Moreover, inflation is stable or even declining; it has been well-behaved throughout the recovery. The appreciation of the dollar may be credited with as much as one-third of the disinflation of 1981 to 1985. This assistance—the one redeeming feature of our high-interest-rate policy mix—was borrowed from our trading partners and will be repaid in extra US inflation as the dollar depreciates. On the other hand, declining oil prices—another striking proof of Reagan's 'luck of the Irish'—have moved US price indexes in a benign direction. We could have hoped to enjoy the reverse of a stagflationary shock, a boost to domestic consumption demand joint with a fall in prices. However, the sharp decline in domestic oil drilling and exploration 1985–6 was a stronger adverse blow to aggregate demand. It seemed, not for the first time, that oil news is bad news, whether it heralds abundance or shortage.

The major question before macro-economic policy makers, in practice the Federal Reserve today, is whether or not to allow or engineer a demand expansion bringing the unemployment rate down to 6 per cent or lower. The Fed seems comfortable with about 7 per cent unemployment, where the economy has been stuck since May 1984. Yet there is little reason to regard 7 per cent as the lowest inflation-safe unemployment rate. No significant bottlenecks, shortages or signs of domestic wage and price inflation loom on the horizon.

The Fed lowered its discount rate in seven half-point steps from 9 per cent in November 1984 to $5\frac{1}{2}$ per cent in August 1986. Other short-term rates fell in concert. Long-term rates also fell dramatically, but they still carry a premium over short rates, fluctuating around 200 basis points as market expectations about deficits and inflation swing between optimism and pessimism. *Ex post* real rates have declined much less because of the continuing fall in inflation; they remain high compared to previous cyclical upswings. Anyway, the interest rate declines have not sufficed to shake the economy out of its doldrums.

The stubborn US trade deficit, $3\frac{1}{2}$ per cent of GNP in 1986, has been an immense drag on aggregate demand. Federal Reserve interest rate policy was instrumental in bringing the dollar down from the heights to which its previous tight policy had raised it. But US exports and imports have been painfully slow to respond. The Fed is afraid of further depreciation, especially of a 'free fall' of the dollar if foreign investors should be turned off, largely because higher dollar prices for foreign foods would show up in US price indexes. However, the high exchange rates of 1981–85 may have done such durable damage to the competitive strengths of numerous American industries that the trade account cannot be corrected without further depreciation. US authorities urge Europe and Japan to fire up their sluggish 'locomotive' economies by expanding domestic demands. But those governments seem unwilling to do enough to make a noticeable difference in trade imbalances. They in turn complain that the dollar's fall is hurting their exporters and their economies. The US is stalled by a domestic political impasse on the budget deficit and by an international political impasse on the trade deficit.

Prospects of deficit reduction
The fiscal–monetary policy mix is still bad, but some correction is gradually occurring. The Gramm–Rudman drama has still to be played out. In summer 1986 the Supreme Court upheld a lower-court decision declaring unconstitutional the provisions of the law that were meant to force automatic spending cuts if Congress and President had not agreed on a budget consistent with the prescribed schedule of deficit reduction by the beginning of the fiscal year. Although both branches of the Federal government profess allegiance to the Gramm–Rudman targets, they seem resigned to missing them. Congress and President are far, far apart regarding the role of defence spending, civilian spending and tax revenues in deficit reductions.

Nevertheless, given the mood in Washington of which Gramm–Rudman was a symptom, the structural deficit is likely to be declining over the next several years. One big help is the decline in interest rates, which is removing one source of explosive deficit growth. Another is the success of Congress in freezing the real size of defence spending.

The Federal Reserve may face the pleasant task of offsetting some withdrawal of fiscal demand stimulus, and one must hope that residual monetarism will not stand in the way. If recession or growth recession should occur in the remaining years of the decade, the Fed will have to act with uncharacteristic boldness, because in the present Washington mood even cyclical deficits are interpreted as reasons for austerity.

The failure of supply-side nostrums

Supply-side effects have been very disappointing. Budget outcomes show that we were not on the wrong slope of the Laffer curve. That is scarcely a surprise. A more credible objective of Reagan policy in 1981 was to shift the composition of GNP from private and public consumption to private investment, particularly business investment in plant and equipment. But comparing real final sales (GNP less inventory investment) in 1985 with 1978, the last pre-Reagan normal year, I find that more than 95 per cent of the increase went into personal consumption and government purchases. In 1981 and 1982 critics of Reaganomics said that the tax cuts would result in more government dissaving than additional private saving; their warnings turned out to be correct. Personal saving in percentage of disposable personal income actually declined from about 7 per cent in the late 1970s to less than 5 per cent in 1985, and to 4 per cent in 1986. Personal consumption in percent of pretax personal income rose by nearly two points between 1978 and 1986, and consumer interest payments by another point.

Business fixed investment did well in the 1983–4 recovery, but, considering that it was starting from rock bottom, not strikingly better than in other cyclical upswings. The strongest gains occurred in equipment, computers, and motor vehicles, for which the incentives added by ERTA were negligible. The investment boom slacked off in the next two years. Growth of private domestic investment during the Reagan years was virtually equalled by the rise in the country's international current account deficit. The decrease in the net claims of the US against the rest of the world, now negative, is as bad for future generations as low domestic capital formation. Private research and development expenditures have slowed down despite new tax incentives. Public expenditures on basic science and on civilian research and development have been victims of federal budgetary stringency.

There is no sign that Reaganomic measures have increased the supply of labour, corrected for normal cyclical effects. The secular downward trend in average hours of work has continued without apparent break. The labour force participation of men has actually declined; the long-time upward drift in female labour force participation has continued, but at a somewhat slower pace.

For supply-side economics the bottom line is productivity growth. Its mysterious decline and disappearance in the 1970s was the most fateful disappointment of that decade. Alas, there is no sign that it has come back to the 2½–3 per cent p.a. characteristic of the economy before 1973. Recession and recovery in the 1980s have had their usual cyclical effects on measured labour productivity; after they are allowed for, the trend growth rate is only 1 per cent or less. The ten million jobs added since the trough of the recession have been good news, though two million fewer than the Administration foresaw in 1981. The bad news is that the added employment has not produced as much GNP as it should have.

Greater poverty and inequality
During the Reagan years poverty and inequality have increased in the United States. The President's promise that supply-side incentives would create a 'rising tide' that 'lifts all boats' has not been fulfilled. Even in 1985, after three years of recovery, 14 per cent of persons in USA were living in households below the official poverty line, the same as in 1981, up from 11.4 in 1978 and 12.1 back in 1969. Inequality has been increasing in the 1980s, reversing modest trends in the other direction since 1960. In the two previous decades families in the lowest quintile consistently received 5.2 to 5.5 per cent of aggregate family money income; the lowest two quintiles together got 16.8 to 17.6 per cent, and the top quintile between 40.9 and 41.6 per cent. In 1984 the share of the lowest fifth is less than 5 per cent, that of the lowest two-fifths below 16 per cent, and that of the highest fifth 43 per cent. These are figures for pre-tax cash incomes. Tax changes in 1981 added to the absolute and relative gains of the higher income groups. The 1986 tax reform of personal income taxes will do likewise, although it will also remove households in poverty from the tax rolls.

Cynics like me are bound to notice that the emphasis of supply-side tax reduction and reform has been on the cutting of top-bracket income tax rates. The emphasis on marginal incentives is reversed in the Administration's policies toward transfer programmes for the poor, where needs tests have been made more stringent and implicit tax rates (benefit losses consequent to additional earnings) have been significantly increased. In the welfare area, the Laffer curve has been matched by Murray's Law, that cutting welfare spending will *reduce* poverty. Thanks to his book *Losing Ground*, Charles Murray has become a popular favourite of the conservative convention speaker circuit, and the President appears to have embraced Murray's philosophy in his proposals for welfare reform.

Income tax reform

Faced with mounting federal and international debts but unable to agree on how to deal with them, President Reagan and Congress spent 1986 reforming personal and corporate income taxes. To most objective observers, the urgent need was to increase federal revenues. But the President insisted that the outcome of tax reform must be revenue-neutral, and Congress aquiesced. Future economic historians will shake their heads in disbelief of this distortion of priorities.

The history of this legislation is confusing and ironic. Before 1984 two tax reform proposals were before the Congress, one a Republican bill sponsored by Congressman Kemp and Senator Kasten and one a Democratic initiative by Senator Bradley and Congressman Gephardt. They were similar in lowering tax rates, broadening the tax bases, attacking loopholes, and purporting to be revenue-neutral. To gain tardily the initiative on this issue in a campaign year, the President asked the Treasury to come up with its own proposal, a task that took almost the whole of 1984 and put the matter on the political back-burner until after the election. The proposal, known as Treasury I, was remarkably apolitical. It was prepared by dedicated experts who were committed to making the system economically neutral, not just revenue-neutral. The distortions they sought to correct were mostly provisions of ERTA, enacted at the behest the same Administration only three years before. The anguished howls from businesses whom those provisions had benefited, and from other interested parties, led in 1985 to Treasury II, a political compromise that sacrificed the purity and incentive neutrality of Treasury I, and to passage in the House of Representatives of a different political compromise, closer to Treasury I.

The Senate took up the matter in 1986. The proposals on the table were variations on a common strategy. A principal objective was to lower marginal tax rates and to reduce the number of brackets. A rule of the game on which the President adamantly insisted was reduction of the top marginal rate of personal income tax from 50 per cent to 35 per cent or less. Before 1981 it had been 70 per cent for 'unearned' income, and before 1971 top tax rates of 70 per cent or higher had applied to all income. Revenue lost by rate cuts was to be regained by broadening the tax base, eliminating or limiting some deductions, exemptions, tax credits, and shelters. The same strategy applied to the corporate income tax. The rates were to be reduced, but the taxable base was to be broadened, principally by phasing out the Investment Tax Credit, accelerated depreciation and expensing of capital outlays, and other incentives for investment. The ITC dated from the Kennedy Administration, but most of the other 'loopholes' were part of ERTA in 1981, when the Reagan Administration and Congress took seriously the promotion of investment. Another common feature was shifting of burden from the personal to the corporate tax. The base-broadening politically feasible in the personal tax was insufficient to render its reform along these lines revenue-neutral, and individuals were unlikely to discern the indirect burden on them of higher corporate taxation.

Even so, it appeared that protests from lobbyists representing taxpayers with vested interests in the provisions slated to be sacrificed to rate reduction would prevent the Senate from agreeing on a bill that the House and the President would also accept. But Senator Packwood, Republican Chairman of the Finance Committee, with help from Senator Bradley across the aisle, pulled off a political miracle. The secret was to reduce personal tax rates so much, the top marginal rate to 32 per cent and the top average rate to 28 per cent, that the bait would disarm opposition from defenders of all but the most invulnerable immunities from the rates. Even so, the sponsors had to buy the votes of many members of Congress by agreeing to an unprecedented number of particularized 'transitional' exceptions, totalling $14 billion in lost revenue, one of the most distasteful episodes in the unsavoury history of tax legislation. The President and Congressmen and Senators of both parties did not deny themselves an orgy of self-congratulation once the Act was passed and signed.

The tax reform of 1986 improves the personal and corporate income tax codes in horizontal equity and in economic neutrality and efficiency. It shuts down outrageous shelters that allowed wealthy operators to avoid taxes that ordinary wage-earners could not escape—for example, claiming paper losses on highly levered real estate investments by deductions of fast depreciation and of interest charges, then selling the property but paying low-rate capital gains taxes. While eliminating concessionary investment incentives in the corporate tax law, the new Act makes effective profits tax rates much more uniform among industries and among different types and durabilities of capital assets. The regressive cuts in tax rates are a high political price for these improvements. There is no evidence that low top rates will stimulate enterprise, innovation, and effort. Our economy and many foreign economies have flourished with progressive rate schedules. Viewing the whole history since 1980, I observe that the 1981 reduction of high-bracket rates was obtained without any compensatory sacrifice of loopholes, indeed with the enactment of provisions further eroding the tax base. Starting from this new *status quo*, in 1986 the wealthy successfully extracted further reduction in top rates as the price of closing loopholes that never were justified.

THE LEGACY OF REAGANOMICS

The crippled public sector

Ronald Reagan will bequeath a crippled federal government to his successor. He tried to squeeze ambitious growth of defence spending into a budget he was simultaneously depriving of tax revenues. Legislators of both parties, most of whom knew better, deserve a share of the blame, for their supine surrender to the President's programme.

President Johnson lost the place in history his domestic social policies could have earned him by his tragic error in embroiling the United States in the Vietnam War. His by-product error in fiscal policy, his insistence on 'guns *and* butter', his delay in asking for taxes to pay for the war, fatefully destroyed the economic stability achieved prior to 1966. The lesson of the Vietnam War may be saving President Reagan and the country from pushing his obsessions with communist threats in Central America to the point of US military intervention. Yet he too is likely to be seen in history as repeating the 'guns and butter' mistake.

President Reagan is right that the country can afford the arms build-up he has asked for. Whether it is needed, and whether it is good national policy, are questions on which an economist has no special expertise. Assuming the build-up is needed, it should not be the victim of budget deficit control. Nor should its burden be placed narrowly on other government programmes and their beneficiaries. A rich country can afford the defence it needs, and it can also afford the Library of Congress, public broadcasting, good statistics, environmental protection, and humane treatment of the poor and disadvantaged. Reagan's 'butter' is different from Johnson's; it consists in the tax reductions he is determined to protect, largely to the benefit of the wealthier citizens of the country. The policy has had the adverse macroeconomic consequences I discussed above notably including the trade deficit. The policy has also brought federal budget-making to the political impasse I described, ending in the colossal irrationality of Gramm–Rudman.

Income taxes have long been the major source of federal revenue. They yielded revenues equal to 11.3 per cent of GNP in 1959, 13.3 in 1969, and 11.6 in 1979. They will yield only 10.7 per cent of GNP in 1989. It is true that payroll tax revenues have risen from 2.4 per cent of GNP in 1959 to 6.8 estimated for 1989. They are, however, earmarked for social insurance benefits, mostly for old age and survivors' insurance. Social security stands on its own feet; it will run surpluses over the next twenty years, building up a Trust Fund that will be needed later in the next century. These accounts are now officially 'off-budget' once more. Regular 'on-budget' governmental activities depend on income taxes—or on deficits. In 1979 defence and debt interest took 6.4 per cent of GNP, and income tax revenues amounting to 4.1 per cent were available for other activities. In 1989 defence and interest will take 8.7 per cent of GNP, leaving income taxes of only 2.0 per cent for other activities.

The social costs and dangers of the resulting austerities in the civilian budget are already evident. Here are some examples:

The federal government is abandoning 'revenue-sharing', federal support of state and local governments' expenditures on infrastructure investments, education, and social programmes. Those governments have responded partly by curtailing those expenditures, as the Administration intended, and partly by raising their own taxes—generally more regressive than the federal income tax.

Secretary of State Shultz is right to complain that Congress does not provide enough funds for foreign aid, for effective diplomatic representation around the world, and for meeting US obligations to international organizations. He should address his complaint to the White House too.

President Reagan promised Prime Minister Mulroney action on acid rain, but the funds are missing from the President's budget. The President and Mrs Reagan made headlines when they solemnly proclaimed an all-out war on drug abuse, but his very next budget cut the funds. American airports and skies are increasingly congested, but there are no funds for expanding facilities, air control personnel and safety enforcement. National highways deteriorate, but petrol taxes supposedly earmarked for their maintenance and improvement remain unspent in order to hold down the deficit. The federal government relies on tax-deductible private donations for more and more purposes: for example, advancing the cause of democracy throughout the world, and enabling the White House and State Department to receive foreign dignitaries in facilities worthy of a great and rich Republic. Cutbacks in federal statistical programmes hamper academic researchers, businesses and others who rely on them. Our national parks deteriorate. Federal support of education and science is short-changed. The federal service is underpaid relative to the private sector, and at the same time reviled by its chief as a parasitic, power-hungry bureaucracy. (As I told an undergraduate class recently; Paul Volcker, the most important economic official in the world, is paid less than green business school graduates hired to guess what Volcker will do next week.)

There never was any reason to believe the Reagan thesis that the trouble with the US economy was that the public sector was too big, either in its real economic activities or in its welfare state transfers. On both counts, the United States had smaller public sectors, relative to the size of the economy, than any advanced capitalist democracy except Japan and Australia. The Administration's view that only formation of physical capital by private business provides for the future of the nation is a vulgar error that sacrificed public investment in human capital (education and health), natural resources, and public infrastructure to the construction of shopping malls and luxury casino hotels.

The current conservative fad is 'privatization'. The Administration's budget-makers have hit upon sales of federal assets as a cute technical way to appear to comply with Gramm–Rudman. Obviously no business accountant would regard asset sales as deficit-reducing current revenue. But privatization is welcome to free market ideologues anyway. Although some privatization may be desirable and cost-effective, current proposals reflect budget cosmetics and doctrinaire principle rather than case-by-case examinations of long-run costs and benefits.

Certainly some federal programmes cut or eliminated over the past six years deserved Stockman's axe, and that is true too of some of the targets of the President's proposed budget for fiscal year 1988. These expenditures would not have been vulnerable under the 'business as usual' budget politics of previous Administrations and Congresses. Yet other cows that deserved slaying under free market principles have remained sacred. The most expensive example is federal agricultural policy; this Administration has spent record amounts for farm price supports and related subsidies. Another example, of interest to Canadians, is our maritime policy. In both these cases costly budgetary subventions are accompanied by regulations restricting competition.

As for deregulation, the major initiatives in energy, air and surface transportation, and finance were begun under President Carter. They have been continued and extended. The Reagan Administration's own initiatives have concentrated less on dismantling anti-competitive regulations than on relaxing those designed for environmental and social purposes. As Canadians know, it has been hard to get the President exercised about acid rain. As Blacks know, the Administration is against 'affirmative action'.

The Administration deserves credit for defending liberal trade policies against the pressures for protectionism, all too tempting to Democratic politicians. But it was the Administration's macroeconomic policies that by appreciating the dollar made American producers uncompetitive in world trade and invited protectionist demands from desperate industries and displaced workers. Moreover, the Administration's rhetoric has been more liberal than its actions. Like his predecessors, the President has arranged import quotas and special duties for particular hard-hit industries.

Missing agenda

Two major economic problems have not been on the Reagan agenda at all. The first is macroeconomic, having to do with unemployment and inflation. The greatest basic obstacle to full prosperity is the fear of policy-makers, at the central bank and throughout the government, and of the influential public, that a return to as low unemployment rates as we reached in prosperities in the 1970s would set off another inflationary spiral. This fear may be obsolete and unjustified, but it is a reality. If it is justified, then the inflation-safe unemployment rate is too high, 6 per cent or more, and we should be actively seeking structural reforms that would lower it. These could include pro-competitive labour market policies, changes in trade union legislation, incentives for employers and workers to adopt profit-sharing or revenue-sharing contracts, and the use of wage-price guideposts with tax-based inducements for compliance. This is not the occasion to discuss specific proposals. I simply observe that this Administration has no concern about this crucial matter.

The second problem conspicuously missing from the Reagan agenda is the pathology of urban ghettoes inhabited by Blacks and other minorities. These neighbourhoods, the people who live in them, and the cities where they are located have been indeed 'losing ground', to use the title of the Murray book mentioned above. The War on Poverty and the Great Society did not prevent or arrest the downward vicious spirals of these areas and populations. Neither did subsequent neglect, or decline in the real public resources channelled to them. Right now the only Administration response is to cut welfare spending further in the belief that this will cut both welfare dependency and poverty. Meanwhile the lower Bronx and Harlem, Roxbury in Boston, Woodlawn and the West Side of Chicago, and similar areas of many other small and large cities are a disgraceful and dangerous contrast to the affluent styles of life displayed in the centres of the same cities and flaunted on national television. President Reagan is fond of likening America to 'a shining city on a hill'. There is a Hill district in my own New Haven, and it does not shine.

At the outset I placed Rondald Reagan in the select class of government leaders who substantially and durably shift the course of policy and the centre of political debate. Yet at the end I do have some doubts about the permanence of the rightward Reagan counter-revolution. Prior to the Iran/contra scandals, opinion polls showed Ronald Reagan's high approval rating to be without precedent for a President in his sixth year; he still is remarkably popular as a person, even among citizens critical of his role in the adventures recently revealed. On very few specific issues, however, have polls shown majorities favouring Reagan's side. In the nature of the case, an anti-government President leaves few public monuments. This President will leave none comparable to Roosevelt's social security or Johnson's civil rights and health insurance.

The awful truth is that Reaganomics was a fraud from the beginning. The moral of its failures and of its legacies is that a nation pays a heavy price when it entrusts its government and economy to simplistic ideologues, however smooth their performances on television.

8 The Conservative Counter-revolution in Economic Policy*

The economic programme of the Reagan Administration, like that of the Thatcher government in Britain, manifests a conservative counter-revolution in the theory, ideology, and practice of economic policy. The aim of the counter-revolution is to shrink the economic influence of government, especially central government, relative to that of private enterprise and free markets. Several kinds of policies are at stake, concerning respectively

- macroeconomic stabilization—the use of fiscal, monetary, and other policies affecting national production, employment, prices, and other variables of economy-wide significance,
- economic inequality—the use of the public fisc to redistribute income and wealth,
- resource allocation—national priorities among various public and private goods,
- regulation of economic activities and markets.

THE EVOLUTION OF STABILIZATION POLICY

I have referred to a counter-revolution, so I should remind you of the revolution to which it is the counter. That took place some 35–45 years ago, just before and after World War II, in this country and in other Western capitalist democracies. Radical changes occurred in the practice of economic policy and in the theory of political economy. Live memory of the Great Depression created a broad consensus that the state must assume responsibility for maintaining prosperity, as well as for protecting individual citizens against the inevitable insecurities

*October 1981, New York University Sesquicentennial Conference. Published in *New York Review of Books*, 3 December 1981. Reprinted with permission from *The New York Review of Books*. © 1981 Nyrev, Inc.

of life in a market economy. The New Deal in the United States and social democratic movements in Europe were the agencies of these changes. They also expanded government investments in schools, housing, transportation, and other public goods, and augmented the market power of workers, trade unions, and farmers *vis-à-vis* business. Over three postwar decades these changes were largely accepted by all mainstream political parties and extended by governments of various political colours. Though rumblings of discontent have been heard in increasing volume over the past fifteen years, only recently have the counter-revolutionaries gained political power.

I shall confine myself mainly to the United States and the first two agenda of the revolution and counter-revolution, macroeconomic stabilization and redistribution of income and wealth. Two acts of Congress symbolize the revolution. The Employment Act of 1946 dedicated federal power to the achievement of 'maximum employment, production, and purchasing power'. Ten years earlier, under the Social Security Act, the federal government recognized an obligation to protect individual citizens from personal economic misfortunes—workers without jobs, aged without funds, children without fathers. The New Deal had already put the federal government in the business of welfare and work relief, the insurance of bank deposits and mortgages, and other 'safety nets'. By 1947 then, the federal government had assumed responsibilities both to maintain general prosperity and to insure and indemnify the worst individual casualties of depression and economic change.

These really were new responsibilities. Fiscal and monetary policies were not significantly dedicated to macroeconomic stabilization before the late 1930s. In 1929–34 both Hoover and Roosevelt raised taxes and sought vainly to balance the federal budget; they were worried about the depression's effect on the budget, not the budget's impact on the economy. Throughout the precipitous decline of 1929–32 monetary policy gave second priority to the American economy, and primary emphasis to defending US gold reserves and the gold value of the dollar—until the disasters of the winter of 1932–3 forced Roosevelt to suspend gold convertibility and devalue the dollar. As for relief of the victims of the depression, Hoover—a Quaker who had earned worldwide fame as a humanitarian in directing relief efforts in devastated parts of Europe after World War I—regarded it on principle as the responsibility of private charity and local government, not the federal Treasury. Roosevelt, fortunately, was a pragmatist.

Similar redefinitions of the economic responsibilities of central government occurred in other advanced democracies in the 1930s and 1940s. In Britain two wartime reports by Lord Beveridge, one on social insurance and one on full employment, set the stage for postwar macroeconomic strategy and 'welfare state' legislation.

To these political developments there were important intellectual counterparts and foundations. A revolution in macroeconomics and in the theory of monetary and fiscal policy began with J. M. Keynes's *General Theory of Employment, Interest, and Money* in 1936 and spread through the English-speaking world and after the war to continental Europe and Japan. This provided the rationale for the full employment commitments of the several countries, along with guidance on how to implement them. The business cycle was no longer to be seen, as both orthodox and Marxist economists saw it, as an inevitable and functional characteristic of capitalism. According to Keynesian theory, economy-wide fluctuations in economic activity are wasteful; they can be avoided by active fiscal and monetary intervention, that is, by so-called stabilization policies.

Keynesian macroeconomics does not logically lead to any position pro or con welfare state measures. But, again in contrast to both Right and Left, it certainly does not say that redistribution of income and wealth by taxation and transfer is fatal to capitalism, or even damaging. In Keynes's personal view, 'The outstanding faults of the economic society in which we live are its failure to provide for full employment and its arbitrary and inequitable distribution of wealth and incomes'. He was confident that both flaws could be corrected without sacrificing the efficiency and progressiveness of market capitalism, for which he had the same respect as his classical forebears and colleagues. Twenty years later, Paul Samuelson, the principal architect of the synthesis of Keynesian and neoclassical theories that became the orthodox mainstream of American economics, expressed this optimistic view very clearly:

A community can have full employment, can at the same time have the rate of capital formation it wants, and can accomplish all this compatibly with the degree of income-redistributing taxation it ethically desires.

Keynes and Samuelson are saying, in other words, that an amalgam of capitalism and social democracy is viable and robust. In contrast, both extreme Right and extreme Left argue that capitalism cannot afford or survive egalitarian policies.

The postwar era, especially its first twenty-five years, appeared to justify the optimism of Keynes and Samuelson. In no other period of similar length have productivity per worker and living standards grown so fast, or aggregate production and employment advanced so steadily, or world trade expanded so greatly. The last ten years were disappointing compared with the 1950s and 1960s. But we should not lose perspective.

The main source of disappointment and disillusionment with the revolution was the stagflation of the 1970s, the combination of high inflation and high unemployment. Even during its era of apparent success, Keynesian policies for full employment and counter-cyclical stabilization aroused chronic anxieties about inflation. Indeed the protagonists themselves, beginning in the 1940s, warned that full employment, by removing the wage discipline exerted by unemployment and the threat of lay-offs, might not be compatible with price stability. Some of them foresaw the need for direct restraints on wages and prices to reconcile the two goals. The economy would have a secular bias toward inflation, they observed, if wages and prices rose freely in expanding industries and during economy-wide booms but fell slowly if at all in declining sectors and during short recessions.

Moreover, inflationary bias was exacerbated by social welfare legislation, extended and expanded as it was by postwar administrations and Congresses of both parties, most dramatically beginning with the Great Society programmes of the late 1960s. Social insurance dulls to some degree the incentive to seek and accept employment, especially the less remunerative or attractive jobs.

Probably more important were developments that fall under the fourth of my initial classifications. The Rooseveltian political coalition opened old-fashioned interest group politics to large groups previously excluded. Like all governments, our federal government has always catered *ad hoc* to private business interests with political clout, as our history of tariffs, 'internal improvements', land grants, bank charters, and subsidies amply illustrates. Beginning in the 1930s trade unions gained federal protection for organizing and bargaining. Wages, hours, and conditions of work became subject to federal standards. Farmers were not only subsidized but organized into federally administered cartels. The promotion of monopolistic powers for unions of workers and farmers was justified by J. K. Galbraith and others as countervailing the monopolistic powers of big business, to the benefit of the society as a whole. This dubious proposition was never congenial to liberal Keynesians devoted principally to full employment and diminished inequality. In any event, these countervailing powers increased inflationary bias. Workers, unionized or not, had more power to gain wage increases in booms or to resist cuts in downturns. Agricultural price supports diminished the downward trends and cyclical declines of food and materials prices that contributed so much to price stability in the 1920s and earlier.

Nevertheless the inflation record of the United States was very good until the late 1960s. That deficit financing of the Vietnam War overheated an economy already operating at capacity was no surprise to any economist, Keynesian, monetarist, or classical. That inflation accelerated in the 1970s, in spite of monetary policies that triggered three recessions, in spite of unemployment higher than in the two previous decades, is the great disappointment to theory and policy that set the stage for the counter-revolution. Many observers would explain the stagflation by the series of external shocks, unprecedented in their severity, that hammered the world economy in the 1970s: the depreciation of the dollar after Nixon proclaimed it inconvertible into gold in 1971, the worldwide commodity shortages and speculative booms in 1973, the two big OPEC shocks, 1973–4 and 1979. Others blame overstimulative monetary–fiscal policies in 1972–3 and 1977–8. The controversy is far from resolution, but the Reagan administration is sure of its diagnosis: the disappointments of the 1970s were the inevitable outcome of mistaken policies followed throughout the postwar decades.

THE COUNTER-REVOLUTION

To the revolution of 35–45 years ago, Reaganomics is, like Thatcherism in the UK, the political and ideological counter-revolution. Just as Keynesian theory enspirited the revolution, so a wave of professional reaction to the synthesis of Keynesian and neo-classical doctrine that became orthodoxy in the 1960s sustains the counter-revolution. In both instances, of course, there are many divergences among economic theory, popular ideology, and actual policy. None the less, in both cases, a common tide of opinion floods academic journals, popular media, political rhetoric, Congress or Parliament, and the guiding philosophies of President or Prime Minister. Rightly or wrongly, the revolution is blamed for the 'stagflationary' disappointments of the 1970s, the high rates of unemployment, inflation, and interest, the depressed stock market, the slowdowns of productivity growth and capital formation. The old doctrines and policies, new forty years ago, are discredited, replaced by new doctrines and policies, old forty years ago.

Respecting stabilization, the new doctrine is that active fiscal and monetary intervention—characterized or caricatured as 'fine-tuning'—is the problem, not the solution. The government should forswear counter-cyclical policies and let the market economy stabilize itself, as it will, given confidence that government policies will be stable. Thus the central bank should tie itself, or be tied to, a fixed-rate rule of monetary growth, independently of the state of the economy. Likewise federal tax and expenditure legislation should not be responsive to business conditions. Various proposals to make macroeconomic policies blind to cyclical fluctuations, including constitutional amendments to require annual budget balance and to restrict government expenditure and monetary growth, are currently before the country and the Congress, and are viewed benignly by the Reagan Administration.

One of the arguments against the counter-cyclical policies of the past is that they fostered inflation by removing from business firms and workers the incentive to lower prices and wages during recessions in order to protect sales and jobs—why not just wait until the government pumps up demand again? In Britain Margaret Thatcher has put her countrymen and women on notice that the only way they can restore the jobs and prosperity lost in the current slump is to disinflate. Her Majesty's Government will do nothing about it.

The same warning has been repeatedly issued in America by Chairman Paul Volcker of the Federal Reserve who, unfortunately for the effectiveness of the warnings, does not quite command the same audience as a head of government. President Reagan has not made Volcker's threat credible to those who determine wages and prices; instead he has undermined it by promising disinflation without tears, an instant spurt of rapid growth, falling unemployment, and declining inflation. Recently, it is true, his Treasury Secretary has lapsed into old Keynesian 'error', urging the Fed to loosen up a bit to forestall incipient recession. On the other hand, the Administration is not fine-tuning fiscal policy in an anti-recessionary direction. Instead its current fine-tuning is aimed in the other direction—trying like Hoover and Roosevelt in the early 1930s to offset the effects of the recession on the budget deficit. (However, recent statements by David Stockman, Director of the Office of Management and Budget, show awareness of the futility of aiming at specific budget deficits in a weakening economy.)

The renunciation of stabilization policy implies, if actually carried through, that the government no longer has meaningful goals for *real* economic variables—for example for employment and unemployment, national production and its growth. Of course, any political administration will publish its projections, scenarios, and hopes. But these will mean nothing if the government eschews measures to make them come true. The Thatcher and Reagan governments both say that they are providing a stable monetary and fiscal framework within which private enterprise and free markets will restore prosperity and non-inflationary growth. Another way to put it is that whatever economic outcomes private agents generate within the framework are by definition optimal. This is how the recent Chairman of the Council of Economic Advisers, Murray Weidenbaum, put the case, even if his client did not yet quite understand it that way.

Clearly this is a 180° reversal of the commitment of the Employment Act of 1946, not to mention the Full Employment and Balanced Growth Act of 1978 (Humphrey–Hawkins). To be sure, employment goals have been slipping for a long time. The unemployment rate was 3 per cent at the end of the Korean War, 4 per cent at the peak of the boom in the mid 1950s when the Fed applied the brakes, and 5 per cent at the next cyclical peak in 1960. The Kennedy–Johnson Administration officially adopted a full employment goal of 4 per cent unemployment, achieved it in 1965, and overachieved it during the Vietnam War. During the 1970s operational unemployment targets were not made explicit, but policy moves revealed implicit targets of 5 per cent, then 6 per cent, now probably 7 per cent or more. The slippage, of course, reflects the primacy given to the frustrating battle against inflation. But if and when that battle is won, I doubt that the Federal Reserve and the Administration would risk re-ignition of inflation by relaxing the monetary screws enough to permit much reduction of unemployment from the 7–8 per cent range. More likely they would settle for a resumption of normal sustainable real growth at prevailing rates of utilization, and would not provide financing for temporarily higher growth to absorb the slack created during the anti-inflationary fight. This scenario is, by the way, explicit in the projections of the UK Treasury.

In the US today macroeconomic policy and prospect are dominated by Federal Reserve monetary policy. The Reagan Administration assigned disinflation to the 'Fed', chided the governors for past mistakes, and urged them to be tough. The Fed is being tough, and as Chairman Volcker has repeatedly made clear, proposes to be gradually but resolutely tougher every year until inflation rates are insignificantly different from zero. As Volcker and his colleagues appreciate much better than President Reagan and his associates, Fed money supply policies will not allow room for real economic growth unless wage and price inflation melts by a point or two a year. Given the stubbornness of built-in wage and cost inflation, there is likely to be considerable economic pain and damage during a transition of several years. The Administration rejects on principle any direct wage and price policies, formal or informal, even diffuse persuasive appeals by the president. In their absence, the only mechanism by which monetary deceleration produces disinflation is by creating sufficient economic distress that workers and employers, desperate to protect jobs and solvency, settle for lower wage and price increases than those currently prevailing. We can see this process at work across the Atlantic, where mid-way in Mrs Thatcher's five-year term the record unemployment rates are in double digits and inflation rates are still in double digits but slowly declining.

A Thatcher scenario was not quite what the Reagan Administration had in mind. The 'supply-side' tax cuts were intended to unleash a surge of investment, enterprise, and productive effort. Supply-siders were impatient with traditional conservative orthodoxies that tax stimuli must wait for budget balance and disinflation. Exploiting the eager competition of both parties in Congress, they succeeded in outdistancing the budget cuts of the redoubtable Mr Stockman. But the tax bill only solidified the firm resolve of Mr Volcker, and he is bound to win a fiscal–monetary tug-of-war. As the securities markets perceived, the situation is catch-22. Interest rates cannot be low enough to sustain expansion unless the economy is in recession.

THE REDISTRIBUTION OF INCOME AND WEALTH

I turn now to a second dimension of the counter-revolution, the distribution of income and wealth as affected by federal taxes and transfers.

Equality of opportunity has been an American ideal and an American excuse. The ideal of capitalism in a democracy is a fair race from an even start. Big prizes go to the swift, but all participants are rewarded— the more, the faster everybody runs. True, economic and social outcomes are highly unequal. The excuses are that the racers all have the same opportunities and that differential prizes generate ever larger rewards for all participants.

Opportunities are actually far from equal. We Americans escaped the feudal castes of the Old World, but erected our own racial, religious, and ethnic barriers. Even as these are overcome, the hard fact remains that children of parents of high economic and social status gain a head start—better education at home and school, better nutrition and medical care, as well as more gifts and bequests of worldly goods. To give children these advantages has indeed been traditionally a strong motivation for work, saving, and enterprise.

Wealth breeds wealth and poverty breeds poverty. Despite legendary examples of spectacular social mobility, the unequal outcomes of one generation are generally the unequal opportunities of the next. Here as in other democracies, governments have sought to arrest the momentum of inequality by free public education, social insurance, 'War on Poverty' measures, and progressive taxation.

US budget and tax legislation of 1981 is a historic reversal of direction and purpose. Existing institutions, commitments, and 'safety nets' can't be rapidly dismantled, but the message is clear enough; inequality of opportunity is no longer a concern of the federal government.

The government has virtually abandoned all pretence of taxing intergenerational transfers of wealth. Capital gains on assets so transferred are excused from income tax, and now most of them will be free of estate and gift taxes as well. In the hasty competition of both parties for the favour of wealth constituents, Congress casually liberalized these taxes without concern for unchecked dynastic wealth and inequality of opportunity.

Capital income, in contrast to wage income, is increasingly free of federal tax. Even before the 1981 tax law, the Treasury calculated that only one-third of capital income showed up as taxable personal income.[1] Taxable capital gains are seldom realized; when they are, the top tax rate will now be only 20 per cent. Deferment of tax on income saved for retirement, easily accessible via employer or do-it-yourself plans, effectively frees the returns on such saving from tax and generally moves the principal into a lower bracket. The new tax-exempt All-Savers' certificates carry no risk and beat the current inflation by several points. The monetary–fiscal policies of the Administration are a recipe for high interest rates; the tax bill eases the pain for upper-bracket taxpayers, who can escape tax on interest receipts, while claiming deductions for interest paid on mortgages, consumer debt, and other loans. The sophisticated rich know how, or know lawyers who know how, to combine depreciation and interest deductions with preferential capital gains rates to shelter salaries and self-employment incomes from taxation. Though many tears were shed in the successful effort to reduce those high bracket taxes alleged to deter saving and investment, especially the 70 per cent rate now abruptly lowered to 50 per cent, few inhabitants of those brackets paid such taxes or will pay them now.

The government is a partner in business enterprise, and recent legislation impairs its equity—almost to the point where the Treasury's share in investment costs and risks exceeds its share in prospective earnings. This is the result of combining greatly accelerated depreciation, '15–10–5–3', with the Investment Tax Credit—its value multiplied by lease-back arrangements—and interest deductions.

At the low end of the economic spectrum, federal efforts to bolster incomes and opportunities are being abandoned. As federal funds for welfare, food stamps, Medicaid, jobs and training, aid to education, and other residues of the War on Poverty are reduced and combined into block grants, the beneficiaries will be at the mercy of local legislators and taxpayers. This process is just beginning. About $150 billion in 1984 tax revenues have been given away, and thanks to bracket indexing, none will be recouped by inflation thereafter. The President has now donned his budget-balancing hat and presses Congress to redeem his promises, by making budget cuts even greater than those enacted earlier. They won't be found in defence, public debt interest, or even in social security. They will be further cuts in social programmes, more doses of the 'new federalism' that devolves these responsibilities and their funding to states and localities.

The Reagan economic programme is advertised to cure inflation and unemployment, to revive productivity, investment, hard work, and thrift. It probably cannot achieve those wonderful results. What it is sure to do is to redistribute wealth, power, and opportunity to the wealthy and powerful and their heirs. If that is its principal outcome, the public will become considerably disenchanted.

Despite its free market ideology, the Administration has done little to dismantle regulations and subsidies that are costly, inefficient, and inflationary. Agricultural programmes still not only subsidize producers but do so in ways that raise prices to consumers. Taxpayers, consumers, and shippers pay for our high-cost non-competitive merchant marine. The Carter Administration deregulated airlines, but analogous measures for surface transport are stalled. The Administration is ready enough to liberalize or discontinue regulations of business when the opposing values are consumer protection or environmental conservation. It is by no means so devoted to market freedom, competition, and consumer interest as to challenge important business, labour, and farm constituencies. These politically sacred cows have been around a long time, and no other Administrations have mustered the will or power to kill them either. But an Administration that claims a popular mandate for counter-revolution should not leave unscathed the most objectionable features of the old order.

THE OUTLOOK FOR THE 1980s

The outlook for the American economy in the 1980s contains some bright spots and some dark prospects. On the bright side, it seems unlikely that the US and the world will be hit by external shocks of the magnitude of the 1970s. Though the present oil glut may not continue, Americans are now much better adapted to high oil prices and much better prepared to cope with future increases. To the extent that productivity and capital formation were held back in the 1970s by energy shocks and uncertainty about how to adapt to them, they should rebound in the 1980s. On the dark side, the purely monetary cure for inflation can hold down the economy for half the decade, with capital formation discouraged either by high real interest rates or by gloomy profit expectations or both. The 'new federalism', as is only beginning to be realized, will have devastating effects on the finances of many state and local governments and on the services they render, especially to the poor. Meanwhile the tax cuts will be widening the gulf between the living standards of the rich and those of the poor, without the promised compensation in the conquest of stagflation. In the end, I think, a democratic polity will not tolerate in its government and central bank an economic strategy of indifference to the real state of the economy.

NOTE

1. Eugene Steuerle, 'Is income from capital subject to individual income taxation?' Office of Tax Analysis Paper 42, October 1980.

9   Reagan: Recovery or Reaction?*

President Reagan appeals for congressional and popular support of his economic recovery programme principally on the ground that this new beginning is the way, the only way, to cut inflation, put the unemployed to work, and speed up economic growth. Stagflation certainly is the debilitating economic disease of the 1970s and 1980s, and we desperately need a remedy. The President says the remedy entails cutbacks of special claims on the federal treasury, and the nation is ready to believe him and to make those sacrifices. Yet it's a mystery how one can get to the rosy fiscal and economic future he promises by pursuing his programme. Even for its authors and proponents, this is a matter of faith. In reality, the programme is largely irrelevant to stagflation and should be judged by the Congress and the people by its true objectives and predictable effects, which are quite different.

The programme consists mainly of Stockman's hit list of budget cuts and of Kemp–Roth tax reductions. Business is to get fast depreciation write-offs, and the Federal Reserve is to keep tightening the monetary screws. The grand macroeconomic strategy is obscure, but the redirection of national priorities is clear enough. Resources are to be shifted from the public sector to private use, from civilian government to defence, from federal to state and local control. Wealth and power are to be redistributed to the wealthy and powerful.

Over the last half century, this country and all other democratic nations have developed a pragmatic mixture of private and public social and economic institutions. Imperfect as they are, these institutions have made capitalism a more equitable and viable system than it was in the preceding century. They have gained the support of a broad political consensus, excluding only extremes on the Left and Right. Those who

*March 1981, published as 'Sleight of mind' in The New Republic, 21 March 1981, pp. 13–16. Reprinted by permission of The New Republic, © 1981, The New Republic, Inc.

value the tradition should defend it. President Reagan's hysterical exaggerations notwithstanding, no imminent economic disaster compels us to turn back the clock.

Evaluated on their merits, many of the proposed budget economies do meet the tests of efficiency and equity. Examples are dairy price supports, subsidized student loans, aid to 'federally impacted' school districts, air and water user charges, trade adjustment assistance. There are more where these came from, and maybe they will be picked up in the next round (for example, other farm price supports and subsidies, maritime shipping and shipbuilding subsidies, veterans' medical care for non-service-connected disabilities). Even Social Security benefits, overindexed and tax free, deserve Mr Stockman's scrutiny; most of them go to people well above 'safety-net' levels. His attention is also invited to the host of other 'tax expenditures', open-ended licences to taxpayers to dispose of potential federal revenues (deductibility of mortgage interest, exclusion of state and local debt interest, charitable deductions, energy tax credits). And a President who bravely proclaims 'The taxing power of the government ... must not be used to regulate the economy or bring about social changes' surely will think twice before proposing tax credits for private school tuitions.

But the cuts in welfare, nutrition, and jobs programmes, in combination with the highly regressive tax reductions, are mean spirited. Marginal tax rates are to be lowered for the rich to provide incentives to work and invest. At the same time, the administration is increasing disincentives for the poor and working poor through needs tests for food stamps and other programmes. Increased autonomy for the states in administration of welfare and Medicaid is a step backward. Regional differences in benefits, eligibility standards, and fairness of administration will become an even greater source of privation, inequity, and migration than they have been. Cuts in federal aid will create serious fiscal crises for state and local governments, which will have to raise taxes, issue more debt, and curtail services.

And some of the Reagan–Stockman budget cuts are narrow minded and vindictive. A wealthy pluralistic nation can afford a few tax dollars for space exploration, for the arts and humanities, for non-commercial broadcasting, and, if I may say so, for basic social science research (targeted for a cut within the billion-dollar National Science Foundation from $40 million to $10 million).

Whatever their direct costs and benefits, these budget and tax proposals are not a cure for stagflation. There are two reasons why this is so. The first is that the tax and spending proposals for 1981 and 1982 virtually cancel each other out in net impact on demand for goods and services and for funds from capital markets. Congress may shift the balance one way or the other, of course. According to administration projections, tax cuts in subsequent years will make the budget expansionary. Whether they will be a welcome stimulus to economic recovery or an unwelcome source of higher prices and interest rates is uncertain today.

The second reason is much more important. It is the failure of the programme to face squarely the stubborn wage and cost inflation in America today. Wage rates and other dollar incomes have been rising at 10 per cent per year. Until this stubborn trend in production costs is broken, inflation will not subside permanently. This is hard arithmetic fact, as true in the through-the-looking-glass world of supply-side economics as in monetarist or Keynesian models.

Actual consumer price inflation, month to month and year to year, is more volatile than the underlying core of wage and cost inflation. It reflects world prices of oil and other commodities, US agricultural harvests and exports, mortgage interest rates, changes of Social Security and sales taxes, depreciation or appreciation of the dollar against other currencies, and a host of other events. Their effects on inflation as measured by the Consumer Price Index occur irregularly and are often transient and reversible. Thus the index shows frighteningly high inflation rates during OPEC shocks and oil supply interruptions, but below average rates when oil markets are quiescent. The CPI spurts during credit crunches and food shortages, and slows down when they are relieved. At various times during the next four years—perhaps if he is lucky, in election years—President Reagan will have good news to report about inflation. But it will not be lasting good news unless wage and cost inflation subside significantly.

President Reagan's economic scenario takes nine points off consumer price inflation in five years. Even an optimist about productivity, food prices, and—despite decontrol and OPEC—energy prices cannot expect so much price disinflation unless at least five points are knocked off wage inflation. It will probably take more. How is the programme for economic recovery supposed to make this happen?

Certainly not by the classical 'cold turkey' cure, involving deep recession and high unemployment, prolonged until workers desperate to protect jobs and employers on the verge of bankruptcy cut wages and prices. The President wants and expects nothing of the kind. He promises 13 million new jobs and reduction of unemployment to 6 per cent in 1985. Prime Minister Thatcher tells unruly citizens they will never enjoy prosperity again until they mend their inflationary ways, and she means it. Ronald Reagan is not Margaret Thatcher.

The President and his advisers assign the conquest of inflation to the Federal Reserve. They urge the Fed to slow money growth gradually and predictably until it is no faster than growth of goods and services, that is until it accommodates no inflation. Federal Reserve chairman Paul Volcker thought he was already on that path. But unless wage, cost, and price inflation subside concurrently, this is the 'cold turkey' recipe, the same one that gave us the last two credit crunches and recessions. The Administration wants a vigorous recovery instead. But as long as the wage and cost inflation proceeds untamed, financing a Reagan recovery will take more money and credit than Volcker wants to provide, and more than the Administration says it wants the Fed to allow. The President may wish to compartmentalize the twin goals of disinflation and recovery, later blaming the Federal Reserve if he doesn't achieve both. But his failure to face the real conflict between them is the fatal flaw of his own programme.

Administration spokesmen say as little as possible about such contradictions. But reporters perceptive enough to inquire have elicited a resolution of sorts. The programme itself, the lower inflation projected in the scenario and the threat-promise of fiscal and monetary discipline, is supposed to diminish inflationary expectations and thus melt the hard core of wage and cost inflation directly, short-circuiting the painful discipline of Thatcherism. We say inflation will subside, so people will expect it to subside, so they will take smaller wage gains and boost prices more slowly, so inflation will subside.

If the strategy is drastic revision of expectations, the President and his economic team are doing their best to keep it secret from those on whose decisions and actions its success depends—not financial wizards in New York, Boston, and San Francisco but business managers, workers, union leaders in Worcester, Milwaukee, and San Diego. They don't know who Paul Volcker is or understand what targets for *M-1A*, *M-1B*, and *M-2* have to do with their sales and jobs. They have heard previous optimistic White House predictions of lower inflation, and they are likely to wait and see before they act. Placing the entire blame for stagflation on federal profligacy, President Reagan in effect has told the people that they have no role or responsibility in its solution except to bear cheerfully the budget cuts he is proposing. Symbolic of this message, one of his first acts as President was to dismantle the Council on Wage and Price Stability.

Our core inflation has resisted the three recessions since 1970 and has ratcheted up in the two recoveries. It is strongly entrenched in long-term wage contracts and perpetuated by catching up and leap-frogging as contracts are sequentially renegotiated. It is whistling in the dark to count on rapid erosion of the institutional patterns and

expectations that sustain this inflation. A policy like Mrs Thatcher's
requires the government to convince the country of its willingness to
endure the 'cold turkey' cure for inflation if necessary and as long as
necessary. The theory and the hope are that wage and cost inflation
will melt quickly in the fact of a 'credible threat'. The policy hasn't
been tried in this country, and I fear its results would be as slow and
uncertain here as in Britain, even if resolutely and clearly announced.
The Administration is not even making a good try.

President Reagan challenged sceptics of his programme to come up
with better alternatives, or else to shut up. He succeeded in muting
criticism. The *New York Times*, for example, publicly shut up. Should
critics of laetrile, alchemy, and astrology be silent because they can't
claim alternative ways of curing cancer, synthesizing gold, and telling
fortunes? Should those who see no clothes on the emperor be quiet
for fear their eyes deceive them? The President vastly overstated
the country's economic plight in his preparatory fireside speech of
10 February, shamefully misusing statistics to make his case. He is
advertising his medicine as a cure for the twin maladies of inflation
and unemployment. Many of his patients would not want to swallow
his pills if they were peddled just as antidotes to the Great Society.

Anyway, there is a better and surer way to attack stagflation. It is
to organize a concerted mutual disinflation of wages, costs, and mark-
ups. Announce a schedule, for a transitional five-year period, of
gradually declining wage-increase guideposts. Reward compliance with
the guideposts by tax rebates to the workers, and to the employer as
well if his mark-up percentage does not increase. These would offset
increased payroll taxes and would be a constructive use of some of
the tax revenue the Administration proposes to give away by
Kemp–Roth. Let the Federal Reserve announce and execute monetary
policies that bring about, on a schedule consistent with the guideposts,
a gradual reduction in the rate of growth of monetary demand for
goods and services. A flexible tax-based incomes policy of this kind
does not confine the economy to the straitjacket of all-out detailed
controls. Concerted with monetary policy, it avoids the fatal flaw of
some past incomes policies; it is not a substitute for monetary discipline
and does not try to suppress inflationary symptoms of excess demand.
It proposes to change embedded expectations and patterns by actual
experience, not by wishful thinking or verbal threats and promises.
Presidential leadership is required to assemble the consensus needed
to support such a policy.

The ideology of the present Administration firmly excludes any
approach of this kind. The new President clearly has capacities for

political leadership that we have not seen in the 'bully pulpit' of the White House for many years. The country is in the mood for a new beginning. It is too bad the rare opportunity is being wasted, and far worse that it is being exploited to engineer a social counter-revolution.

10 The Reagan Economic Plan— Supply-side, Budget, and Inflation*

A speaker who casts doubts on President Reagan's Economic Recovery Program is likely to be as unwelcome as a ghost at a wedding feast. After viewing the euphoria of the joint session of Congress when the President displayed his resilience and his oratorical magic, I hate to be a wet blanket. I wish that his was a cause to which I too could rally. I would like to be enthusiastic about the dawn of the New Beginning.

There are several ways in which we might view the programme. We could examine its *micro*-economics, how it reorders the nation's priorities, reallocates the country's resources, and redistributes income, wealth, and power among individuals, groups, and regions. These may be the most important issues, the most fundamental new directions. The Reagan counter-revolution proposes to shift resources from public sector to private sector, from civilian government to national defence, from the federal government to state and local governments, from beneficiaries of social programmes to the taxpayers, from the poor and the near-poor to the affluent and the very rich. These proposals deserve to be considered in detail, item by item, and evaluated in terms of their economic efficiency and equity.

However, the Administration bills and sells its programme primarily as a *macro*-economic policy. The President and his spokesmen appeal for support of their counter-revolutionary reallocations and redistributions not on their intrinsic merits, but on the grounds that they are necessary and sufficient to solve the problem of stagflation. Here, we are told, is the remedy, the only remedy, for high unemployment, high inflation, low growth, and lagging productivity. We are asked to swallow the microeconomic medicine not because it tastes good but because it is good for what ails us. So far, it appears, Congress, press,

*May 1981, Federal Reserve Bank of San Francisco, published in Supplement to the Bank's *Economic Review*, May 1981, pp. 5–14.

and public readily accept the programme as the necessary remedy of our macroeconomic ills.

It is the macro aspect of the programme that I propose to discuss. I'll begin by reminding you that there is precious little evidence in international experience that successful macroeconomic management is inversely correlated with size of government, tax burdens, public debt, and social transfers. Some countries whose macroeconomic performance we envy have much larger public sectors, more generous social welfare programmes, greater tax burdens, and higher budget deficits.

The Reagan recovery programme, viewed as macro policy, has a fiscal side and a monetary side. Together they are projected to accomplish the disinflation and the real economic growth shown in columns four and five of Table 10.1 and columns one and three of Table 10.2.

A NEUTRAL FISCAL PACKAGE

The fiscal policy, viewed from the standpoint of conventional aggregate demand analysis, does not seem to be a significant factor of either stimulus or contraction over the five years for which it is projected. It is important to judge the impact of fiscal policy against what is and has been going on, last year and this year, and not to use as a hypothetical reference path President Carter's January budget. The Carter budget, since it eschewed tax cuts to offset fiscal drag, would have tightened fiscal policy dramatically over the next few years. The Congressional Budget Office (CBO) compares the Reagan budget programme with a more realistic baseline, the Carter budget modified for 1982 and 1983 by some business tax reductions and by a 10 per cent personal income tax reduction and by unspecified tax cuts to maintain effective tax rates constant after 1983. The CBO projections show little difference between the Reagan budget and this baseline in macro impacts. If anything, the Reagan programme is a little tighter than the assumed baseline. Reagan spends less and taxes less, and the net effect is close to neutral.

Actually the high-employment budget deficit (calculated for, say, 6 per cent unemployment) declines slightly over the next few years under the Reagan proposals, even when the Administration's optimistic inflation scenario is replaced by the more pessimistic price forecasts of the CBO and private model-builders (see Table 10.3). These are conventional Keynesian calculations, without supply-side optimism. (Neither do they apply to the federal government the inflation

Table 10.1: Monetary growth targets vs. Reagan projections of inflation and real growth implications for monetary velocity (per cent per year, yearly averages)

Year	(1) Monetary (M–1B) growth $\left(\frac{\Delta M}{M}\right)$	+	(2) Velocity growth $\left(\frac{\Delta V}{V}\right)$	=	(3) Nominal GNP growth $\left(\frac{\Delta \$GNP}{\$GNP}\right)$	=	(4) Price inflation $\left(\frac{\Delta P}{P}\right)$	+	(5) Real GNP growth $\left(\frac{\Delta Q}{Q}\right)$
1980 actual	6.7		2.2		8.9		9.0		–0.1
	Announced policy		Implied by other columns		Reagan Administration projections*				
1981	3.5–6		7.6–5.1		11.1		9.9		1.1
1982	3 –5.5		9.8–7.3		12.8		8.3		4.2
1983	2.5–5		9.9–7.4		12.4		7.0		5.0
1984	2 –4.5		8.8–6.3		10.8		6.0		4.5
1985	1.5–4		8.3–5.8		9.8		5.4		4.2
1986	1 –3.5		8.3–5.8		9.3		4.9		4.2

Source: Office of Management and Budget, Fiscal Year 1982 Budget Revisions, March 1981, Table 6, p. 13.

Note: Discrepancies between (3) and (4) + (5) are in original sources, and are due to second-order effects $\left(\frac{\Delta P}{P} \cdot \frac{\Delta Q}{Q}\right)$, quarterly compounding, and rounding.

Table 10.2: *Real Gross National Product and Unemployment, 1980–6—Reagan scenario compared with conventional estimates*

	(1) GNP (1980 $billion) Reagan scenario	(2) GNP (1980 $billion) Estimated potential at 6% unempl.	(3) Unemployment (%) Reagan scenario	(4) Unemployment (%) CBO alternative	(5) GNP (1980 $billion) conventional estimate for Reagan unempl.	(6) Reagan scenario GNP relative to conventional estimate
1980	2629	2746	7.2	7.2	—	—
1981	2658	2815	7.8	7.8	2663	.998
1982	2769	2886	7.2	7.9	2802	.988
1983	2908	2958	6.6	7.8	2914	.998
1984	3039	3032	6.4	7.7	3001	1.013
1985	3167	3108	6.0	7.5	3108	1.019
1986	3300	3185	5.6	7.2	3217	1.026

Notes:

(1) and (3) Office of Management and Budget, *Fiscal Year 1982 Budget Revisions*, March 1981, Table 6, p. 13. GNP converted to 1980 dollars by deflator projections given in same scenario.

(2) and (5) Author's estimates, assuming (a) Potential GNP grows at 2.5% per year, (b) $Y^* - Y = Y[.025(U-6.0)]$ where Y^* is potential GNP (2), U is unemployment percentage (3), .025 is the assumed Okun's Law coefficient, and the equation is solved to give Y, 'actual' GNP (5).

(6) = (1)/(5). For 1986, the Reagan scenario gives real GNP 2.6% higher than its unemployment projection would indicate in a conventional Okun's Law calculation.

(4) Congressional Budget Office estimate of unemployment conditional on Reagan budget with less optimistic economic forecast. CBO, *An Analysis of President Reagan's Budget Revisions for Fiscal Year 1982*, Staff Working Paper, March 1981, Summary Table 3, p. xviii.

Table 10.3: The Federal budget, 1980–4—outlays, revenues, deficit, high employment deficit

	(1)	(2)	(3)	(4)	(5)	(6)
	Budget outlays ($billion)			Budget revenues ($billion)		CBO alternative inflation scenario
	Reagan estimates	CBO estimates for Reagan scenario	Estimates for 6% unempl. and CBO inflation	Reagan estimates	Estimates for 6% unempl. and CBO inflation	% increase in GNP deflator
1980	580	580	577	520	554	10.3
1981	655	660	657	600	662	9.2
1982	695	708	716	650	710	8.6
1983	732	740	761	709	765	8.1
1984	770	782	812	771	827	

	(7) Deficit ($billion)	(8)	(9) High employment deficit ($ billion) Estimates for 6% Unempl. and CBO inflation
	Reagan estimates	CBO estimates for Reagan scenario	
1980	60	60	23
1981	55	60	−5
1982	45	58	6
1983	23	31	−4
1984	−1	11	−15

Notes:

(1), (4), (7) Congressional Budget Office, *An Analysis of President Reagan's Budget Revisions for Fiscal Year 1982*. Staff Working Paper, March 1981, Summary Table 1, p. xiii.

(2), (8) Reagan estimates plus subtotal for Alternative Programmatic Assumptions, Spending Rates, and Other Factors, CBO *op. cit.* Summary Table 4, p. xxi.

(6) CBO alternative inflation forecast conditional on Reagan programme, *op. cit.* Summary Table 3, p. xviii. Compare Reagan scenario column (4) of Table 1.

(3) Column (1) plus Total Reestimates from CBO Summary Table 4 *loc. cit.* less author's estimate of reduction in outlays due to difference between CBO unemployment projections in Summary Table 2 and 6%. In principle, column (3) differs from (1) by adding outlays due to higher CBO estimates of inflation and interest rates and by subtracting outlays, mainly unemployment compensation, due to projected unemployment rates above 6%.

(5) Column (4) multiplied by (1 + 1.5(x−1)) where x is the ratio of column (2) Table 2 to column (1) Table 2, i.e., potential GNP to projected actual GNP. The elasticity of revenues with respect to GNP is assumed to be 1.5.

(9) = (3)-(5). Negative figures are surpluses.

accounting we recommend to private businesses, which would of course tell us that even the actual budget is already balanced.)

The composition of the budget, as well as its totals and its balance, affects its macroeconomic impact. Under the Reagan programme, federal purchases of goods and services rise because of the defence build-up. Transfers and taxes fall. The changes in composition are large, but I think they don't change the macro story just told. For the same budget totals, the shift to defence purchases is expansionary. On the other hand, the shift of purchasing power from liquidity-constrained transferees with high marginal propensities to consume to higher-income taxpayers is moderately contractionary. Some economists believe that defence is intrinsically highly inflationary and cite with foreboding the fact that Reagan's projected build-up is comparable percentage-wise to Johnson's Vietnam spending binge. The analogy is far from perfect. This defence build-up starts in an economy with a much larger amount of slack than there was in January 1966. And it lacks the compulsion to disregard costs and budget constraints that an actual war provides.

No observer of the current political scene can forbear comment on the ironies of the political parties' reversals of roles. Now the Republicans defend planned deficits against Democratic attack, advocate tax cuts not just to arrest recession but to sustain incipient recovery, and resist Democratic proposals to tilt tax reduction further toward businesses at the expense of individuals. It was a Democratic President who deliberately declined, ever since 1977, to recommend tax cuts to compensate for fiscal drag and bracket drift, and who sanctimoniously foreswore counter-cyclical fiscal measures to overcome the recent recession. It is the Democrats in Congress who now issue dire warnings of the inflationary effects of stimulating the economy by three years of tax reduction even when the unemployment rate is $7\frac{1}{2}$ per cent and capacity utilization is barely 80 per cent. It is the Republicans—some of them, it is true, without full conviction in their new religion—who say that it is idle and self-defeating to try to balance the budget by higher and higher effective tax rates. The final irony is that it is a Republican budget, proposed by a President who is a free enterprise hero, to which the securities markets are currently registering a vote of no confidence.

The budget is taking a bad rap from those, whether liberal Democrats or conservative investment bankers, who say it is a reckless gamble to reduce taxes so much. To say this is not to agree with extravagant Administration claims that their package increases the national propensity to save, but only to say that it doesn't decrease it; clearly the tax cuts by themselves, without the expenditure cuts, would diminish saving relative to GNP. Nor is it to agree with Lafferite views that the tax cuts will actually maintain or increase revenues. That is most improbable, as I shall explain below.

In judging the fiscal package to be more or less innocuous in its macroeconomic impact, I am not endorsing it. I have serious microeconomic and distributional objections, but I will confine myself here to two macroeconomic reservations. First, I regret that once again opportunities are being lost to use tax reduction to gain ground on inflation. We could cut taxes that directly boost labour costs and prices, for example by reducing payroll levies. We could go further and offer tax inducements for disinflationary wage and price behaviour. Second, we could aim for a different fiscal–monetary mix, one better designed to foster capital formation and growth. In my opinion, that would involve a tighter budget policy compensated by a monetary policy that would give us lower real interest rates.

MONETARY POLICY: DISINFLATION THE FED'S JOB

I turn now to monetary policy, where the greatest inconsistencies in the Reagan recovery programme occur. The President and his Administration have assigned the Federal Reserve responsibility for inflation. You take care of prices, they say in effect, and we'll get the economy moving again. Criticizing imperfect marksmanship of the past, the President and his economic policy makers order the Fed to cut the rate of monetary growth in half over the next five years. This was already the Fed's policy, as anyone who listens to Paul Volcker knows. Now he has Beryl Sprinkel [at the time Under-Secretary of Treasury for Monetary Affairs] and other monetarists looking over his shoulder, if not waiting in the wings.

The monetary targets of the Fed and the Administration are shown in the first column of Table 10.1. The idea that money and prices can be detached and delegated to central bankers while Congress and the Executive independently take care of budget, taxes, employment, and output is the kind of fallacy that makes exam questions for freshman economics, a fallacy now elevated to Presidential doctrine. If Amtrak hitched engines at both ends of a train of cars in New Haven station— we still do have a railroad there—one engine heading west to New York, the other east to Boston, and advertised that the train was going simultaneously to both destinations, most people would be sceptical. Reagan is hitching a Volcker engine at one end and a Stockman–Kemp locomotive to the other and telling us the economic train will carry us to Full Employment and Disinflation at the same time.

This inconsistency is shown in Table 10.1. The third column is the official Administration projection of nominal GNP, equal to the totals of columns four and five, the Reagan scenarios for inflation and real output growth. Subtracting the monetary targets of column 1 from the dollar-GNP projections of column 3 gives the implied growth rates of velocity of *M-1B*, column 2. The two numbers correspond to the two limits of the *M-1B* target brackets.

There has never been a two-year period over which the average growth of *M-1B* velocity has exceeded 5 per cent. It would have to beat that in each of the next five years, hitting 7, 8, almost 9 per cent to make the Reagan scenario come true. These increases in velocity are beyond historical experience, even in the recent decade of unprecedented financial innovation. Finance is one sector where American technology remains the best in the world, and the possibility of even faster progress in economizing cash can't be completely ruled out. But if policy makers were to accept rescue from velocity miracles, or *a fortiori* from further regulatory changes, they would be substituting shadow for substance, appearance for reality. Although the Fed might be tempted by any escape route from the credibility impasse they have painted themselves into, I assume the Fed really means to do literally no more than what their targets say, and to do less if the spirit of the policy so dictates.

This translates, whether the Administration realizes it or not, into significantly lower rates of growth of dollar spending on GNP than the official projections (column three). Of course, another way to achieve high-velocity growth is to engineer even higher nominal and real interest rates than those we're now suffering. But they would surely be inconsistent with the substantial recovery of real and nominal GNP promised by the President (columns three and five). On the other hand, if the inflation and interest rate projections of the Administration were realized, velocity would slow down.

MISSING: A STRATEGY FOR DISINFLATION

As devastating as this inconsistency is to the credibility of the President's programme, the scenario contains a more fatal flaw. This is the division of nominal GNP, column 3, between inflation, column 4, and real output growth, column 5. It defies historical experience to expect price inflation to subside as rapidly as shown in column 4 while output recovers as vigorously as projected in column 5. Experience tells us the combination is a most unlikely one, given the stubborn inertia of existing patterns of inflation. Experience tells us that disinflation requires recessions, prolonged slack, and high unemployment. What entitles this Administration to expect to cut inflation in half while output is growing faster than its sustainable potential for five years?

The only answer that has trickled out of Washington is an appeal to self-fulfilling expectations. The public will read column 5. Observing the decisive budgetary moves of the new Administration, believing them to be the proper medicine for inflation as advertised, the public will act to make the predictions come true. That means they will negotiate lower wage bargains and slow down price increases. Previous optimistic inflation forecasts from the White House have not been self-fulfilling or otherwise fulfilled, but maybe this time will be different.

This is an expectations argument, but certainly not a rational expectations theory. Rational expectations require a model that makes sense, one that truly connects policy actions to results. Rational expectations not only generate but are generated from such a model. In this case no such model exists, and Robert Lucas and Robert Hall [rational expectations economists] are as unlikely as Lane Kirkland and Sam Church [labour union leaders] to believe and act upon the advertised disinflation.

The two major English-speaking democracies are in conservative economic hands, but the policies and public stance of Margaret Thatcher in Great Britain are very different from those of Ronald Reagan in the United States. Their Prime Minister threatens workers, managers, and plain citizens like an authoritarian schoolmistress disciplining an unruly class: you won't have jobs, profits, or prosperity until you stop inflating your wages and prices. Our President promises disinflation without tears, indeed with prosperity. He encourages unions and managements to carry on business as usual. After all, inflation is only the government's fault, and all we citizens are asked to do is to accept tax goodies and stop indulging the poor. The Federal Reserve, it is true, has been following a Thatcher-like policy but in whispers. I am one of the thousand or so Americans who hear and read Paul Volcker and know that $M\text{-}1B$ is not an army rifle. I pay attention to Henry Wallich [Federal Reserve Governor known for hawkish anti-inflation views], too. I believe they will do what they say they will do, and I am duly scared. If *I* were Lane Kirkland [AFL-CIO President], I would take the monetary threats seriously and tell my constituent unions to take it easy.

The Fed's muted threat is quite different from Her Majesty's First

Minister's standing up in Parliament and throughout her country to say that she doesn't care how much unemployment there is for how long, or what is the real rate of growth or decline; she will stick it through whatever the pain, however long it takes to eliminate inflation. Reagan has said nothing like that, and Volcker isn't well known in Peoria or Spokane, in the shops and offices where wages and prices are made. Federal Reserve threats are heard in financial circles all right, but the bond market does not seem to be impressed. In summary, if the Reagan anti-inflation strategy depends on expectations, the Administration has done and said nothing to make expectations work in its favour.

Let there be no illusion. There is no way to reduce inflation in this country so long as wage increases proceed at 10 per cent a year. There is no possible miracle of productivity that can validate such a trend in money wages. Our lost 2 per cent per year productivity trend may reappear as mysteriously as it vanished. If we are very, very lucky, policy to speed investment and research and development might add another half point or full point, not this year or next but some years down the road. But with the best of good fortune we would be left with domestic core inflation of 7–8 per cent unless the money wage pattern is broken—and it may be more difficult to break it when workers can claim to have earned more via improved productivity. We must also expect an adverse trend in the terms of trade between American labour and resource-based commodities imported from abroad or produced within the country. This may be equivalent on average to a half point or full point of decline in worker productivity.

I emphasize the persistent inertial trend of money wages in the central non-agricultural 'fixprice' sector of our economy, because no lasting solution of our inflation is possible unless it is brought much closer to the sustainable trend of productivity. In short runs, especially month to month and quarter to quarter, popular price indexes can vary widely around this core inflation rate, from the weight of flexible prices loosely tied to US wages. In the next eighteen months, for example, the volatile elements in the Consumer Price Index might be favourable, and the Administration might be able to point to some apparent successes in its battle against inflation. If mortgage interest rates stay put or fall, the housing component will contribute less to CPI inflation news than in 1979–80. Perhaps we have purchased a respite on the oil front by selling AWACs to Saudi Arabia, as well as by slowing down our economy and swallowing the decontrol of domestic oil prices in one gulp early this year. Our tight monetary policy, if it does nothing else, is appreciating the dollar against other currencies; this may be bad for the US export–import position but it lowers dollar prices of some imports and world-traded commodities. Food price prospects, always uncertain, are not so favourable, given the end of the grain embargo and the low level of world stocks. My purpose is not to predict prices but to warn that transient luck in the volatile elements of price indexes does not signify final victory, any more than transient misfortune justified panic about runaway inflation acceleration in 1979–80.

At the beginning of my talk, I pointed out that countries with enviable inflation records in recent years are not invariably those with Reagan-like fiscal policies. If the successful countries have a common characteristic, it is that they have some kind of handle on money wage decisions.

Here in the United States whoever was the victor in the November 1980 election had, I thought, the rare opportunity to use the window of good feeling that Americans open at the start of a new Presidential term to gain control over our wage–price spiral. To engineer disinflation without a protracted dose of recession and economic stagnation, I believe it is necessary to give everybody assurance that everybody else is going to disinflate. Otherwise the fear and suspicion of each group that it will lose real and relative income lead it to stick to the existing inflationary pattern. This makes tough going for a Thatcher policy, and even tougher going for a contractionary policy without a clear and credible threat.

For this reason, I have favoured a pre-announced schedule of gradually declining standards for wage increases over a five-year transitional period. Inducements to obey the guideposts would be provided by payroll tax rebates for employees in complying firms, and for employers too if their percentage mark-ups do not rise. The guidepost schedule would be consistent with a macroeconomic disinflationary policy to which the Administration, Congress, and Federal Reserve would be solemnly and visibly committed. Since nominal GNP growth and wage-cost inflation would decline in concert, there would be neither suppressed demand-pull inflation nor the damage to real economic performance caused by cutting monetary demand growth while money cost inflation proceeds unabated.

Such a policy clearly requires a consensus among labour, business, and government, and such a consensus clearly requires strong and persuasive leadership by a popular President. We lost that opportunity this year, just as we lost the chance to follow a 'cold turkey' policy with some chance that inflation would melt faster than previous statistical evidence leads us to believe it will.

SUPPLY-SIDE ECONOMICS: NO FREE LUNCH

But can't we take hope from the recent discovery that the economy has a supply side? This remarkable revelation plays a big role in the rhetoric that rationalizes the Reagan programme, although, as I argued above, the fiscal programme as macro strategy does not really depend on Laffer–Kemp calculus. The official macroeconomic scenario does contain a small bit of supply-side magic. Real GNP five years out is somewhat larger, relative to the projected unemployment rates, than received 'Okun's Law' wisdom would allow. (Table 10.3, column 6) There appears to be on average an extra half per cent per year of real growth, beyond what would normally accompany the unemployment reductions shown. It is not clear from what source these gains are supposed to come.

From labour supply? Supply-side wisdom is that the upward drift of marginal personal tax rates is drying up the supply of productive labour. That there has been such a drift, particularly since 1977, is undeniable, though it is not as great as often alleged. The Brookings Institution tax file permits calculation of the federal marginal rate of personal income tax, averaged over all brackets, faced by a breadwinner with spouse and two children: 1960, 18.8 per cent; 1965, 15.9 per cent; 1970, 18.2 per cent; 1975, 18.0 per cent; 1980, 21.6 per cent. Yet it is hard to find evidence of a weakened propensity to supply labour in recent experience. Labour force participation, overtime hours of work, multiple job holding, weekly hours of work corrected for changes in industry mix—none of these indicators seem out of line with trends and cyclical effects dating from the 1950s and 1960s. Believe it or not, most of our seven million unemployed fellow citizens really do want work, and there are many 'not in labour force' who do also. Finally, I observe that although the Administration's tax bill reduces marginal rates for taxpayers, especially those in high brackets, its budget cuts will seriously impair work incentives for low-income families and individuals dependent on welfare, food stamps, and other transfers.

In the belief that a Curve deserves a Theory, I have derived rigorously a Laffer Curve based on labour supply response to aftertax real wages. Indeed, I have derived two Laffer Curves, one for tax revenues and one for national saving. These are shown in Chapter 11 'Yes, Virginia, there are Laffer Curves'. For reasonable parameter values, the peaks of the two curves are at tax rates of 5/6 and 3/4 respectively. I doubt that we are on the wrong slope of either Laffer Curve now, and I hope we don't go there.

A more credible supply-oriented policy is to stimulate non-residential fixed investment, in the hope that accelerating the growth of capital relative to output and labour supply will raise productivity. As one of the Kennedy team that originated the Investment Tax Credit in 1962, I have some sympathy with this goal. Clearly I do not have time to discuss adequately the Reagan Administration's investment stimuli, so I will confine myself to four short remarks.

First, as I stated earlier, I regret that we cannot adopt a mix of macroeconomic policies, fiscal and monetary, that would shift the composition of output toward capital formation. Why can't we? The main reason is simply the monetarist dogma embraced by the Administration, to which the Federal Reserve is hostage. This locks us into a particular path of a particular monetary aggregate, invariant to fiscal policy and other macroeconomic circumstances.

Second, there are ways to provide investment incentives in the taxation of business that do not make a shambles of economic efficiency and tax equity, as the present proposals for accelerated depreciation do. If the intention is to make amends for the overstatement of taxable profits due to historical cost depreciation, there are straightforward ways of doing so without freezing into the tax code a depreciation system that will still be there if and when inflation abates. Anyway, this investment disincentive is offset, partially or fully, by another inflation distortion in the tax code, the deductibility of nominal interest.

Third, whatever investment incentive is enacted now should be effective immediately. Its impact is diluted by a gradual phase-in such as the Administration proposes, because this gives an inducement to delay investment projects.

Fourth, plant and equipment is not the only social capital. If we wish as a society to make better provision for the future, we should also be concerned with the preservation and improvement of human capital, natural resources, and public sector facilities and infrastructure, all of which are sacrificed in the Reagan budget, pervaded as it is by the ideology that only private business capital is productive.

The outlook, I am afraid, is for continued stagflation, with disappointing results on all fronts—inflation, unemployment, real output, interest rates, and capital formation. We will unwind the Great Society, redistribute income regressively, withdraw the Federal commitment to the environment, and we will have little or no macroeconomic progress to show. The programme will not fulfill the promises that have led the country to support it.

11   Yes, Virginia, There Are Laffer Curves*

INTRODUCTION

The now famous Laffer Curve shows the relationship of tax revenues to the tax rate, allowing for endogenous response of the tax base to the tax rate. In the spirit of its popularizer, I take the response to be variation in *supplies* of factors of production in taxable employment and assume that aggregate demand adjusts or is adjusted to assure full utilization of the supplies. I derive a Laffer Curve based on labour supply only, taking the stock of capital as fixed. These are theoretical calculations, designed to exhibit the strategic behavioural parameters and their roles in determining the shapes of the curves. I do, however, allow myself the luxury of some calculations based on plausible empirical values of the parameters.

The Curve has been used to justify cuts in tax rates on the ground that they will actually raise tax revenues. In principle, as I shall illustrate, the Curve has a maximum (at least one) somewhere between zero taxation and 100 per cent taxation. This obvious fact does not justify the assertion that tax cuts in the US in 1981, or in any other actual economy, will raise revenues. That depends, of course, on where we are on the curve relative to its maximum.

In any event, it is not clear why maximization of tax revenues should be anyone's social objective. Milton Friedman, who favours tax reduction in all economic weather, says he certainly hopes it will *not* raise revenues![1] Economists will generally agree that there is welfare loss in raising distortionary taxes beyond the point of maximum revenue. A political reason for stressing the claim that tax cuts pay for themselves is to disarm opponents who are fearful of enlarging government deficits.

A related 'supply-side' argument for tax reduction concerns inflation.

---

*1981, unpublished, results used in other papers.

The notion that an induced expansion of supply will lower prices is of course a simplistic fallacy of aggregation, refuted by J. B. Say a century and a half ago. Say's Law may have its own problems, but the point that additional supplies in aggregate induce additional demand too is undeniable. A sensible question may be phrased in the following way: Does the additional supply generate additional national saving at an unchanged interest rate? If so, this can be used either: (1) to relieve inflationary excess-demand pressure, if any, by elimination of abnormal or above-natural utilization of resources, or (2) to finance extra investment, with the monetary authority letting interest rates fall as needed to employ the extra saving. In either case, the relevant calculation is to relate full employment national saving, or potential investment, to the tax rate. This will produce a second Laffer Curve for national saving, probably more interesting and relevant for policy than the first.[2]

Note that 'national saving' is private plus government saving, or minus government dissaving. If we are at the maximum of Laffer Curve I, a tax cut leaves government saving unchanged. Since it presumably increases private saving, it increases national saving. So the peak of Laffer Curve II is at a lower tax rate than that of Laffer Curve I. Note also that an increase in *private* saving does not necessarily mean an increase in *national* saving. Failure to remember this elementary point is the main and distressingly prevalent fallacy in current public discussion of tax reduction as stimulus to saving and investment. A tax reduction can increase government dissaving by more than it raises private saving; in this case we are on the low-tax side of the maxima of both Curves.

DIGRESSION TO THE DEMAND SIDE

I digress to remind readers of the Keynesian 'demand-side' answers to the two questions. Assume that tax revenues $\overline{TR}$ are a linear function of national product Y:

$$\overline{TR} = T_0 + TY. \tag{11.1}$$

Assume consumption (C) depends positively on income, negatively on tax revenues:

$$C = c_0 + c_1 Y - c_2 \overline{TR}. \tag{11.2}$$

Recall the national product identity:

$$Y = C + G + I \tag{11.3}$$

where G is government purchase of goods and services and I is private investment. The three equations together give the multiplier equation:

$$Y(1-c_1+c_2T) = c_0 + I + G - c_2T_0 \qquad (11.4)$$

$$\frac{\partial Y}{\partial T} = \frac{-c_2Y}{1-c_1+c_2T}; \quad \frac{\partial \overline{TR}}{\partial T} = \frac{Y(1-c_1)}{1-c_1+c_2T} . \qquad (11.5)$$

The multiplier is positive for government spending and tax reduction if $1-c_1+c_2T>0$. Given this condition, tax reduction increases or leaves unchanged tax revenues only if $c_1 \geqslant 1$, an empirically unlikely value even if induced 'consumption' is reinterpreted to include some investment. In general, the model suggests that lowering tax rates increases Y but lowers tax revenue. As for national saving, equation (11.4) simply says that private saving plus government saving is equal to investment.

$$(Y-\overline{TR}-C) + (\overline{TR}-G) = I . \qquad (11.4a)$$

If investment is a constant, independent of income, then tax reduction simply substitutes private saving for government saving.

A somewhat different question relates to the supply of saving at full employment. If equations (11.4) and (11.4a) are interpreted in reverse, fixing Y at its full employment level Y^* while letting I be endogenous, then tax reduction unambiguously reduces investment in favour of consumption:

$$\frac{\partial I}{\partial T} = c_2 Y^* \qquad (11.6)$$

This review of the Keynesian model is relevant because Kemp–Roth proponents have cited the 1964 Kennedy–Johnson tax cut as a precedent. Sober supporters of this legislation at the time and sober reviewers of the experience have not claimed that it paid for itself. The main rationale was demand stimulus. The 1962 revenue act had introduced the Investment Tax Credit, and the Treasury was liberalizing depreciation guidelines. These measures were intended to stimulate investment demand in short run and increase the economy's capital stock and potential output in the long run.

DERIVATION OF LAFFER CURVES

To return to the Laffer Curves, assume that production is Cobb–Douglas in capital stock, fixed in the short run, and labour:

$$Y = K^\alpha N^{1-\alpha} \qquad (11.7)$$

The pretax marginal product of labour and the pretax wage are equal to $(1-\alpha)K^\alpha N^{-\alpha}$, and the wage bill is $(1-\alpha)Y$ or $(1-\alpha)K^\alpha N^{-\alpha}$. A proportional income tax at rate T collects revenues of $TY=TK^\alpha N^{1-\alpha}$. Labour is supplied in response to the after-tax real wage w, with elasticity of $1/\beta$:

$$N = (aw)^{1/\beta}, \quad N^\beta = aw, \tag{11.8}$$

where a is an arbitrary scale parameter.

The aftertax wage bill is:

$$Nw = \frac{1}{a}N^{1+\beta} = (1-T)(1-\alpha)K^\alpha N^{1-\alpha} \tag{11.9}$$

Therefore, letting $u = 1-T$, we have:

$$\log N = \frac{1}{\beta+\alpha}\log u + \frac{1}{\beta+\alpha}\log(1-\alpha)aK^\alpha. \tag{11.10}$$

Tax revenues are given by:

$$\log \overline{TR} = \log(1-u) + (1-\alpha)\log N + \log K^\alpha \tag{11.11}$$

$$\log \overline{TR} = \log(1-u) + \frac{1-\alpha}{\beta+\alpha}\log u + \text{constants}.$$

We are interested in the response of tax revenues to the rate $T=1-u$:

$$\frac{\partial \log \overline{TR}}{\partial T} = \frac{1}{T} - \frac{(1-\alpha)}{\beta+\alpha}\frac{1}{1-T}$$

$$\frac{\partial \log \overline{TR}}{\partial T} = \frac{\beta+\alpha-T(1+\beta)}{T(1-T)(\beta+\alpha)}. \tag{11.12}$$

This is the slope of Laffer Curve I. Clearly it is positive until $T^* = \dfrac{(\alpha+\beta)}{(1+\beta)}$, where $\overline{TR}$ is a maximum, and negative for higher Ts.

For Laffer Curve II, assume that wage earners consume a fraction c_w of their after-tax wages $u(1-\alpha)Y$ and capitalists consume a fraction c_k of their after-tax profits $u\alpha Y$. Investment is the difference between production and the sum of public consumption G, assumed constant, and private consumption:

$$I+G = Y[1-c_w u(1-\alpha)-c_k u\alpha] = K^\alpha N^{1-\alpha}[1-c_w u(1-\alpha)-c_k u\alpha] \tag{11.13}$$

$$\log(I+G) = (1-\alpha)\log N + \log[1-c_w u(1-\alpha)+c_k u\alpha] + \text{constants}.$$

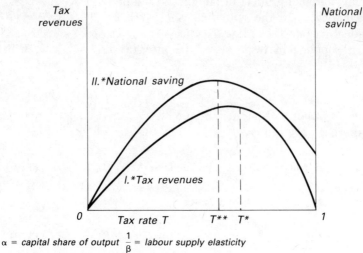

α = capital share of output $\dfrac{1}{\beta}$ = labour supply elasticity

c_k = marginal propensity to consume capital income
c_w = marginal propensity to consume labour income

$$T^* = \frac{\alpha+\beta}{1+\beta}; \quad T^{**} = 1 - \frac{1-\alpha}{(1+\beta)(c_w(1-\alpha)+c_k\alpha)}$$

For $\alpha = \frac{1}{3}$, $\beta = 3$, $c_w = 0.8$, $c_K = 0.4$, T^* would be $\frac{5}{6}$ and T^{**} $\frac{3}{4}$.

Figure 11.1   Laffer Curves

$$\frac{\partial\log(I+G)}{\partial u} = \frac{1-\alpha}{\beta+\alpha}\frac{1}{u} + \frac{-c_w(1-\alpha)-c_k\alpha}{1-u[c_w(1-\alpha)+c_k\alpha]} \tag{11.14}$$

$$\frac{\partial\log(I+G)}{\partial u} = \frac{(1-\alpha)-u(1+\beta)(c_w(1-\alpha)+c_k\alpha)}{u(\beta+\alpha)[1-u(c_w(1-\alpha)+c_k\alpha)]}$$

This slope is zero, and $I+G$ is a maximum when $u=u^{**}$:

$$u^{**} = \frac{1-\alpha}{(1+\beta)(c_w(1-\alpha) + c_k\alpha)} = 1 - T^{**}. \tag{11.15}$$

Suppose, for example, that $\alpha = \frac{1}{3}$, $c_w = 0.8$, $c_k = 0.4$. Let the elasticity of labour supply with respect to the wage be $\frac{1}{3}$, so that $\beta = 3$. Empirical evidence suggests that this is an implausibly high response of labour supply. Then $u^{**} = \frac{1}{4}$, $T^{**} = \frac{3}{4}$. In other words, so long as T is less than 0.75 we know that a tax cut *diminishes* the supply of national saving for private investment.

A fortiori, it will diminish tax revenues. Indeed, with the same parameter values, the slope of Laffer Curve I is zero at $T^* = 0.833$.

Figure 11.1 shows the two Laffer Curves. Figure 11.2 shows their derivation.

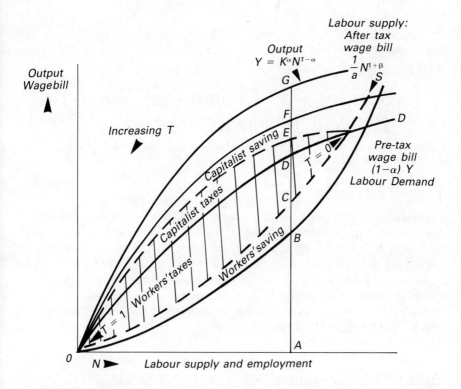

AB: *Workers' consumption*
BC: *Workers' saving*
CD: *Workers' taxes*
DE: *Capitalist taxes*
EF: *Capitalist saving*
FG: *Capitalist consumption*
BF: *Taxes and saving available for government purchases and private investment (G + 1)*
CE: *Tax revenues*
Employment is determined for each tax rate T such that labour supply S, measured by $\frac{1}{\alpha} N^{1+\beta}$ plus taxes is equal to labour demand D, measured by $(1-\alpha)Y$. Here both D and S are in terms of wage bills. The veretical distance in the shaded area is tax revenue, from capitalists and workers combined.

Figure 11.2   Derivation of Laffer Curves

NOTES

1. *Newsweek,* 23 February 1981.
2. Norman Ture, Under-Secretary of the Treasury, is reported to say that the Kemp–Roth tax bill may not pay for itself in tax revenues but it will generate enough taxes plus saving to finance the government without crowding out any private investment. I interpret him, therefore, to be talking about this Laffer Curve II.

12 Supply-Side Economics: What Is It? Will It Work?*

Revolutions and revelations in economics are rare. They have generally occurred at intervals of thirty to sixty years and have taken decades to influence public opinion and policy. The Keynesian revolution, initiated by a forbidding theoretical book in 1935, made its way only gradually through academe to lay intellectuals, media pundits, business and labour leaders, bureaucrats and politicians. When, after considerable resistance and revision, J. M. Keynes's ideas became explicit rationales for American macroeconomic strategy in 1961–5, the press hailed them as the 'New' Economics.

RECENT ECONOMIC COUNTER-REVOLUTIONS

Has the pace of innovation quickened? Since 1965 three counter-revolutions swept through the economics profession, received lavish attention in the media, and powerfully affected influential opinion and the making of public policy. One was monetarism, an ancient doctrine modernized and persuasively propagated by Milton Friedman beginning in the 1950s. When the New Economics appeared unable to explain or control the inflation of the late 1960s and the 1970s, Friedman's alternative attracted hordes of disciples. A second and related counter-revolution was the so-called 'new classical macroeconomics', based on the elegant and appealing theory of rational expectations. In the 1970s under the leadership of Robert Lucas and others, this movement made many theorists and practitioners sceptical of Keynesian hopes that fiscal and monetary policies can smooth out business fluctuations.[1]

The third is supply-side economics, which in just a few years has become not only an obligatory slogan but the philosophy of the federal

*July 1981, *Economic Outlook USA*, University of Michigan Survey Research Center, Summer 1981, pp. 51–3.

government. Though the three counter-revolutions differ, they have in common conservative messages popular in today's political climate. Government interventions, however well-intentioned, do harm, not good. They have led to inflation, instability, inefficiency, and declining productivity. Keynesian policies have failed, and the theories that supported them are discredited.

Supply-side economics, currently the most popular counter-revolution, is also the most amorphous. Without a Keynes or Friedman or Lucas, it lacks a sacred text expounding its theoretical foundations. It is more spirit, attitude, and ideology than coherent doctrine, and its enthusiasts are of many minds. They generally share the view that for forty years, under the malign spell of Keynesian concentration on demand, economic analysis and policy went wrong by neglecting supply. The most common theme is the sensitivity of work, productivity, saving, investment, and enterprise to after-tax rewards. The more exuberant supply-siders, economist Arthur Laffer and Congressman Kemp, expect cuts of tax rates to generate miracles of production and growth. While the more sober architects of Reagan Administration policy do not promise that their tax cuts will pay for themselves in federal revenues, they do predict radical and durable renewal of the vitality of the United States economy.

SUPPLY, DEMAND, AND EQUILIBRIUM

All economics balances supplies and demands, *ad nauseam* of generations of students. Keynesian economics is no exception. Choosing up sides would be a laughable and harmless media diversion were it not taken so seriously. Clearly production and consumption are limited by supplies of labour, capital equipment and other productive resources, and by technical know-how. Almost all economists, Keynesian or classical or eclectic, agree that in the long run these supply factors call the tune and demand adapts. They used to agree also that short-run business cycles are principally fluctuations of demand; economy-wide capacity-to-produce changes slowly and smoothly. Keynes pointed out that when labour and other resources are underutilized, supply responds to demand. The New Economics of the 1960s stressed both demand policies to restore and maintain full employment, and supply measures to accelerate long-run growth. Among the latter were the Investment Tax Credit, accelerated depreciation, and manpower training and retraining.

A serious intellectual challenge to the neoclassical–Keynesian synthesis just sketched is the new classical view that a competitive market economy, to which the United States is taken to be a reasonable approximation, is continuously in demand-equals-supply equilibrium. Unemployment and idle capacity then appear not as pathologies but as voluntary choices at prevailing prices and taxes. The remedies, if any are needed, are not Keynesian demand stimuli but improvements of incentives, for example, less generous unemployment insurance, more take-home pay for workers, businessmen, and investors. Forget about fine tuning, counter-cyclical fiscal and monetary policy. Set up a good stable framework of incentives and price signals and the market, preferably deregulated, will take care of both short-run stabilization and long-run growth. In this spirit a sophisticated economist like Rudolph Penner defines supply-side economics as simply good microeconomics.[2] That involves minimizing or countering the distortions that taxes, subsidies, and regulations inject into market choices—work is taxed but leisure is not, income saved is taxed twice but income consumed only once, etc.—and then accepting whatever short- and long-run outcomes occur.

INCOME AND SUBSTITUTION EFFECTS

As economics students know, those results are not theoretically predictable, even as to direction. Price and tax changes have both income effects and substitution (incentive) effects, and the two often conflict. An increase in real take-home pay is an inducement to work more hours per year, but since it makes workers better off anyway it may encourage them to take more time off. An increase in real after-tax returns is an incentive to save an extra dollar, but the enrichment of wealth-owners may dispose them to consume more both now and in the future. Standard microeconomic theory provides no licence for assuming that substitution effects dominate, and certainly none for declaring income effects null and void, as Under-Secretary of Treasury Norman Ture is bold to do.[3]

Whether supply-side budget cuts, tax cuts, and other measures will, as advertised, lift the American economy from stagflation to a new era of prosperity, productivity, and growth depends on empirical magnitudes of income and substitution effects that are not very well established. Supply-siders' diagnoses of our economic ills do not fit the facts.

THE GOVERNMENT BITE

One allegation is that government has been taking too much of the national product for its own use, leaving too little for private disposition. Actually federal absorption of GNP declined during the 1970s; it was $7\frac{1}{2}$ per cent in 1980, compared with takes of 10 to 11 per cent in the 1950s and 1960s. The reason was the decline in defence spending relative to GNP, a trend the Administration is now reversing. State and local civilian purchases, aided by federal transfers, filled the gap, but all-governments absorption was the same fraction of GNP, 20 per cent in 1980 as in the pre-Vietnam year of 1965. When correction is made for the increasing relative cost of public goods, which are comparatively labour intensive, government purchases are now smaller relative to private purchases than in the 1950s and 1960s.[4]

What did happen since 1965, thanks to LBJ's Great Society as extended by presidents of both parties and Democratic Congresses in the 1970s, was an explosion of transfer payments, largely for retirement and disability insurance, Medicare, and Medicaid. Even so the federal tax burden is lower than in 1969 and only two percentage points higher than in 1956 and 1965. The all-government tax take is the same as in 1969 but because of increases in state and local taxes 4–5 points higher than in 1956 and 1965. Compared with other advanced capitalist democracies, United States taxes are on the low side.[4]

TAXES AND LABOUR SUPPLY

Supply-siders deplore particularly the increase in marginal federal personal income tax rates arising from the interaction of inflation and progressive rate structure. This has indeed happened faster than Congress has reduced rates, especially since 1977. According to calculations from the Brookings Institution tax file, the average rate of federal income plus payroll tax on an extra dollar of income for a breadwinner with spouse and two children was 18.0 per cent in 1960, 15.9 per cent in 1965, 18.2 per cent in 1970, 18.0 per cent in 1975, and 21.0 per cent in 1980.[5] Whatever one may think of the specifics of the personal income tax cuts now before the Congress, it is high time for another tax reduction to arrest bracket creep and fiscal drag.

None the less it is hard to detect evidence of weakened propensity to supply labour. Figures on labour force participation, overtime hours, multiple job-holding, weekly hours of work corrected for industry mix—all are in line with trends and cyclical effects dating from earlier decades. Econometricians have a hard time finding significant effects of real after-tax pay on labour supply.[6] Those they do find are mainly for secondary workers from low-income families, whose incentives will actually be diminished by proposed tax and transfer cuts in combination.

TAXES AND SAVING AND INVESTMENT

Supply-siders also blame high taxes, their bite sharpened by inflation, for low rates of saving and capital investment in the United States. Public discussion of the effects on national saving of general income tax reduction have been confused and confusing. Taxpayers will both spend more and save more. The spending effect will be somewhat mitigated in the administration proposal, which distributes gains in disposable income disproportionately to wealthy taxpayers with higher than average marginal propensities to save the proceeds. But it will not be reversed. From given GNP household saving will be greater by some fraction of the tax cut but government dissaving will be greater by the full amount. Thus the tax cut *by itself* diminishes the national government-plus-private propensity to save. However, in the Reagan economic programme the tax reductions are roughly balanced by budget reductions and implicit tax increases due to inflation and economic growth. The net effect of the programme as a whole is a small increase in national saving for given GNP.

As in the case of labour supply, econometric evidence for incentive effects on household saving is weak.[7] Proposed tax concessions to stimulate saving suffer not only from the usual income effects favouring consumption but also from their restriction to specific kinds and amounts of saving. Most taxpayers will simply shift other savings into the favoured vehicles. This has already occurred as Congress has multiplied tax-free or tax-deferred ways of saving for retirement, home ownership, and posterity, a fact that itself limits the credence of the high-tax explanation of declining household saving.

Business non-residential investment held up much better in the 1970s than the spate of solicitous rhetoric suggests. For its weakness through much of the decade, 1970–2 and 1975–8, recessions, tight money and energy shocks are sufficient explanation. At 11.6 per cent of GNP in 1979, plant and equipment investment surpassed previous postwar cyclical peaks. However, for various reasons, some economic and some tax accounting, investment net of replacement is estimated lower than at previous peaks.

MISGUIDED POLICY PROPOSALS

Spurred by supply-side ideology, the Administration and both parties in Congress are vying to bestow on business and on wealthy individuals tax cuts and subsidies rationalized as investment incentives. These are half-baked proposals, which will introduce more distortions of efficiency and equity than they correct. Reform to diminish tax-cum-inflation distortions is overdue. But neither the Reagan depreciation plan nor the Democratic alternative is the specific remedy, which would be indexing of depreciation and debt. Both propose costly giveaways, subsidies that will still be there if and when inflation subsides. While inflation erodes the real value of tax deductions linked to historical cost depreciation, it also enhances the real value of tax deductions for debt interest. The latter is partially offset by personal income taxation of the same nominal interest payments, but most such income never appears on taxable returns.[8] The proposals distort choices among different types and durabilities of investment projects, and they waste revenue by granting tax relief to income from existing capital and from investment that will occur anyway. The results are likely to fall short of the Administration's goal of increasing the business investment share of GNP by two to three percentage points. One reason is that the supply-side incentives will be bucking an inclement macroeconomic climate, dominated by restrictive monetary policy.

The anti-inflation strategy is to slow down the growth of money stocks while the new incentives expand the supplies of goods the money is chasing. Confidence that this scenario will bring disinflation together with prosperity rather than recession and stagflation is borrowed from the other two counter-revolutions, monetarist and new classical. Keynesians, eclectics, and traditional conservatives are sceptical that entrenched patterns of inflation will melt away so painlessly. Lucky breaks on oil, food, and exchange rates make the price indexes look good for a while, but there cannot be permanent improvement unless and until wage and cost trends give way.[9]

THE ESSENTIAL MESSAGE OF THE SUPPLY-SIDE REVOLUTION

The only sure results of supply-side policies are redistributions of income, wealth, and power—from government to private enterprises, from workers to capitalists, from poor to rich. A revolution is in process all right, social and political more than economic. A capsule symbol is the nearly universal enthusiasm in Washington to rid the federal tax system of all semblance of taxation of intergenerational transfers of wealth. This capitalist democracy was never committed to equality of outcomes. But we were committed to equality of opportunity. And for more than forty years we have shown that an essentially capitalist economy can prosper and grow while the society collectively moderates extremes of wealth and poverty, privilege and deprivation, power and insecurity, boom and depression. Keynes and a generation of economists he influenced believed that capitalism was robust enough to flourish under these compromises with democracy and equality. Both Marxist critics on the extreme Left and conservatives of the extreme Right have always doubted it, and theirs is the essential message of the supply-side counter-revolution.

NOTES

1. For exposition and critique of this counter-revolution *see Rational Expectations*, a Seminar sponsored by the American Enterprise Institute for Public Policy Research, *Journal of Money, Credit and Banking*, November 1980, Part 2, especially the papers by B. T. McCallum, R. C. Lucas Jr, J. Tobin, and A. M. Okun.
2. 'Policies affecting saving and investment', paper presented at the Colloquium on Alternatives for Economic Policy, Washington, DC, 10–12 June 1981, forthcoming in *Proceedings* to be published by the Conference Board, New York City.
3. 'Supply-side analysis and public policy', unpublished paper presented to the Economic Policy Round Table, The Lehrman Institute, 2 November 1980.
4. On the figures and analyses of these two paragraphs *see* my paper, 'Reflections inspired by proposed constitutional restrictions on fiscal policy,' forthcoming in Kenneth D. Boyer and William G. Shepherd, eds., *Economic Regulation, Papers in Honor of James R. Nelson*, East Lansing: Michigan State University Press, 1981. Extension of the tables there compiled to 1980 does not significantly alter the story.
5. I am grateful to Joseph A. Pechman for these calculations.
6. *See* Jerry A. Hausman, 'Labor supply', in Henry Aaron and Joseph A. Pechman, eds., *How Taxes Affect Economic Behavior*, Washington: Brookings Institution, 1981, pp. 27–84.
7. See George M. von Furstenberg, 'Saving', in Aaron and Pechman *op. cit.* pp. 327–402.
8. *See* Eugene Steuerle, 'Is income from capital subject to individual income taxation?', US Department of the Treasury, Office of Tax Analysis Paper 42, October 1980.
9. For discussion of the Reagan administration's macroeconomic and anti-inflation strategy *see* my article 'The Reagan economic program: budget, money, and the supply side', *Federal Reserve Bank of San Francisco Quarterly Review*, May 1981, chapter 11 above.

13 The Fiscal Revolution: Disturbing Prospects*

Long experience has taught me that the subject of government deficits is a particularly difficult one for an economist to discuss with a general audience. Government budgets, deficits, and debts present issues with loud political and ideological overtones. Politicians, journalists, business managers, bankers, union leaders, and just plain voters frequently want simply yes-or-no, good-or-bad answers from economists. Often the answers they want are the firm opinions they already hold. Anyway, they are sometimes impatient with the 'it depends' hedges with which we feel compelled to surround our answers. It's a congenital disability: President Harry Truman, exasperated after his chief economic adviser repeatedly told him 'on the one hand this, on the other hand that', asked his chief of staff to find him a one-armed economist. But the economic effects of government fiscal operations are complex. They do depend, for example, on economic circumstances at home and abroad and on central bank policies, and they can be different in the short run of a business cycle from what they are over decades.

Fiscal policies in the United States are today the target of loud and chronic complaint, both within the country and throughout the world. They are held responsible for all sorts of domestic and world problems, from the plight of Iowa farmers to European stagnation to the debt crises of Third World countries. US policies of the 1980s certainly are a striking contrast to those of previous Administrations and to the current policies of other advanced countries. In the course of this

*October 1984, Conference on Canada–United States Business Perspectives, Montreal, sponsored by the Canada–U.S. Business Conference and the Center for the Study of Canada at the State University of New York, Plattsburgh. Published in the Center's Special Publication No. 1, January 1985, *Canada–U.S. Business perspectives 1984* as 'Government Deficits and the Economy'. The version reprinted here was published in *Challenge*. January/February 1985, pp. 12–16.

article, I shall describe those differences and evaluate the various indictments.

US FISCAL POLICY BEFORE 1981

Much cynical rhetoric to the contrary, US fiscal policy was quite conservative from the end of World War II to 1981. The best and quickest way to see that is to consider the trend of the ratio of federal debt to the Gross National Product. Why is this ratio a good summary statistic? GNP is an indicator of the capacity of the country to save and to pay taxes, and thus to handle the debt. Since the stock of private savings is also in the long run roughly proportional to incomes and consumption, the debt/GNP ratio indicates how much of that stock is absorbed by public debt, 'crowding out' capital investments, foreign and domestic, and other uses of savings.

The war left in 1946 a federal debt equal to fifteen months' national production; thirty years later the ratio had declined from 1.25 to stabilize at about 0.25, three months' GNP. The debt grew, to be sure, but except for short cyclical interruptions GNP grew faster. Deficits were counter-cyclical. They rose in recessions, for two reasons: one, the automatic response of tax revenues and of certain entitlement outlays like unemployment compensation to business activity, and two, the deliberate compensatory tax and spending measures of Congresses and Administrations of both parties. On average, federal deficits were less than 1 per cent of GNP, and GNP itself was growing at an average 3.5 per cent a year in real, inflation-corrected terms. Note that these numbers imply that the debt/GNP ratio will be declining whenever it exceeds 0.285, or 1/3.5.

The many people who are surprised, even indignant, when pre-1981 fiscal policy is described as conservative usually turn out to have in mind trends other than that of debt relative to GNP. They cite dollar figures. After all, the debt quadrupled over the period, and it must have taken lots of deficits to do that. I argued above that the ratio to GNP is the economically relevant measure. The dollar numbers need to be corrected for inflation; in terms of real purchasing power, the debt declined because consumer prices quintupled. But the sceptic might argue that the deficits and the growth of dollar debt caused the inflation, which alone kept the debt manageable, but at the expense of trusting buyers of government obligations. Most economists would say that debt growth is not very inflationary unless it is monetized by the central bank, the Federal Reserve System in the United States. The Fed actually bought much smaller shares of the debt in the 1970s, when most of the inflation occurred, than in previous decades. Much of the inflation of the 1970s was externally imposed by OPEC. The larger deficits of the decades occurred during the recessions the Fed engineered in order to contain those stagflationary shocks.

Another aspect of history sceptics often have in mind is the growth of the federal budget, the absolute size of both outlays and revenues rather than the difference between the two. The budget grew from about 16 per cent of GNP in the late 1940s to about 21 per cent in 1980. A big factor was the expansion of federal transfers for social insurance over the last fifteen years, including the inauguration and growth of Medicare and Medicaid.

The size of the budget certainly is an issue of economic and political importance. Indeed, that issue, rather than deficits and debt, may be what the political and ideological contest in the United States is principally about. It involves social priorities, resource allocation, and the distribution of income, wealth, and power. The budget affects the efficiency of the economy in many ways, positive and negative. These 'supply-side' effects, of course, depend greatly on the composition of expenditures and taxes. I do not dismiss these issues when I say they are separable from those raised by deficits and debt. Obviously, whether society opts for a small budget or a large budget, it can also choose among budget deficits, balances, and surpluses.

THE FISCAL REVOLUTION OF 1981

What was the revolution that occurred in 1981? Since then, the debt has risen to 36 per cent of GNP. With present spending programmes and existing tax and transfer legislation, the ratio will rise to 46 per cent before the end of the decade and will still be rising, with no stopping place in sight. This outlook holds even in optimistic scenarios in which the economy completes its recovery in another couple of years and settles down without recession into a path of sustained growth with 6 per cent unemployment. Thus the previous conservative trend of deficits and debt has been sharply reversed.

What did it? Several initiatives of the Reagan Administration—in most of which, it must be said, most members of the opposition in Congress acquiesced. Corporate and personal income taxes were drastically cut; a rapid and substantial build-up of defence spending was begun. The Administration did go after civilian spending with a fearsome axe, but the cuts fell far short of matching the deficit-increasing items in its programme. Discretionary social spending and needs-tested entitlements were squeezed, but they are just not big enough turnips to yield much blood. The big-bucks entitlement programmes, old-age insurance and Medicare, are not needs-tested but universal; politically they are virtually unassailable. The President might have wished to take them on in his second term, but he made that difficult by his promises during the recent campaign.

Tax cuts, even though partially recouped by subsequent legislation, gave away revenues amounting to 3.5 per cent of GNP as of this fiscal year. The defence build-up added more than 1 per cent of GNP to expenditures, and will ultimately add another 1.5 per cent. The civilian cuts roughly offset the defence increases. The net result is a *structural primary* deficit of about 2 per cent of GNP, which will rise to 3 per cent in another four years. These are magnitudes unprecedented in peacetime. The word *primary* in that concept excludes debt-interest payments and related transactions: a primary deficit is what we would have if there were no outstanding debt. The word *structural* excludes cyclical components, revenue shortfalls, and entitlement excesses attributable to deviations of GNP from a normal reference trend. Specifically, the structural deficit is what existing budget programmes, along with tax and entitlements legislation, would produce if the unemployment rate were 6 per cent. The cyclical component of the actual budget deficit expected in the current fiscal year is 1.8 per cent of GNP.

INTEREST RATES AND DEFICITS

Interest on the debt is also a major factor in the explosive fiscal path I described above. Net debt-service costs have rocketed to 12 per cent of federal outlays and 3 per cent of GNP, and are still climbing. This must be added to the primary deficit, actual or structural, to get the total deficit. There are two related factors in the rapid rise of debt interest costs. One is just the growth of debt itself. The long sequence of cyclical deficits since 1979 is piling up debt on which interest has to be paid. The second is the extraordinary height of the debt interest rate. The relevant rate is *real*, with the inflation rate subtracted; *after-tax*, allowing for return of some fraction of interest outlays to the Treasury; and *after monetization*, allowing for the near-100 per cent return to the Treasury of interest earned by the central bank on its holdings of the government securities.

Before 1980 this measure of debt-service cost was almost always close to zero, often negative, and thus well below the economy's trend rate of GNP growth. The dynamics of compound interest contributed to the gradual decline in the debt/GNP ratio. Now this relationship has been reversed. The net real interest rate cost of debt service exceeds the sustainable rate of growth of real GNP. Compound interest would raise the ratio explosively even if primary deficits were zero, *a fortiori* when they are positive and large. (The arithmetic of this process is exactly the same as describes the foreign debt predicament of a Third World country. When its interest costs exceed the growth of its export earnings it has to run a big 'primary' surplus in its external accounts just to keep its debt burden from getting worse.)

US fiscal policy is by itself not the whole story of how interest rates got so high. They were put up there before the 1980 election by our Federal Reserve in order to bring inflation rates down from the double-digit heights they reached in 1979–80. All major central banks were disinflating together. Those efforts succeeded, but at heavy costs in unemployment and lost production.

The Federal Reserve took mercy on the US and world economies in the late summer of 1982. Engineering a three-point reduction of interest rates, it turned the American economy around. The Fed has been afraid to let them fall further, for fear of adding fuel to an already rapid recovery and reigniting the embers of inflation. The tax and spending initiatives which brought deficits were also fuelling the recovery. In this way, at least, they were contributing to the tightness of monetary policy after 1982. But probably monetary policies would have been much the same, and interest rates would now be much the same, if instead the same recovery had been driven by a spontaneous burst of private spending.

REAGANOMICS AS A CONSERVATIVE DOCTRINE

I have tried to describe what the reversals in fiscal policy were. Why did they take place? Reaganomics in 1981 was a not wholly harmonious blend of several strands of conservative doctrine: a hawkish stance in national security and foreign policy; a general *laissez-faire* view of government's economic role; a monetarism even stricter than the central bank's; a strong commitment to reduce the size of government, on both sides of the budget ledger; a belief that 'progressive' redistribution via taxes and transfers had gone too far; and a 'supply-side' faith that lowering marginal tax rates would invigorate the American economy by inducing more work, saving, investment, and enterprise.

Although most conservatives maintained their attachment to budget–balancing, many—including President Reagan himself—were fed up with the old strategy of postponing tax reductions until they could be matched by simultaneous expenditure cuts. Anyway, cutting the federal government down to size was their prime objective. They deliberately grasped a new political strategy: cut taxes radically first, then use the widespread anxiety to balance the budget to bludgeon Congress into cutting civilian spending, and support an amendment to the Constitution requiring Congress to balance the budget without raising revenues faster than GNP. 'Supply-side' economics, in its more extreme pop versions, added an appealing economic argument to this political strategy. According to its apostles, economist Arthur Laffer, Congressman Jack Kemp, and others, the tax cuts would trigger such a burst of growth in economic activity and federal revenues that the budget would soon balance itself again anyway. They were not, of course, talking about the old, 'discredited' Keynesian demand-side reasons for expecting tax cuts to be expansionary. They were talking about surges in efficiency and productivity.

What happened? The strategy ran afoul on both fronts, political and economic. The defence build-up gave the opposition, especially doves and supporters of the civilian programmes so drastically cut, the opening to use fiscal integrity and government economy on behalf of their priorities rather than the President's. On the economic side, Federal Reserve policies, reinforced by the monetarist wing of Reaganomics, produced the deep recession never envisaged in the 1981 scenarios of the new Administration. As I previously explained, one legacy of high interest rates and recession was the explosive contribution of debt service to the fiscal outlook.

Today, however, the strategy appears marvellously successful. Irony of ironies, the stimulative fiscal measures came into full effect just at the right time, as the recession was ending and powerful demand stimulus was just what the doctor ordered. Of course, this was Keynesian demand-side policy with a vengeance, not the supply-side renaissance intended. Never mind. Voters neither know nor care about subtleties of economic doctrine, and they have short memories. The incumbent basked in the Indian summer of election-year prosperity, and the clouds warning of future fiscal storms seemed far away.

US POLICY AND THE WORLD ECONOMY

US fiscal policy is not only undergoing a reversal of its past; it is also the opposite of the policies of most other economically advanced democratic countries. Their governments are also ideologically conservative, but they give precedence to traditional fiscal discipline over radical supply-side strategy. While their economies declined in the world depression after the second oil shock, they sought valiantly to cut their deficits. While Reagan and Volcker were converting cyclical deficits into structural deficits, their counterparts in Britain, Germany, and Japan—and even in France after the failed go-it-alone expansionism of Mitterand's first year—were converting cyclical deficits into structural surpluses. Their tax increases and spending cuts hit their economies while they were down, reminding this aged observer of similar actions by President Hoover—Roosevelt too, until he learned better—and German Chancellor Bruening, before he gave way to Hitler and fled to Harvard, in the depths of the Great Depression.

Taking the seven 'economic summit' countries together, fiscal policy since 1980 has been neutral, a stand-off between stimulus in North America and anti-stimulus in Europe and Japan. Things worked out as old Keynesian textbooks said. In the United States, Keynesian medicine, demand tonics masquerading as supply-side nostrums, serendipitously administered by anti-Keynesian doctors, revitalized the sick patient. Elsewhere, contractionary fiscal policies prolonged recession and retarded recovery, even as spillover of American demands into foreign markets provided some relief.

Why, then, do foreign governments complain? The high real interest rates the Fed has maintained to temper our recovery were a magnet for foreign funds, appreciated the US dollar more than 30 per cent in real terms against the currencies of our trading partners, and devastated our exports and our import-competing industries. Foreign governments could have captured even more American demand by allowing their local interest rates to fall further below US rates and letting their exchange rates depreciate even further *vis-à-vis* the dollar. They chose not to, mainly for two reasons. Central banks felt constrained by their own monetarist targets. And they feared the inflation effects of further rises in local prices of imports invoiced in dollars, which include oil.

In this way high US interest rates have been transmitted with little relief to the whole world. The consequences for Third World debtors have been especially severe. On the other hand, their exports, too, have benefited from the American-led recovery. Their ultimate salvation hinges on a strong and sustained recovery throughout the developed world, as well as a general easing of interest rates.

Foreign complaints should not be addressed solely to US budget policies but to our mix of monetary and fiscal policies. No nation's interest lay, or lies, in aborting American recovery. Critics at home and abroad should have asked, and should ask now, not for an overall withdrawal of demand stimulus but for a different mixture of medicines, less fiscal tonic and more monetary elixir. A change in the mix requires cooperation between the central bank and the fiscal authorities in the Executive and the Congress. Up to now the Fed's position has been that the responsibility falls entirely on the other players in the game.

Offsetting changes in the two dosages would allow the recovery to continue. At home, the change of mix would have several favourable consequences. Interest rates would fall, and so would the foreign-exchange value of the dollar. The trade balance, now frighteningly negative, would improve, our tottering smokestack industries would get some genuine relief, our debt-ridden farmers would regain some markets, and protectionist sentiment would be weakened. The composition of national output would be improved, as lower interest rates induce domestic investment to replace consumption curtailed by higher taxes. Abroad, an easing of world interest rates would be universally welcome.

THE LONG-RUN CASE FOR FISCAL CORRECTION

The case for a radically different policy mix is greatly reinforced by looking at the long run. Earlier I sketched the dynamics of deficits and debt and explained how the present parameters of fiscal policy, real interest rates, and prospective economic growth are a recipe for rapid and unending increase in the debt/GNP ratio. Why is such a prospect disturbing? Not because it portends an apocalyptic day of reckoning, a sudden calamitous economic and financial collapse neither controllable nor reversible. Too many Cassandras cried warnings about deficits two years ago, and now they have lost their audience.

The reasons for concern are more prosaic: the old story of crowding out. While the economy still has idle labour and capital that can be put to work, crowding out is not a big problem. Taxpayers' consumption, defence procurement, and private capital formation can expand in concert. As incomes rise, so does the saving to finance both investment and government deficits. But when recovery is complete and over a long run characterized, we hope, by high rates of employment and capacity utilization, both national output and saving are limited. Specifically, there is a limit to the amount of wealth relative to GNP that the private sector will choose to accumulate. Public debt is a claim on that limited stock, competing with productive capital—whether business plant and equipment, homes and consumer durables, state highways, or municipal schools—and with income-earning properties abroad. The burden of public debt incurred to permit greater private or public consumption is that future generations inherit fewer productive assets.

There is no need to exaggerate. Private wealth is more than three times the GNP. Even if the debt/GNP ratio rises to 1, the nation will not be impoverished. But the prospect that the debt will rise faster than the economy indefinitely, at an ever faster pace, bringing in its wake higher and higher interest rates, is not a viable future. It will be corrected some day, and since it is a quite unnecessary self-inflicted wound, better sooner than later.

The correction will require tax increases or cuts in defence spending or both. To think that the problem will go away in time with economic growth or that it can be solved by further retrenchments of civilian spending is whistling in the dark. The correction will also require the cooperation of the central bank to realize the welcome reduction of interest rates which a tighter fiscal stance makes feasible. The interest rate reduction, in turn, will make the fiscal correction much easier.

The issues I have discussed seem destined to dominate the domestic agenda of the President and Congress. There is great pressure for policies to improve the fiscal outlook. During the campaign President Reagan, distancing himself from his challenger, reaffirmed his supply-side faith and his adamant opposition to tax increases. He is still wedded to the strategy of lowering taxes and exploiting the budgetary imbalance to trim the size of the federal government. But he has made pragmatic policy shifts in the past. How he and the Congress adjust to fiscal realities over the Four More Years will be interesting, and possibly entertaining, drama. Nothing is more important for the course of the world economy the rest of this decade.

14   The Monetary–Fiscal Mix in the United States*

The mix of monetary and fiscal policies[1] is a central practical issue in the United States today. I shall first review, as background, what macroeconomic theory has to say about the subject. Then I shall describe the policies presently in place in the United States and argue in favour of a very different mix.

REQUISITES OF INDEPENDENCE OF MONETARY FROM FISCAL POLICY

The very concept of a policy mix presupposes that governments and central banks jointly enjoy some freedom of choice, that they can set fiscal and monetary instruments independently one from the other. This condition is not met to any significant degree in most national economies. But it is met in the large developed countries whose policies and performances decisively shape the course of the world economy—the 'locomotives' of North America, Western Europe, and Japan.

Of course, the policy choice of each of these nations is in some degree constrained by international conditions, and thus by the policies of the other major economic powers. But the United States can certainly choose among a menu of differing combinations of fiscal and monetary instruments. And so can West Germany, the key country of the European Economic Community, and Japan. The choices of

*March 1982, revised April 1984, W. A. Mackintosh Lecture, Queen's University, Kingston, Ontario. In the years between the lecture and the revision, both economic projections and policies changed in response to events. The main text of the lecture remains as it was delivered in March 1982. Material added in the revision in the light of subsequent developments is distinguished by enclosure in brackets. In addition, the first five sections come from my Dr C. D. Desmukh Memorial Lecture at the Reserve Bank of India, January 1985, published in French in André Grjebine, ed., *Théories de la Crise et Politiques Economiques*, Paris: Éditions du Seuil, pp. 270–90.

these three locomotives, or more broadly those of the seven governments of the annual economic summit meetings, or still more broadly those of the members of the Organization for Economic Cooperation and Development (OECD), determine the fiscal–monetary policy mix of the advanced capitalist democracies as a group.

The capacity to choose a policy mix obviously requires that government budget deficits need not be financed wholly by printing money, whether base money created by central bank lending to the government or 'low-powered' money created by other banks. There must be instruments of public debt that are neither monetary nor automatically monetizable. Those instruments must not be perfect substitutes for base money as bank reserves or for currency and bank deposits as means of payment. Their prices and interest rates must be variable, not pegged by open-ended commitments of the central bank or the banking system to buy and sell them. By maturity, denomination, and risk of capital loss, these instruments must be differentiated from base money and its close substitutes. Where these instruments and associated financial institutions, markets, and technologies are absent, budget deficits determine the growth of money supplies, and fiscal policy is indistinguishable from monetary policy.

Even when an independent monetary policy is technically feasible, the political means and will to use monetary policy instruments independently of public borrowing requirements may not exist. Quasi-constitutional provisions to insulate central banks from governments frequently provide the means and will to break the fiscal–monetary link. The cost of arrangements which assign fiscal and monetary decisions to separate policy makers is that no conscious coordinated choice of the policy mix is made.

As usual in macroeconomics, it is necessary to distinguish short and long runs. In short-run fluctuations of business activity, the policies affect aggregate demand, production, unemployment and capacity utilization, interest rates, and prices. In longer runs when output is constrained by available resources and their productivity rather than by demand, the policy mix affects the accumulation of capital, the path of economic growth, and the trend of prices. I start with the short run.

EFFECTIVENESS OF DEMAND MANAGEMENT POLICIES

These days any economist who takes seriously the theory of short-run demand management, stabilization policy, must begin by showing awareness of fashionable theories that the economy is not manageable, that systematic demand policies are necessarily ineffective, that business cycles are the tracks of moving equilibria. These are the propositions of the self-styled new classical macroeconomics, logically derived from marrying old-fashioned competitive price-cleared markets to new-fangled rational expectations. This elegant revival of neoclassical economics appeals to professional theorists and sharpens their tools. But the explanations it contrives for the commonly observed facts of business fluctuations are tortuous and implausible.

Recent events have not been kind to the new theories. The theorists had argued that, since only monetary surprises have real effects on output and employment, an announced credible policy of monetary stringency would bring disinflation without tears. But Mrs Thatcher's determined austerity in Britain and Paul Volcker's well-advertised monetary contraction in America, to mention only two examples, inflicted no less real damage to their economies than previous disinflationary recessions in the bad old Keynesian days. Demand management also worked according to Keynesian blueprints in the United States recovery of the last twenty-six months. The contrast with economies of Europe and even Japan, where governments have deliberately eschewed expansionary macroeconomic policies, is striking and instructive. I shall proceed on the assumption that demand management policies do matter and do work.

MEASURES OF MONETARY AND FISCAL POLICIES

To discuss the fiscal–monetary policy mix,[1] one needs in principle to define measures of the two policies. Since there are several instruments for each of the two kinds of policy, it is not strictly possible to describe either of them by a single measure. For monetary policy, however, the supply of base money, or of bank reserves, will do for most purposes.

The problem is more severe for fiscal policy. What we would like is a measure of the direct contribution of the budget programme to aggregate demand, or equivalently to the excess of national investment over national saving. The budget deficit is commonly used for this purpose, but it is a poor measure for several reasons. The deficit is endogenous: the same budget programme, that is, the same legislation authorizing expenditures and levying taxes, will yield higher deficits when the economy is weak than when it is strong. The 'structural' deficit—the contemporary term for what in happier and more optimistic days was called the full employment deficit—is an improvement. It eliminates the cyclical endogeneity by estimating the deficit at a constant reference level of unemployment. But it does not allow for the fact that different items in the budget have different demand impacts even though they contribute equally to the structural deficit. The spending multipliers of tax cuts and transfers are not the same as those of expenditures for goods and services, but generally lower, and within those broad budget categories there are specific differences. A suitably adjusted structural deficit, with items in the budget weighted by their specific multipliers, is the preferable measure, but it has never caught on.

MONETARY AND FISCAL INSTRUMENTS AS SUBSTITUTES IN DEMAND MANAGEMENT

Is it really possible to maintain aggregate demand by different combinations of monetary and fiscal policy? Is fiscal stimulus really an effective substitute for monetary stimulus? The standard Keynesian argument is that fiscal expansion—extra government purchases of goods and services or transfers or tax reductions—will, like any other positive shock to aggregate demand, increase the velocity of base money or any other monetary aggregate. Part of the mechanism is an increase in interest rates, inducing businesses, households, and other agents to economize their holdings of money. My reading, admittedly prejudiced, of the monetarist–Keynesian debate of the 1960s is that professional consensus accepts interest-elasticity of demand for money on both theoretical and empirical grounds. However, the United States financial system is being made more monetarist by the payment of market-determined interest rates on checkable deposits.

Another source of scepticism regarding the demand-stimulating efficacy of fiscal measures is the view that government debts 'are not net wealth' because taxpayers will anticipate future tax liabilities of equal present value to service or pay off the debts. Elsewhere I have listed reasons—liquidity constraints, human mortality, risk pooling, among others—why we should not take the Ricardo–Barro proposition seriously for practical purposes.[2]

Meanwhile macroeconometric models continue to show significant multipliers for fiscal measures over runs of several years. Even more persuasive, perhaps, is the obvious contribution of the Reagan Administration's massive fiscal stimulus to the recovery of the American economy in 1983–4. Though intended and advertised as a package of supply-side incentives, the programme turned out to be well-timed Keynesian demand stimulus on a scale that no Administration sympath-

etic to counter-cyclical demand management would ever have dared.
And it worked.

There are, of course, limits to the possibilities of substituting
monetary for fiscal policy, or vice versa, while keeping the total dose
of demand stimulus or restraint unchanged. If interest rates are at
floors set by Keynesian 'liquidity trap' behaviour or, for a small open
economy in a fixed exchange rate regime, by international capital
mobility, monetary instruments are impotent. If interest rates are
already so high that demand shocks can induce no further responses
in demand for money, then fiscal instruments are impotent. These
extremes will be evident to any student who can manipulate textbook
'*IS*' and '*LM*' curves. There is plenty of room in between them.

HOW THE FISCAL–MONETARY MIX IS DETERMINED IN PRACTICE

Engineering a switch in the policy mix is admittedly a delicate and
uncertain operation. No one can be sure of the exact terms of trade,
or of the speeds of response to changes in the two policies. In practice
nowadays fiscal decisions are made much less frequently than monetary
decisions. Budgets are voted a year at a time, and the tax and
expenditure legislations that determine fiscal outcomes affect budgets
for several years ahead.

In contrast, a central bank operates almost continuously—the decis-
ion-making body of the United States Federal Reserve System meets
regularly nine times a year and can convene more often if necessary.
The central bank can respond promptly to information and projections
about the state of the economy, taking into account along with other
data actual and prospective fiscal policies.

Assuming that the makers of fiscal policy, the Administration and
the Congress in the United States, and the central bank agree about
the desirable macroeconomic path, a policy mix shift would occur as
follows: the projected budget would be altered by tax and expenditure
legislation, and the central bank would then continuously take the
monetary actions necessary to stay on the desired path of output and
prices. Substitution between policies would occur gradually, with some
'trial and error'. This procedure cannot work if the central bank is
committed to purely monetary targets independently of actual economic
events and forecasts.

DEMAND MANAGEMENT POLICIES AND OBJECTIVES

According to Tinbergen–Theil theory of policy, the number of distinct variables for which the government's quantitative objectives can be attained cannot exceed the number of policy instruments it can manipulate. Since we have numerous fiscal and monetary instruments, we might hope to hit many targets at once. We might even, for example, hope to break the short-run link between price inflation and unemployment. By suitable choice of the mixture of monetary and fiscal instruments, could we not achieve and maintain both full employment and price stability? Unfortunately that Utopia eludes our grasp. The Tinbergen–Theil count of instruments is a necessary condition, not a sufficient one. If two or more instruments' effects are distributed among the objective outcomes in identical ways, they are in effect just a single instrument in relation to those objectives. It is the total size of a demand management package, whatever its mix, that determines the combination of employment (or output) and inflation outcomes. Relative to those objectives, monetary and fiscal measures are not independent instruments.

A qualification to this impossibility theorem—I call it the 'common funnel' theorem—occurs in an open economy with a floating exchange rate. A tight monetary policy by the central bank raises domestic interest rates, attracts foreign funds, appreciates the currency, and lowers the domestic prices of internationally traded goods. By itself it also lowers aggregate demand, both by the usual effects of high interest on domestic investment and by the deterioration of the trade balance and net foreign investment due to the currency appreciation. Expansionary fiscal policy could offset the decline of aggregate demand. A tight-money–easy-budget mix might therefore be a way of lowering the path of prices associated with a given path of real output and employment. For any one economy, especially a small economy in a big world, this may well be a feasible tactic. But it is not one that can be repeated regularly. The power of a given differential above foreign interest rates to attract funds diminishes as the portfolio adjustments are completed and only the allocations of new saving flows are at stake. In any event, a lasting effect on the rate of inflation, as distinct from the price level, would require an ever-rising interest rate, a steadily worsening trade balance, a permanently growing government deficit. The gain on the price level from using the tactic once is non-recurrent.

For a country as large as the United States, there are further limitations. The short-term price effects are diluted both by the small

weight of international tradables in relevant price indexes and by
the large weight of the country in determining international prices.
Furthermore, other countries will not stand still as the large country
manipulates its macroeconomic policies. After all, one currency's
appreciation is others' depreciation, and one country's resulting disinflation is others' inflation. The policy mix in question is a 'beggar-my-
neighbour' policy on prices, just as devaluations are 'beggar-my-
neighbour' policies on employment. If all countries together try to use
such tactics, none will succeed.

Expectational effects are a further constraint. The market will
rationally regard the trade deficit achieved by this policy mix as
unsustainable and expect the exchange rate to fall. If so, it will
gradually fall; the decline works against the interest rate advantage as
an attraction to capital inflows.

If we reluctantly discard the hope of using the macro policy mix to
ameliorate the unpleasant short-run link of inflation and employment,
we can split the choice of demand management policies into two
separable decisions. The first decision concerns the total policy impact
needed to achieve the desired path of aggregate demand, considering
its joint consequences for output and employment, on the one hand,
and price levels and inflation rates, on the other. The second decision
is a choice among the various combinations of policies capable of
supporting the desired path. This second decision permits and indeed
requires introducing criteria beyond the objectives of demand stabilization itself.

The additional criteria might include the long-run growth of the
economy. For an open economy, they might include external considerations, the balance of payments on the exchange rate. They might
concern the composition of national output, its division between
governmental and private uses, or between consumption and investment, or between domestic and foreign investment. They might relate
to the distribution of wealth and income.

An important and famous 'neoclassical–neo-Keynesian' manifesto
by Paul Samuelson says: We can take a decision about stabilization,
fixing the total demand management dose to a desired balance of
price and employment objectives. Independently of that choice, we
can respect our priorities regarding resource allocation and the distribution of wealth and income. We don't have to make governmental
claims on resources large relative to GNP in order to have full
employment, because we can obtain the necessary demand from low
taxes, high transfer payments, or low interest rates. We don't have to
slant distribution to the rich to encourage investment and growth,
because we can achieve those goals by other fiscal and monetary tools.

We don't have to rely on the consumption of wage earners or of the poor to employ all our productive resources, because we can stimulate aggregate demand in other ways.

The standard discussion of policy mix has been less general than Samuelson's dictum. It has concerned the composition of output as between capital formation on the one hand and consumption, public or private, on the other. This composition depends on the monetary–fiscal mix in a fairly obvious way: A lower real interest rate achieved by a more accommodative and stimulative monetary policy encourages investment. Its aggregate demand effects can be offset by a tight enough fiscal policy to make room for the investment so stimulated. This, it is alleged, will bring about an output mix heavier on investment and capital formation, lighter on consumption. This result assumes, of course, that the fiscal restrictions apply principally to consumption, either by government itself or by the beneficiaries of transfers on tax reductions. The larger purpose of raising the share of capital formation in national product is to raise, at least for a long intermediate period, the growth of the economy's potential output, or really to substitute future consumption for present consumption.

The reverse policy mix, tight money and easy fiscal policy, has sometimes been advocated or adopted because of balance-of-payments or exchange rate considerations, as I mentioned above. For example, in the early 1960s the President's Council of Economic Advisers was interested in promoting capital formation and economic growth as well as in recovering from the recessions of 1957–8 and 1960. But the United States, committed to an exchange parity that overvalued the dollar, faced a basic deficit in its balance of payments. The perceived need to contain capital outflows limited the degree to which interest rates could be lowered and forced the Administration to rely on expansionary fiscal policy to stimulate aggregate demand. The primacy of the balance-of-payments constraint dictated a policy mix opposite to the growth-oriented mix.

However, the range of choice is somewhat enlarged by the variety of fiscal instruments available. Tax reductions and the incentives they carry for businesses and households can, within limits, be directed either to investment or to consumption. The US dilemma of the early 1960s, just described, was partially mitigated by the investment tax credit, introduced in 1962. It was a stimulus specific to investment; moreover it particularly encouraged home investment, since the credit was not available on foreign investments by United States companies.

Recently Martin Feldstein has advocated a policy mix focused on *the type of investment* favoured by fiscal and monetary policies. Like the sponsors of the Investment Tax Credit twenty years ago, he is particularly concerned to raise the share of business plant and equipment investment in GNP. To this end he has advocated tax concessions beyond the Investment Tax Credit, largely to remove or offset unintended overtaxation of business profits because of inflation. He observes also that inflation has magnified the advantages our tax code provides for residential investment: nominal mortage interest is deductible, 'rental' income in kind to home-owners is untaxed, and capital gains on owner-occupied homes are essentially tax free. These distortions, in his view, justify a tight-money–tax-reduction mix. High interest rates would hold back housing investment or consumption stimulated by capital gains on existing homes. Business investment would be not only spared the deterrent effects of high interest rates but indeed positively stimulated by generous tax concessions. The policies adopted in 1981 conformed in part to Feldstein's prescription.

THE UNITED STATES POLICY MIX TODAY

I now turn to the policy mix in the United States today. I shall argue that both monetary and fiscal policies are extreme, in the sense that the mix has become very tight monetary policy and excessively easy fiscal policy. The late Arthur Okun, a wise theorist and practitioner, said that both policies should stay in the middle of the road, where there is ample room for variation in the interests of demand stabilization and other objectives. Another reason for his recommendation is risk avoidance. We can be more confident of the effects of policy instruments when they are not moved far from actual experience. Ironically our present mix works against widely shared and strongly emphasized goals with respect to the composition of output. The Reagan Administration itself has stressed the need for greater capital formation to increase productivity growth and provide for the future. But the policy mix deters capital formation, both in absolute amount and in proportion to GNP.

At times of high unemployment and excess capacity, the overall stimulative thrust of the package of macro policies is more crucial than the mix. The size of the GNP is more important than its composition. This is true even if the maximization of capital formation were the principal goal of policy. When labour and existing capital are as underutilized as in 1982, capital investment is not limited by the claims of governments and consumers on inelastic supplies of productive resources. Expansion of demand, putting idle resources to work, would both increase incentives for investment and generate the saving to finance them. In the United States, reduction of unemployment by two percentage points would increase GNP by roughly 5 per cent. About 40 per cent of the increase would be in additional national saving, most of which would take the form of additional business investment. The share of such investment in potential GNP would be raised by more than one percentage point. To achieve the same increase at the expense of consumption, with GNP and unemployment unchanged, would require a drastic twist of monetary and fiscal instruments. It might not be possible at all.

At present (March 1982) the overall thrust of macro policies does not promise sufficient expansion of aggregate demand to achieve a decent recovery. At the same time, the threat that the extreme monetary–fiscal mix will hamper capital formation if and when prosperity is restored depresses investment today. Moreover, there is a widespread consensus in financial, business, and political circles that the policy package must be and will be changed, though considerable disagreement as to how and when. The resulting uncertainties themselves diminish the confidence of business investors and weaken the prospects for recovery.

UNITED STATES MONETARY POLICY

The extreme stance of monetary policy has been repeatedly and straightforwardly described by Federal Reserve Chairman Paul Volcker. The growth of the money stock will be gradually but relentlessly diminished until it is no higher than is consistent with the non-inflationary sustainable growth of the economy. Such reduction has indeed been occurring. As Table 14.1 shows the year-over-year growth of *M-1* declined from 1978 through 1981. The table also shows what *M-1* growth may be expected if the policy were to be pursued in subsequent years, 1982–6. In each year target ranges for *M-1* growth are to be lower than in the year before. Table 14.1 shows these target ranges declining by half a point a year after 1981. But Federal Reserve testimony before Congress and other statements have hinted that target ranges should decline by a full point a year.

An important aspect of this stance is that the programme of monetary disinflation be implemented regardless of what happens in the economy. It is a deliberately blindfold policy. According to its rationale, central bankers are not supposed to look out their windows, observe unemployed workers and bankrupt firms, and decide after all to provide more money or to lower interest rates. The strategy depends on public understanding—by borrowers and lenders, unions and employers—that prosperity and jobs depend on the speed with which

Table 14.1: Growth of money supply, nominal GNP, and money velocity 1973–86

	Year	M-1 (ex M-1b)	$GNP	V=$GNP/M-1
		Percentage annual rates of increase, fourth quarter over fourth quarter of preceding year		
Actual	1973	5.8	11.8	5.7
	1974	4.7	7.0	2.2
	1975	5.1	10.0	4.7
	1976	6.2	9.3	3.0
	1977	8.2	12.2	3.7
	1978	8.2	14.2	5.6
	1979	7.5	9.9	2.2
	1980	7.3	9.4	2.0
	1981	4.9	9.3	4.2
Average	1973–81	6.4	10.3	3.7
Projected	1982	2.5–5.5[a]	10.4[b]	7.7–4.6
	1983	2.0–5.0[c]	11.0[b]	9.0–6.0
	1984	1.5–4.5[c]	10.0[b]	8.5–5.5
	1985	1.0–4.0[c]	9.4[b]	8.4–5.4
	1986	0.5–3.5[c]	9.1[b]	8.6–5.6

Notes:
[a] Announced target range.
[b] Projections in the President's budget message, February 1982.
[c] Stated Federal Reserve policy is gradual lowering of targets. The assumption that gradualism means one-half point a year is conservative. The Fed may move down faster. Half a point a year corresponds roughly to the stated wishes of the Administration at its inception in 1981, to cut the monetary growth rate of 1980 in half over a five-year period.

they disinflate prices, wages, and interest rates, that the central bank will not relieve them of this responsibility by validating prevailing patterns of inflation. According to the theory, monetary restriction will purge the economy of inflation more rapidly, more surely, and less painfully if this threat is credible to all.

[In the event, the Federal Reserve departed from the policy beginning in August 1982. By then it had become apparent that the recession was getting much worse, and that the optimistic forecasts of recovery beginning in mid year would not be realized. Interest rates, after declining in late 1981, rose again in the spring of 1982. The incapacity of many domestic and foreign debtors, including a number of foreign governments, to make scheduled payments was a disturbing threat to banks and other financial institutions. The velocities of *M-1* and of *M-2* were turning out to be much lower than the Federal Reserve had anticipated, partly because of increased liquidity preference by an uncertain and pessimistic public and partly because deregulation and innovation were making deposits included in these aggregates more attractive assets. The Federal Reserve took the changes in the meaning and velocity of the *M*'s as the rationalization for allowing those aggregates to exceed their previously announced numerical targets. Chairman Volcker insisted that there was no retreat from the fundamental objective of gradual but firm disinflation. It was clear, however, that the Fed had never expected or intended so severe a decline in the growth of nominal GNP as its money stock targets had turned out to imply.]

Of course, what happens to the economy, how fast the dollar value of GNP grows, does not depend solely on how fast the Federal Reserve allows *M-1*, or any other monetary aggregate, to grow. It depends also on how often a typical dollar of money stock turns over and buys a unit of national output each year—that is, on velocity. Table 14.1 shows in the second column, annual growth of nominal GNP, extended beyond 1981 by the official forecasts of the Administration in the February 1982 Budget Message. (The February 1983 Budget Message contained much lower projections, as a result of the disappointing performance in 1982, when dollar GNP grew only 4 per cent instead of the 10.4 per cent projected. The projections for 1983–6 were lowered from those shown in Table 14.1 to the following: 6.7 per cent, 9.3 per cent, 9.1 per cent, 8.8 per cent.) In the third column of Table 14.1 are shown the growth rates of velocity (*V*) necessary to reconcile the growth of *M-1* (column 1) and the growth of dollar GNP (column 2). There has been an upward trend in *M-1* velocity averaging about 3.7 per cent per year. But this velocity has been quite volatile, as the numbers in the table indicate and as Figure 14.1 depicts.

The projected *M-1* targets are clearly inconsistent with the projected GNP growth unless we enjoy rates of velocity growth very much in excess of the average, very much in the upper range of experience, especially that of the recent past. The record also suggests that large increases of velocity occur only when interest rates rise to extremely high levels and thus induce great economy in holdings of *M-1*. In that case interest rates are likely to be so high that they choke off growth of GNP. [In the event, actual *M-1* growth from the fourth quarter of 1981 to the fourth quarter of 1982 was 8.5 per cent, and velocity actually declined by 4.7 per cent.]

In the absence of a velocity miracle, the situation might be saved by a price miracle—that is, an even more rapid disinflation than the Administration foresees, so that a dollar GNP lower than projected

154

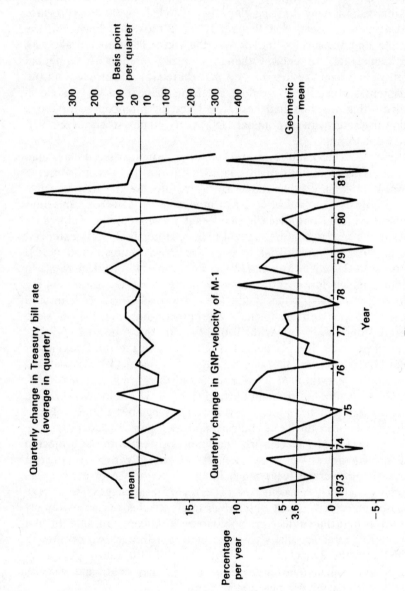

Figure 14.1

is compatible with the same projected growth of real output. The Administration's 1982 projection was 10.4 per cent for nominal GNP, 8 per cent for inflation, 2.4 per cent growth of real GNP. Even if nominal GNP growth fell two or three points short of the forecast, the real GNP forecast could be met if inflation were only 6 per cent or 5 per cent instead of 8 per cent. [The actual outcome for inflation, as measured by the 'GNP deflator' was 4.7 per cent, but this improvement over the forecast was far from enough to offset the error in the projection of velocity.]

Symptomatic of the tightness of monetary policy, given the unrealism of the implicit forecasts of velocity growth, are the high interest rates suffered since the Federal Reserve's policy announcements of 1979. They are high real rates, of an order of magnitude not experienced since the deflation of the early 1930s, when prices were falling at 6 per cent per year and nominal interest rates were 3 per cent. High real interest rates brought on the recessions of 1980 and 1981–2, and they continue even in the depths of recession. A prime bank lending rate of 16 per cent in February–March 1982—it has been higher and may well be higher again—with a projected inflation rate of 8 per cent implies an 8 per cent real rate, somewhat less for borrowers with tax liabilities who can deduct interest costs in calculating taxable income. In contrast, throughout the period since World War II until recently, real prime lending rates generally did not exceed 2 per cent. [Although, thanks to the Federal Reserve policy change, nominal interest rates fell later in 1982, so did the inflation rate. Real rates remained at extraordinary high levels, especially for an economy in deep depression.]

As the brevity of the interlude in 1980–1 between the two recessions indicates, the economy just cannot stand these high rates. They are devastating to interest-sensitive expenditures, for residential construction, non-residential plant and equipment, and inventories. If an upturn begins later this year, as is very likely, then it will run into the high interest rate problem once again. And once again recovery can be stunted or aborted as a result. [Recovery began in November 1982. Interest rates were lower, but remained very high. What will happen to them if and as recovery picks up steam depends on how long the Federal Reserve is willing to accommodate it with above-target monetary growth.]

The narrow money supply *M-1*—publicly held checkable deposits and currency—has been the target aggregate most strongly emphasized by the Federal Reserve, its interpreters, and its critics. Now it is widely recognized that *M-1* has lost the meaning it used to have, if it ever had a stable meaning. Even the President of the Federal Reserve

Bank of Boston has proclaimed the death of *M-1* as a meaningful policy target. The Federal Reserve has officially recognized the mutations of *M-1* by a series of *ad hoc* statistical redefinitions. Their purpose is to preserve a comparable time series in the face of significant changes in financial technologies, institutions, and regulations. For example, the Fed tries to correct its targets to allow for regulatory changes allowing payment of interest at controlled rates on checkable deposits, on the ground that deposits thus attracted do not have the same monetary significance normally indicated by growth of *M-1*. In short, these innovations alter the velocity of *M-1*. Thus the Fed in the end admits that what matters is *M* times *V*, not *M* by itself. [Further regulatory changes in December 1982 and January 1983 allowed payment of uncontrolled interest in checkable deposits, further destroying the usefulness of *M-1* and other *M*'s as targets of policy.]

Although the volatility and unpredictability of velocity constitute the major problem in using money stock growth as the target of policy, it is often the volatility of the growth of the aggregates that attracts the greater attention and criticism. The Federal Reserve is under constant pressure from monetarists, for example those who constitute themselves as the Shadow Open Market Committee, to alter its operating procedures in order to obtain tighter control of *M-1*. In October 1979 the monetarists scored a great victory when the Fed adopted new operating procedures, involving the use of unborrowed bank reserves rather than the Federal Funds interest rate as the instrument guiding week-to-week open market operations. Subsequently both interest rates and money stocks showed greater month-to-month volatility than in the past. The monetarists naturally are still not satisfied. They have persuaded or bulldozed the Fed to base reserve requirements on contemporaneous deposits rather than those of two weeks ago. They want the Fed to index its discount rate to market rates, because the ability of banks to borrow reserves at a fixed rate, moved only occasionally and discretely, allows some slippage between unborrowed reserves and deposits. They favour paying interest on reserves and allowing banks freedom to set deposit interest rates without regulation. [The latter is well on its way to being implemented.]

These changes would no doubt enable the Fed to hit its monetary growth targets more consistently, though other sources of slippage and error would remain, for example the public's choices between currency and deposits. But these concerns are mostly irrelevant. With its present operating procedures, for that matter with its pre-1979 procedures, the Fed can work its will with *M-1* in three or four quarters. That—not the elimination of weekly and monthly variations—is what matters. The Fed does not deserve the criticism that erratic short-term marksmanship is the source of interest rate variability and of high interest rates. No good purpose would be served, and interest rates would be even more volatile, if the monetarist proposals were all adopted. Velocity would be more volatile also, and what really matters is the spending of money on goods and services.

Presumably it is nominal income and spending, *MV*, that the Fed really seeks to control. *M-1* is only an instrument to that end, an instrument to which the Fed sticks because it has in the past staked its credibility on *M-1* targets. As the meaninglessness of *M-1* becomes more apparent and more widely understood, the Fed will move away from it in favour of nominal income. If and when this is explicitly done, it will be important to choose high enough *MV* targets to allow for recovery. Moving downward from a recession number for *MV* growth, even the 9.3 per cent increase shown in Table 14.1 for 1981, would lock the economy into stagnation for several years ahead.

UNITED STATES FISCAL POLICY

Fiscal policy is also extreme—extremely loose. The high-employment budget deficit, standardized to 6 per cent unemployment, is a measure purged of the substantial cyclical effects on revenues and outlays. For some reason, it is now called the structural deficit. It is growing. In fiscal year 1980 it was 0.7 per cent of potential (6 per cent unemployment) GNP. [In fiscal year 1983 it was 2.4 per cent, and in 1988 it will be 5 per cent, on the basis of current or currently planned services, taxes, and entitlements.] The increases are occurring for several reasons.

One reason is the substantial build-up in the defence programme recommended by the President. In the next five years this will raise military spending from 5½ to 8 per cent of GNP. This is not historically high—the ratio exceeded 10 per cent in the peacetime Eisenhower years and in the early 1960s. But the buildup in the 1980s will be rapid; the growth in real defence outlays will be 9 per cent per year on average. Defence will rise from 25 per cent of the budget to 37 per cent.

Second, the Administration and the Congress will do little more to stem the growth of entitlements, principally social insurance. These are expected to grow at 1 per cent a year in real terms. They amount to 45 per cent of the budget. The major outlays are indexed to the cost of living and are protected politically by a strong middle class constituency. [In 1983 a bipartisan Congress–Administration compromise on Social Security finance was enacted, following a report by a

commission chaired by Alan Greenspan. The purpose was to bring
outlays for Old Age, Survivors, and Disability Insurance and payroll
tax contributions into line for the next decade. Thus was preserved a
long tradition that this programme should not run deficits. The
compromise involved both modest reductions of future benefits and
acceleration of payroll tax increases. The same tradition, thus
reinforced, makes it unlikely that Social Security can contribute to
reduction of the overall budget deficit. If benefits are cut, so also will
be payroll taxes.]

Discretionary civilian spending was cut severely in the first year of
the Reagan Administration. The cuts—in food stamps, welfare benefits,
and social services—hit mainly the poorer members of the population.
Little is left to cut. Outlays other than defence, entitlements, and debt
interest account for less than one-fifth of federal expenditures. Congress
has successfully revolted against the Administration's strategy of
making this segment of the budget bear the full burden of fiscal
restraint.

The Economic Recovery Tax Act of 1981 (ERTA) made whopping
reductions in both personal and business income taxes, scheduled to
take effect over several years. [Some of the concessions—notably
about half of the business tax reductions—were withdrawn in the Tax
Equity and Fiscal Responsibility Act of 1982, but even so federal
revenues have been cut below the yield of the previous tax code by
3 per cent of GNP. Actual and projected budget deficits are in the
neighbourhood of 5 per cent of GNP.] ERTA also mandates indexation
of personal income tax brackets beginning in 1985. As a result the
budget will become virtually inflation-neutral; there will be no further
fiscal dividends from inflation.

More serious still, the fiscal dividends of recovery and trend economic
growth are now insufficient to eliminate federal budget deficits or even
to limit them enough to keep federal debt from growing faster than
GNP. The Administration's policies have radically altered the federal
fiscal situation and outlook. For the first time other than major war
years, deficits are no longer self-correcting by passage of time—not
by cyclical upturns, economic growth, or inflation. Until 1981 cyclical
deficits were quickly corrected in recoveries, and the growth trend
created what was called 'fiscal drag' by raising revenues faster than
expenditures. No more.

There are several reasons for this startling change. One of course
is the enormous gap created by the defence build-up and the tax cuts,
as already related. Second entitlements are related to population
growth, and productivity growth has slowed down. Third, the long-
run fiscal outlook is sensitive to the monetary–fiscal policy mix, the

subject of this lecture. The present extreme mix makes the outlook worse. Let me explain.

Why will recovery not eliminate the deficit? [In fiscal year 1982, most of the $111 billion deficit was cyclical. Had unemployment been 6 per cent, the reference point for calculation of high-employment or structural deficits, the deficit would have been only $35 billion. But in 1987 and subsequent fiscal years the *structural* deficits are officially estimated to be around $200 billion. Of course Reagan defence spending and tax cuts were not yet fully effective in 1982, but that is not the whole story.] One big reason is the prospective explosion of interest payments on federal debt, which with present policies will grow by at least 1 per cent of GNP, 4 per cent of the budget, during this decade. Thus cyclical deficits over a long period of excess unemployment pile up debt and are converted into structural deficits due to interest payments. The strength of this perverse effect depends of course on the level of interest rates, which in turn depends on the policy mix itself.

The dynamics of deficits, debt, and interest now for the first time presage a general upward trend in the ratio of federal debt to GNP. The analysis is indicated in Table 14.2, a more arcane table than the previous one. Table 14.2 shows some basic facts about United States deficits and debt, historical for several postwar periods, and projected for the 1980s. The government came out of World War II with a debt 120 per cent of GNP. Gradually this ratio was whittled down to about 25 per cent of GNP. But it will rise to 50 per cent, and perhaps more, in this decade. Moreover, unless the policy mix is changed, nothing will stop it from rising still further.

Row 2 of the table shows what I call the primary deficit, or surplus, in percentage of GNP. The primary deficit is the deficit that would occur if the outstanding public debt were zero. It excludes interest outlays and receipts from taxes on such interest. In both the first two periods, through 1966, we had a primary surplus on average, and in the next three periods, through 1981, the primary deficit was small. Now it is and will remain much higher, for the reasons enumerated above. To the primary deficit must be added interest costs, net of their tax feedbacks. Monetary policy affects those costs in two related ways. First, the fractions of the debt and deficit monetized by the central bank are free of nominal interest. (In the United States the Federal Reserve returns to the Treasury virtually all the interest on its portfolio of government securities.) These fractions are shown in rows 3 and 4. They are clearly smaller in the 1980s than previously, largely because debt and deficit are larger relative to GNP, partly because monetary policy is tighter. Second, the central bank affects

Table 14.2: US fiscal and monetary policy and federal debt dynamics 1952–87

Period: fiscal years (number of years)	1952–7 (6)	1958–66 (9)	1967–74 (8)	1975–9 (5)	1980–1 (2)	1982–7 (6) CBO baseline
1. Federal debt % of GNP, beginning and end of period	64.8–48.5	48.5–35.7	35.7–23.4	23.4–26.5	26.5–27.6	27.6–38.0
2. Federal deficit (+) or surplus (−), excluding interest: % of GNP avg.	−0.58	−0.47	+0.28	+1.38	+0.80	+2.58
3. Share of debt monetized: % range	10.5–11.3	10.7–16.6	16.6–24.0	24.0–18.1	18.1–15.7	15.7–8.0
4. Share of deficit (including interest) monetized: % avg.	0	50	46	12	6	2.6
5. Growth of real GNP: % per yr. avg.	2.8	3.4	3.8	3.5	0.9	3.1
6. Inflation of GNP deflator: % per yr. avg.	2.2	1.9	5.2	7.2	9.1	6.4
7. Treasury ninety-day bill rate: % per yr. avg.	2.1	3.2	5.8	6.7	12.8	10.4
8. Real net interest rate on debt: % per yr. avg.	−0.7	−0.7	−2.8	−2.8	−0.1	1.7

9. Real GNP growth less real net interest rate	3.5	4.1	6.6	6.3	1.0	1.4
10. Hypothetical equilibrium debt/GNP ratio %	−16.6	−11.5	+4.2	+21.9	+80.0	+184.3
Indicated trend of debt/GNP ratio:						
11. Actual, beginning of period	64.8	48.5	35.7	23.4	26.5	27.6
12. After five years	51.9	37.6	27.1	23.0	29.1	38.1
13. After ten years	41.1	28.6	20.8	22.7	31.6	48.0

Notes:

1. Debt held by Federal Reserve and by non-federal owners, par value, at end of fiscal year, relative to nominal GNP for fiscal year, from fiscal year preceding the period to final year of period.

2. Sum of National Income Accounts deficits less surpluses for period, relative to sum of nominal GNP for period. Debt interest outlays (calculated by subtracting Federal Reserve payments to Treasury from 'Net Interest' line of budget) are excluded in calculating deficit or surplus, as are estimated tax receipts recouped from such outlays, estimated at 25 per cent.

3. Monetized debt is the amount held by the Federal Reserve. The denominator of the ratio is, as in line 1, the monetized debt plus the debt held outside the federal government.

4. The increment of monetized debt from beginning to end of period, divided by the increment of total debt as defined in line 1.

8. [line 7 × 0.75 × (100 − line 4)/100] − line 6. The average Treasury bill rate for each period is taken to be the permanent cost of financing new debt and refinancing old debt, which is reckoned at par value, given the conditions and policies of the period. It is multiplied by 0.75 on the assumption that the Treasury recoups 25 per cent of nominal interest outlays in taxes. The third factor reduces the net interest cost for 'seignorage', the fraction of the debt monetized by the Federal Reserve. Subtracting line 6 converts the net nominal interest rate on the debt to a real rate.

9. line 5 − line 8.

10. line 2/line 9. A negative figure means that the hypothetical equilibrium debt/GNP ratio is negative, i.e., the government would be a net lender to the private sector.

12. 13. [line 10 − line 11] × $[(100 + line\ 9)/100]^n$ + line 10, letting $n = 5.10$. See text.

the interest rates paid on the non-monetized part of the debt (rows 7 and 8).

The dynamics of the debt/GNP ratio, call it d, are simple (see also chapter 18):

$$\dot{d} = x + d(r - g). \tag{14.1}$$

Here x is the primary deficit relative to GNP, r is the real rate of interest on the debt, account taken of inflation, of recouped taxes, and of monetization, and g is the growth rate of real GNP. The steady-state solution of (14.1) is:

$$d^* = x/(g - r). \tag{14.2}$$

Values of d^* for the parameters of each period are given in row 10. Combining (1) and (2) gives:

$$\dot{d} = (d - d^*)\cdot(r - g). \tag{14.3}$$

This equation is used to calculate rows 12 and 13. Stability of the ratio d requires that the real net interest rate on debt be smaller than the economy's real growth rate, or equivalently that the nominal net interest rate be smaller than the growth of nominal GNP. Although this condition is still met in the sixth column, the margin is much smaller than before 1980. Quite possibly the interest rate projection in row 8 of that column is overoptimistic. In any event, we are very close to violating the stability condition. Even if the stability condition is satisfied and the steady state debt/GNP ratio is positive, the indicated d^* is so high that the debt/GNP ratio will be rising rapidly in the next decade and continue rising for a long time. [Subsequent projections by the CBO are even more pessimistic than column 5.]

As the public and the Congress come to understand this prospect, the likelihood is that policy will be changed. What is less likely is understanding that both monetary and fiscal policy contribute to the problem, and both must contribute to the solution.

THE NEEDED CHANGES OF POLICY

The combination of extreme policies in effect in 1982 does not seem stimulative enough to support a strong and sustained recovery. With real interest rates so high we might see an incomplete recovery, or perhaps intermittent recessions with short interludes like that of late 1981. Sometimes the problem is described as tug-of-war between monetary and fiscal policies striving to pull the economy in opposite directions. If so, monetary policy has so far been the stronger. But that description is at best a half truth. Current monetary policy, as I argued above in connection with Table 14.1, would restrain expansion of nominal demand whether fuelled by government spending and tax cuts or by a spontaneous burst of private spending and monetary velocity. It is the inconsistency of the monetary targets with demand expansion, from whatever source, that is the threat to sustained recovery. The problem is not specifically a collision of monetary and fiscal policy.

The budget will be giving increasing stimulus to the economy because of the increases in defence spending and the tax cuts. According to the macroeconomics I learned, the macroeconomics I teach, those policies will strengthen, not weaken, recovery prospects. They also, by the same token, will raise the risks of inflation, perhaps especially the risks of sectoral price and wage accelerations in defence-related industries. But general overheating seems a far distant prospect, in both business cycle time and calendar time.

Promotion of capital formation is a widely held economic goal, emphasized in the 'supply-side' foundation of Reagan Administration policy and shared by many of its sceptics and opponents. If and when recovery brings the economy to its threshold of price acceleration, national saving will be the effective constraint on real investment. The fear that absorption of saving by federal deficits will crowd out investment will then be justified. It is premature right now, when investment demand is constrained by high real interest rates attributable to monetary policy and by the excess capacity and low profitability resulting from the recession. These negative factors are overwhelming the generous incentives for business investment given in ERTA.

A side remark: exclusive emphasis on business investment in plant and equipment is misguided. The underlying rationale of a pro-investment policy is concern that society is not meeting its obligations to future generations. But there are several ways to provide for the future. Foreign investment, achieved by current account surpluses, is one, to which the present policy mix is particularly devastating. Public civilian investment, mostly carried out by state and local governments, is another. It is also sensitive to interest rates, as well as to the cyclically sensitive budgets of those governments. Complaints about the decay of the publicly provided 'infrastructure' are increasing. Human capital formation, dependent on public education, training, and on-the-job experience, is also suffering. High interest rates and recession have made residential investment a disaster area, as even Martin Feldstein would admit.

Current conventional wisdom blames interest rates on high current and prospective federal deficits. Federal Reserve Chairman Paul Volcker keeps saying that the key to lowering interest rates is simply tightening the budget. Most commentators and politicians echo this view. But it is only a half truth. Tightening the budget will lower interest rates. Anticipation of tightening the budget will lower long-term interest rates. More saving will be potentially available for investment. But Paul Volcker must do his part too. Without an easier monetary policy, there is no guarantee that investment demand will rise enough to employ the saving to which the federal government relinquishes claim. Without an easier monetary policy, a large part of that potential saving would vanish, wasted in higher unemployment and greater economic slack. The purpose of a policy to prevent 'crowding out' is not to lower interest rates by weakening the economy, but to lower them without weakening the economy. That requires the replacement of fiscal stimulus by equivalent monetary stimulus.

[As noted above, the change of Federal Reserve policy in the second half of 1982 did turn the economy around. Even while budget projections were becoming much more alarming and obsessive, the Fed's moves lowered both short and long interest rates, both nominal and real. Aided substantially by consumer spending stimulated by the second and third instalments of the 1981 ERTA reductions in personal income tax rates and by the beginnings of the defence build-up, the economy recovered at an unexpectedly rapid pace throughout 1983. Fears that deficits would 'choke off the recovery' proved as unfounded as standard macroeconomics would predict. They are still heard, but in sophisticated circles they gave way to more intelligible fears that the budget was over-stimulative. The need for a change in the policy mix remains, even more urgent than before.]

I hope I have made a convincing case for a significant change in the monetary–fiscal policy mix in the United States. It is not easy to bring it about, given the diffusion of macroeconomic responsibilities in the United States among the quasi-independent central bank, the Congress, and the Executive. The Congress itself, moreover, is divided. Democrats control the House, Republicans the Senate. The budget and tax committees are not coordinated with the committees that exercise a loose surveillance of the Federal Reserve. The Administration, which initiates its own budget and tax proposals to the Congress and has diplomatic relations with the Fed, is divided among supply-siders, monetarists, and champions of old-fashioned fiscal orthodoxy. My own proposal for an Accord of 1982—the label is meant to recall the Accord of 1951, a tripartite agreement which liberated monetary policy from its wartime commitment to support government security prices at par—was presented earlier in 1982 in an unconventional way. I claimed to have foreseen a new Accord in a dream in a *New York Times* report. It is reprinted as an Appendix, along with an optional second ending, a newspaper article from the following day's *Times*. [Needless to say, the dream did not come true.]

An Accord among United States makers of macroeconomic policy is not the only agreement needed to set the stage for recovery and prosperity. I have two others in mind, but I can do no more than mention them here. The second would involve private sector labour and management, together with government. Its purpose would be to assure moderation of wages and prices during the recovery. The third one would be international. The United States macroeconomic policy mix has been adopted with indifference—one could say, I am afraid, with an unusual and unseemly conscious indifference—to its international consequences. Our high interest rates are a barrier to recovery and growth in Europe, Japan, and throughout the world. The seven summit countries, which include Canada, should reach a coordinated understanding on their macroeconomic monetary and fiscal policies. We have surely learned by now that floating exchange rates, whatever their virtues, are not a substitute for international coordination of policies.

APPENDIX: A PROPOSAL IN THE FORM OF A DREAM, WITH AN OPTIONAL ENDING

Administration, Congress, Fed, in Major Accord on Money Budget.
Washington, 12 June 1982
A historic 'Accord for Economic Recovery' among the Administration, the Federal Reserve, and Congressional leaders of both parties was announced yesterday in Washington. The Accord plots a new course for fiscal and monetary policy over the next two years. Government spokesmen hailed it as the most important agreement among the makers of federal economic policy since the Treasury–Federal Reserve Accord of 1951, which restored the freedom of the Fed to gear monetary policy to economic conditions rather than to the prices of government securities. The new recovery policy is designed to lower the 9–10 per cent unemployment rates and 18–20 per cent long-term interest rates experienced so far this year.

According to the terms of the 1982 Accord, the President will acquiesce in suspension of the third installment of the personal income tax reduction passed in 1981, a 10 per cent rate cut scheduled for July 1, 1983, and of the indexation of brackets and exemptions scheduled for 1985. Together with other changes in federal revenues and outlays, this suspension will reduce the deficits projected in fiscal years 1983 and 1984 to $80 billion, only half the deficits previously projected.

For its part, the Federal Reserve will relax the 'tight money' policies that have led to extraordinarily high interest rates throughout most of the past three years, even during recessions. Chairman Volcker, speaking on behalf of the Federal Open Market Committee after its special meeting yesterday, said that the 'Fed' will seek to provide a monetary and financial environment for growth of dollar Gross National Product by 11–13 per cent per year over the next four quarters and 9–12 per cent in the succeeding year. Inflation has been declining, and with projections of 8 per cent for the next twelve months declining to 7 per cent in the next year, Volcker explained, the GNP targets will allow room for about 4 per cent per year growth in real (inflation-corrected) production over this period. This is expected to lower unemployment rates by at least two points over the next two years of recovery.

Chairman Volcker emphasized that the Fed remains determined to bring down the inflation that has plagued the economy for the last decade. According to Volcker, the Fed's willingness to accommodate growth in dollar GNP in the period ahead is conditional on measures to improve significantly the budget outlook, as agreed by Administration and Congressional leaders. He said, 'The prospective reductions in federal deficits are a substantial contribution to the battle against inflation and they make it possible for the Federal Reserve to exceed its previously announced money stock growth targets, if this is necessary to accommodate the projected economic recovery.'

Volcker explained that the new Accord should lead to lower interest rates. 'We have said all along that the high deficits previously projected were keeping interest rates excessively high. Now that the federal government will no longer be taking such a large share of the nation's savings, interest rates can be expected to fall. We, for our part, intend to see that real rates are low enough to channel the savings the government will no longer be claiming into productive private investments in business capital and housing construction.'

A corollary of the Accord is that the Fed is abandoning the use of targets for growth of monetary aggregates, of which the most important recently have been *M-1* and *M-2*, as the dominant guides to its operations. Volcker explained that past and expected innovations in financial institutions and regulations alter and obscure the meaning of any particular concept of money stock. 'Our basic objectives, of course, have always been to reduce both inflation and unemployment and to attain stable non-inflationary growths. The monetary aggregate targets were a means to this end, but now they have outlived their usefulness.

We will pursue the same objectives, but without committing ourselves rigidly to any numerical targets either for money stocks or interest rates.'

On the fiscal side, the deficit-reducing budget adjustments include several items in addition to the suspension of personal income tax cuts. These are $10 billion of savings annually in the defense budget, $10 billion in taxation of windfall profits arising from decontrol of natural gas prices, and $10 billion in miscellaneous adjustments of the tax code to close loopholes. In addition, the expected reduction in interest rates due to the Accord will bring some budgetary savings, but neither the Treasury nor the Federal Reserve was prepared at present to estimate these or count them in the economic and fiscal calculations.

President Repudiates Monetary–Fiscal Accord; Sticks to Supply-Side Strategy. Santa Barbara, California, 13 June

Asked at an impromptu press conference at his ranch here about the Accord on money and budget announced Friday in Washington, President Reagan today denied he had agreed to it. After conferring this morning with Congressman Jack Kemp (Republican, New York), the President reaffirmed his faith in the 'supply-side' tax cut of 1981. 'We will not change our course. We will not deny the people the tax cuts they were promised and have every right to expect. Nor will we cut back on the defense build-up the country so desperately needs. Our economic strategy will work, and I call on the Congress and the private sector to make it work. I have asked for non-defense budget cuts to improve the deficit outlook, and the public will know whom to blame if we have high deficits in the next several years.' Later in the conference the President said he had no fundamental differences of view with the officials of his Administration and the Federal Reserve who arrived at the aborted Accord, or with the Senators and Congressmen who participated. There was apparently a slight misunderstanding about tactics, he admitted, but everyone is agreed on goals. Asked if Secretary of the Treasury Regan, OMB Director David Stockman, and Federal Reserve Chairman Volcker will continue in their jobs, the President said 'Of course'.

NOTES

1. *See also* Chapters 3, 7, and 16.
2. *Asset Accumulation and Economic Activity*, Chapter 3.

15   The Reagan Legacy*

Does President Ronald Reagan deserve the credit he is claiming and receiving for the country's prosperity? Not that much, though somewhat more than for Americans' Olympic medals and improved scores on college-entrance tests. He and the country have been very lucky and have deferred serious problems to the future.

Reagan's 1981 fiscal programme—massive tax cuts and a sharp rise in defence spending—injected purchasing power into the economy just when stimulus was needed to promote recovery from the severe recession of 1981–2. By contrast European governments practised fiscal austerity and their economies are still in the doldrums.

Voters have short memories and myopia. They are more impressed by an upswing in an election year than by the level of economic performance, recent history or potential future difficulties.

Strong as it has been for two years, our recovery has still not reduced employment and excess industrial capacity to normal prosperity rates. Reagan's four-year record on real incomes, production and jobs certainly will not surpass Jimmy Carter's (Figure 15.1).

But Reagan's bad news came in his first two years, Carter's during his 1980 campaign. If Presidents are held responsible for whatever happens, then Reagan should be charged for the most severe recession since the 1930s if he is credited for subsequent recovery.

Actually both events owe more to another powerful public official, Paul Volcker, Federal Reserve chairman since 1979. Reagan's recession was in the cards before his inauguration because of the Fed's determined anti-inflationary stance. In late 1982 Volcker relented, stepped up money growth and turned the economy around. Then Reagan's fiscal stimulus took hold.

Better to be lucky than smart! In 1981 the Reagan Administration

---

*October 1984, published in the *Marietta (Ohio) Times*, 26 October and the *Boston Globe*, 20 November.

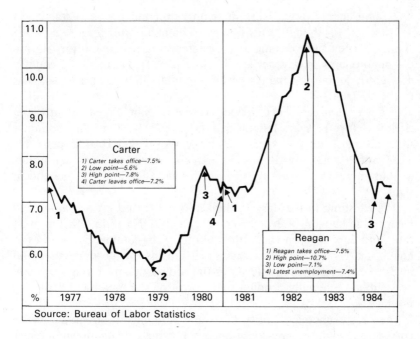

Figure 15.1: Unemployment: Carter vs. Reagan (unemployment rate for civilian labour force, seasonally adjusted)

foresaw no recession ahead and no need for demand stimulus two years later. The big defence build-up was to impress the Russians. The tax cuts, scheduled in instalments, were advertised as supply-side incentives. They were intended to increase saving, not spending, and to speed the growth of the nation's productivity capacity, not to provide markets for its existing capacity.

In fact, the budget primed the demand-side pump. An Administration that disdained John Maynard Keynes and worshipped Arthur Laffer demonstrated that super-Keynesian policies work. The tax cuts have not yet enhanced thrift or accelerated productivity, much less paid for themselves in federal revenues.

On inflation, Volcker's strong medicine did the job. But no supply-side miracle saved us from the recession and other painful side effects.

Our real interest rates remain pathologically high, thanks to our bizarre combination of tight money and loose budget. We attract funds into dollars from the whole world, making foreign currencies and imports cheap. The overvalued dollar helps to hold prices down temporarily. But it prices our farmers and manufacturers out of world markets.

Oil and energy prices were the culprits for inflation and stagflation in the 1970s, though OPEC and Khomeini are forgotten when Jimmy Carter and Democratic Congresses are blamed for all the disappointments of that decade. Lucky again, Reagan and the country now enjoy an oil glut thanks partly to conservation measures adopted in the 1970s.

Reagan's budgets have helped recovery, but they spell trouble ahead. Before Reagan, federal debt declined relative to the economy, from 120 per cent of GNP at the end of World War II to 25 per cent. That ratio has already risen to 36 per cent, will add at least ten points in four more years, picking up speed and exploding with no end in sight.

It is whistling in the dark to think prosperity and growth alone will balance the budget, or even stabilize the debt/GNP ratio. High interest rates and debt feed on each other. As the debt commandeers an even higher share of the public's savings, it crowds out productive capital investments—residential and industrial, domestic and foreign, private and public—gradually eroding the growth of the nation's capacity to produce.

The first economic priority of a new Administration should be to correct our tight-money–loose-budget mix and bring down interest rates. It can be done without inviting either inflation or recession. It is essential to the economic health of the United States and the whole world.

Volcker will have to help mightily. (Indeed he may have to act soon to keep this recovery from burning out, with unemployment and excess capacity much too high.) The fiscal correction is up to the President and Congress.

The debt explosion can't be arrested without raising taxes. Anyone who looks at budget arithmetic knows that. Wall Street knows it. Walter Mondale knows it. Responsible members of Congress of both parties know it.

Reagan doesn't know it. He talks of spending cuts instead, but he exempts defence and Social Security and can't control debt interest. Stockman already mercilessly axed 'discretionary' social spending; he knows, if his boss does not, that there's no blood left in that turnip.

Three Octobers ago I said and wrote:

'The Reagan economic program is advertised to cure inflation and unemployment, to revive productivity, hard work and thrift. It probably cannot achieve those wonderful results. What it is sure to do is redistribute wealth, power and opportunity to the wealthy and powerful and their heirs.'

That is the legacy of Reaganomics.

PART III
Fiscal Policies

INTRODUCTION

These chapters, while inevitably continuing to discuss Reagan's fiscal revolution, set forth some general macroeconomic principles of fiscal policy. I emphasize and illustrate several important points:

1. Distinguish situations of underemployment from those of full employment. Additional public spending and tax reduction can put idle labour and capital to work, provided monetary policy is accommodative. But if resources are already fully employed, fiscal demand stimulus will *crowd out* other uses of national output, particularly interest-sensitive capital investments and, in our world of floating exchange rates, exports net of imports.

2. Distinguish actual from structural budget deficits. Actual budget outcomes are very sensitive to the cyclical state of the economy; deficits are large in recessions. The structural deficit is calculated as if the economy were at a standard reference unemployment rate. It is a measure of the private saving the deficit would absorb in those circumstances; as Chapter 16 argues, it is not a perfect measure and should be adjusted for the differential effects of various budget items on saving. Programmatic changes in the budget, for example new expenditures or reduced taxes, can raise the structural deficit. Cyclical recessions do not, except that the resulting deficits add to future interest outlays.

3. Distinguish passive from active deficits. Cyclical deficits do not expand aggregate demand. The counter-cyclical sensitivity of revenues and the pro-cyclical sensitivity of some expenditures moderate, but do not prevent or reverse, business fluctuations. Active policies, which change *structural* deficits, are required to overcome other sources of cyclical instability.

4. Distinguish primary deficits from debt service. If there were no debt outstanding, debt would arise if other, *primary*, transactions were in deficit. If those transactions were in balance, the debt would rise by the net interest on the already outstanding debt.

5. Pay attention to the size of public debt relative to Gross National Product, a good measure of the economy's capacity to pay taxes and to save. A high and growing debt/GNP ratio leaves less and less room for productive capital in the economy. From 1946 to 1981 federal debt grew more slowly than GNP because the structural primary deficit was close to zero and the debt interest rate was well below the economy's growth rate. The reversal of those conditions

173

in the 1980s threatened runaway increase in the ratio, ever more severe crowding out.

6. Expected future fiscal policies affect the economy today. In Chapter 18 I show how expectation of reduced structural deficits in future may, by lowering long-term interest rates today, raise today's aggregate demand. This is sure to be the case if financial markets also reflect belief that monetary easing will accompany future tightening of fiscal policy.

7. Constitutional or statutory budget rules carry serious economic and political hazards. In Chapters 20 and 21, as in Chapter 3 above, I argue that such rules would make the economy less stable. They would also deprive the electorate and its representatives of the freedom and the responsibility to gear the budget to changing national priorities and circumstances.

16 Does Fiscal Policy Matter?*

Strange propositions are commonplace in macroeconomic commentary these days; the world is turned upside down. The federal government is about to increase real defence spending over the next several fiscal years by 9 per cent annually, to cut personal income tax rates by 10 per cent both this year and next, and to phase in drastic reductions in taxation of business investments in equipment and structures. Similar budgets in the past have invariably made the economy more prosperous, creating jobs and lowering unemployment, speeding the growth of production, raising profits; consider, for example, 1940–1, 1950–2, 1966–9.

But this time the budget prospects are widely regarded as a bad omen. Many forecasters, with or without formal models, would lift their estimates of the strength and longevity of recovery from the current recession if the budgets for fiscal years 1983 and 1984 were revised by cutting spending or raising taxes or both. They would be more optimistic not just about prices and interest rates but about employment and real activity.

It's a puzzle. Suppose the news was that the hundred largest corporations were planning to borrow and spend $100 billion more than previously thought, say on investment projects resulting from research and development breakthroughs. Would that be regarded as a minus in the economic outlook? Suppose then that they announced cutbacks in these plans. Would that news be regarded as a plus?

Policy makers, politicians and pundits, businessmen, bankers and brokers, speak with many voices about the effects and dangers of federal deficits. Economists too. Deficits and public debt are the culprits for inflation. No they aren't—they aren't inflationary unless they are monetized, and the central bank can and should resist political pressures to monetize. Government borrowing raises interest rates and

---

*May 1982, Center for Research on Economic Policy, Stanford University. Unpublished.

preempts saving that would otherwise finance private capital formation.
No it doesn't—rational taxpayers will save enough extra to buy the
government bonds, as a hedge against future taxes or inflation; the
real burden of government is its draft on the nation's resources, no
matter how financed. Tax cuts mean bigger deficits, but stimulate
aggregate demand, employment, and output. No—they're just
inflationary. No—they just raise interest rates. No—they do nothing.
No—if they are well designed they provide such strong 'supply-side'
incentives that tax revenues will actually increase.

To break into this Babel of confusion is foolhardy, but that is what
I've been asked to do.

I. FISCAL STIMULUS, MONETARY POLICY, AND 'CROWDING OUT'

Does fiscal policy matter? I interpret the question to refer to macroeconomic outcomes: output and unemployment, prices and inflation,
investment and growth. Obviously government budgets are major
determinants of the allocation of the nation's resources among various
uses and of the distribution of wealth, income, and consumption. But
it has been alleged that pure fiscal policy—pure in the sense that
variations in government expenditure and tax revenue are fully
absorbed in non-monetary debt—have no significant systematic short-
run macroeconomic consequences. At the same time, fiscal policies
may affect the division of output between consumption and capital
formation, a division of importance for the future growth and level of
the economy's capacity to produce.

We are frequently told that government purchases of goods and
services, using resources that could be employed for other purposes,
is the true and sufficient measure of government's impact and burden
on the economy. What that impact is, in what degree it is a burden,
obviously depends on the nature of the government activities, the
public consumption on investment goods they provide. These are the
difficult agenda of politics at all levels—federal, state, and local. I
don't propose to discuss them today, beyond objecting to the prevalent
idea, unfortunately encouraged by economists, that the size of government relative to the economy can be rationally discussed and debated
without reference to the functions the government is performing and
to the circumstances of the day. Economic calculus does not suggest
that a perceived need for increased defence expenditure, or a national
decision to socialize health care for the aged and the indigent, must
be met wholly from other public outlays.

The major issues concern the financing of a given programme of public expenditure. At one extreme is the Ricardo–Barro equivalence theorem, which says that the mix between taxation and borrowing makes no difference. That is, interest rates, prices, current consumption, investment, employment, and output are the same however large the government budget deficit. Private agents regard debt issues simply as postponement of taxes and are indifferent to such postponements. They simply buy the bonds, the perfect riskless way to provide for future tax liabilities. According to the theorem, deficit spending is impotent—cannot absorb saving in times of slack and excess unemployment—and innocuous—increased supplies of bonds generate their own demands. They do not raise interest rates or crowd out any private demands for resources or saving. Increased government purchases may both directly and indirectly employ otherwise idle resources, or displace other uses of resources already employed. But these effects are independent of their financing.

I have discussed this proposition elsewhere.[1] Although there are grains of truth in the 'theorem', there are not enough for policy makers to take it seriously. Nor is there convincing empirical evidence that the rate of national saving is independent of the amount of government saving, a proposition that contradicts 'Denison's Law' and the findings of David and Scadding that *private* saving is a constant share of national income.

The other extreme position is that substitution of government borrowing for taxation has no effect on prices and inflation, or on output and employment. In short, it has no effect on aggregate demand—but it does alter the composition of national output and generally raises real interest rates. Here government borrowing does absorb private saving, and this is why it completely 'crowds out' other claims for saving. There are two scenarios of 100 per cent crowding out, and they may coincide. One is monetary crowding out. The path of output is independently determined by monetary policy, whether or not unemployed resources are available for a higher path. The second is resource crowding out. Whatever the monetary policy, if the economy is producing at capacity, demands for goods and services by the beneficiaries of tax reductions or transfers can be met only by displacing other demands. If monetary policy is not accommodative, then the mechanism of displacement is the real interest rate. To the extent that it is accommodative, the mechanism may be saving forced by inflation.

The extent of crowding out, and the kinds of demands displaced, depend on the nature of the tax cuts (or increased transfers) which lead to the borrowing. In a world where, contrary to Barro and

Ricardo, current tax reductions have value to taxpayers and therefore make a difference, they almost inevitably lead to some increase in consumption. But 'supply-side' tax reductions may be slanted towards investment. In any case, the rise in real interest rates mainly crowds out investment. The result is substitution of the kinds of investment favoured by the tax incentives for other kinds, for example business equipment and structures benefiting from accelerated cost recovery for residential investment or capital projects of state and local governments. In a floating-exchange-rate world the nation's current account surplus, its net accumulation of foreign assets, is a prime victim of crowding out. The mechanism evident in the US during the past two years is that high home interest rates attract foreign funds, appreciate the local currency, and make exports less competitive and imports more attractive.

Monetary policy could conceivably be made with a target path of real output and employment, to which the central bank tries to hold the economy by adjusting its instrument settings. If this path were considered sacrosanct, independent of the economic objectives of the fiscal policy makers, then full crowding out would occur even though in the eyes of many observers resources would be available to accommodate the demands of the government and its beneficiaries without displacing any other demands. Another way to put it is in terms of saving: the funds to finance the public borrowing could be generated from the incomes associated with expanded production and employment. No rise of real interest rates would be required, and no crowding out would occur, if the monetary authority would accommodate the expansion. This is the essence of the quarrel of Keynes with the Treasury view in 1929. The debate, with all the old misunderstandings and confusions, recurs again and again. Today it seems hardly accurate to charge the federal budget for high real interest rates and for threatening massive 'crowding out'. Rather, the *monetary policy* has crowded out private investment by high real interest rates. The resulting recession has added $60–75 billion to the deficit, absorbing some of the saving that might have gone into the monetarily displaced investment. Most of that saving has simply vanished, lost along with the wages and profits lost in the recession.

Generally monetary policy does not take a real output path as target but some nominal quantity thought to be closer to its jurisdiction and grasp. When the Federal Reserve has staked its credibility on *M-1* targets, presumably it is prepared to allow a variety of outcomes— paths of output, prices, interest rates—without changing those targets. It's hard to believe that the Fed expected or wanted $9\frac{1}{2}$ per cent unemployment today or $9\frac{1}{2}$ per cent real interest rates, or that Fed targets and reserve supplies would be appreciably different if by chance unemployment were only $8\frac{1}{2}$ per cent. The Fed is unwilling to do anything to bring about better real economic performance, while quietly hoping for good luck with velocity.

It makes sense, therefore, to ask what are the effects of fiscal stimuli given the Fed's targets for monetary aggregates. The standard textbook answer is, or used to be, that the paths of output, prices, and real interest rates will all be higher. I don't know why that isn't still the right answer. A forecaster should show a stronger 1983 recovery if federal taxes are not raised and defence spending is not slowed down, just as he would if he learned that Fortune 500 companies were, in an onset of confidence, going to raise in the securities market $50 billion more than previously thought and spend it on new plant and equipment. In both cases the first-order effects are more spending on goods and services, and in both cases the second-order brake is the limited supply of bank reserves. (Actually a government-purchase-driven expansion is slightly less dependent on monetary accommodation because federal cash balances are not included in *M-1*.)

It may be true that the *LM-1* curve is steeper than it used to be. Nominal interest rates are so high, and have been so high so long, that little marginal economy in cash management may be induced by further increase. The spread of interest-bearing NOW accounts, included in *M-1*, works in the other direction. More important is what might be called the Akerlof–Milbourne effect, namely that the elasticity of demand for money with respect to transactions volume is very low in the short run. When business picks up, it can be handled. Later adjustment to more comfortable cash, liquidity, and debt positions raises interest rates.

Does the longer-run *LM* curve actually slope the 'wrong' way? A few years ago this proposition seemed to be implied by complaints that the textbook treatment of fiscal stimulus ignored the wealth and portfolio effects of repeated additions of public debt. Over time, it was argued, these would gradually move the short-run *LM* curve to the left, raising interest rates and eventually overcoming the spending effects of the fiscal policy. The trouble with this argument is that it is hard to see why the demand for money is so high if income has not risen but interest rates have. The rise of interest rates induces people to hold more wealth in the form of government bonds, but why should they demand more money too?

II. MEASURING THE MACROECONOMIC IMPACT OF THE BUDGET

The deficit or surplus is commonly taken as the relevant measure of fiscal stimulus even by economists who know better—witness the current controversy over the budgets for FY 1983 and subsequent years.

For most purposes, the first thing we want to know about the budget programme for a year is how it affects aggregate *excess* demand for goods and services, $E - Y$. Now this is a schedule, not a number. Aggregate demand E is a function of Y, of the variables describing the fiscal programme f, and of other variables x, interest rates, prices, asset stocks, expectations. The relevant comparison of one fiscal programme f_1 with another f_2—that for the previous year or an alternative for the year at hand—is the shift of the schedule: $E(Y, f_1, x) - E(Y, f_2, x)$. Such a comparison is illustrated in Figure 16.1, ignoring or taking as constant the variables x. E_1 and E_2 are aggregate demand functions for the two fiscal programmes f_1 and f_2. Their deviations from the 45° line $E = Y$, positive or negative, are the schedules of excess demand. The government deficit is a function of the same variables $D(Y, f, x)$, also illustrated in Figure 16.1 for programmes f_1 and f_2.

Is there a single number that tells the macroeconomic impact of f_1 compared with f_2? Certainly the predicted actual deficit does not fill the bill. In Figure 16.1, for example, Y_1 and Y_2 are the incomes predicted from the *ex post* requirements $E = Y$, but $D(Y_2, f_2) - D(Y_1, f_1)$ tells us almost nothing of interest. This would be true *a fortiori* if the indicated shift of E, say from one year to the next, arose from differences in x instead of f, especially if those differences had little or no effect on the D function.

The concept of the high-employment deficit (HED) was invented decades ago in order to eliminate the endogenous response of the deficit to Y. In Figure 16.1, Y^* is the assumed 'high-employment' level of Y; $D(Y^*, f_1)$ and $D(Y^*, f_2)$ are the corresponding HEDs. Actually any reference Y^* in the range of normal experience will do for the purpose, whatever the rate of employment or unemployment to which it corresponds. The high or full employment tag may have confused politicians and public and aroused their suspicions. The idea that the budget should be balanced at Y^* and the idea that it need not, should not ever, be balanced for $Y < Y^*$ are normative propositions quite separable from the analytical objective of correcting for endogeneity. In any event, for comparisons of budget programmes over time presumably the reference Y^* should grow at the economy's

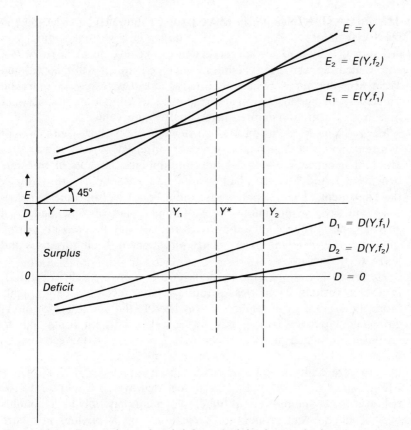

Figure 16.1: Excess demand and deficit schedules for two budget programmes

trend and the HED should be expressed as a fraction of Y^*.

Although HED corrects for the Y-endogeneity of the deficit, it is not the contribution of the budget programme to excess demand $E - Y$. In Figure 16.1 this comparison, as between f_1 and f_2, would be illustrated in the *upper* panel as $E(Y^*, f_2) - E(Y^*, f_1)$. Though this is generally positively correlated with $D(Y^*, f_2) - D(Y^*, f_1)$, it is not the same thing. But it is $E^* - Y^*$, not D^*, which tells how much spending must be increased or decreased by non-fiscal policies or events (e.g. by monetary measures affecting investment and saving) if Y^* were to be realized along with the fiscal programme. Thus it is $E^* - Y^*$ that is relevant to the much-discussed issue of 'crowding out'.

Differences between the two comparisons arise, of course, because the several fiscal instruments affect aggregate demand and deficits differently. One example is related to the famous balanced-budget multiplier theorem. An increase of a dollar in government purchases accompanied by a lump-sum increment of tax revenues will leave D^*, and indeed the whole D schedule, unchanged. But it will raise E^* and the E schedule uniformly by $\$(1 - b)$ where b is taxpayers' marginal propensity to spend. Government purchases of goods and services have a bigger multiplier than taxes, in absolute value.

More generally, items on the two sides of the budget—purchases of different goods and services, taxes of different types, transfers to different beneficiaries—vary in their multipliers. Tax cuts or transfers benefiting liquidity-constrained low-income households are virtually the equivalent of direct purchases, while liquid high-income benefici-aries will save significant fractions. Grants-in-aid of state and local governments, to the degree they are fungible, may induce only partial spending; the recipient governments will augment their surpluses and lower their own taxes.

These considerations suggest the use of an adjusted deficit, AHED, in which various categories of outlays and receipts bear weights proportional to their multipliers, normalized to the multiplier for direct government purchases of goods and services. It is important not to use HED, adjusted or not, for the wrong purpose. If the economy is not at Y^* when a new budgetary programme is introduced, but at Y_1, the measure of fiscal stimulus needed by a forecaster is $E(Y_1, f_2) - E(Y_1, f_1)$ not $E(Y^*, f_2) - E(Y^*, f_1)$. A tax cut which would total \$100 billion if the economy were at full employment may only be a stimulus of \$50 billion to an economy in recession. This is obvious in Figure 16.1, but some reduced-form tests of the efficacy of fiscal and monetary policies have used HED as the measure of fiscal stimulus. The weighted measure would approximate $E^* - Y^*$ more closely than D^* does. Adjustments and the procedures for making them were pointed out long ago in Gramlich's doctoral dissertation.[2] Yet they have still not made their way into official budget documents, or into public debate on fiscal policy.

III. PROSPECTIVE FEDERAL BORROWING REQUIREMENTS: THE CURRENT DISCUSSION

Weighting adjustments are crucial in assessing the potential 'crowding-out' effects of the federal deficit in prospect over the next several years. Clarity in approaching this confused and confusing discussion is served by separating two issues. One is the path of real output Y the economy will or should follow over the next several years, and how it depends on fiscal and monetary policies. This is the more important issue.

The second issue, which I take up now, assumes the Y path as given and asks how much room the fiscal programme would leave for non-federal investment. This question, which can be asked and answered comparatively for various budget proposals is one for which the AHED analysis is designed. To avoid misunderstanding, I emphasize that we leave open at this point whether and how private investment will be forthcoming in just the amounts to fill the room left for it.

Alarmists about 'crowding out' see huge federal debt issues coming on to the securities markets, commandeering saving that would otherwise flow to corporations, other businesses, farmers, home purchasers, state and local governments, and other borrowers. They look at prospective deficit numbers unadjusted, and include also off-budget and agency borrowing. These alarms are crude, the Administration correctly points out, because they ignore increases in saving, in supplies of funds to buy securities or to replace borrowing, by-products of the same fiscal programme that generates the deficits. The Administration, though sympathetic in spirit with supply-side theories of the beneficial consequences of tax rate reductions for the economy and the tax base, never committed itself literally to the view that the US was on the inefficient slope of the Laffer Curve. But the Treasury did argue that the saving generated by tax cuts would be enough to buy debt securities covering the resulting deficit. This argument envisaged that supply-side tax incentives move the economy to a higher output path. A Laffer Curve can be constructed for taxes plus saving (see Chapter 11), and it is quite unlikely that we are at its peak or on the wrong slope. Some outside observers agree; Albert Wojnilower, for example, says that deficit-reducing proposals will lower the supply of saving to the capital markets almost as much as they lower federal demands. In short the proper concern is, as argued above, $E - Y$, not D. In this context, several features of the budget and prospective federal borrowing requirements deserve comment.

Capital transactions and off-budget borrowing
Budget accounting in the national income and product accounts eliminates these in principle. Selling more oil leases adds to cash revenue, but unless the buyers are liquidity constrained the transactions do not reduce $E^* - Y^*$. The buyers will in effect borrow in the market what the government does not, while maintaining their demands for goods and services. They may indeed increase borrowing and demand by undertaking investments to develop their new leaseholdings.

Although many analysts add net off-budget borrowing to the budget deficit, this procedure exaggerates 'crowding out'. Here the government is acting as an intermediary, relending to eligible non-federal borrowers. The borrowers thus served will not be in the regular capital markets. Some of them, it is true, would not have been there anyway, or would have borrowed less. The government is accommodating borrowers at rates below what private lenders would have charged. The intermediary operations add to net demands on the markets, but by only a fraction of the gross federal borrowing they entail.

Business investment incentives

Accelerated capital recovery and other tax concessions increase the cash flow of businesses. What the government is borrowing businesses need not. The balance of aggregate demand and supply is worsened only to the extent that stockholders enjoying increased dividends or capital gains raise their consumption.

Debt interest has become a major budgetary outlay, more than 10 per cent of the total budget, 2 to 3 per cent of GNP. As interest rates have risen beyond expectations, upward revisions of net interest outlays have significantly worsened the budget outlook. But it is by no means clear that interest payments have the same stimulative or 'crowding-out' effects as, for example, defence purchases. While some pensioners may simply spend whatever interest flows they receive, at the other extreme there are younger savers who accumulate in illiquid retirement accounts whatever interest they earn. Those who believe that the incentive effects of higher real interest rates on saving dominate the income effects should not regard a government budget as expansionary just because those rates entail higher outlays.

The 1982 Economic Report echoes many other economists in applying inflation accounting to the federal budget and eliminating interest outlays which merely compensate creditors for inflation. This procedure is relevant for calculations of stimulus and crowding out if savers rationally and automatically buy enough bonds to maintain their holdings in real value—indeed to increase them *pari passu* with the growth of the economy. Unfortunately there is not much recent evidence of such behaviour. Households have allowed real wealth to decline, absolutely and relatively to real incomes, without much sign of saving extra to make up for real capital losses suffered in the past.

The significant fact about the longer-run budget outlook is that if the parameters of the federal budget are not changed the federal debt will grow relative to the economy, for the first time since World War II. (On the dynamics of the debt see Chapter 14.) 'Crowding out', a worry of little operational significance at present, could become important in more prosperous years ahead.

NOTES

1. *See* my *Asset Accumulaton and Economic Activity*, Oxford: Blackwell, 1980, Chapter 3.
2. E. M. Gramlich, 'The behavior and adequacy of the United States federal budget', *Yale Economic Essays*, Spring 1966, vol. 6, no. 1, 98–159.

17 Make Jobs, Cut Deficits*

Twelve million unemployed. A $200 billion budget deficit. Congress doesn't know what to do. Raise taxes? Lower taxes? Spend less? Spend more? The ugly truth is that no fiscal measure will both create jobs and cut deficits. Tax increases and spending cuts, social or military, destroy jobs; tax cuts and spending for public jobs and infrastructure enlarge deficits. Budget-neutral measures, like funding roads with gas taxes, are virtually employment-neutral too.

Establishment orthodoxy, however, blames deficits for the depression and urges fiscal austerity to lower interest rates and promote recovery. These propositions were not valid in the 1930s and are not today. The economy suffers, now as then, from weak markets for goods and services; curtailing any demands, including those of governments and taxpayers, is counter-productive. Interest rates might decline, reviving some demands for cars and houses. But could the increase in demand induced by lower interest rates more than compensate for the loss of demand induced by lower spending or higher taxes? And if so, wouldn't such demand push interest rates higher than they originally were? The contradiction exposes the flaw in the orthodox argument. Experience also refutes it, as in 1982 when interest rates fell while actual and projected deficits ballooned.

In panic, the Administration and Congress are heeding wrong-headed diagnoses and prescriptions. Though President Reagan, to his credit, remembers what even most Democrats forget, the perversity of raising taxes in hard times, he echoes his orthodox critics in urging expenditure cutbacks. Leaders of both parties should welcome a strategy to restore prosperity and fiscal stability simultaneously.

That strategy is at hand. Monetary stimulus can put the nation back to work and concurrently trim federal deficits to manageable size. No other strategy can achieve these goals.

---

*8 February 1983, *New York Times*. © 1983 by The New York Times Company. Reprinted by permission.

Recovery and long-run fiscal stability both require low real interest rates. The Federal Reserve, and only the Fed, can lower rates to levels that sustained prosperity through most of the period since 1946. Real rates on Treasury bills were normally below 2 per cent, even negative at recession troughs. Last summer, the Fed suspended its self-imposed constraints on money growth. Interest rates fell significantly, confounding monetarist warnings that easier policies would raise them. They must fall still further to stimulate recovery from this stubborn and demoralizing slump. The economy hungers for assurance that the Fed's relaxations were more than transient and technical.

Jobs? Vigorous recovery is imperative. Given normal increases in the labour force and productivity, the real Gross National Product must grow at 2.5 to 3 per cent per year just to keep unemployment from rising. To lower unemployment to 7 per cent in four years, an unduly modest target, requires real GNP growth averaging 4.5 to 5 per cent. The Administration's scenario for slow recovery is a recipe for permanent disability.

Deficits? The frightening numbers reflect mainly economic weakness, actual and projected, implying depressed revenues and large safety-net outlays. Every point by which a money-fuelled recovery reduces unemployment cuts the deficit by $30 billion. Lowering interest rates also relieves the budget directly by saving debt interest costs, now more than 10 per cent of the budget. A reasonable fiscal goal is to stabilize the ratio of federal debt to the GNP. Federal debt exceeded a year's GNP right after World War II; it gradually declined to one-quarter of the GNP in the early 1970s. Now the ratio is rising, but it can be stabilized around one-third—lower than in the prosperous 50s and 60s—on two conditions: first, trim the 'primary deficit' on transactions other than debt service, from the 4 per cent of GNP expected in 1983 to 0.5 per cent. This is feasible with—and only with—strong recovery. Congress could nail it down by enacting now both the proposed Social Security compromise and other budget corrections contingent on restored prosperity, not on deficits symptomatic of prolonged stagnation. Second, move the real after-tax interest rate on federal debts well below the growth rate of the economy. Otherwise interest costs alone will raise deficits and debt faster than the GNP. Thus, the low-interest monetary strategy essential for recovery also brings fiscal stability.

The knee-jerk objection to the strategy is, 'It's inflationary'. This is really an objection to recovery itself. Any recovery, whether fuelled by the Fed or by extraordinary luck, will induce some price increases. Recovery inevitably carries more inflation risk than does prolonged depression. But the main response to demand expansion starting with

11 per cent unemployment and 33 per cent idle capacity will be more production, not higher prices. The Fed has ample opportunity to counter future, inflationary pressures. The time has come for the Fed to claim and receive credit for a signal victory in its war on inflation, and to concentrate on reconstruction before economy and budget suffer irreparable damage.

18 Unemployment, Interest, Deficits, and Money*

I. INTRODUCTION: THE CURRENT CONTROVERSY

The conference is titled 'The Interest Rate Dilemma'. I wasn't exactly sure what the dilemma is. The word seems to refer to two clear choices, but they are hard to find. The dilemma that I think is the main issue in the United States today is whether lowering interest rates is a responsibility of fiscal and budget policy or of the monetary policy of the Federal Reserve System.

Now let me give you a little background on the state of play in this controversy, so very prominent in the public arena recently. On 26 January 1983, on the same day as the report of the President's State of the Union message, there appeared in national newspapers all over the country a two-page advertisement called the Bipartisan Appeal, sponsored by a committee headed by former Secretary of Commerce Peter Peterson and containing as founding members five former Secretaries of the Treasury of both parties and several administrations. The Appeal was signed by some five hundred people, a veritable 'Who's Who' of what irreverent people call the Establishment—prominent business executives, financial leaders, university presidents, and former government officials. The ad was repeated just the other day.

The message of the Appeal is that we simply must take steps to cut these horrible budget deficits in order to get interest rates down.

*March 1983. Conference on the Interest Rate Dilemma, Duke University. Terry Sanford, ed., *The Interest Rate Dilemma*, New York: KCG Productions, 1983, pp. 1–25. The final part has been replaced by similar material from 'Budget Deficits, Federal Debt, and Inflation in Short and Long Runs', presented at The Conference Board Public Policy Research Program Conference, Washington, December 1983 and published in its *Proceedings, Towards a Reconstruction of Federal Budgeting*, New York: Conference Board, 1983, pp. 51–9. Title slightly changed, adding 'Deficits'.

Table 18.1

	1983	1984	1985	1986	1987	1988
Bipartisan appeal:						
Fiscal policy	0	0	–	–	–	–
Monetary policy	0	0	0	0	0	0
Total dose	0	0	–	–	–	–
Tobin:						
Fiscal policy	0	0	0	–	–	–
Monetary policy	+	+	+	+	+	+
Total dose	+	+	+	0	0	0
Zero-dose forecasts of unemployment:						
Administration (OMB)	10.7	9.9	8.9	8.1	7.3	6.5
Data Resources, Inc. (DRI)	10.7	9.6	8.5	n.a.	n.a.	n.a.

Otherwise we won't have a recovery because the high deficits are raising interest rates and crowding out private investment. At least they will be doing so in 1985 and subsequently. The Appeal calls for a drastic set of austere fiscal measures, including tax increases and spending cuts of all kinds, to take effect in 1985 and thereafter.

I found only one obscure mention of the word 'monetary' in the whole text. Some signers, it said, as much as they agreed with the Appeal, might have various other proposals in mind too: for example, research and development, social security, export policies, and monetary policy. Even a careful reader would come away with the idea that monetary policy was mostly irrelevant, that interest rates are a problem to be conquered solely by fiscal austerity.

After the Appeal first appeared I wrote an Op-Ed piece in the *New York Times* of 8 February 1983 (Chapter 17), which argued the case for a monetary approach to the high-interest-rate problem for some years to come, while suggesting that reducing structural deficits later in the decade would help. In *The Times* of 27 February 1983, Fred Bergsten and Fred Kahn affirmed their support of the Appeal and said all reasonable persons should join them. Table 18.1 gives schematic representations of their policy proposals and mine.

In the upper part of Table 18.1 are the recommendations for changes from currently prospective and planned policies by the authors of the Bipartisan Appeal. Zero means no change recommended; plus means give more stimulus. That means, as far as the budget is concerned, spending more money or lowering taxes. Minus, as far as the budget is concerned, signifies recommendations of austere measures—cutting expenditures and raising taxes in comparison to present projections.

For monetary policy, zero means the same thing—just go along with the policy, whatever it is now, with no recommendation for change. Minus means a tighter policy—cutting down on the supply of bank reserves and stocks of money; plus means recommendation of easier policy—providing more bank reserves and presumably more *M-1, M-2*, etc. Those are the differences between the 500, including Kahn and Bergsten, and me, as I understand them.

My problem with the Bipartisan Appeal, in summary, is that it proposes no larger dose of stimulus for the economy by either monetary or fiscal policy. It proposes, indeed, to take some away beginning in 1985, on the fiscal side. As I read the recommended policies, they do nothing to strengthen the recovery of the economy from the current depression. (I use the word 'depression' these days because George Stigler paved the way. He's a Nobel economist of impeccable conservative reputation. Right there in the White House itself he told the press it is a depression. So I consider the word a legitimate description now.)

The Bipartisan Appeal said it's too late to do much of anything about fiscal years 1983 and 1984, but after that let's restrict budgetary stimulus a lot. What I say to do is to get a stronger recovery via a more stimulative monetary policy over the next three years. For years after 1985, the 'out years' in horrible budget jargon, let's plan some fiscal corrections. But let's offset them by monetary stimulus, which maintains the overall dose so that fiscal restrictions do not retard the economy. That is, we need to change the mix of monetary and fiscal policy. At the bottom of Table 18.1 are forecasts of unemployment for the years in question, both by the Administration's Office of Management and Budget, and by Data Resources Inc. The year 1985 doesn't look prosperous to me with 8.9 or 8.5 per cent unemployment. We used to consider unemployment rates that high as symptoms of deep recession, or maybe depression, and not of booms which need to be cut short or reversed.

II. REAL INTEREST RATES AND THEIR VARIOUS MEANINGS

Interest rates are too high. That is about the only point generally agreed in current debate on fiscal and monetary policies. Why are they too high? How can and should they be lowered? Controversy rages on these questions. The orthodox view—as in the Bipartisan Appeal—blames federal deficits in prospect in fiscal years 1985 and thereafter. The Appeal urges massive spending cuts and tax increases to reduce the deficits. Other voices, including my own, stress the role of the Federal Reserve and call for stimulative monetary policy. Some economists do not share these concerns about interest rates, trusting the markets to set them right if policies soundly geared to other objectives are pursued.

What does it mean to say interest rates are too high? The distinction between real and nominal rates, long stressed by economists, is now widely understood and respected. Real rates are the relevant focus for economic recovery and capital formation, the objectives motivating today's anxieties about interest rates. Of course nominal rates could be regarded as too high simply because they mirror high actual and expected inflation; in that case the focus would be on policies for disinflation.

Real interest rates are unfortunately not observable. They are conceptually ambiguous. They depend on subjective price expectations, which may be ill defined for any one individual and vary widely across individuals. Moreover, the particular prices whose future paths are relevant, and the time period that matters, depend on the transactions the individual is contemplating. How prevailing nominal interest rates affect her decisions depends also on her tax status, her balance sheet, and many other individual circumstances. It is necessary to mention these obvious and annoying reservations because it is all too easy to slip into the habit of treating expectational variables as objective and single-valued.

Let me be more specific and topical. A business manager considering the accumulation of inventory of raw materials will compare the nominal interest on a commercial loan from her bank with the expected rise in price of those goods, adjusting both for their effects on her tax liability. Her real interest rate is not the same as that of a couple considering buying a home, who will be interested in the aftertax nominal mortgage rate compared with their estimates of future appreciation in the values of the property and of their own labour. A consumer–saver on the margin between consumption now and next year will be concerned with nominal after–tax yields of money-market accounts compared with the expected rise in prices of the specific market basket of goods she consumes. Her real rate of interest is not necessarily that of the corporate executive contemplating an issue of bonds and stocks to finance the building of a new plant. In the 1970s two spurts of inflation and expected inflation were associated with oil imports and energy prices. These made real interest rates low for consumer–savers balancing current spending against consumption a short time later. But low CPI-adjusted interest rates were not a good indicator of the climate for capital investments by most domestic industries. The inflation was in their operating costs, not their selling prices.

Differences of these kinds may not be of great significance when there are large and pervasive swings in inflation and inflationary psychology. But they can be important at times like the present, when the future is cloudy and when savers, business investors, lenders, and borrowers apparently vary significantly in what they see ahead.

The complaint that real interest rates are too high today has several meanings:

1. They are too high to balance national savings and investment in prosperity, that is, at rates of unemployment and capacity utilization that represent a viable social compromise between risks of inflation and unemployment. There is uncertainty and disagreement on where that point is located; the Council of Economic Advisors says it is in the range of 6 to 7 per cent unemployment, and the Administration officially aims for 6.5 per cent in 1988. Anyway few would deny that 'prosperity' means much lower unemployment than we suffer now. National saving would be much greater if unemployment were four points lower; with higher incomes, households and businesses would save more and governments would dissave less. By itself, the four-point reduction of unemployment would raise real GNP 10 to 12 per cent (equivalent in 1982 to $300–60 billion), of which 40 to 50 per cent would be saved (equivalent in 1982 to $120–80 billion, considerably more than actual net national saving during that year). Recovery would also, of course, raise investment demands, now depressed by excess capacity, but by less calculable amounts. The question is whether real interest rates would be too high to induce enough investment to absorb the higher flow of saving. If so, the assumed recovery would be aborted for lack of markets for the goods and services the economy could produce at prosperity rates of unemployment and capacity utilization. Table 18.2 presents some estimates of real rates in previous years of prosperity.

2. A related but distinguishable question is whether real interest rates are too high right now to permit sustained recovery to get under way. The rates needed now are presumably lower than those needed for saving–investment equilibrium in prosperity. The reasons are that investment demands are currently depressed by excess capacity, liquidity shortages, and pessimistic appraisals of the economic outlook. Moreover, responses to improvement in the financial climate take time. Table 18.3 presents some estimates of real rates in recession troughs, including the present one.

3. The danger disturbing the authors of the Bipartisan Appeal is that real interest rates are or will be too high to sustain the capital

Table 18.2: Real interest rates in years of low unemployment

	1956–3 to 1957–2	1965	1972–4 to 1973–3	1978
In terms of GNP deflator:				
Treasury bills	0.7	1.0	−0.9	−1.7
Treasury bonds	0.7	1.3	−1.0	−0.8
Corporate bonds	1.0	1.6	0.7	0.3
Municipal bonds	−0.3	−0.3	−1.8	−2.7
Prime bank loan	1.1	1.5	−0.4	0
In terms of CPI:				
Treasury bill	−0.1	1.5	−2.2	−1.9
Municipal bond	0	0.9	−3.0	−3.5
In terms of PPI:				
Prime bank loan	1.7	0.9	−8.3	−0.6
In terms of non-residential fixed-investment deflator:				
Corporate bonds	0.1	2.0	1.9	1.1
In terms of residential investment deflator:				
Mortgage yield	4.3	2.4	−1.0	−1.6

Note: Rates for each quarter of a year were calculated in the manner described in the Note to Table 18.3. The entries in this table are simple averages of the four quarterly estimates for each year.

formation, particularly the business plant and equipment investment, which the country needs for long-run economic growth. In this view, the problem in prosperity will be a shortage of national saving relative to investment demands—just the opposite of the problem posed in item 1. Indeed the Appealers expect this problem to arise as early as fiscal year 1985, before anyone expects the recovery to be anywhere near complete. They fear that the federal government will be making such heavy demands on the nation's resources and on private savings that its deficits will 'crowd out' private investment. The mechanism of crowding out will be high real interest rates resulting from federal deficit financing.

4. The final sense in which real interest rates may be too high now and in the future has to do with the dynamics of federal deficits and debt (*see* section IV of this chapter and Chapter 14). Rates may be too high to permit the ratio of debt to GNP to be stabilized. To see this, imagine that the 'primary deficit' is zero, that is, the budget is balanced on transactions other than debt service net of offsetting

Table 18.3: Real interest rates at cyclical troughs

	1954–2	1958–2	1961–1	1970–4	1975–1	1980–3	1983–1
In terms of GNP deflator:							
Treasury bills	0.3	−1.0	0.6	0.2	0.4	−2.0	3.8
Treasury bonds	1.8	1.0	2.2	0.9	0.6	−0.2	6.5
Corporate bonds	2.2	1.6	2.9	3.4	3.1	1.5	7.2
Municipal bonds	1.8	0.9	1.7	0.7	0.7	−1.8	5.4
Prime bank loans	2.3	1.7	2.8	1.8	4.0	1.5	6.7
In terms of CPI:							
Treasury bill	1.3	0.9	2.1	2.4	−1.3	−1.9	5.4
Municipal bonds	2.7	2.7	2.3	2.9	−1.0	−1.9	7.1
In terms of PPI:							
Prime bank loan	5.3	4.5	6.6	3.0	5.6	−3.5	6.8
In terms of non-residential fixed investment deflator:							
Corporate bonds	1.3	0.6	3.8	3.6	1.4	5.3	8.5
In terms of residential investment deflator:							
Mortgage yield	2.5	5.1	6.0	1.4	4.6	6.2	12.1

Note: The rates are nominal rates at the beginning of the quarter corrected for inflation over the subsequent six months, or over the next two quarters for price indexes available only quarterly. (No allowance is made for taxes or for appreciation or depreciation of prices of longer term assets.) Inflation expectations at the time the bills, bonds, or mortgages were priced may, of course, have been different from the prices actually realized. 1983–1 figures are necessarily based on extrapolations of recent inflation rates to the near future.

receipts from the Federal Reserve and from taxes paid on receipts of interest in federal securities. Then the debt will grow each year by the net interest outlay. If this interest rate exceeds the GNP growth rate, the debt will grow faster than GNP, and so will the deficit. Of course, if the primary deficit is positive the rise in the ratio will be accelerated. Long-run growth in the debt/GNP ratio threatens 'crowding out'. More and more of the nation's stock of private wealth will be diverted to federal debt away from real capital, and likewise more and more of the flow of private saving will be absorbed in federal deficits. Fiscal stability, in the sense of a constant debt/GNP ratio, requires a real net interest rate on federal debt lower than the economy's trend rate of real growth. Because this condition was nearly always fulfilled from 1946 to 1980 and the primary deficit was a small fraction of GNP, the debt/GNP ratio actually declined from more than 100 per cent to around 25 per cent. The question now is what will happen during this decade.

The particular real interest rate on which you focus depends on which of the four concerns makes you think the rate is or will be too high. If it is the first or second or both, your main worry is the rate relevant to real investment decisions. Investment demand, not saving, is the principal constraint on recovery and on capital formation. If it is the third, crowding out, your main worry is the rate relevant to private saving decisions, because you foresee a shortage of saving. If it is the fourth, fiscal stability, it is of course the net interest cost of federal debt.

III. ARE REAL INTEREST RATES BEYOND THE REACH OF POLICY?

Before proceeding to discuss measures of macroeconomic policy to lower real interest rates, I should pay my respects to various arguments asserting they are beyond the reach of policy.

First, it is alleged, financial and capital markets are international; savings and investments are mobile across frontiers and currencies. Thus interest rates in any single country cannot deviate from those in world markets. This is a decisive inhibition on the monetary and fiscal policies of a small country, but not on those of a nation that plays so dominant a role in world markets as the United States. Our markets and policies affect world interest rates, and capital mobility is not so perfect as to eliminate variable deviations of our rates from those elsewhere. An important mechanism by which tight monetary policy brought disinflation and recession since 1979 has been to attract funds into dollar assets by high interest rates relative to those available in other currencies. The resulting appreciation of the dollar lowered US exports and raised imports.

Second, it is asserted, real interest rates are invariant to policies even in a closed economy. They reflect the national equilibrium of the time preference of consumers–savers and the marginal productivity of capital. Sometimes these are regarded as such stable parameters that intertemporal substitutions in consumption and investment hold the real rate close to a fairly constant natural level. Even if they vary over time, the equilibrium real rate could be independent of government policies. For example, private agents and taxpayers could adjust their saving to compensate for variations in governmental dissaving; then postponement of taxes by deficit financing would not affect interest rates, and crowding out would never be a problem. Likewise, variations of monetary policy could be completely absorbed in prices, expected future prices, and nominal rates in ways that leave real rates unaffected. These propositions arise in theories that also deprive government policies of power to affect other real outcomes: output, employment, relative prices. Since those theories have great difficulty accounting for observed fluctuations in real interest rates, output, and employment, particularly those of the amplitude recently experienced, I do not think it necessary here to review all the theoretical reasons for rejecting them.

Scepticism that monetary policies can affect real interest rates is supported by a long and strong tradition in neoclassical economics, the neutrality of money. It says that real outcomes are the same whether the stock of money is large or small, whether it is growing fast or slow. Variation of money stocks changes only absolute prices, leaving relative prices, including real interest rates, unchanged. The proposition gains credence from the obvious truth that a 'currency reform' which just changes the monetary unit, say from dollars to half dollars, thus doubling the money stock, will do nothing real to the economy. But central bank monetary operations are not units changes. They change some money stocks, alter some other stocks of promises to pay money in the future in the opposite direction, and leave most contracts to pay or receive dollars intact. Whether they are neutral or not cannot be settled by a simple appeal to the fact that economic behaviour is motivated by real rather than nominal quantities.

IV.   MONETARY POLICY, REAL INTEREST RATES, AND RECOVERY

Certainly the immediate impact of increasing the supply of reserves to banks and of reducing the central bank's lending rate is to reduce nominal interest rates in money markets, inducing banks to offer loans at lower rates and to bid up the prices of securities. Banks don't like to hold idle cash. The declines in short interest rates will spread to longer-term assets unless the market expects the Fed to reverse the operations in the near future. These will be reductions in real rates which stimulate borrowing and spending. It happened this way when the Fed eased up in 1982.

What can go wrong? One conceivable scenario is that prices quickly rise until the augmented nominal stocks of reserves, deposits, and bank assets are not larger in real, purchasing-power terms than they were initially. Interest rates too return to their higher original levels.

This scenario is most improbable in an economy with as much idle labour and capacity as the US will have for several years.

Another possible scenario is that expansionary Fed policies this year arouse expectations of higher inflation and of higher nominal short-term rates next year or subsequently. These expectations raise long-term interest rates today and discourage long-term investments. Fear of this sequence of events, it is fair to say, is the principal inhibition on the Fed's willingness to promote recovery.

The rationality of this scenario and the expectations it assumes is suspect, for several reasons. First, a monetary expansion to promote recovery, and to accommodate the increased demand for deposits and bank reserves due to disinflation and deregulation of deposit interest, by no means implies a permanent shift to faster growth of reserves and money. Only the latter would justify expectations that the Fed had turned inflationary. As in 1982, the 'financial markets' should be able to make the distinction.

Second, it is possible, to be sure, that the 'bond markets' are suspicious of recovery *per se*, whether fuelled by the Fed's increasing the stock of money or by spontaneous ebullience of investors and consumers, boosting the velocity of money. The anonymous pundits who make the market's view prefer to minimize inflation risk by keeping the economy in the doldrums. Recovery undeniably carries more risk of price increases and acceleration of inflation than does continued depression. But, as argued above, the risk will be low for several years in an economy with so much unemployment and idle capacity.

Third, contrary to the myths of financial pages, lenders cannot unilaterally raise long-term interest rates to match their worst expectations and fears. There are two sides to the market. Borrowers clearly do not share those inflation expectations. (If they did, nominal long rates would rise, but there would be no increase in long-term *real* rates and no deterrence to investment.) Neither do borrowers anticipate sales and earnings that would make them willing to pay the rates which, according to the scenario, lenders would desire. Moreover, the same uncertainties about inflation and recovery and the same risk aversions that motivate lenders to seek a positive premium for lending long motivate borrowers to seek a negative premium for borrowing long. The only clear outcome is that both borrowers and lenders will move toward shorter maturities, where there will be net new lending as a result of the assumed expansion of bank reserves. Or they will employ long-term instruments with variable interest rates.

Even if lenders stubbornly persist in irrational expectations, the Fed's expansionary moves would achieve a net reduction in real interest rates. Whether the long/short premium would increase is not clear; that depends on whether borrowers or lenders are the more ready to shift to shorter maturities in response to rate differentials. The Federal Treasury could help by refraining from borrowing long when the rates are unfavourable. The improbable worst scenario is that institutions—pensions funds and insurance companies—dump their existing holdings if long rates fail to give them protection commensurate to their expectations and fears. Low short rates would then drive the recovery until they changed their minds.

Monetary tightness was the principal cause of the high real interest rates that brought the severe recession, and monetary stimulus is the way to bring the rates down and promote recovery. Fortunately the Fed, having achieved a considerable disinflation at heavy cost to the real economy, now appears to give recovery high priority. Fortunately the Fed no longer feels bound to targets for growth of monetary aggregates, which have lost whatever meaning they ever had because of deregulation, institutional innovation, and new financial technology. Fortunately, as market responses last year and last month to announcements of the new Fed priorities indicate, the credibility of the Fed in the markets no longer is tied to those money growth targets. But real rates are still too high for recovery. It is still not clear whether the Fed will move actively to lower them further, or whether it is simply prepared to accommodate a recovery if and when one gets under way from other sources.

V. FISCAL POLICY, REAL INTEREST RATES, AND RECOVERY

Fiscal austerity is not a recipe for recovery. The economy is suffering from weak demand for goods and services, of which high unemployment and excess capacity are the obvious symptoms. Even if recovery is now beginning, these conditions will persist for several more years, perhaps most of this decade. The first-order effect of cutting government expenditures for goods and services, defence or civilian, is to reduce demand. Likewise, cutting government transfers diminishes the consumption demands of their beneficiaries, and raising taxes lowers the spending of taxpayers. Curtailing demand is not the way to raise demand.

True, fiscal austerity will lower interest rates, real interest rates. Federal borrowing to finance deficits will be somewhat less. The lower rates will revive some interest-sensitive expenditures, for houses, durable goods, business plant and equipment, and even state and local capital projects. But these positive secondary effects on aggregate demand cannot exceed the negative first-order effects. If non-federal borrowing more than replaced federal borrowing, interest rates would end up higher, not lower. But then there would be no inducement for increased non-federal borrowing! That exposes the fallacy in the reasoning so often and prestigiously repeated these days. Most likely, the secondary effects will be smaller than the initial reductions of demand. Real interest rates will be lower, but that is not an end in itself. The name of the game is to lower interest rates as a means to prosperity and growth, not to lower them by weakening the economy.

Fiscal austerity could be accompanied by monetary stimulus. Indeed with enough monetary stimulus, the net result would be an expansion of demand. But of course the Federal Reserve could administer that same stimulus anyway, without the fiscal measures, achieving larger pay-offs in output, employment, and general recovery. The argument for the fiscal measures would be psychological. The 'bond markets' whose views scare the Fed might be more tolerant. Chairman Volcker and his colleagues might be more willing to step on the monetary gas if they saw concrete signs that the budget was being brought 'under control'.

A shift in the fiscal–monetary mix is desirable to shift the composition of national output from private and public consumption toward capital investment. But the more urgent task right now is to raise total output, not just to alter its composition, therefore to enlarge the total dose of fiscal–monetary stimulus, not just to alter the mix of the medicine. In a depressed economy with excess capacity and pessimistic outlooks, it is a difficult and chancy manoeuvre to boost investment enough to offset fiscally induced declines in consumption. After all, private consumption is two-thirds of gross national expenditure, while gross private investment is only one-seventh.

'Crowding out' worries about the deficit make sense in reference to the composition of national output when the recovery is mature and prosperity is restored. Anticipation that high deficits in the second half of the decade will collide with buoyant investment demand, generating high enough *real* interest rates to discourage such demand, could raise long-term rates now and in the early stages of recovery. Note that this interest rate expectation is different from the one previously discussed, which concerns future inflation and its reflection in nominal rates. This one concerns future real rates and assumes a successful recovery, not prolonged stagnation with expansion dissipated in inflation. If shared by borrowers as well as lenders, this expectation might slow down the revival of investment demand so crucial for early recovery.

The Administration has proposed tax increases contingent on the state of the economy and the budget beginning in fiscal year 1986. The rationale of the proposal is to limit 'crowding out' when prosperity is restored and to overcome the earlier negative impacts of the anticipation of such crowding out. Unfortunately the Congress does not understand the rationale and gives the proposal short shrift. The Congress has never looked favourably on surrendering the prerogatives of future Congresses over taxes either to the Executive or to formulas; there are legitimate political and constitutional grounds for this attitude. Moreover, the Administration has added, to the other conditions required to trigger the new taxes, one that is particularly hard for Congress to swallow, namely enactment of the Administration's preferred cuts in federal civilian spending. None the less the idea that future fiscal austerity could be constructive, while current austerity is counter-productive, is in some form a sound guide for both the Congress and the Administration. For example, from a macroeconomic standpoint it would be preferable to schedule cuts in defence spending later rather than to improve current budget cosmetics by postponements and stretchouts.

It is also important to coordinate future fiscal policy and future monetary policy, in fact and in anticipation. No one can be sure now that fiscal austerity by itself will be appropriate macroeconomic policy in 1986 and in subsequent years. The Administration's official forecast does not envisage complete recovery until 1988. Fiscal contractions will weaken demand then, just as they would now, and might be premature and unwelcome. Anticipations of such weakness have negative effects on future-oriented investment and consumption expenditures today. These work against the favourable advance effects of anticipated fiscal contraction on real interest rates. But if the Federal Reserve stood ready, and were perceived to stand ready, to offset the negative effects, a future fiscal contraction would be unambiguously helpful to recovery this year and next. In other words, what is needed is a change in the future fiscal–monetary mix, to insure not just that the federal government will claim less of the potential private saving in prosperous years but also that the saving it does not claim will actually be channelled into capital formation. As argued above, the re-channelling cannot be expected to happen automatically. It requires the active assistance of the Fed.

A number of people in the audience are economists or students of economics. They are entitled to a diagram that will make them glad they took economics courses, so I am going to provide one. Those of you who are not in tune with this kind of thing—that is, have not taken a course in macroeconomics in the last quarter of a century or have attended a university which represses this kind of analysis—can skip the next few minutes.

Here in Figure 18.1 we have two periods. Period 2 is the counterpart of the latter years of the decade. Period 1 means 1983 and 1984, at least. I would include 1985, as I argued at the outset. The *IS* curve represents the balance of savings and investments in period 2 and the *LM* curve the balance of demand and supply for money, under present plans for fiscal and monetary policy. The famous equilibrium of the two curves is at point *a*, period 2. And now come along the Administration, the Congress, and the Bipartisan Appeal, and we all agree on a fiscal programme that cuts the deficits, raises taxes, cuts expenditures in those years of period 2. Standard curve shifting says that the *IS* curve shifts left, so we slide down the *LM* curve which the Federal Reserve plans to give us in those years to the equilibrium *b*. Now what are the effects of that slide, correctly anticipated, on demand for goods and services today in period 1.

I suggest that there are two effects, at least two that you can put on the diagram. One occurs through the change in the expected real short interest rate, and the other through the change in the expected level of real output. These are shown in the diagram as the functions of E_{1r} of r_2 and E_{1y} of Y_2, respectively. The lower the interest rate, the bigger is the demand effect transmitted to period 1 via the interest rate. The lower is period 2 output, the smaller is the demand effect transmitted to period 1 via expectations of sales, profits, and other incomes. The question is, which one of these two effects on period 1 demand predominates? It might be either one. That depends on the shape of the *LM* curve itself. Were monetarists running things, it would be vertical. Then there wouldn't be any output effect at all, because output in period 2 would be and would be expected to be the same even after the fiscal change. Then we would have only the interest effect. If *LM* were quite flat, however, the output effect might be much greater. Look in the lower diagram, for period 1. Here is shown the optimistic possibility, by which the anticipated fiscal contraction shifts the *IS* curve in period 1 upward and raises output in period 1, although raising short-term interest rates. Period 1 equilibrium moves from *a* to *b*. But *IS* could have shifted the other way. If we wanted to be sure that it is not going to shift the wrong way, then we could adopt the policy I recommended above. Let the Federal Reserve offset the fiscal contraction of period 2 so as to maintain the output level. This would be done by shifting LM_2 so as to achieve equilibrium *c*. In that case, we get only the favourable expected interest rate effect, and it would be an even stronger one than is shown in the diagram for period 1.

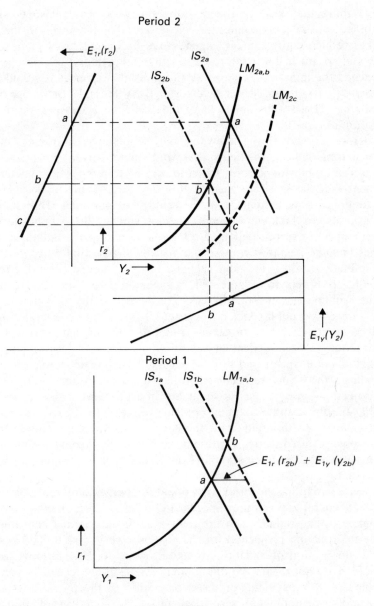

Figure 18.1

Tightening period 2 budget shifts IS_2 and lowers Y_2r_2 from a to b, $E_{2r}(r_2)$ and $E_{2y}(Y_2)$ (both zero at a) are effects on aggregate demand in period 1. Their sum at b is the horizontal shift of IS_2 in the period 1 diagram below. It raises Y_1r_1 from a to b. Imagining a flatter LM_2 through a_1 you can see how the IS_1 shift could be reversed.

To avoid any negative effect on period 1 aggregate demand, Fed could maintain Y_{2a} by shifting LM to LM_{2c}.

I think that kind of diagram, by the way, would also enable a student of macroeconomics to expose the fallacy involved in the idea that reducing government expenditures or raising taxes in period 1 would so much lower interest rates that the demand response would exceed the initial reduction in demand. That is a result you could not extract from these curves unless you drew the *LM* curve backward sloping. Those who tuned out of the academic digression are invited to tune in again.

How serious will the 'crowding out' problem be? Estimates of the 'structural' deficit—the deficit that would under current policies remain at 'high employment', now taken to mean 6 to 6.5 per cent unemployment—are designed to answer this question. Table 18.4 gives the Administration's estimates, in percentage of potential GNP standardized also to 'high-employment' unemployment. The Administration's estimates are surprisingly high. One reason is that the Administration has become pessimistic about the growth of potential real GNP. But the main reason is the large increase in debt interest costs due to the build-up of debt from large deficits expected during the slow recovery the Administration now foresees. This is also shown in Table 18.4.

Interest on public debt now exceeds 10 per cent of federal outlays. It is a major factor in actual and projected deficits, cyclical and structural. Actual deficits and debt issues expected during periods of high unemployment, most of this decade in current economic forecasts, enlarge the structural deficits projected for all future years. Those projections also are sensitive to the interest rates assumed. I think that the fiscal and economic problems connected with federal interest payments are different from those arising from other budget transactions. Consequently, I present in Table 18.4 some estimates of deficits that treat interest outlays differently from conventional budget accounting.

One variation, shown in rows 6 and 9, charges only real interest as a net federal expenditure. Specifically, it reduces the nominal interest outlay by the reduction in the real value of outstanding debt implied by the inflation projection for the year, shown in row 3. The logic of this application of 'inflation accounting' is as follows: rational wealth holders do not regard the full nominal interest they receive as income; some of it is payment for the depreciation of the purchasing power of dollar-denominated securities, in effect a return of principal. Consequently they will 'save' to maintain their wealth intact in real value. Deficits inclusive of full nominal interest outlays exaggerate the federal government's claim on private saving and overstate 'crowding out'. It is true that there is no guarantee that wealth-owners will consistently behave in this rational manner. But the same logic that

Table 18.4: Federal deficits and debt 1983–6—primary, structural, and total, with and without inflation corrections (based on administration (OMB) projections)

	Fiscal years			
	1983	1984	1985	1986
1. Debt/GNP ratio (%) average for fiscal year	31.9	35.8	39.5	42.8
2. Interest outlays:				
as % of GNP	3.5	3.7	3.9	3.9
as % of Debt	11.0	10.3	9.8	9.2
3. Inflation-accounting correction:				
as % of GNP	1.6	1.6	1.7	1.8
as % of Debt	5.0	4.5	4.4	4.1
4. Primary deficit, % of GNP	3.4	3.3	3.0	2.8
5. OMB total deficit, % of GNP	6.9	7.0	6.9	6.7
6. Total deficit after correction, % of GNP	5.3	5.4	5.2	4.9
7. Structural primary deficit, % of potential GNP	1.2	1.3	1.4	1.8
8. OMB structural total deficit, % of potential GNP	4.3	4.7	5.1	5.5
9. Structural total deficit, after correction, % of GNP	2.7	3.1	3.4	3.7

Notes: All calculations are based on the economic and fiscal projections in the Budget of the United States Government, Fiscal year 1984.

Row 1. Average of debt held outside the government, including Federal Reserve holdings, at beginning and end of fiscal year, divided by GNP projected for the fiscal year.

Row 2. Interest payments projected for fiscal year, divided by GNP projected or by average debt outstanding. Interest payments are net of the Federal Reserve repayment to the Treasury. No allowance is made for payment of federal taxes on interest by other debt holders.

Row 3. The correction on the projected increase in the GNP price deflator for the fiscal year multiplied by the debt at the beginning of the year.

Row 4. The primary deficit excludes the interest payments described in (2).

Rows 7,8,9. The structural deficit is OMB's estimate for 6.1 per cent unemployment, and potential GNP is OMB's estimate for the same unemployment rate.

says nominal interest rates include inflation premiums and dictates our focus on real rates argues for this correction, especially for long-range forecasts.

Second, I show in rows 4 and 7 estimates of the actual and structural primary deficits. This calculation removes from the structural deficit the effects of interest rates and of the accumulation of debt from projected actual deficits after fiscal year 1983. The reason for this separation is that the two components, primary and debt service, play different roles in the evolution of the debt.

VI. THE SIMPLE DYNAMICS OF DEFICITS AND DEBT

I present now a simple framework for discussing the long-run dynamics of deficits and debt, with particular reference to the current situation in the United States. I focus on the magnitudes of deficits and debt relative to GNP. Scaling to GNP gives a rough measure of their size relative to the capacity of the economy to generate saving and taxes. Moreover the society's total demand for non-human wealth is roughly proportional to its annual permanent income from work. The market for federal debt, monetary and non-monetary, can be expected to grow with the economy, other things equal. Those other things are numerous, including the real returns expected on federal obligations and other stores of value.

A few numerical orders of magnitude will help keep things in perspective. At the end of 1981, federal debt, monetary and non-monetary (at book value), to non-federal holders was 27 per cent of GNP. The ratio *is* projected to be 30 per cent by the end of FY 1983. Total non-federal net worth runs about four times GNP. Thus, federal debt is 7 to 8 per cent of total non-federal wealth. In a steady state that maintained these ratios, with real GNP growing at 2.5 per cent, increase of federal debt would absorb at most three-quarters of 1 per cent of GNP, while total non-federal net saving would be 10 per cent of GNP.

Under what conditions does total debt grow faster, or slower, than the GNP? Let x be the primary deficit as a fraction of Y, the nominal GNP; let i be the nominal interest rate, after federal taxes, on the non-monetary debt; let D be the total debt outstanding and d, equal to D/Y, its ratio to GNP; and let γ be the fraction of the debt in non-monetary form. Then the deficit $\dot{D}$, in dollars, given by:

$$\dot{D} = xY + i\gamma D \qquad\qquad (18.1)$$

the proportionate rate of growth of the debt is:

$$\dot{D}/D = xY/D + i\gamma \qquad\qquad (18.2)$$

Suppose that nominal GNP is growing at rate n. Then the growth of debt/GNP ratio d is:

$$\dot{d}/d = \dot{D}/D - \dot{Y}/Y = x/d + i\gamma - n \tag{18.3}$$

For example, take the situation projected for FY 1984 in CBO's September Update. I calculate the primary deficit as 1.7 per cent of GNP, the total previously outstanding debt as 30 per cent of GNP, the non-monetary share 86 per cent, bearing an after-tax interest rate of 8 per cent. The debt will be growing at 12.5 per cent per year while, according to the CBO projection, nominal GNP will be rising at 9.8 per cent. Equation (18.3) tells us that the debt/GNP ratio will be rising at 2.7 per cent per year, that is, from 0.30 to about 0.31 in one year.

Formula (18.3) can be made more informative and more relevant to the subject of this session by separating real and inflation effects in interest rates and growth rates. Thus the interest rate i can be written as the real rate r plus the inflation rate π, and the growth rate n can similarly be split between real growth g and inflation π. The result is:

$$\dot{d}/d = x/d + [r\gamma - \pi(1 - \gamma)] - g \tag{18.4}$$

Note that the expression in brackets is the average real interest rate on the debt, call it r_D. It is the sum of the real rate on non-monetary debt r weighted by its share γ, and the real rate on monetary debt $-\pi$ weighted by its share $1-\gamma$. If, as CBO forecast in September, inflation of the GNP 'deflator' is running at 6.1 per cent in FY 1984, the real rate on the debt would be only 0.8 per cent, while real GNP growth would be higher, 3.7 per cent.

The significance of the comparison of r_D with g can be seen as follows: Suppose the various parameters in (18.4) remained constant, for example at the FY 1984 values assumed in the numerical illustration. Would the debt/GNP ratio ever stop changing—rising in the illustration—and, if so, at what value? By setting $\dot{d}/d$ equal to zero in (18.4), we can calculate that hypothetical stationary value of d, call it d^*:

$$d^* = x/(g - r_D) \tag{18.5}$$

In the example d* is $0.017/0.029 = 0.61$. That is, if and when the debt/GNP ratio would reach 61 per cent, it would stop rising. Using (18.5), we may rewrite (18.4) as:

$$\dot{d} = (g - r_D)(d^* - d), \tag{18.6}$$

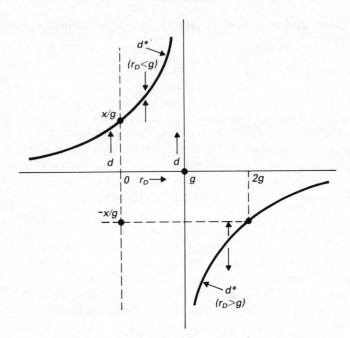

Figure 18.2: Steady-state debt ratio and interest rate

from which it is clear that d moves in the direction of d^* provided $(g - r_D)$ is positive, and moves away from d^* when it is negative. The former case is stable; the latter unstable. The illustrative case is stable. The indicated rise of d from 0.31 at the end of FY 1984 to 0.61 would be quite slow. After ten years, d would reach 0.385.

Figure 18.2 summarizes the conceptual framework just presented. The horizontal axis measures r_D the real interest rate on the debt. As noted, the economy's real growth rate g is a crucial watershed for r_D. The vertical axis measures d, the debt/GNP ratio. Its steady state value d^*, as shown in (18.5), falls along the hyperbola in the northwest quadrant or on the hyperbola in the south-east quadrant. As the arrows indicate, points on the north-west hyperbola are stable and points on the south-east hyperbola are unstable. (Hyperbolas in the other two quadrants are not shown. They correspond to primary surpluses, negative values of x.)

What if r_D and g were exactly equal? The outcome would then have to fall on the vertical axis through g. Equation (18.4) says that in this event $\dot{d}$ is equal to x. In the example, d would rise by 1.7 percentage points a year indefinitely, reaching 0.48 in ten years. To stop the rise, x would have to be reduced to zero. Given that condition, balance in the primary budget, any point on the vertical line above g is a stable d^*.

Which of the many possible d^* is the economy's long-run equilibrium? How is the steady-state value of r_D determined? This is a very complicated matter, and I cannot treat it here.[1] The outcome depends on the economy's long-run demand for wealth and on how wealth-owners wish to divide their wealth among capital, non-monetary public debt, and monetary debt. An increase in the primary deficit x shifts the north-west hyperbola up (and the other one down), but without specifying saving and portfolio behaviour we cannot determine whether this raises or lowers the steady-state r_D and its constituents r and π.

Calculations like those in the example above are sensitive to the assumed parameters. A real growth rate of 3.7 per cent is modest for recovery from deep recession but too high to be sustained indefinitely; 2.5 per cent is a better guess for g. Although 14 per cent of past deficits were monetized on average, Fed policy now implies monetization of only about 5 per cent of current deficits. The inflation rate will be lower than the CBO projection, if not in 1984 then subsequently. It is not hard to construct frightening scenarios, with r_D equal to or greater than g. In the next section, however, I shall argue for a more optimistic view.

Table 18.5, which is Table 14.2 repeated here for the convenience of the reader, gives calculations, based on the framework described in this section, for five periods of the three decades 1952 to 1981. At least to 1979, fiscal policy looks pretty benign. The primary deficit was, on average, negative in the first two periods, to 1966, and the combination of fast real growth and negative r_D brought rapid reduction of the high debt/GNP ratio inherited from World War II. Even after the primary deficit turned positive, the real interest rate was very favourable. Consequently the debt/GNP ratio remains well below its levels of the 1950s and 1960s. It is true that inflation contributed to that result in the 1970s, while policies to contain inflation worked in reverse, increasing unemployment and raising the average primary deficit.

VII. A RECIPE FOR FISCAL STABILITY AND NON-INFLATIONARY PROSPERITY

Can the United States economy later in this decade find a path of non-inflationary growth with a stable ratio of federal debt to GNP not far from its present value? I believe it is feasible, given suitable fiscal and monetary policies. The recipe includes: (1) reduction of the primary deficit, mainly by recovery of the economy to normal rates

Table 18.5: US fiscal and monetary policy and federal debt dynamics 1952–87

Period: fiscal years (number of years)	1952–7 (6)	1958–66 (9)	1967–74 (8)	1975–9 (5)	1980–1 (2)	1982–7 (6) CBO baseline
1. Federal debt % of GNP, beginning and end of period	64.8–48.5	48.5–35.7	35.7–23.4	23.4–26.5	26.5–27.6	27.6–38.0
2. Federal deficit (+) or surplus (−), excluding interest: % of GNP avg.	−0.58	−0.47	+0.28	+1.38	+0.80	+2.58
3. Share of debt monetized: % range	10.5–11.3	10.7–16.6	16.6–24.0	24.0–18.1	18.1–15.7	15.7–8.0
4. Share of deficit (including interest) monetized: % avg.	0	50	46	12	6	2.6
5. Growth of real GNP: % per yr. avg.	2.8	3.4	3.8	3.5	0.9	3.1
6. Inflation of GNP deflator: % per yr. avg.	2.2	1.9	5.2	7.2	9.1	6.4
7. Treasury ninety-day bill rate: % per yr. avg.	2.1	3.2	5.8	6.7	12.8	10.4
8. Real net interest rate on debt: % per yr. avg.	−0.7	−0.7	−2.8	−2.8	−0.1	1.7

9. Real GNP growth less real net interest rate	3.5	4.1	6.6	6.3	1.0	1.4
10. Hypothetical equilibrium debt/GNP ratio %	−16.6	−11.5	+4.2	+21.9	+80.0	+184.3
Indicated trend of debt/GNP ratio:						
11. Actual, beginning of period	64.8	48.5	35.7	23.4	26.5	27.6
12. After five years	51.9	37.6	27.1	23.0	29.1	38.1
13. After ten years	41.1	28.6	20.8	22.7	31.6	48.0

Notes:

1. Debt held by Federal Reserve and by non-federal owners, par value, at end of fiscal year, relative to nominal GNP for fiscal year, from fiscal year preceding the period to final year of period.

2. Sum of National Income Accounts deficits less surpluses for period, relative to sum of nominal GNP for period. Debt interest outlays (calculated by subtracting Federal Reserve payments to Treasury from 'Net Interest' line of budget) are excluded in calculating deficit or surplus, as are estimated tax receipts recouped from such outlays, estimated at 25 per cent.

3. Monetized debt is the amount held by the Federal Reserve. The denominator of the ratio is, as in line 1, the monetized debt plus the debt held outside the federal government.

4. The increment of monetized debt from beginning to end of period, divided by the increment of total debt as defined in line 1.

8. [line 7 × 0.75 × (100 − line 4)/100] − line 6. The average Treasury bill rate for each period is taken to be the permanent cost of financing new debt and refinancing old debt, which is reckoned at par value, given the conditions and policies of the period. It is multiplied by 0.75 on the assumption that the Treasury recoups 25 per cent of nominal interest outlays in taxes. The third factor reduces the net interest cost for 'seignorage', the fraction of the debt monetized by the Federal Reserve. Subtracting line 6 converts the net nominal interest rate on the debt to a real rate.

9. line 5 − line 8.

10. line 2/line 9. A negative figure means that the hypothetical equilibrium debt/GNP ratio is negative, i.e., the government would be a net lender to the private sector.

12. 13. [line 10 − line 11] × [(100 + line 9)/100]^n + line 10, letting n = 5. 10. See text.

of utilization of labour force and plant capacity; (2) reduction of real interest rates on federal debt to their normal historical range, around 1 per cent after tax; (3) sufficient expansion of the monetary base, relative to GNP, to accomplish (1) and (2) and to satisfy the increased demand for money due to decline in inflation and in nominal interest rates.

Frightening deficit projections, I cannot emphasize too strongly, arise from gloomy forecasts of the economy and of interest rates. Although CBO's September Update estimates a deficit of 4.2 per cent of GNP in FY 1984, as already noted the projected primary deficit is only 1.7 per cent of GNP, and this at an assumed 8.2 per cent unemployment rate. Each point of unemployment increases the deficit in that year by about 0.8 per cent of GNP. With unemployment two points lower, there would scarcely be any primary deficit at all. Even if, as I am not ready to accept, the inflation-safe unemployment rate is now taken to be 7 per cent, at that rate the primary deficit would be only 0.75 per cent of GNP. That amounts to 4 per cent of federal tax revenues under existing law. And it would be further reduced by real growth, even at sustainable rates rather than cyclical recovery rates, because growth still raises revenues faster than outlays. Modest 'revenue enhancements' and slowdown of the defence build-up would do the job faster.

Given decent recovery, the major long-run fiscal problem is to keep the real interest rate on the debt below the trend growth of the economy, as it has been throughout the period since World War II. This objective coincides with the necessity to restore low real interest rates to encourage non-federal capital formation to absorb savings the government will not be borrowing. This is at least as much a responsibility of Federal Reserve monetary policy as of fiscal policy. I stress that it is the real interest rate that matters. Reduction of nominal interest rates *pari passu* with disinflation does not improve either fiscal dynamics or investment incentives.

To be concrete, suppose that the after-tax real rate on non-monetary debt needs to be 1 per cent, a figure not exceeded through most postwar history before 1979. Suppose that a 2 per cent price trend, as in 1952 to 1966, is low enough to proclaim victory in the anti-inflation crusade, I suspect that any lower rate would make it difficult to obtain the adjustments in relative wages and prices needed in a dynamic economy, especially one vulnerable to external price shocks. Nominal after-tax interest rates will then have to come down to about 3 per cent, a reduction of the order of 60 per cent. Assuming an interest-elasticity of money demand of 0.2, this will entail a one-time increase of 12 per cent in the monetary base. That would raise it from

5.6 per cent of GNP to 6.3 per cent, still below the 8 per cent ratio of the 1960s. It would require a 15 per cent increase in Fed holdings of federal debt, raising them from 4.6 per cent to 5.2 per cent of GNP. (I assume that other components of the base, mainly gold and SDRs, do not change.)

I take the fiscal objective to be to stabilize the debt/GNP ratio at 30 per cent. After the required monetary injection, Federal Reserve monetization of debt and future deficits would be 17 per cent, a fraction much closer than current policy to earlier historical practice. The bottom line of this calculation is that the nominal interest cost of the debt will be 0.83×1 per cent, while nominal GNP will be growing at 4.5 per cent (2.5 per cent real plus 2 per cent inflation), 2 points higher than the interest cost. Recall formula (18.5), which says that $(g - r_D)d^* = x$. Our $(g - r_D)$ is 0.02 and our desired d^* is 0.30. Consequently, x must be 0.006. The primary deficit must be held to 0.6 per cent of GNP. As argued above, a primary deficit lower than 1 per cent of GNP is within reach, even with conservative objectives for unemployment and without significant contractionary fiscal policy.

These considerations underlie the fourth concern about high real interest rates suggested at the beginning of the paper, that they will be too high for long-run stability of the debt/GNP ratio at a value not far above the current ratio. The net real interest cost on the debt must be below the economy's sustainable real growth rate, now estimated at about 2.5 per cent per year. From this standpoint, a further advantage of a monetary strategy for recovery and for the revival of capital investment is that it will contribute to long-run fiscal stability. Of course it is also necessary to hold the structural primary deficit to a low fraction of GNP, probably below 1 per cent. This is the reason for making budget corrections effective in the latter years of the decade.

VIII.   CONCLUSIONS

Let me summarize my conclusions. Real interest rates are actually and prospectively too high, in all four of the meanings distinguished at the beginning of the chapter: too high for recovery, too high to sustain prosperity once it is restored, too high for the capital formation needed for long-term economic growth, too high for fiscal stability. Both fiscal and monetary measures are required to lower them. Now and in the near future, the ball is in the Federal Reserve's court. When prosperity is restored, lowering the federal deficit will be desirable to channel saving to capital formation. Continued action by the Fed will be needed to keep real interest rates low enough to assure that the saving thus released will actually be invested. Anticipation of this improvement in the future fiscal–monetary mix will help the economy recover from the present depression. This recipe will also promote longer-run stability in the ratio of federal debt to GNP, which requires both a low 'primary deficit' and a real debt interest rate below the sustainable real growth rate of the economy.

NOTE

1. *See* my paper 'The monetary–fiscal mix: long-run implications'. *American Economic Review*, May 1986, pp. 213–18.

19 Who is Crowding Out What?*

Administration economic officials are in well-publicized panic over a prospective capital shortage in American industry, a fear widely echoed by articulate financial and business leaders and writers. Recent and projected rates of private investment in plant and equipment, it is alleged, are insufficient to sustain US economic growth, especially when the extra capital requirements of environmental protection and of energy conservation and development are considered. A concerted campaign is under way to sell this message to the American people.

The worriers call attention once more to the fact that faster-growing economies like Germany and Japan report larger fractions of GNP devoted to capital formation than the United States. They draw two major morals for US economic policy. One is that the supply of saving available for business investment must be increased. Federal deficits must be reduced or reversed, so that government borrowing does not divert saving from private use. The claim that large-scale deficit spending will 'crowd out' private borrowers and investors has been the major intellectual excitement of public economic controversy in 1975.

The second lesson of the campaign is that after-tax profits must be vastly improved, to provide both incentive and funds for the capital expansion the country needs. This is the rationale for bigger permanent Investment Tax Credits and faster write-offs, reduction or elimination of corporate income taxation, and further tax concessions for capital gains.

A Treasury Secretary who solemnly warns of capital shortage when industry is operating at 70 per cent of capacity is like a hotel keeper who frets about financing an expansion when 30 per cent of his rooms are chronically empty. Plant and equipment investment, down 17 per cent in real volume since the second quarter of 1974, is indeed

---

*November 1975, *Challenge*, November/December 1975, pp. 56–7.

dismal. Capital appropriations, intentions surveys, and cancellation announcements indicate continued weakness.

But the problem is not the supply of saving. In the current underemployed economy new investment would generate saving to match, by familiar Keynesian processes. At 5 per cent unemployment the GNP would be more than $150 billion per year higher and provide about $75 billion in additional private saving or reduced public deficits to finance private investment (including housing and inventories as well as business facilities). We're far from 5 per cent unemployment, and the saving and investment lost by recession and stagnation may never be made up.

Would full employment saving be adequate? Estimates differ, but even the cautiously optimistic projections of the Brookings study require the government to eschew budget deficits at full employment. Crowding out will then be a legitimate concern. But an Administration which does not intend to move the economy even to 5 per cent unemployment before 1980 is wasting the saving potential of the nation while complaining that it is too low.

The current weakness of investment demand is easily explained: excess capacity; scepticism about the strength and duration of the recovery of sales and profits; high cost of debt and equity finance. The last is not a symptom of shortage of real savings or of productive resources preempted by a profligate government at the expense of private business. No such shortages exist. Tight money reflects the single-minded policy of the Federal Reserve, determined to fight inflation by keeping recovery slow and unemployment high. Chairman Burns helps to make the capital shortage he helps to deplore.

The main thing wrong with current fiscal and monetary policies is that they don't add up to a rapid and complete recovery. More stimulus, whether fiscal or monetary, is needed. There is a second objection, important to anyone interested in capital formation and productivity growth. The present policy *mix*, fiscal stimulus braked by tight money, overemphasizes public and private consumption. If Secretary Simon wants to shift the emphasis toward investment, he should talk to Chairman Burns as well as to Congress.

Meanwhile, the current weakness of business investment should not be the occasion for permanent concessions in taxation of business and property income (beyond reforms to correct inflationary exaggerations of taxable income). Sometimes these concessions are advocated as measures to increase saving; but the advocates forget that, since the beneficiaries would consume a fraction of their gains, the loss of tax revenues and government saving would exceed the extra private saving induced. The case for investment incentives is stronger than for saving incentives. But generous incentives, in the form of tax credits and accelerated depreciation, have already been built into the tax system. It is not these that have failed. *Macroeconomic* policies are the cause of the present inhospitable investment climate, and changed macroeconomic policies are the remedy.

20   Against the Balanced Budget and Tax Limitation Amendment*

The Amendment to the Constitution proposed by the Senate (Senate Joint Resolution (SJ Res.) 58) last 4th August has two aims. One is to force future Congresses to balance every year's federal budget. The second, equally significant but less widely noticed, is to limit the growth of federal revenues and outlays. Let me review the provisions of SJ Res. 58.

First, the Congress would be required to adopt prior to each fiscal year a statement of receipts and outlays in balance or surplus. There are two escape valves. A deficit budget may be adopted whenever a declaration of war is in effect or in peacetime by a three-fifths vote of the whole numbers of both Houses.

Second, the President and the Congress would be required to 'ensure' by legislation that actual outlays do not exceed those budgeted. This appears to permit an actual deficit due to a shortfall of receipts. But Section 6, the last-minute Armstrong–Boren addition to the Joint Resolution originally under consideration, blocks this escape route.

Thus, third, by Section 6 of SJ Res. 58, the public debt limit cannot be raised unless another three-fifths vote of the memberships of each House passes a bill which, unlike the other three-fifths vote, requires Presidential assent. One effect is to require such a bill whenever an unplanned deficit arises, whether by excess of outlays or shortfall of revenues.

Fourth, budgeted receipts shall not rise faster than 'national income' rose in a prior base period. The original intent of this provision, Section 2, was to clinch the second aim of the amendment, freezing the size of the federal budget relative to the economy. The escape hatch here is another extraordinary vote of both Houses. This one requires majorities of the memberships and assent of the President.

---

*December 1982, Tax Foundation 34th National Conference, New York City. Published in its *Proceedings, The Federal Fiscal Dilemma: Is There a Solution?*, 1983, pp. 21–4.

In SJ Res. 58, unlike the original proposal HJ Res. 350, the base period is not pinned down; the latitude Congress would have in choosing it could somewhat loosen the rigidity of this provision.

To me it seems incredibly ironic that anyone would take this proposal seriously at this time. This President and this Congress do not have budget balance in sight, even at long distance. Every advocate of the Amendment—the President, Senators, Representatives, and other supporters—should be required to tell concretely how he or she would comply with it if it were in force for fiscal year 1984 or 1985.

Outlays for FY 1984 are, according to the September Update of the Congressional Budget Office, expected to be $844 billion. Budgeted receipts for FY 1984 would not be allowed to exceed those in FY 1983 by more than the growth of national income in a prior base period. For a concrete illustration, let's calculate this limit as provided in HJ Res. 350, the growth of Gross National Product for the preceding calendar year over the year before. In the case at hand, calendar 1982 GNP will not exceed 1981 GNP by more than 4.5 per cent. CBO's September projection of FY 1983 receipts is $633 billion; this already seems optimistic, but let's accept it. Thus, under the Amendment, budgeted receipts for FY 1984 would be limited to 104.5 per cent of $633 billion, namely $661 billion. The Amendment would then require Congress to cut budgeted outlays by $183 billion from the $844 billion now projected. How and where would this 22 per cent cut be made? Defence? Entitlements to social insurance?

If the President and the Congressional supporters of the Amendment were prepared to take these draconian steps, nothing in the Constitution prevents them from doing so now. Of course, the effects on the economy would be disastrous, converting the present depression into a great depression.

For this and other reasons, the most likely practical outcome in my hypothetical story is that the escape valves would be opened. The necessary extraordinary majorities would be mustered to allow revenues to exceed the arithmetic limit, to permit adoption of an unbalanced budget, and to raise the public debt limit. The necessary Presidential signatures to bills for the first and third would be reluctantly granted. But these would occur only after lengthy political and parliamentary manoeuvres. Small minorities in either House could delay the budget, just by being absent, and hold the budget and the very operation of the government hostage to their favourite causes, however extraneous. The President too could play this game.

The example for FY 84 also applies to FY 85. It may seem extreme, but cases of this kind are likely to occur frequently. They will occur every time a recession depresses federal revenues and growth of national income during the base period. Routine resort to the escape valves would negate the spirit and intent of the Amendment, while making budget procedures more cumbersome, more political, and more drawn out than they already are.

Cosmetic accounting would be a real temptation. The terms in the Amendment, 'outlays', 'receipts', 'national income', are fatally ambiguous, conceptually and statistically. They can be redefined to facilitate apparent compliance. According to present budget practice, some receipts are counted as negative 'outlays'; the size of the budget and its growth depends on how much netting of this kind is done. Programmes which swell the budget can be otherwise achieved by tax expenditures, by setting up off-budget public or semi-public corporations, by mandating activities of state and local governments (a provision forbidding this escape was in early drafts of the proposed Amendment but has disappeared), or by regulations compelling private actions and expenditures. To keep the ostensible size of government within limit, Congress would be tempted to use the military draft rather than to pay market wages to volunteers.

The ambiguities also open the door to litigation. Citizens may allege that their tax liabilities were unconstitutionally imposed or that federal disbursements should be blocked because they exceed Constitutional limits or that the President and Congress have defaulted on their obligation to 'ensure' that actual outlays do not exceed the budget.

My FY 1984 exercise dramatizes, I think, the motive of some proponents of the Amendment. It is to lock into place the 1981 tax cuts, or what is left of them after the revenue enhancements of 1982, and to force future Congresses to dismantle not only discretionary social and welfare programmes but also entitlements to retirement, health, and unemployment insurance. This would still be the immediate transitional problem even if the Amendment came into effect several fiscal years later. Note, by the way, that the Amendment would inhibit a tax solution to the financial difficulties of the social security system, whether higher payroll taxes or, what I and many other economists would favour, counting half the benefits as taxable personal income. These solutions might well run foul of the proposed limitation on revenue growth.

I do not wish to rest my case against the Amendment on the hypocrisy and inefficiency of writing into the Constitution language whose intent will be negated by chronic resort to the escape votes or by ingenious cosmetic budgeting and accounting. The worst consequences, I believe, would ensue if the intent of the Amendment was fully realized and no escapes or evasions were used. Let me explain.

I would like to make clear at the outset that, although I believe, and shall argue, that federal deficits are economically desirable in some circumstances, I also think that there are many situations, many fiscal years, in which budget balance or surplus would be the outcome of appropriate policy. Until very recently federal debt had been declining relative to GNP ever since World War II. I would prefer to see a stable or declining trend in this ratio rather than the rise which, thanks to the recession, high interest rates, the 1981 tax cuts, and the upsurge of defence spending, is now in prospect. But these personal views about current monetary and fiscal policy are not today's subject.

Like other opponents of the Amendment, I am frequently asked why the federal government should not be subjected to the same requirements of living within means that other economic agents, households, businesses, state and local governments, must obey. The first answer is that the Amendment would constrain the federal government much more severely than most of those entities are constrained. For one thing, they are not as a rule legally limited in increasing their receipts. More important, they generally do not have to hold their outlays to their receipts every year. If the Amendment applied to a household, the family would not be able to spend more than its income any single year, to borrow to buy a house or a car or a college education. A business would not be allowed to sell securities to invest more than its retained earnings in plant and equipment. State and local governments would have to finance capital as well as current outlays from current tax receipts. Evidently there is widespread semantic misunderstanding on this point.

But it is not the main point. The central government *is* different from other economic agents. It is entrusted with the ultimate taxing and monetary powers and responsibilities of the society. Its horizon spans the generations. It can and should gear its fiscal and financial policies to the needs of the nation and economy as a whole.

Making deficits unconstitutional would increase economic instability. It would force ill-timed expenditure cuts or tax increases, as in the FY 1984 example. These would make recessions worse. The federal budget has been, on the whole though not always, a stabilizing influence these past thirty-five years. Outlays were fairly stable, moving moderately counter to business cycles. Tax revenues were pro-cyclically sensitive, sustaining private spending in bad times and restraining it in booms. These stabilizing features are automatic, built in to the structure of the budget and the tax system. In addition, discretionary changes in budget and tax programmes have been made in all Administrations to combat recessions and inflations. In both these ways, the budget is a major reason why cycles have been much less severe than before World War II. It is foolish, it is reckless, to discard this essential balance wheel.

Evidently many people just do not realize how sensitive budget outcomes are to the state of the economy. The unemployment rate is a cyclical indicator, and every extra point of unemployment adds to the deficit some $25–30 billion as of FY 1983, about $\frac{3}{4}$ of 1 per cent of GNP. The deficit outcomes and projections that currently arouse such consternation are mostly the result of poor economic performance, actual and projected. To force the Congress to cut expenditures or raise taxes to offset cyclical deficits would further depress the economy. The deficits perform a useful function in absorbing saving that would otherwise be wasted in unemployment, excess capacity, lower production. The cyclical sensitivity of the deficit comes not only from the tax revenue side but also from outlays, principally unemployment compensation and welfare benefits. The Amendment, however, commands President and Congress to keep outlays within the budget, even if the economy turns sour.

'Crowding out' of private investment by federal borrowing is a legitimate concern in times of prosperity, a good reason why the budget should come into balance or surplus in those times. The natural cyclical sensitivity of the budget has worked in this direction. Well-timed tax increases, whether automatic or discretionary, counter inflation and avoid 'crowding out', but they may actually be inhibited by the Amendment.

Absent the stabilizing contributions of fiscal structure and fiscal policy, the entire burden of economic stabilization would fall on the monetary policies of the Federal Reserve. It is by no means sure that the Fed would or even could offset destabilizing shocks from the private sector or from overseas, augmented by the destabilizing fiscal responses mandated by the Amendment. What is sure is that there would be much greater volatility of interest rates than in the past, at least before 1979. Considering the effects of recent interest rate volatility on the economy and on the federal budget too, I doubt that this consequence of the Amendment is a healthy one.

Underlying the proposal is an unsubstantiated and dubious diagnosis of the disappointing economic performance of our economy in the last decade. It is that growing federal outlays, taxes, deficits, and debt were responsible for the stagflation. Past fiscal policies were not always the best, to be sure, but this diagnosis is a vast and simplistic misreading of the facts.

Neither our history over the decades nor international comparisons support the diagnosis. Though the economy performed less successfully in the 1970s than in the previous quarter century, that earlier period was an exceptional and spectacular success story, both in the high growth trend and in the moderation of cyclical fluctuations. The postwar period stands out, relative to periods of comparable length in statistically recorded history, even when extended through the 1970s. Most of the things the government was doing in the 1970s were continuations of postwar practices and trends, yet the conservative condemnations cover the last 20, 30, 40, 50 years. Why did policies that were apparently successful, certainly no worse than harmless, for years and decades, suddenly fail and damage the economy? Clearly there were other causes, particularly the unprecedented supply and price shocks, the OPEC blows of 1973–4 and 1979.

And there's the other side of the coin. Before World War II the federal government was tiny, spent little and taxed little, generally balanced the budget, kept out of the way of private business and finance, didn't try to tame the business cycle, took no responsibility for the aged, the sick, and the poor. The economy was a lot less stable, even before the Great Depression.

In international perspective the US is one of the smallest-government countries in the advanced democratic capitalist world. Compared with the democracies of Western Europe (including West Germany, so often held up as a model of capitalist progress and stability) the US has a small government sector—even though we have much greater defence responsibilities—and a small welfare state. Moreover, our public sector has not been growing as rapidly as those of other advanced countries, including Japan. Foreigners who see our statistics on the size and growth of government regard the thesis underlying the Amendment as laughable for the US.

Is our federal government a Leviathan with an insatiable appetite for the resources of the nation? Is the record one of spend and spend, tax and tax, borrow and borrow? The statistics do not support the description. Certainly government is a bigger factor in the economy than before 1940. Defence is a big federal item; it has varied from a peace-time high of 11 per cent of GNP in the 1950s to 5.5 per cent recently, and now will rise to 8 per cent under the Reagan programme. This is about the only purpose for which the federal government buys goods, services, and labour. Civilian government purchases have risen since the war, but they are largely made by state and local governments—schools, roads, streets, sewers, parks, etc.—with some federal aid. In total about 20 per cent of GNP is taken for government use, for collective consumption or public investment; this ratio has been quite steady for a quarter century.

Total government outlays have risen from about a quarter to around a third of GNP over the same period, and total tax revenues a comparable amount. This increase has been in transfer payments.

There is no analytical justification for including transfer payments or the taxes that fund them in a ratio to GNP intended to indicate the size of government and its growth. The numerator and the denominator of such a ratio are not comparable, any more than numbers of apples and oranges. Gross National Product is the volume of goods and services; transfers do not absorb goods and services for government rather than private use. They re-allocate the goods and services from some private, or non-federal, agents to others. The tax-transfer process does absorb some real resources, to the extent that the modes of collecting taxes and making transfers distort incentives and generate inefficiencies. But these 'deadweight losses' are not 100 per cent of the amounts transferred; they are much less. Redistribution is a legitimate political issue, but the ratio of government receipts or outlays, inclusive of transfers, to GNP is not the way to analyse it or debate it. More important, freezing that ratio by constitutional amendment is not the way to resolve the issue.

Three points in the increase of federal outlays, relative to GNP, since the mid 1960s are due to increases in social insurance benefits, of which a major part is due to the inauguration of federal and state health insurance programmes in 1966—Medicare and Medicaid. Everywhere, whether medical care is paid publicly or privately, health outlays become a larger share of national expenditure. Very little of the growth of transfers is 'welfare' in the conventional and sometimes derogatory sense; most of it is to the benefit of the great middle class. It is certainly true that our social insurance systems have serious financial problems, but they can be solved without the Amendment and the Amendment will not help.

Deficits and debt? I already mentioned, perhaps to the surprise of some of you, that the US federal debt declined relative to GNP until the mid 1970s—specifically from more than a year's GNP to 25 per cent, one-quarter's GNP. Since then it has remained pretty stable, though it is now rising to about 30 per cent by the end of the current fiscal year. US deficits are very much smaller relative to GNP than those of other major economies, including Germany and Japan. In general, international comparisons show no correlation between deficits and inflation or deficits and economic growth.

I stressed at the beginning the tax limitation provisions of the Amendment. These are designed to freeze the size of the budget relative to the economy. There is no justification in political economy for freezing this statistic for all time, independently of the nature and cost of government outlays, or of economic circumstances, or of state and local activities, or of perceived national priorities. Now, for example, President and Congress agree that peacetime defence spending should for a time rise faster than GNP. No principle of economics or of equity dictates that the needed resources must be shifted to defence from other federal programmes or from beneficiaries of social insurance and other transfers, rather than from the personal consumption of taxpayers. We elect representatives in a democracy precisely to make national decisions of this kind about priorities and allocations of burdens.

The great and wise men who framed our Constitution thought so too. They designed a framework of rights and procedures that has stood the test of time. They prudently refrained from substantive legislation. They did not prejudge the choices of succeeding generations in unforeseeable circumstances. They wrote an elegant and concise charter, uncluttered by trivia, certainly uncluttered by strictures of economics and book-keeping. I do not think the advocates of this Amendment are wiser than they.

21 Comment from an Academic Scribbler*
(on *Democracy in Deficit*)

Polemics is fun to write and read, more fun than analytics. The Buchanan–Wagner (BW) attack on Keynesian economics in theory and practice will be on lots of reading lists. Sometimes polemical controversy sharpens and illustrates issues, but this seems unlikely to be one of those times. The authors carry their righteous anger toward professional colleagues to outrageous extreme: Keynesian economics is, they say, undemocratic and elitist, and leads ultimately to 'our own version of "national socialism" ' (p. 73). The 1964 tax reduction, the pride of Keynesian economics in operation, led to 'The Great Society—Vietnam spending explosion of the late 1960s' (p. 35). Thus, like Joan Robinson on the Left, BW blame American Keynesians for the Vietnam War. They also blame the economics of the Democratic Camelot for the disasters of the Nixon–Ford years: inflations, recessions, bloated government, under-investment, wage and price controls, dollar devaluations, budget deficits. 'Can we seriously absolve the academic scribblers from their own share of blame?' (p. 35).

The scribblers are rarely named, cited, or quoted; but positions are confidently attributed to them anyway. Aside from Keynes himself, and Abba Lerner for the sin of 'functional finance', the main targets are the American Keynesians who brought the 'New Economics' to Washington in 1961 and, according to BW, destroyed politicians' inhibitions against deficit spending and thus opened the floodgates to endless disaster. Now the 1962 *Economic Report of the President*, prepared by the Heller–Gordon–Tobin Council of Economic Advisers with help from Solow, Okun, Schultze, Samuelson, Pechman, and other staff members and consultants is surely the most complete and authoritative statement of the doctrines of the economists BW are

*1978, Symposium on James M. Buchanan and Richard E. Wagner, *Democracy in Deficit: The Political Legacy of Lord Keynes. Journal of Monetary Economics*, 4, 1978, pp. 617–25.

attacking. It is cited only once in their entire book.[1] Very few of the positions which BW characterize as Keynesian can be found in that *Report*, and on most of the issues the *Report* says the opposite.

Let me speak for myself. I must assume that, as a member of the Kennedy CEA, I am one of the 'Keynesians' under attack, and BW's passing references to me (pp. 80, 84) certainly convey that idea. Presumably that's why the editor invited me to contribute to this symposium. I have certainly derived a great deal of inspiration from Keynes, and from other great economists too. I have written some things very critical of Keynes and many things which substantially modify the macroeconomics of the *General Theory*. I have made my share of errors of analysis, empirical interpretation, and policy recommendation. Often I disagree with friends and colleagues, including partners in the BW indictment. I thought I was just an *economist* struggling, like Buchanan and Wagner in their soberer moments, to understand how the economy works and perhaps how to make it work a bit better. Controversy and reasoned debate are part of that process. Labelling 'schools' is not. The BW book is one more symptom of the increasing doctrinal and, yes, ideological polarization of the economics profession in recent years. It is a shame, and it should stop.

BW attribute to 'Keynesians' the following positions, among others: impossibility of shifting burden of government expenditure from present to future by debt finance; optimality of full employment budget balance; likelihood that deficits can be reduced by lowering taxes; Galbraithian view that the public sector is systematically and chronically undernourished; indifference between monetary and non-monetary financing of deficits; lack of concern for inflationary danger of high employment and growth. I do not hold these positions, and neither did the authors of the 1962 *Report*.

'Intellectual error of monumental proportion has been made. The academic scribbler of the past who must bear substantial responsibility is Lord Keynes himself, whose ideas were uncritically accepted by American establishment economics' (p. 4). That is surely nonsense. If grown men of normal intelligence made errors of analysis and policy in the 1960s, if they suspended their critical judgement about the contents and relevance of a book written in 1936, that is in no way the responsibility of the book's author, deceased in 1946. Likewise, Heller and his 1960s colleagues are not responsible for views of others whom BW choose to label as Keynesian, certainly not Hugh Dalton (p. 9) and not even Abba Lerner or Keynes himself.

Monumental intellectual error? The book is very aggressive in asserting it and deploring it, but attempts very little rigorous theoretical or empirical argument. The main issues in the forefront of macroeconomic discussion today, much the same as in Keynes's debate with his orthodox contemporaries, are not elucidated.[2] These are: Is the economy best understood as a moving equilibrium with labour and product markets continuously clearing, or is it subject to protracted disequilibria with excess supplies or demands removed only slowly by wage and price adjustments? Is the economy intrinsically stable against exogenous shocks, adjusting promptly without assistance from policy? Are policies responsive to economic conditions destabilizing? useless once understood? inflationary? Is the Phillips Curve essentially vertical with respect to monetary or fiscal stimulus no matter how high the rate of unemployment when the stimulus is administered? On the empirical side, what explains the general improved performance of the United States and world economies since World War II? Has the retreat from 'fine tuning' in monetary and fiscal policy in the 1970s produced better and more stable economic results? BW make no serious contributions on these crucial questions.

Their chief analytical complaint is the 'Keynesian' theory of burdenless public debt. According to BW, the academic scribblers convinced themselves and persuaded politicians that interest-bearing public debt burdens neither present nor future generations. The charge is factually false for the generation of American economists whose malign influence in the 1960s is the main subject of the book.[3]

As BW note, many of those economists subscribed to what Samuelson called a 'neoclassical synthesis'. What was its doctrine about public debt? True enough, it distinguished internal from external debt. True enough, it was not the Ricardian view, currently revived under the banner of rational expectations, that debt and tax finance are essentially the same because rational taxpayers' behaviour will not be altered by deferring their taxes. BW also reject this view, according to which deficit financing is both ineffectual and innocuous. The standard American Keynesian doctrine has been, I believe, that economy-wide burden on future generations is to be measured by the reduction, if any, in stocks of physical and human capital bequeathed to them. Government obligations differ from their counterpart in future tax liabilities in several respects: liquidity, uncertainties, distribution among citizens. Moreover, taxes are not lump-sum levies; an individual's future liability depends partly on his own behaviour. For these reasons public debt absorbs some savings that in the long run would otherwise go into productive capital. For the same reasons, in short-run underemployment circumstances, a deficit can absorb some saving that would otherwise be lost in lower income and employment.

This doctrine clearly is not one that 'denies that debt finance implements an intertemporal shift' or views 'the existence of opportunities for cumulative fiscal profligacy ... as impossible [because] there are no necessarily adverse consequences for future taxpayers' (p. 19). BW are just wrong in saying that selling the myth of burdenless debt-financed expenditure was 'a necessary first step' (p. 19) to the 'dreams of Camelot' (pp. 34–5). Again I invite BW and their readers to read the 1962 *Economic Report*. There they will find considerable attention to choices among government purchases, private consumption, and private investment both at times of full employment and at times of underutilization. They will find high priority given to policies and policy mixes which benefit future generations via capital formation, private and public. They will even find that the authors of the *Report* were just as familiar as BW with the concept of opportunity cost.[4]

The other major analytical point in this book is, like the public debt discussion, an offshoot of previous work by the authors. This one concerns public choice. BW argue that deficit finance underprices government programmes and thus induces public and politicians to 'buy' them in excessive amounts (pp. 104, 141–4).[5] The point is logically valid if and only if the marginal tax cost of government programmes is, and is perceived to be, the same as the average. As an empirical proposition about the attitudes of Presidents and legislators, the condition appears improbable. The balanced budget ethic remains stronger than BW think. In deficit times new spending proposals encounter stiff resistance in the Office of Management and Budget, the White House, and the Congress; this is true even though the deficit reflects cyclically depressed economic activity and the high-employment budget is in surplus. On the other hand, in times of budget balance or actual or prospective surplus, spending proposals are less rigorously screened. This model, the opposite of BWs, is the usual argument of conservatives who favour tax reduction in all seasons and advocate indexing and other reforms to deny government automatic gains in revenue from inflation and growth.

The new Congressional budget procedure, it should be noted, requires Congress to determine an overall budget, including a projected deficit or surplus. Once this is decided, new proposals for spending and taxes must be neutral in their effects on the deficit. Thus the perceived marginal cost of an incremental programme is the same whether the budget is projected to be in balance or in deficit. Indeed under this procedure the marginal cost is effectively higher in a slack economy than in a full employment economy, because it takes a higher tax rate to collect a dollar of revenue when the tax base is low.

Social insurance outlays (including extraordinary unemployment compensation) have risen by more than $100 billion in the past decade; they account for 42 per cent of the 'explosion' in federal outlays that

BW deplore. Social insurance taxes and contributions have risen by $75 billion; they are below par because of recession, and substantial increases are about to be enacted to keep the reserve fund in the black. Congress feels strong compulsion to keep the social insurance budget actuarially balanced. If benefits have been expanded too liberally, it is not because Congress has deceived itself or the public regarding the tax cost.

Although BW regard Keynesian theory as erroneous economics, their critique is largely directed at its political implications and their consequences. Their subtitle is 'The political legacy of Lord Keynes'. Until 1960, they argue, the balanced budget norm kept federal spending and deficits in check. The taboo on deficits was the only fiscal discipline. Even if the taboo was not rational in all economic weather, economists should not have imparted this dangerous knowledge to politicians, who had and have every motivation to misunderstand it and misuse it.

Thus BW raise the interesting question who is the economists' audience in a democracy. BW seem to think that rational policy advice can only be given to elitist and authoritarian governments, and they single me out as naive about democratic politics. I think our audience is the public and its servants in Congress, White House, Federal Reserve, and other agencies. Our responsibility is to provide as accurate a description as we can of the economic structure in which policies operate, and of the consequences for the nation and its constituents of alternative courses of action, with candour about our considerable margins of uncertainty. We have no duty, we have no right, to shade our message because we judge that there are some things the people and their representatives should not be told. Do BW propose to censor the professional and popular media to keep potentially dangerous information and ideas from voters and politicians and policy makers?

In economic analysis meant for policy advice, it is quite proper to take policy decisions as exogenous. As positive social scientists we also aspire to a purely descriptive political economy, in which politicians are endogenous and their decisions are to be explained. BW and their colleagues have contributed greatly to this task. But a fully closed model is not useful as a policy guide; it doesn't make sense to tell voters or Congress or President: 'Don't do X because our descriptive model says that you will not do X and will do Y later'.

Let us turn to the authors' main charge, that Walter Heller was the serpent in the 1961 Garden of Eden, enticing the innocent to partake of the forbidden fruit of fiscal knowledge—source of sin and calamity for years to come.

The 1961–5 recovery, sustained by the 1962 and 1964–5 tax cuts and by supportive monetary policies, brought unemployment to the Kennedy 4 per cent target without inflation. BW do not dispute this record; they contend, however, that the 1966–9 excess demand inflation was the inevitable political, economic, and intellectual sequel.

They know that LBJ's economic advisers urged him to raise taxes in January 1966; the economists, they say, should have realized from the outset that politicians would follow Keynesian fiscal precepts only in one direction. Should physicians never recommend aspirin—which is in any case obtainable without prescriptions—because some patients might overdose themselves and their children?

President Johnson's escalation of the Vietnam War certainly was a disaster in every dimension, and his decision not to ask for a tax increase to finance it was a momentous economic error. Was Keynesian economics to blame? Were the economic advisers of Kennedy and Johnson responsible? They advised a tax increase before they even guessed the full magnitude and speed of the military build-up. Had they previously taught the President Keynesian fiscal doctrine all too well? He had non-economic considerations in mind: disclosing only gradually the full extent of the new military commitment, protecting his domestic programmes from Congressional cutbacks. Would he have been unaware of the deficit–financing alternative to higher taxes if he had never met Heller, Ackley, and Okun? Wars have been financed by borrowing or printing money throughout history, long before 1936 or 1961. Does exposure to Keynesian advisers invariably addict politicians to inflationary finance? Harry Truman, following the advice of economists at least as Keynesian as Johnson's, courageously and successfully insisted on paying for the Korean War by taxation. Would the Constitutional amendment BW propose to require annual budget balance have prevented the Vietnam disaster or the fiscal mistake? Possibly it would have compelled the President to be more candid with the public and the Congress in the early stages of the escalation. But a Congress which would vote the Tonkin Gulf resolution would also declare a national emergency to escape fiscal restrictions. The more appropriate remedy, already partially and belatedly adopted by Congress, is to obey existing constitutional provisions on making war.

Although economists inside and outside the government, Keynesian and non-Keynesian, opposed deficit financing of Johnson's war, few if any foresaw the extent and persistence of the Vietnam War inflation. BW are wrong to ascribe to deliberate macroeconomic policy the economy's ride up the Phillips Curve to 3 per cent unemployment. None the less, as a by-product of LBJ's war finance, the ride was taken. High production and low unemployment had the expected benefits, especially for the poor and disadvantaged. But the inflation trade-off encountered was worse than expected. Speaking only for myself, an outsider then and now, I acknowledge that I had been overoptimistic about the trade-off and too sceptical of accelerationist warnings.

But let us not exaggerate. In 1969–70, when Administrations, economic advisers, and Federal Reserve Chairmen changed, price inflation was 5 per cent per year, wage inflation 6.6 per cent. The subsequent history should arouse at least as much disappointment and intellectual humility among monetarists and other anti-Keynesians as among BW's Keynesian targets. Inflation accelerated when excess demand pressure ceased and was followed by deliberate recession in 1970–1; inflation bulged to a degree disproportionate to fiscal and monetary stimulus in 1973–4; inflation abated in 1975 once the OPEC and commodity shocks were absorbed but remained stubbornly insensitive to slack in labour and product markets during three years of slow recovery.

BW are appalled by the growth in governmental outlays since 1960 and the almost unbroken string of federal budget deficits. They blame the 'New Economics' of the 1960s for this history. They say (p. 57) that government spending as a percentage of national income increased from 32.8 per cent in 1960 to 43.5 per cent in 1975 and that increases in government spending have 'absorbed' nearly 50 per cent of increases in national income. They complain of a cumulative deficit exceeding $230 billion for 1961–76. These figures merit some comment.

1. Government outlays include both purchases of goods and services and transfers. Only purchases use resources and 'absorb' national product. Moreover, purchases are made at market prices and should not be compared with national income at factor cost. Total purchases by all governments were 19.8 per cent of GNP in 1960, 22.4 per cent in 1975. However, the 1975 figure is exaggerated by the deep recession of that year. In terms of full employment GNP, re-estimated by the Ford CEA, the percentage was 18.9 per cent in 1960, 20.2 per cent in 1975. Even this small increase is more than accounted for by the increase in the relative price of government purchases. In 1972 dollars, the government share fell from 22.4 per cent to 19.8 per cent. State and local governments accounted for 46 per cent of the total in 1960, but for 63 per cent in 1975. Of course, federal transfers to those governments are partly responsible. Between 1965 and 1976, government purchases have 'absorbed' 21 per cent of incremental GNP.

2. Transfers, other than intergovernmental, tripled in real amount

between 1960 and 1975, while full employment GNP grew by 70 per cent. As a share of personal income, transfers rose from 6.8 per cent to 13.5 per cent, three-quarters of the rise occurred after 1969. The present or future taxes needed to achieve this redistribution impose some distortions and efficiency losses on the economy, but this burden is certainly a lot less than the gross amount of the transfers.

3. Of the $238 billion cumulative federal deficit 1961–76, only $57.4 billion occurred before 1970, most of that in the Vietnam War period discussed above. Nearly half of it, $111.6, came in the last two fiscal years, largely as the result of the severe recession. BW make no distinction between deficits due to deliberate increases in spending and reductions in taxes and those which result from cyclical changes in tax collections and legislatively mandated outlays. Over 1961–76 the cumulative full employment (5 per cent unemployment) deficit is $91.6 billion. For the two fiscal years 1975 and 1976 the full employment deficits totalled $26.7 billion.

In this perspective the explosion of a debt-financed public sector looks a good deal less alarming than BW's rhetoric. Moreover, the deficits that triggered their book in fiscal years 1975 and 1976 were largely due to the deep recession of 1974–5, which in turn was caused by some non-linear combination of OPEC and Arthur Burns, surely not by anything Walter Heller *et al.* did or said in the early 1960s.

BW object to deficits primarily because they are both cause and symptom of growth of government. They have other objections too. One is of course the inflationary effect of debt finance. This makes very good sense for 1966–9, some sense for 1973, and almost none for 1974–6. BW are ambivalent about monetarism. They like its anti-interventionist stance, but they don't like its implication that deficits are not inflationary unless monetized. They argue that political pressure forces the Fed to monetize more public debt when deficits are bigger. The statistical table they offer (p. 115) in support of this thesis is not very convincing. It looks more like 'leaning against the wind', a moderately anti-cyclical monetary policy which makes money growth loosely and non-causally correlated with deficits. In any case this Friedmanesque claim is not consistent with the authors' warning that deficits 'crowd out' private investment by raising interest rates; if the Fed behaved as BW contend, investment would not be displaced by government obligations.

The bottom line of this account of 'democracy in deficit' is the recommendation of two Constitutional Amendments. The first would require annual–why not quarterly or monthly or daily?—balance in the projected federal budget. 'In the event that projections prove in error, and a budget deficit beyond specified limits occurs, federal outlays shall be automatically adjusted downward to restore projected balance within a period of three months' (p. 180). During a five-year transition, the same sanction would compel deficit reduction of 20 per cent per year. The only escape from the transitional and permanent provisions would be declaration of national emergency for a year, voted by two-thirds of each house of Congress and approved by the President. The second Amendment would limit growth of the monetary base to 'a rate roughly equivalent to the rate of growth of real output in the national economy' (p. 182).

The language leaves lots of loose ends. How can outlays be '*automatically* adjusted downward'? Which ones? Social security benefits? Federal wages and salaries? Payments on defence contracts? Who decides, and how? Does the monetary base grow ('*roughly*') with actual output or with potential output? And so on. It will take a few more hours or years at the economic and legal drawing boards before these proposals are ready for Congress and the States.

The main purpose is to outlaw discretionary macroeconomic policy, fiscal and monetary. Annual budget balance does more. It wipes built-in stabilizers out of the fiscal system. The 1974–5 recession, for example, increased the fiscal 1975 deficit by $24 billion. The Buchanan–Wagner Amendment would have compelled a $24 billion reduction in annual rate of expenditures in the third or fourth quarter of 1975, when recovery had barely begun, unemployment was 8.9 per cent, capacity utilization lower than 80 per cent. (The $10 billion discretionary tax rebate and reduction of 1975, not counted above, probably would not have occurred, or it would have been matched by additional expenditure cuts.) The result would certainly have been deeper and longer recession.

The old-fashioned multiplier measures, among other things, the susceptibility of the economy to aggregate demand shocks, like the rise in cost of imported oil in 1974. Gearing government expenditure to tax receipts raises the multiplier. Indeed in some circumstances— as when current sales and profits are considered strongly indicative of the future and investment therefore is responsive to contemporaneous business activity—the budget balance rule would make the multiplier process unstable.[6]

Under the second BW amendment, monetary policy would be powerless to help. This is true even if we generously assume that the authors mean their monetary rule to refer to potential not actual output. If the downward demand shock were also an upward price shock, as was the case in 1974, then the rule would automatically contract the real monetary base.

Having eliminated discretionary policy and built-in fiscal stabilizers, the authors place the entire burden of stabilization on market adjustments of prices, wages, and interest rates. Yet they provide no arguments or evidence that these adjustments will work more satisfactorily than the mechanisms they discard, or at all. Perhaps their new economic constitution would induce much more responsive price and wage flexibility than we have observed in the present regime, but that is just faith.

Anyway BW don't really care about economic outcomes. Process is what matters, not results (p. 171). The kind of process the authors like is one in which government does the minimum and follows simple predictable fiscal and monetary rules uninfluenced by feedbacks from economic events. As realistic students of public choice, BW must know that our own nation and other peoples will judge our democratic capitalist society by performance.

NOTES

1. On a tangential issue, in reference to the 4 per cent unemployment target and 'Okun's law,' p. 162.
2. For a survey of these, *see* my article, 'How dead is Keynes?', *Economic Inquiry*, October 1977, pp. 459–68.
3. As representative exponents of Keynesian public debt theory, the authors cite Hugh Dalton and Abba Lerner. As BW note on p. 33, fn. 11, a lively discussion of public debt theory took place in the late 1950s and early 1960s, stimulated by Buchanan's writings. They cite J. M. Ferguson, ed., *Public Debt and Future Generations*, University of North Carolina Press, 1964. This book contains a number of Keynesian contributions which do not follow Dalton or the early Lerner, e.g. by Modigliani, Musgrave, Mishan. In a review of the Ferguson book (*Journal of Finance*, December 1965, pp. 679–82), I endorsed the 'capital stock' approach of these authors, as summarized in the next paragraph. BW can scarcely help knowing they are attacking a straw man.
4. On these fiscal issues *see* in particular pp. 81, 85–6, 130–1, 138–9, 142–3. In a 1960 article, 'Growth through Taxation', *New Republic*, July 1960, I advocated high employment budget surpluses as a way of generating additional saving for private capital formation and growth. Since memories are short, perhaps a reminder that the Investment Tax Credit was enacted on recommendation of the Kennedy Administration in 1962 is timely.
5. Also: 'After the 1964 tax reduction, the "price" of public goods and services seemed lower. Should we not have foreseen efforts, to "purchase" larger quantities. Should we not have predicted the Great Society–Vietnam spending explosion of the late 1960s?' (p. 50).
6. Let *b* represent the non-federal marginal propensity to spend, *t* the marginal

Fiscal Policies

net tax share of national product, h the marginal propensity to import. With stable government expenditure, the multiplier is $[1 - b(1 - t) + h]^{-1}$. Under the budget balance rule it is $[(1 - b)(1 - t) + h]^{-1}$. If $t = 0.3$, $h = 0.1$, $b = 0.86$, the first multiplier is 2, and the second is 5. If $b = 1.21$ the first multiplier is 4 and the second is negative, implying that decline due to a negative shock has no stopping point.

PART IV

Monetary and Financial Policies

INTRODUCTION

Monetary policy has been discussed in previous Parts, particularly in reference to the extreme tight-money–easy-fiscal policy mix of recent years in the United States. Here I am concerned more specifically with the conduct of monetary policy.

In Chapters 22 and 24, I argue against monetarism and in favour of conducting monetary policy to achieve desirable macroeconomic performance rather than gearing it to targets for *M-1* and other money aggregates. In Chapter 24 I detect considerable movement by the Federal Reserve in this direction. More recently, however, as indicated in Chapter 3, I find the 'Fed' overcautious in its objectives for macroeconomic performance, especially the rate of unemployment.

Technological innovation, institutional change, and deregulation have complicated the task of the central bank, as described in Chapter 23. I believe the monetary authorities can maintain control, but their modes of operation will have to adapt to their new environment. I suggest means, including optional 100 per cent-reserve deposits, for protecting the payments system without obliging the central bank and other government agencies to bail out imprudent or unlucky banks and all their depositors.

In Chapter 25 I warn, as in Chapter 18, of the fallacy of assuming that nominal interest rates simply register expected inflation. Here I show how 'q', the ratio of securities market valuation to replacement cost of the business capital stock, can be a barometer of the financial climate for capital investment. If 'q' is falling, *real* interest rates relevant to investment decisions are most likely rising, whatever is happening to current inflation rates.

Finally, Chapter 26 is a sceptical look at the overall contributions to the economy made by our highly developed system of financial institutions and markets. In his famous Chapter 12 of the *General Theory*, Keynes was likewise sceptical, so this chapter too is in a Keynesian mode.

22 Monetary Policy in an Uncertain World*

Power attracts advice and criticism. These days central banks are the most powerful actors in the economic drama. Polls of American leaders rate Paul Volcker the second most powerful person in the United States. Outside military and diplomatic contexts, Chairman Volcker probably plays a more decisive role than the President himself. So if central bankers are receiving ever larger quantities of conflicting advice from citizens in general and economists in particular, that is testament to their recognized power. And if the counsels of the various critics cancel one another out, as may happen even at this conference and even in this session, then the central bankers can continue in good conscience to do what they would do anyway.

This conference is well timed, for several reasons. First the world economy is, in 1983, just beginning to recover from its worst depression since the 1930s; a strong and sustained recovery is still not assured. The monetary authorities of the leading economic powers, the United States, Japan, and the European Community, bear proximate responsibility for the depression, the by-product of the severe counter-inflationary measures they felt compelled to take at the end of the 1970s. The immediate practical question is what role monetary policies should play in accommodating or promoting recovery.

Second, intellectual developments in macroeconomics converge with real world events in raising just now some fundamental issues about the conduct of monetary policy. Monetarism, having won the hearts and minds of many economists and central bankers in the 1970s, may now be losing some adherents and influence—partly because of the depression, partly because regulatory, institutional, and technological changes have so clearly altered the meanings and velocities of monetary

*June 1983, Keynote Paper, First International Conference of The Institute for Monetary and Economic Studies, Bank of Japan, Tokyo. Published in Bank of Japan *Monetary and Economic Studies*, October 1983, vol. 1, no. 2, and in Albert Ando *et al.* eds., *Monetary Policy in Our Times*, Cambridge, Mass.: MIT Press, 1985, pp. 29–42.

aggregates. Last summer and fall Chairman Volcker and his colleagues suspended their monetarist targets, to nearly universal relief. But no coherent philosophy of monetary control, no systematic strategy, has yet replaced them. What responsibility central banks should assume for recovery in this decade is a specific instance of a general issue, the weight that real macroeconomic performance should have in monetary policy decisions. A currently influential view is that monetary policies can and should aim solely at nominal, not real, outcomes.

Third, both recent experience and contemporary theory underscore the international dimensions of monetary policies. Recent events in the United States played out with remarkable accuracy the textbook scenario for the effects of restrictive monetary policy in a world of floating exchange rates. High interest rates attracted funds to dollar assets and appreciated the home currency; deterioration of the US trade balance was the major component of decline in final demand. Other countries have not welcomed the impacts on their interest rates, exchange rates, and prices. Rhetoric at Versailles and Williamsburg summits recognized the interdependence of our economies and financial markets and the need for coordination of macroeconomic and monetary strategies. But very little concrete progress is evident. In consonance or dissonance the major central banks together determine the international monetary environment and the general levels of interest rates throughout the world. None of the three 'locomotives' can claim it is too small to influence the world economy. If in my discussion I fall into the old American habit of talking about one closed economy with one monetary authority, please interpret me as referring to the OECD as a whole and to the several leading central banks as a group.

My remarks are divided into three parts. Part I takes up the fundamental issue mentioned above, the place of real economic objectives in the making of monetary policy. I argue against the proposition that only nominal variables should concern the central bank. Part II discusses the hierarchy of ultimate objectives, intermediate targets, and instruments in relation to uncertainties monetary policy makers face over various horizons. Part III discusses some current issues of policy connected with recovery from the world depression.

I. REAL AND NOMINAL VARIABLES AS OBJECTIVES OF MONETARY POLICY

Should monetary authorities consider the real economic performance of their countries in setting policies? Should their objectives include real outcomes of national and international importance—employment, trade, production, capital formation—as well as nominal variables—prices, nominal incomes, monetary aggregates?

Today many economists and central bankers answer 'No'. Monetary authorities' capacities and responsibilities, they argue, cover only nominal variables. After all, they have only nominal instruments. Dedication of those instruments to real objectives has, they allege, not improved but if anything actually worsened real performance, while destabilizing prices and causing inflation. Chastened by the stagflation of the last fifteen years, central banks should be content to provide a stable, credible, predictable non-inflationary nominal path and to accept whatever real outcomes occur along that way. Devotees of the new classical macroeconomics assure us that those outcomes will be optimal. Knowing that the central bank will neither confuse them nor rescue them from the consequences of imprudent wage and price increases, private agents and free markets will achieve the natural equilibrium values of real variables, quantities and relative prices.

The issue is an old one, and the answer has oscillated over the history of central banking. The primacy of nominal objectives was well established before the Great Depression. Central banks and governments were expected to place defence of a fixed parity of their currency with gold or foreign currencies ahead of domestic economic performance. Today some economists, statesmen and commentators—frustrated by exchange rate instabilities these past ten years—advocate restoration of an international gold standard. They believe that the discipline of gold convertibility will create and maintain anti-inflationary expectations and behaviours.

Monetarists concur with this objective but prefer the discipline of monetary rules to that of gold. They would commit central banks permanently and publicly to specific numerical rates of growth in monetary aggregates of nominal income. Some would impose such rules by legislative or constitutional mandate. The purpose and effect are the same as intended by advocates of the gold standard. Monetary operations will be, and will be seen to be, independent of actual economic performance, in particular independent of paths or real outcomes.

I believe that purely nominalist monetary strategies are neither feasible nor desirable, for several reasons.

The first reason is political. The responsibility of the central government for real macroeconomic performance is strongly entrenched in the politics of democratic societies. This has been true at least since the Great Depression of the 1930s and especially after World War II. In the United States, for example, the Employment Act of 1946 and the Full Employment and Balanced Growth Act of

1978 ('Humphrey–Hawkins') commit the federal government, including the Federal Reserve System, to the pursuit of real economic goals. More important realistically, unemployment, real growth, and related variables are significant factors in public opinion and in electoral campaigns.

Central banks cannot stand aloof from objectives highly valued by the societies they serve. Central bankers and their constituencies frequently dismiss the priorities of elected officials, for example reduction of unemployment, as 'political', hence unworthy of respect. The legitimacy of such a value judgement is as doubtful as its welfare economics.

A purely nominal stance of monetary policy, wilfully blindfold to real developments, is not likely to be credible. Sooner or later the central bank of a democracy will rescue the economy from the worst unintended real by-products of a fixed nominalist line, just as Paul Volcker did last summer. Expectation that this will happen is bound to undermine policies whose effectiveness depends on public belief that it never will.

The second point is economic. The dichotomy between real and nominal policy operations, by which monetary instruments are classified as purely nominal, is not valid theoretically or empirically.

Nominal price and wage paths are sluggish, some more sluggish than others. Prices and wages which are administered or negotiated change less rapidly and readily than the prices of financial assets and commodities traded in auction markets. Because of such inertia, fluctuations in aggregate nominal spending resulting from monetary operations have important real consequences over fairly long short runs. The 1980–3 recession and depression confirm this obvious fact once again. Nor is it confined to downturns. Cyclical recoveries, stimulated or at least accommodated by monetary expansions, generate real as well as nominal gains. It is disingenuous, to say the least, for central bankers to pretend that their actions have no effects on real interest rates, unemployment rates, and other variables of concern to the populace.

The claim that monetary policies, since they necessarily rely on nominal instruments, can have only nominal effects trades on an analogy between altering monetary stocks and changing the unit of account. Switching the unit of account from dollars to half dollars would, everyone agrees, have no real consequence. Why shouldn't doubling the stock of dollars by other means be likewise neutral? The analogy is false. Actual central bank operations do not, while units changes do, change the public's stocks of all nominal assets in the same proportion. Actual operations effect exchanges of some assets for others, usually obligations to pay currency on demand for obligations to pay currency in future. Since future currency is not a perfect substitute for present currency, these exchanges are not neutral. They generally affect real interest rates, real exchange rates, saving, investment, and other real variables. Price changes affect private wealth and its distribution. Changes in inflation rates and in the distribution of price expectations necessarily alter real rates of return on currency and other assets with fixed nominal interest, and therefore influence the whole structure of asset prices and returns.

Some of these effects vanish in principle in long-run steady states, but others do not. Time will eliminate the inertia of price and wage adjustments. But there are no long-run steady states whose properties are independent of the paths by which they are reached. For example, depressions and high real interest rates irreversibly interrupt the accumulation of physical and human capital.

History does not support, in my opinion, the verdict that counter-cyclical monetary and fiscal policies failed. Today they are blamed for the inflation and stagflation of the 1970s, and for the greater amplitude of business fluctuations in that decade. Against this currently fashion-able interpretation of history I would make two points.

First, a somewhat longer historical perspective is desirable. Govern-ments accepted responsibility for macroeconomic stabilization after the Great Depression, and began practising counter-cyclical monetary and fiscal policy after World War II. Compared with previous periods of comparable length, the last thirty-five years and of course especially the period before 1970 look very good, both in their high trends of real growth and in the limited severity of cyclical fluctuations. Maybe there is no causal connection, but neither is there a prima-facie empirical case for abandoning the policies on account of recent disappointments.

Second, we should be careful not to draw the wrong lessons from the 1970s. After 1965 there were three bursts of inflation, each followed by recessions deliberately provoked by anti-inflationary mon-etary policies. The first acceleration of inflation, associated with the Vietnam War, was a classic demand-pull episode. President Johnson, contrary to the advice of his own economists, loaded his increased war spending on to an already fully employed economy without raising taxes, and the Federal Reserve was overaccommodative. The two bursts of inflation in the 1970s were associated with extraordinary supply and price shocks, the first in 1973–4 by the Yom Kippur War, the oil embargo, and OPEC's fourfold increase in the dollar price of oil, the second in 1978–80 by the Iranian revolution, restriction of Middle East oil supplies, and a further tripling of the OPEC price.

These events happened to occur in the late stages of cyclical recoveries, to which conscious stimulative and accommodative policies in the United States and other countries had contributed.

The lessons pundits and policy makers commonly draw from these experiences are that recoveries are dangerous, especially if they are promoted by policy. Accordingly central banks are most reluctant now to adopt expansionary policies even when their economies are as severely depressed as they are today. But these are wrong lessons if the frightening bursts of inflation were due not to recoveries *per se* or to policies that fostered them, but to the extraordinary exogenous shocks. Vietnam, OPEC, and the Ayatollah Khomeini were not the endogenous consequences of normal policy-assisted business cycle recoveries. Nor should governments and central banks be paralysed and our economies kept chronically stagnant for fear of similar recurrences.

I have argued that monetary authorities should not, indeed cannot, escape responsibility for real macroeconomic outcomes. To avoid misunderstanding, I stress that I certainly am not advocating that they disregard nominal outcomes, price levels and inflation rates. Professor Friedman told us in his Presidential Address some fifteen years ago that monetary policy could not *peg* real variables like unemployment and real interest rates and should not try. If 'peg' meant to seek a particular unchanging numerical value forever, I think no one wanted or wants to peg. Permanent pegging of unemployment is one thing: taking account of the state of the labour market is quite another. Trying to move unemployment down in some circumstances, up in others, is not pegging.

II. OBJECTIVES, TARGETS, AND OPERATING RULES

Central bankers cannot, I have just argued, hope for easy lives administering mechanical rules independent of actual and prospective economic conditions. In the end there is no substitute for stochastic dynamic models of the economy linking policy instruments to contemporaneous and future outcomes. Policy makers use at least implicitly their models of the way the world works—better to make them explicit. They can and should regularly consider and evaluate various feasible deviations from a 'current policies' reference path. New information about exogenous variables, stochastic disturbances, and structural equations is always flowing in. New observations tell whether current instrument settings are having their intended and expected effects.

Periodically policy makers must reconsider whether their policies are achieving to the degree possible the desired mixture of basic economic objectives.

Instrument settings and targets for intermediate variables are not locked in forever. It is important that their subordination to more fundamental objectives be generally understood. To simplify a complex decision process and to aid public understanding, the central bank could use a hierarchical structure. For example, the objective for several years ahead could be described as ranges of outcomes the bank seeks in paths of variables of basic concern: unemployment, real GNP, prices, capital formation. For a year ahead, an intermediate target like nominal GNP growth would indicate how the bank would allow price and productivity shocks to affect output and employment, while allowing complete freedom to offset velocity of money surprises with money supplies. For shorter periods, one month to two quarters ahead, the bank could indicate targets or operating rules relating to intermediate money stocks, bank reserves, and short-term interest rates. For each horizon, the target ranges or rules would remain constant for the period. The policy makers are thus deciding and announcing how, if at all, instruments will be changed in response to surprises that occur during the interval.

Obviously monetary and fiscal policies should be coordinated, consistent in their assumptions and their aims. It is likewise desirable to coordinate macroeconomic policies, at a minimum to exchange information about them, among the principal economic powers of the non-communist world. I do not try here to say how these difficult tasks are to be achieved.

The policy-makers' model will also tell how stochastic disturbances of various kinds, not directly and immediately observed, produce surprises in observed variables and displace the economy's path from its intended and expected course. Disturbances relevant to monetary policy take several forms: surprises in aggregate real demand— consumption, investment, net exports; portfolio shifts, especially those affecting demands for monetary base or bank reserves and the net demand for foreign-currency assets; supply-price shocks, for example unexpected movements in nominal wages or labour productivity or import prices.

The structure of the economy combines with the rules that guide the policy instruments themselves to determine how those shocks are translated into observable macroeconomic outcomes, that is, into deviations of variables from their intended paths. The observed variables that absorb the shocks include real national product, employment, interest rates, foreign-exchange rates, and monetary aggregates.

An essential function of the model is to estimate these linkages and how they vary across different operating targets and rules.

Different structures and operating rules distribute the shocks quite differently among the macroeconomic variables. For example, as is well known from William Poole's analysis,[1] pegging nominal interest rates converts real demand shocks into unexpected and presumably unwelcome deviations of output and/or price level, but prevents pure portfolio shifts from having such effects. Pegging unborrowed reserves, by comparison, makes real output and prices quite vulnerable to portfolio shifts (velocity shocks) but relatively immune to real demand disturbances, which will be mostly absorbed in interest and exchange rates. On these lines monetarism could be characterized by the conviction that real demand disturbances are much more likely than financial surprises. If so, an ultramonetarist rule—reducing reserves or money supplies in response to positive interest rate surprises— would logically be preferable to pegging those quantities, unless money demand is wholly insensitive to interest rates.

Of course the central bank need not peg anything for very long; our Federal Open Market Committee convenes monthly and knows how to telephone between meetings. As soon as the nature of a shock can be identified, the central bank will know how to alter any peg, whether for interest rates or for monetary quantities, to get back on track. Meanwhile the evidence may be ambiguous; nominal interest rates, net borrowed reserves and monetary aggregates may rise or fall either because of real demand shocks or because of purely financial shifts. During that ambiguous meanwhile the appropriate operating rule depends on the probabilities of the different kinds of shocks. A formula relating reserve supplies to nominal interest rates, taking account of those probabilities, is generally better than pegging either of the two variables. The relationship might be positive, 'leaning against the wind', or negative, 'pushing the wind back', as in the ultramonetarist case mentioned above. The interim rule should be the more accommodative the greater the probability that observed interest rate deviations reflect portfolio shifts rather than real demand shocks. But no such formula should be followed once the nature of the disturbance can be diagnosed.

Targeting of monetary aggregates amounts to a rule calling for restricting reserves when *M-1*, let us say, exceeds the intended path and expanding them when *M-1* falls short. Like interest rate deviations, *M-1* deviations sometimes reflect undesired strength or weakness in nominal income, and sometimes reflect innocuous shifts in money demand or in intermediation. In the first case they should be opposed, in the second case accommodated. It is hard to make a case for *M-1* constancy as the optimal interim rule. It is even harder to see why *M-1* targets should be maintained in the face of subsequent evidence on the nature of the disturbances. Interest rates carry much the same information sooner and more accurately. Indeed considerable evidence on the sources of disturbance becomes available as soon as or even sooner than reliable *M-1* statistics. Monthly series of personal income, retail sales, industrial production, unemployment, and price indexes anticipate quarterly reports of real and nominal GNP. The central bank is in a position to know quite promptly a great deal about purely financial sources of *M-1* surprises. Decisions on how much to accommodate should rely on these kinds of information. What usefulness monetary aggregates have comes from their informational content, not from their semantic monetary character. Central banks should ask their research staffs to devote more effort to obtaining and utilizing alternative and supplementary information.

Those of you who follow the American financial press are familiar, only too familiar, with the obligatory weekend news story about the latest, two-week old, *M* figures. The reporter feels a professional obligation to explain to the innocent reader who wanders to that page of his newspaper why these numbers are so important. Nowadays the standard formula—maybe it's the Fed's own publicists who supply it— is that *M-1* 'measures money readily available for spending'. We economists know that is nonsense. *M-1* does not begin to measure the funds that could conceivably be mobilized and readily spent for goods and services. An increase in *M-1* may indicate or presage an increase in spending, or the contrary.

A target for nominal GNP or *MV* (money stock times its income-velocity) makes much more sense over periods of several quarters, long enough for the central bank to detect and offset velocity surprises. This is what the Federal Reserve has been groping toward these last few years, explaining its departures from monetary aggregate targets as corrections for identifiable changes in the 'meaning' of the measures, that is, their relation to nominal income. A nominal GNP target implies for the duration of its tenure a one-for-one trade-off between price and quantity. An upward supply price shock will mean commensurately smaller real GNP growth. These terms of trade may not accord with national priorities; separate ranges for price and quantity would allow an extra degree of freedom. But a nominal GNP target range is simpler to understand. In any case it can be reset annually, taking into account price and wage developments, unemployment and excess capacity, estimates of sustainable real growth rates, and other circumstances.

Adherence in recent years to money growth targets, reinforced by the Fed's feeling that its credibility was at stake, has prevented the Federal Reserve from accommodating promptly and fully some changes in money demand which, on the Poolean principles sketched above, should have been accommodated as soon as the sources of the shocks were clear. I refer to increases in liquidity preference for precautionary motives bred by the depression, to shifts of lending transactions from open markets into financial intermediaries and thus into monetary aggregate statistics, and to deregulations that made deposits more attractive interest-bearing assets than before.

At the same time structural changes are making the system less automatically accommodative than it used to be. Deregulation allowing payment of market interest rates on deposits makes velocities less sensitive to interest rate levels than they were previously. In consequence, given the same monetarist policy rules, the economy is less vulnerable to real demand and price shocks and more vulnerable to purely financial shocks. A related result is greater volatility of interest rates and exchange rates. It is also likely that the probability of financial shocks to the demand for moneys and reserves has been increased. These consequences were probably unintended; the reforms were made largely for standard microeconomic reasons. But the macroeconomic effects should be explicitly considered in a review of the hierarchy of goals, targets, and rules. Because of the structural changes any operating rule that was optimal before is no longer optimal and should be replaced by a more accommodative rule.

III. MONETARY POLICIES AND RECOVERY FROM THE WORLD SLUMP

Not everybody thinks recovery is a good idea right now. Some believe it is premature because victory over inflation is not yet complete. They would continue the relentless process of disinflation, at the cost of high unemployment and prolonged stagnation, until core inflation rates are dependably reduced to zero. That could take several more years. This is a coherent and candid position, whatever one may think of the cost–benefit calculations implicit in it.

It is not, I think, the prevailing sentiment, anyway outside the United Kingdom. Most governments and central bankers, most business managers and financiers, and certainly most of the general public would welcome recovery. The question is what, if anything, macroeconomic policy, in particular monetary policy, should do to bring recovery about. Many who would welcome a spontaneous-combustion recovery—energized for example by a miraculous burst of business investment—are afraid of a recovery driven or even accommodated by monetary expansion. In their view a recovery powered by a spurt of velocity would be fine, while one generated by commensurate increase of money stocks would be dangerous.

The argument that recovery driven by monetary stimulus is more inflationary than recovery otherwise fuelled but of the same shape and strength is not one that I understand. Standard macroeconomic theory says that, as a strong first approximation, price and output paths depend on the interaction of aggregate spending flows, nominal GNP or MV, with the economy's capacity to produce goods and services. The division of demand impulses between prices and output, between wages and employment, depends on the ongoing inertial patterns of wage and price inflation, on the degree and composition of underutilized productive resources, and on the wage- and price-setting institutions of the society. The relevant demand variable is MV, regardless of its factorization between M and V. Prices do not depend directly on policy instruments, monetary and fiscal. Macro policy influences are indirect, channelled through the determinants enumerated, principally through aggregate demand. I am aware of some qualification of this standard doctrine, but they are of second order.

What opponents of monetary stimulus generally have in mind, to the extent that they are not really objecting to recovery *per se*, is an expectational response to monetary expansion. Perception of expansionary policy will, they allege, lead the public to expect inflation. Expecting it, businesses and workers will raise prices and wages at once, and no improvement in output and employment will occur. The expectations will be self-fulfilling. No such inflationary expectations would block a recovery which started and rolled on its own steam, without monetary accommodation. In the case of a spontaneous-combustion recovery unemployment and excess capacity would discipline wages and prices. In the case of money-fuelled recovery they would not. The scenario does not make sense. It certainly violates the canons of rational expectations, particularly if the standard model outlined above is correct. If the story had been true for monetary disinflation, similar self-fulfilling expectations would have unwound the inflation of 1978–80 quickly and costlessly.

A less extreme story focuses on the effects of inflationary expectations, generated by perceptions of expansionary monetary policy, on interest rates rather than on actual prices and wages. The 'financial markets' will expect inflation in future if not now. The resulting high long-term interest rates will hinder recovery.

One source of such psychology is the monetarist habit of defining monetary policy by growth rates of aggregates. This leads to undiscrimi-

nating extrapolation of currently announced targets for one quarter or
one year or of deviations from targets. In the United States Chairman
Volcker needs to convince his nervous financial constituency, now
relieved by his re-appointment, that the economy needs and can safely
absorb a change in the *level* of money stock, and that this by no
means signifies permanently higher rates of growth. The level change
is needed for three reasons. First, recovery itself requires larger money
stocks, to make up for the restrictions of the past three years and to
bring real interest rates down to levels consistent with recovery and
sustained prosperity. Second, disinflation itself has made monetary
assets more attractive. Third, as already noted, payment of market-
determined interest rates on deposits has increased the demand for
moneys. Events since the Fed adopted its more pragmatic stance in
1982 give cause for optimism. Money growth accelerated, but contrary
to repeated monetarist warnings interest rates, long as well as short,
moved down, not up.

Lenders' expectations and fears do not set rates unilaterally; there
are two sides to all markets, even bond markets. If long-term rates
were to rise on expectations of inflation held by borrowers and lenders
alike, real rates would not have risen and the high nominal rates
would not be a deterrent to current investment and recovery. More
likely borrowers and lenders differ in their expectations and calculations
of risk. Long rates high enough to compensate lenders for their fears
of inflation would be high real rates for borrowers, certainly high
relative to their current appraisals of earnings prospects. The effects
of these asymmetries on term structure are ambiguous. The predictable
result is that both sides shift to short maturities, or to long-term
contracts carrying variable short-term rates. In short markets central
bank supplies of base money, expanded by hypothesis, are decisive
for interest rates. Neither banks nor other lenders will sit on idle
cash.

Central banks should not be paralysed in fright of bond market
psychology. Let them educate the public by words, deeds, and
experience. World recovery, with real growth of production exceeding
long-run sustainable rates for several years, is essential to bring
unemployment down, to raise the utilization of industrial capacity, to
generate the saving and capital formation needed for long-run progress,
and not least to provide the Third World with the markets and export
earnings which alone can resolve their critical financial difficulties.
High real interest rates, especially in the United States, are a major
obstacle to world recovery. It is true that prospective structural budget
deficits are part of the problem, though cyclical deficits now and in
the fiscal years immediately ahead are not. But whatever contributions

future fiscal corrections can make, interest rates cannot be lowered without substantial help from monetary policy. To bring them down will require a period of above-normal monetary growth in the United States and in the other locomotive economies. If monetary policy is to be made on the assumption that it cannot expand real economic activity even after monetary restriction has depressed it for several years, we are doomed to a downward ratchet or to a mix of fiscal and monetary policies unfavourable to capital formation.

Everyone agrees that in this recovery it is important to avert inflation accelerations such as occurred at the ends of the two previous recoveries in the 1970s. I have argued above that it is unduly conservative to frame policy on the assumption that the extraordinary supply price shocks of those periods are bound to recur. There remains the serious question how much employment and general economic slack to maintain as insurance against another acceleration. In concluding this talk, I wish to address this issue briefly as a problem of policy making under uncertainty.

The serious question of macroeconomic policy today is how much unemployment and general economic slack to maintain as an insurance against another acceleration of inflation. According to a widely accepted model of inflation there exists at any time a minimum unemployment rate consistent with non-acceleration of inflation, sometimes called the natural rate of unemployment or more neutrally the non-accelerating-inflation-rate-of-unemployment, NAIRU. Here the unemployment rate is serving as a barometer of general slack, of the overall pressure of aggregate demand on productive capacity. Unfortunately no one knows what the NAIRU is. Current estimates for the United States vary from 8 per cent to 5 per cent. For policy makers this doubt is compounded by uncertainty about the translation of their instruments via aggregate demand into unemployment. The decision problem is to balance, given these uncertainties, the costs of unemployment and lost production against the risks and costs of accelerating inflation. Those costs and risks can be made commensurate by estimating the extra unemployment necessary to eliminate the bulge of accelerating inflation should it occur.

A conservative solution is to minimize expected unemployment subject to the constraint that the probability of trespassing the NAIRU threshold and accelerating inflation does not exceed some epsilon, perhaps even zero. Thus if there were any non-negligible probability that policies designed to bring expected unemployment down to, say, 9 per cent would generate acceleration—either because the NAIRU may be at least that high or because the policies might actually bring a lower unemployment rate—then conservative policy makers would try to keep unemployment higher than 9 per cent. This solution is the spirit of macroeconomic strategies prevailing today, and it is a recipe and rationale for stagnation.

An optimal solution would not apply so absolute a constraint. A marginal dose of stimulus is justified if, and only if, the expected gain from reduction in unemployment exceeds the expected loss due to inflation acceleration. The latter is the cost of the unemployment correction times the probability that such correction will be necessary, that is, the probability that the NAIRU threshold will have been crossed. If, for example, the correction costs two unemployment points for every point by which the NAIRU threshold was crossed, then the median estimate of the NAIRU is the proper target of policy. A higher relative correction cost implies a higher unemployment target, a lower appraisal of the cost a more ambitious unemployment goal.

Permanently high unemployment and excess capacity are costly insurance, and quite possibly self-defeating in the long run, as the same problems of reconciling price stability and prosperity recur at lower levels of output and employment. Incomes policies, for all their allocational inefficiencies, may be a much less costly mode of insurance. But to discuss that non-monetary alternative would take me beyond my subject and my time.

I have argued that the recoveries of the 1970s are not relevant models for the 1980s, in so far as they suggest that double-digit inflations are the inexorable outcome. Uncritically accepted, that reading of history could lock our economies in stagnation for another decade. A better analogy is to the recovery of 1961–5. In 1961 as in 1983 fears of inflation persuaded many influential people in and out of government that the United States must settle permanently for higher unemployment and slower growth. At that time too a pair of recessions back to back had at considerable social cost diminished inflation and inflationary psychology. Building on that foundation, expansionary fiscal and monetary policies—assisted by an informal incomes policy in the shape of wage–price guideposts—successfully generated recovery. The unemployment target of the day, 4 per cent, was achieved with negligible increase in inflation. There were even supply-side policies, notably the Investment Tax Credit, designed to foster investment and long-run growth. Events belied and dissipated the initial pessimism, and the stock market soared.

NOTE

1. *See* 'Optimal Choice of Monetary Policy Instruments in a Simple Stochastic Macro Model'. *Quarterly Journal of Economics*. Vol. 84, No. 2, May 1970, pp. 197–256.

23 Financial Innovation and Deregulation in Perspective*

Deregulation of financial industries is popular these days for the same reasons that recommend it elsewhere—the perceived gains in microeconomic efficiency from unfettered competition. However, banks and other depository institutions are not just like other industries. They supply the exchange media used in the bulk of transactions in the economy. They are the institutions through which central bank operations of monetary control are transmitted to the economy at large. We need to consider how much regulation, and what kind of regulation, is needed to protect and foster the payments system and to maintain the effectiveness of monetary control.

These questions arise at a time when technological and institutional innovations are changing costs, opportunities, and competitive relations in financial industries. Some of the regulations of the past are being abandoned simply because they are no longer enforceable, or because they stand in the way of new opportunities of obvious merit.

The important trends are these:

1. Transactions, whether for financial assets or for commodities, are less and less expensive of time and resources. Electronic payments networks are making possible instantaneous payments via computer from one account to another.
2. The issuance of obligations payable on demand and transferable to third parties by check or wire is not confined to government and commercial banks and other depository institutions regulated by government.
3. Legal ceilings on interest rates payable on deposits are vanishing.
4. Financial supermarkets and conglomerates are blurring or erasing

*May 1985, Keynote Paper, Second International Conference, Institute for Monetary and Economic Studies, Bank of Japan, Tokyo. Published in Bank of Japan *Monetary and Economic Studies*, September 1985, vol. 3, no. 2, pp. 19–29.

distinctions between banks, other depositories, mutual funds, brokers, insurance companies, investment bankers, securities dealers, and other financial agencies.

THE MIRAGE OF PRIVATE MONEY

Contemporary literature applying general free market principles to monetary theory suggests that competitive private enterprise could supply the economy's 'money'. I must say that I was not surprised by this development. I had wondered about the marriage of monetarism and 'Invisible Hand' doctrine, and figured that some day the exception which assigns government the responsibility to limit the supply of money would be challenged. I doubt that my fellow keynoter, Milton Friedman, is any happier about the challenge than I am.

Currency is the physical embodiment of the monetary unit of account defined by the sovereign. Currency is the sure and perfectly liquid store of value in units of account. It is legal tender, for the payment of taxes and for the discharge of private obligations enforceable in courts of law for payments in units of account. Consequently it is generally acceptable in payments.

I find it difficult to imagine a system in which there is no governmentally issued store of value in the unit of account. Some discussions of 'private money' in the literature seem to suggest that the government can define the 'dollar' as the unit of account without printing and issuing any dollars. Private agents could issue promise to pay dollars, and these would circulate. But what are they promising to pay? Of course, if the government sanctified the issues of a particular bank or private firm or individual by agreeing to accept them in payment of taxes and by granting them legal tender status, those issues would be currency. The sovereign would be delegating its fiat to the favoured private institution. History suggests that such an institution would eventually be nationalized and made politically responsible. The idea of a disembodied fiat unit of account, with embodiments of it freely and competitively supplied by private agents, seems to me to be a fairy tale.

Private monetary issue makes more sense for commodity money. The government can define a dollar in terms of gold or silver, or plywood or wheat, or some combination of goods. Experience suggests that societies will find it more convenient to handle transactions with promises to pay the *numéraire* commodity than to circulate the commodity itself. Whose promises? Just those of competing private agents? Of unregulated private agents? Once again, the government cannot escape the question what IOUs it will accept from citizens in payment of taxes and other obligations, or avoid deciding whose IOUs will be regarded as discharging private debts. Neither can the government take a *laissez faire* attitude toward the ability of private issuers of such IOUs to redeem their promises, especially if the government gives them the cachets of acceptability and legal tender.

Free market enthusiasts may say that the judgements of private agents will price, that is, discount, issuers' IOUs in proper relationship to their quality and their backing. Rational market pricing may not be feasible, even conceptually, because self-fulfilling prophecies are involved. Reserve ratios that suffice when there is 'confidence' will not avail when there is not. In any case, a payments system, like any other communications network, derives efficiency from universality, standardization, and predictability. It is not efficient to have competing currencies with varying rates of exchange one for another.

Some writers have envisaged commodity moneys without stocks of the commodities held to back the currencies, whether private or governmental. They appeal to analogy of the unit of account to a unit of measurement: as a yard is a length of a certain stick at the Bureau of Standards, so the dollar used to be by definition a certain weight of gold or silver and could be similarly defined in commodities again. It is not a good analogy. Those who promise to pay on demand 'dollars' so defined must have stocks on hand to enable them to fulfil their promises. That is the only way to assure the defined equivalence.

I conclude that there must be store-of-value embodiments of a monetary unit of account, and that basically these will be and should be designated and supplied by the central government. Once this is done, private initiatives will generate all kinds of promises to pay basic currency, on demand and at future dates. The question is how much and how those initiatives should be regulated by the state. I have an uneasy suspicion that in the general enthusiasm for deregulation we are in danger of re-establishing the conditions and problems which generated financial regulations in the first place.

BANK DEPOSITS AS INSIDE MONEY

Paper currency and coin are not very convenient media of exchange, except for small items of consumption, vending machines, and certain transactions among total strangers. Where they are useful in large payments, it is for discreditable reasons, tax avoidance or crime. Currency is too bulky for large legitimate transactions, awkward because it comes only in a few denominations, vulnerable to loss or theft, unsuitable for remittance by mail. It is in fact used for a very small fraction of transactions weighted by value. This is true whether currency and coin are fiat money or governmental promises to pay on demand commodities in which the monetary unit is defined.

Some writers complain of the government's monopoly in currency supply. Whatever inefficiencies there may be in payments systems, they surely would be mitigated very little by allowing private issue of currency and coin. Maybe some banks would put out notes in more, and more convenient, denominations than the government does. Against that gain would be the difficulty of handling and sorting different kinds of notes and coins.

Demand deposits, bank's promises to pay currency on demand or on order to third parties are more convenient than currency itself. Historically commercial banks exploited this opportunity to obtain funds to meet borrowers' demands for commercial loans. Their incentive was the interest gap between deposits, which were competing with zero-interest currency, and loans. Many of the deposits come from the same businesses to whom the banks on occasion lend. Commercial banks serve as intermediaries for businesses with temporary surpluses, seasonal or cyclical, to lend to businesses with temporary deficits. The lending depositors and borrowers change roles frequently. Commercial banks administer this circulation of deposits and credit. In addition, they transfer saving from household depositors to the business and public sectors.

Obtaining loanable funds via demand deposits, banks borrow very short to lend longer, and borrow liquid to lend illiquid. The risks in such intermediation do not fall solely on the managers and shareholders of the banks; their leverage is immense. Even if bank managers act with normal perspicacity in the interests of their stockholders, even if all temptations of personal gain are resisted, sheer chance will bring some failures—insolvency because of borrowers' defaults or other capital losses on assets, or inability to meet withdrawals of deposits even though the bank would be solvent if assets' present values could be immediately realized. The probability is multiplied by the essential instability of depositor confidence. News of withdrawals triggers more withdrawals, *sauve qui peut*, at the same bank, or by contagion at others. For these reasons the banking business has not been left to free market competition but has been significantly regulated:

1. Minimum reserves of currency or other liquid assets held against deposits have been legally specified. The original purpose was to protect depositors, in particular to prevent imprudent erosion of reserve ratios by competition among banks. Paradoxically, once

reserves are required, they are not available to be paid out on depositors' demand. Required reserves have turned into an instrument of central bank monetary control.

2. The function of protecting banks and depositors against illiquidity falls to the central bank as 'lender of last resort'. By lending $7 billion to one troubled bank, Continental Illinois, the Federal Reserve showed how seriously it takes this responsibility. To put this number in perspective, recall that normal lending by the Fed to the whole banking system rarely exceeds $1 billion. Thus the 'lender of last resort' function can seriously distort the customary use of central bank instruments for purposes of monetary control. In the instance cited, the Fed offset its extra lending by open market sales of similar magnitude.

3. Regulations govern the capitalizations, accounting, asset portfolios, types of liabilities, deposit interest rates, ownership, and other business activities and interests of banking firms. They are enforced by periodic reports, inspections, and audits. New firms can enter the industry only with government charters. It is mainly these regulations that critics advocate relaxing or repealing in the name of competition and efficiency.

4. Governmental deposit insurance has been by far the most effective measure to prevent bank failures. In the US it virtually eliminated the unstable run, the contagious panic. However, it has not been altogether successful, especially during recent years of heightened competition, international in scope, among banks and other financial enterprises. These years were also characterized by severe gyrations of economic activity, prices, interest rates, and foreign-exchange rates. The United States authorities found it necessary to extend the insurance guarantees to all deposits of large banks, even though the statutory protection covered only the first $100,000 of each account.

Deposit insurance, like other regulations, has been criticized on grounds of efficiency. It diminishes the incentives of the insured institutions themselves to assess and limit risks, throwing more of a burden on bureaucratic surveillance by regulators, reinforced by the insurance agency itself. It also diminishes whatever incentive depositors themselves might have for assessing the riskiness of banks where they might deposit funds. Deposit insurance, moreover, is a massive extension and delegation of the government's monetary fiat—a blank cheque, so to speak, which might be an enormous obligation in certain contingencies. The federal deposit insurance agencies have reserves less than 1 per cent of the deposits they have guaranteed. Any big bank failure would wipe them out and require Congress to appropriate additional funds.

It *is* important to provide economic agents a convenient substitute for currency, usable in payments and riskless as a store of value in the unit of account. It *is* important to protect the society's payments system from interruptions and breakdowns due to bank failures. The problem is that this provision and this protection cannot be accomplished by unregulated competition for checkable demand deposits and loans. Bank deposits are *inside* money, which has the macroeconomic advantage that no net national saving is tied up in its accumulation. However, the accident of history that made the principal medium of exchange inside money also made it vulnerable to events that impair the value and liquidity of the assets backing the money. Striking a balance between competitive efficiency and the protection of depositors seems to be increasingly difficult and costly. Perhaps some other ways of meeting the problem deserve consideration.

DEPOSITED CURRENCY

Perhaps we need means of payment like currency but without its disadvantages. Deposited currency—100 per cent-reserve deposits— payable in notes or coin on demand, transferable by order to third parties, secure against loss or theft, would be a perfect store of value in the unit of account. One way to provide it would be to allow individuals to hold deposit accounts in the central bank, or in branches of it established for the purpose and perhaps located in post offices. Or any bank or depository institution entitled to hold deposits in the central bank could offer deposited-currency accounts to customers. One question, of course, would be how to pay the costs of managing such accounts. The government could subsidize them, in the case of private retailing, by paying some interest on the 100 per cent reserves. The argument would be that the payments system is a public good which taxpayers at large should provide. Or user charges could be levied; after all, individuals bear most of the costs of the use of ordinary currency in transactions and can afford to pay something for the greater convenience of checkable deposits.

It might be argued that no interest should be paid on these deposits, just as none is paid on ordinary currency. Banks and other depositories could compete for these deposits in the terms of costs and services. On the other hand, the government could pay the banks a low interest rate, indexed perhaps to the Treasury bill rate. The banks could then compete for the business in interest payable to depositors as well as in service and service charges. Since interest-bearing deposits would be more popular, the Treasury might save taxpayers money by making them possible. In any case, no institution would be licensed to retail currency in deposit form without meeting certain standards of service and convenience, and without participation in a common national clearing network.

BANKS AND SEGREGATED FUNDS

Present deposit insurance in the US protects not only means-of-payment deposits but all other deposits in eligible institutions, including non-checkable savings accounts and time deposits. Similar obligations of mutual funds and other debtors not covered by deposit insurance are not guaranteed. It is not clear why all kinds of liabilities of covered institutions should be insured, except that the assets are so commingled that withdrawals of non-insured deposit liabilities would imperil the insured deposits. That indeed is why the insurance guarantee was *de facto* extended beyond the statutory limit.

This problem could be avoided by segregating and earmarking assets corresponding to particular classes of liabilities, permitting a depositor in effect to purchase a fund which could not be impaired by difficulties elsewhere in the institution's balance sheet. In this way, a bank would become more like a company offering a variety of mutual funds, just as those companies—which are not insured—are becoming more like banks. The 100 per cent reserve deposit proposed above would be one such fund, but there could be others. For example, many households of modest means and little financial sophistication want savings accounts that are safe stores of value in the unit of account. These can be provided in various maturities without risk by a fund invested in Treasury securities. They can be provided as demand obligations either by letting their redemption value fluctuate with net asset value or by crediting a floating interest rate to a fixed value. These options need not displace, but could supplement, standard insured savings deposits and time certificates. The total amount, wherever deposited, insured to a particular person (identified by Social Security or tax identification number) would be strictly limited to the $100,000 in current legislation.

Perhaps an even more important addition to the menu of assets, especially for small and unsophisticated savers, would be savings accounts or certificates indexed to cost of living. The index should be purged of terms-of-trade effects and indirect taxes, contingencies against which the nation as a whole cannot be insured. This reform should apply to all public or publicly sanctioned indexations. To enable financial intermediaries to offer indexed liabilities in safe, convenient and flexible form, the government would have to issue some indexed securities.

The advantage of the 'segregated funds' approach is to limit the scope of intermediaries' liabilities that need to be protected by deposit insurance, and by the same token the scope of intermediaries' assets that need to be continuously scrutinized and regulated. If there were a clear and clean line between the two kinds of intermediary activity, *caveat emptor* could apply to the uninsured and less regulated business, where banks and depository institutions would be vigorously competing with each other and with other market participants. If some of them fail from time to time in the process, that would not impair the value or even the liquidity of the segregated funds they were administering. We could expect the businesses of managing liabilities, certificates of deposit and the like, and of seeking profitable lending opportunities to continue to occupy the managerial and entrepreneurial skills of banks and other financial firms. But we would not have to undergo a monetary crisis every time big depositors became suspicious of a large bank, or save either those depositors or the bank from the consequences of mistakes or misfortunes.

NEW TRANSACTIONS TECHNOLOGY AND MONETARY POLICY

Withdrawals and payments to third parties can easily be made from any demand account, and there is no reason to restrict this convenience. Some demand accounts will be 'deposited currency' or other segregated funds. Some will not be. Of these, some will be insured and others not. Some will have fixed unit-of-account values; others will not. In the brave new world of electronic payments, all can be linked in a computerized payments network.

On the initiative of the payer, payments will be made at time of purchase or settlement or scheduled to be executed at a designated future time. They will be made from stations connected to banks and to the central bank, located at banks themselves but also in stores, offices, and homes. I suppose plastic cards will be used, as at interactive teller stations today. When the payment is executed, the accounts of payer and payee at their banks or other intermediaries will be debited and credited, and so will their banks' accounts at the central bank. There will be no float, either for depositors or for banks, and no opportunities for adventurous cheque-kiting cash management as recently practised by E. F. Hutton. This is a greatly accelerated version of the European giro system, a more efficient flow of information than the cheque system.

In this payments system, it will be natural and almost inevitable that banks allow overdrafts up to established credit lines like those now defined by bank credit cards. Extensive use of overdrafts may be the principal monetary innovation of the new system for the United States. A transaction will be completed if and only if it would not result in an overdrawn balance beyond the pre-arranged limit. Likewise the central bank, on whose computerized 'books' the clearings between banks and other institutions takes place, would need some rules about overdrafts.

The likely extensive use of overdrafts would make it necessary to revise the present base for calculation of bank reserve requirements. Evidently it will not be practical to stick solely to reserve requirements against liabilities. If 'deposited currency' accounts are set up, there would be of course 100 per cent reserve requirements against them. But other types of deposits will also be transferable through the network, and overdrafts will be allowed in those accounts. I propose gearing reserve requirements to the corresponding bank assets, including overdraft advances. Assets covered by capital liabilities would be exempt from required reserves, as would be assets covered by liabilities which are neither insured nor eligible for transfer through the network. Any financial institution or firm which wants to use the network for transfer of ownership of its liabilities or equities would have to become a 'bank' subject to reserve tests and associated regulations.

The central bank will still have effective monetary control in the new system. In the United States, and in many other monetary systems, the fulcrum of monetary control is the reserve test. Monetary control via reserve tests is effective if and only if the government, via the central bank, monopolizes and controls the aggregate supply of eligible reserve assets, the monetary base. This the central bank does by open market operations and by setting the rates and other terms on which it will lend reserves to the banks. I am assuming also, of course, that the 'banks' subject to reserve tests are in aggregate weighty enough participants in financial and capital markets so that central bank operations affect the quantities, prices, and interest rates determined in those markets.

So far as I can see, nothing in the system of the future that I have sketched vitiates the conditions for effective control via reserve tests. Monetary aggregates will not be very interesting statistics, for the same reasons that deposits will not be entirely suitable as the base for reserve requirements. They will not be useful targets either. But variation of the Fed's instruments, open market operations and discount rates, will still affect the monetary base and will be transmitted to macroeconomic variables of importance.

INTEREST-BEARING MONEY

Payment of market-determined interest rates on deposits, as I have argued elsewhere,[1] diminishes the sensitivity of demand for money to the level of nominal market rates. In old-fashioned textbook terms, it makes the '*LM*' curve steeper. If the rates the central bank charges on its loans and pays on reserves deposited with it are also indexed to market rates, the 'money multiplier' is also made less sensitive to interest rates. Consequently, variations of central bank instruments will have bigger effects on national income than in previous regimes where these nominal interest rates are fixed by legislation or administrative decision. So will shocks in the demands for deposits by the public and for reserves by banks. I think, moreover, that those demands will be more variable in the new regime; when there is little to gain from sharp-pencil cash management, people will accept without prompt correction large swings in their cash balances.

The lesson I draw for the conduct of monetary policy is that it should be more accommodative in the new regime; that is, the supply of reserves should be more responsive to interest rates. Thus accommodation by the central bank would replace the accommodation now built in to the system by the control of deposit interest rates and of rates on reserves and central bank lending. This replacement is appropriate for macroeconomic reasons, while the abandonment of the interest rate controls is justified on grounds of microeconomic efficiency.

NOTE

1. 'Financial structure and monetary rules', *Kredit und Kapital*, 1983, vol. 16, pp. 155–71.

24 Monetarism: An Ebbing Tide?*

Monetarism became influential doctrine in the late 1960s and the 1970s. Economists, financial pundits, central bankers and legislators flocked to its banner, disillusioned with the eclectic synthesis of Keynesian and neoclassical economics that had become mainstream macroeconomics after World War II. Inflation displaced unemployment as the salient economic evil. Keynesian theories and policies were blamed, justifiably or not, for the Great Stagflation. Monetarism offered the way out. Thus were the tables turned. The Keynesian revolution of the 1930s succeeded because the orthodoxy of the day, including the essentials of monetarism without the label, appeared to offer neither explanation nor remedy for the mass unemployment of the Great Depression.

Now that inflation has subsided and unemployment has soared in most economically advanced democracies, will there be another switch? What are the legacies of monetarism to doctrine and to policy in this decade and the next? It is too soon to know the answers, but the questions provide a background for a review of the present status of monetarism.

Monetarism has several meanings, variously emphasized by its adherents.

THE ALTERNATIVE TO 'FISCALISM'

The word 'monetarism' was coined as antinomy to 'fiscalism' in the 1960s. Professor Milton Friedman had long been fighting endemic scepticism of the efficacy of monetary policies, inherited from the Depression and perpetuated by some Keynesians. Particularly in Britain, the view that money and financial markets are a self-contained

---

*April 1985, *Economist*, London, 27 April, pp. 23–6.

sideshow to the main macroeconomic performance held sway for much too long. Mainstream American Keynesians did not dispute Friedman's contention that 'money matters'. But we also advocated and practised fiscal management of aggregate demand, and resented the popular monetarism/fiscalism dichotomy. We opposed Professor Friedman's stronger contention, that money is all that matters in the sense that fiscal policy has insignificant effects on such macroeconomic outcomes as real GNP, employment and prices.

Like Keynes himself, we believed that generally both policies work. The mix of monetary and fiscal measures is open to choice, and some mixes are better than others. The non-monetarist theory of policy mix is very relevant today; the United States has stumbled into a bizarre and extreme mix, hazardous to its health and to that of the world economy.

To talk about the efficacies of the monetary and fiscal instruments and their proper mixture in demand management presupposes, of course, that they are technically and politically separable. If, for lack of markets for non-monetary government debt or of political will to pursue an independent monetary policy, the central bank automatically finances government deficits, monetary and fiscal policy are essentially one. The debate on the efficacy of fiscal measures concerned pure fiscal policies, with budget deficits not monetized by the central bank.

In theory, this debate turned on the question of whether fiscal stimulus can systematically raise the velocity of money. We Keynesians said, Yes, by raising interest rates and inducing businesses and households to manage their transactions with smaller holdings of cash. Both theory and evidence supported this view, and monetarists shifted ground to the more basic propositions reviewed below.

The patent success of fiscal stimulus in promoting recovery in the United States in 1983–4 (Figure 24.1) reinforces the Keynesian side of this old debate, as does the stagnation of European economies under restrictive fiscal policies reminiscent of the early 1930s. Of course Mr Reagan's deficits, if not corrected, bode serious trouble ten or twenty years hence. The same logic that says deficits absorb saving and stimulate spending when it is needed to pull the economy out of recession says that they crowd out productive domestic and foreign investment when saving and output are limited by productive capacity. Mainstream Keynesians say that the United States could have had—should have had—the same recovery with a different policy mix, tighter budget and easier money, yielding lower interest rates and a less expensive dollar.

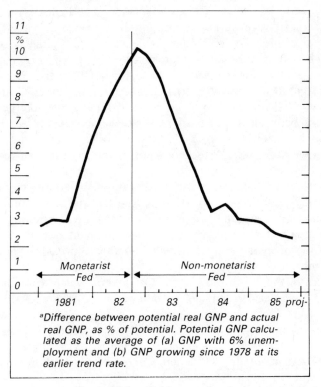

ªDifference between potential real GNP and actual
real GNP, as % of potential. Potential GNP calculated as the average of (a) GNP with 6% unemployment and (b) GNP growing since 1978 at its
earlier trend rate.

Figure 24.1: Taking up the slack

MONETARY TARGETS

During the 1970s monetarists persuaded most major central banks to gear their operations to announced targets for one or more intermediate monetary aggregates. The word 'intermediate' denotes a variable which the authorities can control only indirectly and imperfectly, via the effects of their market interventions on the behaviour of banks and the general public. At the same time, the economic and social importance of an intermediate target is not intrinsic but is derived entirely from its indicative or causal relation to measures of macroeconomic performance that really matter: production, employment, and prices.

Adoption of intermediate monetary targets downgraded central banks' attention to interest rates, 'credit conditions', international reserves, exchange rates, and the many other kinds of financial and economic information to which central banks formerly responded with discretion and imprecision.

In the United States, Congress requires the Federal Reserve to report targets twice a year to committees in both houses. The Fed obliges with three Ms for money, one L for liquidity, and one D for total debts. Its mechanics of monetary control have also changed in response to monetarist pressure. In October, 1979, the Fed stopped targeting interest rates altogether, abandoning the practice of setting a narrow band for the overnight 'Federal Funds' rate for the five or six weeks between meetings of its open market committee. Instead, the traders at its New York desk were to be instructed to supply certain quantities of bank reserves, letting interest rates move as they will.

Money targets and quantitative operating procedures prevent the central bank from accommodating unexpected and unwelcome shocks in demand for goods and services. To this virtue corresponds a vice. When the same targets and rules prevent accommodation of unexpected shocks to monetary velocity, they generate unwelcome booms or recessions.

Generally the central bank cannot discern which kind of shock, demand for goods or demand for money, is the source of upward or downward pressure on interest rates. Then its best bet is a compromise between (a) sticking to a money stock target and (b) holding to the interest rate that target was expected to imply. In premonetarist days, the Fed's vague policy of 'leaning against the wind' was a rough compromise.

In principle, the degree of partial accommodation in response to an interest rate surprise should be smaller the greater the likelihood it came from a shock to goods demand rather than to money demand. One article of monetarist faith is that goods-demand shocks are much more likely than money-demand shocks. Non-monetarists do not assert the opposite, but observed instabilities in monetary velocities (see Figure 24.2, 24.3) vindicate their scepticism of the monetarist claim.

Money-demand shocks have been particularly disturbing recently, as the pace of technological, institutional, and regulatory change in fnancial industries has quickened. The Fed has had to redefine its aggregates repeatedly and re-interpret its targets accordingly. Even so, 1982 was a disastrous year. Velocity not only fell far short of its expected growth trend; it actually declined (Figure 24.2). The money stock targets supported much less nominal GNP than the Fed had expected (Figure 24.1). In desperation the Fed suspended its monetary growth targets, allowed a surge of money creation that lowered interest rates three points, turned the American economy around, and saved the world from financial disaster. The strict monetarist regime of October 1979 had lasted just three years (Figure 24.1).

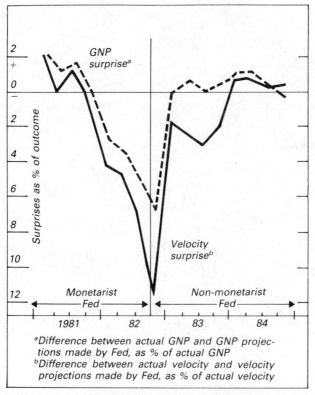

*Figure 24.2: Less surprising
(GNP and velocity surprises)*

The rationale for targeting intermediate monetary aggregates never was convincing. The most popular aggregate, *M-1*, gains semantic appeal as 'transactions money', immediately usable to buy goods and services. But that has never meant that fixing its total supply is either necessary or sufficient to control aggregate spending. Its speed of turnover is quite volatile. Near-monies quickly and easily convertible into *M-1* cash are abundant, and the ingenuity of financial entrepreneurs armed with modern technologies is endless. A different rationale for *M-1* and the other *M*s is that they give advance information on GNP and other truly important variables. Yet any expert forecaster knows better leading indicators.

None the less, recent reforms in the United States have sought to identify *M* more closely with 'transactions money', and to enhance the Fed's technical capacity to control *M-1* so defined (by imposing uniform contemporaneous reserve requirements on all depository institutions and only on those liabilities transferable by cheque or wire on demand).

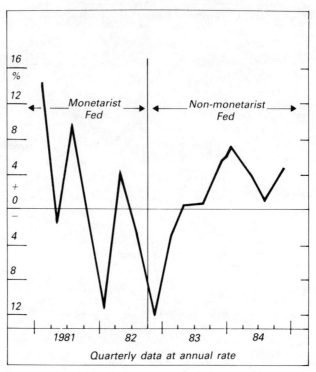

Source: Federal Reserve.

Figure 24.3: Less variable now: (volatility of velocity, % change M−1 velocity)

The irony is that these technical changes are occurring just when their purpose, closer control of *M-1*, is losing favour both at the Fed and outside.

There are two ways to go. One is to move closer to instruments under the direct control of a central bank—central bank liabilities, base money, or bank reserves. This direction appears to be the latest preference of Mr Friedman and other monetarists. The other is to target the growth of nominal income, or of output and prices in some other combination, making explicit the objectives that logically guide the settings of intermediate targets anyway. Both approaches could be used: macroeconomic goals for a year or two ahead and instrument targets consistent with those goals for one to three months. The intermediate targets, neither fish nor fowl, are at best redundant and at worst destructive.

PRIORITY FOR ANTI-INFLATION GOALS

Price surges accompanying the second oil shock in 1979–80 provoked major governments and central banks to launch in concert the single-minded anti-inflation crusades that dominated the world economic scene of the early 1980s. The crusades certainly succeeded in breaking the back of inflation, but at great costs in production, employment, and investment, costs that have scarcely abated in most of the OECD outside North America. The United States broke ranks from the anti-inflation war in October, 1982, in effect declaring victory even though the inflation rate remained above 4 per cent. Perhaps the Fed chairman, Mr Paul Volcker, heeded the wise counsel of the late Senator George Atken on the war in Vietnam: declare victory and get out.

The recessions of 1980–2 were a blow to the 'credible threat' strategies of modern monetarists. Their idea was that a determined policy of monetary restriction, accompanied by warnings that the authorities would not relent even to save jobs and businesses, would induce faster and less painful wage and price disinflation than previous bouts of tight money. This time, they alleged, workers and businesses would not wait for the government to reflate. Experience under Mrs Thatcher and Mr Volcker did not confirm these hopes.

ENDING COUNTER-CYCLICAL MANAGEMENT

The 1979 commitment to disinflation exemplifies the monetarist approach to policy. Active variation of fiscal and monetary instruments in hope of taming the business cycle is taboo. Derided as 'fine tuning' and blamed for the ills of the 1970s, counter-cyclical demand management is replaced by commitments to hold those instruments steady, in faith that the economy will then be stable too. Rules replace the discretion of policy makers—and blind rules at that, not to be altered in response to new information or second thoughts every week, every committee meeting, or every legislative session.

Professor Friedman always questioned the wisdom, motivation and backbone of central bankers and politicians, and doubted that even the wisest, best-intentioned and firmest of them could outguess and improve nature. Better to rely, he said, on the capacity of the economy to adjust to shocks and to adapt to predictably steady policies. In his famous Presidential Address to the American Economic Association in 1967, he warned against dedicating monetary policy to any unemployment target. The target might be too low, and then the result would be spiralling inflation. If not—well, the economy will gravitate to its own 'natural rate' of unemployment without the help of the central bank or the government budget.

Although Mr Friedman advised against demand management, his theory did not completely shut the door. Stimulative measures when unemployment was surely unnaturally high could hasten the economy's return to the natural rate without adding to inflation.

Newer monetarists, more royalist than the king, did slam the door. In their theories, buttressed by 'rational expectations' logic, monetary policies can never alter unemployment—except temporarily when the central bank's moves surprise and confuse the public. Once any monetary policy is generally understood and expected, it will have no real effects at all; it will just be absorbed in prices.

These ideas and prescriptions are now orthodox over most of Western Europe. The architects of policy probably do not read Professors Lucas, Sargent, Barro and other apostles of the new classical macroeconomics; these new-monetarists are not popular evangelists like Mr Friedman. But the spirit of their ideas is in the air. Policies are to be governed by rules: balance the budget, and fix money growth at a non-inflationary number; disregard the state of the economy, especially the unemployment rate.

Prime ministers and central bankers wait and watch for their economies to adjust, recover and prosper. They have been waiting and watching for half a decade already, and their constituents have been remarkably patient. Yet every month of high unemployment sharpens the challenge to the new orthodoxy.

In the United States, in contrast, new monetarist doctrines and policies, fashionable though they are in academic economics, have lost in practical influence. Since October, 1982, the Fed's policy has been orientated to macroeconomic performance, responsive to the actual and projected state of the economy, designed to guide the economy to a 'soft landing' at the natural rate of unemployment (Figure 24.4). The Fed has been willing to encourage and finance unemployment-reducing cyclical growth so long as it is not too exuberant and inflation is not increasing. Yes, they have been 'fine tuning'.

The Fed's report to congress of 20 February 1985, confirms this policy. As much attention is paid to velocity as to money supplies. Although the upper limit of the *M-1* target range for 1985 is one percentage point lower than for 1984, the Fed states clearly its intention to offset velocity surprises by adjustments of money stocks within their target ranges and, one may infer, outside them if necessary.

In effect the Fed is targeting 'velocity-adjusted' monetary aggregates. That amounts to targeting nominal GNP. Consequently the regular summary of the GNP, price, and unemployment 'projections' of the

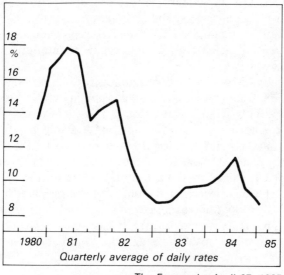

The Economist April 27, 1985

Figure 24.4: After the change: federal funds rate

seven Federal Reserve governors and the 12 Federal Reserve Bank presidents assume major importance. These projections, for the fourth quarter of 1985, follow the 'soft landing' recovery track. Their reported 'central tendency' is a 7.5–8 per cent growth in dollar GNP from the final quarter of 1984; a modest 3.5–4 per cent inflation rate; a 3.5–4 per cent growth of real GNP, and, consistent with that, an unemployment rate of 7 per cent or just below. These 'projections' may well be the true targets of Fed policy. In summary, Mr Volcker has announced that the Fed will continue to support recovery, but more cautiously than in the past two years.

The Fed has pursued this course in an economy receiving massive fiscal stimulus, no less effective in creating demand because it was labelled 'supply-side'. Consequently the Fed, in order to stay near its desired path, has had to brake the economy much more and keep interest rates and the exchange value of the dollar much higher than if moderate pre-Reagan fiscal policies had remained in effect. On this crucial issue—the fiscal/monetary policy mix and its correction— monetarisms new or old are no help.

Monetarism, in its several meanings and messages, has greatly influenced economic thought and government policy over the past twenty years. Much of its influence is durable. Central banks' duty to hold in check the inflationary institutions and proclivities of their societies is widely understood and accepted. But this duty allows large scope for choice among alternative operating procedures, targets and short-term goals. It definitely does not exclude counter-cyclical demand management.

Mechanical monetarism, stressing targets for intermediate monetary aggregates, is waning in professional opinion and in central-bank practice, especially in the United States. History since 1979 has not been kind to the monetarist prescriptions of stable policies blind to actual events and new information. In the United States the Fed appears to have subordinated monetary targets and rules, and oriented its month-to-month decisions to macroeconomic performance. While the Fed has not become soft on inflation, it seems prepared to engineer further recovery so long as prices do not threaten to accelerate. European governments and central banks remain wedded to non-interventionism. The resulting stagnation must be counted as an unhappy legacy of monetarism.

25 Inflation, Interest Rates, and Stock Values*

These days 'inflation' is the catch-all scapegoat for all economic evils—energy crisis, the troubles of Con Ed, world food shortage, even recession and unemployment. It is also popularly blamed for high interest rates and for the sag in equity prices.

Is it in fact true that interest rates have been pulled up to double digits primarily by double-digit inflation? Or is a substantial part of the rise in interest rates due to Federal Reserve policy? Has Arthur Burns tightened credit relative to realistic opportunities to invest in homes, plant and equipment, and inventories?

In the main I believe the answer can be found in restrictive monetary policy. Indeed, I shall argue that the behaviour of the stock market this year confirms that the recent run-up of interest rates is not just inflationary froth but has real substance.

The performance of the securities market clearly is evidence that the financial climate for capital investment in the United States has deteriorated. Since 1966 aggregate market valuations of corporate securities (bonds and stocks) have not kept up with the replacement cost of corporate inventories and fixed capital. Figure 25.1 shows for the years 1951–73 the ratio of the securities market valuation of US non-financial corporations to the replacement cost of their tangible capital. A high value of this ratio means that the market thinks well of the earnings capacity of the capital assets and/or applies a low discount factor to future earnings. A low value means that the market is pessimistic about future profits and/or discounts them heavily.

During the 1950s and early 1960s this ratio was generally increasing. For corporations this meant that funds for expansion and investment were easy to come by, and also that managements were generally doing their shareowners a favour by re-investing profits. The decline in the ratio since 1966 indicates a worsening of the financial climate

---

*July 1974, *Morgan Guaranty Survey*, New York, pp. 4–7.

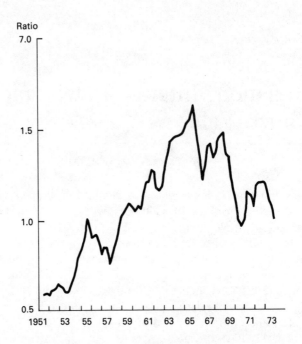

Figure 25.1:   An indicator of the changing financial climate for business capital investment[a]

[a]*Ratio of the aggregate market valuation of the bonds and stocks of US non-financial corporations to the replacement cost of their tangible capital. I am indebted to Jack Ciccolo of the Federal Reserve Bank of New York for the calculations.*

for business capital investment. In 1974, obviously, equity financing has become a laughable idea, internal funds are scarce, and companies are risking their shareholders' future by undertaking huge fixed-interest commitments.

One reason for the worsening climate, no doubt, is the well-known profit squeeze. William Nordhaus estimates that corporations' after-tax rate of return on replacement cost has fallen from 10 per cent in 1965 and 1966 to 5.4 per cent in 1973. To have maintained the same climate for investment and growth, it would have been necessary for real after-tax financial interest rates—that is, market rates corrected for inflationary expectations—to have declined correspondingly. That has not happened.

It is true that inflation has something to do with the profit squeeze. Taxable profits are swollen by fictitious inventory gains and by reckoning depreciation at historical cost. Partly in response to the capricious tax penalties of inflation, increasingly favourable treatment of depreciation has been provided for in the tax laws. But, despite such relief, the effective tax rate on true economic income, as estimated by Nordhaus, rose from 38 per cent in 1965 and 1966 to 42 per cent in 1972 and to nearly 49 per cent in 1973. Significantly, however, this rise in the effective tax rate accounts for only a part of the steep fall-off in the rate of after-tax return since the mid 1960s. Had the rise in the effective tax rate not occurred, the after-tax rate of return on replacement cost would have been 6.5 per cent in 1973 rather than 5.4 per cent. Thus, a substantial part of the decline from 10 per cent remains.

Profits before taxes have been depressed in recent years of recession and 'stagflation'. The sluggish economic climate was not the automatic or natural result of inflation. Rather it was deliberately engineered by Washington policy makers to control inflation.

Yet the decline in profitability exceeds what might be expected on cyclical grounds. Among other possible explanations are: price controls; foreign competition; increased relative costs of materials imported from abroad or purchased from the non-industrial sector of the US economy; environmental controls; slowdown in productivity growth; diminishing returns to the heavy capital accumulation of the long investment boom of 1946–66.

The main point is that the facile and complacent assertion that inflation is the culprit for the trauma of the stock market is a dangerous exaggeration. It is dangerous because it gives the impression that the conquest of inflation by restrictive monetary policy is both necessary and sufficient to revivify the stock market. It is dangerous not because strength in the market is a goal *per se* but because weakness indicates a general financial climate unfavourable to investment needed for recovery and growth. And it is dangerous because it diverts attention from the role of current monetary policy and interest rates in perpetuating that unfavourable climate.

A related strand of the new conventional wisdom is the theory that market interest rates fully reflect inflationary expectations. Interest rates, it is commonly argued, are not high in any real sense if they do not exceed the contemporary rate of inflation. Why have commercial paper rates risen from 5 per cent to 12 per cent since 1965? A widely accepted explanation is that price indexes, which were then rising at less then 3 per cent per annum, are now rising at 10 per cent per year.

In 1896 in his book *Appreciation and Interest* Irving Fisher formalized the theory that the nominal interest rate (dollars yielded by dollars) is the real rate (commodities yielded by commodities) plus the anticipated rate of inflation. Fisher's insight, long neglected, enjoyed

spectacular renaissance in the 1960s. Monetarists in particular have
seized upon inflationary expectations as the principal source of variations of nominal interest rates, both the upward postwar trend and
shorter-term fluctuations around it. The premise, usually tacit, is that
the real rate moves little and slowly. The conclusion is that a rise of
nominal interest rates simply to mirror heightened expectations of
inflation is neutral, that it is not a meaningful rise of rates in any real
economic sense.

Applied to the current American scene, the two theories—that
inflation is responsible for the stock market decline and that increases
of interest rates have been neutral reflections of inflation—are in
logical conflict. If observed increases in market interest rates simply
mirror general expectations of inflation, why do equities fall in value?

A correctly anticipated general inflation, *neutrally* embodied in
interest rates, would not change equity values. Upward corrections in
interest rates to allow for general inflation would not drain money
from the stock market; they would simply maintain the attractiveness
of bonds relative to stocks. The real value of equities would reflect
real economic conditions, independent of price levels and rates of
inflation. As time and inflation marched on as anticipated, equity
prices would rise in step with commodity prices. The charted statistic
in Figure 25.1, the ratio of the securities market valuation of companies
to the replacement cost of their tangible capital, would remain stable.
When, as has been true in recent years, the ratio of paper claims to
capital goods declines in value while the goods themselves rise in
price, we must conclude that actual and expected inflation is a very
inadequate explanation of events in financial and capital markets.

A principal concern of these markets is to anticipate future government policies: monetary, fiscal, wage–price control. Why is inflationary
news deflationary these days? Not because of the effects of inflation
per se but because of the anticipated anti-inflationary responses of the
federal government. As experience since 1971 has taught, these
responses may include price freezes and controls. They may include
new taxes that restrict consumer demand and business profit. They
may include restrictions on foreign trade and capital movements, or
new exchange rate policies.

But perhaps the market's most consistent concern is the response
of the Federal Reserve to inflationary developments. The market
knows that Arthur Burns, an announced, determined enemy of
inflation, reads the newspapers too. News of more inflation is taken
as a signal that the Fed will further and longer restrict the growth of
the economy, with uncertain impact on inflation but obvious damage
to the real earnings prospects of American business. News of increased

interest rates—to which the market has become acutely sensitive—is read as a signal that the Fed is in fact pursuing a strongly restrictive policy.

MAKING THE WIND

The acute sensitivity of the stock market to interest rates is a relatively recent phenomenon. Before 1966, stock and bond prices frequently moved in opposite directions. Booms and expectations of booms pulled up stock prices but raised interest rates; recessions did the opposite. Firmness in interest rates was a signal of prosperity to come, reflecting strength in business-loan demand more than restriction of credit supply. The Fed's practice, well understood, was to 'lean against the wind'. The Fed did not generally tighten strongly enough in booms to nullify the improvement in the climate for earnings and investment. Nor did it ease credit so drastically as to overcome the pessimism about profits induced by recession. Now, however, stock and bond prices move together. Interest rate movements drive the stock market, both because high yields on dollar-denominated assets attract funds and because they signal the intentions of the authorities to make the wind, not just lean against it. This market behaviour is strong evidence that the interest rate variations we have been experiencing have real bite; they are not simply Fisher-like adjustments for expected inflation.

To substantiate the point, Table 25.1 shows some correlation coefficients computed on quarter-to-quarter changes of the indicated variables.

It is not really surprising that current interest rates can be low and

Table 25.1:

	1951: II to 1965: IV	1966: I to 1973: IV
Stock prices (S & P 500) and corporate bond rate (AA new issues)	+0.11	−0.43
Stock prices and prime rate	−0.04	−0.53
Dividend yield (S & P 500) and corporate bond rate	−0.06	+0.49
Dividend yield and prime rate	+0.21	+0.57

high at the same time—low relative to contemporaneous inflation in general price indexes, high relative to operational investment opportunities. The explanation is twofold. First, recent price indexes contain dramatic one-shot price increases in fuel, food, and—thanks partly to the depreciation of the dollar since 1971—internationally traded goods. Rational investors would not expect recurrent shocks of equal magnitude. Second, much recorded inflation, especially in consumer prices, occurs in items in which net speculative investment is impossible or very costly—services, perishable goods, imports, taxes, even interest rates themselves. Many recent price increases have added to corporate costs but not to corporate revenues. Although business loan demand has been strong during the 1974 slowdown, it seems to reflect more the scramble for liquidity to carry out existing commitments and plans at higher prices than the financing of real economic expansion. The inflation of 1973–4 has affected asset values unevenly. For some categories of reproducible assets, it has merely trickled through. But it has strongly favoured non-reproducible assets—mineral deposits, agricultural land, precious metals, old coins, objets d'art. The prosperity and progress of the United States economy, however, is crucially dependent on financial incentives for the accumulation of reproducible productive capital.

TOO MUCH COMPLACENCY

That is why I think the Federal Reserve, and the articulate voices of the business and financial community, are much too complacent about today's double-digit interest rates. The Fed, of course, is not responsible for the very real economic difficulties besetting the nation—the shortages of food, fuel, and materials; the apparent decline in the productivity of capital investment; the strains of the international monetary system; the crisis of confidence in political and economic institutions. But these are maladies which tight money does not cure and only aggravates. The stock market's weakness, the recession in residential construction, and the general sluggishness of the economy are warnings of the dangers in our present course. I realize that the objective of the policy is to weaken aggregate demand enough, and long enough, to reduce significantly the rate of inflation. Experience does not, I think, justify much optimism about the success of this policy, but I have not argued that point here. I have only tried to indicate that the policy contains more bite and cost and risk than one might suspect from superficial comparisons of interest rates and rates of inflation.

NOTE

1. *Brookings Papers on Economic Activity*, 1974, vol. 2.

26 On the Efficiency of the Financial System*

The United States, as befits the major capitalist economy of the world, has the largest, most elaborate, most sophisticated financial industry in the world. New York is rivalled only by London, which thanks to long-standing international connections and experience, maintains a financial role disproportionate to Britain's declining position in world trade and production. Moreover, finance is one of America's rapid growth sectors.

Just the other day, the *New York Times* listed forty-six business executives whose 1983 compensation (salary and bonus, exclusive of realizations of previously acquired stock options) exceeded one million dollars. What struck me was that sixteen members of this elite were officers of financial companies.[1] No wonder, then, that finance is the favourite destination of the undergraduates I teach at Yale, and that 40 per cent of 1983 graduates of our School of Organization and Management took jobs in finance.[2] Their starting salaries are four times the poverty threshold for four-person families. All university educators know that finance is engaging a large and growing proportion of the most able young men and women in the country. Later in the lecture I shall present further information on the economic size of our financial industries.

Fred Hirsch, gifted economist and social critic, took all institutions, private as well as public, to be fair game for analysis and evaluation. He was not willing to assume on faith or principle that 'markets' work for the best, or to blame distortions solely on government interventions and regulations. Nor did he have illusions that legislatures and bureaucracies work for the best. In the same spirit I decided to use the rostrum which you have given me as Hirsch lecturer to voice some sceptical views of the efficiency of our vast system of financial markets

*May 1984, Fred Hirsch Memorial Lecture, New York. Published in *Lloyds Bank Review*, No. 153, July 1984, pp. 1–15.

and institutions. These views run against current tides—not only the general enthusiasm for deregulation and unfettered competition but my profession's intellectual admiration for the efficiency of financial markets. Finance theory itself is a burgeoning activity in academia, occupying more and more faculty slots, student credit hours, journal pages, and computer printouts, both in management schools and in economics departments. And as the newspapers have been reporting, finance academics are finding their way to the street.[3]

EFFICIENCY

Efficiency has several different meanings: first, a market is 'efficient' if it is on average impossible to gain from trading on the basis of generally available public information. In efficient markets only insiders can make money, anyway consistently. Whatever you and I know the market has already 'discounted'. The revealing standard anecdote goes like this: finance professor is walking on campus with his research assistant, who says, 'Professor, I see a twenty-dollar bill on the sidewalk. Should I pick it up?' 'No, of course not, if it were really there, it would already have been picked up.' Efficiency in this meaning I call *information arbitrage* efficiency.

A second and deeper meaning is the following: a market in a financial asset is efficient if its valuations reflect accurately the future payments to which the asset gives title—to use currently fashionable jargon, if the price of the asset is based on 'rational expectations' of those payments. I call this concept *fundamental valuation* efficiency.

Third, a system of financial markets is efficient if it enables economic agents to insure for themselves deliveries of goods and services in all future contingencies, either by surrendering some of their own resources now or by contracting to deliver them in specified future contingencies. Contracts for specified goods in specified 'states of nature' are called in economic theory Arrow–Debreu contracts. Kenneth Arrow and Gerard Debreu showed rigorously that a complete set of competitive markets of this kind is necessary and, given some other conditions, sufficient to guarantee the existence of an equilibrium with the optimal properties intuitively perceived by Adam Smith and succeeding generations of free market theorists.[4] I call efficiency in this Arrow–Debreu sense *full insurance* efficiency.

The fourth concept relates more concretely to the economic functions of the financial industries. They do not provide services directly useful to producers or to consumers. That sentence is an overstatement, because some people enjoy gambling *per se*, and prefer the securities markets to casinos and race tracks. But the resources devoted to financial services are generally justified on other grounds. These include: the pooling of risks and their allocation to those most able and willing to bear them, a generalized insurance function in the Arrow–Debreu spirit just discussed; the facilitation of transactions by providing mechanisms and networks of payments; the mobilization of saving for investments in physical and human capital, domestic and foreign, private and public, and the allocation of saving to their more socially productive uses. I call efficiency in these respects *functional* efficiency.

Before discussing the American financial system in terms of those four criteria of efficiency, I want to point out that the services of the system do not come cheap. An immense volume of activity takes place, and considerable resources are devoted to it. Let me remind you of some of the relevant magnitudes.

Item: The Department of Commerce categories Finance and Insurance generate $4\frac{1}{2}$–5 per cent of GNP, account for $5\frac{1}{2}$ per cent of employee compensation, and occupy about 5 per cent of the employed labour force. They account for $7\frac{1}{2}$ per cent of after-tax corporate profits. About 3 per cent of personal consumption, as measured by the Commerce Department, are financial services. These figures do not include the legal profession. It amounts to about 1 per cent of the economy, and a significant fraction of its business is financial in nature.[5]

Item: The measures just reported do not tell the complete story. They cover only the value added by the labour and capital directly employed. If the inputs of goods and services purchased from other industries are included, Finance and Insurance use about 9 per cent of the GNP.[6]

Item: Thirty billion shares of stock, valued at a thousand billion dollars, changed hands in 1983. The turnover was 60 per cent of the outstanding shares. Thus the average holding period is about ninteteen months. Assuming conservatively that costs are $1\frac{1}{2}$ per cent of dollar volume, traders paid US$14 bn. In fact, the expenses and after-tax profits of New York Stock Exchange member firms were in 1982 US$22 bn, $3\frac{1}{3}$ per cent of the value of transactions. The securities industry employed 232,000 persons, including 61,000 sales representatives, out of approximately 5,000 sales offices.

The turnover of stocks in the United States is greater than in any other country. The closest competitors are Japan, 35 per cent, Germany, 24 per cent, and Britain, 16 per cent.

Our secondary market in bonds, in contrast to stocks, is very inactive. Annual transactions of $7.2 bn on the New York Stock

Exchange are less than 1 per cent of the par value or market value of the listed bonds. For another comparison, consider one-family homes. Annual sales, of which one-sixth are new homes, amount to $4\frac{1}{2}$ per cent of the existing stock.[7]

Item: Stocks and bonds are by no means the only instruments traded on organized markets. The pages of the *Wall Street Journal* report markets in options as follows: 4,000 contracts on 475 common stocks varying in date and striking price; 100 contracts on 15 stock indexes; 60 contracts on 5 foreign currencies, 11 contracts on 3 interest rates. There are also some 500 futures contracts traded, varying as to future date, covering 400 commodities, 5 foreign-exchange rates, 10 interest rates or bond prices, and 6 stock indexes. There are even 100 'futures options' contracts. Transactions volumes in all these markets are substantial but difficult to measure in terms comparable to transactions in primary securities.

Item: Our 15,000 commercial banks do business from 60,000 banking offices, one for every 3,800 persons. The operating expenses of commercial banks were $61 bn in 1982. Of these $10 bn were annualized 'occupancy expenses', $170,000 per office,[8] In addition 4,250 savings institutions with 25,750 offices had operating expenses of $14 bn.[9]

INFORMATION ARBITRAGE EFFICIENCY

The long-standing judgement of almost all academics in economics and finance is yes, securities markets are efficient in this sense. The first study to indicate this result was by Alfred Cowles, the founder of the Cowles Commission, now the Cowles Foundation at Yale. An investment adviser himself, chastened by the stock market's gyrations from 1928 to 1933, he showed statistically that an investor would have done at least as well choosing stocks at random as following professional advice.[10] His conclusions have been confirmed many times in different ways. As a statistical matter actively managed portfolios, allowance made for transaction costs, do not beat the market. Prices are a random walk in the sense that their correlations with past histories are too weak to be exploited profitably.[11] These findings contradict the claims of 'technical' analysis. They suggest, in general, that the mathematical expectation of return from resources used in active portfolio management is zero for the clients of brokers and investment advisers and for the owners of mutual funds.

Efficiency in information-based arbitrage does not come free. It requires resource inputs from arbitrageurs, specialists, market makers.

Random walking does not, of course, mean that prices are unresponsive to new information. To the contrary, it means that they respond promptly and fully—and conceivably with little or no trading.

FUNDAMENTAL VALUATION EFFICIENCY

This brings me to the second kind of efficiency, the accuracy with which market valuations reflect fundamentals. Efficiency in this sense is by no means implied by the technical efficiency just discussed. There are good reasons to be sceptical. The fundamentals for a stock are the expected future dividends or other payouts, or what amounts in principle to the same thing, the expected future earnings. The stock's value is the presented discounted value of either of these streams. Casual observation suggests that the market moves up and down much more than can be justified by changes in rationally formed expectations, or in the rates at which they are discounted. This suspicion has been rigorously verified by my colleague Robert Shiller.[12] Evidently market speculation multiplies several fold the underlying fundamental variability of dividends and earnings.

Shiller has also demonstrated the analogous empirical proposition for the bond market.[13] The yield of a long-term bond is in principle a kind of average of the short-term interest rates expected to prevail in sequence from now to the bond's maturity. Bond prices fluctuate much more than the variability of short rates can justify. Stephen Golub and others have shown that foreign-exchange rates are excessively volatile relative to fluctuations in trade balances.[14]

Equity prices have been a puzzle for the last decade, falling well below the replacement value of the underlying capital assets and the present value of the pay-outs those assets could be expected to earn.[15] Among the hypotheses advanced was one by Modigliani and Cohn, that the market was not allowing for inflation in the streams of earnings and dividends but was discounting real streams by interest rates containing substantial premiums for expected inflation.[16] The authors made a convincing statistical argument for such irrational downward bias, and corroborated it by quotations from professional market advisers displaying the misunderstanding. The Modigliani–Cohn thesis is controversial and is probably not the whole story. Whatever the sources of the chronic undervaluation, it is evidently nothing that arbitrage could or did correct.

Takeover mania, motivated by egregious undervaluations, is testimony to the failure of the market on this fundamental valuation criterion of efficiency. A takeover mobilizes enough capital to jump the price of the target stock to levels much closer to the fundamental value of the underlying assets, for example Gulf's oil reserves. Ordinary investors might have detected the same undervaluations, but could not expect to profit from them unless and until other ordinary investors agreed—or a takeover materialized. Takeovers serve a useful function if they bring prices closer to fundamental values. But the fact that markets fail to do so on their own is a serious indictment of their efficiency.

J. M. Keynes likened the stock market—and he referred particularly to the American market—'to those newspaper competitions in which the competitors have to pick out the six prettiest faces from a hundred photographs, the prize being awarded to the competitor whose choice most nearly corresponds to the average preferences of the competitors as a whole; so that each competitor has to pick, not those faces which he himself finds prettiest, but those which he thinks likeliest to catch the fancy of the other competitors, all of whom are looking at the problem from the same point of view ... (We) have reached the third degree where we devote our intelligences to anticipating what average opinion expects the average opinion to be. And there are some, I believe, who practise the fourth, fifth, and higher degrees.'[17]

Speculations on the speculations of other speculators who are doing the same thing—those are 'bubbles'. They dominate, of course, the pricing of assets with negligible fundamentals, zero or vague or non-transferable returns in consumption or production. Gold and collectibles, for example, derive value almost wholly from guesses about the opinions of future speculators. But bubbles are also, as Keynes observed, phenomena of markets for equities, long-term bonds, foreign exchange, commodity futures, and real estate.

Keynes, himself an active and experienced market participant, despaired of 'investment based on genuine long-term expectation'. 'There is no clear evidence from experience', he said, 'that the investment policy which is socially advantageous coincides with that which is most profitable'. He noted that professionals who bet on long-term fundamentals, while everyone else is engaged in short-term attempts 'to guess better than the crowd how the crowd will behave', run greater risks. Not least of these is criticism for unconventional and rash investment behaviour. Keynes's views would be confirmed today if he observed how professional portfolio managers seek safety from criticism in short-run performances that match their competitors and market indices.

Keynes's pessimism on the long-term rationality of securities markets led him to the view that the liquidity these markets provide is a mixed blessing. 'The spectacle ... has sometimes moved me towards the conclusion that to make the purchase of an investment permanent and indissoluble, like marriage, (sic!), except by reason of death or other grave cause, might be a useful remedy ...' But he concluded that illiquidity would be the worse evil, because it would push savers towards hoarding of money. Today that disadvantage seems less serious than when Keynes was writing, during the Great Depression. Anyway, he advocated as a halfway measure a 'substantial ... transfer tax ..., with a view of mitigating the predominance of speculation over enterprise in the United States'. For similar reasons, I have advocated an international transfer tax on transactions across currencies.[18]

FULL INSURANCE EFFICIENCY

My third concept is drawn from the purest of economic theory. Arrow and Debreu imagined a complete system of markets in which commodities are defined not only by their physical characteristics but also by the dates and contingencies—'states of nature'—at which they are to be exchanged. Such a market, for example, would enable me to contract now for an umbrella on the day of the Harvard–Yale football game in 1990 if it is raining that day and if a Republican is in the White House. In exchange, I could sell a promise to give an economics lecture in New York City in 1994 if I am still in good health and the unemployment rate exceeds 8 per cent. Prices set in such markets would clear supplies and demands in advance for all such commodities, with each participant constrained by his or her budget to promise no more than he or she can deliver. Arrow and Debreu showed that this system would realize the claims for the economy-wide efficiency and optimality of competitive markets.

It can be shown further that securities and insurance markets can mimic the Arrow–Debreu system, provided that the menu of available securities 'spans' the space of 'states of nature'.[19] That is, there must be as many different independent securities as there are states of nature. I could get my umbrella with the proceeds of a security that would pay off in the medium of exchange under the specified contingencies at the time of the 1990 Harvard–Yale football game. At a price, I would be insured against those risks.

Our actual institutions fall far short of the Arrow–Debreu vision. There are good reasons. Markets require resources to operate; given their costs, it would be inefficient to have a complete set. Many of them would in any case be too thin to be competitive. 'States of nature' are difficult to define and observe. Lawyers and judges would be even busier than they are already on disputes over whether contingencies specified in contracts have occurred. Many relevant contingencies are not independent of the actions of the parties; as insurance carriers know, 'moral hazard' is a real problem.

Nevertheless the Arrow–Debreu ideal provides a useful way to look at our actual institutions and markets. The system does some things very well, for example life and disability insurance, even health insurance. It enables individuals and families to trade earnings in their productive years for consumption in retirement and old age. Futures markets allow businesses and farmers to hedge against events that might alter spot prices of commodities they will be buying or selling. Capital markets enable fundamental risks of business enterprise to be taken by the adventurous, while risk averters content with lower average returns are protected from many possible sources of loss. Our financial system allows individuals and households considerable facilities to shift the time pattern of their spending and consumption to accord with their needs and preferences, rather than slavishly conforming to the time profile of their earnings. But it could do better.

For example, the long-term level payment mortgage was a great invention. But mortgage instruments with payments that conform more closely to typical earnings profiles and are flexible in maturity would be helpful to young families, especially in inflationary times. Likewise, older households whose equity in homes is the major part of net worth do not find it easy to consume such wealth while retaining occupancy and ownership. It should not be difficult to devise instruments which would meet their needs. Consumer credit also permits households to advance consumption in time and age, though at what seem exorbitant interest rates. Borrowing against future earnings, against human capital, is much more difficult than against negotiable financial or physical assets. Educational loans would not be generally available without government guarantees and subsidies. They could be longer in term, and lengths and even amounts of repayment could be contingent on the debtors' actual earnings.

The obvious major contingency which our system leaves uncovered is inflation. Twenty-five years ago we thought equities, which are after all titles to real capital goods and real returns earned by their use, were good hedges against inflation. Subsequent experience turned out otherwise, partly because inflation hit us from unexpected sources like OPEC, partly because policies to stem inflation lower profits and raise interest rates. Short-term nominal interest rates are better correlated with inflation; consequently variable interest instruments provide rough protection to both debtors and creditors. But the correlation is imperfect. It is not clear why private financial institutions cannot take the next step and develop price-indexed instruments for both savers and borrowers. Those institutions are better placed than the general public to assume the risks of deviations of interest rates from inflation rates. Of course, if the federal government were to issue indexed bonds—Her Majesty's Government has done so—it would be easy for financial intermediaries to offer indexed assets tailored in maturities and denominations to the needs of small savers.

The development of indexed financial instruments, with or without government initiative, would be facilitated by the construction of a price index more appropriate than the present Consumer Price Index. This would exclude the effects of changes in the country's external terms of trade, from shocks to prices of oil or other imports and from movements in the foreign exchange value of the currency. It would also exclude changes in indirect taxes. These CPI movements are essentially uninsurable for the nation as a whole. An index purged of them is preferable for wage contracts and social insurance benefits as well as for new financial instruments.

New financial markets and instruments have proliferated over the last decade, and it might be thought that the enlarged menu now spans more states of nature and moves us closer to the Arrow–Debreu ideal. Not much closer, I am afraid. The new options and futures contracts do not stretch very far into the future. They serve mainly to allow greater leverage to short-term speculators and arbitrageurs, and to limit losses in one direction or the other. Collectively they contain considerable redundancy. Every financial market absorbs private resources to operate, and government resources to police. The country cannot afford all the markets that enthusiasts may dream up. In deciding whether to approve proposed contracts for trading, the authorities should consider whether they really fill gaps in the menu and enlarge the opportunities for Arrow–Debreu insurance, not just opportunities for speculation and financial arbitrage.

FUNCTIONAL EFFICIENCY

I turn finally to what I call *functional* efficiency, the services the financial industries perform for the economy as a whole.

Very few securities transactions are sales of new issues. They amounted to only $100 bn in 1983, and one-third of these were issues of financial businesses themselves.[20] Of the issues of non-financial corporations, a large share will have represented refunding and restructuring of debt and equity rather than raising funds for new real investments. Even in recent years of high investment, 1978–9, 86 per cent of aggregate gross capital expenditures by non-financial corporations could have been financed by internal funds, retained after-tax earnings and depreciation. Retained earnings were in aggregate sufficient to cover two-thirds of investment net of capital consumption charges. In the recent recession, internal funds exceeded capital expenditures.[21]

These overall figures, it is true, understate the role of the capital markets. Some businesses with surpluses of internal funds over investment requirements finance the deficits of others, either directly by purchases of securities or, much more usually, indirectly via financial intermediaries. There are no statistics on the gross amount of this activity. However, suppose half of the new non-financial securities issues financed capital expenditures by deficit companies—this seems a conservatively high proportion. Then internal funds would be credited with two-thirds of gross 1978–9 capital expenditures instead of 86 per cent, and only with one-sixth of net capital expenditures instead of two-thirds. The calculations include as external funds bank loans and short-term paper, 68 per cent of the total, twice as much as the funds raised in securities and mortgage markets. They also include, on the investment side, corporate-owned residential structures and inventories.

What is clear is that very little of the work done by the securities industry, as gauged by the volume of market activity, has to do with the financing of real investment in any very direct way. Likewise, those markets have very little to do, in aggregate, with the translation of the saving of households into corporate business investment. That process occurs mainly outside the market, as retention of earnings gradually and irregularly augments the value of equity shares. Capital markets and financial intermediaries assist this process by facilitating transfers from surplus companies to deficit companies.

Financial markets, of course, play a much bigger role in financing public capital investments of state and local governments and government deficits in general. Through the markets government securities find their way into the portfolios of individuals and, more importantly, of financial intermediaries.

The traditional role of commercial banks is to facilitate the circulation of funds among businesses, channelling the temporary seasonal and short-run surpluses of some businesses to those businesses with temporary deficits. This circulation is closely connected with the diverse rhythms of accumulation and decumulation of inventories of finished goods, raw materials, and work in process, and of interbusiness accounts receivable and payable. Some of the surpluses show up, almost automatically, in excesses of bank deposits over borrowings from banks, while the deficit companies are drawing down their deposits and using more fully their lines of credit.

Banks' intermediation between businesses is mixed with their borrowing from and lending to other types of economic agents—households, governments, and foreigners. As banking has become increasingly generalized, the word 'commercial' has become less appropriate. Likewise, other financial firms and institutions, new credit markets, and even non-financial companies have invaded both sides of the banks' traditional commercial intermediation business.

I have noted above that there is little net aggregate transfer of household saving into business investment. Indeed most household saving goes into household investments in residences and consumer durable goods. Commercial banks, savings institutions, insurance companies, and pension funds are vehicles for channelling the surpluses of some households to finance the deficits of others. This is done mainly by mortgage lending and by consumer credit. Since houses, in particular, are beyond the capacity of all but a very few families to purchase from current or accumulated savings, intermediation between surplus and deficit households is a great service to the economy.

A by-product of traditional commercial banking was the provision of a payments mechanism; checkable demand deposits became the predominant means of payment in modern economies. This function, too, is now increasingly shared with other financial institutions and businesses. The link between commercial banking, supplying money, and operating a payments mechanism was more a historical evolution than a planned design. It is logically possible to think of different arrangements, ranging from on the one side a public monopoly in the provision of this public good to complete deregulation and *laissez faire* at the other extreme. We seem likely to stay in the middle of the spectrum, moving in the direction of deregulation.

Total debits to deposit accounts—cheque clearings, wire transfers, etc.—amount to more than 100 *trillion* dollars a year. A dollar of demand deposits turns over an average of once a day. The bank-operated payments mechanism does a lot of work. From the fact that more than 40 per cent of national clearings are in New York City alone we may infer that more than half of cheque payments are for the financial transactions described above—the flip side of them, so to speak. Transactions directly connected with the flow of goods and services probably amount to no more than a quarter of aggregate debits.[22]

Our financial intermediaries are decentralized and competitive. But they hardly fit the textbook model of pure competition, where firms too small to affect prices compete in supplying homogeneous products. The applicable model is that provided fifty years ago by Edward

Chamberlin, monopolistic competition.[23] Like Chamberlin's firms, banks and other financial intermediaries actively seek the custom of depositors and borrowers by trying to differentiate their products as well as by offering attractive interest rates and terms. Product differentiation takes many forms, among them locational convenience, comfortable premises, personal attention, packaging, and advertising.

Symptoms of monopolistic competition are readily apparent. Like gas stations clustered on the same intersections, competing banking offices are adjacent to each other. Like the products of those gas stations, the financial services differ only trivially. To persuade us of the contrary, monopolistically competing firms resort to a great deal of advertising. In 1981, banks and savings institutions spent US$158 m on local TV advertising. Financial advertising in newspapers of 64 cities amounted to $387 m, $5\frac{1}{2}$ per cent of advertising other than classified.[24] Another symptom is the prevalence of conventional pricing based on the leadership of large firms in the industry—the prime rate is an obvious case in point.

Many optimistic advocates of financial deregulation attributed the 'wastes of monopolistic competition'—Chamberlin's phrase—to the legal ceilings on deposit interest rates. They correctly observed that banks and other intermediaries were led to fill the profitable gap between lending rates and those ceilings by advertising and by non-price competition. They predicted that abolition of the ceilings would eliminate wasteful forms of competition. I doubt that, because the system remains monopolistically competitive even without the regulation of deposit interest and because deregulation itself vastly enlarges the opportunities for product differentiation. One by-product of the regulations was to standardize the deposit instruments banks could offer. Since proliferation of non-standardized products is costly, beyond a certain point it is not necessarily a service to the consuming public.

In other countries, where branching and merging of banks and other financial enterprises are not restricted, the industry is highly concentrated.The US is probably moving inexorably in this direction. The number of distinct firms, though not the number of offices, will shrink drastically. Competition will be oligopolistic rivalry rather than Chamberlinian monopolistic competition. There will be some economies of scale in the operations of the payments mechanisms, and some improvements in the management of small banks which have comfortably enjoyed local monopolies sheltered by anti-branching laws. But there will be some losses too. The local commercial banker knew his community; at his best, he was a good judge of personal and business risks. Branches of large nationwide lenders following bureaucratic rules are all too likely to deny credit to small new entrepreneurs while their national headquarters take immense billion-dollar risks with foreign countries and big-time operators.

CONCLUSIONS

Any appraisal of the efficiency of our financial system must reach an equivocal and uncertain verdict. In many respects, as I have tried to indicate, the system serves us as individuals and as a society very well indeed. As I have also tried to say, however, it does not merit complacency and self-congratulation either in the industry itself or in the academic professions of economics and finance. Nor are its shortcomings entirely attributable to government regulations and likely to disappear as deregulation proceeds apace. Here as elsewhere many regulations have been counter-productive. But the process of deregulation should be viewed neither as a routine application of free market philosophy nor as a treaty among conflicting sectoral interests. Rather it should be guided by sober pragmatic consideration of what we can reasonably expect the financial system to achieve and at what social cost. My lecture today presents some of the problems, but I regret I have no sovereign solution to propose.

I confess to an uneasy Physiocratic suspicion, perhaps unbecoming in an academic, that we are throwing more and more of our resources, including the cream of our youth, into financial activities remote from the production of goods and services, into activites that generate high private rewards disproportionate to their social productivity. I suspect that the immense power of the computer is being harnessed to this 'paper economy', not to do the same transactions more economically but to balloon the quantity and variety of financial exchanges. For this reason perhaps, high technology has so far yielded disappointing results in economy-wide productivity. I fear that, as Keynes saw even in his day, the advantages of the liquidity and negotiability of financial instruments come at the cost of facilitating nth-degree speculation which is short sighted and inefficient.

The casino aspect of our financial markets was the subject of a thoughtful and devastating article on commodity future markets by John Train in the *New York Times* Sunday 12 May. The author, himself in the investment business, pointed out that speculation in these contracts was a negative-sum game for the general public, thanks to the large 'win' of the brokers, estimated at several billions of dollars annually. Only 5 per cent of the contracts exchanged entail actual deliveries of the commodities. Mr Train berated brokerage houses for misleading amateur clients into this particular casino.

The case points out the general dilemma. Commodity futures contracts serve a significant Arrow–Debreu function for traders with business interests in the commodity; and since hedging will seldom balance supply and demand, some risk takers, speculators are needed in the market too. But Arrow and Debreu did not have continuous sequential trading in mind; when that occurs, as Keynes noted, it attracts short-horizon speculators and middlemen, and distorts or dilutes the influence of fundamentals on prices. I suspect that Keynes was right to suggest that we should provide greater deterrents to transient holdings of financial instruments and larger rewards for long-term investors.

NOTES

1. *New York Times*, 2 May 1984, p. D1. The representation of financial executives would be larger except that a corporation is required to disclose compensation only for its five highest-paid officials. The *Wall Street Journal*, 21 May 1984, p. 33, guessed that as many as fifteen to twenty officials of Phibro-Salomon, in addition to the five listed, would have been eligible. Furthermore, most Wall Street firms are partnerships or private corporations and do not report. The *Journal* said it was 'a safe bet' that the senior executives or partners of several leading firms belonged on the list, very likely at the top.
2. Information on job placements from the School's office of Career Planning and Placement; categorization of positions by the author.
3. Recent names in the news include William Silber and Fisher Black, who left New York University and Massachussets Institute of Technology respectively. Many others, who have not made the full leap, serve as consultants. They serve not only during vacations from classes; a day a week free for consulting during terms is standard in business schools.
4. Their seminal article is 'Existence of an equilibrium for a competitive economy', *Econometrica*, vol. 22 (1954), pp. 256–90. *See also* Debreu, *Theory of Value, An Axiomatic Analysis of Economic Equilibrium*, New York: Wiley, 1959.
5. Figures from US National Income and Product Accounts Tables, *Survey of Current Business*, US Department of Commerce, July 1983.
6. The 9 per cent assumes the same proportion between direct and indirect expenses on labour and capital as estimated in the 1972 input–output table for the US economy. *See* 'The input–output structure of the US economy 1972' and 'Dollar value tables for the 1972 input–output study', *Survey of Current Business*, February and April 1979.
7. Figures derived from statistical reports in *SEC Monthly Review*, US Securities and Exchange Commission, and from *1983 Fact Book*, New York Stock Exchange.
8. Figures based on *Federal Reserve Bulletin*, July 1983, Table A.1, p. 501.
9. Figures from *'83 Savings and Loan Sourcebook*, US League of Savings Institutions, and *1982 Fact Book of Savings Banking*, National Association of Mutual Savings Banks.

10. Alfred Cowles, 'Can stock market forecasters forecast?', *Econometrica*, 1933, vol. 1, pp. 309–24, Alfred Cowles and Herbert E. Jones, 'Some a posteriori probabilities in stock market action', *Econometrica*, 1937, vol. 5, pp. 280–94.
11. Burton G. Malkiel, *A Random Walk down Wall Street*, New York: Norton, 1973. John G. Cragg and Burton G. Malkiel, *Expectations and the Structure of Share Prices*, Chicago: University of Chicago Press, 1982. (A National Bureau of Economic Research monograph.)
12. Robert J. Shiller, 'Do stock prices move too much to be justified by subsequent changes in dividends?', *American Economic Review*, 1981, vol. 71, pp. 421–36.
13. Robert J. Shiller, 'The volatility of long-term interest rates and expectations models of the term structure', *Journal of Political Economy*, 1979, vol. 87, pp. 1190–219.
14. Stephen S. Golub, 'Exchange rate variability: is it excessive', Chapter 4 of unpublished Ph.D. dissertation, *International Financial Markets, Oil Prices, and Exchange Rates*, Yale University, 1983.
15. William C. Brainard, J. B. Shoven, and L. Weiss, 'The financial valuation of the return to capital', *Brookings Papers on Economic Activity*, 1981, vol. 2, pp. 453–502.
16. Franco Modigliani and R. Cohn, 'Inflation, rational valuation and the market', *Journal of Business, University of Chicago*, vol. 35, pp. 24–44.
17. This and the quotations and paraphrases that follow come from Keynes's *General Theory of Employment, Interest, and Money*, New York: Harcourt-Brace, 1936, pp. 156–60. The whole of his Chapter 12, 'The state of long-term expectation' deserves reading and re-reading by anyone interested in these subjects.
18. James Tobin, 'A proposal for international monetary reform', *Eastern Economic Journal*, vol. 4, 1978, pp. 153–9. Reprinted in *Essays in Economics, vol. 3, Theory and Policy*, Chapter 20.
19. Roy Radner, 'Competitive equilibrium under uncertainty', *Econometrica*, 1968, vol. 36, pp. 31–58.
20. Figures on new issues from *SEC Monthly Review*.
21. Figures for 'Sources and uses of funds, nonfarm nonfinancial corporate business', from the Board of Governors of the Federal Reserve System, published *inter alia*, in *Economic Report of the President* 1984, Washington: US Government Printing Office, Table B–87, p. 320.
22. Statistics of Bank Debits and Deposit Turnover are published monthly in the *Federal Reserve Bulletin*, Table 1.20.
23. Edward Chamberlin, *The Theory of Monopolistic Competition*, Cambridge: Harvard University Press, 1933.
24. *Statistical Abstract of the United States* 1982–1983, Tables 966–8, pp. 567–8.

PART V

Inflation, Stagflation, Unemployment, and
Incomes Policies

INTRODUCTION

Inflation and stagflation were the salient economic evils and disappointments of the 1970s. The apparent incompatibility of price stability and
full employment had long been recognized as the central macroeconomic dilemma of modern capitalist democracies, a dilemma beyond
the power of fiscal and monetary policies of demand management to
resolve. In the 1970s this old problem was magnified by new sources
of inflation, dramatic external supply shocks, notably sharp increases
in the price of oil contrived by the OPEC cartel. Central bank attempts
to control inflation by customary tightening of money and credit
brought the deep recessions of 1974–5 and 1979–82. The word
'stagflation' was coined to describe the unprecedented combination of
high inflation, high unemployment, and slow economic growth.

The chapters of this Part concern both the chronic difficulty of
reconciling high employment with tolerably low inflation and the
special problems created by supply shocks like those of the 1970s. In
Chapters 27–29 I try to sort out various sources of inflation, arguing
that the indicated treatment differs among them. I criticize the common
view that inflation is always a symptom of excess demand and thus
always an occasion for tightening monetary and fiscal policies. In these
chapters and especially in Chapter 30 I argue for a cost–benefit
approach to anti-inflationary policies, because contractionary demand
management generally imposes heavy costs in unemployment and lost
production.

The disinflationary monetary policies adopted by all major central
banks and governments in 1979–80 have significantly lowered inflation,
but at heavy costs. As Chapter 35 argues, those costs are still being
paid, especially in Western Europe. Chapters 31 and 32 concern
strategies of disinflation and their sequels. I advocated incomes policies,
guideposts for wage and price increases with penalties or rewards to
induce compliance, as a means of achieving disinflation with less cost
in unemployment and real economic growth.

In fact, I believe that some types of incomes policy should be a
permanent tool of macroeconomic policy, in order to arrest the dismal
upward trend in unemployment, apparently regarded by policy makers
as essential to avoid risk of new surges of inflation. At this writing
inflation does not seem to be a serious problem, perhaps because
unemployment and excess capacity remain high. Incomes policies and
other measures to reduce the real costs of stabilizing prices are not
popular in today's political and ideological climate. None the less most

of the chapters of this Part argue my case. The cruel dilemma is likely to recur, and we should be ready.

Is this too in a Keynesian mode? I believe so, because Keynes argues for stability of money wage rates, both in the *General Theory* and elsewhere, in a way that suggests he regards wages as a proper and important item in the government's agenda of policy.

27 Inflation*

Inflation means generally rising money prices of goods and services. To understand what inflation is and is not, consider the above definition in detail:

Goods and services—this refers not to stocks or bonds or other financial assets, but to the tangible and intangible commodities economic agents produce and sell to one another. These are commodities to be consumed or held for future use: for example, food, haircuts, shelter, houses, health care, schooling, cars, tractors, machine tools.

Money prices—this refers to amounts of money, dollars, and cents in the United States, per commodity unit, for example, per pound of butter, gallon of gasoline, haircut, bus trip, kilowatthour, or diesel engine. In contrast, imagine the barter prices at which one commodity trades for another: for example, three gallons of gas for one hour of labour, two bus fares for one pound of butter, one haircut for 100 kilowatthours. From the money prices for any two commodities can be calculated their implicit barter price, their relative price in economists' language. Inflation does not refer to movements of relative prices, but to movements of absolute prices, that is, money prices.

Rising—this does not mean 'high'. By some measures, money prices in the United States were twice as high at the end of 1978 as in 1967. Thus, in the interim the annual average inflation rate was 5.8 per cent. (If a dollar deposited in 1967 earned this rate, compounded continuously, it would have doubled after twelve years.) If by some miracle prices had ceased to rise and were the same at the end of 1979 as twelve months earlier, the inflation rate would have been zero for the year 1979. But a dollar would still have bought only half as much and could have been obtained by selling only half as much, as in 1967.

*1982, in Douglas Greenwald, ed., *Encyclopedia of Economics*, New York: McGraw-Hill, 1982, pp. 510–23. © McGraw-Hill 1982. Reproduced with permission.

Generally—inflation refers to pervasive, widespread increases of money prices. A rising price for a single commodity, even beef or oil, is not *per se* inflation, any more than declining prices of pocket calculators or digital timepieces represent deflation.

MEASUREMENT OF INFLATION

To measure inflation over a month or a year or decade, it is necessary to average the diverse changes in thousands and thousands of specific prices. This is not easy, and it is bound to be arbitrary. If prices all moved together in proportion, there would be no ambiguity about the direction and amount of change in the price level. But they do not; relative prices are always changing. In practice, statisticians, usually in government agencies, calculate price indexes. In these indexes commodities are weighted by their importance in consumer budgets, or in the GNP, or in other aggregates. Indexes with weights differing in concept or in base data give different results.

Averaging and weighting are not the only problems. Products change in design and quality, for better or worse. A truck, a computer, a pair of skis, a subway ride, are not the same as a year ago, let alone ten years ago. Wholly new products are introduced; others vanish from the scene. According to the US Consumer Price Index, prices were 365 per cent higher in 1978 than in 1940. But television was not available then at any price, and new 1940 Ford cars are not available now. The physician may do more or less for the patient in an hour than formerly, but statisticians cannot measure units of health and can only enter in the index the rise in the fee per visit.

Though the measurement of inflation is inevitably imprecise, the standard price index numbers capture the big changes. For example, the years 1974 to 1978, when the GNP price index increased on average 6.8 per cent per year, were very different from 1965 to 1969, when it rose 1.8 per cent per year.

MONEY AND INFLATION

Inflation is by definition a monetary phenomenon, a decline in the commodity value of the monetary unit of account, the dollar in the United States. Deflation too is monetary, a rise in the commodity value and commodity cost of a unit of money. (From 1929 to 1933, for example, prices fell at, on average, 6.7 per cent per year.)

To understand inflation and deflation, therefore, it is necessary to review the role of money in economic life. An economy where goods and services are always bartered directly for each other would be spared inflation or deflation. It would also be terribly inefficient. Perhaps the village cobbler can trade shoes for the farmer's eggs, and even promise shoes tomorrow for eggs today. But imagine the difficulties if steel plants had to pay their workers in steel ingots, or else trade the ingots for eggs and shoes and other goods more to their employees' tastes. Without money, much time and effort would be spent seeking and executing mutually advantageous trades, and much capital would be tied up in inventories. To escape these inefficiencies the people of even primitive societies have agreed among themselves on a common trading commodity, a money.

The money of a society serves as a commonly accepted medium of exchange and as a unit of account and calculation. Goods and services can be traded for money rather than directly for other goods and services. The cobbler can sell shoes for money and use the money later to buy eggs, as well as leather, nails, and the services of an apprentice. The steel plant can sell ingots for money and pay employees in money, and the workers can find and buy what they individually want. Prices can be quoted and values calculated in units of money. Imagine the difficulty of keeping track of barter prices for all possible pairs of commodities.

These are money's functions. But what is money? It is whatever the society collectively fixes upon, by convention and tradition and in modern nations by law. The substances chosen have differed widely, including cattle, land, rocks, silver, gold, and engraved paper. Some, so-called fiat moneys, have had no value except that conveyed by their status as money. Others have been commodities with intrinsic value in consumption (such as cigarettes among prisoners of war) or production. Even commodity moneys have had, thanks to their monetary designation, more value in terms of other goods and services than they would have had on their own. Some things make more convenient moneys than others, but the vast advantages of money to the society are gained by agreeing on a common medium of exchange and account, whatever it is. In this respect, money is a social institution comparable to language. In both cases, the immense contribution to social cooperation and communication depends on the general currency of whatever medium is chosen.

Money is also a store of value, in which individuals can save and hold wealth for future use. Otherwise, it would be useless as a medium of exchange. The farmer parts with eggs for the cobbler's money only because the farmer expects the money will later be acceptable payment for shoes or seed or fence wire, tomorrow or next week or next year.

Everyone who accepts fiat money—or commodity money such as cigarettes or silver in excess of consumption needs—is counting on its future acceptability to others.

But money is not, of course, the only store of value available to savers and wealth owners, or even the principal form of wealth. Even in primitive societies, land, livestock, and other commodities are more important vehicles of wealth. This remains true in modern economies, where ultimate ownership of real properties is often indirect, expressed through a network of financial claims.

In a modern national economy, many assets and debts are denominated in the monetary unit of account. Some of these are media of exchange, but most are not. In the United States, for example, the basic physical manifestation of the dollar is the fiat issue of currency—paper bills and coin—by the federal government. The federal government also has outstanding obligations to pay specified amounts of these dollars, some on demand (notably the deposits of commercial banks in Federal Reserve banks), some on stated future dates (Treasury bills, notes, and bonds). Currency and demand deposits do not bear interest: time obligations do. In addition, non-federal debtors have issued an immense volume and variety of dollar-denominated obligations, some payable on demand, others at future dates. The debtors include banks, savings institutions, state and local governments, business firms, individuals (home-owners, car buyers, department store customers, students, etc.), and foreigners. Most of these IOUs bear interest, but demand obligations (e.g. bank checking accounts) generally do not.

In addition to currency itself, some promises to pay currency on demand are generally or frequently acceptable instruments of payment. These include not only checkable deposits in banks and savings institutions but also the obligations of credit card and travellers' cheque companies and of some mutual funds.

When inflation or deflation alters the value of the dollar, it affects the real values of all dollar-denominated obligations, whether private or public, whether demand or time, whether media of payment or not. For this reason, both the causes and consequences of changing values of the dollar *qua* unit of account extend far beyond government issues of basic dollar currency and beyond the dollar means of payment supplied by banks.

Throughout history, the value of monetary stores of value has been variable and unpredictable. Considering the nature of money, this is not surprising. The notion that price stability or predictability is natural and normal, while inflation and deflation are pathological aberrations, is an abstraction with little realistic foundation. People save for future consumption, for their old age, or for their children. But whatever form of wealth they accumulate, they can never be sure what value it will have when they or their heirs need it. Since they cannot store precisely the commodities they will want to consume, they are always dependent on what other people will be prepared to pay for their assets. This is true of land, houses, personal skills (human capital), machines and tools, and common stocks. It is certainly true of money, the value of which depends not on its intrinsic utility in consumption or production, but always on what others expect its value will be to them. Investors are always speculating about the relative values of goods and titles to them, on the one hand, and money and titles to money, on the other. Fluctuations in the value of money are costs societies have to pay for the efficiency that monetary institutions contribute in trade and division of labour. The problem is to keep the fluctuations from being so violent that they negate those positive contributions.

ANTICIPATED AND UNANTICIPATED INFLATION

In a hypothetical pure case of anticipated inflation everyone correctly foresees the future path of the money price of every commodity. In deciding how many dollars to borrow or lend, for how long, and at what interest rates, everyone can correctly calculate the depreciation of the dollar *vis-à-vis* the commodities consumed and produced. Lenders expecting more inflation demand more interest in compensation, and borrowers likewise are able and willing to pay it when they expect to repay their debts in depreciated currency. As Irving Fisher observed sixty years ago, in these circumstances market interest rates would adjust point for point of expected inflation, leaving unchanged all real interest rates (those implicit in the expected future amount of each commodity purchasable directly or indirectly by a unit of the commodity today). The path of the real economy—relative prices, physical quantities—would be independent of the rate of inflation anticipated. The inflation would make no difference and would do no one either harm or good.

This abstraction contains a valuable practical lesson. The more thoroughly adjusted an economy becomes to an ongoing inflation, the less consequential is the inflation.

However, there are a number of economic institutions that adjust slowly, if at all, to changes in actual and expected inflation rates. One crucial rigidity is the zero nominal interest rate on base money, currency, and its equivalents. Legal or conventional interest limitations often apply to demand and savings deposits and to loans and mortgages, though these rate ceilings can be and have been changed at intervals. Their ceilings prevent the Fisher adjustment of nominal interest rates to expected inflation. With higher inflation, the real rate of return from holding currency becomes lower (more negative). As owners of wealth seek to substitute other assets for money, the reduction of real rates spreads to them. Since it modifies the structure and level of real rates of return, expected inflation is not neutral. One effect of higher expected inflation is to induce economies in cash management; holding periods are shorter, money turns over faster, more costs are incurred, and more resources are diverted in order to avoid losses on depreciating assets uncompensated by interest. Against these social costs are possible gains from greater capital formation. In some circumstances, it may not be possible to get real interest rates low enough to encourage a socially desirable degree of accumulation of productive capital unless the attractiveness of holding monetary assets is diminished by expectations of inflation.

Unanticipated inflation is different. People have made monetary commitments on the basis of price expectations that in the event turn out wrong. Examples of such commitments are loans of a few weeks, wage contracts of one to three years, life and retirement insurance contracts, thirty-year mortgages, and long-term bonds and leases. The economy is always carrying heavy baggage of contracts made at various dates in the past, with various expectations about prices today and in the future. Deviations of inflation rates from past expectation will bring capital gains to some, capital losses to others. As every history student knows, unexpected inflation is good for debtors, who borrowed at low rates, and bad for their creditors. By the same token, farmer–debtors revolted against the deflations of 1879 to 1896 and 1926 to 1933; it wasn't possible to pay off 6 per cent loans when grain prices were steadily declining. Pensioners and civil servants enjoyed the deflations but suffered from wartime and postwar inflations.

Redistributions of this kind are painful disappointments and often cruel disasters for the losers. But several points should be remembered:

1. There are winners as well as losers. The nation as a whole does not lose except as its foreign debts become unexpectedly onerous or its foreign loans yield disappointing real returns.
2. Gains and losses occur whenever events fail to confirm the expectations held when contracts and commitments were made, not from inflation *per se*. The culprit could be deflation, or any deviation of actual prices up or down from previously expected paths. For example, in the 1970s many companies incurred debts at double-

digit interest rates premised on the continuation of inflation at 8 to 12 per cent per year. Many householders assumed mortgages at rates they expect to pay from inflation in their wages and in real estate values. If the inflation were dramatically curbed in the 1980s, these debtors would be in trouble.

3. Inflation and deflation are by no means the sole sources of unexpected income redistributions. Most capital losses and gains are related to mistakes and surprises that afflict forecasts of relative prices and of real economic phenomena. Consider, for example, current or imminent retirees who in the 1960s and 1970s sought protection from inflation by investing in common stocks rather than fixed-dollar securities. Consider enterprises that built glass office buildings or bought gas-guzzling cars just as OPEC was raising prices. Consider young people who committed themselves to teaching careers in the 1960s and 1970s and later found education to be a declining industry.

INFLATION AND THE QUANTITY OF MONEY

As media of exchange, currency circulates from hand to hand and chequing balances from account to account. At any instant of time, however, every dollar of money in circulation is in someone's hands or someone's account. At the end of any business day, it is possible in principle, though not in practice, to account for the entire stock by a census of the amounts held by everybody. At the end of the next business day, the census would find quite a different distribution even though the total stock was virtually unchanged.

How big a stock does it take to handle the business of the nation? The answer clearly depends on, among other things, prices. If all prices were halved, would it not be possible to execute the same trades with a money stock half as large? If all prices were doubled, would it not take a circulating stock twice as large to make the same real transactions? Affirmative answers are plausible, and they are the kernel of an ancient and important doctrine. Although it is commonly known as the quantity theory of money, a more descriptive label is the quantity of money theory of prices.

The doctrine goes back at least to David Hume, and in its modern form of monetarism its leading protagonist is Milton Friedman. In its starkest form, the proposition is that prices are proportional to the quantity of money. Suppose, for example, the stock of money in dollars were doubled. Having more than needed to handle transactions at prevailing prices, households and businesses would try to get rid of excess money holdings by buying more goods and services. But the excess money would not be extinguished, merely transferred to other households and businesses, which would act in the same manner. In the process the money prices of goods and services would be bid up until they are high enough so that the stock of money would no longer be excessive. That occurs when prices have doubled. In summary, there is a certain amount of purchasing power that the society needs and wants to hold in the form of money. Whatever the nominal, or dollar, stock of money, prices will adjust until the purchasing power of this stock is the needed and desired amount. By extension, the quantity theory says that the rate of inflation depends on the rate of increase in the nominal money stock.

History provides at least some rough confirmations. As Hume observed, European inflation in the sixteenth and seventeenth centuries was associated with the discovery, importation, and monetization of gold from the New World. In the late nineteenth century, a gold shortage produced deflation in Europe and North America, reversed at the turn of the century when new technology and discovery flooded the world with South African gold. History is full of inflations resulting from undisciplined issues of fiat moneys, for example, Continentals by the rebellious American colonies, Civil War greenbacks, German marks in the 1923 hyperinflation, the currencies of almost every Latin American country again and again.

Nevertheless, the quantity theory is an incomplete explanation of inflation in advanced capitalist democracies in the late twentieth century. The sources of inflation are more complex and diverse, and the cures less obvious and sure than the theory suggests.

A popular capsule explanation of inflation is 'too much money chasing too few goods'. Now money chasing, or 'money on the wing' in the words of the English monetary economist D. H. Robertson, is not the same as what Robertson called 'money at rest'. The stock of money enumerated in the hypothetical census above is at rest in its holders' pockets, vaults, and accounts at the end of the business day. Money is chasing or on the wing when it circulates during the day, moving from one holder to another as goods are bought and sold and other transactions are consummated. Irving Fisher expressed the relationship of circulation to stock in the concept of velocity, or turnover, the average number of times a dollar is transferred within a period. (This can be measured for checking accounts by calculating the ratio of the aggregate dollar value of cheques drawn to average balances in the accounts debited. The ratio averaged twelve per month for the United States as a whole in 1978, and forty-five for New York banks alone.) But the bulk of these transactions are not for purchases of the final goods and services counted in the GNP, whose prices are those relevant for inflation. A more restrictive concept, GNP velocity, tells the average number of times a dollar of money stock buys GNP goods and services during a year. (This figure was 5.9 in 1978, for the so-called narrow money stock concept *M-1*, consisting of publicly held currency and demand deposits.)

The Equation of Exchange
Fisher provided a framework for analysis, the equation of exchange. For the purpose at hand it can be written $MV = PQ = Y$, where M is the stock of money, V its GNP velocity per year, P the GNP price index, Q the real (constant-price) GNP per year, and Y the dollar GNP per year. The equation is actually an identity, since V can be estimated only by dividing GNP in dollars per year (PQ) by M. In this framework the quantity theory holds if V and Q are constants, independent of M and P. Then P must move proportionately to M. However, both theoretical reasoning and empirical evidence cast doubt on the two premises of the quantity theory, at least during short-run cyclical fluctuation in economic activity.

The equation of exchange may also be written in terms of year-to-year rates of growth; the following is a close approximation:

$$\left(\begin{array}{c}\text{\% growth} \\ \text{of } M\end{array}\right) + \left(\begin{array}{c}\text{\% growth} \\ \text{of } V\end{array}\right) = \left(\begin{array}{c}\text{\% growth} \\ \text{of } P\end{array}\right) + \left(\begin{array}{c}\text{\% growth} \\ \text{of } Q\end{array}\right) = \left(\begin{array}{c}\text{\% growth of} \\ \text{dollar GNP}\end{array}\right). \qquad (27.1)$$

$$\frac{\Delta M}{M} + \frac{\Delta V}{V} = \frac{\Delta P}{P} + \frac{\Delta Q}{Q} = \frac{\Delta Y}{Y}$$

As an illustration of equation (27.1) consider 1978 relative to 1977, Dollar GNP Y rose by 12 per cent from \$1900 billion to \$2128 billion. But the real volume of goods and services produced, Q, increased by only 4.4 per cent. The difference was the inflation rate, 7.6 per cent. On the left-hand side of the equation, the money stock grew by 7.3 per cent, from \$335 billion average in 1977 to \$360 billion in 1978. Velocity rose by 4 per cent from 5.7 to 5.9.

If the changes in velocity $\Delta V/V$ and in real output $\Delta Q/Q$ are constants, independent of the other terms in equation (27.1), the inflation $\Delta P/P$ and money growth $\Delta M/M$ must vary together point for point. In this dynamic form, the quantity theory does not require that velocity V and output Q be unchanging—they may have non-zero trends and vary unsystematically around them. The trend of output Q is constrained by trends of labour force and productivity, which change slowly and gradually. In the United States since World War II, these trends have yielded average growth of real GNP of 3 to 4 per cent per annum. As a result, the average inflation rate has been three or four points less than the average growth of Y, dollar spending on GNP. In cyclical short runs, there are considerable deviations from the trend; year-to-year values of $\triangle Q/Q$ vary from -2 to 8 per cent. During business cycles, fluctuations in Y and in $\triangle Y/Y$ are generally registered in output Q and $\triangle Q/Q$, at least as much as in prices P and $\triangle P/P$.

Velocity V is not a mechanical property of money, but the outcome of the decisions and behaviours of millions of individuals. A way to interpret velocity is to notice that its reciprocal $1/V$ is roughly the average length of time an individual holds a dollar between transactions. (In this context the relevant measure of velocity refers to all transactions, not just to GNP purchases and sales. The figures given above imply holding times of $2\frac{1}{2}$ days for the United States, and of $\frac{2}{3}$ day for New York City.) But holding periods are economic decisions. In between necessary transactions, funds can be taken out of cash and placed in interest-bearing assets. The incentive is the interest earned. Against the interest gains must be set the inconveniences, costs, and risks of keeping cash balances low by making frequent conversions into and out of other assets. The incentive becomes relatively stronger when interest rates are high. The downward trend of velocity in recent decades of rising interest and inflation rates, and the pro-cyclical movements of both velocity and interest rates, are empirical confirmations. Inflation itself heightens the incentive to economize cash holdings and shorten holding periods, to acquire either real assets rising in price or financial assets with interest rates reflecting the inflation. Interest rates also reflect monetary policies. In business cycle short runs, active restriction of monetary growth will, other things being equal, be associated with tight credit markets and high interest rates, and thus with high velocity of money. On these systematic effects are superimposed more volatile changes in liquidity preferences and expectations, as well as innovations in financial markets, institutions, and technology.

The following sections discuss some sources of inflation in the late twentieth century in industrial societies with democratic and capitalist institutions. Monetary factors are always important, though in some instances their role is accommodative rather than initiative. In any event, it is always necessary to ask why monetary expansion is occurring given that modern governments and central banks have the capacity to prevent it. The answer may be that the government finds printing money and consequent inflation the expedient way of mobilizing resources for war or other government purposes. Or the answer may be that the government regards the economic consequences of severe anti-inflationary monetary policies, with their political and social by-products, as the greater evil.

EXCESS-DEMAND INFLATION

In the classic inflation drama, government is principal actor and villain. It needs more goods and a larger work force, typically for war. The economy is already operating close to its normal capacity. If government is to buy more, private citizens will have to buy less. Higher taxes are the straightforward way to achieve this shift, but government cannot or will not levy them. Instead, the sovereign simply prints the money needed, or at least enough new money so that the rest can be borrowed cheaply. New government demands accumulate in addition to undiminished private demands, and the economy cannot supply both. In terms of the equation of exchange, the higher growth of dollar spending induces little extra GNP and spills into higher inflation. The government gets what it wants. The price rise squeezes out private citizens caught by surprise, especially those dependent on fixed-dollar incomes and assets. Thus, inflation earns its reputation as the cruellest tax.

The drama has played many times throughout history, in the United States as elsewhere. The most recent performance, subdued compared with most previous wartime inflations, accompanied the Vietnam War. In 1966 President Johnson, against his economists' advice, chose not to ask Congress for higher taxes to pay for his escalation of the conflict. By 1968, defence spending had increased more than 50 per cent and had thrown the budget into a $12 billion deficit at a time when unemployment was well below the official 4 per cent target. The economy was overheated for most of four years, and the inflation rate rose from 2 per cent per year to 5 per cent. Comparing 1968 with 1965, money-supply growth had accelerated from 4.7 to 8.1 per cent, and GNP velocity increased from 4.1 to 4.5 per cent.

Excess demand need not be so striking as in wartime, and it need not be government spending that initiates the acceleration of dollar GNP. A dollar chasing goods is a dollar, whoever the spender. A boom in business investment or housing construction or purchases of consumers' durable goods could outrun the economy's productive capacity. Worldwide private speculative stockpiling of materials was a significant inflationary factor in 1973, as it had been in 1950 at the outset of the Korean War. (Thereafter, President Truman kept Korean War procurement non-inflationary by insisting on a stiff dose of taxation to pay for it).

Easy monetary and credit policies may be the source of excess demand. Business investment, home building, purchases of cars and appliances, and inventory building may be overstimulated by opportunities to borrow at interest rates low relative to anticipated returns in dollars or in use. One symptom of such policies will be high rates of monetary growth $\triangle M/M$. The period 1972–3 is a widely cited example. Monetary growth in 1972 was 9.1 per cent. Dollar GNP rose by 10.1 per cent, real GNP by 5.7 per cent. The inflation rate accelerated in the following year to 6 per cent, the highest year-over-year rate since 1948.

INFLATION WITHOUT EXCESS DEMAND: 'STAGFLATION'

Excess demand is not the only inflation story. Simultaneous inflation and excess supply afflicted the world economy through much of the 1970s. The symptoms of excess supply are abnormally high unemployment of labour and underutilization of productive capacity. In the United States in 1975, for example, unemployment averaged 8.5 per cent of the labour force, compared with an average of 5.4 per cent over the previous five years. Industry was operating at 74 per cent of capacity, compared with 83 per cent on average from 1970 to 1974. Inflation, at 9.7 per cent according to the GNP Price Index, could scarcely be attributed to contemporaneous excess demand.

The lesson of stagflation, and of earlier experience as well, is that inflation has a life of its own, in several senses.

1. Historical patterns of wage and price increase have a strong momentum during periods of excess supply. They respond slowly and erratically to economic circumstances reflected in monetary spending, unemployment, excess capacity, and GNP growth.
2. A modern economy appears to have an inflationary bias. Inflation rates rise more easily and more quickly in response to excess demand than they fall in response to excess supply.
3. Accidents may occur; events not connected with the state of the economy or with monetary and fiscal policies can change price levels as well as relative prices, and affect inflation rates at least temporarily. Recent examples are union wage push (1970–1), world food shortages (1973), good harvests (1976), and, of course, OPEC (1973).

The inertial inflation continues because it is self-consistent and because it becomes habitual and expected. Workers, unionized or unorganized, look at the wage gains of their peers and seek to do as well or better. They seek to catch and overtake the cost of living too, and cost-of-living adjustment (COLA) clauses help. Employers pay the pattern wage increase in their labour markets and industries, knowing they will not jeopardize their competitive position by doing so. Industrial pricing is strongly cost based. If hourly labour costs are rising by 9 per cent per year, and productivity is increasing by 2 per cent, the average industry will raise prices by 7 per cent, and this will be reflected in the workers' cost of living. The same real outcomes would occur if wage inflation was 4 per cent and prices were rising by 2 per cent, as in the early 1960s. Only if dollar wage rates rise, on average, no faster than labour productivity can there be stability in price levels. But a higher pattern, once built in, is very stubborn.

The pattern can change, for better or worse. Wage inflation is not wholly insensitive to economic conditions. Econometric estimates are that the difference between a 7 per cent unemployment year and a 6 per cent unemployment year is a quarter to half a percentage point of inflation. Even on the more optimistic estimate, it would take six years of the higher unemployment rate to wring three points from the inflation rate. It is this dismal calculus that leads governments here and abroad to seek more direct solutions—wage and price controls or less drastic and less mandatory interventions in private wage bargains and price decisions.

The inflationary bias is that wages and prices respond faster to demand pressure than to excess supply. Expanding firms and industries in tight labour markets are ready to bid above pattern for the labour they need; their existing employees are delighted. But it's not so easy for employers in less prosperous industries and regions to pay less than the prevailing pattern. Queues of job seekers at the factory gate, willing to work for less than those inside, seldom force rapid wage reduction. Existing employees, even if not under union contract, have considerable collective power; wage patterns give way only when the financial plight of the employer is a credible threat to their jobs. Minimum wages and unemployment insurance benefits limit downward movements of wages. Similarly, industrial firms raise prices when demand for their products is strong but are reluctant to compete by price cutting when demand is slack.

Inflexibility and inflationary bias appear to be developments of our twentieth-century amalgam of industrial capitalism and social democracy. In nineteenth-century Britain and the United States prices and money wages moved freely down and up. Periods of deflation were not prosperities, especially for farmers in debt, but output growth continued. As late as 1919, a sharp postwar inflation of commodity prices in the United States pulled money wages up; but both promptly fell just as sharply, and the setback to output and employment was small and shortlived. In the 1920s and 1930s, however, deflation of wages and non-agricultural prices occurred very slowly in both countries in spite of prolonged mass unemployment and idle capacity. The deflations that did occur did not seem to ameliorate the situation.

These observations led John Maynard Keynes to challenge the orthodox economic view that flexibility of wages and prices would restore full employment equilibrium after monetary or non-monetary disturbances. His challenge is still relevant, though it may be a pattern of inflationary increase of wages and prices, not just their level, that resists competitive pressures.

The modern economy does not behave like a world of atomistic competition among small shops, farms, and unorganized workers. True, there is still a 'flex price' sector as well as a 'fix price' sector. Not all sellers can set their own prices. In agriculture and mineral extraction, in which there are numerous producers of identical commodities, prices are determined in impersonal auction markets. But the flexible price sector has declined relative to the economy. In any case farmers and other competitive producers have obtained government-supported price floors making their prices, too, less flexible down than up.

In these circumstances large increases in individual prices become sources of inflation for the whole economy. Food prices rise because of bad weather. Oil prices rise because of OPEC. Hospital prices rise because of Medicare. Such events require changes of relative prices: scarcer goods naturally become more expensive. In a world of flexible prices, this could happen without inflating economy-wide price indexes. Dollar prices of other goods would fall enough to balance the increases in food energy, and medical care. In our world that does not happen. Instead, as in the years 1973–4 and 1978–9, large upward adjustments of prices of important commodities bring double-digit inflation.

THE UNEMPLOYMENT–INFLATION TRADE-OFF

In a striking empirical study published in 1958, A. W. Phillips showed that in the United Kingdom from 1861 to 1957 unemployment among trade union members was negatively correlated with rates of increase in money wages. The relationship was curvilinear: the rate of wage inflation appeared to be much more sensitive to variation in the unemployment rate when unemployment was low than when it was high. This shape embodies the asymmetries that lead to inflationary bias. Phillips Curves fit for other countries and to modern statistics told the same story. Moreover, a Phillips Curve relationship appeared to describe price inflation as well as wage inflation, as could be expected if prices are essentially marked-up labour costs.

Macroeconomic theorists warmly embraced the Phillips Curve, for several reasons. Keynesian economics contained no theory of inflation except for an economy operating at full employment with excess demand. According to the model of Keynes' *General Theory*, there should be no continuing inflation when the economy is operating below its full employment capacity. For that situation, which he regarded as usual in peacetime, Keynes provided a theory of the price level (it would move upward as employment and output increased) but not a theory of inflation (the price level should be stable or maybe declining if employment and output are stable). But there were plenty of cases, especially after World War II, when inflation kept going although employment and other measures of utilization were stable or declining. The concept of full employment itself was troublesome in peacetime. Did the occurrence of inflation mean the economy was fully employed, even though employment did not look full according to unemployment rates and other statistics? The Phillips Curve appeared to solve, or to finesse, these problems by making the inflation rate, rather than the price level, an increasing function of employment and capacity utilization, and by making fullness of employment a matter of degree rather than a yes-or-no condition.

Elevated from an empirical scatter diagram to a functional macroeconomic relationship, the Phillips Curve also implied that monetary and fiscal policy makers faced a usable trade-off, by which lower unemployment rates could be obtained at the cost of higher inflation rates and vice versa. Whether any government explicitly made policy on this basis is doubtful, but the notion of trade-off certainly has been indirectly influential.

In 1967 and 1968, Edmund Phelps and Milton Friedman independently raised serious theoretical questions about the Phillips Curve and the reliability of the Phillips trade-off as a basis for policy. They argued that rational workers, unions, and firms will take account of inflation and expected inflation in setting wages and prices, so that only deviations from the expected trend will be related to unemployment rates. Thus, the eventual inflation effects of a reduction in unemployment would be much greater than the initial impact. Events after 1966—inflation rates increasing while unemployment rates were low, but stable—supported these arguments.

According to Phelps and Friedman, there is in principle only one unemployment rate—Friedman's natural rate—at which wages and prices will continue on their anticipated path, whatever inflation rate that may imply. (Thus, full employment reappears in new guise, but with considerable residual mystery as to why it involves so much unemployment.) If unemployment is held by policy below the natural rate, inflation will be ever accelerating. Symmetrically, if unemployment is held above the natural rate, inflation will decelerate and eventually there will be ever-faster deflation. The latter implication may seem empirically doubtful, but the theory does not exclude the possibility that downward adjustments are slower than upward adjustments.

A common synthesis is to combine a short-run Phillips Curve with the natural rate. Even though there may be no long-run trade-off, the short-run relationship tells how hard or easy it is to diminish the prevailing inertial inflation by running the economy for a time with unemployment higher than natural. Once this has been done, once price expectations have been revised downward or eliminated, the economy can return to the natural rate without re-igniting the previous inflation.

But how can policy makers know what the natural rate is? The new classical macroeconomists, Robert Lucas, Thomas Sargent, and others, say they cannot and should not try. These theorists take the old Phelps–Friedman argument a long step farther. They regard the economy—labour markets included—as always in equilibrium, with neither excess supply nor excess demand. Prices and wages adjust to clear markets, subject to the expectations that the actors form with the information they have. In this sense, the economy is always at its natural rate, but this rate itself varies. Future policies are an important dimension of economic expectations. So the predictability or capriciousness of policy makers is crucial for the stability or volatility of the economy. The recommendation is that the makers of monetary policy simply announce and stick to non-inflationary rates of monetary growth. Workers and employers will then expect zero inflation and behave accordingly. The economy will then gravitate quickly to its correct-information natural rate of unemployment. To put it another way, whatever rate it moves to will be that natural rate.

MONETARY ACCOMMODATION

Inertial inflation and increases in important specific prices confront central banks and governments with cruelly difficult choices. Shall they accommodate these price movements or not? That is, shall they permit a growth of monetary spending Y sufficient to sustain normal increases of output and employment at the rising prices? If they do so, they are doing nothing to arrest the inflation itself, and indeed they are in a sense ratifying the behaviour and the institutions that bias the economy toward inflation. (With accommodation, incidentally, $\triangle M/M$ and $\triangle P/P$ may be positively correlated, as quantity theory suggests, but the causation runs in reverse, from prices to money stock.) If they do not accommodate, then as in 1974 to 1975 they will depress output and employment, while the counter-inflationary effects are uncertain and slow at best.

The makers of monetary and fiscal policy in democracies are always seeking politically acceptable compromises. Their natural bent is to lean against the evil wind of the day, to fight inflation when it is the most vivid popular complaint and to combat recession and unemployment when they become the uppermost concerns. Business cycles due to stop–go alternation of policies are the result. Some economic observers believe that a resolute irreversible commitment of non-accommodation would melt the rock of inertial inflation much faster than previous experience under counter-cyclical and semi-accommodative policies would suggest. Others believe that non-accommodative policies will eliminate inflation only at great and prolonged cost in lost output and employment, and quite possibly not at all. They are reconciled either to living with inflation, possibly accelerating inflation, or to limiting wage and price increases directly by more or less formal controls.

INFLATION AS SYMPTOM

Inflation is, as emphasized above, a monetary phenomenon. But inflation may also be the symptom of some real economic, social, and political difficulties. The monetary authorities may choose accommodation in the belief that inflation is one of the less painful manifestations of the underlying disease.

It is an economic burden on a society to fight a war, and usually to lose one. Inflation is probably not the most orderly or just way to distribute the burden. But doing it differently would not avoid the basic social cost, the diversion or loss of productive resources. After World War I, the victorious Allies imposed punitive reparations on the German people. The German government mistakenly tried to pay the victors by printing marks and selling them in the foreign-exchange markets for the francs and pounds they were required to deliver. As the mark depreciated in the exchange markets they had to print more and more, and the result was the most famous hyperinflation of history. As disastrous as the inflation was, the original burden on the German economy, which had to be shouldered one way or another, was still the reparations. In the 1970s the OPEC cartel inflicted a heavy social loss on oil-importing countries, whose residents had to work harder and longer to import a barrel of oil. This is the true and unavoidable cost. The OPEC price boosts also inflated US price indexes, but that is a symptom rather than the cause of losses of real income. Even if sufficient wage reductions were absorbed to keep the price indexes from rising, US citizens still would be losing to OPEC.

A more disquieting possibility is that inflation is the symptom of deep-rooted social and economic contradiction and conflict, between major economic groups persistently claiming pieces of pie that together exceed the whole pie. Inflation is the way that their claims, so far as they are expressed in nominal terms, are temporarily reconciled. But it will continue and indeed accelerate so long as the basic conflicts of real claims and real power continue.

There are a number of possible scenarios of conflict inflation in the 1970s. A common story is that a combination of misfortunes—OPEC, long-run energy shortage, environmental dangers and costs—has sharply lowered the paths of potential output, real wages, and real returns on capital investment. But it has not lowered the standards of real income progress to which employed workers are accustomed, or the profit rates that managers and share-owners expect. The relative price shocks of the mid 1970s are the source of serious and lasting conflict, not simply of a temporary bulge of inflation statistics.

REFERENCES

Fisher, Irving, *The Purchasing Power of Money*, rev. edn., New York: Macmillan, 1926; Friedman, Milton, and Anna Schwartz, *A Monetary History of the United States*, National Bureau of Economic Research, Princeton, NJ: Princeton University Press, 1963; Friedman, Milton, 'The role of monetary policy', *American Economic Review*, March 1968, vol. 58, no. 1, 1–17; Hume, David, 'Of money', in T. H. Green and T. H. Grose, eds, *Essays, Moral, Political, and Literary*, vol. 1, 1977; New York and London: Longman, 1912; Keynes, John Maynard, *The General Theory of Employment, Interest, and Money*, London and New York: Macmillan,1936; Lucas, Robert and Thomas Sargent, 'After Keynesian macroeconomics', *After the Phillips Curve*, Federal Reserve Bank of Boston Conference Series, no. 19, Boston: Federal Reserve Bank of Boston, 1978, pp. 49–83; Phelps, Edmund S., 'Phillips curves, inflation expectations, and optimal employment over time', *Economica*, August 1967, vol. 34, pp. 254–81; Phillips, A.W., 'The relation between unemployment and the rate of change of money wage rates in the United Kingdom, 1861–1957', *Economica*, November 1958, vol. 25, pp. 283–99; Robertson, Dennis A., *Money*, 4th edn., Chicago: University of Chicago Press, 1959.

28   There are Three Types of Inflation: We Have Two*

Three decades of experience tell us that inflation is endemic to modern democratic industrial societies. Fortunately the same record indicates that these economies are nonetheless capable of yielding their citizens substantial gains in well-being decade after decade. But hysteria about inflation may lead to policies that keep economic progress well below its potential.

The United States inflation of 1973–4 is a complex and difficult case, unique in our history. In general we may distinguish three types of inflation: (a) excess-demand inflation, popularly summarized as 'too much money chasing too few goods', (b) the wage–price–wage spiral, and (c) shortages and price increases in important commodities. Our current inflation is a combination of (b) and (c). But public discussion generally ignores these distinctions and identifies every inflation, including the present case, as the classical type (a). From this diagnosis, mistaken in my opinion, follows the classical remedy, the 'old-time religion' of restricting aggregate demand by tight monetary policy and by fiscal austerity.

With some oversimplification, we can say that the US suffered a severe case of excess-demand inflation (a) in 1966, when President Johnson and Secretary of Defence Robert McNamara piled war demands onto an economy already operating close to its capacity, and ignored their economists' pleas to raise taxes. Reinforced by a lesser dose of excess demand in 1968, the 1966 outburst left in its wake a surprisingly stubborn case of inflation type (b), the wage–price–wage spiral. Attaining a momentum of its own, this inflation first accelerated and then abated somewhat under the deliberately recessionary policy of 1969–71, assisted by phases I and II of the controls introduced in August 1971.

At the end of 1972 the ongoing wage–price dynamic was producing overall inflation of $3\frac{1}{2}$ per cent per year, down from 5 per cent in 1969 and 1970. However, it was obvious, as events confirmed that some of the improvement was transient window dressing which would not survive relaxation of controls and completion of the recovery from recession.

Some observers view the 1973 expansion of the American economy as another case of excess demand and blame the Federal Reserve and the Nixon budget for overheating the economy once again. But unemployment never fell below 4.6 per cent, and the Government cooled off the boom pretty quickly after midyear. In any case, the underlying wage–price–wage dynamic was proceeding at year-end with wage increases of 7 to 8 per cent, which with normal productivity gains would mean price inflation in the neighbourhood of 5 per cent per year.

But meanwhile the United States was hit by a severe type (c) inflation, a spectacular increase in commodity prices. For the first time since the Korean War, external events sharply increased the prices facing American producers and consumers. Everyone knows about the world shortages of food and energy, and about the aggressive new policies of the oil-producing nations, who have in effect imposed an excise tax of $10 to $15 billion a year on American consumers of their products. What may be less well undertood is the role of the 16 per cent depreciation of the dollar in foreign exchange since 1970. Working precisely as the architects of the policy hoped, dollar depreciation made imports about $10 billion a year more expensive to Americans. Combined with booms in Europe and Japan, depreciation also increased foreign demand for US products, notably basic agricultural and industrial commodities. Foreign demands for our export created shortages and price increases for American buyers.

Now there are two important differences between types (b) and (c) inflation. First, the wage–price–wage spiral keeps going of its own momentum. Wage increases are covered by price boosts, and subsequent wage settlements respond both to past wage patterns and to price inflation. The type (c) commodity price increases, however, are once-and-for-all adjustments to new supply–demand situations: those prices won't necessarily fall, but all that is needed to improve the rate of inflation is that they stop rising.

Second, the wage–price–wage spiral does not of itself impose any collective loss on the nation or on the urban non-agricultural sector of the economy in which it occurs. One man's price is another's income; when buyers pay more, sellers receive more. The inflation may proceed unevenly, so that some workers, consumers, and property owners lose while others gain; such relative distributional changes are always occurring, inflation or no inflation. But it is simply vulgar nonsense—no less for constant repetition by economists, politicians, bankers, and journalists—to say that an internal self-contained inflation causes *per se* a loss of economic welfare in aggregate.

The commodity price increases are a different matter. They are symptoms of a real national economic loss, and in particular a loss to urban wage earners and consumers. In current circumstances, we are paying more for oil and other imports. We're not just paying more dollars but more work and resources; under our new foreign-exchange rate policy we can no longer buy foreign goods with paper dollar IOUs. We are also paying more, about $25 billion a year gross, to our own farmers. Recorded declines of real wages are the painful and unavoidable consequences. To attribute them indiscriminately to 'inflation' is superficial and misleading.

The economy is currently in recession, and the prospects are for abnormally slow growth in output and for rising unemployment. The Federal Reserve is administering the classical medicine for excess demand inflation (a), because that is the only medicine it has. Some of its spokesmen, supporters, and critics regard every inflation, almost by definition, as the excess demand type—on the ground that whatever the proximate origins of inflation, it could be avoided by sufficiently resolute restriction of demand. The idea is that the wage–price–wage spiral will unwind if enough slack—idle capacity and unemployment—is created. Extreme advocates of the old-time religion even argue that determined disinflation of demand could have yielded big enough reductions in prices of other goods and services to offset or average out the recent price increases of food, fuel, and basic materials.

The trouble with this prescription is that it will not succeed without years of economic stagnation, high unemployment, and lost production, with much more severe consequences for real economic welfare than the inflation itself. Experience shows that the wage–price–wage spiral is extremely resistant to unemployment, recession, and economic slack. The unpleasant fact of life is that the wage- and price-setting institutions of our economy, and of every other non-communist economy, are biased toward inflation. Wages and prices rise when and where demand is strong much more readily than they decline when and where demand is weak. While the classical medicine would have prevented the Vietnam burst of inflation, it will take much more time and pain than its advocates admit to overcome the wage–price–wage inflation now built into our economy.

The main inflationary threat this year is that the temporary inflation of type (c) will be permanently built into the ongoing wage–price–wage spiral. The setbacks to real wages reflected in higher prices in food, fuel, and other commodities cannot really be reversed. General attempts to 'catch up' by escalated wage settlements will simply be defeated by accelerated price inflation. So Washington is right to be alarmed by this year's wage settlements.

But there is very little the Federal Reserve can do about them, even if the Fed provokes a full-blown recession. The settlements are already in the works; and they depend much more on the recent history of wages and prices than on the current strength or weakness of demand. The budget makers of the Executive and the Congress are in much the same position. They too can be nobly and resolutely austere, pretending they are fighting a classical type (a) inflation. But the results of budget cutting will be measured more in lower employment and production statistics than in wages and prices. Present anti-inflation hysteria may well yield policies that bring us the worst of several worlds.

Is there a more promising and less costly way to confront the unique inflationary problem of 1974? If ever there was a time for what the Europeans call 'incomes policy', the time is now. It may be that the Nixon experiment with wage and price controls was never a good idea, and the stop-and-go alternation of phases certainly didn't help. But the total abandonment, in April of this year, of every legal or informal restraint was incredibly untimely.

What was needed was Presidential leadership—in open, candid understanding with business, labour, agriculture, and consumers—to establish realistic moderate guideposts for wages and prices. We still need what some of us have called a new social contract for the economy, along the following lines: (1) Monetary and fiscal policy would be geared, not to increase unemployment, but to keep it from rising, and to achieve, not to thwart, the 4 per cent a year growth in production of which our economy is capable. (2) Workers' take-home pay would be increased by cutting Social Security payroll taxes and by making the structure of those taxes more equitable and progressive. This tax cut would provide part of the demand stimulus needed under (1). (3) Labour, for its part, would consent to a general wage guidepost of 8 or 9 per cent, and Washington would expect an exact comparable moderation in business and agricultural price setting.

The hour is late. But the long national nightmare is over. Our new President has the trust and good will of the American people. If the economic problem he confronts is unique, he also enjoys a unique opportunity to seek a new direction.

29 Inflation: Monetary and Structural Causes and Cures*

I. YES, INFLATION IS A MONETARY PHENOMENON

Inflation is always and everywhere a *monetary* phenomenon. Milton Friedman says so, and I stipulate my agreement at the beginning in order to avoid misunderstanding. By definition, *inflation* is a decline in the purchasing power of the monetary unit of acount. To say that inflation is a monetary phenomenon is not to say that excessive monetary expansion is always its sole or principal cause. There are, I shall argue, several varieties of inflation. The inflations observed at various times and places often differ in their origins, their effects, and their possible remedies. The monetary nature of every inflation does not imply that it is always easy to disinflate by turning off the monetary spigot.

Reconciling the invariable monetary nature of inflation with my thesis that there are various sources and species of inflation is not difficult. There are two points in this reconciliation. First, the velocity of the money stock—however it is defined, whichever of the concepts *M-0, M-1, M-A* or *-B, M-2, M-3* is adopted—is variable and elastic. Consequently, some sources of inflation may work by increasing velocity rather than by increasing the stock of money. The second and more important point is *accommodation* by the monetary authorities. The central bank, instead of being the initiator and prime mover of inflationary expansion of money supplies, responds to upward price movements and provides the money to finance them. No central bank does so because it likes inflation. Monetary policy makers accommodate ongoing inflationary trends, usually reluctantly and grudgingly, because

*March 1980, Conference on Inflation, Brooklyn College. In Nathan Schmukler and Edward Marcus, eds., *Inflation Through The Ages: Economic, Social, Psychological and Historical Aspects*, New York: Brooklyn College and Columbia University Presses, 1983, pp. 3–16.

the consequences of not accommodating appear to them, rightly or wrongly, as the greater evil.

For example, in the United States in recent years aggregate dollar spending on final goods and services, that is, nominal GNP, was growing at 11 to 12 per cent per year. This was financed by an 8 per cent per year growth in the *monetary base*—currency outstanding and bank reserve deposits at the Federal Reserve—and by an even smaller rate of growth in *M-1*, the most common measure of the stock of transactions money. These numbers indicate how fast velocity has been increasing.

The upward trend of velocity is partly rational response to the upward trend of nominal interest rates, which induces economies in cash management. It is partly the result of innovations in financial technology which, however induced, will persist even if and when interest rates fall. Closer examination of the quarter-to-quarter and year-to-year relations between monetary stocks and spending on goods and services would show that velocity and its rate of growth have been highly variable. Their variability is partly random; for example, cash management innovations don't occur smoothly. The variabiity also reflects systematic responses to short-term variations in interest rates.

In any case, the 11 to 12 per cent per annum growth of nominal income obviously exceeds the sustainable growth in real output in the United States economy, which is only about 3 per cent. It has also exceeded even the high rates of growth of real output, 5 or 6 per cent, typically attained during cyclical recoveries. Such a rate of growth of dollar spending is in that sense obviously inflationary. But it does not follow that the growth in the monetary base or in the transactions money stock that supports such growth in dollar spending is the spontaneous cause of the accompanying inflation. Presumably the monetary authorities could have reduced the growth rate of spending on goods and services whether that was the result of increases in velocity or of increases in monetary stocks. Indeed they have done so this year (1980). They did not do so two years ago because they estimated the costs of non-accommodation of the existing inflation to be very high.

This brings me to the basic point. Reducing the rate of expansion of money stocks is *necessary* for disinflation but not *sufficient*. Confusion between necessary and sufficient conditions is an endless source of confusion in economics, as in many other aspects of national and personal life. In the long run, if an economy were to experience an era of zero inflation, we would observe a rate of growth of nominal spending on goods and services equal to the rate of growth of real output. In the United States, therefore, we would observe trends in both money spending and real output of about 3 per cent per year. That obvious fact, however, does not entitle anyone to believe that a sudden reduction of the rate of monetary spending from 11 per cent to 3 per cent, engineered by the instruments available to the monetary authorities, would eliminate inflation tomorrow, or this year, or next. Certainly some fraction of the reduction in spending growth would show up in output rather than in prices; I shall argue that output contraction will normally be much the larger share. Neither our Federal Reserve nor any other central bank has any power to channel the effects of its policies into prices and output in the proportions it would like. The institutions of the economy—business enterprises and trade unions—determine those proportions. At this moment, our Federal Reserve has succeeded in contracting sharply the growth of money stocks and of money spending. The result is, as it was in 1974, a sharp recession, a precipitous fall in production and employment. When the authorities choose accommodation, it is because non-accommodation would result, not in price disinflation, but in substantial and costly reverses in real economic activity.

The main point of this introduction is that those of us who, in examining problems of inflation, look at real events and non-monetary institutions are not committing a vulgar fallacy. Knowing that inflation is a monetary phenomenon, we carry the analysis one layer deeper when we ask why monetary expansions occur and why they continue.

II. VARIETIES OF INFLATION

I hope therefore that even the monetarists will let me proceed to enumerate three varieties of inflation: (a) excess-demand inflation, (b) inertial inflation, and (c) conflict inflation.

a. Excess-Demand Inflation

By *excess-demand inflation* I mean the classical scenario, often popularly described as 'too much money chasing too few goods'. More precisely, it is the inflation that results when aggregate demand at existing prices chronically exceeds the capacity of the economy to produce goods and services. Many episodes of wartime and postwar inflation meet this description. Frequently, but not always, excess demand arises when governments pile their demands for resources into an economy already operating at, or close to, capacity and finance their purchases by printing money or borrowing rather than by taxation. A recent example in the United States was the Vietnam War (1966–9). Orthodox policy prescriptions—restriction of money and credit,

increased taxation, and reduced public spending (to balance government budgets) are just what the physician orders for excess-demand
inflation.

b. Inertial Inflation

The second type, which I call *inertial*, is inflation without excess
demand. The word coined in the 1970s is 'stagflation'. Inertial inflation
has several characteristics.

First, inertial inflation, as the name implies, is inherited from the
past, very often from past excess-demand inflation. In the United
States, the Vietnam War period left a legacy of inertial inflation that
we found in the 1970s very difficult to erase. Second, inertial inflation
is perpetuated by contracts and commitments, particularly with respect
to wages. In the United States the setting of money wage rates is
decentralized. It occurs either in negotiations of employers with trade
unions or in unorganized labour markets in periodic administrative
decisions by individual employers. The timing of these negotiations
and decisions is staggered, not synchronized; every week some contracts
are expiring and being renegotiated, and some administered wage
settings are being reconsidered. Contracts are long, often for three
years; non-union employers usually change their wage scales annually.
In addition to formal contracts and scales, both organized and
unorganized workers have implicit assurances and expectations as to
the wage treatment that they will receive from their employers. In a
modern industrial economy of this kind, wage setting is greatly
influenced by workers' concern for their positions relative to other
workers. They want above all to keep up with, catch up with,
possibly leap ahead of workers with whom they regard themselves as
comparable.

Third, the inertia in wages that results from this system supports
and is supported by the mark-up pricing conventions of employing
firms. Labour and materials costs per unit of normal output are the
principal basis for industrial prices; mark-ups vary with demand, but
by no means sufficiently to avoid substantial adjustments of output
and employment. Together these institutions lead to the sluggishness
in wage and price responses in the face of recession and excess supply
with which we are all familiar. These inertial wage and price patterns
are internally consistent. That is, if each employer follows the going
pattern of wage increases, workers will find their relative positions
maintained and employers themselves will maintain their competitive
positions not only in their labour markets but also in their product
markets. If they raise their prices in accordance with the prevailing
wage increase they will not lose markets to their rivals. The circle is

closed as the price increases feed back into the workers' cost of living, reinforcing the pattern of wage increase itself.

Fourth, the continuation of an entrenched self-consistent pattern of wage and price increase can be described as the establishment and realization of expectations. Expectations are certainly important. It is the employer's expectation that other firms will be following the same pattern that leads him to follow the pattern too. Workers' expectation that prices will rise by the pattern and that other workers will receive similar wage increases leads them to demand and to accept the pattern wage increase. This is true, but the phenomenon is not simply a matter of expectations. Adjustment lags are intrinsic to the contracts, institutions, and conventions of wage and price setting. These provide inertia in the adjustment of wages and prices to economic slack, even when expectations change.

Fifth, inertial inflation has taken a new and particularly troublesome form in the 1970s as a result of price and supply shocks external to the industrial economies of the United States and other developed countries. The principal examples are the two big increases in OPEC prices, first in 1973–4 and then in 1978–9. Our inflation as measured in Consumer Price Indexes is a combination of the built-in core of wage–price inflation and of more volatile elements. These more volatile components are the prices of imports, either from overseas or from the flexible price sectors of our own economies. In recent years the United States has suffered several unpleasant surprises in the prices of food and raw materials and, of course, in the price of oil. These shocks not only increase actual inflation rates while they are being diffused and absorbed; they may also feed into wage demands and settlements and thus accelerate the inertial inflation. Indexation of wages and other prices by the cost of living automatically ratchets the basic inflation rate upward. In the United States, however, this effect has been less severe than in several European economies. Indeed, our wage earners have swallowed significant cuts in their real wages.

Monetarists typically deny that movements in the prices of individual commodities, relative to wages and other prices, can affect overall inflation rates. They stress the dichotomy between specific relative prices, real phenomena, and economy-wide absolute prices, monetary phenomena. The answer, the resolution, is again accommodation and inertia. Relative price shocks would *not*, it is true, affect the economy-wide inflation rate even temporarily if wages and prices were highly flexible. In such an economy we could imagine an increase in the relative price of a particular commodity occurring partly via reduction in the absolute money prices of all other goods and services. We could imagine those prices falling sufficiently that the average price level, the overall Consumer Price Index for example, remains unaffected. In such an economy an OPEC shock like that of 1973–4 or 1979 would not have boosted inflation rates to double digits. The adverse shift in terms of trade would instead have been reflected in reductions of wages and prices in domestic industry. Clearly, we do not live in that kind of economy. In the economy we do live in, the monetary authorities are faced with the unpleasant choice to accommodate the external price shock or to force a monetary contraction that will result not in immediate disinflation but in recession and unemployment. Hence, the prevalence of unfavourable price shocks in the 1970s has pointed up the difficulties created by inertial inflation.

c. Conflict Inflation

The third type of inflation I wish to distinguish I call *conflict inflation*. Inflation of this type is symptomatic of a fundamental disharmony within the society. There is no consensus on the division of the pie. Neither the mechanisms of the competitive market nor the political process work with sufficient authority to reconcile the several economic interests to the rewards they receive for economic activity, or inactivity. The constituent economic and social groups claim collectively more 'pie' than there actually can be. Moreover, each group has the economic or political bargaining power to raise its money income. As the rival interest groups strive in turn to gain larger shares of the pie by claiming higher money incomes, inflation is the outcome.

Of course, this process cannot continue without ratification, accommodation, by the monetary authorities. On the other hand, as long as consensus is lacking, as long as fundamental conflicts continue regarding the distribution of real income and wealth, monetary contraction will not solve the problem. It will not eliminate the inflation, but will simply result in reduction of real economic activity, as in the case of inertial inflation. Hence monetary contraction will just shrink the pie, the total social product over whose division the contestants are fighting. It is not clear that diminishing the size of the rewards in dispute will mitigate the conflict or diminish the inflation symptomatic of the conflict.

Distributional conflict may be exacerbated by losses of real national income, such as payments of 'tribute' to OPEC, and by slowdowns of productivity growth, such as we have recently experienced. Even a nation that previously had enjoyed a fairly harmonious consensus about distribution might at least temporarily experience conflict inflation, induced by disagreements about sharing the costs of national reverses in terms of trade and productivity. In this way the relative price shocks of the 1970s may have created conflict inflation.

III.   ON THE COSTS AND BENEFITS OF ANTI-INFLATIONARY POLICIES

The natural approach of economists to issues of public policy is to balance costs and benefits. In the case of inflation, as in other applications of this approach, it is essential to consider operationally realistic alternatives. That is, we cannot really make a cost–benefit appraisal of 'inflation' in the abstract, as if we had a free choice whether to have inflation or not. Disinflation is not a free good. I have given some reasons why it is not, reasons embedded in the institutions of wage and price setting of a modern democratic, capitalist nation like the United States. The supposed costs and discomforts of inflation are not always the same, nor are their distributions among individuals and groups. They vary with the nature and source of the inflation. Most textbook generalizations on these matters are wrong— for example, that inflation always hurts wage earners, always hurts creditors, always benefits debtors, always aids entrepreneurs. We cannot make such generalizations if the inflations that we experience and observe are the results of a variety of causes, different at different times and places. Moreover, the supposed costs of inflation are deeply entangled with the costs of those real economic and political events of which inflation is a joint symptom. Those costs are usually not avoidable; at any rate they are not avoidable by the usual macroeconomic instruments of anti-inflationary policy. They are not avoidable even if it were somehow possible to eliminate or suppress the inflationary symptoms of the basic causes.

In recent years, in the United States and elsewhere, 'inflation' has become a scapegoat, a universal shorthand explanation for all disappointments and reverses in economic status. When men and women respond in public opinion surveys that inflation is their number one problem and the number one problem of the nation, probably they mean that they are disappointed by losses in their real incomes, losses relative at least to previous trends and expectations. They use the term *inflation* to register those losses and disappointments.

OPEC raised the cost of oil, and the true loss to an importing nation is that it must work harder and longer; we must give up more of our product and our toil to purchase a barrel of oil. That cost in terms of trade would still be there, even if we could have deflated domestic wages and prices enough to avoid the aggregate inflationary impacts of the OPEC shocks. It is muddled thinking, therefore, to attribute to inflation the costs of paying more for imported oil. Those economic statisticians who seek in the record of the 1970s generalizable clues to the national, international, sectoral, and distributional burdens of inflation engage themselves in an inquiry that is doomed from its very conception. When we assess anti-inflationary policies, we should recognize that the measures available to our monetary and fiscal policy makers do not include forcing the oil-exporting countries to reduce the price of oil and return us to the happy days before 1973.

The elementary point I am making applies even to classical excess demand inflations. Most of those have occurred historically in connection with wars—for our country in the last half century, World War II, Korea, Vietnam. Wars inevitably levy large real costs. They consume resources, real resources. We have no right, therefore, to charge the costs of wars to 'inflation'. The economic approach is to compare inflationary finance with other methods of extracting the resources needed for war. Maybe, even probably, inflation is 'the cruellest tax' that could be used for this purpose, but that is not a self-evident conclusion. The gains, if any, from anti-inflationary financial policy consist of the differences in social output and consumption and in income and wealth distributions from financing by explicit taxation instead.

Another example is the notorious German hyperinflation of 1923. We have all heard about the serious economic and social costs of that inflation. At the same time, we must remember that the basic burden on the German people was the levy of reparations. Those reparations—like the tax levied by OPEC on foreign consumers of its oil—the German nation had to pay one way or another. Probably the manner in which the Weimar Republic tried to pay the victorious Allies was foolish and socially destructive. But the true comparison is with some other method of taxation, some other mechanism for transfer to the Allies of the real tribute exacted by the treaty.

In short, optimal taxation theory is the proper way to go about examining the desirability of anti-inflation policies, as Professor E. S. Phelps has pointed out many times. Even today we may note that a 10 per cent inflation in the United States gives the federal government annually $15 billion of equivalent revenue from expanding the monetary base. Taxpayers benefit also from reduction of the real federal debt, since the debt service now is mostly repayment of principal. These effects on federal finance need to be balanced against the costs of other taxes that could and would be used to pay the government's bills.

a. Anticipated Inflation
In assessing the costs and benefits of anti-inflationary policies we need to distinguish between anticipated and unanticipated inflation. By *anticipated* I mean inflation rates to which the private economy has

adjusted. What are the costs of anticipated inflation? That is, what are the benefits of reducing it? The main costs that economists have found are the so-called 'shoe-leather' costs of economizing holdings of transactions money. These are the costs of making frequent transactions between means of payment on the one hand and interest-bearing assets on the other, in order to avoid the losses of interest incident to large balances of idle cash. Now it is difficult to make shoe-leather costs appear very large and their reduction yield great benefit to the economy. In the United States about $400 billion of transactions balances are used by the nation's households and businesses. If we assume that a ten point increase in nominal interest rates goes along with a 10 per cent inflation, then our 10 per cent inflation has meant a shoe-leather cost of $40 billion, which is one-sixtieth of GNP. Moreover, given an elasticity of demand for cash balances with respect to the interest rate of 1/2, a generously large estimate, one more point of the inflation rate would increase the aggregate cost by $2 billion, namely 1/1,200 of the GNP.

Martin Feldstein has, it is true, argued that even this small cost on an annual basis has a very large and possibly infinite present value. The reason he advances is that, with the growth of the economy, the shoe-leather costs of inflation and anticipated inflation will grow at the economy's natural rate of growth. He argues further that the revealed discount rate on future consumption by American households is smaller than the growth rate of the economy. Therefore, he finds, the gain from a reduction in shoe-leather costs has an infinite present value.

This argument is not very convincing. If the operational discount rate for the future is really lower than the economy's growth rate, then all kinds of investments, however costly at the outset, will be justified, if they produce gains that grow with the economy. One cannot really make welfare economics arguments with divergent integrals.

Furthermore, it is necessary to consider the possible stimulus that anticipated inflation gives for capital formation. Anticipated inflation does have the redeeming feature of making investment in real productive assets attractive relative to monetary saving, and this may offset its shoe-leather cost. To put the point another way, a developed capitalist economy may need a real interest rate on safe assets that is close to zero and at times negative; as Keynes pointed out, this is difficult to bring about in the absence of inflation because of the zero floor interest rate on basic money.

The central issue is whether social investment in sufficient unemployment for sufficient time to bring the inflation rate down pays off subsequently in the real advantages of permanently lower inflation. The investment in disinflation reduces current real output and employment, and consequently, it also reduces capital formation. The lost capital formation would have bestowed on the economy an evergrowing benefit, a benefit that is an offset to the evergrowing shoe-leather costs of the inflation. Moreover, the inflation may substitute in public finance for explicit taxation of capital, an investment deterrent Feldstein himself emphasizes in other contexts. We cannot be sure that we have chosen the optimal combination of the inflation tax and income taxation.

Another cost of anticipated inflation often mentioned is the cost of calculation and planning when price changes are more frequent. This, of course, would be a cost of deflation no less than inflation. It is hard to quantify—we don't know how much additional trouble higher inflation rates make for companies that establish price lists or catalogues for the goods they have for sale. We don't know how much confusion between relative and absolute prices arises because prices in general are rising. Remember that relative prices are always changing, even when price indexes are fairly stable. It is not proper to compare an ideal situation of complete certainty and stability of individual prices with a realistic situation in which relative prices vary and attribute the difference solely to inflation. Empirically it has been observed that the variance of inflation rates is greater when the general level of inflation is higher. One reason is that changing price quotations is costly; if prices are changed in discrete jumps on unsynchronized schedules, relative prices do get out of line, the more so the higher the inflation rate. Higher volatility in the movement of prices makes planning and calculation more difficult. But there is a serious problem of identification in the observed correlation of price variances with mean inflation rates. As I have previously observed, a possible source of higher inflation is extraordinary movement in relative prices, of which the OPEC shocks are an example. There the causation runs the other way, given the bias of our institutions toward making relative price adjustments by increases in the one price rather than decreases in the multitude of others. Periods of considerable relative price volatility will be periods of higher inflation and also periods of greater volatility of inflation.

Finally, anticipated inflation is a problem because people think it is a problem. Its social disutility is apparent from people's discontent, even though their distaste for the process may reflect misunderstandings and misperceptions. Their discontent is a fact we must confront.

b. Unanticipated Inflation

As for unanticipated inflation, the costs are well known. They have to do with the distribution of income and wealth. There are many old clichés about the redistributions resulting from inflation, but they do not apply systematically and regularly. Inflations are not all alike. The redistributions that occur in war-related excess-demand inflations are not the same as those that occur in stagflation. We can no longer say with as much truth that inflation hurts older people, retired people, people on so-called fixed-money incomes. Social Security is now fully indexed. During inflation of the type we have recently been having, beneficiaries of social insurance are better protected than young workers. There aren't many fixed incomes any more; civil servants, even teachers, no longer fall in that category. Interest rates are adjusting to inflation and compensating those who now save in interest-bearing assets for the inflation. Those of us who invested in common stocks, formerly regarded as the natural hedge against inflation, have suffered more than people who in the recent decade of put their funds in short-term interest-bearing dollar claims. Altogether, one can see little change in the size distributions of income and wealth, or in the shares of labour and property. They have remained much the same throughout the postwar period, in both periods of inflation and periods of relatively stable prices.

It is easy to forget that economic life is always risky, always generating capital gains and capital losses, always producing surprising changes in economic welfare both for individual workers and for savers and investors. Fortunes are made and lost mainly by relative prices and relative wages. It is an illusion to believe that a non-inflationary environment would be one in which people could feel secure in their careers and their investments. The major losses of recent years are traceable to real causes, not to the process of inflation *per se*. Consider the owners of gas-guzzling cars, energy-intensive equipment, glass buildings, and ski chalets with electric heat. Consider members of our own academic profession, who as university students choosing careers misread the prospects of supply and demand. Their plight is not really due to inflation.

In weighing unemployment and its costs as against inflation and its costs, we should not forget that unemployment has both global and distributional effects. Many of the losses are concentrated on a small segment of the population. The distributional effects of stagnation and unemployment deserve to be added to the economy-wide losses of production, just as inflation is charged with both social costs and distributional inequity. We should also remember, and remind our students and our lay audiences, that unexpected disinflation would be tough on many people. Consider those who have borrowed long term at high nominal interest rates. It is not just unanticipated inflation that gives rise to unexpected capital gains and losses; surprises come from all unanticipated developments. Remember—at least some of us *can* remember—the redistributions due to deflation in the past, notably in the Great Depression of the 1930s.

In suggesting that we use some perspective in calculating the costs of inflation, in suggesting that we apply our usual apparatus of cost–benefit calculus to the appraisal of anti-inflationary policy, I do not want to be misinterpreted. I agree that the deliberate use of inflation for the finance of government is a symptom of social and political failure, failure to reach explicit consensus on how the burden of government activity should be borne. I, too, would deplore the distributional effects of inflationary finance. If it is not the cruellest tax, at least it is an arbitrary and random one, and its consequences are not deliberately debated and assessed by the legislature. At the same time, when our inflation is not the result of deficit finance and excess demand, but the lingering consequence of past events and shocks, or when it is the result of temporary or enduring social conflict, I believe that we must be cautious in recommending the classical cures. As I have suggested, popular discontent with inflation probably reflects disappointment with the progress of real wages and real standards of life. It is ironical that such discontent should be the basis in public opinion of policies that will further reduce incomes and standards of living.

IV. POLICY CHOICES TODAY

I turn now to the choices that confront us today. There are really only three choices, hard as it is to face the unpleasant fact. None of the feasible choices is pleasant. Maturity for a nation and its government, as for an individual, consists in willingness to face up to budget constraints.

The three choices are first, 'muddling through' as we were doing, at least until recently; second, severely disinflationary monetary and fiscal policies; third, combining monetary disinflation with an effective incomes policy directly reducing the rate of increase of wages and prices.

a. Orthodox Monetary Disinflation

The second course, monetary disinflation alone, is the one in which we have recently embarked. As I suggested earlier, monetary contraction is a necessary, but unfortunately not a sufficient, condition for successful disinflation. Suppose that we do reduce the 11 per cent or 12 per cent rate of growth of nominal GNP to 4 per cent or 5 per cent, an amount consistent with 1 per cent or 2 per cent inflation along with normal sustainable growth of real production. That will not, all of a sudden, bring the desired result. Federal Reserve Chairman Volcker, President Carter or Reagan or Anderson, and the Congress do not control the division of the rate of growth of nominal income as between price inflation and output growth. Past evidence says that the institutions of our economy will divide nominal spending about one-tenth for prices and nine-tenths for output. That is, reducing the rate of increase of nominal spending by one point would reduce inflation that year by only one-tenth of a percentage point. Another way to look at it is this. Every additional point of unemployment, maintained for a year, will reduce the built-in core of inertial inflation by at most a half a point. And, when external shocks, OPEC, for example, are working the other way, an extra point-year of unemployment may not do that well. In these circumstances, the prospect ahead of us, if we adopt and maintain a policy of monetary disinflation, is a long period of stagnation, a deep recession with high unemployment, low output, and uncertain success in reducing the core inflation rate.

Some economists say that if the government makes unmistakably clear that it will stick with this draconian remedy, the costs will be less and the cure will be more rapid and less painful. They say that statistical evidence on the past stubbornness of inflation rates in the face of monetary contraction is misleading, because the response was conditioned by the expectation that the government would reverse course quickly and bail out firms and workers hurt by recessions. Wage and price patterns will melt faster, they say, if the government resolutely forswears the compensatory anti-recession measures customary in the past. Is a 'credible threat' of this kind possible in a democracy? Can our central bank and government say with conviction and truth that come what may they will not accommodate any OPEC shocks, they will not adopt any counter-cyclical policies—no matter how bad the news of unemployment, production, and profits? Would the remedy, even if adopted and relentlessly maintained, work? I noted before that in our country wage and price decisions are highly decentralized, wage negotiations occur on a staggered schedule, contracts last for as long as three years.

It is hard to be confident that a global macroeconomic threat will have meaning in the local markets, sectoral labour negotiations, and particular enterprises that matter for the course of wages and prices. At these microeconomic levels, employers and employees are concerned with what other unions and other firms have been doing, are doing, and will be doing. They cannot be sure that their rivals and their reference groups will disinflate in response to the threat of unrelenting contractionary macroeconomic policies. If one group obeys the threat while others do not, it will lose relative position. If it does not obey the threat, while others do, it will gain relative position. This is an $n + 1$-person game, n agents and 1 policy maker, and the outcome is not predictable.

In other countries, where labour negotiations follow synchronized annual schedules and are more centralized, there is more coordination between macroeconomic demand policies and the wage and price decisions of management and unions. In Germany, for example, the leaders of the labour federation and the employers' groups meet with representatives of the central bank and the government and discuss the whole macroeconomic picture, including the policies of the central bank and the government for the coming year. It is clear to the firms and to the unions what will be the consequences of a wage and price development inconsistent with the intentions of the monetary authorities. The threat is also a promise—that with moderation in wages and prices, employment and sales will be favourable. Lacking similar mechanisms, we cannot confidently bet that a firmly announced and executed course of restrictive demand management will accelerate the disinflation of wages and prices. But if our policy makers are going to follow that course, they should make it more evident to the whole economy. At the moment it is really difficult for anyone in the private economy to interpret the rather esoteric signals and targets that emerge from statements of the Federal Reserve and discussions of the federal budget between the President and Congress.

b. The Role of Incomes Policy

More important, I think, is the patent need for an incomes policy— yes, for controls of some kind—to supplement any demand management firmly oriented to disinflation. A consistent schedule of declining guideposts for wage and price increases for the next few years would limit the damage which gradual reduction of monetary aggregate demand would otherwise cause. We already have standards for wage and price behaviour, but without teeth to make them stick. Indeed, currently our flimsy institutions of incomes policy are relaxing those standards. The core inflation rate will probably increase even while the guns of monetary and fiscal policy take aim at the present inflation. Collision is imminent between contracting monetary demand guided by the Federal Reserve, the President, and the Congressional budget makers and the accelerating trend of wages and prices contemplated by unions and managements and accepted by the Council on Wage

Price Stability. These two policies must be made consistent if we are serious about accomplishing disinflation without a long period of stagnation.

We should make the standards effective by creating inducements to comply with them. These could be either 'carrots' or 'sticks', either rewards for employers and employees in economic units that comply with the guideposts or penalties for those that do not. The rewards and penalties would be given in the tax system. There are, of course, costs in any kind of wage and price controls, even of the flexible variety just mentioned. Economists' trained instincts are against controls that alter the relative prices thrown up by the market and interfere with the accompanying allocation of resources. Here again we need to apply the perspective and power of cost–benefit calculus. Against the well-rehearsed costs of controls weigh some benefits. Absent controls, we face very heavy macroeconomic losses, and these too violate optimality and efficiency. Indeed, I think the potential losses from disinflation by demand management alone are larger by orders of magnitude than the allocational distortion that would occur during several years of a transitional programme of flexible tax-based disinflationary guideposts.

We have only unpleasant choices. Perhaps the choice we are making, consciously or unconsciously, is the first of the three I mentioned, muddling through. Perhaps the society does not have the will to accomplish a disinflation. Perhaps most of the rhetoric against inflation is simply rhetoric and will not lead to any constructive actions. Unfortunately, it can lead to some destructive actions—another deep and long recession, with permanent damage to the future of our economy, permanent damage arising from the losses of physical and human capital resulting from sustained periods of underproduction and underemployment.

It is not easy to detect the nature of the inflations and stagflations that afflict nations today, to tell whether they fall under the rubric of inertia or of conflict. In either case it is doubtful that application of the remedies appropriate to excess demand inflation is a constructive solution. The instincts of the man in the street are correct: there must be more rational solutions than recession and unemployment. An economist can add that there must be less costly ways to save energy than to arrest the economic progress of the globe. The better ways demand social and political consensus, and that in turn depends on leadership that will face squarely the underlying economic realities from which obsession with inflationary symptoms alone diverts attention. To wind down our inertial inflation in an orderly way, we need incomes policies that are supported by the understanding and consent of the major economic interests. To resolve possible conflicts among their claims, we need the same policies, understanding, and consent. It is often said, too often, that the conquest of inflation demands 'sacrifices' from us all, but that is only a half truth. Our real incomes and consumption possibilities will not be less if we achieve the consensus that will allow disinflation without stagnation. They will indeed be more. The task is a severe test of democratic institutions, to be sure, but the stakes are high.

30 Inflation Control as Social Priority*

THE EMPEROR'S CLOTHES?

The President of the United States made his priorities clear when he declared to a cheering Wall Street audience, 'After all, unemployment affects only 8 per cent of the people while inflation affects 100%'. At the time the country was barely emerging from the depths of its worst recession since the 1930s, a downturn deliberately engineered by government policies triggered by 'double-digit' annualized rates of increase in prices in 1974.

To many, perhaps most, Americans—not just the security analysts in his immediate audience but even some of the 8 per cent—the President's declaration had the ring of truth. To ordinary citizens *inflation* connotes increasing prices of things they buy, notably at the time of the speech gasoline, fuel oil, and food. Real incomes had indeed shrunk. Dollar devaluations, OPEC, and world food shortages had turned terms of trade against American wage earners and city dwellers. The same events, as recorded in price indexes, had produced a bulge in inflation statistics. It was all blamed on 'inflation', and served as the justification for anti-inflationary monetary and fiscal policies. It was a persuasive justification; people don't like their real incomes to shrink.

Hardly anyone—not the President, not the Federal Reserve Chairman, not their economists, very few other economists—told the people that anti-inflationary macroeconomic policies could not restore favourable terms of trade. Hardly anyone told the people that these measures will, if they succeed in holding down the prices of things people buy, also hold down the prices of labour and other things they

---

*October 1976, Conference on the Political Economy of Inflation and Unemployment in Open Economies, Athens, Greece. Published in Hebrew in *The Economic Quarterly*, vol. 24, no. 92–3, April 1977.

sell. Certainly hardly anyone told them that the anti-inflationary policies they were asked and led to support in expectation of higher real incomes would, at least over a long transition period, actually depress real incomes.

Today recovery in the United States is slow, and it is faltering. Official doctrine, almost universally echoed in business and financial circles and press commentary, is the slower the better. The reason always given is that faster recovery would re-accelerate inflation and thus lead to another and probably even more severe recession. This orthodox view appeals to three widely accepted interpretations of recent history: that overexpansionary policy and too strong a boom in 1972–3 led to the double-digit inflation of 1973–4, that the inflation itself brought on the recession, and that cautious fiscal and monetary policies caused the inflation rate to subside by 50 per cent and the recovery to begin. As against these standard interpretations it can be argued: that only the dramatic deterioration of terms of trade took inflation rates into two digits, that anti-inflationary monetary policy rather than inflation *per se* caused the recession, that the inflation rate has subsided mainly because the extraordinary price shocks of 1973–4 were by nature non-recurrent.

In my opinion, popular support of anti-inflationary fiscal and monetary policy in the United States is based on a huge misundertanding, probably a 500 billion dollar misunderstanding if the GNP losses due to excess unemployment and industrial capacity are cumulated.

A PLEA FOR WEIGHING COSTS AND BENEFITS

Now perhaps I should apologize for the introduction. It is parochial; the American scene is what I know most about. It is somewhat churlish, and it is intentionally provocative. I wish to make a serious general point.

The control of inflation—limiting it or reducing it to zero or any other number—should not be an objective of absolute priority, to be pursued by central banks or other policy makers regardless of costs. At any moment the paths open to an economy are limited by its resources, institutions, and history and by the environment it faces at home and abroad. Policy makers' choices among these paths are further limited to the capacities of the instruments they command. Within the set of feasible policy choices, path A may imply lower inflation rates than path B. The differences between path A and path B in real incomes, in the immediate and more distant futures, for the society as a whole and various groups within it, are the relevant economic considerations in choosing between them. Generalized costs of 'inflation' are not a sufficient argument against path B, unless it can also be argued that path A avoids these costs without incurring, relative to B, other losses of equal or greater social moment. The point is quite symmetrical, of course. Advocates of expansionary macroeconomic policies have no right to claim on their behalf the general virtues of high real growth of output in circumstances in which such policies will in fact deliver not that result but only inflation.

The point is trivial, and deserves emphasis and elaboration only because it is so often ignored. Discussions of the 'costs of inflation', among economists as well as among laymen, are usually flawed by a fundamental error: namely the implicit assumption that societies, and on their behalf central banks and legislatures, have a free choice whether to inflate or not to inflate, other things remaining equal. This is the premise of usual discussions and evaluations of the distributional damage traditionally attributed to 'inflation'—the losses of capital and income suffered by pensioners, investors in fixed-money-value assets, and wage earners dependent upon them, the gains to debtors, land speculators and some taxpayers. It is also the assumption in reckonings of the inefficiencies of induced efforts to economize cash holdings and of the costs of sending and receiving information about price increases.

In the introduction I alluded to a recent dramatic example of a fairly frequent phenomenon. Changes in the relative scarcities of goods, or in the relative market powers of their producers and consumers, dictate changes in relative prices. These occur, at least in the first instance, by increases in the nominal prices of the goods which are rising in relative value. As a by-product, general price indexes rise faster than before, yielding a higher inflation rate for a time. I do not want to see solemn statistical studies of such episodes charging to 'inflation' instability of relative prices and unanticipated redistributions of income and wealth. I don't want to see them, but I am sure I will.

Economists and policy makers should never forget that assessments of costs and consequences of inflation are operational only as they relate to practicable choices among alternative policies. Usually, always so far as central banks are concerned, these choices relate to macroeconomic management of aggregate demand. The tools are generic—money supply, interest rates, public debt management, government spending, taxes, exchange rates. These tools provide no handle for altering the conditions of relative scarcity and bargaining power that affect relative prices, or for preventing or reversing changes in these conditions even if it were desirable to do so. With respect to the feasible set of demand management alternatives, whatever damage is done by shifts in terms of trade, international or interregional, is quite irrelevant. World recession is not a cost-effective way to fight OPEC.

INSTRUMENTAL AND ULTIMATE GOALS

In the hierarchy of ends which guide economy policy the control and reduction of inflation are logically at the instrumental end of the spectrum. The pay-offs of economic activity to individuals and societies are real, not nominal, quantities; basically the pay-offs are goods and services and leisure consumed now and in the future. Prices in dollars or drachmas and their rates of change are not among the arguments of utility functions or social welfare functions. It does not really matter how many tokens it takes to buy a bus ride, or even how many coins it takes to buy the tokens. It does matter how many minutes of work or pints of milk it costs to take the trip.

The justification for inflation control is, therefore, necessarily indirect. Six per cent inflation between now and 1980 is not *inherently* better than 12 per cent or 2 per cent inherently better than 6 per cent. Anyone who says that the lower rates are better must argue that they have socially preferable real consequences and specify what those consequences are. Nor may he mark against the higher rates the consequences of policy actions taken to reduce them, for that is circular logic—like opposing legalization of marijuana on the grounds it is harmful and listing among the harmful effects the hazard of arrest.

In the United States a Discomfort Index, the sum of the rates of inflation and unemployment, is commonly cited as a gauge of overall economic performance. The implicit social trade-off is that it is always worth an additional point of unemployment to reduce the inflation rate one point. Yet there is certainly a difference between accustomed and expected inflation and unaccustomed, unexpected inflation. The annual output loss for a point of inflation is very small. An extra point of steady and anticipated inflation means, let us say, a 20 per cent increase in nominal interest rates, from 5 per cent to 6 per cent; one-sixth of GNP is held in demand deposits and currency on which no nominal interest is paid—an institutional fact, but not immutable; the interest elasticity of demand for these assets is not less than -0.5; thus the annual extra effort to economize money due to an extra point of inflation is at most 1/1200 of GNP, that is, 1/10 of the original cost, which is 5 per cent of 1/6 of GNP. The loss due to one point of unemployment is, conservatively, 1/100 of GNP, a different order of magnitude. Perhaps some small part of the difference can be made up by the costs of making and announcing more frequent changes in nominal prices; I have yet to see an estimate of these.

Unanticipated inflation, like other erroneous expectations, has unwelcome distributional and allocational consequences. But so does unanticipated deflation, or unexpected reduction of inflation from a rate to which the economy is adjusted. And so also does unemployment, *in addition* to global deadweight loss of production. In the United States, the recession pushed 2.5 million more people into poverty, that is, below an officially chosen standard of real income, in 1975. The Shah of Iran was not among them. Much is quite properly made of the losses of pensioners, retired persons, widows, and orphans dependent on past fixed-money-value investments made at interest yields which underestimated inflation rates. Likewise many investors in the 1950s and 1960s staked their future and that of their dependents on equities, expecting them to be an inflation hedge and not realizing that anti-inflationary monetary policies would drastically impair their real value.

The lesson is that neither the Discomfort Index nor any other simple weighted sum of inflation and unemployment statistics is a meaningful guide to policy. There is really no good substitute for the prescription offered above: compare the real distributional and aggregative consequences of alternative feasible paths. In such a comparison it is typically the case that less inflationary paths show losses in the short run, which must be justified by later gains. To this end it used to be asserted, though without convincing empirical evidence, that inflation deterred saving. Today the conventional wisdom is the contrary, but it may be equally unfounded. Those who ask society to make large sacrificial investments now for a later stream of permanent benefits should specify and evaluate those long-run gains.

DISEASES AND SYMPTOMS

I suspect that opposition to inflation is often really revulsion from societal maladies of which inflation is one symptom. A country where labour unions and other organized groups have the economic and political power to press exorbitant claims for real income on their employers and customers and on the state is certainly in trouble. The inability of any society to find orderly ways to resolve conflicting claims is certainly alarming, no doubt about it. (In our own country New York City is an example and a warning.) Disorder of this kind is deeper than the inflation to which it contributes. Indeed the problem would still be there even if the currency were converted to a commodity-bundle standard on which inflation would be by definition impossible. This is not a disease a central bank can cure, though no doubt monetary policy can help when the needed fundamental structural reforms are undertaken. In the absence of such reforms, deflationary macroeconomic policy will frequently punish the innocent and power-less for the sins of the greedy and powerful.

INFLATIONARY PUBLIC FINANCE

From what I have already said it will be clear that I think there are a number of possible sources of inflation in the modern world. I know full well that inflation is a monetary phenomenon—after all it is a change in the purchasing power of the monetary unit of account—and accordingly I recognize that the central bank is an accomplice, willing or unwilling, in any ongoing inflation, whatever its source. Rarely, I am sure, do central banks make a free choice to have more inflation rather than less. To accommodate or not to accommodate, that is the question. Shall they provide the finance for price and income move-ments which they did not initiate, when to deny it will be costly, at least temporarily, in output and employment? It is for this dilemma that I have been recommending a careful and pragmatic cost–benefit calculus.

The dictum that inflation is always and everywhere a monetary phenomenon is often a stronger proposition, namely that existence of inflation, or certainly of accelerating inflation, is *per se* evidence of excess real aggregate demand. If so, anti-inflationary policy is always costless, in the sense that it is restoring real equilibrium. This proposition, I think, is at worst a tautology—*defining* equilibrium as the absence of inflationary pressure—and at best an unproved and dubious assertion. Eight per cent unemployment and 25 per cent excess capacity just don't have the feel of equilibrium, whatever is happening to price statistics. But I certainly don't deny that excess-demand inflations sometimes happen; the most notable recent clear example in the United States was the financing of the Vietnam War in 1966.

Even in such a case cost–benefit calculations are the appropriate way to choose among alternative methods of finance. Suppose that the economy is close to capacity operation and that an increase of government expenditure must be financed. The choice is between a tax increase and deficit financing, the latter partly with interest-bearing debt and partly by printing currency or borrowing from the central bank. Explicit taxation will provide the government with the real resources it needs by inducing or forcing taxpayers to curtail their own consumption and investment. Deficit financing will, if the events are unexpected, provide the resources mainly by inflation-forced reductions in purchases by those whose incomes or spending budgets respond slowly or whose holdings of money and money-denominated assets are eroded in real value and yield. If the events are anticipated, deficit spending will release the needed resources by a price increase which reduces the real value of money balances and a real interest rate increase which deters investment and consumption.

Both methods of finance inflict deadweight losses on the economy. There is no explicit tax which does not distort incentives. Unanticipated inflation distorts consumer and producer allocations of resources. Anticipated inflation and real interest rate increases induce socially unnecessary expenditures of resources to economize cash balances and other fixed-interest rate assets. Both methods of finance redistribute income and wealth, though in different directions. So the choice is not black or white. In political rhetoric inflation is the 'cruellest tax', but one can imagine taxes that are crueller.

However, I am not arguing for inflationary public finance. Personally I prefer that in such circumstances governments face squarely and explicitly the burden of their expenditures, and I am offended by the deceit involved in selling ill-informed savers obligations that will have lower real interest rates than the buyers are led to expect. The thematic point nevertheless remains: the policy choice involves not only totting up the costs of one action but weighing them against those of the other.

INCOMES POLICIES

Suppose that a society which has inherited from the past a high persistent inflation rate is determined to reduce it or eliminate it. Macroeconomic demand management will do so at the cost of protracted stagflation, with substantial losses of output, employment, and capital formation. No wonder that statesmen, politicians, and ordinary citizens refuse to believe that there is no other solution. Americans don't like inflation, but their instincts, repeatedly expressed in opinion polls, are to control prices and wages directly.

In circles of economics and finance, however, the most determined foes of inflation are also the most determined opponents of incomes policies. (By the conveniently evasive term 'incomes policies' I mean to include everything from full-fledged wage and price controls to wage/price guideposts and 'open mouth operations' without legal sanction.) The opposition is often one of principle or ideology. It is hard to argue with absolutes, but most citizens would not agree that this principle must be maintained regardless of cost.

A more pragmatic approach would be one in the spirit of this paper: compare the costs of reducing inflation by one route with the costs of the others. There is no doubt that effective controls, compulsory or persuasive, distort resource allocation and create inequities. But the costs of macroeconomic stagflation are enormous, and one would have to cumulate a vast sum of allocational and distributional damage to equal them. It takes a heap of Harberger triangles to fill an Okun gap.

Of course if incomes policies won't work at all, there is no argument. The propitious time for incomes policies is not in periods of excess demand, when they confront an irresistible tide, but in periods when inflation is fuelled by its own momentum of experience and expectation rather than by contemporary demand pressures. Under the Kennedy–Johnson guideposts and persuasive Presidential interventions, a five-year recovery occurred with negligible increases in price levels or their rates of change. Today's stagflation may provide a similar opportunity. At the moment both government and private sector seem immobilized by the possibility that recovery might eventually hit some bottlenecks and cause some prices to rise.

A number of 'gimmicks' for breaking the entrenched pattern of wage and price increases have been suggested, but they have attracted very little support. Wallich and Weintraub have independently suggested a corporate profits tax surcharge equal to the percentage points by which the year-to-year growth in the company's average hourly wage exceeds an official guidepost. Okun has suggested a carrot instead of a stick: a tax rebate for employees and employers if they comply with the guidepost. He has also proposed an insurance scheme; in return for respecting a guidepost workers would be given income tax rebates by the number of points actual inflation exceeded the guidepost. Arthur Burns has been on record in support of a notification and waiting requirement for major wage contracts and price increases.

But anti-inflation hawks generally ignore or denounce remedies other than the classic prescription of austere budgets and restrictive monetary policies. It is almost as if they think, like old-time physicians, the more unpleasant the medicine the better it is for the patient.

31   After Disinflation, Then What?*

The 1970s will be the Age of Stagflation in the economic history books, and the 1980s are likely to be the Age of Disinflation. Today conquest of the stubborn inflation inherited from the previous decade is the dominant priority of economic policy throughout the democratic capitalist world. In Britain under Margaret Thatcher, in the United States under Federal Reserve Chairman Paul Volcker, and less dramatically in other advanced economies of Western Europe and Japan, relentlessly restrictive monetary and macroeconomic policies are gradually grinding down world inflation rates.

These efforts, I believe, will eventually succeed. They are taking a longer time and exacting a greater toll than their protagonists expected or promised. But the patience of the public, even of the victims of the deep recession the policies produced, remains remarkably robust. So firmly entrenched is popular distaste for the inflation of the late 1970s that dramatic reversals of direction are unlikely even if the present leaders of the crusade are displaced.

The key to success in disinflation is bringing the pattern of wage increase down to the trend of growth in labour productivity. The weapon now in use is severe economic slack, unemployment of labour and excess industrial capacity, prolonged until businesses, workers, and trade unions give way on wages and prices in desperate and often vain attempts to save jobs and avert bankruptcies. It is no surprise that the strategy works. It will continue to work as long as large margins of slack persist, even if the 1981/2 recession comes to an end.

There is still considerable distance to go. Inflation rates are now in the upper single digits in the major advanced economies of North America, Western Europe, and Japan. The anti-inflation crusades aim at rates well below 5 per cent, if not actually zero. After all, inflation

---

*October 1982, Killam Lecture, Dalhousie University, Halifax. In John Cornwall, ed., *After Stagflation: Alternatives to Economic Decline*, Oxford: Blackwell, 1984, pp. 20–40.

control was a major concern of policy before OPEC shocks brought double-digit rates. In the United States, for example, 5 per cent inflation caused consternation both in the mid 1950s and in the Vietnam era. At the present and foreseeable pace, it seems, victory over inflation will take a couple more years at least, more if events in the Middle East inflict a third shock to oil supplies and prices.

Nevertheless I think it is not too soon to look forward to V-I (victory over inflation) Day, to think about what the economic landscape will look like, and to consider where we will go from there. Like any victorious war, this one will leave in its wake difficult problems and important issues of policy. We should start working on them now. Moreover, thoughtful consideration of the prospects after V-I Day relates to some current issues about how vigorously and by what weapons we prosecute the war.

THE ECONOMIC LANDSCAPE AFTER DISINFLATION

After two or more additional years of monetary disinflation, our economies will be badly wounded. Unemployment and excess capacity will still be high, compared with the norms of the 1950s, 1960s, and 1970s, even if modest recovery from the recession does occur. In the United States today, for example, two years of real growth of $4\frac{1}{2}$ per cent per year, rates that forecasters would regard as extremely optimistic, would barely suffice to reduce unemployment from 10 to 8 per cent—a figure higher than that of business cycle troughs prior to 1975. Protracted high unemployment destroys human capital, especially among cohorts of youths and young adults who during their crucial formative years are denied the training and experience of holding jobs. Prolonged excess capacity likewise deters physical capital formation; business firms lack the actual and prospective profits that would induce them to make, and enable them to finance, new investments. Recession and stagnation also squeeze public sector budgets; in the United States, the overhead capital—roads, streets, sewage systems, parks, schools—provided by state and local governments is not even being maintained and replaced, much less expanded to meet future requirements.

These are the irreversible and durable costs incident to the hundreds of billions of dollars of lost production during the war to subdue inflation. Our economies, stocked with less capital and less up-to-date technology, will be less productive even when and if prosperity restores more normal rates of utilization of labour and other resources.

These social costs are accompanied by symptoms of financial distress painful to thousands of business enterprises and millions of households. Personal and corporate bankruptcies are epidemic; nations too have to beg for 'restructuring' of their debts. In chain reactions, banks, other financial institutions, and other lenders are threatened too. In part these difficulties are intrinsic to disinflation. Those who borrowed long at interest rates they could cover only if their wages or profits or the values of their properties grew in dollar value at high rates of inflation are bound to be in trouble when inflation unexpectedly subsides. Fifteen per cent mortgages, with interest deductible from taxable income, were a bargain if the debtor's wages would rise at 10 per cent per year and the value of his house at 15 per cent per year; they are a heavy burden when wages are rising only 5 per cent and real estate prices are flat. The same is true of a company or municipality that expected to service high-interest bonds from sales or tax revenues regularly swollen by inflation.

The consequences are shifts of income and wealth, in the opposite direction from the gains to borrowers at the expense of lenders characteristic of unanticipated inflation. We are learning, or re-learning, that such shifts occur in both directions and cause serious social strains both ways. Economists are prone to say that these financial shocks are 'merely' redistributions; factories and houses and farms are still there even if their ownerships change and their fruits are differently divided. But the adjustments are often costly. Moreover, in the present difficulties more is involved than unexpected disinflation burdening borrowers who contracted to pay too high interest. Most debtors have also been hit by the real by-products of the disinflation. The unemployed car worker, Braniff and International Harvester, and Mexico all lost their markets. The resulting financial distress is symptomatic of the real social costs previously discussed, the immense sacrifices of real income due to the idleness of productive resources.

THE DUBIOUS PROSPECTS FOR FULL RECOVERY

I have suggested that when victory over inflation is achieved considerable slack will remain in the world's advanced capitalist economies. Unemployment will be high, excess capital capacity too, by comparison with previous years of prosperity. What will be the prospects of restoring more normal rates of utilization? To be concrete, suppose that in the United States inflation has been brought down two or three years from now to 2 or 3 per cent, while unemployment remains at 8 per cent or higher. Could we then expect to reduce unemployment even so far as 6 per cent, where it stood in 1978/79? One could ask a similar question for Britain: when and if Mrs Thatcher's determined policy succeeds in getting inflation down, will unemployment then be brought down too?

Let me give some reasons for a pessimistic answer to those questions. V-I Day is a figure of speech, and a somewhat misleading one. No one, least of all the victorious generals, can be sure the war is over and won. There is no palpable enemy commander to yield his sword, disarm his troops, and sign a document of surrender. There are only price statistics and their changes over time. Maybe the next month, the next quarter, or the next year will bring bad news again. The anti-inflation crusaders will be very cautious. After all, they will say to themselves and to us, we have paid dearly for this victory; let us not throw it away now. We did that before, they will remind us, losing in subsequent expansions the gains against inflation won in 1957–60, 1970–1, and 1974–5. We must not rekindle inflationary psychology this time. Further recovery is bound to raise some sensitive commodity prices, and to encounter some bottlenecks in domestic and world supplies. Oil prices might shoot up again if prosperity expands world demand for energy too much and too fast, and one can never tell when there will be political disruptions of supply. Moreover, some important cost-based prices in our economies are still rising excessively, partly because they are still absorbing cost increases from the previous inflation—public utility rates and medical care fees are prime examples.

Reasoning thus, these policy makers will be content to let the economy resume a track of normal sustainable growth in production, that is, one which keeps the margin of slack, as measured in unemployment and excess capacity, roughly constant. Real GNP would grow as much as the expansion of the labour force and the growth of productivity would permit, but not enough, even temporarily, to take up the residue of slack. Permanently higher unemployment, perhaps at least 8 per cent in North America, will be insurance against the resumption of inflation.

THE LEGACY OF MONETARISM

The likelihood of this scenario is reinforced by central banks' commitments to monetarist targets. Their strategy in the crusade for disinflation is gradually to reduce growth rates of monetary aggregates until they do no more than finance sustainable growth of real GNP at stable prices. In the United States, for example, the Federal Reserve has been cutting the year-to-year growth of transactions money, *M-1*, its principal target, since 1977, and has strongly emphasized its determination to follow this course since its well-publicized change in operating procedures in October 1979. The Reagan Administration, shortly after coming into power in 1981, endorsed the policy and asked that *M-1* growth targets be cut in half by 1985, that is, to around 2 per cent per year. The end of the process could be 0 per cent, because the upward trend in the velocity of transactions money, due to innovations in financial technology, might be sufficient to handle sustainable inflation-free growth of GNP, 2.5–3 per cent per year.

The monetarist view underlying policy in the United States and elsewhere stresses the crucial role of expectations. Declining and ultimately stable money growth, with actual performance confirming announced intentions, is regarded as essential for cooling inflationary psychology and preventing its re-ignition. Achieving and maintaining 'credibility' is the watchword, and credibility is thought to be attached to monetary aggregates even more than to prices and nominal incomes. This is a strong additional reason why central banks will be reluctant to allow the burst of monetary growth, albeit temporary, needed to finance a slack-reducing economic recovery even when inflation has abated.

The transition from a monetarist strategy of disinflation to a monetarist recipe for stable growth involves another and somewhat more subtle difficulty. Successful disinflation will itself increase the demand for money, which will become a more attractive asset when its purchasing power is not depreciating. To put the point another way, nominal interest rates on substitute assets—time deposits, Treasury bills, commercial paper—will fall with disinflation, lowering the opportunity cost incentive for economizing holdings of transactions money, currency and checking account balances. Given an interest-elasticity of demand for *M-1* estimated conservatively at 0.15 in absolute value, a nominal interest rate decline of 67 per cent as a result of disinflation would raise money demand by 10 per cent. The central bank would somehow have to accommodate this one-shot, non-recurrent, demand just to finance sustainable zero-inflation growth, quite apart from any period of exceptional real growth designed to diminish unemployment. But accommodation of extra money demand by temporarily higher money growth targets—5 per cent more in each of two years or 3 per cent more for three years— would endanger the central bank's hard-earned credibility.

The problem is even further exacerbated in the United States because legal ceilings on deposit interest rates are gradually being phased out. In a few years, we may expect, checkable deposits counted in *M-1* will bear market-determined interest rates, differing from rates available on substitute assets only by costs of intermediation and transactions services. This reform too will augment the demand for *M-1*, as payment of controlled interest on checkable savings deposits ('NOW accounts') has already done, and as the popularity of checkable money-market funds, not included in *M-1*, indicates. The Federal Reserve recognizes that accommodating extra money demand from this source is innocuous, appropriate, even desirable, and has struggled to do so to date without exceeding its year-to-year targets. In future this may not be possible, so the credibility dilemma looms still again. Somehow the 'Fed' will have to persuade its constituencies that upward departures from its austere path of money growth are healthy, and do not signal retreat from its basic anti-inflationary stance.[1]

There is, to be sure, a way that extra monetary demand from any of the sources discussed, could in principle be satisfied without any departure, either in form or substance, from announced monetarist strategy and tactics. That is to prolong and extend the disinflationary transition to include a period of actual deflation. During that period the price level would have to fall enough to accommodate the extra demands for money. Some of you—especially any whose memory like mine includes the deflation of the 1930s—may find even the contemplation of such a scenario incredible. Remember, however, that in monetarist theory it is as easy for nominal wages and prices to fall as to rise, as easy to lower inflation from 1 per cent to −1 per cent as from 8 per cent to 6 per cent.

If this recital makes any of you feel that it is silly and dangerous for central banks to stake their credibility on targets for monetary aggregates whose velocity and meaning change both systematically and randomly, I would be pleased and not surprised. Elsewhere I have advanced other arguments to the same effect,[2] which I will not repeat here. Anyway the monetary authorities, at least the Federal Reserve, will some day have to extricate themselves from the monetarist trap they set for themselves. The best time is now, during the disinflationary transition.

THE UPWARD DRIFT OF THE 'NATURAL RATE' OF UNEMPLOYMENT

A basic issue of macroeconomic policy after V-I Day is what has happened to the 'natural rate of unemployment' or as it is sometimes more neutrally called the 'non-accelerating inflation rate of unemployment' (NAIRU). If it is 4, 5, or 6 per cent, then policy makers should not be content with steady sustainable growth while unemployment is stuck at 8 per cent. But maybe they believe that the NAIRU is now

8 per cent, that no smaller unemployment rate is compatible with stable prices or with any stable, non-increasing, rate of inflation. No one can be sure. Policy makers might, for example, estimate the expected value of the NAIRU to be 6 per cent but assign some probability to lower and higher values. They might then aim at 8 per cent because they consider the costs of inflation resulting from going lower than the NAIRU to exceed the costs of running the economy chronically with 'unnaturally' high unemployment.

How low an unemployment rate can the economy, with the help of macroeconomic policy, achieve and sustain? Over the past thirty years views of economists and policy makers have become more pessimistic, almost monotonically. In 1952/3, after the Korean War build-up and inflation, prices stabilized with unemployment as low as 3 per cent. In the mid 1950s, however, inflation of 4 per cent plus seemed to be heating up with unemployment at 4 per cent plus, inspiring monetary and fiscal policies that led to two recessions in rapid succession and lowered inflation to the 1–2 per cent range. The official unemployment target of the Kennedy–Johnson administration was 4 per cent, and it was reached with negligible inflation cost in 1965. President Johnson's decision, against his economists' advice, to spend for his Vietnam adventure without raising taxes led to an excess-demand inflation, lowering unemployment to 3 per cent while raising inflation to 5 per cent. After the anti-inflation recession of 1969–71 yielded disappointing results, President Nixon imposed wage and price controls and macroeconomic policies turned expansionary. This time the boom was deliberately ended by restrictive policy with 5 per cent unemployment, and with inflation accelerating in frightening degree, led by international commodity markets and by OPEC oil prices. The next United States recovery, from 1975 to 1979, was deliberately cut off with unemployment around 6 per cent, again as a result of an alarming surge of inflation, featuring the second OPEC shock.

What accounts for the apparent high level of 'natural' unemployment and for its secular increase? If measured unemployment is not Keynesian involuntary unemployment, capable of being reduced by demand expansion without unleashing pressure for higher real wages, what is it? The other adjectives are frictional, search, voluntary, and classical; they are not exclusive, one of the others.

Frictional unemployment is matched by job vacancies. Data on vacancies comparable to those for unemployment are not available for the United States, but two conclusions would be generally accepted. One is that meaningful vacancies in aggregate do not begin to match the number of unemployed even in prosperous times. The other is that in America, as in countries where vacancies data exist, the vacancy rate has risen secularly relative to the unemployment rate. This is indicated in the United States by the trend of the index of help-wanted advertising.

Frictional unemployment may represent active voluntary search between jobs by unemployed workers, especially youth and young adults. In the 1960s and 1970s the demographic composition of the labour force shifted in this direction, though now it is moving the other way. Voluntary unemployment, whether for selective search or not, is fostered by unemployment insurance and by other transfer benefits available to the unemployed. As these benefits have become more generous—partly indeed in response to higher unemployment rates—they may well have dulled incentives to stay employed and to seek and accept new jobs.

'Classical' unemployment may be due to restraints of trade that fix real wages too high, union monopolies, or minimum-wage legislation. These restraints can make individual workers involuntarily unemployed, but the remedy is more effective competition in labour markets rather than demand stimulus.

THE UNEMPLOYMENT–INFLATION TRADE-OFF; ALTERNATIVE DIAGNOSES

From this history several different lessons could be drawn, with radically conflicting policy implications. The orthodox conclusion, the accepted diagnosis supporting current policy, is that the NAIRU has been chronically and over-optimistically overestimated, so that policy has consistently erred on the inflationary side. The NAIRU has been steadily increasing, so that attempts to restore the unemployment rates of previous prosperities have blown up in inflation. Maybe unemployment is too high, but that is a problem for microeconomic structural policy, not for macroeconomic demand management.

A variant of this position, a modern version of classical economic doctrine, is that a market economy will find equilibrium on its own, in unemployment as in other variables. Whatever unemployment the economy settles into, under stable policies like monetarist rules described above, will be the equilibrium, natural and non-accelerating inflation rate. Economists and policy makers cannot know what it is numerically and should not aim at any particular value of unemployment or of any other real economic variable. These diagnoses and prescriptions are pessimistic about unemployment, placing it beyond the reach of macroeconomic demand management by monetary and fiscal measures.

An alternative reading of recent history, for want of a better word let us call it a neo-Keynesian analysis, is in one sense more optimistic and in another more pessimistic. The stagflation of the 1970s and especially the double-digit inflations at the peaks of the two prosperities were not endemic. They were the results of supply and price shocks of unprecedented severity. History, from the Vietnam escalation in 1966 through the Iranian revolution, has bequeathed us a high inflation rate; monetary efforts to contain and conquer inflation have brought high unemployment rates. Though the inflation is accidental in origin and arbitrary in magnitude, it has become embedded in habits, patterns, and expectations and has acquired a stubborn momentum of its own. That is why disinflation is so time consuming and so costly in employment and production.

But once the process is completed and new lower patterns of wage and price increase are established, they too will tend to persist in the absence of a new sequence of extraordinary shocks like those of the last sixteen years. Restore the initial conditions of 1961 and we can enjoy the prosperous and non-inflationary expansion of 1961–5. Maybe the NAIRU is now a point or more higher than 4 per cent, though that cannot be proved by the experience of 1973 or 1979. In some measure the NAIRU follows actually experienced unemployment. Thus the high unemployment of the 1970s, by destroying human capital and by deterring investment and lowering excess capital capacity relative to human unemployment, has temporarily raised the NAIRU. By the same token, prudent expansionary policies will lower both actual unemployment and the 'natural rate'.

At the same time, there is a more pessimistic strand in this American neo-Keynesian tradition. Long before the stagflation of the 1970s, indeed as early as the 1940s, its adherents detected an inflationary bias in the wage- and price-setting institutions of modern capitalism. Wages and mark-ups are, they perceived, more responsive upward to demand stimuli than downward to demand reductions. As a result, inter-industry and inter-regional shifts in demand and business activity tend to be inflationary in aggregate, and likewise cyclical fluctuations generate a higher inflationary trend than stable growth. It is difficult to combine price stability and full employment in the sense of 'natural' labour market equilibrium. The NAIRU is not full employment in any equilibrium or welfare sense; some margin of involuntary unemployment is necessary to contain inflation. The bias was especially severe in the face of the supply and price shocks of the 1970s; it took an inordinate amount of slack to make non-energy costs and prices compensate for the large increases in oil prices.

This view of the world has led some of its exponents to advocate incomes policies. In the placid early 1960s, informal wage–price guideposts were invoked to keep the expansion free of inflation and, one might say, to make the NAIRU coincide with full employment. Recently neo-Keynesians have advocated incomes policies, for example tax rewards or penalties to induce compliance with guideposts, in order to speed disinflation and limit its damage to employment and production. Conceivably incomes policies could be used, as in 1961–5, as insurance against resumption of inflation during recovery from the current disinflationary slump, substituting for the insurance provided by maintaining a permanently large margin of slack.

A third view, sometimes called post-Keynesian, is more pessimistic about the wage- and price-setting mechanisms of modern capitalism. These mechanisms, far from being competitive markets, reflect conflicts among groups with significant economic and political power. Their effective claims on the national product add to more than the total product, and there are no natural market processes capable of resolving this fundamental disharmony. Of this unreconciled conflict, inflation is one symptom. But macroeconomic restriction by monetary and fiscal policy cannot overcome either the struggle or its inflationary symptoms. It can only shrink the size of the pie, and that will not make the claimed shares add up, or rather add down. From this standpoint, the substantial content of Mrs Thatcher's policies in Britain, and to a much lesser degree of President Reagan's, is to destroy the power of trade unions, relative to those of other players. In America the characteristic post-Keynesian recommendation is the imposition of permanent price and wage controls on major corporations and unions, as long advocated by J. K. Galbraith.

POLICIES TO IMPROVE THE TRADE-OFF

As divergent as these viewpoints are, they concur on one point: V-I Day will merit only one or two cheers. Of stagflation the 'flation' will be subdued, but the 'stag' will remain. Reconciliation of a tolerably stable trend in the value of money with satisfactory performance in employment and production will be, as before, a terribly challenging task. Moreover, it may well be beyond the capacity of the conventional fiscal and monetary tools of macroeconomic management by themselves. Auxiliary measures are likely to be necessary, at least prudent. Even monetarists and born-again classical economists, who are complacently confident of the ability of competitive markets to find equilibrium employment and production, would generally agree to microeconomic reforms to improve the efficiency of markets and in the process to diminish unemployment. Economists of other schools have other auxiliary policies and reforms in mind.

I propose now to review the major proposals. At one extreme are structural reforms designed to make markets more competitive, more consonant with the classical model. At the other extreme are permanent wage and price controls, whose advocates take concentrations of economic power as ineradicable features of modern capitalism. In between are pragmatic suggestions that defy doctrinal or ideological categorization. In discussing this spectrum my stress will be on the great macroeconomic dilemma, unemployment and inflation, not on the entire range of issues involved in various proposals. That is why the discussion will focus principally on labour markets and wage determination.

CENTRALIZED AND SYNCHRONIZED COLLECTIVE BARGAINING?

Wage-setting institutions and the behaviour of employers, workers, and unions determine the position of the NAIRU and the responses of money wage rates to expansions and contractions of monetary demand and to price movements. Are there structural and institutional changes which would ameliorate the trade-offs between unemployment and inflation? In North America nominal wages respond more slowly both to unemployment and to price movement than in most European economies. Could we, should we, make them more responsive? Some of our problems apparently arise from asymmetries in short-run response; wages, prices, and their rates of change move up more readily than they move down. Could we engineer greater symmetry, or even reverse the asymmetry? Do our institutions of collective bargaining, which also differ from those of other economies, make macroeconomic stabilization more difficult?

In the United States and Canada wage setting is decentralized; there is no national bargain, not even an advisory guide agreed by national employers' and trade unions' federations after consultation with government. The advantage of a centralized bargaining institution is that the parties can understand the macroeconomic situation of the country, the monetary and fiscal policies of the government, and the consequences of greater and lesser wage settlements. The consultations can be a two-way street, in which the parties also influence macro policies. Remote economy-wide considerations are not prime considerations in decentralized local bargains. Economy-wide bargaining cannot work and may yield dangerously explosive results if there is an irreconcilable conflict of power and interest between the parties. Nor can it work if the bargaining federations lack or lose influence over their constituents. In the United States national organizations with the requisite legitimacy do not exist. Neither does the community of interest in international competitiveness that has facilitated agreement in smaller and more open economies. Wage setting in North America will remain decentralized, with any national 'guideposts' to which leaders of industry and labour lend moral support depending on government initiatives, that is, incomes policies.

Wage setting in our economies is not only decentralized but also unsynchronized. Collective bargaining contracts vary in duration from one to three years, with irregularly staggered dates of renegotiation. Employer-administered wage scales are generally adjusted annually, but at diverse times of year. A centralized system is necessarily more synchronized, with uniformly annual contract reopenings and wage settings concentrated in one season of the year. The American system, it is widely agreed, contributes to the sluggishness of nominal wages and prices in the face of fluctuations in economic activity and unemployment. Multi-year contracts work in this direction. Staggered wage setting does too, by accentuating emulative patterns of behaviour designed to maintain relative wages—catching up with or leap-frogging over settlements in other industries and unions.

Some observers, therefore, suggest legislation to impose greater synchronization on our decentralized system, forbidding contracts longer than one year, perhaps even prescribing uniform dates. The idea is to make wages respond more promptly to current realities of the economy and labour markets. Like most recommendations on this subject, this one is double edged. Less sluggish, more responsive, nominal wages would clearly be macroeconomically advantageous in periods like the present. Recession would do its anti-inflationary job more quickly and with less contraction of employment and production. But cyclical upswings might generate more inflation, and sooner. Moreover, the sluggishness of nominal wages in America, in contrast to most European countries, facilitated the adjustment of real wages to the oil price shocks of the 1970s. This was accomplished in true Keynesian fashion, as the money wage trend fell behind cost-of-living inflation even while employment and activity were rising. In Europe there was greater rigidity of *real* wages, a major reason why recovery there after 1974 was weaker and slower.

There are, of course, microeconomic objections to the synchronization proposal, major intervention into 'free' collective bargaining and even into employer-administered wage setting. Multi-year contracts were adopted to give both sides more security against work stoppages, more certainty in future planning, and more relief from the costs of negotiation. I should interject that I think objections of this kind should be judged pragmatically, not accepted as matters of principle. Unions and collective bargaining are protected and governed by the state, by a complicated code of rights and procedures; correspondingly the state has the right to regulate in the public interest the process and the contracts that result.

INDEXATION

Indexation is a related but separable issue. It too is double edged. When macroeconomic policies and events are bringing disinflation, when flexible commodity prices are weakening and even falling, when exchange rate appreciation is lowering the domestic prices of internationally traded goods, wage indexing speeds the process of disinflation and limits its damaging real consequences. In the opposite circumstances, it accelerates inflation and restricts real economic expansion. In 1974 and after, full indexation common in Europe was another obstacle to adjustment to the oil shock, while the incompleteness of wage indexing in America facilitated the real wage adjustment previously mentioned.

Asymmetric indexation, for example uncapped up but limited on the down side, yields the worst of both worlds. Even when agreements on base wages are frequently reopened, the spirit of indexation can introduce perverse asymmetry, rendering unthinkable any downward adjustment of real wages. Given the asymmetries, a case could be made for forbidding wage indexation in collective-bargaining contracts. Short of that extreme, government could withhold its sanction and enforcement from non-symmetrical indexing provisions of contracts. In any case, the government should construct and publish, recommend, perhaps even require a suitable price index. One thing we learned in the 1970s is that the customary Consumer Price Index is not suitable. It includes items—notably adverse shifts in terms of external trade and indirect taxes—against whose increase neither government nor employers can be expected to insure workers or other citizens. Some countries, Austria and Sweden to my knowledge, have purged the index used in wage agreements and transfer payments of such items. In the United States short-term movements of the CPI were also distorted by faulty technical procedures that exaggerated the effects of increases in nominal interest rates on home mortgages and in residential real estate prices.

GAIN SHARING?

Japan these days is the envied model economy, and Western observers naturally wonder whether we could emulate institutions of labour relations that apparently combine low unemployment and low inflation. Flexibility of wage costs in Japanese industry is obtained by making a significant fraction of labour compensation contingent on the firm's sales and earnings, paid as annual bonuses rather than as contracted or pre-set wages. Daniel Mitchell of UCLA proposes a similar system— he calls it 'gain sharing'—for the United States, though the contingent compensation would be spelled out in formulae in advance, rather than left to employers' discretion.[3] The recommendation is addressed more to unions and managements than to legislators, although presumably some tax incentives could be offered as encouragement, at least initially. The US tax code already encourages profit sharing, but it has never been popular with either management (except for managers) or organized labour. The bonus system fits better the all-encompassing paternalism and the lifetime employment commitments in Japan than the strictly business-like spirit of American labour–management relations. But we shall see. *In extremis*, where many American firms and workers find themselves as a result of Japanese competition, Mitchell's proposal may appear quite attractive.

TRADE UNION POWER

Reforms congenial to many economists would diminish or break the bargaining power of trade unions, which they view as monopolies restraining trade with government support. But many of the same economists have also denied that labour monopolies, any more than product monopolies, have significant *macro*economic consequences. I suspect that they do, if only because administered and negotiated wages and prices contribute to the stickiness and sluggishness of wage and price adjustment discussed above. It is true, however, that in the United States these phenomena antedated both widespread labour organization and the legislation encouraging and protecting it.

Another channel by which union power has macroeconomic effects could be by increasing the NAIRU, as follows. When unions impose higher than market-clearing wages in organized industries, workers are thrown into competitive sectors, lowering market-clearing real wages there. But minimum wages in force by legislation or custom may prevent their employment. Or the lower wage available to them may make unemployment more attractive while waiting and seeking for a high-wage job, especially for those eligible for unemployment compensation.

Unions have sometimes been accused of initiating 'cost-push' inflation, though it seems irrational for them to postpone for a 'push' the exploitation of any monopoly power they possess. The worldwide wage explosion of 1970–1 seemed like wage push, because it was hard to explain by previous wage or price inflation or by contemporaneous tightness of labour markets. Possibly the struggle for relative wage positions, to which union rivalries contribute, becomes on occasion dynamically unstable—at least that happened in those years among construction trades in the United States. The unusual gains of union wages relative to non-union wages in the later 1970s in the United States may indicate another push.

Finally, in a wholly syndicalized society, collective union power claiming the lion's share of national product is a macroeconomic problem far exceeding in gravity its inflationary symptoms. I do not place Canada and the United States in this category of hopelessly conflicted societies.

In our countries, I think, the problem is that the unemployed, especially the never-employed and the non-union, have precious little voice in the determination of wages, in the local and national trade-offs of wages and jobs. The insiders, the employed, and among them the senior workers, control union policies; indeed they have the greatest influence on employers in unorganized shops as well. Workers at the factory gate, willing to replace those inside at lower wages, have little direct effect on wages. Recession and depression generate unemployment, but their main effect on wages comes via the financial and market pressures that impair employers' ability to pay and stiffen their backbones. Big wage concessions come, as we have observed recently in the automotive industry, when employers facing bankruptcy can credibly threaten senior workers with losses of jobs and pensions, via wholesale permanent closings. Cheap labour eventually disciplines the wages of established workers through competition from new products, new technologies, new firms, new regions, and foreign countries. Our economy would function better, both microeconomically and macroeconomically, if the discipline of wages by unemployed workers were exerted more directly and more quickly.

Writing about these issues sixteen years ago, I observed:

. . . [The] bargaining powers of unions are in considerable degree granted to them by federal legislation. In return for these privileges, it seems to me, the public could require unions to be effectively open to new members and apprentices. It is especially important to eliminate racially discriminatory barriers to entry.[4]

This still seems reasonable, indeed minimal. Certainly the federal government should not reinforce and extend union power by measures that require union scale wages to be paid on projects directly or indirectly, wholly or partially, federally financed, even to non-union workers in locations where no union scale is otherwise effective. The infamous Davis–Bacon Act has been on the hit list of every Council of Economic Advisers and Budget Office in living memory.

MINIMUM WAGES AND UNEMPLOYMENT INSURANCE

Minimum wage legislation probably does make the NAIRU higher, especially increasing youth unemployment. But the evidence is that its effects are greatly exaggerated in conservative rhetoric. United States law allows many exceptions and exemptions. Since the minimum wage did not rise in real terms or relative to median wages in the 1970s, it can hardly be blamed for the increase in unemployment. Similar remarks apply to unemployment compensation. No doubt it increases the NAIRU, the more so the more liberal the standards of eligibility, the duration of benefits, and their size relative to prevailing wages. Quantitatively the effects are small relative to observed unemployment; moreover, liberalizations during the 1970s, many of them in response to high unemployment in the recession of 1974/5, cannot account for more than a few tenths of a point of unemployment. Recently unemployment compensation was made taxable as income for taxpayers with incomes inclusive of this compensation exceeding $20,000. Further reforms would be possible without impairing the 'safety net' the system provides. They would include tightening the connection between an employer's contribution rate and the claims attributable to lay-offs by the employer. At present employers and employees, especially in seasonal businesses, can collude tacitly or otherwise and shift to other taxpayers part of the employees' annual wage.

MANPOWER POLICIES

I referred above to the rise in frictional unemployment indicated by the rise in vacancies relative to unemployment. Measures which make unemployment and prolonged search less attractive would reduce this contribution to the NAIRU. So should a host of labour market policies, some of which have been tried for at least two decades with little evident effect. These include improving the exchange of information about jobs and available workers; training and retraining on and off the job; assistance in relocation. Martin Baily and I have shown how government programmes to create jobs for low-wage and unskilled workers, either by direct employment or by subsidies, could 'cheat' the Phillips Curve in the short run and lower the NAIRU in the long run.[5]

OTHER STRUCTURAL REFORMS

I have spoken too long about labour markets and unions. There are other targets of structural reform. Government support of agricultural prices imparts another perverse asymmetry to the macroeconomy; the prices go up without impediment when demand–supply conditions are favourable, but supports hinder their fall when the dice roll the other way. Businesses raise prices when their sales, production, and employment are declining; the anti-trust lawyers in the Department of Justice should take notice. In Washington, Ottawa, and other capitals knowledgeable economists have well-known lists of 'sacred cows', inflation-increasing and efficiency-reducing laws and regulations with unassailable political support. Unfortunately one consequence of economic distress of the present virulence is that more and more claims for protection against competition, foreign and domestic, become irresistible in Congress or Parliament.

INCOMES POLICIES

It is easier to enumerate possible structural reforms than it is to muster confidence that much will actually be done or that they would greatly change the situation. That is why discussions of this kind always come in the end to incomes policies. These range from Kennedy–Johnson guideposts—open-mouth policy, without teeth—to full-fledged Nixonian or Galbraithian controls. They include economists' favourites, Abba Lerner's negotiable ration vouchers legally required of firms raising their average wages, and tax-based incomes policies (TIP) advocated by such diverse authors as Weintraub, Wallich, and Okun, which induce compliance with guideposts by rewards or penalties.[6] Those are my favourites too. I would embellish usual TIP proposals, if possible, by special penalties for increases of wages or mark-ups by firms whose employment and production are declining.

As in 1961, it is important to pave the way for a non-inflationary recovery from years of stagnation. Nervousness about resumption of inflation is more acute now, both among private agents and among policy makers, than twenty years ago. Consequently guideposts need more teeth, such as TIP could provide, than the Kennedy guideposts had then. They also need the understanding and support of leaders of business and labour. The promise of genuine and full recovery, promoted by monetary and fiscal policy, would be a strong inducement, a welcome change from vaguely threatening indifference to private sector wage and price behaviour. Without strong leadership from Presidents and Prime Ministers, the climate of opinion necessary for successful incomes policies cannot be created or maintained.

Incomes policies have a bad reputation because they are difficult to administer and because they inevitably distort market allocations of resources. TIP is designed to minimize these inefficiencies and to allow flexibility. When market signals are strong, firms can exceed guideposts, foregoing some rewards for themselves and their employees or incurring some penalties. These costs can be justified by the externalities incident to the value the society places on the avoidance of inflation. The economy-wide costs of incomes policy must be weighed against the social costs of avoiding inflation by macroeconomic policies that run the economy at chronically low speed. Those, in my view, are orders of magnitude greater. Let me emphasize also that it is not proposed to use incomes policies to contain and suppress excess demand inflation; we know from experience that you can not keep the lid on a boiling pot. The purpose rather is to guard against the revival of an inflationary dynamic, arising from the structural biases of the economy or from cost pushes or from expectations, even while the economy is operating within the bounds of full employment and normal capacity utilization.

My fear is that the purely monetary strategy of disinflation now, and inflation control thereafter, condemns our economies to chronic excess unemployment and to permanent weakness. Indeed I would not wait for V-I Day to engineer a recovery, preferably assisted by incomes policies to assure continued disinflation. Since World War II our pragmatic amalgam of capitalism and democracy in North America, Western Europe, and Japan spectacularly refuted the indictments and prophecies of Marx and other opponents. It would be ironic, maybe fatal, if we were now to concede by thought and deed that our system cannot function without an industrial reserve army of unemployed.

POSTSCRIPT

In the fourteen months since I wrote this Killam lecture, the main macroeconomic event has been the upswing of economic activity in

North America. The United States recession reached bottom in November–December 1982; production and employment recovered briskly throughout 1983. The turnabout was due to a deliberate change in Federal Reserve policy in the late summer and fall of 1982. Alarmed by the severe economic decline in America and elsewhere, by the possibility of a further collapse more difficult to reverse, by threatened financial insolvencies at home and abroad, Federal Reserve Chairman Volcker and his colleagues relented. It was not quite V-I Day, but the rate of inflation of the comprehensive 'GNP deflator' price index was below 4 per cent per year, six points below the years 1979 and 1980. The 1983 recovery was fuelled not only by interest rate reductions following the easing of monetary policy but also by fiscal stimuli from tax cuts effective in July 1982 and July 1983 and from defence procurement. By ironic accident, budget policies adopted in 1981 motivated by 'supply-side' economics and national security considerations, turned out to be well-timed counter-cyclical demand management.

The Federal Reserve is, however, very nervous about the pace of recovery and the possibility of new inflationary consequences. Real interest rates are still very high, and the Federal Reserve is clearly prepared to slow or stop the recovery, even at unemployment rates one to three points higher than those achieved in the two recoveries of the 1970s, whenever wages and prices seem to be accelerating. Moreover, Europe and Japan have not shared in the 1983 recovery. The governments of those countries have not adopted actively expansionary monetary policies, and their fiscal policies are actively restrictive. Unemployment and other indicators of economic slack are still rising throughout most of the advanced economies of the free world. Incomes policies are still anathema. The dismal prospect described in the text— stagnation due to the risk of inflation and the absence of any other means of insuring against it—is still all too probable.

NOTES

1. Beginning in late summer of 1982, the Federal Reserve did suspend its targets for monetary aggregates, particularly *M-1*, for the reasons given above. In July 1983 the 'Fed' announced new targets for 1983 and 1984 monetary growth, de-emphasizing *M-1* and re-basing its *M-1* targets to make clear that no effort would be made to eliminate the above-target bulge of *M-1* during the previous two quarters. Financial markets took these pragmatic moves in their stride.
2. J. Tobin, 'Stabilization policy ten years after', *Brookings Papers on Economic Activity*, 1980, vol. 1, 50–2; 1983, vol. 16, 'Financial structure

and monetary rules', *Kredit und Kapital*, 2, 155–71; 'Monetary policy in an uncertain world', *Bank of Japan Monetary and Economic Studies*, 1983, **1**, 2, 15–28, 'Monetary policy: rules, targets, and shocks', *Journal of Money, Credit, and Banking*, 1983, xv, 4, 506–18.

3. D. J. B. Mitchell, 'Gain sharing: an anti-inflation reform', *Challenge*, 1982, **25**, 3, 18–25.

4. J. Tobin, 'Unemployment and inflation: The cruel dilemma'. In Almarin Phillips, ed., *Price Issues in Theory, Practice, and Policy*, Philadelphia: University of Pennsylvania Press, 1967, pp. 101–7. Reprinted as Chapter 25 in my *Essays in Economics*, vol. 2, Amsterdam: North-Holland Pub. Co., 1975, pp. 3–10.

5. M. Baily and J. Tobin, 'Macroeconomic effects of selective public employment and wage subsidies', *Brookings Papers on Economic Activity*, 1977, vol. 2, 511–41.

6. For a general survey and criticism of these proposals, *see* A. M. Okun and G. L. Perry, eds., *Curing Chronic Inflation*, Washington: Brookings Institution, 1978.

32 Strategy for Disinflation (Fellner on 'The State of Monetary Policy')*

I. WAGE DISINFLATION IS A NECESSARY CONDITION OF PRICE DISINFLATION

United States inflation cannot be permanently reduced to the 2 per cent of 1961–5 unless money wage inflation is brought down by six or seven points from its current rate of 10 per cent per year. Wage inflation of 3–4 per cent a year would allow for a 2–3 per cent trend in the productivity of labour, partially offset by an adverse trend, possibly as much as 1 per cent per year, in the terms of trade of the products of American labour for agricultural and mineral products domestically produced or imported.

Please understand that I am not blaming labour for the inflation of the 1970s. I know that money wages have not even kept up with the Consumer Price Index in recent years. It is just a fact of life that lasting price disinflation cannot occur without wage disinflation.

Another necessary condition for disinflation is to reduce the growth of monetary demand for goods and services (dollar GNP, equal to MV, the money stock times its annual circuit velocity). Fellner's target for dollar GNP, 5 per cent a year, would accommodate 2 per cent inflation, plus an estimated sustainable real growth of 3 per cent from an expanding labour force with rising productivity.

Both wage disinflation and monetary disinflation are necessary. Without disinflation of aggregate monetary demand, wage disinflation would not slow prices down and would not last very long. Employers enjoying rising mark-ups and profit margins would bid up money wages. Without wage disinflation, reduction in the growth of dollar

---

*June 1981, The Conference Board Colloquium on Alternatives for Economic Policy, Washington. In its *Proceedings*, 1981, pp. 54–7.

spending on goods and services will be dissipated in low and maybe negative rates of increase in output and in increasing unemployment of labour and capital.

The conquest of inflation, I emphasize, requires a slowdown of wage gains and price increases in the central industrial sector of our economy. Food, materials, and oil prices are more volatile. Just as the prices of these commodities, together with home-financing costs, made for frightening inflation statistics fifteen to eighteen months ago, now they are generating good news. Such respites are transient. Given natural scarcities, the likely trend is adverse.

Likewise, the course of foreign-exchange rates sometimes makes short-run inflation statistics worse, sometimes, as in recent months, better. The dollar has been appreciating because our interest rates are high relative to those abroad. But that cannot be a permanent source of inflation relief.

No supply-side miracle can raise productivity growth enough to render wage increases of 10 per cent a year, or anything close to that, non-inflationary. Labour productivity may rebound on its own, and some years hence the incentive policies of the Administration may make a perceptible difference. I'm sceptical, but that doesn't matter for my present point. The wildest supply-side optimist could not expect to add more than a point a year to productivity growth. That is not in the same ball park as the present wage inflation.

II. ALL STRATEGIES OF DISINFLATION ARE INCOMES POLICIES

The preceding argument leads me to the proposition that every policy for disinflation is an incomes policy, and specifically a wage policy. This is true of demand management and of monetary policy in particular, whether or not it is accompanied by direct measures to disinflate wages and the prices associated with them.

In this spirit I distinguish four strategies:

1. Monetary disinflation unassisted.
2. Monetary disinflation assisted by well-advertised credible threat.
3. Gradual monetary disinflation concerted with gradually declining wage and price guideposts and tax-based inducements to comply with them.
4. Abrupt monetary disinflation concerted with abrupt scaling down of existing commitments and entitlements to future dollar payments.

How does unassisted monetary disinflation work? By monetary

disinflation I mean Fellner's 'gradualism with perceptible speed', reducing nominal GNP growth by a point a year for four or five years, until it gets down to 5 per cent. I note in passing that this is *not* the expressed policy of the Reagan Administration, whose economic scenario envisages double-digit growth of nominal GNP for several years, a forecast that can be reconciled with Federal Reserve money supply targets only by an unprecedented and improbable burst of velocity.

Monetary disinflation brings wage, cost, and price disinflation by generating enough unemployment among workers and enough idle capacity and financial distress among businesses so that the existing pattern of wage–price inflation gives way. The availability of workers outside the factory gate willing to replace those with jobs inside at lower wages has, experience tells us, very little effect by itself. But the spectre of bankruptcies, plant closings, and permanent lay-offs is eventually persuasive. Fellner thinks it will take about four years, a full business cycle and, yes, a full Presidential term. He is not, after all, much more optimistic than those of us he criticizes for extrapolating the disappointing results of the brief 'stop' phases of previous stop–go cycles. As he says, the response should be faster than in those recessions and slowdowns if businessmen, union leaders, and workers understand that this time there will be no 'go' until inflation is defeated.

This point brings me to the second strategy in my list. In his paper today, and even more in previous writings, Fellner has stressed the importance of *credibility* for the success of gradual monetary disinflation. In his view, policy makers must demonstrate 'willingness to expose the economy to the difficulties of a transition period'. In plainer language, they must convince businessmen, workers, and union leaders who set or negotiate prices that unless and until they disinflate they will lose sales and profits, jobs and wages. They must convince price and wage setters that the government will not again save them from disaster by anti-recessionary monetary and fiscal stimulus. Fellner recognizes that even a 'determined and credible policy of demand disinflation' will take time, because it takes time to establish credibility and to unwind contracts and commitments that built in and perpetuate past inflationary patterns.

Announced monetary disinflation, combined with the threat and promise to persevere regardless of the consequences for unemployment and production, is clearly an incomes policy. It is Margaret Thatcher's strategy in Britain. Whether she will achieve disinflation without severe and lasting damage to her economy it is still too early to judge. Anyway this is not Ronald Reagan's strategy. The President has not threatened American labour and business. He has told us all we will have disinflation without tears, and with business as usual, if only we accept his budget.

The Administration has taken the view that prices are a mechanical, arithmetic consequence of money supplies, which the Federal Reserve can control if it only will. The Reagan economic scenario undermines the threat implicit in the Fed's own targets—gradual reduction of money supply growth by half a percentage point a year—even though the Administration endorses and even mandates these targets. Paul Volcker's plans for *M-1B* mean little to businessmen and labour leaders who have scarcely heard of Volcker, don't understand the intricacies of monetary aggregates, and certainly have no way to translate those targets into their own prospects for sales and jobs.

A rare opportunity to adopt a credible threat strategy has already been lost. President Reagan could have put his inaugural prestige behind a Thatcher-like strategy, but he did not. Instead he pushed the Fed out front to fight inflation with monetary weapons alone, without the psychological support that might bring victory faster and with fewer casualties. My explanation of the President's stance is that the Administration places much higher priority on its allocational and distributional objectives—reducing the economic size and power of the federal government, and dismantling the 'Great Society'—than on the conquest of inflation.

III. DIRECT INCOMES POLICIES ARE NEEDED

The two other strategies involve direct intervention in the wage and price decisions of private agents. Both are discussed in Fellner's paper.

Neither strategy, I hasten to make clear once more, is a substitute for disinflation of aggregate demand. Both are complements to monetary disinflation, and to the credible threat. Both are intended, like the credible threat, to speed the transition and limit the damage.

Direct incomes policies are premised on the view that the principal obstacle to price and wage disinflation is the fear of each economic group—workers, unions, firms, industries—that its unilateral disinflation will not be matched by others. Thus workers resist departures from the standard pattern, because other workers who settled last month got higher wage increases and so, they suspect, will those who settle next month. Firms and industries resist unilateral price concessions, fearing that the prices of the inputs they buy will continue to rise at the accustomed pace. The impasse can be broken by an organized, concerted disinflation, by multilateral rather than unilateral disarmament. One of the two policies is gradualist, the other is abrupt shock treatment.

The particular gradualist mechanism I have advocated contains the following elements: (a) pre-announced guideposts for wage increases for five years ahead, declining annually on a schedule consistent with the announced monetary disinflation; (b) price guideposts based on the principle that percentage mark-ups should be stable; (c) compliance with the guideposts by an employer voluntary, but rewarded by tax rebates to both compliant employers and their employees, with bonuses in the degree that they do better than the guideposts; (d) claims of compliance and entitlement to rebates made by declaration in tax returns, subject to usual surveillance by the Internal Revenue Service; (e) termination of the plan at the end of the transition period, when both monetary policy and ongoing wage and price increases under the guideposts will be consistent with the target, say 2 per cent inflation.

Tax-based incomes policies of this kind seek to avoid the mistakes of the past that have given wage–price controls a bad name. They would not put the economy in a straitjacket but allow flexibility. For example, expanding firms that need to bid for labour could do so; although they would forgo some tax benefits, the distortion is justified by the common national interest in disinflation. These policies would not be a substitute for demand management: they would not try to hold a lid of controls on a pot boiling with excess demand. They would not be permanent, but neither would they be removed until the inflationary legacy of expectations and commitments had been removed by experience under the guideposts. These features should avoid the snapback that occurred on the ill-timed release of controls in 1974.

The shock strategy, associated with an abrupt monetary disinflation, would wipe out in one fell swoop the expected-inflation component of existing commitments to pay and entitlements to receive dollars. This would be done by emergency legislation scaling down the payments whose tender will satisfy pre-existing obligations to pay dollars in future. Fellner suggests but does not describe in detail a less surgical alternative, in which renegotiation is voluntary but encouraged by strong incentives. The more radical and universal shock treatment seems to me more reliable. In either case, the transition would be quick. There would be no restrictions on subsequent contracts. The parties would know however that pre-existing contracts have been rescaled to a non-inflationary future, to which demand management policy is firmly committed.

Forceful and persuasive Presidential leadership would be indispensable in obtaining the political, social, and economic consensus to support either of these incomes policies. President Reagan evidently has, or had, the personal magnetism and popularity to pull off coups of this magnitude. But this opportunity too has probably been lost, at least for several years.

IV. THE FED SHOULD TARGET NOMINAL GNP, NOT MONETARY AGGREGATES

The issues I have been discussing, addressed in the first part of Fellner's paper, are vastly more important than the technicalities of monetary aggregates and their control, discussed in the latter part of this paper. I think Fellner himself agrees.

I will state my view very bluntly. The long-run targets of the Federal Reserve should be expressed as a path of nominal GNP, the annual rates of increase in the flow of spending on goods and services. Since fiscal as well as monetary policies affect this path, the targets should be adopted and announced in concert with the Administration and the Congress. These targets should take precedence over any short-run instrument targets for monetary aggregates or interest rates. It should be made clear that both the Fed's instruments and those intermediate targets will be varied so as to keep nominal GNP on track—not of course month to month or quarter to quarter but on average year to year.

Since the path of dollar spending is the true objective of demand management, it has been and it is now extremely foolish to waste credibility on marksmanship in hitting targets of purely indicative and instrumental significance. The velocities of monetary aggregates vary in predictable and unpredictable ways, as interest rates vary and as financial technologies, regulations, and institutions change. The present confusion over M-$1B$ is an instructive example. The current overblown debate on whether by various technical tinkerings and by one short-run control procedure or another the Fed can keep M-$1B$ on target is really quite irrelevant, given the loose, unpredictable, and uncontrollable relation between M-$1B$ and nominal GNP.

During a transitional period of disinflation it is particularly unwise to stake the Fed's credibility on a monetary aggregate rather than nominal GNP. The very success of disinflationary policy will, other things equal, lower the velocity of transactions money. It will increase the demand for money, measured in purchasing power, because money balances will be depreciating less rapidly and alternative assets will have a small interest advantage. It will be not only be proper but necessary for the Fed to accommodate this increase in demand, but they will be unable to do so without raising doubts about their determination if they are tied to a mechanical schedule of declining *M-1B* growth.

33 The Case for Incomes Policies*

THE MACROECONOMIC RATIONALE

The principal obstacle to a recovery strong enough to lower unemployment to 6 per cent, its rate in 1978–9 before the two recent anti-inflationary recessions, is the fear that so full a recovery would ignite a new inflationary fire. This is not a new concern. The main problem of macroeconomic policy in the last forty years has been the difficulty of reconciling goals for employment and for prices. Their inconsistency became acute, of course, in the stagflation of the 1970s.

Those who regard the outbreak of accelerating inflation as itself a sufficient signal that the economy is at or below its 'natural rate' of unemployment, its full employment rate of unemployment, the rate consistent with Walrasian labour market equilibrium, deny that there is any dilemma. The only problem they see is the mistaken propensity of policy makers, abetted by politicians and by Keynesian economists, to aim for unnaturally low unemployment rates.

The identification of accelerating inflation with over-full employment seems to me a poor guide to macroeconomic policy, for the following reasons:

1. Prices and wages in our economy are not determined in competitive auction markets. Most of them are administered or negotiated. The institutions of wage and price setting are biased in the sense that wages and prices rise more in response to excess demands than they fall in response to equivalent excess supplies. This is true across markets and sectors of the economy, as well as for the economy as a whole through time.

*July 1983, Western Economic Association Symposium, Seattle. In 'A Symposium: Incomes Policy', *Challenge*. March/April in 1984, pp. 49–57.

2. Empirical estimates of 'natural rates' defined by the absence of price acceleration are just too high to be credible indicators of labour market equilibrium. Those rates are too high to be explained by voluntary search or preferences for leisure among respondents reporting job-seeking activity to Census interviewers. They are much too high to be attributed to 'friction' and to mismatching of jobs and idle workers. At unemployment rates alleged to be 'natural' there is ample evidence that jobs are scarce.

3. Some prices always rise in business cycle upswings, as flexible commodity prices recover and businesses restore mark-ups shaved in recessions. In the 1970s, these normal cyclical price increases were swamped by enormous exogenous oil price shocks at the ends of both cyclical recoveries. Whether endogenous or exogenous, price increases make for high inflation rates while they are occurring. It is hard for analysts and policy makers to tell whether they are observing one-shot events and temporary bulges of inflation or signals of permanently higher inflation rates.

4. Both econometric estimates and policy-makers' views of the current natural rate are greatly coloured by the record of the last decade. That experience, however, tells us very little about the relation of inflation to unemployment of labour and capital in the American economy. World commodity scarcities, Middle East wars and revolutions, and oil cartels are not intrinsic to the United States Phillips Curve.

5. Since policy makers are today extremely nervous about inflation, they are likely to resolve their uncertainties about the natural rate by aiming for unemployment rates one, too, or three points above their actuarial expectation of the natural rate.

Extra points of unemployment—carrying with them, as Okun's law tells us, multiple extra points of national output lost—are very costly insurance against accelerating inflation. The macroeconomic role of incomes policy is to provide much less costly insurance. Any incomes policy imposes microeconomic costs well known to economists, the allocational distortions our profession loves to tell the world about. That exercise is not sufficient. It is hard to imagine, and hard to argue empirically, that those costs could come close to those of insuring against inflation by permanent excess unemployment.

GUIDEPOSTS AND INCENTIVES

Inflation control is a public good, as the public's distaste for inflation, registered in polls and politics, testifies. Employers and unions who contribute to inflation by their price and wage behaviour are imposing costs on the rest of the society. These are standard welfare economics externalities, and the remedies are well known—devices to force or induce agents to internalize the social costs.

It is not surprising, therefore, that such eminent welfare economists as William Vickrey and the late Abba Lerner have suggested systems of negotiable rations. Essentially, the government would issue to employers vouchers allowing designated increases in payrolls per person hour and/or dollar value added per unit of output. The total issue of vouchers for any year or period of years would be calculated to hold prices in aggregate to the desired path. But the vouchers could be bought and sold; firms with the stronger microeconomic reasons for raising prices and wages could buy them from others.

As is often true, what can be done by negotiable rations can be approximated by taxes and subsidies. A tax-based incomes policy (TIP) may be more feasible administratively and more understandable politically than a Vickrey–Lerner system. Guideposts for wages and prices in what Hicks calls the 'fixprice' sectors of the economy would be announced yearly. Compliance with the guideposts would not be compulsory but would be encouraged by rewards or penalties. Weintraub and Wallich suggested extra corporate taxes for transgressions of a wage guidepost. Arthur Okun and others suggested rewards for compliance with the guideposts.

A carrot is likely to be more acceptable than a stick. For example, both employers and employees of an entity which complies with the wage guidepost could be rewarded by tax credits. Eligibility for the tax credits would be claimed by declaration, as in the case of other credits and deductions in the income tax codes. Employees' claims would be based on certification by the employer. The employer's reward would be contingent on his compliance with a mark-up guidepost; without this feature labour would be reluctant to agree to the programme. Enforcement by the IRS would be similar to enforcement of other provisions of tax law; the employer must be prepared to defend the validity of his claims.

Incomes policies of these types have two purposes. One is to diminish the price increases associated with any level of unemployment—to shift down the Keynesian Aggregate Supply Curve in (p, Y) space and the short-run Phillips Curve in $(\Delta p/p, Y)$ space. A second purpose is to lower the unemployment rate at the threshold of accelerating inflation: the after-tax marginal productivity of labour is raised for many workers. There are several things these policies are not intended to do. They cannot suppress an excess demand inflation, fix prices in auction markets, or evade the direct consequences of shifts in the real terms of international trade.

Incomes policies are usually dismissed by the facile generalization that they never have worked in the past. Certainly they have failed when they were overwhelmed by excess demand, when they were swamped by overpowering external price shocks, and when they were lifted before they had tamed inflationary psychology. But the Korean war price and wage controls, assisted by suitable fiscal policy, succeeded admirably. The Kennedy guideposts had no legal teeth, though they engaged the President and his Administration in opposing inflationary outcomes to important wage negotiations and related price decisions. In retrospect it does not seem far-fetched to assign them some credit for the inflation-free recovery of 1961–5, which reduced unemployment from 7 per cent to 4 per cent. They could not, of course, withstand the excess demand which followed, when President Johnson escalated the Vietnam War without raising taxes. The Nixon wage–price controls, despite the inconstancy of their application, mitigated wage and price increases during the recovery of 1971–3. The world commodity boom and OPEC were beyond their reach, and the controls were abandoned at the worst possible time in 1974. Even the Carter incomes policy worked during the recovery of 1975–8. Unfortunately it was scuttled by President Carter's political treaty with the AFL–CIO even before the Iranian revolution and the second oil shock brought a new acceleration of prices. Table 33.1 gives the history of wage and price inflation in the United States from 1961 to 1982.

The success of an incomes policy depends on a national consensus, and it takes Presidential leadership to create that consensus. The economic climate today is favourable. Chastened by ten years of stagflation and depression, both business and labour are hungry for sustained resumption of non-inflationary prosperity and growth. They should be ready for a social compact in which all would agree to restrain wage and price increases in return for jobs and markets.

The Federal Reserve's 1980–2 disinflationary monetary policy was also an implicit incomes policy. The announced commitment to gradual but relentless slowdown of monetary growth was intended to threaten unions and managements with unemployment and bankruptcy if they did not disinflate fast enough. The theory was that the 'credible threat' itself would take the place of realizations of the threatened events. Things didn't work out that way—the severe real consequences of the monetary disinflation were about what could have been expected from cyclical experience in previous policy regimes.

There were two probable reasons. First, the threat was not well understood by business managers and labour leaders; Paul Volcker is heard in financial circles, but it would have taken Presidential leadership to make sure that producers throughout the nation heard the message. Second, no one group could have any confidence that other groups would heed the message. What was needed was mutually assured disinflation, and the mutual assurance was lacking. The threat was no more effective than, say, a threat by the state highway police to close down a road if the *average* speed on it continues to exceed 55 m.p.h. The strategic advantage of an explicit incomes policy is to provide the essential mutual assurance. It is as important for the prevention of inflation during recovery as it was for limiting the real damage of monetary disinflation after 1979.

I realize that at the moment Presidential leadership to develop an incomes policy and the consensus to support it is quite unlikely. It goes against the grain of official ideology, supported by the bad memory of Nixon controls. It goes against the national mood now that inflation seems to be under control. If it isn't raining, why fix the roof?

But the American people have never really believed that unemployment is the way to prevent or remedy inflation. They instinctively believe there must be a better way, and they are right. Incomes policies are the better way, and their time may yet come.

Table 33.1: Price and wage inflation in the United States 1961–1982

	GNP deflator	Consumer Price index	Hourly earnings	Unemployment rate	GNP deflator	Consumer Price index	Hourly earnings	Unemployment rate
	(Year-to-year increases, %)			(%)	(Inflation increments, %-points)			(Changes, %-points)
1961	0.9	1.0	3.0	6.7				
1965	2.2	1.7	3.6	4.5				
1965–1965: Recovery and guideposts					+1.3	+0.7	+0.6	−2.2
1969	5.1	5.4	6.7	3.5				
1965–1969: Vietnam boom					+2.9	+3.7	+3.1	−1.0
1971	5.0	4.3	7.2	5.9				
1967–1971: Recession					−0.1	−1.1	+0.5	+2.4
1973	5.8	6.2	6.2	4.9				
1971–1973: Recovery and controls					+0.8	+1.9	−1.0	−1.0

1975	9.3	9.1[a]	8.4	8.5				
1973–1975: OPEC I decontrol, recession					+3.5	+2.9[a]	+2.2	+3.6
1978	7.4	7.7	8.1	6.1				
1975–1978: Recovery and guideposts					−1.9	−1.4	−0.3	−2.4
1980	9.3	13.5	9.0	7.1				
1978–1980: OPEC II					+1.9	+5.8	+0.9	+1.0
1982	6.0	3.6	6.8	9.7				
1980–1982: Recessions					−3.3	−9.9	−2.2	+2.6
1961–1982	av. 5.4	av. 5.7	av. 6.3	av. 5.9	+5.1	+2.6	+3.8	+3.0
1961–1982 omitting OPEC periods					−0.3	−6.1	+0.7	
1969–1980	av. 6.8	av. 7.6	av. 7.5	av. 6.1	+4.2	+8.1	+0.1	+3.6
1969–1980 omitting OPEC periods					+1.2	−0.7	−3.0	

[a] Peak year was 1974, 11.0%, 4.8 points higher than 1973.

34 Incentive-Based Incomes Policies: Foreword*

Our economy seems repeatedly to be on a tightrope, precariously negotiating a narrow passage between spiralling inflation and higher unemployment. Sometimes the fine line between them is called the NAIRU, for non-accelerating inflation rate of unemployment. The word is as unattractive as the condition, and the physical analogy it suggests is misplaced. But it has become part of the macroeconomists' vernacular.

No one can ever infallibly predict how the NAIRU will fluctuate. Expanding the economy in order to lower unemployment always entails some risk of generating faster inflation. The risk is greater as the actual unemployment rate is lower. But it is always hard to evaluate. Experts will disagree about the odds. Economists, and also politicians and the general public, will differ in their priorities, in how much risk of higher inflation they are willing to accept in the interest of reducing unemployment.

How do we as economists advise policymakers who are trying to steer the economy between the two hazards? Most of the contributors to this volume have concluded that the predicament of conventional macroeconomic policy is intolerable. We believe that two or three extra points of unemployment—running the economy at 7 or 8 per cent unemployment instead of 4 or 5 per cent—is too costly a way of ensuring against crossing the NAIRU and triggering faster and faster inflation.

Our alternative is simple. We must find a less costly insurance policy, one that will greatly diminish the risk of accelerating prices at low unemployment rates. Of course, there are dissenters from this consensus, even at this conference.

In my opinion, there is nothing *optimal* about the NAIRU. Indeed

*1984, Conference on Economic Affairs, Middlebury College, Vermont. In David Colander, ed., *Incentive-Based Incomes Policies: Advances in TIP and MAP*, Cambridge, Mass.: Ballinger, 1986, pp. xvii–xv. © 1986 Ballinger Publishing Company. Reprinted with permission.

it is the connotation of optimality in the word 'natural' that leads me to use the acronym in place of 'natural rate of unemployment'. By any name, it does not smell as sweet as a Walrasian equilibrium. It is not the result of intersections of marginal productivity schedules with labour supply curves. Whether you call it equilibrium or disequilibrium, it is not a situation in which prices have cleared markets but rather one in which excess supplies of labour and productive capacity persist.

Our economy is dominated by non-Walrasian institutions. Most wages and prices are decision variables determined by negotiation or administrative choice rather than by impersonal auction markets. Collective bargaining is not a way of life contemplated by Walras or by Arrow and Debreu. Even in the absence of unions, unemployed workers have very little of the influence on wages that they should and would have in competitive markets.

During the fall semester 1984–5, my own university was torn by a labour dispute between the administration and a newly organized union of clerical and technical workers. To me as an observing economist, it was striking that the supply/demand balance in the relevant labour markets was hardly ever mentioned by the two sides or by their partisans among faculty, students, and townspeople. It would have been considered 'an inappropriate issue' for the university to raise, and it would have been unwise for the union to mention. At prevailing wages, benefits, and working conditions there seemed to be an excess supply of potential employees. In a Walrasian world, this would have led to a fall in wages. In the actual circumstances it was irrelevant. The existing employees had obtained the power to ignore such competition, and debates on the campus concerned the 'justice' of their claims on the university's resources. The example is quite typical.

Our wage- and price-setting institutions respond asymmetrically to micro- and macroeconomic shocks. Prices and wages rise more readily and quickly than they fall, not only absolutely but relative to their ongoing inertial trends. The asymmetries apply over both time and space. Sectoral shifts of demand and supply, like the energy shocks of unhappy stagflationary memory, are on average inflationary, because they raise prices and/or wages more in excess-demand sectors than they lower them in excess-supply markets.

Given the institutions that generate these results, individual decisions to raise prices or wages damage third parties; they inflict on society at large costs that the price makers or wage negotiators do not take into account. Just as markets fail to impose on those who pollute air and water the social costs of their acts, so inflation pollution is an externality neither felt nor considered by businesses and unions. Just as we seek by public intervention to internalize the costs of actions that damage the natural environment, so we can try to internalize the macroeconomic costs of decentralized price and wage decisions. That, too, will require government intervention.

Two general strategies of intervention are available. One is to make the world more Walrasian, more competitive. We can revamp our institutions toward the model Poole has in mind when he says, in effect: 'Let the economy adjust to monetary and fiscal policies, rather than adapting those macro policies to the state of the economy. Accept as natural whatever unemployment rate comes out of those processes of adjustment.' I don't think that dream can be made to come true. But I certainly do not exclude pro-competitive reforms from the agenda.

Every Council of Economic Advisers, Republican or Democratic, has had a list of pro-inflation 'sacred cows' deserving of slaughter, much the same list year after year: Davis–Bacon, farm price supports, subsidies and restrictions of competition for the American merchant marine, and on and on. Economists are virtually unanimous in favouring reforms of this kind, but they are politically difficult to obtain.

The second and more controversial approach is *incomes policy*. It is by no means inconsistent with the agenda of pro-competitive reform. This approach aims to create new institutions to offset the inflationary biases of existing price- and wage-setting institutions, recognizing that the latter are entrenched for many reasons, often for good social purposes. The tax- and market-based incomes policies proposed and discussed in this volume are designed precisely to restrain and correct the inflationary biases of existing institutions.

Advocates know that these measures inevitably entail administrative inefficiencies and inequities, and that they are bound to distort in some degree the allocation of resources among economic activities. However, we live in an imperfect world, and we have to make 'second-best' judgements. Ultimately the decisive consideration is that the macroeconomic losses of running the economy with chronic excess unemployment of labour and capacity are greater by orders of magnitude than the social costs of incomes policies.

For example, if the federal corporate and personal income tax codes are used to induce compliance with guideposts for wage and price increases, we have to expect and tolerate slippages of the same kind and degree that characterize other provisions of these codes. Despite these shortcomings, we know from experience that tax incentives and disincentives do work in the intended directions, even though they are administered and enforced largely by self-declaration and selective surveillance.

The design of incomes policies is still a worthy challenge to the imagination and ingenuity of economic architects. We need not rely exclusively on tax systems; we should be able to exploit other governmental programmes and laws. Consider, for example, unemployment compensation. Some critics contend that its benefits increase the NAIRU by promoting voluntary unemployment. They probably exaggerate these effects, but reforms could diminish the disincentives for seeking and taking jobs without impairing benefits. A more important and unconventional reform of the unemployment compensation system would be to strengthen and extend the 'merit rating' feature of its financing. Tax penalties could be levied on employers who have raised wages beyond guidepost ceilings during periods of high or rising unemployment.

In the current political and economic climate one cannot be optimistic about the prospects of reforms and innovations to diminish the inflationary risk of full employment. When the sun is shining no one cares to fix the leaky roof. Both inflation and unemployment are lower than they were early in the 1980s. Their relative improvement blinds the nation to the fact that on both counts we did much better in the 1950s and 1960s. Certainly we will never have effective incomes policies without presidential leadership of the highest order, and we cannot expect such a commitment in the present ideological mood of the country.

What is most disheartening is that the labour movement, which has the most to gain from full employment, has still learned nothing from the macroeconomic disappointments of the last fifteen years. Like business managers, labour leaders and their economists continue to discuss incomes policies myopically, in terms of burdens and sacrifices and their distribution. The larger picture is not one of sacrifice; from a national viewpoint there are immense gains to be achieved. Economy-wide restraints on *nominal* wages and prices will make nobody worse off. Labour will be better off because there will be more jobs.

This volume will be a helpful contribution to the public policy debate, especially if it attracts more economists to this important and challenging subject. The essays here collected cover the major proposals now on the table, specifically tax-based incomes policies (TIP) and market anti-inflation plan (MAP). History tells us that intellectual, ideological, and political fashions change. The cruel unemployment/ inflation dilemma is not going to disappear. Those who regard its resolution as the basic economic problem of modern capitalism must be ready with concrete remedies when the need and opportunity arise.

35 Unemployment in the 1980s: Macroeconomic Diagnosis and Prescription*

I. UNEMPLOYMENT AND AGGREGATE DEMAND

Unemployment in the twenty-four nations of OECD rose from 5.5 per cent of the labour force in 1979 to 10 per cent in 1983. The number of unemployed persons rose from 18 million to 32 million. This development was the second upward ratchet in unemployment in the decade following the first oil shock. (Table 35.1 summarizes the recent history of unemployment in the advanced economies of the non-communist world.)

The prospects of reducing unemployment to 1979 rates, let alone 1973 rates, are dismal for the remainder of the 1980s. For the governments of the major locomotives of the world economy—the seven countries of the annual economic summit conferences (Canada, France, West Germany, Italy, Japan, the United Kingdom, and the United States)—significant reduction of unemployment is not a high joint or individual priority. Nor is it apparently a big concern of the electorates of these democracies. The prevailing attitudes, among both governors and governed, are fatalism and complacency; not much can be done, not much needs to be done, about unemployment. The fiscal and financial plans of most governments contemplate adjustment to permanently higher unemployment rates.

Europeans seem more resigned to the intractability of unemployment than North Americans. In the United States, return to unemployment rates less than a point above those of 1978 and 1979 is considered possible and desirable. The strong economic recovery which began in late 1982 buoyed optimism on this side of the Atlantic; unemployment

*1984, in Andrew J. Pierre, ed., *Unemployment and Growth in Western Economies.* (With other contributions by Marina V. N. Whitman, Raymond Barre and Shirley Williams.) The Project on European-American Relations, no. 2, New York: Council on Foreign Affairs, 1984, pp. 79–112.

has subsided from a cyclical peak of 10.7 per cent in December 1982 to 7.8 per cent in February 1984. Recovery in Europe has been later and weaker; unemployment is still rising, and common projections envisage a 'recovery' which leaves joblessness on a new higher plateau. Japan is a special case. Overt unemployment is always low, but the measured increases since 1973 and 1979 none the less are symptoms of large and growing margins of economic slack. Recent improvements in Europe and Japan reflect mainly export demands due directly or indirectly to the American recovery.

Half a century ago, four years of precipitous decline in world economic activity generated mass unemployment. Most of this persisted through the six years of recovery prior to World War II, which brought with it shortages of labour and everything else. The depression of 1979–83 was much less severe, and now society treats the jobless more generously than in the 1930s. Yet there are disturbing parallels. Then as now, governments and central banks eschewed active measures to create jobs in favour of austere fiscal and financial policies designed to win the confidence of international bankers and bond holders. Their efforts, individually and collectively, made depression and unemployment worse; and in the end they failed to balance budgets, protect currency parities, or prevent exposed banks from falling like dominoes.[1] Chancellor Heinrich Brüning adhered religiously to the canons of sound finance, and within a year after he left office, the Weimar Republic fell to Hitler. France, the leader of the gold bloc, eventually succumbed to the disasters it helped to inflict on its neighbours. Weakened by economic strife, political chaos, and class warfare throughout the 1930s, France was no match for Nazi Germany. Capitalism, democracy, and Western civilization barely survived.

Such momentous dangers seem remote today. But passive acceptance of prolonged high unemployment cannot be taken for granted either. Another decade of poor economic performance can undermine allegiance to the institutions of democratic capitalism, especially among successive cohorts of youth who fail to find jobs. Macroeconomic disappointments can also erode support for the international economic and political order on which the security and prosperity of the free world have been based since 1945. They have already triggered autarchic measures and proposals in nearly every nation, *sauve qui peut* expedients that protect some jobs and businesses at the expense of others and sacrifice the gains from efficient trade in the process. Stagnation in the developed 'North' is devastating to the less developed and debt-burdened 'South'. The austere prescriptions of the International Monetary Fund are politically risky in many countries friendly to the West. They may be inevitable when sick economics are treated

Table 35.1: *Selected macroeconomic data for OECD economies*

	(1) Unemployment rates (%) (average for year)			(2) Capacity utilization indexes		
	1973	1979	1983	1973	1979	1983
United States	4.8	5.8	9.5	88	86	75
Japan	1.3	2.1	2.7	100	90	83
West Germany	0.8	3.2	8.5	87	84	78
France	2.6	5.9	8.3	85	82	77
United Kingdom	3.3	5.6	11.5	43	42	32
Seven summit countries	3.4	5.0	8.3			
Fifteen OECD countries	3.3	5.1	9.0			

	(3) Real growth (% per yr.) GNP or GDP			(4) Output gap: % shortfall of 1983 GNP/GDP below 1979, projected to 1983 by	
	1965–73	1973–79	1979–83	1973–79 trend	Mean of 1973–79 and 1965–73 trends
United States	3.8	2.8	0.9	7.1	8.9
Japan	9.8	3.7	3.6	0	11.2
West Germany	4.1	2.4	0.5	7.5	10.4
France	5.2	3.1	1.1	7.7	11.3
United Kingdom	3.8	1.4	0	5.3	9.8

	(5) Money wage inflation (%)			(6) Unit labour costs (% Increase over prev. yr.)		
	1973	1979	1983	1973	1979	1983
United States	7.1	8.4	4.6	3.4	6.9	3.7
Japan	23.4	7.4	4.5	2.3	−2.5	1.2
West Germany	10.7	5.5	2.7	5.4	2.0	−1.2
France	14.6	13.0	11.0	7.2	6.1	8.0
United Kingdom	12.7	15.5	8.0	5.4	12.8	1.2
Total OECD	13.0	9.6	6.0			
Seven summit countries				4.6	5.3	3.5

	(7) Price inflation, GNP/GDP deflator (% rise over prev. yr.)		
	1973	1979	1983
United States	5.8	8.6	4.2
Japan	11.9	2.6	1.0
West Germany	6.5	4.1	3.0
France	7.1	10.4	9.0
United Kingdom	7.1	15.1	5.2
Total OECD		8.4	4.7
Seven summit countries		7.9	5.2

Notes: Except for the United States, figures for 1983 are OECD estimates from incomplete information. The seven summit countries include Italy and Canada. The fifteen OECD economies are the advanced countries, for which employment data are meaningful.
(1) Unemployment rates are standardized by OECD to United States definition.
(2) Estimates of utilization of manufacturing capacity. For Japan, the Ministry of International Trade and Industry index is normalized to 1973. For the United Kingdom, figures are percentages of firms reporting full utilization.
(5) Hourly earnings in manufacturing for the United States and West Germany. Monthly earnings for Japan. Weekly earnings for the United Kingdom. Hourly wage rates for France.
(6) Labour costs per unit of manufacturing output. For Germany, includes mining.

Sources: *Economic Outlook, OECD No. 27, July 1980 and No. 34, December 1983*; *Main Economic Indicators, OECD; International Financial Statistics, International Monetary Fund; and Economic Report of the President, 1984, US Government Printing Office.*

one by one. But in aggregate the medicines, like the belt-tightening national policies of the Great Depression, make the world situation worse.[2] Moreover, neither the examples nor the effects of current performance and policies in the advanced countries are likely to win the contest for the hearts and minds of the Third World.

The Great Depression taught the world that mass unemployment in advanced capitalist economies was a *macroeconomic* problem. That revelation means several things: first, when millions of people become unemployed, it is not because of their individual characteristics. They have not suddenly become lazy or unruly or unproductive or untrainable. The jobs are just not there. When jobs reappeared in the late 1930s and the 1940s, as in all subsequent cyclical recoveries, the unemployed were willing and able to fill them.

Second, mass unemployment is not due to shortages of capital equipment, land or other productive resources complementary to human labour. Indeed, industrial capacity is underutilized too. Table 35.1 shows for the most recent decade how measures of capacity utilization have fallen, while unemployment has risen.

Third, unemployment and underutilization of capacity both vary inversely with aggregate production and real income. This relation also is illustrated in Table 35.1, where shortfalls of Gross Domestic Product (GDP) from trend have risen parallel to unemployment.

Fourth, short-run fluctuations in production, employment, and capacity utilization are principally fluctuations in aggregate demand for goods and services. Potential aggregate supply, the productive capacity of a national economy or group of national economies, varies little from year to year. Of course, supply is the determinative constraint over horizons longer than business cycles. Growth of productive capacity is the source of secular progress in standards of living.

Fifth, mass unemployment is not technological in origin. New technologies do, of course, displace particular workers and impose hardships upon them, and upon whole industries and regions. But human labour in general has never yet become obsolete. Despite the dire science fiction prophecies that accompany every period of high unemployment, revival of aggregate demand has always created jobs in numbers vastly beyond the imaginations of the pessimists—or to put the point the other way round, productivity has not spurted to the heights imagined by the optimists. Given a buoyant macroeconomic climate, market capitalism has repeatedly demonstrated its capacity to adapt to new technologies, new patterns of demand, and new structures of comparative advantage in interregional and international trade.

Sixth, governments' monetary and fiscal policies are powerful influences on aggregate demand. They can be used to reduce unemployment due to deficiencies of demand. After World War II, every economically advanced democracy resolved not to allow unemployment to become again the scourge it had been in the 1930s. The next quarter century was an era of prosperity, growth and stability without parallel in economic history. Compared with prewar experience, even excluding the Great Depression of the 1930s, unemployment rates were low and fluctuated in a narrow band. The use of monetary and fiscal policies contributed to the favourable macroeconomic climate. The perverse policies so disastrous in the early 1930s were not repeated. But they are being repeated now.

Aside from its macroeconomic instruments, a modern democracy governing a decentralized economy has almost no tools to cope with unemployment. So-called structural, manpower, or labour-market policies are by no means new. Almost every advanced country has pursued them for decades. They can, as their successful use in Sweden in particular suggests, smooth and speed movements of workers displaced by technological and industrial change to new jobs. They can, therefore, reduce the minimal frictional unemployment inevitable in a dynamic economy. But they cannot do so unless the jobs are there, and thus they are virtually helpless when the macroeconomic climate is inclement. They are a useful complement to, but no substitute for, macroeconomic policies that assure adequate effective demand.

To be sure, our governments have the responsibility to educate our youth, but one can scarcely argue that today's young people are more vulnerable to unemployment than their fathers and mothers were because they are less educated—the contrary is the truth. Government programmes can train or retrain workers in skills relevant to contemporary technology and industrial practice. It is futile and even demoralizing if the graduates of those programmes cannot be placed, or if they simply displace workers whom those programmes passed by. In any case, evidence and common sense indicate that the best training is generally on-the-job experience itself. Governments can help to match job openings with available candidates by collecting and disseminating information on job specifications and workers' qualifications. But there is no reason to think that more than a tiny amount of unemployment is due to inefficiencies in these matchings at present. There are vastly more unemployed than vacancies today. Governments can sharpen incentives for encouraging the unemployed to search for jobs and to accept less attractive offers by diminishing the compensation paid to them and by instituting other reforms. Several governments are currently doing just that. This may help, but the fact remains that low unemployment coexisted with generous unemployment compensation for a long time. Governments can spread more evenly the work opportunities available by encouraging or mandating shorter hours. This does not really reduce unemployment, except by the illusion of the statistical conventions that do not allow even fractionally for persons involuntarily working short hours. A fairer distribution of the burdens may ease the pain to the affected workers, but it does not diminish the overall economic waste.

An all too common misconception about unemployment is that its social cost is negligible when the incomes of the unemployed themselves are substantially maintained by the welfare-state subventions to which they are entitled. For one thing, those payments are not compensation for the stigma and demoralization of enforced idleness in a society where achievement at work is a principal source of esteem and self-esteem. Economists are wrong to think that most people positively dislike work and engage in it only for the pay. In any case, the cost of unemployment and of excess capital capacity to the society is the shortfall of GDP. The lost output could have augmented not only private and public consumption but also accumulation of national wealth, either productive capital at home or net claims on the rest of the world. That loss is the burden; unemployment insurance and work sharing redistribute but do not eliminate it. The substantial size of the burden is shown in Table 35.1, the percentage shortfalls of GDP from trend. Economists generally use the unemployment rate as a barometer of macroeconomic performance and of cyclical fluctuation. In this sense, reduction in unemployment is valued not just in itself but as the symptom of economy-wide gains of output and income.

Those who expect structural labour market policies to make a significant dent in current unemployment are, I believe, whistling in the dark. Many who propose them are probably rationalizing conscious preferences for continued slack in labour markets. Macroeconomic stimulus is necessary to lower unemployment to rates comparable to those of the late 1970s. It is probably sufficient as well. Structural labour-market policies can make only marginal improvements.

A long-standing constraint in all advanced economies on the reduction of unemployment by expansion of aggregate demand for goods and services, whether from stimulative policies or from other internal or external sources, is the possible inflationary by-product of such expansion. The extents to which inflationary risks are, and can reasonably be, the basic reasons for the reluctance of major governments to employ their macroeconomic policy instruments to lower unemployment will be discussed below. Structural policies to diminish those risks and loosen the constraints they impose on macroeconomic policies will be discussed below as well. They are to be distinguished from direct labour market policies.

II.   UNEMPLOYMENT, THE PERMANENT CURE FOR INFLATION?

The principal intellectual obstacle to the use of policies of demand stimulus, monetary or fiscal, to reduce unemployment is fear of inflation. Demand management was discredited in the 1970s by the surges of inflation that terminated two cyclical recoveries in 1973–4 and 1979–80, recoveries driven or accommodated in degrees varying among countries by expansionary macroeconomic policies. The lesson learned by many policy makers, influential citizens, and economists is that unemployment cannot be cured in this way without unacceptable risk of inflation. This view is more solidly entrenched in Europe than in North America.

Reconciling high employment and price stability has been a chronic dilemma in advanced democratic economies for nearly four decades, most pronounced in the stagflationary decade of the 1970s. Economists generally recognize that the occurrence of price and wage acceleration at low rates of unemployment limits the possibility of reducing unemployment by management of aggregate demand. But to estimate where the limit is, to give a numerical value to the minimal inflation-safe unemployment rate for a specific economy at a specific time, is very difficult. The implicit consensus view of that threshold—often called the 'natural rate' though there is not necessarily anything natural about it, sometimes called the 'non-accelerating-inflation-rate-of-unemployment' or NAIRU—has appeared to rise secularly, for example, in the United States from 4 per cent in the 1960s to 5 per cent in the mid 1970s to 6 per cent or higher now. (President Reagan's Council of Economic Advisers pronounces it to be 6.5 per cent for the 1980s.) Governments and central banks who consider stability of prices, or at least stability of low inflation rates, their paramount goal, to which employment and production objectives are subordinate, are inclined to take no risk of crossing the threshold. In this view they are supported by a new generation of anti-Keynesian economists who believe essentially that labour markets are always in equilibrium, so that actual unemployment is always natural.

Overlearning the Lessons of the 1970s
The dismissal of expansionary macroeconomic policies is in my opinion a misreading of, at least an overreaction to, the events of the 1970s.

The frightening inflations accompanied two external price shocks without parallel in modern peacetime history. The Yom Kippur War, the oil embargo, and the first price hike Organization of Petroleum Exporting Countries (OPEC I) were not endogenous consequences of the 1971–3 recovery or of the major policies that fostered it. The Ayatollah Khomeini, the Iran–Iraq War, and OPEC II were not endogenous results of the recovery of 1975–9 or of the policies that supported it. Those two shocks would have been seriously inflationary and stagflationary even if demand policies had been more restrictive and unemployment higher before, when, and immediately after they occurred. This is not to exonerate demand policies of all responsibility for the inflations of the 1970s. It is to say that those events tell us little about the natural rate of unemployment and the safe limits of demand expansion in the 1980s.

It is true that the growth of American oil demand after 1974, due both to macroeconomic expansion and to continued controls on domestic oil prices, helped to bring world oil demand into collision with limits on OPEC's willing supply. It increased the vulnerability of oil-importing economies to the political interruptions of supply which occurred and to the hoarding of oil in anticipation of them. But if the inflation at the end of the 1970s tells us about any 'natural' rate, it was not that of unemployment but of oil consumption at the time.

Today the oil and energy situation is much improved. Abundant new non-OPEC supplies are available. Oil producers both within and outside the cartel are pumping far below capacity and far below their desired rates of exploitation. Thanks to decontrol of prices by Presidents Carter and Reagan and to other incentives for conservation and substitution, Americans have, like consumers elsewhere, substantially reduced consumption of energy in general, and oil in particular. These improvements continue as producers and consumers put into use energy-efficient machinery, structure, and appliances. We have found less costly ways to economize petroleum than economy-wide, worldwide recession and stagnation. It is estimated that recovery will restore only one-quarter of Americans' reduction in oil consumption since 1979. A third oil shock cannot be ruled out, but we are much better prepared. It cannot make sense to run our economies at low speed permanently just because another oil shock would be somewhat less inflationary in those circumstances than if the world economy were prospering.

In other respects too the inflation outlook is pleasant. Table 35.1 includes figures showing the impressive progress in disinflation of prices and wages in the major economies. The hardships of the past four years did accomplish something. The considerable slack in all economies should continue to discipline wages and prices even while utilization rates improve. Growth of productivity is reviving and holding down unit labour costs.

The Classical Unemployment Diagnosis

In Europe the restrictive stance of macroeconomic policy in the face of the highest unemployment and deepest depression in half a century is rationalized by a pessimistic diagnosis of the maladies. They are not the type, it is argued, that management of demand can cure; hence expansionary fiscal and monetary stimuli will just be dissipated in inflation. In effect, the inflation threshold rate of unemployment is close to the current rate.

Specifically, the argument goes like this: in the jargon of economics, the unemployment is classical, not Keynesian, that is, the culprit is not low demand but rigidly high real wages. Wage rates, relative to the prices employers receive for their products, are too high to make expansion of employment profitable. Trade union power, exercised on behalf of senior employees, defends uneconomically high real wages against the potential competition of the less privileged workers whom they render involuntarily unemployed. Raising mark-ups and prices will not relieve the profit squeeze because money wage rates will promptly and fully follow prices up. The process may or may not be formalized by indexation; in either case, the convention that money wages should rise with the cost of living is strong. It is especially damaging to profit margins and employment when, as in the cases of oil price shocks or exchange depreciations, cost of living indexes are rising relative to the prices of local products. Unless the real wage impasse is broken, demand stimulus is impotent to raise employment and production. Misdiagnosing and treating unemployment as Keynesian will only release an inflationary wage–price spiral.

According to this theory, classical unemployment arose in Europe after the first oil shock.[3] Organized labour was accustomed to the pre-OPEC growth of real wages and resisted departure from the trend. But employers could no longer afford to pay those wages, and the 'wage gap' grew as the growth of labour productivity slowed down. Countries like the United Kingdom, which none the less tried to restore high employment, suffered from inflation, while West Germany, the most important example, recognized the new situation and kept inflation under control. This scenario makes some sense through 1979 or even 1980 but strains credulity for the subsequent rise of unemployment. For the later period, structural disturbances due to new technology and foreign competition are said to have rendered much existing human and physical capital obsolete.

It is difficult to tell by inspection whether unemployment is Keynesian or classical, or in what proportions it is the one or the other. It is difficult to tell whether real wages are above those which would be consistent with a lower unemployment rate, and if they are, to say whether or not they would naturally fall during a demand-driven recovery. And even if all those doubts are resolved on the pessimistic, classical side, it is gratuitous to assume that governments can do nothing to modify the recalcitrant path of real wages.

Squeezed profit margins are characteristic of cyclical lows of business activity, and sometimes but not always reflect high real wages. Recoveries generally restore profit margins, and not necessarily by lowering real wages (relative to trend).

In retrospect no one doubts that mass unemployment in the 1930s was Keynesian. But an observer of the world scene in 1933 would have noted a severe profit squeeze. Real wages had risen in terms of labour's product from 1929 to 1932 in West Germany, Sweden, and the United Kingdom; they had fallen in the United States. Labour's share of product had risen by 38 per cent, 9 per cent, and 16 per cent in the first three countries respectively, and also by 11 per cent in the United States.[4] It would have been easy to call unemployment in the Great Depression classical. Indeed most economists rejected monetary and fiscal solutions at the time.

Keynes pointed out how real wages could be high and profits squeezed because of the same deficiency of aggregate demand that caused the unemployment.[5] In recession and depression businesses cut prices competitively but lay off workers and cut production until their (marginal) costs at existing wages are lowered as much as their prices. During reflations and recoveries they reverse the process, enjoying higher profit margins as prices rise relative to wages, while increasing employment and production. Workers gladly accept additional employment even though their real wages may be falling. The Keynesian mechanism envisages cyclical price movements around relatively stable money wages. Keynesian adaptations of real wages occurred in the recoveries of the three European countries in the 1930s. In the United States real wages gained as production, employment and profits recovered.

Almost immediately after publication of the *General Theory*, empirical investigations challenged Keynes' unquestioning acceptance of the conventional view that real wages, because they must be equal to the marginal productivity of labour, will vary counter-cyclically.[6] Those and many subsequent studies concluded that both labour productivity and product wages more usually rise than fall during cyclical upswings, as was true in the United States in the 1930s. The classical theory of marginal cost pricing is not a reliable guide to the cyclical behaviour of prices and real wages. In an imperfectly competitive economy in disequilibrium, relief of profit squeeze is provided by higher volume, increasing returns to scale, and efficient utilization of both overhead labour and redundant employees. As aggregate demand expansion shifts out firms' product demand curves, employers with constant or declining marginal costs will raise employment without any reduction of product wages.

For these reasons, observations of high real wages and squeezed profit margins do not *per se* show that unemployment is classical and not susceptible to Keynesian remedies. Rigidly high real wages may be the effective constraint on expansion of output and employment in particular economies in particular circumstances. Credible recent examples are the United Kingdom and Sweden in the 1970s, where export industries unprofitable at internationally competitive prices could not be made competitive by devaluation because of wage indexation. The immediate question is the applicability of the classical unemployment thesis to the 'locomotive' economies today, discussed in the next section.

One other point of macroeconomic theory deserves emphasis. Even if real wage reduction is necessary for expansion of output and employment, it may not be sufficient. Suppose, for example, that workers economy-wide give up one annual cost-of-living increase of money wages to allow business profit margins to increase. The redistribution of purchasing power does not obviously increase aggregate demand, and may indeed diminish consumption. A positive outcome can come from net exports. This will benefit any one open economy at the expense of others, but it is not a solution for all countries together. In a closed economy, or in the world as a whole, the hope would centre on business investment. Will it be encouraged enough by the improved outlook for profit margins to overcome the disincentives of current excess capacity and sales prospects? Maybe, if the profit improvement is expected to be permanent. Maybe not. The safest course would be to combine durable wage corrections with assurances of accommodative and, if necessary, stimulative demand policies.

Policies to Improve the Inflation–Unemployment Trade-off
By far the most formidable barrier to monetary and fiscal stimulus to recovery and jobs is the risk of reacceleration of wages and prices. The danger seems remote today, when OECD economies are performing so far below capacity. But any business cycle recovery raises some prices. The prices of raw materials and foodstuffs traded in world commodity markets, sensitive to demand and supply, fell precipitously in the

recent depression. Flexible upwards too, they are bound to rise in recovery. Likewise, businesses will have to restore to normal profitable rates the mark-ups they shaved in hard times. These reversals are one-shot price increases, but they worsen month-to-month inflation statistics temporarily while they take place. Nervous policy makers cannot know for sure that they do not presage a more stubborn escalation of inflation.

Central banks and governments are so sensitized to inflationary dangers that they will resolve on the side of caution and restriction their uncertainties about the location of the minimal inflation-safe unemployment rate. They will buy insurance against a new spurt of inflation at the cost of extra points of unemployment. For their economies and the world, this insurance is very expensive. It may well be increasingly expensive, and ultimately self-defeating, in the long run. Experience suggests that prolonged high unemployment becomes 'natural' and structural—a self-fulfilling prophecy. The mechanisms are obvious: unemployed workers lose, or never acquire, the skills and habits imbued by actual job experience. Businesses lack the profits and prospects that spur investments in new capacity and technology, the advance of productivity falters, and bottlenecks loom at ever higher unemployment rates.

The obvious desiderata are policies to diminish the inflation risks of demand expansion and to lower the inflation-safe unemployment rate. The candidates fall into two somewhat overlapping categories: *institutional reforms* and *incomes policies*. The prospects and the particulars differ widely from country to country. Here it is possible only to indicate general principles, with illustrative examples.

In most countries the institutions of wage and price setting are biased upwards. That is, wages and prices—other than those commodity prices set continuously by supply and demand in auction markets—rise more readily than they fall. Consider government-supported floors on farm prices, minimum wages, asymmetrical indexation. Consider the inexorable ascent of costs of health care, undisciplined by market forces when payments are by third-party insurers, governmental or private. Consider the limited sensitivity to excess capacity of 'administered' industrial prices, and the stubbornness of negotiated wages in the face of unemployment. When government interventions are responsible for these biases, they are obvious, though politically elusive, targets of legislative reform. When governments grant private agents and groups—trade unions or trade associations—immunities from competition, the public has at the very least the right to insist that the privileges are not exercised in ways that inflict inflation or unemployment on the whole society. For example, if indexing is permitted at all, it should be symmetrical; and the price index used should exclude cost-of-living increases that are burdens to employers and to the whole society as well as to workers, like import price boosts and increased sales taxes.

In most countries, collective bargaining procedures are sanctioned, protected and regulated by legislation. A general problem is that no one represents workers laid off or never hired. All too often the wages of senior employed workers take precedence over the number of jobs. Remedies are hard to find. Perhaps official recognition as bargaining agents could be denied to unions that restrict membership and deny voice to the unemployed. Perhaps employers who raise wages while curtailing employment, or while qualified workers are in excess supply in their industry or region, should have to pay penalty surcharges into unemployment insurance funds. Perhaps legislation should provide incentive subsidies for employers and workers to agree on compensation systems which, like the Japanese model, condition some payments to workers on the profits or revenues or productivity gains of the firm.

Incomes policies are an alternative more readily available. In one form or another, they have on occasion been practised by almost every country. They range from the full-blown detailed price and wage ceilings of wartime mobilization to advisory guideposts dependent on persuasive interventions by government leaders. In a sense, threats, promises, and conditions respecting monetary and fiscal policies are also incomes policies. Their recent use in the United States and United Kingdom was not encouraging. They work better where wage bargains are synchronized in time, and in significant degree centralized; where government officials, union leaders, and business representatives can annually discuss wage and price patterns in their macroeconomic contexts.

Explicit incomes policies have failed when they attempted to suppress inflation in overheated peacetime economies; when they were removed before inflation expectations were damped; when they lacked or lost the consensus of the parties; when they were overwhelmed by uncontrollable price shocks, as in the oil crises of the 1970s. Past failures have made incomes policies unfashionable, but *faute de mieux* they deserve to be reconsidered.

Today conditions are favourable in several major economies. There is plenty of economic slack; inflation and expectations of inflation have been receding; both workers and employers can see how much they have to gain from a sustained non-inflationary recovery. In similar circumstances from 1961 to 1965 the Kennedy–Johnson guideposts, though without the teeth of legal compulsion, helped to keep recovery free of inflation. Today they probably should be strengthened by incentives for compliance, either the stick of tax penalties or the carrot of tax rewards. Tax-based incomes policy (TIP) is designed for decentralized, unsynchronized institutions of wage and price setting, and designed to avoid the rigidities and inefficiencies of absolute controls. It may not be necessary in economies with institutions for economy-wide bargaining. Whatever the institutions and the policy, the indispensable ingredient is the leadership of Presidents and Prime Ministers to develop and sustain the underlying consensus. Unfortunately, this leadership will never come from governments whose *laissez-faire* ideologies tell them that market economies will on their own achieve full employment without inflation.

Ordinary citizens never believe economists and bankers who tell them unemployment is the only cure for inflation. They think there must be a better way, and they are right.

III. THE CASE FOR DEMAND EXPANSION IN EUROPE AND JAPAN

Among the seven summit countries, the United States, West Germany, and Japan are the decisive actors in the macroeconomic drama. They have the opportunity and responsibility to restore prosperity and growth for the whole world. Canada must willy-nilly follow in the footsteps of its large neighbour to the south, amplifying its world impact. In Europe, West Germany is the key economy. Its macroeconomic performance and policy set the tone for the European Economic Community and for the whole area. Of the three other large economies of Western Europe, only the United Kingdom has much room for independent manoeuvre just now. France is still paying the penalties of deviating from the deflationist ranks of its trading partners in the first year of Mitterrand's socialist government. The Italian economy is too unruly and uncontrollable to be a significant force in the world economy. The discussion here will focus on West Germany, the United Kingdom, and Japan.[7]

As recorded in Table 35.1, West German inflation is enviably low and still falling, despite the adverse effects of the Deutschmark depreciation against the dollar and in lesser degree against the yen and the pound sterling. Since 1980 unemployment has more than doubled and is still rising. Job vacancies have virtually vanished. In the late 1970s, with unemployment at 3.5 to 4 per cent, there were four unemployed for every vacancy. Now there are 40! Money wage increases have slowed to 3.5 per cent per year. After allowance for productivity trends, labour costs per unit of output are stable or declining. Could anyone seriously contend that macroeconomic expansion is now barred by rigidly high real wage rates? Surely at least half of current unemployment is Keynesian, not classical.

The view that West Germany was afflicted by classical unemployment, that its 'natural rate' rose after 1973, gained currency during the post-OPEC stagflation. The onset of expensive energy coincided with immigration restrictions that limited the role of potential *Gastarbeiter* as an uncounted reserve army of unemployed. One signal of structural deterioration is that during the last ten years unemployment of labour rose more than underutilization of capacity. Another signal was the rise in the 'wage gap', a measure of unit labour costs relative to prices, compared with a base year, specifically one of normal pre-OPEC prosperity, 1969. An increase in the wage gap is a squeeze on profit margins. The gap rose significantly, perhaps as much as 10 per cent, in the early 1970s, but it has since declined to its 1969 norm. In any event, labour costs relative to after-tax net incomes to capital are low in West Germany compared with the United States. (In 1974 and 1982 the West German ratios were 3.1 and 3.0 respectively, while the American ratios were 3.6 and 3.4.) The wage-gap theory of the post-OPEC West German slowdown through 1979 is plausible, though debatable. It is not a credible explanation of the rise of unemployment in the 1980s.

The trend of potential real output in West Germany, that is, output at a constant unemployment rate, is lower than before 1973, but still appears to exceed 3 per cent per year. The bulk of it is productivity growth; the labour force is virtually stationary. A conservatively high estimate of the present inflation-safe rate of unemployment is 4.5 per cent. The 'Okun's Law' coefficient, relating percentage shortfalls of real GDP to excess unemployment, seems to be 2 or 2.5. Thus the loss of GDP at 9.5 per cent unemployment is 10 to 12 per cent. Eliminating it would take five years of growth in real GDP averaging around 5 per cent per year. With so much room and time, the Bundesbank and government would have plenty of chance to apply the brakes on evidence of price acceleration before unemployment fell the full amount.

There is another reason why fatalistic acceptance of the classical unemployment thesis is especially puzzling for West Germany. The history of wage determination in the Federal Republic is by and large not one of confrontation but one of moderation and 'codetermination'.[8] Realities of international competitiveness, macroeconomic trade-offs, and monetary and fiscal policies have influenced collective bargaining more successfully than in most other countries, including the United

States and the United Kingdom. This has been true even after 1977, when the unions withdrew from the annual summit sessions with representatives of employers, the central bank, the government, and the Council of Economic Experts. Rigidities are not built into the system. Contracts last only one year, and indexation is outlawed. Government, unions, and employers have recognized that wage setting is a matter of national political economy and economic politics. The West German government has actively pursued incomes policies, using macroeconomic policies and the wage–employment trade-offs they imply as both threats and promises.

If, as the influential economist Herbert Giersch has argued,[9] West Germany needs a *Lohnpause* (pause in wage increases) to clear the road for macroeconomic expansion, the record does not suggest, at least to an outside observer, that it could not be negotiated in return for a promise that policy will assure the expansion. If, under its new conservative government, West Germany is in the process of reforming its system of labour relations in the direction of decentralization, non-intervention, and confrontation, the outsider may be excused for observing 'if it ain't broke, don't fix it'.

The situation of the United Kingdom is similar to that of West Germany, except that unemployment and inflation are both about three points higher. Both wages and unit labour costs have been decelerating, while a modest recovery—enough to raise capacity utilization and employment but not to stop the unemployment rate from rising—has been under way for two years. Of course, labour relations and wage behaviour have been throughout Great Britain's postwar history a much greater source of macroeconomic difficulty than in West Germany. Evidently a major objective of the Thatcher government has been to break the unions' grip on the economy. The question is whether, after five years of disinflationary policy and rising unemployment, the groundwork for expansion without wage and price acceleration is finally in place. And if not yet, when? Maybe by now even British trade union leaders would be ready to offer wage stability in exchange for jobs.

Japan absorbed the two OPEC shocks of the 1970s and the subsequent world slumps with remarkable success. Real growth was interrupted only mildly in 1974–5. But growth rates after OPEC I were less than half the double-digit annual rates common previously, and they fell still farther in the 1980s. These slowdowns have opened a wide GNP gap, suggested by declining indicators of capacity utilization but not easy to discern in unemployment statistics. The 1983 unemployment rate, though under 3 per cent, is twice the rate of 1972. In Japan, far more than in Western economies, slack demand is absorbed by keeping redundant workers on the payroll—in effect a system of private unemployment insurance. As a result, the Okun coefficient for Japan is estimated to be from 13 to 25.[10] The lower number indicates that an extra point of unemployment in Japan signifies the same degree of slack as an extra five points in the United States or West Germany. Today, therefore, Japanese production is far below potential trend.

Like West Germany's, Japan's inflation is low and declining. With the help of a one-shot reduction of real wages, Japan overcame the inflationary consequences of the first oil shock by 1978. The second one Japan took pretty much in stride. Wage pressure is a minor problem in a country where unions are weak and the bonus system makes labour costs move up and down with employers' ability to pay—the workers' *quid pro quo* for immunity from lay-offs.

IV. DEMAND MANAGEMENT POLICIES IN THE MAJOR OECD ECONOMIES

The severe decline in world economic activity since 1979 was the result of restrictive macroeconomic policies deliberately and concurrently adopted in almost all major countries. The common goal was to overcome the price acceleration accompanying the second oil crisis, when oil demands enhanced by the 1975–9 recovery confronted supplies interrupted by the Iranian revolution and the beginnings of the Iran–Iraq War.

The firm, unanimous and single-minded dedication of macro policies to the conquest of inflation reflected experience after the first OPEC shock in 1973–4. Then too, restrictive policies brought severe recession and disinflation throughout the world. But subsequent experience differed from country to country. The most striking differences were between the United States and the two other big locomotives, West Germany and Japan. In the United States, fiscal and monetary policies turned stimulative or accommodative in 1975, and the subsequent recovery lowered unemployment rates by more than three percentage points. In West Germany and Japan, the macro brakes were relaxed very little. Unemployment and economic slack in those countries, indeed throughout the OECD outside North America, remained much higher than before. But the more austere governments preserved more of the disinflationary gains of the mid-decade recession and were less vulnerable to inflation following the second oil price shock. The United States and Canada, together with those European countries (notably the United Kingdom, France, and Italy) with chronically high inflation, were also vulnerable to crises of confidence in foreign-exchange markets. The lesson perceived by all central banks was applied as the second OPEC shock hit: tighten promptly, tighten hard, and stay tight.

Disinflation, Depression, and Recovery in the United States
In the United States, Federal Reserve Board Chairman Paul Volcker announced in October 1979 a policy of relentless gradual reductions in the growth rates of monetary aggregates to continue until monetary growth would accommodate only sustainable non-inflationary rates of increase in GNP. The policy differed from the restrictive measures taken in mid 1974 by Chairman Arthur Burns and his Federal Reserve colleagues in Volcker's explicit disavowal of counter-cyclical monetary policy. This time the 'Fed' would not rescue the economy from recession by accommodating continuing inflation, as the Burns regime was perceived to have done from 1975. In the United States, as in the United Kingdom and Europe, many economists, financiers and policy makers believed that the effectiveness of recession as therapy for inflation was diluted and rendered transitory by the expectations of workers, unions, and businesses that anti-recessionary policies would save them from hard times whether or not they gave way on nominal wages and prices. The same theory predicted that if the private sector were convinced that policy makers would 'stay the course', a disinflationary recession would be shorter and do less damage than past recessions to employment and production.[11] The theory has influenced fiscal as well as monetary policies in most major economies: the Thatcher and Reagan governments forswear counter-cyclical macro policies as a matter of principle, and others act in the same spirit.

The Federal Reserve nevertheless relented in the late summer and fall of 1982. United States inflation rates had by then fallen dramatically. But the side effects, in unemployment, business failures, lost production, and low investment, were much more damaging to the American and world economies than had been intended. The advertised commitment to 'stay the course' had not noticeably speeded the disinflation or limited the damage. Third World debtor countries, notably Mexico and Brazil, could not earn enough hard currency in export markets to carry debts at the high interest rates resulting from restrictive monetary policies in the United States and elsewhere. Their difficulties threatened the solvency of their creditors in North America and Europe. A sharp decline in the velocity of money in the United States, partly because deregulation was making checking accounts in banks more attractive vehicles for saving and partly because general pessimism increased preference for safe, government-insured liquid assets, was making the Federal Reserve's money supply targets even more restrictive of nominal GNP than had been expected. When those targets were suspended to allow higher money growth, interest rates of all maturities fell sharply, and interest-sensitive expenditures, for residential construction and consumer durable goods, revived. The economy turned up in November, assisted strongly by the usual cyclical rhythm of inventories as businesses stopped liquidating them and began restocking.

The strong recovery of final sales of goods and services (GNP less net inventory accumulation) throughout 1983 was powerfully assisted by consumers spending the proceeds of two 10 per cent cuts of personal income tax rates, one in July 1982 and one in July 1983. These were the second and final instalments of the three rate reductions scheduled in the Economic Recovery Tax Act of 1981. Likewise the build-up of defence spending, also planned in 1981, began to provide markets and jobs, more via the placement of orders than by actual outlays.

By pure serendipity the Administration carried out a classic well-timed Keynesian anti-recession fiscal policy complementary to the counter-cyclical change in monetary policy in late 1982. Neither of the deficit-increasing measures was intended to be a demand stimulus. In 1981 no recession clouded the officially projected scenario, and the Administration was on principle opposed to counter-cyclical demand management. The tax cuts were supply-side incentives, intended to encourage saving, work, and risk taking, not spending. The defence build-up was for national security and diplomatic strategy, not for any economic purpose.

Whatever their motivations, expansionary monetary and fiscal policies worked as traditionally expected in the United States in 1983. Three or four million new jobs[12] were created, and the unemployment rate came down from 10.7 per cent to 7.8 per cent. As recently as the summer of 1982, the air was full of pessimism about the intractability of unemployment: the feeling then was that even as business activity recovers it will not create jobs. Congress, in a desperate attempt to do something, raised gasoline taxes to fund additional public jobs. The programme was to create at most 300,000 jobs, but at least an equal number were probably lost by diversion of private spending to tax payment. Also as recently as early 1983 the air was full of dire predictions that federal deficits would 'choke off recovery', even while pragmatic business forecasters correctly knew they would do the opposite.

The 1979–82 episode achieved a substantial but incomplete victory over inflation in the United States. The 'core' inflation rate, which excludes patently non-recurrent price changes, has fallen four or five points, from 9 to 10 per cent per year to 4 to 5 per cent per year.

Wage inflation has fallen similarly; what this portends for price inflation depends on the productivity trend of the 1980s, which is not yet clear. In any event recovery has not reversed, or even arrested, gradual progress on inflation to date. This was to have been expected given the slack in utilization of labour and capacity still remaining. It was not to have been anticipated by those who expect price inflation to follow monetary growth regardless of the economic climate, because the Federal Reserve allowed double-digit growth of *M-1* (currency in circulation plus demand deposits) from July 1982 to June 1983. (Since then *M-1* growth has slowed to 4 per cent, leading some monetarists to predict an early recession.)

The Federal Reserve has by no means abandoned its anti-inflation objective. After the initial drop of interest rates in 1982, the Federal Reserve raised them about 100 basis points in June 1983 and has held them steady to date. Paul Volcker and his colleagues will probably be content so long as, on the one side, no new recession begins and, on the other side, the expansion is well behaved. A well-behaved recovery in this context means that the pace is slowing and approaching sustainable growth; prices and wages are not accelerating; unemployment is safely above the 6 per cent rate of 1978–9; and monetary aggregates are within the target ranges for their growth, lower for 1984 than for 1983. In the absence of any one of those conditions, Chairman Volcker has made clear that the 'Fed' is ready to apply the brakes and raise interest rates. Continued recovery will not receive the benefit of the doubt against the risk of accelerating inflation.

Interest rates in the United States are still by historical standards very high in relation to actual inflation and to reasonable expectations of future inflation. These rates are a formidable obstacle to accumulation of domestic capital—residential and non-residential, human and physical, private and public, fixed and working. They are even more devastating to United States foreign investment; here indeed the nation is disinvesting, running large deficits on current account because of enormous merchandise trade deficits. How long the sheer momentum of the recovery, the general optimistic mood, and the fiscal stimulus can prevail over these obstacles is the main near-term uncertainty about the strength and duration of the recovery.

United States Interest Rates and the World Economy
The mechanisms by which American interest rates crowd out the nation's net exports is a striking illustration of textbook analysis of the workings of macroeconomic policies in today's international monetary environment, a world of floating exchange rates and closely connected financial markets. As differentially high interest rates have attracted

funds into dollar-denominated assets, the dollar has appreciated against the yen, Deutschmark, franc, and other currencies—actually by 52 per cent on average since 1980, 45 per cent when account is also taken of differences in national inflations over the period. The appreciation handicaps American exports and encourages imports.

The unique strength of United States recovery in 1983, and prospectively in 1984, also raises American imports while the sluggishness of foreign economies continues to depress their demands for American exports. Dollar appreciation since 1979 has, on the other hand, contributed to disinflation in the United States by making imported goods less expensive in dollars—US inflation is estimated to be one or two percentage points lower as a result.[13] But this effect is only a transitory contribution to disinflation. It cannot be repeated without further appreciation, and it is more likely to be reversed.

While interest rate differentials are the major source of the dollar's strength in exchange markets, they are not the only factor. International political developments and longer-run assessments of economic prospects may have improved the dollar's standing as a safe haven. There is no assurance that continued interest differentials will maintain the dollar's exchange value. Portfolio adjustments to exploit the perceived advantages of dollar assets in risk and return are not endless; most of them may have already occurred. United States' current account deficits shift wealth to foreigners who tend to prefer their home currencies. Those deficits also raise doubts about the long-run viability of America's heavy reliance on foreign borrowing to finance its budget deficits and domestic investments.

High American interest rates and the high exchange value of the dollar have been and still are important determinants of the world macroeconomic environment in several respects. First, because of the weight of the United States in international financial markets, high interest rates in the United States make interest rates high everywhere. In this way they contributed to the universal world depression, and they are still an obstacle to world recovery. Second, they intensify Third World debt burdens, especially in a period of disinflation and depression. Third, the appreciation of the dollar has exacerbated trade frictions, particularly between the United States and Japan, and inspired protectionist measures and proposals in the United States. Fourth. American interest and exchange rates have constrained macroeconomic policy options in Europe and Japan, although not as tightly as those governments claim. This point will be discussed in the next section.

Monetary and Fiscal Policies Outside North America
The 1983 recovery was unique to North America, and so were the shifts to expansionary macroeconomic policies. Europe and Japan lag far behind, benefiting from the spillover of American demand into their economies but doing nothing else to stimulate domestic demand. Their certainties that active policies of expansion would be futile and inflationary should be reconsidered in light of the American example.

As stated above, monetary policies in those other countries are in some degree constrained by American interest rates. Major foreign central banks have lost some control of their own interest rates and exchange rate, but not all. The more expansionary their domestic monetary policy is, the lower their own interest rates will be, and the more their exchange rates will depreciate. Such depreciation is advantageous to exports and to domestic economic activity and employment. In effect, foreign central banks could capture for their own economies even more of the expansion of demand in North America than they already have. In particular, this is a realistic opportunity for Great Britain, whose international competitive position is still less favourable than in the 1970s.

There are several reasons they do not exploit this opportunity. It would raise the local prices of imports invoiced in dollars, not just goods of American origin but other internationally traded goods, notably oil. Inflation statistics would be temporarily worsened. Moreover, central banks impose on themselves monetarist targets and are determined to stick by them. A special reason applies to Japan, the fear of increased trade friction with the United States.

What about fiscal policy in the major economies outside North America? Demand stimulus by tax reductions or government spending would not lower interest rates and further depreciate currencies against the dollar but would have the reverse effects. Those effects, indeed, would create room for additional monetary expansion at existing interest and exchange rates, if monetary targets were adjusted accommodatively. In fact, however, fiscal policies outside North America are severely restrictive, not stimulative. All major governments are trying to reduce their budget deficits by fiscal economies and tax increases.

The depression itself has, of course, automatically increased actual budget deficits, both by drastically reducing revenues and by requiring increased outlays for unemployment compensation and for relief of economic distress. Those features of modern fiscal systems, which raise deficits in cyclical recessions and lower them in recoveries and prosperities, are 'built-in stabilizers'. They sustain incomes and spending during downturns and restrict them in booms. Cyclical deficits are passive consequences of bad times. They buffer the decline in demand but do not actively stimulate demand.

Table 35.2: Fiscal policies and outcomes in major OECD economies

	(1) Increases in surplus (decreases in deficit), % of GNP or GDP, cumulative 1981–4			(2) Budget deficits relative to GNP/GDP, and to net private saving (%)	
	Actual	Cyclical	Non-cyclical	1983	1984
United States	−2.5	−0.9	−1.6	3.8, 67.8	3.7, 58.3
Japan	+2.0	−0.9	+2.9	3.4, 28.3	2.5, 22.2
West Germany	+1.0	−3.7	+4.7	3.1, 37.3	2.1, 26.1
France	−4.1	−3.8	−0.3	3.4, 47.0	3.8, 52.9
United Kingdom	+1.2	−3.4	+4.6	2.7, 54.8	2.3, 46.1
Seven summit countries	−1.4	−2.0	+0.6	4.1, 56.1	3.8, 48.4

Notes: OECD calculations and estimates for 1983 and 1984. Figures cover both subordinate and central governments.
(1) The figures shown are sums of four annual figures. This approximation is not strictly accurate but is indicative. Non-cyclical changes are discretionary actions on taxes and outlays. Cyclical changes are passive responses to economic fluctuations, given the tax legislation and the budget programme. Actual changes are the sum of the two.
Source: *Economic Outlook*, OECD, December 1983, Tables 9, 10 and 13.

Measures to overcome cyclical deficits are actively contractionary, intensifying recession or retarding recovery. This lesson was supposedly learned long ago, for example in the early 1930s from the counter-productive efforts of Presidents Herbert Hoover and Franklin D. Roosevelt to balance the US federal budget and from the disastrous consequences of Chancellor Brüning's sacrifice of German unemployed to fiscal orthodoxy. The fiscal policies of major European governments and Japan in the 1980s are similarly perverse, if less extreme.

Table 35.2 summarizes the effects on budget deficits of recent fiscal actions in the seven summit economies and the OECD as a whole, and compares them with the passive cyclical components of recent deficits. The Table shows remarkable 'success' in wiping out the built-in stabilizers. Another way to interpret these policies is to consider their effects on the 'structural' or 'high-employment' budget deficits, that is, those that would hypothetically occur if economic activity were on its normal growth trend. Those deficits are being significantly reduced, in some countries transformed into surpluses. The Thatcher government, for a notable example, has moved the budget into substantial structural surplus, a remarkable 'achievement' during a long and severe economic decline. Evidently the general objective is to raise the unemployment rate and lower the GDP level at which permanently acceptable budget outcomes will be achieved. In other words, these governments have lowered their sights and are adapting their budgets to macroeconomic performance chronically weaker than in the past.

Almost all of these countries have higher national propensities to save than the United States. Even in prosperous times, when private investment demands are strong, they have less reason to worry about the 'crowding out' consequences of government deficits. In these slack times, their saving is ample to finance both public and private borrowers, and indeed to acquire dollar claims as well. Table 35.2 also shows deficits in various economies relative to national saving.

The tightening of fiscal policies in the locomotive economies of Europe and Japan has serious international ramifications. Fiscal stimulus would not only increase domestic demands and employment but raise imports, spilling badly needed demand into the rest of the world—the smaller countries of Europe and Asia, the Third World in general, and North America. By putting their fiscal engines into perverse gear, Europe and Japan are setting back recovery throughout the world.

Appropriately stimulative policies need not, by the way, commit any country to high budget deficits in times of prosperity because tax cuts or job-creating expenditures could be designed to terminate at a scheduled date or contingent on economic circumstances. They need not favour consumption, public or private; they could take the form of tax incentives for investment or of public investment projects. They need not commit governments to larger public sectors than they desire in the long run. Whatever the national priorities of the country and its social philosophy with respect to the roles of public and private economic activity, they can be reconciled with fiscal policies appropriate to macroeconomic circumstances.

The contrast in macroeconomic policies between the United States and the other locomotives of the world economy is striking. The United States is pursuing a tight high-interest monetary policy, albeit one that was sufficiently relaxed a year and a half ago to avert economic and financial collapse and start recovery. American fiscal policy is easy and becoming looser every fiscal year. The combination has produced a vigorous recovery at home and arrested economic decline throughout the world. But the extreme policy mix portends serious problems for the United States in the future, and the contagious high interest rates retard recovery elsewhere. Other countries have a right to complain, though they should address their complaints to American monetary authorities as well as the fiscal policy makers in the White House and the Congress. With unchanged monetary policy, tightening of the US budget would worsen, not relieve, the economic predicaments of other nations. Europe and Japan, in contrast, are pursuing tight monetary and tight fiscal policies both. Their monetary policies are tight because of US interest rates and their own monetarist principles. Their fiscal policies are, for the most part, difficult to understand and justify.

Both West Germany and Japan have traditionally enjoyed and depended on export-driven growth of demand and have eschewed demand management for either domestic or international objectives. Both governments have plenty of room for expansionary fiscal policy and have high-saving citizens to whom to sell bonds. The continued series of budget austerities of these governments seem quite misguided. Both countries have domestic needs, individual and collective, to which their unused potential product could be devoted. Both could expand their assistance to the less developed countries. It is high time for these reluctant locomotives to pull their shares of the weight of the world economic train.

Macroeconomic expansion is the key to progress against unemployment. It will not solve all the problems, to be sure. In the US, the pathology of urban neighbourhoods that condemns nearly half of black youth to unemployment cannot be cured by monetary and fiscal policy. The same is true of growing youth unemployment in Europe. Macro policies and general prosperity will not restore the old high-wage jobs in smokestack industries in the American Midwest or the Ruhr. There is plenty of room and need for intelligent public policies to treat these difficult cases. But they will be hopeless unless general prosperity and growth are restored. That is the first and highest priority.

V.   INTERNATIONAL COORDINATION OF MACROECONOMIC POLICIES: THE CHALLENGE TO THE LEADERS OF THE SUMMIT ECONOMIES

From an international standpoint, policy corrections are needed both in the United States and in the other locomotives of the world economy. These require international cooperation. Monetary stimulus by any single country acting alone expands home demand and at the same time depreciates its currency to the benefit of its exports and to the detriment of its trading partners. Internationally concerted monetary stimuli that lower interest rates simultaneously everywhere can give the whole world economy a boost, expanding everybody's exports and imports and creating no trade imbalances. The United States is in the position to take the lead. Since our interest and exchange rates are too high, other countries could lower interest rates by smaller amounts, narrowing the differential and engineering an orderly decline in the exchange value of the dollar. Continuing on the present course may at any time provoke a disorderly decline of the dollar.

In fiscal policy, the United States would be shifting to a tighter budget while other countries would substitute for their fiscal restrictions expansionary measures appropriate to the economic situations in their own economies and in the world at large. These monetary and fiscal actions should be the major agenda of the next economic summit conference; no topics deserve higher priority.

Can the major economic powers effectively coordinate their macro-economic policies? On the record, the prospects are not good. It is true that central banks agreed, after the second oil shock, on single-minded disinflationary policy. The heads of the seven economic summit governments affirmed the priority at their Venice and Ottawa meetings in 1980 and 1981 respectively. Since that was the disposition of each country individually, agreement and synchronization were not difficult to achieve. At Williamsburg in 1983 unemployment and stagnation were clearly the pressing macroeconomic problems of the day. The best the group could do was to commit their governments to attack their structural budget deficits. President Reagan, the target of this vote, did not take it seriously. Unfortunately, his peers did.

The nine annual economic summits[14] have usually concentrated on energy, trade, and commerce with the Soviet bloc. At the Bonn summit of 1978, however, the United States succeeded—in return for pledging decontrol of its domestic oil prices, a long overdue reform—in persuading reluctant allies to fire up their locomotives. Several governments promised increased growth of output. West Germany and France agreed to specific amounts of extra fiscal stimulus, 1 per cent and 0.5 per cent respectively. Japan and the United Kingdom had already instituted expansionary budget measures—Japan in response to American diplomatic pressure prior to the summit. The United States, whose recovery had been running ahead of the others, promised modest fiscal contractions. Six months later the Shah of Iran was overthrown. The world was hit by the second oil shock, a new spurt of inflation and international financial disarray. The locomotive theory of the Carter Administration was discredited, along with demand management in general. That legacy stands in the way of any internationally coordinated recovery programme, even though the locomotive theory seems quite correct in today's circumstances.

Perhaps our leaders could be inspired by an earlier example. As the decade of the 1960s began, the world economy had been beset by a slump, by an unpleasant history of inflation, and by international monetary disturbances. The United States had suffered two recessions in quick succession, designed to bring down an unacceptably high inflation rate and to protect the dollar. As recovery from the slump began, the Ministerial Council of the OECD announced that the member nations (which did not yet include Japan) had pledged themselves to aim for a 50 per cent growth of output by the end of the decade for the group as a whole. The Council noted that this growth would not only increase the welfare and strength of the member countries but would lead to an increased flow of resources to developing countries.[15] Though this declaration was a statement of hope and intent, it was taken seriously by member governments both individually and in their consultations with each other on specific macroeconomic issues. In the event, the growth target was fulfilled with room to spare.

The present situation is more serious and more difficult. It will take statesmanship and imaginative leadership to turn the 1980s from a decade of unemployment and stagnation to one of prosperity and progress, from a period of discord in the alliance over competition and trade to one of cooperation and mutual benefit. Alliances are strengthened not just by resolving conflicts of interest but by undertaking together enterprises that offer substantial benefits to all. Macroeconomic policy coordination is a good place to begin.

I am greatly indebted to Gabriel de Kock for his capable research assistance and instruction, but the opinions and errors are my own responsibility. I have benefited greatly from the expertise of Sylvia Ostry, both from personal conversation and from her article, 'The world economy: marking time'. Foreign Affairs. America and the World, 1983.

NOTES

1. For the tale well-told *see* Charles P. Kindleberger, *The World in Depression*, Berkeley: University of California Press, 1973, especially Chapters 6 to 8 and 11. It should be required reading for the economic statespersons of the 1980s.
2. For analysis and projection of Third World debt problems, *see* William R. Cline, *International Debt and the Stability of the World Economy*, Washington, DC: Institute for International Economics, 1983. Cline shows how solvency depends on export volume and terms of trade highly sensitive to OECD economies' real growth, and on restoring a positive margin between debtor countries' export growth rates and the interest rates at which they borrow.
3. Herbert Giersch, 'Aspects of growth, structural change, and employment—a Schumpeterian perspective', and Michael Bruno and Jeffrey Sachs, 'Supply versus demand approaches to the problem of stagflation', in *Macroeconomic Policies for Growth and Stability: A European Perspective*, ed. Giersch, Symposium 1979, Tübingen: Mohr, for the Institut für Weltwirtschaft an der Universität Kiel, 1981.
4. Jeffrey D. Sachs, 'Real wages and unemployment in the OECD countries', *Brookings Papers on Economic Activity*, No. 1, Washington, DC: Brookings Institution, 1983; Sheila Bonnell, 'Real wages and employment in the Great Depression', *Economic Record*, September 1981, pp. 277–81.
5. J. M. Keynes, *The General Theory of Employment, Interest, and Money*. New York: Harcourt, Brace & Co., 1936.

6. J. T. Dunlop, 'The movement of real and money wages', *Economic Journal*, No. 48, September, 1938.

7. The OECD *Economic Outlook* series and *Economic Surveys* of particular countries are indispensable sources. The Bruno–Sachs paper cited in Note 3 and the Sachs paper cited in Note 4 are very important in advancing the argument that supply limits and the 'wage-gap' were the important constraints on output in OECD economies outside North America after OPEC 1. However, in the second paper Sachs concludes that a large component of European unemployment in 1981 was Keynesian, and presumably an even larger proportion of 1983–84 unemployment is attributable to deficient demand. In a study for the Center for Economic Policy Studies of the European Community, R. Dornbusch, G. Basevi, O. Blanchard, W. Buiter, and R. Layard, 'Macroeconomic prospects and policies for the European Community', Brussels, April 1983, argue the case for a coordinated expansion. *See* Wolfgang Franz, 'German unemployment and stabilization policy', *European Economic Review*, No. 21, 1983, for a careful econometric analysis leading to the conclusion that the German natural rate of unemployment is now around 4 per cent or 4.7 per cent, according to an amendment by R. J. Gordon in the same issue.

8. R. J. Flanagan, D. W. Soskice, and Lloyd Ulman, *Unionism, Economic Stabilization and Income Policies: European Experience*, Washington, DC: Brookings Institution, 1983, Chapter 5.

9. Cited and quoted in translation by Dornbusch *et al., op. cit.* in Note 7. Giersch's article is 'Kaufkraft and Lohne', from Deutsche Bundesbank, *Auszüge aus Presseartikeln*, 6 November 1982.

10. Koichi Hamada and Yoshio Kurosaka, 'The relationship between production and unemployment in Japan: Okun's Law in comparative perspective', paper presented at International Seminar on Macroeconomics, Paris, Maison des Sciences de l'Homme, June 1983.

11. The theory is associated in the economics profession with the 'new classical macroeconomics' and the 'rational expectations' revolution. Independently the late William Fellner set forth the 'credible threat' policy in several papers and in his book *Towards a Reconstruction of Macroeconomics*, Washington, DC: American Enterprise Institute, 1976. For exposition and criticism of these ideas *see* the papers of McCallum, Fellner, Tobin, and Okun in *Journal of Money, Credit and Banking*, November 1980, part 2. For tests of the theory against the recent disinflationary recession, *see* papers by George Perry and by Fellner and Philip Cagan in *Brookings Papers on Economic Activity*, No. 2, Washington, DC: Brookings Institution, 1983.

12. The ambiguity arises from an unusual discrepancy between the gains in employment reported in the household survey by workers and those reported in the establishment survey by employers. The former is the higher number; possibly the reduction of unemployment, remarkably large considering the growth of output, is an overstatement.

13. Otto Eckstein, 'Disinflation', *Data Resources Economic Studies Series*, No. 114, October 1983.

14. For a useful review of economic summitry, *see* George de Menil and Anthony M. Solomon, *Economic Summitry*, New York: Council on Foreign Relations, Inc., pp. 30–4 and 78–9.

15. Reported in *Economic Report of the President*, 1962, Washington, DC: US Government Printing Office, 1962, p. 38.

36 Okun on Macroeconomic Policy*

On the last page of Arthur Okun's posthumously published book *Prices and Quantities* he says:

I expect the era of chronic inflation to end in the eighties. I am not particularly optimistic, however, that the era will be terminated by a coordinated program that combines a deceleration of nominal income growth with the cost reducing elements and the incentives to wage and price restraint that the analysis of this book has highlighted. Viewing the world objectively, I believe it is more probable that the era of chronic inflation will end with a deep and prolonged recession or with a protracted period of rigid mandatory price and wage controls. I am not resigned to that conclusion, and I hope economists will work hard to prevent it.[1]

The United States, like the United Kingdom, has embarked on the course of disinflation via gradual destruction of monetary demand. Like Okun, I would expect the process to be lengthy and costly, characterized by deep recessions, stunted recoveries, and high and rising unemployment. The external environment is likely to be more benign in the 1980s than in the previous decade, when our economies suffered external shocks of severity unprecedented in peacetime. Therefore the orthodox cure, monetary starvation, will probably triumph in the end, at least if the political and social fabric holds together.

I think the experience, under Paul Volcker as well as Margaret Thatcher, will also vindicate Okun's scepticism, and my own, of claims that threatening advertising can make the process quick and painless. Our profession is in no small measure responsible for the confidently held view that public announcement of resolute irreversible monetary disinflation will so alter expectations in the private sector that our

*September 1981, Columbia–Yale–Brookings Symposium in Memory of Arthur M. Okun, New York City. In J. Tobin, ed., *Macroeconomics: Prices and Quantities: Essays in Memory of Arthur M. Okun*, Washington: Brookings Institution, 1983, pp. 297–300.

415

inherited wage and price inflation will melt like snow in spring sunshine. This proposition is not based on empirical evidence, of which there is precious little, but on the a priori view that only misinformation prevents labour and product markets from arriving at market-clearing wages and prices. If in the past monetary disinflation has had a disappointingly small impact on prices and a large impact on output, the reason given is the expectation, based on experience over the postwar decade, of countercyclical reversals of monetary and fiscal policy. These make it unnecessary for workers and firms to disinflate in order to protect and restore their jobs and sales. Although Okun agreed that public perception of abandonment of compensatory policy would work in the direction claimed, he was sceptical of the quantitative magnitude of the shift.

He had several reasons. First, he doubted that a democratic government could make very credible a stance of indifference to the real state of the economy—unemployment, production, bankruptcy, and other symptoms of distress. In confirmation we may note that, unlike Mrs Thatcher, President Reagan has not risked his prestige on the strategy of credible threat. He has promised disinflation without tears, along with simultaneous reduction of unemployment, rapid and full recovery, accelerated growth, and balance in the budget, to boot. Chairman Volcker is firm and clear enough, but his message may not penetrate to the level where wage and price decisions are actually made. Okun himself regarded a Volcker–Thatcher policy as indefensible:

I would be morally outraged by a local ordinance designed to promote fire prevention by prohibiting the fire department from responding to any alarms in a month. This is a strong analogy to attempting to prevent inflation by committing the government not to deal with a recession no matter how deep it becomes. A democratic society must have better cooperative ways to instil such socially desirable efforts than by threat and fear.[2]

Second, Okun's whole book explains why and how there are business reasons for price and wage stickiness, for absorbing variation in demand in quantities rather than in prices and wages, at least in the first instance. The phenomenon is not solely due to misinformation and to errors of forecast perpetuated in contracts. There is some tangency between Okun's approach and that of Lucas and company. Rules of behaviour adopted for local microeconomic reasons affect the response of a decentralized economy to macroeconomic events and policies, and will indeed be modified when the macroeconomic environment appreciably changes. The difference is that Okun was considering monopolistic rather than pure competition. (It is, by the way, both puzzling and unfortunate that Keynes, in spite of the

Chamberlin–Robinson revolution that was occurring in microeconomics at the same time he was making his macro revolution, chose to challenge orthodoxy on its own microeconomic ground of competitive markets.) In 'customer markets' with administered or negotiated prices, the micro rules of behaviour leave room for quantities to adjust to demand, anticipated and unanticipated, and thus leave room for macro policies that control monetary demand.

From his unparalleled command of the facts of real world business fluctuations, Okun was able to muster a list of observations that contradict the implications of so-called equilibrium business cycle theory. See his marvellously cogent paper in the American Enterprise Institute Symposium on Rational Expectations, the last one of his published.[3] Nowadays theorists are busy trying to amend and elaborate rational expectations models to reconcile them with Okun's facts. I suspect that this process will result in a synthesis in which rational behaviour and rational expectations are divorced from competitive markets simply and continuously cleared by price. When this synthesis matures into a new mainstream theory, I suspect it will be capable of explaining Okun's observations and will also allow room for compensatory stabilization policies.

Third, Okun saw the conquest and control of inflation as a problem of externality. What we need today, for example, is mutually assured disinflation. Resistance to departures from the existing inflationary pattern is due to the fear of each group, workers and firms, that others will not disinflate simultaneously or subsequently. If these fears are correct, the group will lose real and relative terms of trade for very little gain in demand. But if everyone disinflates, no one will lose in terms of trade, and everyone will gain the benefits of low inflation or price stability. Those benefits, I must say, Okun rated more highly than I do. But it is sufficient now to say that inflation has serious social costs because society, for reasons some of which are valid and some invalid, regards it as a prime social malady, and its continuation cripples society in dealing with other serious economic problems.

Coordinated and mutually assured disinflation is difficult to arrange in an economy with decentralized and staggered wage setting. The tax-based incomes policies that Okun, I, and many others have advocated have their own costs and distortions, but their justification is the public good of achieving disinflation without severe cost in employment and production. At the same time, a supportive consensus of labour and management must be engineered by presidential leadership, fostered more by the promise of real economic gains than by the threat of disaster. The incomes policies must be in place during a transition long enough to unwind the previous history of contracts, patterns, and expectations. Monetary and fiscal policy must not, of course, overheat the economy during the transition and, indeed, should err on the cautious side. But Okun would certainly not approve a game plan that I fear will be the likely sequel to any successful monetary campaign against inflation, namely, that the economy will be run permanently at the high transitional unemployment rates in order to avoid all risk of the resurgence of inflation.

I have devoted this comment to recalling what Arthur Okun thought and said about the issues of science and policy discussed in this book. I have done so not only because the book is the result of a conference held in his memory and honour, but also because I think he was wise and right.

NOTES

1. Arthur M. Okun, *Prices and Quantities: A Macroeconomic Analysis*, Brookings Institution, 1981, p. 359.
2. *ibid*. p. 358.
3. 'Rational expectations with misperceptions as a theory of the business cycle', *Journal of Money, Credit and Banking*, vol. 12, November 1980, pt. 2, pp. 817–25.

PART VI
Political Economy

INTRODUCTION

This final Part contains seven essays on various aspects of political economy. The first two mostly continue the major emphasis of the book on macroeconomic strategies. Chapter 37 is about the Kennedy–Johnson years, on which I, having played some role at the beginning, am not a disinterested witness. The next chapter is a broader review of United States stabilization policies for the thirty years from the end of World War II.

Chapters 39 and 40 are excursions into energy, which preoccupied the nation in the late 1970s. Events have, I think, justified my 1974 view that the oil crisis would not lead to the drastic changes in American life that many people foresaw at the time. The second energy chapter explains the impact of energy scarcities and prices on macroeconomic events and policies.

Throughout my career I have believed that a democratic state must moderate the inevitable inequalities of market capitalism, and since the 1960s I have advocated improvements in our systems of income assistance to our poorer fellow citizens. In this volume these interests emerge in the final three chapters. The conservative counter-revolution of the 1980s has taken policy in the opposite direction. But the Catholic bishops' pastoral letter is helping to awaken renewed interest in economic equity; public opinion polls now show majorities in opposition to cuts in federal welfare spending and other social programmes. Although the bishops underestimated the difficulties in meeting some of their objectives, I thought their timely reminder that economic policies should serve ethical values deserved reinforcement.

37   The Political Economy of the 1960s*

I shall concentrate on the general macroeconomic design and strategy of the Kennedy and Johnson Administrations, especially during the period 1961–5 before the Vietnam War and its financing dominated the scene. The macroeconomic strategy of those years was, I think, the indispensable foundation for the important advances in domestic social policy of the two Presidents. As those innovations are the main subject of this book, I shall allude to them only in the briefest and broadest terms. At the outset I should also confess the obvious. I come to this subject with the bias of an economist who served on President Kennedy's Council of Economic Advisers in 1961–2 and was associated with the Council for some years thereafter.

KENNEDY–JOHNSON MACROECONOMIC STRATEGY

Over the five years from 1961 to 1965 the Kennedy and Johnson Administrations developed, preached, and practised a remarkable coherent macroeconomic strategy. The theme was steady economic growth at full employment, avoiding cycles of recession and inflation. The Administrations regarded growth in national production and income not only as an end in itself but as the fount of economic and fiscal resources for meeting national needs. With new resources unendingly provided by growth, public services could be expanded and upgraded, social insurance and income assistance extended, a war on poverty launched—all without divisive conflicts over taxes, the size of the public sector, defence spending, and the distribution of income and wealth. Stable, rapid, non-cyclical, non-inflationary growth was

*September 1976, Conference on the Social Policies of the Kennedy and Johnson Administrations, Lyndon B. Johnson School of Public Affairs, University of Texas, Austin. In David C. Warner, ed., *Toward New Human Rights: The Social Policies of the Kennedy and Johnson Administrations*, Austin: University of Texas, 1977, pp. 33–50. Reprinted with permission.

to be the underpinning of the Great Society.

I must now make an academic but important distinction, one which the Council taught from the outset in 1961, not always successfully. The distinction is between the growth in the economy's capacity to produce goods and services and the short-term growth in actual output and real income. The growth of capacity is limited by the growth in the labour force and its productivity, determined by trends in the size of the population, its availability for work, its skills and education, and in the rate of technological advance, capital accumulation, and the supply of land and other natural resources. The trend growth rate of potential output changes very slowly; in the United States since World War II it has been between $3\frac{1}{2}$ and $4\frac{1}{4}$ per cent per year, of which $1\frac{1}{4}$ to $1\frac{1}{2}$ points are attributable to the growth of labour input and the remainder to the various factors raising the productivity of labour. On the other hand, the short-term—quarter-to-quarter or year-to-year—growth of actual output has varied drastically, from rates as high as 10 per cent per year to negative figures. Accompanying these variations are extreme changes in the rate of utilization of the labour force, reflected in fluctuations of unemployment rates, and of industrial plant. These oscillations are due to instability in the growth of aggregate demand for goods and services; while potential supply grows quite smoothly, actual demand advances unevenly and sometimes indeed falls.

In the short run, if there is a lot of slack in the economy in the form of unemployed labour and underutilized plant and equipment, production can respond to rapidly expanding demand and grow more rapidly than its long-run trend. This is what happens in a recovery from recession; indeed there cannot be a true recovery unless output does grow faster than capacity, for otherwise unemployment and extreme capacity will not be reduced. But rates of growth greater than the growth of capacity cannot be sustained; once the recovery is complete and the economy is again operating at potential, output will be limited to the capacity growth rate, 4 per cent more or less in this country.

The distinction is essential to understanding the macroeconomic design of the Kennedy–Johnson Administrations. There were basically three objectives. (1) Taking office at the trough of the fourth postwar recession, with unemployment at 7 per cent, the Kennedy Council naturally saw rapid and full recovery, with high short-run growth of actual output, as its prime goal. (2) Once that was achieved, moreover, the Council aimed to keep the economy operating at its potential, with demand expanding fairly steadily at the sustainable rate of growth of supply. (3) But the Council and the Administration also hoped to accelerate the growth of capacity, not of population and labour force, of course—that would be determined by demographic and social trends and individual tastes—but of productivity, output per hour of work.

The government's handle for the first objective, recovery, is much more obvious than its ability to achieve the other two. And the second goal is probably easier for government to realize than the third. That is because the first two tasks involve the manipulation of demand, for which the Federal Government has some powerful direct and indirect tools. Influencing supply—technology, efficiency, human and physical capital—was and is a much more uncertain enterprise.

The recovery strategy of 1961–5 was quite successful, and it was popularly perceived as even more successful than it really was. Five years of uninterrupted advance brought the unemployment rate down to 3.9 per cent in January 1966, achieving the Kennedy Administration's explicit 'interim goal' of 4 per cent. Real GNP, that is, production measured in constant prices, grew more than 5 per cent per year over the same period, and employment by 2.5 per cent per year. The percentage of the population living in poverty, as it came to be officially measured, declined from 22.4 per cent in 1960 to 14.7 per cent in 1966. Corporate profits after taxes rose by 80 per cent. Other economic indicators performed just as spectacularly. Meanwhile the inflation rate remained below 2 per cent per year.

For the reasons already explained, growth at the 1961–5 pace could not continue, as the Kennedy–Johnson economists knew and said. Of the total GNP advance, about 27 per cent was cyclical recovery, associated with the three-point reduction of the unemployment rate. The remainder was growth in the economy's capacity to produce, which could be expected to continue. The aim of macroeconomic policy was to slow demand in 1966 to the sustainable rate of capacity growth, to keep unemployment close to 4 per cent, to avoid both recession and inflationary overheating of the economy. Meanwhile manpower and labour market policies were to pave the way for gradual reduction of unemployment below the interim 4 per cent target, and policies fostering the formation of physical and human capital and the advance of technology were slowly to raise the sustainable growth rate.

We will never know whether this was a feasible scenario. The sudden escalation of Vietnam War spending in 1965–6, without compensating tax increases or spending cuts, destroyed the prospects of stable growth not only for the remaining years of the Johnson Administration but for the 1970s as well. Although economists inside and outside recognized in January 1966, that deficit financing of Vietnam spending was a serious error, no one foresaw how dreadful and durable the consequences would be. The new fiscal stimulus pushed unemployment down as far as 3 per cent, with predictably desirable effects on the employment and income of the disadvantaged and poor. But it also generated waves of wage and price inflation of unexpected virulence and persistence. In any case macro policies in 1966–9, in contrast to 1961–5, were a scramble to restore stability—a well-managed scramble, but a scramble.

RECOVERY POLICY AND ITS OBSTACLES 1961–5

I have attributed to the Kennedy and Johnson Administrations a coherent macroeconomic strategy, but this was not in place on inauguration day in 1961. The Heller Council of Economic Advisers and its allies in the Bureau of the Budget had a clear conception of the task ahead, but this was far from fully accepted in the White House, Treasury, or Labor Department, much less in the Federal Reserve, the Congress, or influential public opinion. It took sixteen to twenty-four months for the Council's diagnosis and prescriptions, modified in internal and external debate, to become dominant Administration policy. Not until 1964 did the centrepiece of New Economics fiscal policy, the $12 billion tax cut, take effect.

As a result, the 1961–5 recovery was, for worse or better, slower— and at times more fragile and uncertain—than its economist architects desired. I point this out today because the 1961–5 episode is widely cited as a model for the current recovery, in particular to support the view that slower is better and longer. The fact is that there were some anxious days in 1962–3, when luck, together with whatever fiscal stimulus could be smuggled into conservative budgets and whatever monetary support a gold-conscious central bank could be induced to provide, kept recovery from petering out.

The Council's prime objective was to restore full employment, defined for the time being as 4 per cent unemployment. According to Council estimates, which proved correct in the event and are known to all economics students as Okun's Law, the requisite three-point reduction of unemployment would yield a 10 per cent increase in GNP, on top of the normal annual increment from growth of labour force and productivity. In the Council's view the country had the labour power, skills, technology, and plant to produce the extra 10 per cent, and failure to utilize these resources was an inexcusable massive waste.

The Council was, of course, concerned by the human predicaments of people who could not find jobs. But unemployment was also seen as a general barometer of the country's economic health. Business profits, state and local finances, farm incomes, real wages, stock market value—all would look much rosier if prosperity were restored and maintained. Because of the 1957–8 recession, the aborted recovery of 1959–60, and the recession of 1960–1, the economy had not achieved 4 per cent unemployment since 1957 and was in danger of prolonged stagnation.

To the Kennedy economists the means were as obvious as the end. Federal fiscal policy and Federal Reserve monetary policy should stimulate aggregate spending, public and private, by some combination of new government expenditure, tax reduction, and easing of credit and interest rates.

Fiscal expansion meant, in the short run at least, larger budget deficits. But these were innocuous and appropriate in an under-employed economy, even one commencing a cyclical upswing. Indeed one of the reasons for the post–1957 stagnation, in particular the 1960 recession, was 'fiscal drag'—the natural growth of the economy was raising the potential Federal tax take at full employment faster than Federal expenditures were increasing. Yet the potential revenues were not realized because the taxes detracted from private spending and depressed the economy. The Council pointed out, with emphasis if not originality, that the budget should be judged not by the actual deficits yielded in recessions but by the deficit or surplus it would produce at full employment.

Although the New Economics remains identified in the public mind with the active use of fiscal policy for stabilization, the Council also strongly advocated the use of monetary measures. The Federal Reserve was urged to lower interest rates, especially long-term bond yields, and to abandon its self-imposed rule of intervening only in the market for Treasury bills. The Treasury was urged, unsuccessfully, to adopt debt management tactics that would lower long-term rates. The Council was not monetarist, but it was not 'fiscalist' either, if that term has the symmetrical meaning that the other tool is viewed as useless. The Council recognized the efficacy and importance of both kinds of macroeconomic policy, not only for promoting recovery but for restraining aggregate demand if the economic situation were reversed.

Regarding the mixture of public spending, tax reduction, and easy monetary policy as recovery instruments, there was some disagreement in the Administration. J. K. Galbraith's prime concern was to nourish the public sector; the only expansionary measures he favoured were those that increased government spending. He opposed the tax cut of 1964, and he had little faith in monetary policy. Some of us took quite seriously the expressed objective of raising the long-run growth rate of the economy's capacity to produce. We stressed the importance of public and private investments in human skills, technology, and physical capital. Encouragement of capital formation, as a contribution both to recovery and to long-term growth, was a major motivation for the Investment Tax Credit enacted in 1962. For the same reasons, we stressed the importance of monetary policies which would stimulate investment with low interest rates. We hoped to have a Federal budget surplus, augmenting the saving available for capital information, once full employment was restored. Walter Heller was, I think, somewhat sceptical of the economic, as well as the political, feasibility of a policy mixture strongly oriented to investment. He thought the surest road to recovery was direct stimulus by public spending or private consumption induced by tax cuts.

These differences of emphasis were largely resolved by practical constraints on the policy mix. No Galbraithian burst of Federal civilian spending was in the political cards. To be sure, the Kennedy Administration made use of opportunities to increase some Federal spending. Social Security benefits were increased ahead of schedule and ahead of the matching payroll taxes; at the time this could be done without cosmetic damage to the administrative budget. No one wanted to use defence spending as a demand stimulus. But when the Berlin crisis of 1961 evoked a modest increase of military outlay, the Council successfully blocked the instinctive urge of many high Administration officials to raise taxes to match. Monetary policy was also constrained. Because of anxieties about the US balance of international payments, the Federal Reserve could not or would not pursue an aggressively easy monetary policy. For major expansionary stimulus, tax reduction for private consumers and business investors was the only avenue open.

INFLATION AND THE WAGE/PRICE GUIDEPOSTS

The major serious justification of the restrictive monetary and fiscal policies that led to the two recessions of 1957–8 and 1960–1 was the need to cool off the 4 per cent inflation rate reached in the mid 1950s. Inflation had subsided to a negligible 1.5 per cent per year. The Kennedy Council did not regard revival of inflation as likely early in the recovery. But it did not want to take any risks, and the mid 50s were a warning of what might happen as unemployment was reduced again to 4 per cent. To be quite candid, the Council feared rises in price index less for their own sake than for the damage they would do to the credibility and acceptability of a full recovery and full employment policy within the Administration, the Federal Reserve, the Congress, and in general public opinion. To the customary objections to inflation would be added the deterioration of the US competitive position in world markets and of the US balances of trade and payments.

Like most economists, the Council members were well aware that full employment in an advanced democratic capitalist economy was likely to give wages and prices an inflationary tilt. By themselves, monetary and fiscal policies to regulate aggregate demand cannot be sure to achieve both full employment and price stability. This is definitely not a recent revelation.

The Council's answer was the 'guideposts for non-inflationary price and wage behaviour' set forth in the 1962 Economic Report. The guideposts were standards for management and labour. Perhaps more important, they were standards for government officials in their inevitable interventions in labour disputes. We did not want industrial peace at any price level. The guideposts had no legal force. But the President, the Council, the Secretary of Labor, and cabinet officers deployed their persuasive powers to keep announced prices and wage bargains of national importance in approximate compliance.

This policy began as early as 1961, when the President—largely on the initiative of the late Kermit Gordon, a member of the Council at the time—began urging restraint on the steel industry and its union. These contacts culminated in the moderate steel wage contract of 1962 negotiated with the active participation of Secretary Goldberg. President Kennedy's confrontation with the industry, when major steel companies announced price increases before the ink was dry on the union contract, is an oft-told tale.

Through 1965 the recovery was virtually free of inflation. Whether the policy of guideposts supported by moral suasion deserves any credit remains debatable. Perhaps the slack in the economy sufficed to restrain wages and prices. In comparison with subsequent periods, however, the stability of the early 1960s now appears exceptional. History has vindicated the Council's view that some kind of incomes policy is an essential complement to fiscal and monetary management of demand. Without it—pessimists will say with it too—full employment and inflation control are all too likely to be incompatible. The experience also suggests that incomes policies should be in place when there is still slack in the economy, not imposed when the pot is already boiling.

A weakness of the guideposts is that they were not developed with the participation of business and labour leaders; they were indeed opposed by most of them. This was not because the Administration did not try. It was intended that the President's Labor–Management Advisory Committee, with business, labour, and general public members, would seriously confront the problem. But the climate was not favourable; the Committee preferred to debate general issues of economic policy among themselves and with Federal officials. After the disheartening experiences of the last decade, I suspect the climate today is much more favourable for joint formulation and support of guideposts.

The outbreak of excess-demand inflation in 1966 put impossible strains on the 'open mouth' operations of the Johnson Administration. Under such pressures even full-fledged controls would have given way.

FISCAL CONSERVATISM AND THE NEW ECONOMICS

The principal obstacles to the macroeconomic design of the Kennedy economists were conservative fiscal and financial tenets prevalent in the Administration itself, the Congress, and influential public opinion. At the beginning of a new Democratic Administration, after an uncomfortably close election, with an unreliable majority in Congress, highly suspect in the business and financial community, JFK was not ready to do battle for New Economics. Planned deficit spending was taboo, especially after the recession had 'bottomed out'. Budget deficits initially were okay only if they could be blamed on Eisenhower. Even when minds were later liberated, Ike's $12 billion deficit in fiscal 1958 became an upper limit.

The 4 per cent unemployment target was widely challenged, from the Right and from the Left. Federal Reserve Chairman Martin attributed the growth of unemployment in the 1950s not to demand inadequacy but to structural maladjustments in labour markets. For different reasons this view also appealed to the top leadership of Kennedy's Labor Department. Prophets like Robert Theobald laid the increase of unemployment to automation and detected a trend toward technological obsolescence of human labour. These issues are discussed further below.

Conservatives contended that the count of the unemployed was swollen by undeserving cases, and even deliberately exaggerated by the government. JFK was moved to appoint a blue-ribbon committee to defend the purity and intertemporal comparability of the statistics.

Re-enforcing the grip of conservative fiscal opinion was the suspicion and hostility of the business and financial community toward a new Democratic Administration after eight years of Eisenhower. It was easy to read the confrontation with Big Steel as confirming their worst fears. The extent of mistrust was exemplified by the organized opposition of industry to the Investment Tax Credit proposed by the Administration, a bonanza now highly prized and resolutely defended. These political attitudes accentuated a general failure of confidence in the American business future, initially bred by the stagnation of the late 1950s and the nation's international economic difficulties. The mood of 1962 was very similar to that of 1975. But there was less reason for discouragement then, and pessimism was quickly transformed into euphoria in 1963–5.

THE DOLLAR, GOLD, AND THE BALANCE OF PAYMENTS

Potentially the external position of the dollar and defence of the country's dwindling gold stock were serious constraints on domestic economic policy. As it was, they constrained the mixture of demand management policies more than the overall thrust, and they compromised the traditional liberal position of the United States in international economic relations.

Convertibility of dollars held by foreign governments into gold at the established price was considered, in the Federal Reserve and the Treasury and in private financial circles, a sacred commitment and absolute priority. Its precedence over other policy objectives was never to be questioned, even behind closed doors, lest doubts arise at home and abroad regarding the Administration's determination to defend the parity, doubts which could trigger further speculation against the dollar. Like non-conservative governments in other countries—the first Administration of Harold Wilson is a notable and notorious example—the Kennedy–Johnson Administration felt particularly vulnerable to charges of softness and amateurism in international finance. To demonstrate soundness and firmness, such governments overreact. Just as, for similar political reasons, it eventually took a Republican President and Secretary of State to crack open the door to China, so it took Nixon and Connally to cut the tie between dollar and gold. When they did it in 1971, it was heralded as a famous victory.

In the early 1960s gold and the balance of payments constituted a powerful argument against all expansionary policy, but particularly against expansionary monetary policy. Our friends in Europe, notably in the influential Working Party Three of OECD, came to understand and to accept the value to the world as well as to the United States itself of a strong sustained American recovery. They thought it should be fuelled by fiscal policy, and their acceptance of deficits along the way defused some of the domestic opposition and official hesitation. However, they supported the Federal Reserve's view that US interest rates should rise, certainly not fall, in order to avoid outflows of funds in search of higher yields in Europe. This position stood in the way of the policy mixture preferred by some Kennedy economists, which featured easy monetary policy for a high-investment recovery oriented to long-run growth. The Investment Tax Credit, and the largely futile effort to twist the interest rate structure toward higher short-term rates, to keep funds at home, and lower long-term rates, to encourage domestic investment, were attempts at reconciliation.

Once fears of deficits and inflation were neutralized, the balance of payments was not a serious inhibition on economic expansion *per se*. The reason was a variety of *ad hoc* measures: direct controls to limit foreign-exchange demands by government and private citizens, and international arrangements to defend the dollar against speculation and to limit actual conversions into gold (except by de Gaulle) while maintaining formal convertibility.

Throughout the period the Council argued, mostly unsuccessfully, that the gold–dollar parity should not be allowed either to interfere with domestic recovery and growth or to erode the historic American commitment to unrestricted international trade and capital movement. With one hand, the Kennedy and Johnson Administrations were ostentatiously carrying forward the thirty-year-old policy of negotiating mutual reduction of tariffs and other trade barriers. These efforts encountered increasing domestic resistance, as more and more American industries and workers found themselves no longer competitive at the established exchange rates. Organized labour, especially resentful of the 'export of jobs' by overseas investments of American corporations, became increasingly protectionist. With the other hand, the Administrations were busy defending the exchange rate and American producers by informal quotas on textile imports and other products, by insisting that foreign aid be tied to purchases in the US, by discriminatory rules on military procurement, and other devices. Likewise the Treasury was compromising the position of the United States as an international centre of finance and capital by restrictions on foreign lending by American banks, flotations of foreign securities, and direct investments abroad by US companies.

The Council's argument was that the risk of dollar devaluation and exchange depreciation should be accepted, because the consequences would be anything but disastrous if these events ever came to pass. When they finally did, in 1971, the truth of the argument was demonstrated. Meanwhile, the Council thought, the US should use more of its diplomatic weight to negotiate improved international

monetary arrangements, augmenting international liquidity and assigning a proper share of adjustment responsibilities to the surplus countries
of Europe and Japan. In retrospect it really is a shame that our
government did not have the courage and foresight to float the dollar
in 1961, instead of ten years later.

POLICIES TO REDUCE UNEMPLOYMENT AND POVERTY

The Kennedy–Johnson Council economists were from the beginning
confident that the American economy, adequately stimulated by
policies to expand aggregate demand, could create enough jobs to
restore 4 per cent unemployment. Jobs were required not only for the
two million workers representing the excess of unemployment over
the target but also for the growth of the labour force from demographic
trends and from the increased availability of jobs. In fact the economy
generated nine million new jobs in the five years 1961–5.

Critics inside and outside the Administration thought that the
Council overstressed its macroeconomic remedies for unemployment
and underplayed microeconomic cures. The Council's main concern
was to refute the influential views in vogue at the time, that the
economy had undergone a change of life rendering macroeconomic
stimuli ineffective against unemployment. I recall an Undersecretary
of Labor, later Secretary, who argued that there was no *general*
unemployment problem, but as many specific problems as there were
unemployed individuals. Of course no specific programmes oriented
to particular jobs and individual workers could ever have generated
nine million new jobs in five years.

Actually the Council always recognized that there were limits to
macro policies, that 4 per cent unemployment overall implied excessive
rates for some demographic groups and geographical regions, and that
general prosperity left all too many people either out of the labour
force—not even counted as unemployed but discouraged or unemploy-
able because of discrimination, disability, location, lack of skill or of
education—or for similar reasons employed sporadically at substandard
jobs and wages. The Council always supported the Administration's
microeconomic employment policies: development assistance to
depressed areas like Appalachia, equal employment opportunity,
improvement of labour exchanges to match jobs and workers more
quickly and efficiently, federal assistance to urban schools, youth
employment, training on and off the jobs.

The hope was that these programmes would eventually make it

possible for macro policies to aim at lower rates of unemployment than 4 per cent. Unfortunately the hope has not been realized. Whatever their individual successes, labour market policies collectively have been a disappointment. Certainly they have not lowered the feasible non-inflationary unemployment rate. Meanwhile demographic trends have worked the other way, raising the fractions of the labour force of workers—young, female, non-white, single—who whether through discrimination, disqualification, or personal preference are highly susceptible to spells of unemployment. The structuralists who in 1961 claimed this had already happened were premature, but it has happened since 1966. Likewise urban pockets of unemployables, chronically outside the mainstream of American economy and society, have grown. It is even more evident today than in the 1960s that general prosperity and growth will not by themselves solve these problems. The economy cannot be stimulated to such a pitch that jobs are created for those at the end of the queue or beyond it, without igniting inflationary fires that the society at large will not tolerate.

This truth does not justify today, any more than in the 1960s, the discard of macro policies of expansion. Anaemic recovery and stagnation will surely worsen the plight of disadvantaged workers and add new cohorts of adults who cannot get a job because they never had one. In spite of the disappointments of the past, specific job programmes are even more essential today than fifteen years ago. But they will have two, maybe three, strikes against them if macro policies hold the economy at 8 per cent unemployment, or 7, or 6 per cent.

That in 1959 nearly a quarter of the population lived in abysmal poverty was a disgrace to the affluent society. Kennedy–Johnson economists knew that general economic expansion and progress were the most powerful forces for reduction of poverty. The two Presidents knew that it was much less divisive to aid the poor from the fruits of economic expansion than from explicit redistribution of the existing pie. The unpopularity of redistributive programmes today, in an economy stalled for several years, confirms the soundness of their instincts. Yet Presidents Kennedy and Johnson agreed with Walter Haller and his colleagues that overall recovery and growth, essential as they were, would not diminish poverty fast enough. The War on Poverty embodied their determination to enable all Americans to share the general prosperity of the country.

I shall confine myself to two comments about the War on Poverty. First, in the grand design, the maintenance of prosperity, full employment, and growth was always regarded as necessary though not sufficient. The necessity is confirmed by the increases in incidence of poverty accompanying recent macroeconomic reverses. Second, I regret that the Johnson Administration never supported systematic universal income guarantees and income-conditioned cash transfers—yes, a 'negative income tax'. This reform was not inconsistent with War on Poverty programmes, and it would have brought victory in the war appreciably closer. In eschewing this approach—belatedly endorsed by the Heineman Commission appointed by President Johnson—the Administration carried to extreme its reluctance to face squarely the issue of income redistribution. Moreover, Democratic fears of conservative backlash almost defaulted this innovation, like the overture to China and the floating of the dollar, to the next Republican administration, in the form of Nixon's Family Assistance Plan.

STABLE GROWTH AT FULL EMPLOYMENT

The Kennedy–Johnson Administration hoped to break permanently the postwar cyclical rhythm of the American economy. The Council was confident that fiscal and monetary management of aggregate demand, supported by incomes policies, could hold the economy within a fairly narrow band around its full employment growth track. 'Fine tuning' was, I believe, not Walter Heller's own phrase but a journalistic caricature, but it did succinctly capture the faith of the New Economics in the efficacy of discretionary macroeconomic policies and in the wisdom of policy makers.

However, the policy-making apparatus was inadequate. As for fiscal policy, Congressional procedures for appropriations and taxes were too slow, too decentralized, too preoccupied with issues extraneous to economic stabilization. They seldom added up to rational overall fiscal policy, or provided prompt and measured counterweights to fluctuations of private spending. The long delays in enacting the tax reduction of 1964 are a case in point.

A remedy proposed by Presidents Kennedy and Johnson was limited Presidential discretion to make temporary changes of income tax rates in a pre-arranged format, or, failing such a delegation of power, agreed streamlined procedures for speedy consideration of Presidential requests for temporary tax changes for purposes of economic stabilization. These proposals got nowhere—unfortunately in my view. However, other ideas for making fiscal policy more responsive to economic conditions—notably extension and enlargement of unemployment benefits in recession—have been adopted. Moreover, the new Congressional budget procedures and staffs promise greatly to increase the rationality of Federal fiscal policy.

As for monetary policy, the tools are generally adequate, flexible, and capable of quick response. The problem is the independence of the Federal Reserve, which can follow a macroeconomic policy quite different from that of the Executive and the Congress. The Fed does read the election returns, and informal relations with the President, Council, and Treasury were generally good during the Kennedy–Johnson years. (The big exception was in December 1965, when a restrictive move by the Fed surprised the Administration. In retrospect, I think the Fed was right in substance, although I did not think so at the time.) Yet its independence, and the exclusion of other economic officials from its deliberations, gives the Fed's position a greater weight in overall policy than other government agencies, and for that matter foreign central banks, enjoy. Independence is a sensitive political issue. The Kennedy Administration could not even get Congress to make the Federal Reserve Chairman's term coincident with that of the President, although that reform was endorsed by Chairman Martin and his colleagues. Recent efforts for reform have also lost to the lobbies of banks and financial interests. But Congress and Committees have been making the Federal Reserve accountable; and now that Congress makes fiscal policy with explicit economic objectives and forecasts, it probably will not tolerate Federal Reserve policies which pull the economy off course.

The Keynesian views of the Kennedy–Johnson economists regarding the need and efficacy of discretionary policy stand in contrast to what may now be once again the prevailing orthodoxy of economists, a doctrine that certainly exerts heavy influence in Washington today. This is the faith that the private economy is intrinsically stable, that cycles and fluctuations are mainly the reflection of instability in government fiscal and monetary policies themselves, that discretionary variation of these instruments, fine tuning or coarse, is unnecessary and counter-productive. The prescription of the new–old orthodoxy is to follow a steady fiscal and monetary course, unvarying with economic conditions and outlooks, in the beliefs that the economy will settle down in adjustment to the fixed policy and that wherever it settles, whatever the rate of unemployment, is the optimal outcome.

I point out the contrast, but I do not debate the issue here. I remain of the view that the economic vessel has been, will continue to be, buffeted by many strong winds and currents other than those of the pilots' own making. Poor helmsmen steer wavy courses, but that is not a convincing reason to lock the rudder. Nothing in the history of capitalist economies suggests that they are inherently stable or that they can unguided achieve and maintain a tolerable volume of employment.

LONG-RUN ECONOMIC GROWTH

The third objective I mentioned at the beginning was to raise the sustainable rate of growth of productivity. Like the reduction of unemployment and poverty, this was to be attempted by a combination of general and specific measures. As I have already explained, a growth- and investment-oriented mixture of macro policies was for the most part ruled out by the international constraints on monetary policy. While the Investment Tax Credit undoubtedly accelerated capital formation during the recovery, nothing was done to augment the saving available for capital formation at full employment. The tax cut of 1964 worked in the opposite direction, and so, of course, did the deficit financing of Vietnam War expenditure, only partially mitigated by the belated temporary tax increase of 1968. Consequently tight monetary policy, discouraging to investment, bore the brunt of anti-inflationary restraint. As for specific pro-growth policies, there were modest efforts to speed up technological and scientific advances and their diffusion, and I am afraid that no perceptible success can be claimed for them. Agriculture is the model here, but no one knows how to copy the successes of agricultural experiment stations and extension services in other industries.

Of course, under the best of circumstances it would be difficult to detect policy-induced changes in long-run growth trends for the economy as a whole. We are talking about fractions of percentage points; measurement is imperfect, and other influences, probably more powerful than policies, are at work. The trend of productivity is probably much the same now as in the 1960s.

In the early 1960s, the vision of economic growth as the source of ever improving material well-being for ever larger majorities of the population was unclouded by the concerns prevalent today over environment, energy, and resource limitations. Growth is no longer a popular word. To many persons, especially among the young, the Kennedy–Johnson enthusiasm for growth seems misguided and insensitive. The failure of those Administrations to develop environmental, energy, and resource policies was certainly a grievous omission.

Yet the 1960s commitment to growth was motivated by the same considerations as the conservation movement, namely giving future generations a fair deal or better. Overall economic slowdown is a terribly wasteful way to diminish pollution, conserve energy, and husband natural resources. The problems are microeconomic, not macroeconomic. The solution is not to cut back in production and employment indiscriminately, as the advocates of zero economic growth suggest. The solutions are incentives, regulations, and programmes that prohibit or limit the use of processes and products which damage the environment and waste scarce resources. With specific remedies in place, the case for full employment and for overall progress in technology and productivity is as strong as ever. The composition of national output will be different from the past, and the nation's capacity to produce may grow more slowly, at least temporarily.

ECONOMIC ASPECTS OF THE VIETNAM TRAGEDY

The 1960s began with high promise for American life, but much of it was lost in Vietnam. The economic dimension is perhaps the least important, but serious enough. The War on Poverty petered out, the dream of the Great Society was not fulfilled, the grand macroeconomic design was discredited. The economy resumed an unstable course, with stubborn inflation and, in the 1970s, excessive unemployment too.

Lyndon Johnson bravely fought to combine guns and butter, to prevent his Great Society programmes from being sacrificed for military spending. In a sense he was quite right: the society could well afford both. Vietnam War spending was never a large fraction of GNP, and at its height the total defence budget was smaller relative to the economy than in the 1950s. But in 1966 the economy could not finance both without an increase in taxes. Deficit financing overheated the economy and began the era of inflation and instability still afflicting us.

The President's motive was to save his domestic programmes from the cuts which a request for higher taxes would, as experience later showed, surely have invited. But in the longer-run politics of the country, his aim was not achieved. The standard mythology today, erroneous in my opinion, forgets the war and its financing and blames inflation and instability on the economic design itself, on Great Society programmes, on government spending and deficits *per se*.

The war tragically rent the fabric of American society, the bonds of trust and compassion among citizens and between citizens and governments. The political economy of the 1960s did not expect citizens to be altruistic. But it did assume a widespread popular faith that government and the economy would give all individuals and groups a fair deal, and a fair share of the fruits of a growing economy. The willingness of the tax-paying majority to help less fortunate citizens depended on such attitudes. But the faith has been eroded by the war and its economic consequences, as well as by Watergate and other betrayals of trust and justice. The 1970s display more selfish, group-interested, militant behaviour of every kind—economic, social, political. Today the people yearn for leadership to restore the spirit of community to American life.

38 Economic Stabilization Policies in the United States*

The economic future of the United States and of the world looks considerably dimmer at the beginning of 1976 that it did ten years ago. Until 1966, the economies of the non-Communist world appeared to be doing very well indeed. North America, Western Europe, and Japan had enjoyed two decades of unparalleled progress in production, employment, trade, and living standards. They had recovered spectacularly from World War II; they had banished the spectre of the Great Depression of the 1930s; and they seemed to have tamed, if not killed, the age-old business cycle. The future promised steady growth, bringing ever larger social and material benefits and at last diffusing the fruits of modern technology to all classes and all peoples.

An unrelenting sequence of economic shocks has shattered the tranquility and optimism of 1965. These include:

The Vietnam War
Relative to World War II, Korean War, or even cold war budgets, Vietnam was not an expensive adventure. But the sudden escalation of 1966 was financed in ways that left the United States and the world a legacy of inflation that still persists. Less concrete but perhaps more important, the war severely damaged the fabric of consent and trust essential to effective democratic government within the United States and to American world leadership, an erosion of confidence massively reinforced by Watergate and subsequent disclosures of misconduct.

Environmental damage
Evidence has accumulated that some advanced technologies of production and consumption damage and deplete the natural environment or risk the health and livelihood of present and future generations. For this and other reasons, many citizens have questioned the value,

---

*1976, *The Great Ideas Today 1976*, Encyclopaedia Britannica Inc., pp. 40–55.

for themselves and their societies, of conventionally measured economic progress.

Third World
Less developed nations have expressed with growing militancy and unity their dissatisfaction with their economic relationships with advanced countries. The gap in standards of living between the two worlds has widened throughout the past quarter century, and recent setbacks have deepened the mood of frustration and rebellion in the poorer nations. Though many of the barriers to economic progress are endemic to those nations, the institutions and policies established by the advanced countries to foster trade, aid, and investment in the Third World have fallen far short of their objectives. Negotiation, in the United Nations and elsewhere, of new economic relationships between haves and have-nots has barely begun. The passage will be stormy, full of political hazards for the West.

Energy shortage
The world won't be the same again, after the Arab oil embargo in October 1973 and OPEC's quadrupling of oil prices. The sources of energy on which industrial economies increasingly depend are no more finite than before, but now everyone is conscious of the limits. More immediate consequences have been an enormous shift in world distribution of wealth and power, severe hardship for most poor countries, sudden bulge in price inflation throughout the world.

Inflation, recession, unemployment
Prices have increased chronically ever since World War II. But since 1965 inflation has sharply accelerated. Although the Vietnam War, the energy crisis, and food shortages are recognized as contributing sources, recent inflation has brought to the fore some fundamental questions of economic and social direction—the viability of the 'full employment' and 'welfare state' objectives of modern democratic capitalist countries. In 1974 strong anti-inflationary measures in the United States and other major countries triggered or accentuated the worst postwar economic recession and lifted unemployment to rates unprecedented since the Great Depression. Now, in 1976, major governments hesitate to stimulate rapid recovery of employment and production for fear of igniting another burst of inflation. Some thoughtful observers wonder whether the unemployment/inflation dilemma, compounded with the problems of energy, environment, and international inequality, is a veritable crisis of the regime.

This essay concerns the last of the listed problems—economic stabilization. The other formidable economic shocks of the last decade enter the story in so far as they have complicated and confused the task of stabilization. I shall review in particular the policies of United States authorities toward unemployment and inflation. United States policies are strategic, if not decisive, for the world economy; and the difficulties, controversies, and dilemmas besetting economic stabilization here are shared by nations throughout the world.

DEMAND MANAGEMENT AND POSTWAR PROSPERITY

In the optimistic early 1960s Andrew Shonfield, a reflective observer of modern capitalism, wondered, 'What was it that converted capitalism from the cataclysmic failure which it appeared to be in the 1930s into the great engine of prosperity of the postwar Western world?'[1] His answer was that in all economically advanced democracies, government had undertaken responsibility for the overall management of the economy. This did not mean detailed planning and controls as in Eastern Europe and China. But Shonfield himself thought that direct government intervention in private industry was a necessary part of the management of capitalism.

Most economists disagreed. Democratic governments could, they thought, steer and stabilize their economies by a few general and gentle instruments of policy—their budgets, their taxes, their issues of money, and public debt. These powers were not new interventions into the realm of private business and free markets. They were intrinsic and traditional functions of government, and the only change was the discovery that they could be dedicated to broad economic objectives as well as to governmental housekeeping. We could hope to enjoy the best of several worlds, mastering our economic destinies without surrendering free enterprise, assuring overall stability without losing individual initiative and innovation.

Demand management is one of the great ideas of economics and one of the most significant innovations of modern government. Both are due in large measure to John Maynard Keynes's diagnosis of the Great Depression and his prescription of policies to restore and maintain full employment. Business cycles are typically fluctuations in the aggregate demand for goods and services and for the labour to produce them. Supply, the capacity of the economy to produce, moves slowly and smoothly. In recession and depression, demand falls short of capacity, and both workers and machines are unemployed. In booms, unemployment declines, along with margins of reserve plant capacity.

Through fiscal and monetary policies, government is well placed to keep aggregate demand in line with supply. Fiscal policies relate to the budget. The government is a big purchaser of goods and services for its own use. (Federal purchases in 1975 were 8.2 per cent of all expenditures for Gross National Product in the United States.) Other fiscal measures affect demand indirectly but no less powerfully. The federal government transfers spendable funds to other governments, to businesses, and to individuals (15 per cent of GNP in 1975), and limits the spending of businesses and households by taxes (19 per cent of GNP in 1975).

Monetary policy arises from the central government's monopoly of the issue of coins and currency. Nowadays the historic monetary power of the sovereign is exercised by the central bank's control of the lending capacity of banks. In the United States, commercial banks are required to hold reserves, in currency or on deposit in Federal Reserve banks, against their deposits. The Federal Reserve System, our central bank, controls the supply of such reserves. In its day-to-day operations the 'Fed' can make reserves abundant, credit accessible, and interest rates lower, or reserves scarce, credit tight, and interest rates high.

Monetary control affects demand for goods and services via several channels. Residential construction is particularly sensitive to the availability and cost of mortgage credit. Business capital projects respond to the cost of raising funds by bank borrowing or by public issues of securities. Consumers find it easier and cheaper to buy 'on time' when the Fed fosters easy credit conditions. State and local governments defer or cancel capital projects—schools, roads, etc.— when interest rates are high.

Until the 1930s recession, inflation, and unemployment were popularly regarded as natural disasters. Business cycles seemed as inevitable as the rhythm of the seasons. Thanks to the Great Depression and to Keynes, the overall performance of the economy has become a responsibility of government and a perennial election issue.

DEMAND MANAGEMENT IN THE UNITED STATES TO 1965

The revolution in expectations came to the United States later than to European countries. True, in the Employment Act of 1946, a bipartisan monument of national determination to avoid recurrence of massive unemployment, Congress resolved to concert federal policies to achieve 'maximum employment, production, and purchasing power'. But rhetorical commitment is not self-fulfilling practice. Fiscal and monetary policies have always responded to many political and economic pressures other than the Act. Indeed, the dominant ideology of the Eisenhower Administration, 1953–61, was unfriendly to the whole idea of a government-guided and stabilized economy. In 1953–4, 1957–8, and 1960 the economy suffered three sharp recessions, and throughout the period unemployment rose more in recessions than it fell in recoveries.

The New Economics, a modern American adaptation of Keynesian ideas, triumphed in the next five years. President Kennedy broke new ground by committing his administration to a concrete goal for federal economic policy, 4 per cent unemployment. The rate was 7 per cent on his inauguration in January 1961 and 5 per cent at the previous business cycle peak in May 1960. But, uncertain of its political ground, the Kennedy administration moved cautiously in extracting stimulative fiscal and monetary policies from a sceptical Congress and a reluctant Federal Reserve. When the recovery threatened to falter in 1962, President Kennedy decided to ask Congress for a major tax reduction, deliberately budgeting a deficit in order to increase purchasing power, production, and employment. Enacted in early 1964 under President Johnson, the tax cut, combined with an accommodative monetary policy, carried the economy nearly to the 4 per cent unemployment target by the end of 1965.

Five years of uninterrupted recovery contrasted favourably with the cyclical instability of the 1950s, and the public perceived demand management as a great success. Thanks to the 'fine tuning' of the New Economics, the business cycle was replaced by a track of stable growth. Advances of employment, production, real wages, and profits had exceeded all expectations, and the stock market was euphoric. Contrary to some earlier fears, inflation, at 1 or 2 per cent per year, was scarcely noticeable.

Although unemployment was clearly the major failure of capitalism in the 1930s, avoidance of inflation has always been a major objective of United States economic policy. Moreover, economists and policy makers have long recognized that full employment and price stability are often conflicting goals. An economy with low unemployment rates is likely to be inflationary, and those fiscal and monetary measures which abate inflation are also likely to increase unemployment. An aphorism common to economists in the late 1940s was that a democratic capitalist society could enjoy at most two of the following three objectives: full employment, price stability, and freedom from wage and price control.

During World War II, with unemployment between 1 and 2 per cent and industry operating at full blast, inflation was suppressed by price and wage controls and by rationing. The country experienced two bouts of inflation after the war, in 1947–8 after controls were removed and pent-up wartime demands and savings poured into consumer markets, and in 1950 in a speculative binge of commodity hoarding set off by the Korean War. Yet, thanks to the tax increases imposed to finance the war and to a temporary spell of price and wage controls, the country emerged in 1952 and 1953 with negligible ongoing inflation and with unemployment as low as 3 per cent.

It was a shock, therefore, when inflation rates accelerated to 4 per cent per year and more during the peacetime boom of 1955–7, even though unemployment did not fall below 4 per cent. The alarm of the Eisenhower Administration and the Federal Reserve led to policies which helped to throw the economy into recession in 1957–8 and again in 1960. In their view these recessions were necessary to eliminate inflationary psychology. The same scenario, with the same rationale, was to recur in 1974.

The 1955–7 experience was the main reason that Kennedy Administration economists set the unemployment objective of demand management at 4 per cent rather than a lower figure. Fearing that any revival of inflation would undermine the support for expansionary policy in Congress and in the Federal Reserve, the Administration set forth 'guideposts for non-inflationary wage and price behaviour'. The guideposts had no legal sanction, but the White House wheedled, scolded, and arm-twisted visible unions and companies into compliance. How much credit this policy deserves for keeping the 1961–5 expansion inflation free is still unclear.

DEMAND MANAGEMENT AND INFLATION 1965–73

During 1966, federal defence purchases increased by 25 per cent. Ignoring the advice of his economists and the example of his predecessor Truman in the Korean War, President Johnson did not ask Congress for a corresponding increase in taxes. The Federal Reserve's credit crunch in the spring of 1966 only temporarily dampened a boom which by the end of 1968 had lowered the unemployment rate to 3 per cent and raised the inflation rate to 5 per cent. The president finally did ask for temporarily higher taxes, and Congress finally did enact them in June 1968. But their anti-inflationary effect was disappointing: overestimating the impact of the tax surcharge, the Federal Reserve eased monetary policy too much. Meanwhile, under the pressure of shortages of goods and labour, the wage–price guideposts had become ineffectual and obsolete.

Although the experience vindicated the 4 per cent unemployment target, the degree and the persistence of the inflation triggered by pushing the rate below 4 per cent were an unpleasant surprise. The three or four points added to the inflation rate during 1966–9 have so far proved impossible to shed.

The demand management policies of the Nixon Administration in 1969 were intended to cool the economy gradually. They succeeded in engineering a recession, which raised unemployment to 6 per cent by December 1970, a level that prevailed throughout 1971. Meanwhile, the inflation rate continued to rise. The main burden of restricting demand fell on the Federal Reserve. Fiscal policy became less restrictive as outlays under the social programmes of the 1960s grew with their own momentum and taxes were lowered by president and Congress in 1969 and 1970. During this period the White House ostentatiously withdrew from any attempt to influence wage bargains and price decisions in the private sector.

Frustrated by 'stagflation', the Administration abruptly reversed field in August 1971. Formal wage and price controls were introduced, and monetary policy encouraged, or at least permitted, a brisk recovery through 1972 and most of 1973.

Controls were virtually suspended in January 1973, reimposed in June 1973, then phased out and finally terminated from December 1973 to April 1974. In spite of their on-and-off character, the controls did appear to slow the pace of wage and price inflation. But they did not achieve a lasting abatement of inflationary pressures and expectations. As controls were phased out, 'catch-up' increases in wages and prices frequently occurred. The timing of decontrol may have contributed to this outcome, because the general climate of 1973 and 1974 was for other reasons inflationary.

Recovery from the 1970–1 recession picked up speed during 1972, and unemployment was reduced to a plateau just below 5 per cent throughout 1973. Inflation accelerated from 4 per cent per year in the last quarter of 1972 to double-digit figures at the beginning of 1974. Although a list of possible contributing sources is easy to compile, the assessment of the blame is highly controversial. The explanations include:

1. The 1972 recovery overshot the mark. Although 4 per cent unemployment may have been non-inflationary in 1965, now the safe target for demand management is at least 5 per cent, possibly much higher. This is demonstrated by the acceleration of inflation

with unemployment rates around 5 per cent in late 1972 and 1973.
2. The 1972 recovery was badly paced. As the economy approached capacity ceilings, demand was accelerating. If demand management had applied the brakes earlier in 1972 and contrived a soft landing, some bottlenecks and shortages could have been anticipated and avoided. A slower recovery, gradually decelerating, would have been less inflationary.
3. The US expansion in 1972–3 coincided to an unusual degree with vigorous cyclical expansions in other industrial countries. The result was an unusual and unexpected spurt in world demands for metals and other basic materials. The pressure of these demands on limited capacity led to sharp price increases, magnified by speculation.
4. Beginning with the 'new economic policy' of August 1971, the United States deliberately depreciated the dollar with respect to foreign currencies. The purpose, to make American goods more competitive at home and abroad, was abundantly fulfilled. The inevitable by-product was that the dollar prices of internationally traded goods, whether Japanese cameras, German cars, Pennsylvania steel, or Illinois soybeans, increased.
5. Failures of land and marine food supplies abroad led to sharp increases in world and American agricultural food prices in 1973. In that year and the year after came OPEC's quadrupling of oil prices. As these price increases spread through the economy, annualized inflation rates rose to double digits.

DEMAND MANAGEMENT SINCE 1973: RECESSION AS ANTI-INFLATIONARY POLICY

Not since 1929 had the Federal Reserve faced such momentous decisions as at the end of 1973. Historians and economists will long debate the demand management policies of 1973–5. Should the Fed 'accommodate' the increases in prices of materials, food, and fuel— that is, provide the economy with enough money and liquidity to buy the nation's growing production at the higher prices? Or, should the Fed resolutely restrict money supply growth to rates inconsistent with double-digit inflation? The Federal Reserve, with administration blessing, chose the second course in the final months of 1973 and pursued it dramatically by engineering in the spring of 1974, a half year after the onset of recession, a credit crunch which raised interest rates to double digits. Reeling from this blow, the economy plunged into the deepest slump since the 1930s, culminating in unemployment rates as high as 9 per cent in 1975. United States policy, reinforced by similarly drastic anti-inflation measures in Western Europe and Japan, spread recession and unemployment throughout the world.

The recession, if not its severity, was inevitable once the Fed and other central banks set their faces against accommodative policy. The OPEC price increase *per se* curtailed aggregate demand in the oil-importing countries, as only a fraction of the tribute exacted from them by the oil producers returned as demand for their exports. Moreover, monetary restriction could neither reverse the specific price increases—materials, food, oil—which caused the frightening bulge in inflation statistics, nor force very quickly offsetting reductions in other prices. Impotent to alter directly the course of prices, monetary restriction could only contract production and employment. Eventually, the competition of unemployed men and machines may moderate wage and price inflation, but experience suggests that this process is very slow.

The deliberate use of recession to counter inflation is not a new policy. As noted above, it was followed in 1957, 1960, and 1970, but never on so grand and global a scale as in 1974. Note also that the recession was—contrary to many official explanations and popular beliefs—the consequence not of inflation *per se* but of anti-inflationary policy.

Were these hardships necessary to conquer double-digit inflation? At the beginning of 1976, as measured by the GNP price deflator, the US inflation rate, 13.7 per cent at its peak in the fourth quarter of 1974, had fallen back to 6.5 per cent. Was this the result of the policy, or would it have happened anyway? We will never know. Critics of the policy give little credit to the recession. They said from the beginning that the double-digit bulge would pass on its own—after all, OPEC will not quadruple prices every year.

The same controversy carries over to the speed and extent of recovery. Thanks largely to a tax cut forced by Congress on a reluctant Executive, recovery began in the spring of 1975. But the Ford Administration and the Federal Reserve favour a slow and cautious expansion of demand, reducing unemployment by less than two points in three years and taking five years to return unemployment to prerecession rates. Anything faster, they argue, would accelerate inflation, if only by rekindling the inflationary expectations of those who associate the 1973 burst of commodity price inflation with overstimulus in 1972. Critics argue that so slow a recovery costs the nation hundreds of billions of dollars in output which idle men and machines could be producing, and all for negligible gain in inflation

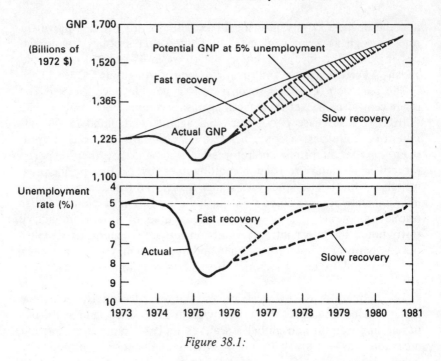

Figure 38.1:

abatement. The government hopes to reduce the inflation rate to 4
per cent per year by 1980. (Ironically, it was to avoid 4 per cent
inflation that the Federal Reserve provoked recession in 1958 and
1960.) Advocates of more rapid expansion of demand, employment,
and production believe that under their policies inflation rates will
continue in the 5–6 per cent range. No one, on either side of the
argument, can be very confident of predictions about inflation.

The debate is displayed graphically in Figure 38.1. The curve
'potential GNP at 5 per cent unemployment' represents the real
output–goods and services valued always at their 1972 prices—which
the United States economy is capable of producing with 5 per cent of
the labour force unemployed. This potential grows steadily at 4 per
cent per year, thanks to normal growth of labour force and productivity.
Unemployment exceeds 5 per cent in proportion to the shortfall
between actual GNP and potential. Actual GNP is shown to 1975,
continued by two projections through to 1980. 'Slow recovery' is the
Administration's projection of 6 per cent per year growth of output.
'Fast recovery' is an illustrative alternative designed to restore 5 per
cent unemployment in 1978. The shaded area is the cumulative
difference in national output between the two paths, amounting to

$240 billion in 1972 dollars. In the lower panel are the corresponding paths of unemployment.

THE POLITICS OF DEMAND MANAGEMENT TODAY

No more momentous issue of domestic policy faces the United States than the strategy of demand management for the rest of the 1970s, involving as it does the nation's priorities between inflation control and growth of employment and output. As opinion polls indicate, inflation and unemployment are dominant popular concerns, and the electorate holds the federal government responsible for meeting them. Yet the governmental and political process of the United States is unlikely to reveal clear and effective guidance to the makers of demand management policies. There are several reasons.

First, the mechanics of inflation and unemployment, and their relations to government fiscal and monetary policies, are difficult to understand. The uncertainties, confusions, and disagreements among experts are magnified among politicians and voters. No politician cares to admit that one evil can be ameliorated only if another is aggravated. Administration spokesmen say that their austere anti-inflation policies are the only way to increase employment and output in the long run. Democrats advocating public employment, job guarantees, and Congressional commitment to a 3 per cent unemployment target either dodge the inflation issue or claim, unconvincingly, that greater production will itself dampen inflation. Many voters likewise regard inflation and unemployment as twin consequences of unfortunate events or mistaken policies; they think that good remedies will solve both problems together.

Second, the natures of inflation and unemployment are popularly misunderstood. Public distaste for inflation arises mainly from resentments at *paying* higher prices, not receiving them. Yet the price A pays is, of course, B's income. In a self-contained economy. B directly or indirectly pays higher prices to A too, but both of them complain of inflation. In the US inflation of 1966–70, the same process which raised prices also raised wages and other incomes. Redistributions of wealth and real income accompany inflation, of course, but they may be cause rather than effect. In 1973–4, for example, urban American workers lost real income to oil producers, foreign exporters, and American farmers. These losses were always attributed to 'inflation', but they were due to fundamental changes in world supply–demand conditions for specific commodities. No demand management policies could have avoided them, but the price increases that accomplished these redistributions undoubtedly increased the acceptability of anti-inflationary demand management.

The national losses associated with unemployment are popularly underestimated at times, exaggerated at other times. Underestimation arises from focusing on the unemployed alone. Even in recessions, they are a small minority of the population, and in most cases their personal losses are mitigated by unemployment compensation. The vast national losses of output depicted in the graph, diffused through the whole economy, are indirect and invisible. In prosperous times, on the other hand, some reported unemployment represents neither social problem nor economic loss. Individual spells of unemployment are of short duration and represent voluntary searches which help to match workers and jobs.

Third, the federal government as a whole cannot now adopt and execute a coherent demand management strategy. Fiscal policy is the outcome of the annual budget process. The President proposes a budget in January for the next fiscal year (now to begin 1 October, formerly 1 July). His proposal embodies the Administration's overall fiscal policy for the economy, as well as recommendations for specific appropriations and taxes. Until 1975 the Congress acted on the budget piecemeal, without explicit consideration of its overall economic impact. Now, under the Congressional Budget and Impoundment Control Act of 1974, Congress is to consider and adopt early in its session a resolution on the budget as a whole, to which the actions of the several appropriations and finance committees must conform. This historic reform enables and requires the Congress to decide upon a fiscal policy for the economy, accepting or modifying the President's recommendation.

The missing component is monetary policy. The Federal Reserve, as currently organized, has a large measure of independence from both the President and the Congress. So far there is no procedure to ensure that Federal Reserve policy will aim at the same economic objectives as the budget. Moreover, the Fed has the last word. Once fiscal policy is set, it is difficult to change it for another twelve to eighteen months. But monetary policy is made and remade continuously.

Although the political process is ill-designed to reach a clear-cut decision, the tilt of demand management will undoubtedly respond to public attitudes on unemployment and inflation. These attitudes affect the outcomes of specific legislative issues, for example, public employment programmes, grants to state and local governments, welfare benefits, and taxes. They even affect the tone of congressional scrutiny of Federal Reserve actions and the vulnerability of the Fed to attacks on its independence. Slow recovery policies, which keep unemployment above 6 per cent for two years and above 5 per cent for two or three years, may not be politically sustainable—especially and paradoxically if those policies, aided by good luck, succeed in their objective of making inflation a less salient concern for ordinary citizens.

If, on the other hand, both unemployment and inflation continue to be regarded as serious problems, popular and political pressures for wage and price controls may become irresistible. Controls are now out of favour, as they usually are with businessmen and unions who have recently suffered through them. But the public at large probably shares neither the ideological antipathy to controls of the present Administration nor the worries of many economists about their ineffectiveness and inefficiency. Eventually the nation might decide that controls in some form are preferable both to inflation and to the use of high unemployment as a cure for inflation.

DEMAND MANAGEMENT AND THE WORLD ECONOMY TODAY

Today no one can share the pre-1965 confidence that demand management policies can move democratic capitalist economies along a steady path of economic growth. In the last ten years, full employment and stable prices, or even stable rates of increase of prices, have turned out to be much more difficult to reconcile than almost anyone expected. The unemployment rate that can be achieved without accelerating inflation in the US has risen to at least 5 per cent, and by some estimates to 6 per cent or more. At those rates, millions of people are unemployed, not because they are voluntarily and constructively seeking better jobs or because they prefer leisure, but because there are not enough jobs. This is disproportionately true of young, old, female, and non-white workers. High unemployment through 1979 may actually produce a further adverse shift in the safe non-inflationary unemployment rate, as an increasing fraction of potential workers are deprived of experience to make them employable and employers design an increasing fraction of jobs for experienced and trained personnel.

Demand management cannot wholly solve this stubborn problem. The answer may involve wage and price controls or some other form of social consensus which mutually limits claims for increasing incomes. It may involve structural reforms, designed to increase competition and to promote downward price flexibility in product and labour

markets. It may involve changes in our systems of unemployment
compensation, minimum wages, farm price supports, and collective
bargaining. It may involve better and larger programmes of public
employment and vocational training than we have yet tried.

Demand management itself went wrong at several junctures in the
past decade. Fiscal policy was overstimulative in 1966; monetary policy
was too easy in late 1968; recovery was allowed to pick up steam in
1972; the policy-induced recession of 1973–4, whether or not it was
at all appropriate, was certainly unnecessarily deep.

Some observers conclude, from this record and from similar histories
in other countries, that discretionary demand management should be
abandoned. They allege that 'stabilization' policy itself has been the
major source of instability. They would substitute obligatory rules, for
example, that the quantity of money should grow at a fixed rate every
year; that government expenditures and taxes should always be set at
levels which would balance the budget if the economy were producing
its potential output.

But even if such rules were technically, administratively, and
politically feasible, evidence does not justify the verdict that they
would perform better. Outside shocks like the Vietnam War, currency
devaluation, food shortages, and OPEC have been important sources
of instability. Although a fiscal rule would have neutralized with higher
taxes much of the inflationary impact of Vietnam, there is no reason
to think President Johnson would have followed the rule more steadily
than he followed his advisers' counsel of the same course. Certainly
fiscal and monetary policies constrained by rules would have produced
an even worse recession than actually occurred in 1973–5.

For the next several years the tone of the United States and world
economies is likely to be one of austerity. The onset of belt tightening
may appear to vindicate the warnings of environmentalists and conservationists even more suddenly and dramatically than they foresaw.
This appearance is superficial. The economic machine is not stalled
out of respect for the environment. On the contrary, environmental
outlays and regulations are likely to be casualties of recession and of
austere remedies for inflation. Nor is the economy stalled for lack of
fuel. Plenty is available, at least for the time being, at current prices.
Recession has reduced petroleum demand, it is true, but at an
unnecessarily extravagant cost. Indeed, stagflation has impeded adoption of rational measures to conserve energy. One reason Congress
has rejected decontrol of domestic petroleum and natural gas prices
is to hold down inflation statistics, an understandable precaution
when Fed policy might again translate extra inflation into extra
unemployment. Depressed profit rates and risk-shy capital markets do

not generate the funds needed for investment in energy exploration and conservation.

It may be that, as environmentalists and conservationists warn, the postwar pace of world economic growth cannot continue. But recession and unemployment are not the rational way to slow it down. Selective, not generalized, austerity is the proper approach—specific regulations, taxes, and price controls to protect the environment from the specific technologies and activities at fault and to limit the use of exhaustible natural resources. Labour *per se* is neither a scarce exhaustible resource nor a hazard to the environment. It should not be idled but employed in activities that circumvent or overcome environmental hazards and resource limitations.

Third World nations other than those endowed with oil have been dealt a double blow. Their costs of importing oil, food, fertilizer, and capital goods have increased sharply. Recession in the advanced countries has constricted the markets for their exports. In consequence, they have increasing difficulty in servicing their debts and in attracting private and public capital from overseas. They have a strong interest in rapid recovery of their markets in the advanced economies, and, meanwhile, those countries have both an obligation and an interest in easing the financial strains of the less developed nations.

The vulnerability of the United States economy to world events— oil cartels, Soviet harvests, commodity speculations, currency crises— has been dramatically demonstrated since 1971. But interdependence runs both ways, and the United States is still the biggest economy. The economic health of the world depends once again, as in the 1940s and 1950s, on American leadership. Prolonged stagnation will evoke, as it did in the 1930s, increasing pressures everywhere for autarchy, protection of home industry, bilateral deals, and other restrictions of trade and international flow of capital. At Rambouillet in November 1975 President Ford rebuffed European statesmen who were urging more vigorous concerted policies to expand world demand. Other countries fear the balance of payments deficits or currency depreciations they will suffer if they expand out of step with the United States. In 1961 US recovery policies were constrained by fears of balance of payments deficits and losses of gold reserves. Today, in contrast to 1961, international considerations reinforce the domestic case for expansionary policies of demand management.

NOTE

1. Andrew Shonfield, *Modern Capitalism*, London: Oxford University Press, 1966.

39   Does the Energy Crisis Endanger the American Life-Style*

The proposition I have been asked to discuss is: 'the greatest crisis in the energy problem may come in choosing compatible technologies and life-styles'. I am no expert on energy, technology, or styles of life. I can offer only a few general observations on adaptation of the American economy and society to the news that energy is scarcer than we thought. I am somewhat puzzled by the formal proposition, but as I understand it I guess I am taking the negative. The compatibility of new technologies to generate or conserve energy with American styles of life seems to me about the least of the problems we face. Given the proper price incentives and reasonable time, the American economy and consumer can cut energy use well below the recent trend without severe economic or social cost.

Darkened service stations, weekend scrambles for gas, cold houses, winter shutdowns of schools and colleges, and January daylight saving time will forever symbolize the coming of the energy 'crisis' to America in 1973. But these are misleading and transient symptoms. Empty pumps and long queues are not portents of an era of chronic shortages. They reflect a failure of markets to function and of oil companies and governments to plan, shocking failures to be sure but not epic disasters. While we expect our grocer sometimes to be out of ketchup and our bookseller not always to have the latest Galbraith in stock, I never thought that service stations would run dry of that single homogeneous commodity they dispense for the oil companies. I never thought the companies would do that to the stations or to us, after all these years when we gave them tax privileges, import quotas, and exploration concessions to keep the gas flowing. But they did, and even before the Arabs gave them an excuse.

The drama of 1973–4 was the coincidence of special events: the

*January 1974, Forum on Energy, National Academy of Sciences, Washington, January 30, 1974 and published in *Business and Society Review*, Spring 1974, No. 9, pp. 60–4. The final paragraph has been added.

jelling of the oil countries' cartel; the Yom Kippur War and the Arab embargo; United States price controls; the oil companies' unexplained failure to anticipate expanding demand and to build adequate tanker, port, and refining capacity.

I say the symptoms of this winter are transient because I think experience with the current non-system will in time convince the most sceptical that energy, like most commodities, is best rationed by price. Centralized administrative allocation of fuel, queuing and informal rationing, irregular interruptions of supply, regional shortages and surpluses, limitations on home temperatures, never-on-Sunday restrictions, and constant appeals to patriotism for no clear national purpose— these are not the way to run an economy, at least for long. These devices do not allocate fuel to the most valuable uses; they waste time, effort, and even fuel; they strain the society's capacity for voluntary self-restraint and cooperation. Nor is there anything especially fair in distributing petroleum to those with the patience, leisure, and fortitude to wait in line, or to those with the closest ties to filling station proprietors, heating oil distributors, oil company executives, and politicians, or to those who are able to take more because their neighbours heed Presidential appeals.

The price of a commodity is usually the best way to signal its scarcity. Considering the bite into his budget, the consumer can decide for himself whether to drive on weekdays, weekends, or not at all, whether to economize in commuting in favour of a vacation trip, whether to keep his home at 65° or 75°, whether to skimp elsewhere in order to fuel a snowmobile or a boat, and even whether to cut energy consumption or other things instead. Whatever the scarcity value of gasoline is, we should be able to buy it at that price without advance appointment, privileged status, waiting, and guilt.

Does rationing by price favour the rich? They were already consuming more fuel than the poor and doubtless will continue to do so. If the rich choose to maintain their fuel consumption, they will pay heavily for their preference. Current and prospective inequalities in energy consumption mirror pretty faithfully general inequalities of income and wealth. These inequalities are excessive, but the answer is not a double standard which forces 'equality' in gasoline use while maintaining or even accentuating inequalities in income and in other items of consumption—food, housing, medical care, education, etc. The answer is a fairer and more progressive system of taxes and income assistance.

Preference for allocation by price is not an argument against coupon rationing but an argument *for* 'white market' rationing in which coupons are negotiable. Given the dollar price of gasoline at the pump, the dollar price of coupons will adjust to clear the market. This is one method of balancing supply and demand without enriching suppliers with windfalls that elicit little or no increase of supply. Another method is an excise tax. They are essentially equivalent if the proceeds of the tax are distributed to the populace on the same criteria as the ration coupons.

The durable message of the so-called energy crisis is that the social cost of energy to the present generation of Americans is higher than we previously thought, higher than the market prices of a year ago (though probably not nearly as high as OPEC now pretends). A few people already knew this. It took the Arabs to deliver the message to the rest of us.

There is some doubt whether the message is really true, whether petroleum reserves really have the scarcity value their owners now think they have.[1] For the world as a whole, that seems to depend on the eventual availability of a 'backstop' technology for generating electricity which does not depend on exhaustible resources. If nuclear or solar energy will become available, even many decades from now and even at high cost in labour and reproducible capital, its shadow limits the true scarcity value of fossil fuel today. Of course, it could happen that Arab rulers and other owners of oil continue to overrate the value of their reserves for years and decades. Moreover, the need to conserve deposits is increased for any country which, like the United States, either aspires to self-sufficiency in energy or resolves to move in that direction for reasons of bargaining or foreign policy. At any rate, I shall proceed in this paper on the assumption that the bad news is at least partially true, that the nation faces not just temporary shortages of imported supplies and of capacities for extraction, transport, and processing but also a lasting shortage—at pre-1973 prices— of basic fuel.

One implication is that we have suffered a loss in real national income. Our additional oil import bill, assuming we are allowed to import, will be around $10 billion per year in 1973 dollars, between $\frac{1}{2}$ and 1 per cent of national income. That is not a trivial blow. But it is not *per se* a catastrophe in a country where the normal annual growth of output is around 4 per cent and cyclical fluctuations range from zero or negative growth to annual increases of 8 or 9 per cent. Consumers who are not simultaneously owners of oil or oil company stock will feel a bigger loss. The national bill for petroleum products will rise in 1974 by $20–40 billion; most of that is not a national loss but an internal transfer from energy users to owners of oil and coal reserves. Much of it, I feel sure, could be captured in taxes without blunting incentives for exploration, investment, research, and development.

More important, especially in the long run, is the incentive which the higher social cost of energy gives us to shift the pattern of national production and consumption to less energy-intensive processes and products. The easier the substitution, the more ingenious the new technologies, the smaller will be the ultimate loss to the nation. The higher social cost must be translated into prices that enter the calculations, decisions, and plans of users of energy everywhere in the country.

I would like to say a word in defence of the maligned American public, so furiously indicted in hindsight for profligacy in the consumption of energy. An energy-intensive style of life was a perfectly natural response to the prices that confronted American producers and consumers. What else was to be expected when gasoline was twenty or thirty cents a gallon and electricity a penny a kilowatt hour? If those prices did not reflect true scarcity values, that was not the fault of Joe Consumer or Detroit or the electric utilities.

We are told it was a horrendous thing for 6 per cent of the world's population to account for some 30 per cent of the world's energy consumption. It was a horrendous thing if and only if it were horrendous for the United States to achieve much greater productivity and living standards than most of the rest of the world. We have not done our duty to the poor of the world any better than our duty to the poor at home. But our own resources and products, including fossil fuels and finished goods made with their help, have been available for export and have in fact been exported. It is true that we have recently become a net importer of oil, but it is not true that we supply nothing in exchange.

It is not true, either, that Americans of this and past generations have been neglectful of their successors. Leaving oil and coal and other minerals in the ground is not the only way to provide for future generations, nor obviously the best way. We have been equipping our children and their children with ever larger and more productive stocks of capital equipment, with more widespread and intensive education, with growing scientific and technological knowledge. We have found a lot of mineral deposits, but we haven't just consumed them in riotous living heedless of the future. We have, directly and indirectly, converted them into other forms of social capital.

Have we overdone the conversion of below-ground capital into above-ground capital? The simple principle for optimal balance is that the two kinds of capital yield the same rate of return to the society. The return for leaving a barrel of oil in the ground, extracting it next year rather than this year, is the increase in its price. So if the social rate of return on reproducible capital investments is, say, 10 per cent per annum, then supplies of exhaustible resources should be exploited at a pace such that their prices (*before extraction*) likewise increase, relative to other prices, at 10 per cent per annum. If these prices are already so high that their expected rate of increase is slower than that, then the resources should be exploited faster. And vice versa—the signal that the pace of exploitation is too fast is that prices are expected to rise faster than the rate of return available on other investments. If $6 per barrel is the right royalty for petroleum under the Arabian desert today, the royalty in dollars of 1973 purchasing power will become $15.50 per barrel in 1983 and $40 in 1993. Is that plausible?

Perhaps future energy scarcities were underestimated in the past and the value of keeping oil and other minerals in the ground was underrated. The course of market prices did not give that signal, but the human beings who make markets could be just as myopic as the rest of us. Now the Arab countries, and other OPEC members, have abruptly changed their view. They may, as I observed earlier, have overdone the correction. Their price now appears to be so high relative to the prices at which alternatives will be economical in the future that the OPEC rulers may earn less appreciation on oil in the ground than they could by investing the proceeds of oil sales. Once the cartel realizes this, more oil will flow and the prices will fall—temporarily— so that it can rise thereafter at the proper rate.

But let us assume that things will not be the same again. Technological processes and consumption patterns will have to adjust to higher cost energy, and probably to steadily rising prices of fossil fuels relative to other prices. One useful role our government could play is to provide some authoritative guidance to the market on future prices. If the country knew for sure, for example, that the price of gasoline inclusive of tax would be no less than a dollar a gallon in 1980 and no less than $1.50 in 1985, Detroit and its customers would shift spectacularly to small economical cars. The market cannot be very good at such forecasts, especially when governmental actions in diplomacy, taxation, and research and development are themselves crucial to the outcomes.

The technologies and facilities for saving energy will take some time to put in place, and considerable capital investment. In the interim we are substantially committed to the technologies, equipment, and tastes of our energy-using past. We will pay a lot for the fuel to operate our big and powerful cars, heat our poorly insulated homes, and air-condition our glass offices. If high prices draw the supplies, from the Arabs or elsewhere, it is entirely reasonable to consume them—*provided* that we are simultaneously making the investments and adaptations that will eventually limit fuel consumption and energy use. To stage this scenario the government must resolutely assure the country that charges for energy use will be held permanently above 1972 levels.

I don't really know how much consumers' budgets of money and time must change before a social historian would declare a change of 'life-style'. To me the economies and substitutions that will be induced by scarcer and more costly energy do not seem revolutionary. The major changes of life-style of this century were connected with the massive shift of population from country to city, and from farm to factory and office; with the vast spread of education; with electricity, automobiles, telephones, radio and television, and home appliances.

None of these changes is about to be reversed. People are going to do much the same things they do now—though in different, less energy-using ways. It may well be that teenagers of the later 70s and the 80s will not enjoy, even in suburbia, the same random access to cars, for trips of any distance and duration, to which their elder brothers and fathers were accustomed. They will find other ways to be mobile and other patterns of dating and courting. Some other contemporary developments may be changing the American way of life more significantly than the energy shortage. I refer to the liberation of women, the decline in the birth rate, and the attrition of family institutions.

Adaptation to energy scarcity entails two kinds of technological substitution, one in the production of energy, the other in the use of energy to produce goods and services. The new sources and processes for producing energy have been discussed at earlier sessions of this forum. I see no reason why they should significantly alter American life-style for good or ill. Electricity is electricity however generated; automobilies are automobiles however powered. No doubt there will be changes in the location of economic activity, in the skills and occupations required of the labour force, and in the nature of energy-using installations. But these do not seem out of proportion to the adjustments which dynamic capitalist economies make decade after decade.

As for the measures of substitution and conservation, some will be at the expense of consumer comfort, convenience, flexibility, and leisure; in many cases human energy will replace other sources: fewer, more purposeful trips; more telephoning, walking, bicycling; more hiking, hitch-hiking, sailing, cross-country skiing; more car pooling, gear shifting, train travelling; colder and hotter and darker buildings; smaller and slower cars. Other measures will provide by less energy-

using means roughly the same services consumers now enjoy. Typically
the new processes will be more capital intensive than the old: better
insulation; more finely controlled heating and cooling systems; more
railway freight and passenger traffic; engines more economical of fuel;
more houses and other buildings designed with sun and weather in
mind. In the still longer run, the pattern of residential and business
locations will gradually change to diminish transport and weather costs;
central cities and temperate climates will gain.

The changes are forced but not all bad on that account. In saying
that I am not simply expressing my personal preference for slower
and safer highways speeds, for fewer Detroit monsters threatening my
small foreign car, for skis rather than snowmobiles, for sails and oars
rather than outboard motors, for the decent train service we used to
have between New Haven and Washington, for public buildings which
are not colder in July than in January, and so on. That would be
presumptuous, and so would be the paternalistic observation that more
exercise would do Americans good. There is a more substantial and
less personal point. Even before the supply crisis, we knew that the
market was pricing fuel too cheaply. Consumers of fuel do not take
account of the costs their usage imposes on others, in congestion,
danger of accident, noise, and pollution. Higher fuel prices are a blunt
instrument for correcting the failure of the market to handle these
'external effects', but in practice they work in the right direction.

On the other hand, there is a clear conflict between standards of
environmental protection and the development of new energy sources
and fuel-saving technologies. This is the greatest technological challenge—to minimize the environmental risks and costs of new sources,
coal, shale oil, and nuclear power, and to minimize the fuel penalties
of anti-pollution devices in automotive engines and elsewhere. If he
thought that the society had, by 1973, reached the optimal degree of
environmental protection, an economist would be tempted to say that
in adapting to the bad news about energy supplies the society should
give a little on this front as well as on all other margins. But we were
still considerably short of this goal in general, in spite of particular
cases where environmental arguments were overdone. The energy
crisis is not a reason for abandoning hard-won environmental gains or
goals. Let the consumer's cost of energy, from old and new sources,
reflect the cost of generating and delivering it in 'clean' ways. In the
search for fuel economy in automobile motors, let the engineers and
drivers give up weight, power, speed, automatic transmission, etc.
before sacrificing emission control.

The United States faces an exceedingly difficult long-range problem,
arranging an orderly transition from reliance on petroleum to other

sources of energy, ultimately to renewable sources. This is not merely a scientific and technological challenge. It demands longer foresight and more planning than our political and economic institutions customarily display. The job cannot be left to private enterprises and markets, important as their role must be. Even if they were capable, without government assistance and guidance, of accomplishing the research and development necessary and raising the massive risk capital needed, inescapable responsibilities for national security and public safety place the federal government in the central role. The task is not the moral equivalent of war. It will take a lot longer than most wars, it makes more demands on intelligence and organization than on moral fibre, and unlike some wars it is not an endeavour that either can or needs to invoke the patriotic and altruistic motives of the citizenry. Just charge American consumers the economically rational price for energy and the American life-style will take care of itself. Like our political and economic system, it is adaptable and robust.

NOTE

1. For a negative answer *see* W. D. Nordhaus, 'The allocation of energy resources', *Brookings Papers on Economic Activity*, 1973, vol. 3.

40 Energy Strategy and Macroeconomic Policies*

I. THE BAD NEWS

In 1970 United States oil production reached its peak, and during the subsequent seven years import volume rose $2\frac{1}{2}$ times. By 1977 imported oil had reached 46 per cent of our oil consumption and accounted for 23 per cent of US energy use. In 1973–4 the major oil-exporting nations, in the most momentous *coup d'économie* of modern history, took control of their production and prices away from the international oil companies. The dollar price of imported oil quadrupled in 1973–4 (OPEC I) and tripled in 1979-80 (OPEC II). Both episodes accompanied political conflict and instability in the Middle East— OPEC I the October 1973 Egypt–Israeli war, OPEC II the revolution in Iran and its armed conflict with Iraq. Although the increases in OPEC's dollar prices of oil have been eroded by US inflation, the rise in the real price of such a basic commodity in so short a time is a shock for which it would be hard to find a parallel in peacetime economic history. In 1972 an average American could buy a barrel of imported oil by less than one hour of work; now it would take more than four hours.

These events carried bad news for the United States, and of course for most other countries. The bad news went beyond the immediate impacts of price boosts and supply cutbacks. The items were as follows.

The costs of dependence: vulnerability to temporary interruptions of supply
The 1973 embargo, and in lesser degree the 1979 gasoline shortages, vividly illustrated how the daily life of Americans has come to depend

---

*January 1981, McNaughton Symposium, Syracuse University, New York. In its *Proceedings*, pp. 17–24.

on ready and universal access to petroleum. Temporary interruptions, originating overseas, scarcely endanger national security, but they generate disproportionate economic annoyance, social friction, and political discontent.

The costs of dependence: the shift of wealth and power
The embargo, the OPEC coup, and the events in Iran showed how oil could be used for international political objectives, how US foreign policy could be constrained by dependence on oil imports, and how supplies and prices could be affected by political instability in exporting countries. Our growing dependence on imported oil placed us at the mercy of the OPEC cartel.

With the value of oil in the ground relative to other commodities multiplied six or seven times, its national and private owners, already rich, have suddenly become fabulously wealthy. Since 1974 the OPEC countries ran current account surpluses that added $265 billion to their external real and financial assets. The political implications of this shift of wealth to the oil-rich countries are potentially enormous and quite uncertain. Some of these countries are thinly populated Arab monarchies or oligarchies, some are poor and backward developing nations, some are governed by revolutionary and Western regimes, some are advanced capitalist democracies, and the Soviet Union is a big producer, with unknown but vast reserves.

The exhaustibility of fossil fuels and the long-run transition to other sources of energy
We always knew that world supplies of petroleum and coal were finite, but earlier warnings of their depletion were regularly falsified by new discoveries. Now the reminder carries more conviction. The age of petroleum, even a second age of coal, cannot last forever. Anyway, the extraction and use of fossil fuels entail environmental costs and risks. Somehow we must engineer a transition to other sources of energy, employing technologies yet undeveloped.

The increased and increasing real price of oil and other sources of energy
Clearly oil became vastly more costly, and its cost in terms of human labour and other goods and services would continue to rise. The prices of substitute forms of energy, present and potential, could be expected to rise in concert, as needed to draw forth and use additional supplies in safe and environmentally acceptable ways.

The worsening in the terms of trade of US labour and its product for imported oil is a loss in American economic welfare. To buy the imports of 1973 suddenly cost about $25 billion more. The imports of 1980 cost about $75 billion more than if the 1972 price had risen at the US inflation rate. These amounts are respectively 1.9 per cent and 2.8 per cent of the US Gross National Product. It is as if the productivity of American labour and capital had been reduced by similar amounts. Further deterioration—though not a smooth trend—in terms of trade is to be expected, a loss in our effective productivity averaging between one-fifth and two-fifths of 1 per cent a year (see Appendix). However, these losses can be diminished by substitution of domestic energy for imports and especially by substitution of domestic labour and capital for energy.

Internal redistributions of wealth

Within the United States a large redistribution of wealth is also occurring. Valued at the world price, domestic oil and gas reserves have appreciated by $2500 billion, a capital gain that is gradually being realized by production and sale, as domestic prices are decontrolled. Concern and conflict over the equity of the redistribution have greatly complicated the nation's adjustment. A host of secondary capital gains and losses is also occurring, notably the differential advantages of regions and localities as sites for industrial activity and residence.

The foreign-exchange value of the dollar and the international monetary system

Those oil-exporting countries whose receipts exceeded their capacity or willingness to absorb imports gained not only wealth but financial clout. Their portfolio decisions could and did affect exchange rates—for example—as between dollar, sterling, yen, Deutschmark, and Swiss franc—to the extent that the currency distribution of their asset purchases differed from the sources of net demand for their exports. They also affected the prices of particular assets, notably gold. In the beginning of OPEC portfolio preferences seemed favourable to the dollar *vis-à-vis* other currencies, but later their currency tastes worked the other way. Evidence of unabated US dependence on imported oil was a factor in the speculative 'runs' on the dollar in 1978 and 1979.

Stagflation, present and future

Stagflation was already the recognized macroeconomic malady of the decade before the oil embargo of 1973 and the initial hike of OPEC prices. But OPEC I was the prototypical stagflationary shock. The higher cost of imported oil siphoned $25 billion a year from the circular stream of income and expenditure in the US. It was like a mammoth excise tax on products of inelastic demand, only levied by foreign governments rather than our own and only fractionally matched by foreign demands for US products. Simultaneously, the boost in energy prices and its gradual absorption in other prices temporarily lifted inflation indicators to double digits. Here, as in other importing countries, central banks and governments faced an unpalatable dilemma. To what extent should they 'accommodate' energy-related price increases—accepting the risk that the bulge of increased inflation becomes permanent—in order to limit their adverse consequences for production and employment? The compromise answers have differed among countries, but the general outcome is worse stagflation—higher rates of both inflation and unemployment—than in the pre-OPEC years of the 1970s.

How should the United States adapt to these substantial changes in its economic circumstances? We have had a hard time diagnosing the problems, finding solutions, and agreeing on policies. But in our muddled and imperfect democratic way, we are slowly adapting. Energy use per constant (inflation-corrected) dollar of GNP is at last declining. The year 1977 was probably the peak for volume of petroleum imports. I shall discuss strategies of adaptation under two headings: microeconomic and macroeconomic.

II.   RE-ALLOCATING RESOURCES AFTER OPEC[1]

The social cost to the nation of consuming an additional barrel of oil, from whatever source, is no less than the world price, the price at which we import and could conceivably export. Moreover, this price may be expected to rise in future, relative to US wages and other domestic prices. Possibly the marginal social cost is even higher. As a major factor in the world market, the US affects the price; it will be lower in future if we hold down our demand. Moreover, there are non-pecuniary gains from diminishing our dependence. These considerations suggest a tariff on imported oil, or what amounts to much the same thing, restriction of imports to quotas enforced by licences sold at auction.

In any event, one point on which virtually all economists agree is that the social cost of oil should be 'internalized' by all domestic users, so that they make decisions about current and future consumption of gasoline, heating oil, and other direct and indirect products of petroleum on the basis of its true scarcity. Controls that have kept prices below the world price have encouraged individuals to consume oil that the country has to replace at the world price. Decontrol is belatedly ending this perverse incentive.

However, it is a mistake to think that prices are the only way, or even a sufficient way, to steer consumers to socially rational choices. Although economic theorists' professional conceit is to identify the 'market system' with the 'price system', common observation tells us that private markets utilize many non-price signals and incentives—advertising, salesmanship, product design—and that public interventions cannot always be taxes or subsidies but frequently take the form of education, information, and quantitative limitations or prohibitions. Oil and energy conservation needs promotion, organization, and education, along with rational prices. Automobile fleet fuel consumption requirements, 55-m.p.h. speed limits, and temperature standards for public places have helped and can continue to help.

Evidently there are vast opportunities for conserving energy, for reducing the energy content of national production and consumption. Some are virtually costless: production can be maintained or consumer utility kept unimpaired with almost no additional inputs (turn off motors, lights, heat when not needed; keep oil burners and auto engines in better tune and adjustment). These would have been desirable economies even at pre-OPEC prices; anyway they would not be reversed if by some miracle those prices were restored. Most involve the substitution of non-energy resources—labour, land, capital. Some such substitutions can be made at once: colder interiors in winter, warmer in summer; slower, shorter, and more crowded trips. Some require retrofitting: storm windows, insulation, sophisticated heating controls. But many require new capital equipment, designed to use less energy: fuel-efficient vehicles, solar homes, cogeneration plants, heat pumps.

The full potentials of conservation and substitution will take a long time to realize as the existing stock of energy-intensive capital—cars, refrigerators, homes, commercial and industrial buildings, electric generating plants—is gradually retrofitted or replaced. Gradualism is *not* inefficient. We can't replace everything at once. Even a gas-guzzling car should not be scrapped until the variable cost of driving it a mile exceeds the full cost, fixed plus variable, of a mile with a new model.

Clearly the same price signals and expectations that will promote conservation and substitution will also encourage the development of domestic energy resources—oil, coal, and other forms. Every bit helps, but it seems unlikely that domestic supplies will be a major factor in reducing our dependence on imports. There seems little prospect that the decline in US oil production can be reversed. The price of new domestic oil has risen sharply since 1973, exploration and drilling have responded, but 'in spite of dramatically higher rewards ... US proven reserves have continued to decline'. (Stobaugh and Yergin, p. 42, see Note 1.) Enhanced recovery processes and exploitation of shale-rock are unlikely to fill the gap, anyway in the next decade. The US has vast coal reserves, and it is reasonable to expect substitution of coal for oil to be an important phase of our long-run transition. This substitution will be mainly in electrical generation and in heating, saving oil for transportation, in which it has comparative advantage. But the process is going to be slow, depending as it does not only on conversions but on meeting standards of safety and environmental protection.

Our economy-wide strategy should have been, and should be now, to focus capital investments on both conservation and substitution and on expansion of domestic supplies. Meanwhile we have to buy imports to keep our existing, and now obsolescent, capital stock operating. Since the Saudis and other exporters are in effect willing to lend us the oil, deferring their demands for our goods in exchange, we should make sure that the resources thus released are channelled into the investments we need. In other words, our import surplus should represent neither extra consumption nor waste of productive capacity and labour in unemplyment. Unfortunately we did not follow this strategy in the period 1974–80.

The nation's higher energy costs have to be paid by someone. Most of the burden must fall on the owners of the capital that costly energy has made obsolescent, on their employees, and on final consumers of energy and of energy-intensive products. Companies stuck with the capital cannot expect to earn the profit it was designed to yield when oil and other energy were cheap. Indeed their inability to do so is the market signal to replace it sooner or later with energy-saving designs. Those investments are economic and promise normal profits, but it is a fallacy to expect to finance them from the earnings on the uneconomic equipment they will replace. This discrimination is a challenge to our capital markets, but they are paid to be forward looking and sophisticated. In addition, the higher cost of energy and the diversion of investment from labour-augmenting to energy-saving design is likely to reduce the marginal productivity of labour, and to diminish employment unless real wages fall commensurately. In Britain, Sweden, and some other European countries, maintenance of real wages after OPEC I squeezed profitability and deterred employment and investment. In the United States, however, real wages declined, relative to their previous trend, by more than enough to pay the additional tribute to OPEC.

Many Americans, many members of Congress, were reluctant to let domestic producers of oil and natural gas earn the world price, even more reluctant to see them earn the world price augmented by a US tariff. Their capital gains would indeed be enormous. But for reasons already discussed, holding the domestic price below the world price distorts the allocation of resources. The case is a dramatic example of the age-old difficulty of reconciling equity and efficiency. The combination of decontrol and 'windfall' tax was a pragmatic political compromise. I would stress two points in its favour. First, the important thing is to give the right incentives on the margin, for the finding and development of new supplies. This can be done without giving intramarginal producers and owners the full capital gains. Second, even if marginal rewards are somewhat diluted, they will be so fabulously high that making them still higher will make very little difference. Remember, moreover, that what is not found or drilled or produced today is still in the ground, for use tomorrow.

III. ENERGY, OIL, AND MACROECONOMIC POLICY

The importance of effective rational policies for reducing both total energy consumption and dependence on foreign oil was underscored by the events of 1979–80. In their absence, recovery from the 1974–5 recession and normal growth in the US and other advanced economies raised oil import demands beyond the limit of OPEC's willing supply, itself unexpectedly diminished by the revolution in Iran. Oil prices shot up on the spot market; contract prices followed, and with OPEC II came another inflationary bulge along with speculative disarray in currency, credit, and bond markets. In response, the Federal Reserve and other major central banks produced a recession (maybe two recessions), just as they had in 1974 in the wake of OPEC I. On both occasions recessions checked the demand for oil. In a very real sense, that was their true purpose and function.

In comparison with specific measures of conservation and substitution, recession and stagnation are terribly wasteful means of saving energy. They 'save' labour and capital too, creating unemployment and excess capacity. Yet rational resource allocation is to use those resources more intensively, to make up for the scarcity and costliness of oil. We must indeed stay below OPEC supply ceilings, but we must find a better and more discriminating way.

In 1974 and again in 1979 the 'Fed' refused to accommodate OPEC shocks and actively opposed their inflationary by-products. Thus the demand-reducing effects of restrictive monetary policy were superimposed on those of paying tribute to OPEC. In 1974–5 the result was the deepest recession in postwar history, taking unemployment to 9 per cent, and incidentally adding some $50 billion to the federal budget deficit. The 1980–1 story is not quite as dismal, but it is still in process.

In each case inflation receded from its frightening peak. Was recession necessary to achieve this result? Or did inflation subside simply because OPEC dollar oil prices stabilized after the shock, and in 1975–6 other commodities which had contributed to the 1972–3 inflation actually fell in price? These volatile components aside, the moving average of US price inflation is closely related to the rate of increase of dollar wage rates, corrected for the trend growth of productivity. Wages accelerated much less than prices during the two OPEC bulges—and in 1974 the acceleration may have had less to do with oil prices than with the ill-timed end of controls. Likewise wages decelerated much less than prices during both recessions.

Accommodation of an OPEC shock would have entailed an easy enough monetary policy to permit the existing real output to be bought at the higher prices. This would have required lower, not higher, real interest rates—real rates computed not from transient CPI movements but from realistic investment opportunities—in order to employ in productive and adaptive investment the funds recycled from the oil exporters. But the Fed and other major central banks attached higher priority to minimizing the risk that the price shock would permanently ratchet the inflation rate up one more notch.

Opponents of accommodation also argue that it would delay the necessary and ultimately inevitable adjustments of real wages and other incomes to the bad news about energy. To the extent that accommodation encourages workers, capitalists, and other groups to seek recompense for losses to OPEC in higher money incomes, not only is inflation perpetuated but adjustment is deferred. On the other hand, it is quixotic to expect that any monetary policy, no matter how austere and non-accommodative, could prevent price indexes from showing the effects of big shocks to specific prices. In the cases of OPEC I and II, the bulk of non-oil prices and wages would have had to move down while oil prices were moving up.

A macroeconomic climate dominated by stop–go and stagflation is not favourable to the energy-saving, energy-producing, and productiv-ity-improving investments in physical and human capital the country needs. Neither is our mixture of monetary and fiscal policies. After tight money brings recessions, easy fiscal policies are adopted to stimulate recoveries. This happened in 1975–7, and, it appears, is about to happen in 1981–3. The overall result is to shift the composition of resource use toward unemployment and toward private and collective consumption, at the expense of capital formation.

IV. CONCLUSION

Our dependence on foreign oil is very costly, and it is gratifying that we are making progress in reducing it. Daniel Yergin estimates that we now use 10 per cent less energy to produce a unit of final output than in 1973, and President Carter's promise that we will never again import as much as in 1977 now seems a feasible prospect. We should, however, not take credit for or comfort in that part of the reduction— roughly 50 per cent—that is due to our economic slowdown and recession.

In addition to price decontrol and to other incentives and regulations designed to reduce energy consumption and increase domestic energy production, a tariff on foreign oil deserves serious consideration. This probably makes more sense than extra gasoline taxes: our problem is the scarcity of crude oil and the national cost of importing it, not gasoline specifically. Indeed gasoline is a product for which it is particularly difficult to find non-petroleum substitutes.

OPEC has made stagflation much worse, and macroeconomic policy was forced to make up for the deficiencies of our energy strategy. But the preoccupation of macro policy, particularly monetary policy, with inflation has worked counter to rational energy strategy, especially by creating an inclement climate for capital investment. It may not be possible to remedy this situation until the inflation rate has been reduced to 5 per cent a year or lower. Decontrol of energy prices and their inevitable upward trend, desirable on grounds of efficient allocation, make the conquest of inflation even more elusive than it would be anyway. In my personal opinion, a purely monetary fiscal attack on inflation, even if carried out with Thatcher-like resolution, will not succeed without several years of trauma and permanent economic damage. That is why pragmatists will not dismiss as unthinkable a transitional period in which incomes policies are concerted with monetary disinflation.

APPENDIX

Economic theory says that, as a first approximation, the owners of an exhaustible resource will schedule its supply over future time so that the rate of return they can earn from deferring extraction and sale is equal to the return they can earn from investing the proceeds of production and sale. If owners of oil reserves produce too little now, they will have to sell oil at low prices in future: the oil left in the ground will earn a low or negative return. If they produce too much now and sell it at low prices, they won't have it available to sell at high prices later. This principle suggests that the real price of oil will rise at the real rate of interest OPEC countries can earn by selling oil and investing the proceeds either in their own industrial development or in other assets, that is, properties, securities, or gold.

Assuming OPEC follows a rational strategy and can earn 6 per cent real interest on investments, we can expect their royalty prices to rise roughly 6 per cent faster than our inflation. Of course this may occur not smoothly but in a series of jumps like OPEC I and OPEC II. With US oil imports about $3\frac{1}{2}$ per cent of GNP, this adverse trend in terms of trade means a loss of effective productivity averaging two-tenths of 1 per cent a year. If we assume OPEC will require a 12 per cent real return, the trend loss is about four-tenths of 1 per cent per year. While this is a significant drag, it is not an unmanageable disaster.

OPEC does not appear to act like a monopolistic cartel, but the members, especially those with the larger reserves and especially Saudi Arabia, take into account interaction between their supply decisions and prices. For them, it is real marginal revenue, not price, that should grow at the real interest rate, which of course may be different for different producers, say Nigeria, Venezuela, and the Emirates. The price would rise more slowly, and therefore be higher at the outset, if they expect—as would seem realistic—demand to become more elastic with the passage of time. The analysis concerns the pure royalty, and if costs of extraction, transportation, and processing do not rise faster than general inflation, that is another reason to expect prices to consumers to rise more moderately. But risk considerations work the other way. Immense wealth is concentrated in oil reserves and subject to military, political, and physical hazard, as well as the economic risk that the customers will find relatively cheap alternative energy sources. For these reasons the owners might be in a hurry to diversify, to lodge their wealth in safer form.

It is insufficiently recognized that monopoly and competition are not so different for exhaustible resources as for the replicable operations of textbook cases. The resource owners must end by selling the same cumulative amounts whether they are cartelized or competitive. The only difference is the timing of the sales. A cartel cannot make its customers pay more than competitive prices in every single period from now to eternity. The best it can do is to soak us when our demands are particularly inelastic.

NOTE

1. For much of the material of this section, I am indebted to Stobaugh and
   Yergin. *Energy Future* (Robert Stobaugh and Daniel Yergin, editors,
   Energy Future: Report of the Energy Project at the Harvard Business
   School, Cambridge, Mass.: Random House, 1979).

41   Sowell on Race and Economics*

The Civil Rights revolution of the 1960s radically improved the legal
and civic status of Blacks and other minority citizens of the United
States. Laws denying them on account of race the rights and privileges
of other citizens were struck down. The powers of the state and its
courts of law were redirected toward assuring equality of treatment
and opportunity in many private, as well as public, transactions. Indeed
'affirmative action' goes further and aims to redress past inequities;
paradoxically, it is now challenged on the constitutional ground that
it denies equal protection of the law to individuals who are not
members of 'minorities'.

The dramatic developments of the past fifteen years have not, of
course, created *de facto* parity of condition or opportunity among
individuals or among races and ethnic groups. Racial prejudice and
discrimination have not been completely expunged. More important,
economic opportunity is in general very unequally distributed, and
conditions that would handicap anyone of any race are heavily
concentrated on minorities. Since an individual's access to legal remedy
depends in fact on his social position, economic circumstances, and
educational attainment, *de jure* impartiality is not as great an achievement as it seems.

Blacks have made significant economic gains during the same period,
but their slow pace and uneven distribution have fallen far short of
the aspirations of both the Civil Rights revolution and the War on
Poverty. This disappointment is the main subject of the book under
review. Thomas Sowell views it from the perspectives of an economist
and historian. That he himself is black must also give perspective, but
the writing leaves this fact implicit and virtually irrelevant.

In Sowell's view, militants who argue for more militancy because

---

*1977, review of Thomas Sowell, *Race and Economics*, New York: McKay, 1975. In
Journal of Economic Literature, vol. 15, no. 4, December 1977, pp. 1391–94.)

past militancy has not yet achieved their economic goals are badly mistaken. So are liberals who use the disappointing pay-offs of past governmental programmes to argue for more and bigger programmes.

Sowell counsels patience: the history of ethnic minorities shows that their economic assimilation and success take several generations, while Blacks have been in urban America only two generations at most.

Sowell counsels self-reliance: politics is a treacherous route to economic advancement. Jews and Japanese–Americans, who could not depend on political strength and governmental favour, made greater and more durable progress than Irish and Negroes, who in different ways and at different times depended on political clout.

Sowell counsels individualism: Conscious efforts to develop group identity and image did not serve Irish and Negroes well. Ethnic groups with internal social divisions and with weak resistance to 'Americanization' have been more successful economically than those with strongly cultivated group identities. Even so, the successful groups have quietly maintained ethnic pride, cultural tradition, and institutions of mutual assistance.

Sowell counsels economic integration: the members of ethnic groups and neighbourhoods cannot achieve American standards of life by taking in each other's washing. They must trade with the larger society; to do so, they must have something to sell, to export. 'Black capitalism' cannot be created by acts of will or Congress.

Sowell counsels realism: moral and political crusades against 'racism' are limited in their effects on majority attitudes. America has gradually accepted the ethnic, national, and religious differences of past waves of immigrants, and eventually the country may even become colour blind. But acceptance has been based less on generalized appeals for tolerance and justice—cf. the continuing plight of the American Indians—than on respect earned by economic performance and cultural assimilation. Nor has acceptance been a precondition for economic advancement. Several minorities—Jews, Orientals, West Indian Negroes, even free American Negroes in the nineteenth century— have progressed in spite of discrimination and hostility. Especially today, with all the doors recently opened to Blacks, their leaders do their people disservice by giving them the easy excuse of White racism for their own economic shortcomings.

Sowell counsels tough educational standards: lowering of academic expectations, automatic promotion, toleration of disruptive behaviour and absenteeism, credit for non-intellectual activity—all these adaptations of school and college to the least able and motivated pupils deprive academic credentials of meaning and induce students to seek ever higher credentials at excessive cost to themselves, their families, and society. The content of education, and the incentives, expectations, and values it generates, are what matters—not the racial composition of the classroom. As proof the author repeatedly (the book is well written and concisely, perhaps even cryptically, argued in the small; it is not well organized in the large; one symptom is frequent repetition of facts, arguments, and phrases) cites the extraordinary record of some all-black schools, notably Dunbar High School in Washington, DC.

A litany like the foregoing never appears in the book, and in fact Sowell does not offer much explicit 'counsel'. His general stance is analytical rather than moral, positive rather than normative. The problem, he says at the outset, 'needs to be dealt with in *cause-and-effect* terms' (p. v). Lessons are largely left to readers to infer for themselves. Nevertheless the message is clear. Sowell concludes as follows:

Perhaps the greatest dilemma in attempts to raise ethnic minority income is that those methods which have historically proved successful—self-reliance, work skills, education, business experience—are all slow developing, while those methods which are more direct and immediate—job quotas, charity, subsidies, preferential treatment—tend to undermine self-reliance and pride of achievement in the long run. If the history of American ethnic groups shows anything, it is how large a role has been played by attitudes—and particularly attitudes of self-reliance. The success of the antebellum 'free persons of color' compared to the later black migrants to the North, the advancement of the Italian–Americans beyond the Irish–Americans who had many other advantages, the resilience of the Japanese–Americans despite numerous campaigns of persecution, all emphasize the importance of this factor, however mundane and unfashionable it may be. (p. 238.).

In between, the book contains three parts: The first is a brief history of American slavery and the economic evolution of Black Americans. The second is a survey of the experience of immigrants and ethnic groups. The third contains the economic analysis. 'There is no racial economics in the sense of a different kind of analysis for Black people than for White people, or for Jews and Gentiles, but there is an economics of race in the sense that the basic principles of economics can be applied to deepen our understanding of the social problems that revolve around race' (p. v).

In his application of 'the basic principles', Sowell argues that competitive markets will not exploit or discriminate against minority workers and consumers, in the sense of paying them less than their marginal social product or charging them more than marginal cost for goods and services. Attempts to do so could be at best only temporarily successful, as they would yield abnormal profits and profit opportunities

to be competed away. Of course collusion, monopoly, and monop-
sony—ranging from legal enslavement of minorities to restrictive trade
unions and real estate covenants—may, historically, have perpetuated
exploitation and discrimination. But Sowell alleges that significant and
enduring deviations from the competitive result depend on barriers
erected or protected by state power. He argues, moreover, that
governments, non-profit institutions, and regulated industries, where
the absence of competition permits the luxury of substituting prejudice
and preference for profit maximization, have had a much worse record
in hiring and serving minorities than ordinary businesses. Consequently,
he finds it unsurprising that those are the realms where minorities
made the greatest gains once public opinion and political incentives
changed in their favour.

From this analysis Sowell concludes that the overwhelming cause of
poverty among Blacks is not that they are cheated but that their
marginal social products are low. Why are they low? Sowell firmly
rejects any genetic explanation and also denies that current disadvantages are an inevitable residue of slavery. West Indian Blacks are a
counterexample to both hypotheses. His negative arguments are
convincing, but he leaves readers with little positive explanation. He
recognizes, of course, that Blacks long received inferior education and
public services. But mainly, it appears, their current problem is an
accident of history and culture. Peasant peoples—accustomed to nature
and fate, rather than input, as the principal determinants of their well-
being, oriented to gratification and self-expression in the present rather
than planning and preparing for the future—always adjust poorly and
slowly to urban and industrial life.

Sowell has an easy time disposing of the crude ideologies of
exploitation and discrimination espoused by many Black leaders and
White reformists, as well as of many of their favourite remedies like
rent controls, minimum wages, and slum clearance.

Yet his confidence in the benign outcomes of unfettered markets
and social adaptation seems excessive, on several counts. First, pure
competition is not a good model for most of the US economy,
which is more accurately described as monopolistic competition or
differentiated oligopoly. These forms of market organization emphasize
non-price competition in both product and factor markets, and stress
long-term relations with customers, suppliers, and workers. As can be
readily observed, firms tend to converge at the modes of public
preferences, differentiating their products only enough to capture
profitable shares of majority markets. Set-up costs and risks are
substantial barriers to catering to minority tastes or to deviating from
conventional employment practices. These barriers do not necessarily

protect profits; abnormal profits are eaten by competitive advertising, promotion, and image building, and by in-group employees. In this kind of economy, doors will not open to minority customers and workers nearly so readily as Sowell assumes.

Second, it is surely naive, especially in the course of a hard-nosed 'cause-and-effect' analysis, to attribute discrimination by regulated enterprises, non-profit institutions, and governments simply to the attitudes of their administrators as reflections of diffuse public opinion. These institutions are all responsive to pressures and demands from the markets they serve. When Blacks could get into professions, they could get into professional schools. When they could buy houses in decent neighbourhoods, they could get mortgages and insurance from mutual and regulated enterprises. When they became acceptable in positions of contact with the general public, they were placed there by existing profit-seeking businesses, not by new firms seeking obscure corners of unexploited profit previously overlooked.

Third, the nagging question remaining unanswered at the end of Sowell's book is whether the market, the government, and sociological evolution can provide escape from the morass of social and economic pathology that currently entraps so many Blacks and other minorities in urban America. The awful thought is that the 'vicious cycle' is an equilibrium, pessimal not optimal. Sowell himself gives some reasons for this fear: the high birth rates of poor Blacks; the immunity of people who have nothing to lose to the normal instruments of socialization—legal penalties and moral inhibitions, educational and economic incentives; demoralization resulting from protracted welfare dependency; the destruction of family ties and the absence of constructive adult role models for children, particularly males; the ravages of drugs and violence.

Sowell is right that people, who move, fare better than physical neighbourhoods, which don't. He is right that other ethnic groups overcame comparable, in many respects worse, urban situations in the past. Yet, though the overall economy is much wealthier now, conditions are less favourable in several respects. The majority is losing interest in full employment and economic growth, and appears quite willing to let youth and poor and minorities bear the brunt of anti-inflationary policy. The widespread diffusion of luxury is painfully evident, via TV and direct observation, to those who don't enjoy it. The trappings of the majority life style are terribly vulnerable to extralegal acquisitive instincts. The egalitarian ethic, re-enforced by consciousness of racial injustice, makes passive acceptance of poverty or of personal responsibility for it as unnatural today as it was natural for earlier urban immigrants. So does the general assumption that governments are responsible for the economic well-being of their constituents. Meanwhile, older cities are becoming obsolescent anyway; they still have plenty of places to live but fewer good jobs. Their educational systems, swamped with pupils lacking in motivation and home support, do well to maintain reasonable order, but can rarely succeed in their real purpose in the social environments in which they operate.

No one, including Sowell, has the solution for urban pathology. Throwing money at the problems didn't solve them, as the saying goes. The implication that neglecting them will be benign is wrong too. Sowell's book contains a great deal of wisdom, punctures many myths, illusions, and wishful thoughts. But the long historical view and dispassionate analytical approach come through as cold hearted. The author leaves us in a predicament without a programme. The book can easily be used to justify complacency both by Blacks who are 'making it' and by Whites. That would be a tragic misuse of a valuable and stimulating work.

42 Considerations Regarding Taxation and Inequality*

I

The case for a progressive income tax is still as uneasy as when Blum and Kalven examined it in 1953.[1] So, for that matter, is the case for a proportional tax, regressive tax, 'degressive'[2] tax, of any proposed schedule of tax rates. The 'proper' or 'optimal' tax schedule cannot be ascertained either by rational argument or by empirical inquiry. Although reason and fact can help, the question is in the last analysis ethical and political. Any individual's answer, any citizen's vote, will depend on his personal interests and values, and society's answer will be the outcome of the political process of choice among conflicting interests and values.

In saying this, I am consciously giving short shrift to attempts, whether as ancient as Plato or as recent as Rawls,[3] to deduce rules of economic justice from first principles. Rawls' maximin criterion, for example, has no compelling intuitive appeal. I doubt that the 'haves' of contemporary society would find convincing the contention that they voted for redistribution in a constitutional convention held before the random drawing of endowments of human capital, and other wealth in which they were so fortunate. 'There but for the grace of God ...' is a reflection which has evoked more verbal humility than material charity over the years.

Blum and Kalven traced many other principles of just taxation and always found arbitrary assumptions at the end of the path. Henry Simons said, 'The case for drastic progression in taxation must be rested on the case against inequality—on the ethical or aesthetic

*May 1976, American Enterprise Institute Income Redistribution Conference, Washington. In Colin D. Campbell, ed., *Income Redistribution*, Washington: American Enterprise Institute for Public Policy Research, 1977, pp. 127–34. Reprinted with permission.

judgment that the prevailing distribution of wealth and income reveals a degree (and/or kind) of inequality which is distinctly evil or unlovely.'[4] I don't think we can do better.

Let us, however, be careful not to prejudice cases by implicit but arbitrary assignments of burden of proof. The very title of the Blum–Kalven classic and of this session suggests that proportional taxation gets the nod unless someone can advance a convincing case for progressive deviation from it. I don't see any obvious presumption for proportional taxation. One could as well say that the burden of proof is on those who would depart from a quadratic schedule, or from the Revenue Act of 1975. A confidence interval may include zero, but that fact alone does not validate the null hypothesis against any other parameter value in the interval. Why *shouldn't* tax schedules be progressive?

And why should I continue? I am only going to express my views as one citizen of a democratic society and advance considerations which I think and hope other citizens might find relevant to their views and votes. In such a discussion, I guess that what is really going on is an appeal to shared—perhaps widely shared—tastes and values. But there is no way such appeal will convince listeners who do not share them. Last fall I joined a group of undergraduates discussing economic inequality and redistribution. One of them asked me if I didn't believe in the Tenth Commandment. For him, that clinched the matter. For others it was just as obvious that presumption favours strict equality of income.

I fail to see how the issue of progressivity is essentially different from the issue of equality. Progressive taxation may not be the only way for government to mitigate economic inequality. But surely it is one way, a very important way. Certainly the overriding purpose of progressive taxation is to achieve a less unequal distribution of income and wealth than proportional taxation. After a moment's examination, this is what principles like 'ability to pay' and even 'benefit assessment' come down to. For any given programme of government purchases of goods and services and the net revenues required to pay for them, progressive taxation will leave after-tax income and consumption less unequally distributed than proportional taxation.

Note that I said *net* revenues. Let us not be gratuitously constrained by the arbitrary assumption that taxation is a one-way street. The government can and does pay out transfers, negative taxes, to some citizens, and these payments can be an important source of progressivity. Utilizing transfers, a small government—as measured by its substantive or exhaustive expenditures—can be as redistributive as a large government. We need not assume, as so many earlier writers on public finance did, that pro-egalitarian taxation is limited by the net revenue requirements of the government. There is no difference of moment between taxing a citizen nothing rather than a dollar, and transferring to him a dollar rather than nothing. (The Blum–Kalven book, in fact, is vitiated by failure to treat transfers and positive taxes symmetrically. The 'degressive' system they apparently favour—a flat rate tax on income above an exemption—is flawed by their failure to imagine paying low income citizens the implicit tax value of their unused exemptions.)

We would agree, I suppose, that the inequality of concern is that of *lifetime* income *within* a cohort, not of annual or monthly or daily income. Differences of *lifetime* income between cohorts of different vintages do not transgress egalitarian standards. There are indeed difficult issues of intergenerational equity, but it is best to keep them separate.

I can imagine some grounds for opposition to a presumption for lifetime equality, although I don't find them attractive. One argument is the claim that some people are better utility machines than others. Even if interpersonal utility comparisons were meaningful, we have no reason to believe that the capacity for utility is correlated with initial endowments. The propensity of some of the rich to support arts and sciences and their applications is often advanced as a reason to tolerate inequality. No matter who the rich are, the argument goes, it takes concentrations of wealth to divert resources from more prosaic and transient items of consumption.

The argument is not convincing. Modern governments are perfectly capable of mobilizing the necessary resources, or of encouraging their private mobilization by tax concessions and subsidies. We do not have to pay huge costs of inequality for the chance that, without any tax incentive, some fractions of some accumulations of wealth will be devoted to purposes of enduring social value. Moreover, the argument that the rich spend well is countered by the distaste many observers feel and express for their consumption habits. Blum and Kalven and many other defenders of inequality tell us that the vulgarity and frivolity and arrogance of some life-styles are irrelevant to the issues of inequality and progressive taxation. We should neither complain of personal tastes, they say, nor infer from them anything about the marginal utility of consumption and income. Maybe so, but then let us not hear about art collections, architecture, and ballet either. And let us apply the same principle to welfare recipients and other consumers at the low end of the income spectrum.

I think Abba Lerner[5] is right. Human beings are human beings—

at least that is the faith underlying our modern democratic societies. We do not ascribe social and economic status by caste or class or race. Lacking any other basis for assessing capacity to enjoy life we must assume it is randomly distributed, independently of endowments. This provides a probabilistic presumption for equality. Any other assumption would founder not only on the uncertainty of measurement but on the obvious self-interest every individual would have to display more utility potential than his neighbour.

II

If we agree so far, then we agree that the failure to equalize resource endowments, by taxation or otherwise, is only *instrumentally* justified. We don't know how to equalize without inducing tax-reducing or tax-avoiding behaviour which deprives both society and tax collector of some of the potential productivity of the resources. If we could assess the value of every individual's native talent in its most productive use and tax him on that basis, he could not escape by loafing instead of working, taking comfortable jobs instead of responsible ones, consuming instead of saving, hoarding instead of risk taking, imitating instead of innovating. Human endowments, like land, would be assessed and taxed at the value of their highest use. For better or worse, this cannot be done. The assessment procedure would have to rely on observations obtained with the cooperation of the taxpayers themselves, and the incentive structure would be like that of intelligence and medical tests for the military draft during the Vietnam War.

Society necessarily taxes the individual outcomes of endowments-cum-behaviour, not of endowments alone. It's pretty clear that the controversies arise from differences of emphasis as between the two components. Advocates of equalization usually attribute observed inequality mainly to endowments, and opponents emphasize the role of behaviour. These differences affect judgements both about 'justice' and about 'social efficiency'.

We can, I suppose, imagine an economy of disjoint individual economies, with Robinson Crusoes of equal endowments of physical and human nature, each satisfying all his needs from his own effort and ingenuity, without specialization or trade or cooperation. It will then seem unjust and inefficient to tax the industrious and ingenious in favour of the lazy and improvident. Indeed even proportional taxation of measurable income or wealth does not seem to fit the case. However, even these Crusoes may be subject to chance fortunes and misfortunes, for example of weather and health and technology.

They may wish to join each other in an insurance scheme, even though the inevitable moral hazard imposes some deadweight loss and injustice.

But endowments are not equal, and individual economies are not independent. Even if endowments were initially equal, they would not remain so in the next generation. The children of successful, industrious, fortunate, wealthy parents have a head start. There seems no way to avoid this fact so long as the family is the child-rearing institution of the society, and we certainly don't have an alternative at hand. Indeed provision of a good environment for children and family is a principal motivation of economic performance. In this sense, as Marshall pointed out, the most ardent and ruthless profit-seeking businessmen are generally altruistic.

Here is a great dilemma. One of the slogans of our casteless democratic society is equality of opportunity, and this equality is our excuse and consolation for inequality of wealth. After all, the unequal prizes are won in a fair race. But if the starting advantages in the next race are correlated with the order of finish of the last one, is opportunity equal, is the race really fair? As we know, the same problem arises in socialist societies. Mao has a drastic solution for it, periodic levelling by 'cultural revolution'; how costly this may be we don't yet know. In our own society we can only hope to mitigate the problem, by a progressive tax transfer system and by public education.

A work ethic is essential to a society. We have a great stake in maintaining the view that performance pays off, that indolence and inefficiency do not. Since we cannot disentangle the elements of endowment and effort in performance, we must tolerate considerable reward for endowment, in large measure undeserved and redundant. But those of us who benefit from this circumstance should not delude ourselves. When I as Chairman of my Department tell the Dean and the Provost and the President that economists' salaries should be raised so that we can attract a better department than we have now, I am making a self-serving argument. When the National Association of Manufacturers tells us that we need to tax high incomes less in order to sustain the supply of capital and management, the NAM is making a self-serving argument.

The interdependence of modern economic life is another consideration. After all, this is not a society of isolated subsistence farmers. Anyone's earning capacity is dependent on a complex web of interdependence, on economic, locational, professional specialization, and trade; on a highly developed legal and governmental system that enforces contracts, protects life and property, fosters markets; on a shared accumulation of culture, learning, science, and technology. Market prices are probably a good way of allocating resources, even when the competitive conditions which would justify identifying factor prices with marginal productivities do not obtain. What is not justified is the presumption that these prices or marginal productivities are just deserts. It is not unreasonable to attribute part of the national product to the general societal overhead capital and to allocate it as a social dividend for equal division.

How much inequality can a society stand before the legal, social, and political foundations of its economic productivity are undermined? These foundations depend on consent, expressed not only in formal collective political action but in the informal daily actions of individuals and groups. A complex interdependent market economy is extremely vulnerable to disaffection. It is a great illusion to rely on legal compulsion to sustain the rules of the economic game—to protect every property, enforce every contract. As Weber, Schumpeter, and other thoughtful analysts of the sociology of capitalism long ago pointed out, the framework must be sustained by a widely shared and internalized ethic, an ethic which differs from feudal explanations of inequality precisely in *not* ascribing differences of income and power to differential birth rights. It is too much to expect that loyal consent to the rules of the game will be forthcoming regardless of the outcomes of the game. We don't know the extent to which the disquieting problems of crime, corruption, demoralization, and anti-social behaviour which beset our cities are due to highly visible—probably more so than ever, thanks to TV—and dramatic differences of opportunity and consumption. It would be imprudent, to say the least, to ignore the possible connection and to rely wholly on police and prison.

III

I return now to the trade-off between the egalitarian gains of progressive taxation and the losses due to the disincentives of such taxation. This is a matter on which utilitarian calculus can conceivably shed some light, although for the reasons I gave at the beginning it can never be conclusive. Unfortunately our empirical knowledge of the strength of the disincentives is terribly thin.

Even a voter who places no social value on the utility of those above him in the income scale, or more accurately in the endowment scale, will not as a rule rationally favour taxation to bring them all the way down to his level. There is a point beyond which higher surtax rates collect less revenue, not more. If the voter–taxpayer pushed the surtax on wealthier citizens beyond this point, he would have to impose more taxes on himself. This is because the surtax will induce the wealthier citizens to divert resources to leisure or other untaxed employments. A further possibility is that the diversion will reduce the marginal productivities and values of the majority voter's labour and other resources. This, however, is not certain: the withdrawn resources may be substitutes for, not complements of, the voter's resources.

On the other hand, there is no presumption that proportional taxation is the way to minimize deadweight loss. Consider, for the moment, a system which includes no per capita tax or transfer (negative or positive demogrant). If revenues must be raised for public purposes, there are bound to be some distortions. Roughly speaking, the average of marginal tax rates—weighted by the total incomes in the brackets to which the marginal rates apply—must equal the ratio of the revenue requirement to the tax base. The higher the marginal rate for any bracket, the less effort and taxable income are generated by the taxpayers of the bracket, but the more revenue (up to a point) is obtained from that bracket and higher brackets. The same tax schedule must apply to everyone; we cannot, even if we thought it was equitable, practise price discrimination and tailor tax schedules individually to endowments and preferences, because these are unobservable.

Given these constraints, there is advantage in assigning high marginal tax rates, on the one hand to those brackets whose labour supply is relatively inelastic and, on the other hand, to increase the average take from brackets with relatively low marginal utilities of consumption. It's a complicated problem, and there is no reason at all to believe that the solution is proportional taxation. There is no such presumption even if all individual utilities are equally weighted, and *a fortiori* if the median voter–taxpayer consults only his own utility.

Furthermore, as I stated earlier, we should not confine ourselves to the assumption of zero demogrant. A flat-rate tax coupled with a positive per capita demogrant—the guaranteed minimum disposable income for anyone with zero taxable earnings—is a progressive system in the sense that the ratio of tax, negative or positive, to income rises algebraically with income. If there are some individuals with zero or near-zero endowments, and if the marginal utility of consumption approaches zero, then any utilitarian calculation which counts their utility will dictate a positive demogrant. To pay this, and to credit it against the gross tax liabilites of more fortunate citizens, will increase the rate of a flat-tax schedule or the average marginal rate of a variable-rate schedule. But the utility losses on this account will be balanced by the gains at the bottom.

In this country we have been struggling to dodge this problem for many years, hoping to avoid the costs of a universal demogrant by restricting the payments to citizens who can be observed or reasonably inferred to have zero or minimal endowments. The categorical systems ran into formidable problems of inequity and disincentive themselves. I have discussed them on several occasions, including a previous 'rational debate' with Allen Wallis under the same sponsorship as today's session.[6] I will only repeat here my conviction that the opportunities for innocuous and fair categorical discrimination are quite limited.

On what characteristics of endowments and utility funcitons does the desirable degree of progressivity depend? It is always hazardous to propose generalizations, since so many formulations of the problem and so many sets of parameter values are conceivable. But the following seem reasonable. First, the utilitarian case for progressivity clearly depends on declining marginal utility of total consumption, and is stronger the steeper the decline. Of course, declining marginal utility across individuals may be imposed by the valuations of the observer or voter, whatever the shapes of individual functions may be. Second, the case is stronger the weaker is the substitutability of leisure for work—or in general of untaxed utility-producing activity for taxed activity. Weak substitution means that it is easier to obtain surtax revenues from high-endowment taxpayers and to transfer them to low-endowment citizens in the form either of demogrants or of low marginal rates. Third, the case is stronger the smaller the non-redistributive revenue requirement. The reason is that a high net revenue requirement already means a high marginal rate in a proportional tax system. Consequently there is less room to raise rates for any bracket without inducing substitution that actually lowers revenue or, in any case, gains little revenue for the utility loss imposed.

The utilitarian approach to optimal taxation implies that, contrary to the premise of the Blum–Kalven book, ethical principles and interpersonal valuations, although necessary, are not sufficient to determine even the general shape of the optimal tax schedule. The answer will differ as between economies, and for the same economy at different times. It will depend on a number of circumstances and parameters of behaviour, some of which could be empirically derived. Following this line of inquiry, economists may yet contribute to this subject.[7]

NOTES

1. Walter J. Blum and Harry Kalven Jr, *The Uneasy Case for Progressive Taxation*. Chicago: University of Chicago Press, 1958.
2. The Blum–Kalven label for a single-rate tax on income minus a subsistence exemption, apparently their preferred schedule.

3. John Rawls, *A Theory of Justice*, Cambridge, Mass.: Harvard University Press, 1972.
4. Henry Simons, *Personal Income Taxation*, Chicago: University of Chicago Press, 1938, pp. 18–19.
5. Abba Lerner, *The Economics of Control*, New York: MacMillan, 1946, pp. 29–32.
6. Allen Wallis, *Welfare Programs: An Economic Appraisal*, Washington, DC: American Enterprise Institute for Public Policy Research, 1968.
7. There is a flourishing literature. *See*, for example, J. A. Mirrlees, 'An exploration in the theory of optimum income taxation', *Review of Economic Studies*, April, 1971, pp. 175–208, and A. B. Atkinson, 'How progressive should income tax be?' in M. Parkin and R. Nolsay (eds), *Essays in Modern Economics*, London: Longman, 1973.

43 Running the Economy with Less Unemployment and Poverty[1]
(Comments on the Bishops' Pastoral Letter on Catholic Social Teaching and the Economy)

As an economist and citizen, I welcome the bishops' pastoral letter. The bishops are doing our nation a great service by raising moral and ethical questions about our economic institutions and policies, in particular by insisting on the priorities of reducing unemployment and poverty. Addressing those of us who are, by accidents of birth and fate, spared these evils, they remind us that we are the beneficiaries of a highly interdependent social, economic, and technological system that magnifies the fruits of our labours many times the rewards of the most talented individuals of other ages and other nations. They are right to remind us of our obligations to those to whom our system has not provided the opportunities and lucky breaks that we have enjoyed. The present climate of opinion in this country stresses individuals' responsibilities for their own economic fates, implies that wealth and poverty are both individuals' just deserts, and promotes the comfortable, complacent reassurance that competition magically transmutes personal greed into social beneficence. The pastoral letter is a timely antidote.

Actual economic policies result from confrontation of values and priorities with the limits of feasibility. Many economists and men and women of affairs are criticizing the draft pastoral letter as lacking in appreciation of the achievements of our system and in understanding of the realistic requisites for its successful operation. There are plenty of cheerleaders for the *status quo* these days, indeed for the *status quo ante* 1933. Economic policy does have to respect feasibilities. Too often these words are none too subtle rationalizations for simple greed, voiced by those who want to pay less taxes or receive larger benefits.

*March 1985, Statement to US House of Representatives Subcommittee on Economic Stabilization. Ninety-ninth Congress first Session, *Hearing* of the Subcommittee, 19 March 1985, Washington: Government Printing Office, pp. 26–34.

But realistic policies to implement the bishops' agenda will have to provide incentives and disincentives that so far as possible work for rather than against their objectives.

The values expressed in the pastoral letter are presented as derived from Catholic theology. I, a nonCatholic and indeed an unrepentant 'secular humanist', find them of universal appeal, striking responsive chords among persons of all religious faiths and of none. The ethics of equity and equality are very American, just as much as the ethics of individualism heard so exclusively today. The two are married in general adherence to the principle of equality of opportunity.

If our economy is a competitive race, the contestants should have an even start. True, as many opponents of redistributive tax and transfer programmes say, equality of opportunity does not imply equality of outcome—an even start does not mean an even finish. But what those critics forget is that today's inequality of condition is tomorrow's inequality of opportunity. In all kinds of ways the children of successful and affluent parents have a head start; the children of poverty have too often lost the race before it begins. That is why democratic governments have stepped in, should step in, to modify the extreme outcomes of market economies. That is why we have public education, progressive taxation, and social insurance. We cannot expect to guarantee absolutely even starts. Indeed the desire of parents to give their children better starts in life has itself moral worth, and practical importance as economic incentive. But we can do better. A social and political democracy cannot survive the extreme inequalities of unmitigated market capitalism.

The pastoral letter rightly deplores the upward trend of unemployment in the United States and the complacency of policy makers towards unemployment. During the last thirty-five years unemployment rates at cyclical peaks and troughs, and averages across cycles, have generally risen. The makers of federal fiscal and monetary policy, especially the Federal Reserve, have found higher unemployment a necessary by-product of measures to contain or reduce inflation. What is not so clear is why, especially in the 1970s, it took higher and higher unemployment rates to accomplish these tasks.

The upsurge of inflation during the Vietnam period 1966–9, when unemployment fell as low as 3 per cent, is understandable. The failure of the policy-induced recession of 1970–1 to bring inflation back down remains a puzzle and a disappointment. The subsequent recovery was killed in 1974 with unemployment around 5 per cent at the cyclical peak of production, and with inflation touching double digits. The next recovery was killed in 1980; unemployment had fallen just below 6 per cent at its lowest, and inflation was again in double digits. In both cases therapeutic recessions brought inflation down to 4–5 per cent, but at the cost of much higher unemployment rates than had occurred in previous postwar business cycles.

Of course, spectacular increases in world prices of oil and other commodities led to the two inflationary bulges of the 1970s. There is great disagreement in assigning blame, as between the supply-price shocks and a structural increase in the inflation-safe threshold of unemployment. Optimists, observing that similar supply shocks are now quite improbable, believe that unemployment can now be reduced to 6 per cent or lower. Pessimists more inclined to blame the 1970s on failures of policy makers to recognize how much structural changes had raised the threshold, are afraid of unemployment rates much below 7 per cent—the worst rates experienced in cyclical recessions in 1950–60.

The Federal Reserve is determined not to allow a repetition of the price accelerations that accompanied the last three cyclical recoveries. The Fed is cautiously allowing the present recovery to proceed, alert to signs of price acceleration but in their absence apparently willing to let unemployment slowly decline below 7 per cent, maybe to 6 per cent, maybe eventually below that if the price environment of the 1980s remains benign.

The unemployment objectives of the pastoral letter are, however, like those of the Humphrey–Hawkins Act, far below any levels that most economists and, more important, the Federal Reserve would find realistic inflation-safe rates. They are not unreasonable objectives, but experience these last twenty years suggests that they are not attainable by macroeconomic means alone, that is, by overall fiscal and monetary policies. They are not attainable by those policies without risks of heightened inflation that are generally regarded as socially and politically unacceptable.

Reducing unemployment to 4 per cent or lower will require structural policies to diminish and limit the inflationary risks. I emphasize that requirement. We know how to create more jobs, and so does Paul Volcker. But that is not enough. Jobs have to be provided in ways that do not have chronic inflationary by-products. The structural problem is twofold. In booms and prosperities prices and wages tend to accelerate at unemployment rates still too high. In the recessions designed to cool off inflations, the rates of wage and price increase do not subside until unemployment has been raised by three to five points and held high for a long time.

The bishops' call for direct job creation by government makes sense. Anyone who observes and experiences the deterioration of public facilities—parks, streets, schools, and so on—and knows at the same time the numbers of jobless in the same communities is bound to wonder why the two social needs cannot be met at the same time. This may be possible if the jobs are targeted to the disadvantaged persons who need them, mostly teenagers and others whose unemployment is not helping to contain inflation anyway. But there are structural problems. We must get round the claims of unions, aided by Davis–Bacon Act and similar legislation, for those jobs at prevailing wages. Likewise on-the-job training can be subsidized for target populations, provided other employees and their unions can be persuaded or forced to allow what they regard as competition.

As the bishops say, the government can try to reduce structural unemployment by helping to retrain and relocate, occupationally and geographically, workers displaced from declining industries. This will be of limited help if there are not enough jobs in expanding industries and regions. There will not be if the Federal Reserve is afraid that expansion risks more inflation.

The United States has had federal, state, and local programmes in all these areas for at least two decades. We cannot say that in aggregate they have significantly arrested the upward trend of unemployment. Probably the best long-run manpower policy is a general and generous investment in upgrading public education, designed to make sure that new generations of youth will be functionally literate—not so much trained for specific vocations as capable of absorbing the on-the-job training they will get in future, whatever the economic and technological trends. It is often said that our youth and our schools must adapt to the revolutionary technological complexities of the day. But not everybody can be or needs to be a computer whiz. Employers need to adapt their jobs and techniques to the labour supplies we have. The host of investment tax concessions and subsidies by all levels of government, often the result of interstate and interregional competition, give too much incentive for labour-saving technologies. The more neutral provisions of the Treasury's tax reform proposal would be an improvement in this respect.

To achieve the bishops' unemployment goals, I am afraid, we will have to attack the inflation problem head on. The availability of unemployed workers willing to work at prevailing wages or lower has too little effect in limiting wage increases, and the existence of excess capacity has too little effect inconstraining price increases. Those who already have jobs, the insiders, have too much power to raise or defend their own wages and benefits, at the expense of the outsiders. That is why it takes extreme economic distress, threatening bankruptcies and plant closings, to bring disinflation. Wage and price increases by individual firms and unions are like pollution; they impose costs on others, on the whole society, which those who decide them, negotiate them, and benefit from them do not consider. The solutions are incentive devices to make them feel and consider those costs.

Here are some possible devices. In the 1960s we had 'guideposts for non-inflationary wage and price behaviour' enunciated by the government, with the persuasive powers of President and cabinet behind them in applications to specific wage and price settlements and decisions. They had some success before everything fell apart in 1966 with the inflationary financing of the Vietnam War. A number of economists of different viewpoints have advocated guideposts plus incentives to obey them, provided either by tax penalties or tax-reduction rewards. Another idea is to impose extra unemployment–compensation taxes on employers who have raised wages above guidepost when they were reducing employment or when unemployment in their occupations and localities were high.

Collective bargaining is regulated and protected by federal law, under which both employers and employees have rights. The federal government could legitimately take more interest in the contents of the contracts that result. For example, if COLAs were required to be symmetrical, wages and prices would disinflate faster during downturns, or when world commodity prices were falling. Similarly, competition, foreign as well as domestic, is a powerful anti-inflationary medicine. We should certainly insist that any industries and workers who are protected by tariffs or quotas should not take advantage of the protection by inflating wages and prices. Finally, a number of economists[1] have proposed new forms of worker compensation, sharing of profits or revenues or productivity gains, which could mitigate the painful unemployment–inflation trade-off. They might be encouraged by suitable provisions of tax law.

I do not have a magical solution or a specific package. The main thing is to keep the objective of lower unemployment before us, not to give up on it as we seem to have been doing in our concentration on anti-inflationary macroeconomic policy.

Poverty in the United States is a problem distinct from unemployment. Many unemployed are not poor by the official definition, Many of the poor are not unemployed. Some are working, and some are not in the labour force because of disabilities, home responsibilities, discouragement by the unavailability of jobs, or life-styles. Nevertheless the overall performance of the economy, of which unemployment rates are a good barometer, is the main reason for recent disappointing reversals of the previous downward trend in poverty. By the same token, the overall prosperity and growth which would lower unemployment rates would also yield improved poverty statistics.

But macroeconomic performance is not the whole story or the whole remedy. Budget stringencies at all levels of government in recent years have cut the purchasing power of needs-tested transfers. Although cuts in federal tax rates were rationalized as needed to increase incentives for work and enterprise, the analogous incentives have been reduced for persons partially dependent on welfare benefits, food stamps, and other transfers. Measures to economize by confining assistance to the 'truly needy' imply heavy taxes, in the form of reduced benefits, on earnings that would move recipients out of the eligible categories. This is a reversal of policies of the 1960s and 1970s.

Any income transfers that provide adequate support to the truly needy are bound to provide some perverse incentives. But our various assistance programmes can be better designed and better integrated with each other, so that the working poor and some above the poverty line will not be heavily taxed on the fruits of their own efforts to escape poverty. Discrepancies among states and localities in benefit levels and eligibility rules still provide uneconomic incentives for residence in the more generous jurisdictions. The absence of adequate programmes of assistance to husband–wife families before retirement is a gaping hole in our anti-poverty programme. We need to provide incentives to form and to maintain intact families; Aid for Families of Dependent Children does the opposite now. Too many people in this society have no health insurance and are not eligible for Medicaid or Medicare. Not all of them are technically poor, but neither can they withstand the costs of catastrophic illness.

The ghettos of our cities are a problem most Americans prefer to forget. Foreigners who see these neighbourhoods are shocked and incredulous that they exist in the wealthiest economy of the world. These urban neighbourhoods are caught in vicious circles, in which poverty, decay of the physical environment, broken families, illegitimacy, unsuccessful schools, street crime, violence, drugs, joblessness, poor health, and functional illiteracy feed on each other and perpetuate themselves. While 'throwing money at the problems' didn't solve them, not throwing money at them doesn't solve them either. We really must launch a renewed effort to find and finance constructive solutions.

Your letter of invitation asked whether policies to reduce unemployment and poverty are consistent with economic growth. They are. There is no reason to believe, either in economic logic or in experience, that capitalism must be inhumane and unjust in order to function successfully. The quarter century after World War II was a period of unprecedented growth and prosperity in this country and in all democratic capitalist nations. It was also the period of expansion of public programmes of social and economic security.

NOTE

1. Notably Martin Weitzman in *The Share Economy*, Cambridge, Mass.: Harvard University Press, 1984.

Acknowledgements

The publishers are grateful to the following for their kind permission to reproduce articles in this book:

American Economic Association, American Enterprise Institute, Ballinger Publishing Co., Bank of Japan, Basil Blackwell, *The Boston Globe*, The Brookings Institution, Brooklyn College Press, Cambridge University Press, Center for the Study of Canada, The Conference Board, Council on Foreign Relations, *Economic Outlook USA*, *The Economist*, Encyclopaedia Britannica, Federal Reserve Bank of San Francisco, *Harper's Magazine*, KCG Productions, *The New Republic*, *New York Review of Books*, *The New York Times*, North Holland Publishing Co., McGraw-Hill Book Co., Macmillan, Morgan Guaranty Trust Co., ME Sharpe, Syracuse University, Tax Foundation, University of Chicago Press, University of Texas at Austin.

Index